Mutual Accommodation

Ethnic Conflict and Cooperation

Mutual Accommodation:

Ethnic Conflict and Cooperation

Robin M. Williams, Jr.

in collaboration with Madelyn B. Rhenisch

UNIVERSITY OF MINNESOTA PRESS □ MINNEAPOLIS

Library of Congress Catalog Card Number 77-90060

ISBN 0-8166-0822-9

The University of Minnesota is an equal opportunity educator and employer.

The author acknowledges permission to reprint passages from the following: *Achieving Effective Desegregation* by Al Smith, Anthony Downs, and M. Leanne Lachman, pp. 1, 22, 23, 25, 26, 29, reprinted by permission of the publisher (Lexington, Mass.: D. C. Heath and Company, 1973). *Administrative Justice* by Philippe Nonet (New York: Russell Sage Foundation, 1969), pp. 67, 87. © 1969 Russell Sage Foundation. *A Behavioral Theory of Labor Negotiations: An Analysis of a Social Interaction System* by R. E. Walton and R. B. McKersie, pp. 10, 14-15. © 1965 McGraw-Hill Book Company. Used with permission of the McGraw-Hill Book Company. *Community Conflict* by J. Coleman, pp. 1, 21. © 1957 The Free Press. Used by permission of the Macmillan Publishing Co., Inc. *Equal Opportunity in the U.S.: A Symposium on Civil Rights* by E. Warren, pp. 20-22. Edited by Robert C. Rooney and published by the Lyndon B. Johnson School of Public Affairs. © 1973 Board of Regents, The University of Texas. *The Functions of Social Conflict* by L. A. Coser, p. 65. © 1956 The Free Press. Used by permission of the Macmillan Publishing Co., Inc. *Human Behavior: An Inventory of Scientific Findings* by B. Berelson and G. A. Steiner, pp. 150-152, 536, 541, 543, 548. © 1964 Harcourt Brace Jovanovich. *International Encyclopedia of the Social Sciences.* © 1968 Crowell Collier and Macmillan, Inc.: Vol. 3, 246-53, R. A. Falk, "Conflict of Laws," p. 2; Vol. 8, 341-47, E. Cahn, "Justice," p. 344; Vol. 11, 117-120, F. C. Ikle, "Negotiation," p. 120. "Mankind at the Turning Point" by K. E. Boulding, pp. 1188-89, *Science*, vol. 187, 1188-89, 28 Marsh 1975. © 1975 by the American Association for the Advancement of Science. *The Negotiation of Desegregation in Ten Southern Cities* by L. W. Jones and H. H. Long, p. 37. © 1965 Fisk University Library. *Political Violence, The Behavioral Process* by H. L. Nieburg, pp. 9, 80-81. © 1969 St. Martin's Press, Inc. *The Politics of Nonviolent Action* by Gene Sharp, p. 902. Hardback edition, 1973; paperback edition in 3 volumes, 1974. Porter Sargent Publishers, Inc., 11 Beacon Street, Boston, Mass. 02108. "The Problem of Arbitration — the Resolution of Public Sector Disputes," by William Gomberg, p. 413, in *Proceedings of the American Philosophical Society*, vol. 118, No. 5, 1974, originally published by the American Philosophical Society. *Race and Authority in Urban Politics* by J. David Greenstone and Paul E. Peterson (New York: Russell Sage Foundation, 1973) pp. 197, 290, 313, 314. © 1973 Russell Sage Foundation. *The Resolution of Conflict* by M. Deutsch, pp. 267, 352, 378, 386. © 1973 by Yale University. *Resolving Conflict in Africa* by L. W. Doob, p. 2. © 1970 by Leonard W. Doob. *Social Change in a Metropolitan Community* by Otis Dudley Duncan, Howard Schuman, and Beverly Duncan (New York: Russell Sage Foundation, 1973) pp. 102-3. © 1973 Russell Sage Foundation. "Violence and Civic Responsibility: Combinations of 'Fear' and 'Right'" by Tony Duster, p. 5, in *Our Children's Burden, Studies of Desegregation in Nine American Communities*, 1-39, edited by R. W. Mack. © 1968 by Raymond W. Mack, published by Random House, Inc. "What's Wrong with Politics" by Joseph Lee Auspitz and C. W. Brown, pp. 52, 59. © 1974 *Harper's Magazine*, vol. 248, 51-61. "White Students' Evaluation of a Black Student Protest Organization, a Test of a Model," p. 701, *Social Science Quarterly*, 1974, vol. 55, 691-703. © 1974 The University of Texas Press.

Foreword

Americans can no longer be reproached for their lack of a tragic sense. On all sides we are regularly reminded of the awesome disparity between the magnitude of our problems and our uncertain repertoire of countervailing strategies. Who now in the face of recent international felonies, constitutional crises, and chronic unemployment dares speak of an American Century or a Great Society except with irony or despair? The rhetoric of failure is especially marked in discussions about intergroup relations. Since the heroic period of freedom rides, the Montgomery bus boycott, the surrender of George Wallace at the University of Alabama, and other triumphs that preceded the enactment of the Civil Rights Act of 1964 we have witnessed the rediscovery of militant ethnicity, the politics of confrontation, and massive disorders in the cities. At the end of nearly three decades of recurrent crises and intermittent violence many now wonder aloud if free democratic institutions can endure the strain of protracted intergroup conflict. No latter-day H. L. Mencken could easily find current occasion to mock the ingenuous boosterism that once hailed the inevitability of progress.

The prevailing *Zeitgeist* for all its apparent high moral concern and unblinking realism is nevertheless ultimately self-indulgent. Virtuous gloom, no less than Panglossian complacency, is the enemy of understanding and the will to overcome. At bottom, "nothing can be done" and "nothing needs doing" are the same. We are, therefore, beholden to Robin Williams for insisting that the verification of "difficulties, evils, recriminations, liabilities and obstacles" is a necessary, but insufficient, condition for intelligent social diagnosis and

v

action. Accordingly, in the present volume Williams declines to cry havoc and seeks instead to systematize existing knowledge that suggests "workable solutions of problems and avenues of favorable change" in the area of interracial and interethnic relations.

Professor Williams's definition of his task would have been thoroughly congenial to the late Sydney Spivack whose estate established the Cornerhouse Fund, a foundation devoted to social research and social policy, which provided financial support for the current inquiry. Spivack, a gifted sociologist whose own commitment to social justice and cultural pluralism was reflected in his posthumously published study, *The Unequal Elites*, written in collaboration with Robert Althauser, was even more than Williams given to accentuating the positive. Like all men who have absorbed the modern sensibility Spivack was occasionally haunted by frightening visions, but always some combination of historical perspective, broad learning, and direct observation intervened to restore his faith in the capacity of diverse groups in America to reach acceptable modes of mutual accommodation.

Robin Williams's similar brand of qualified optimism has persisted through more than thirty years of grappling with the complexities of intergroup behavior. By common consent he is at once one of the most diligent, sophisticated, and responsible of all sociologists who are active in this field. His propositional inventory, *The Reduction of Intergroup Tensions*, published in 1947 is an acknowledged classic, for it was in this monograph that Williams first revealed his unrivaled talent for converting great masses of data into parsimonious empirical generalizations. These formulations were so impressive because of their respect for evidence, and Williams's reading of more recent data likewise command respect. He is now persuaded that the convergence of increasing minority gains and declining majority recalcitrance offers the real prospect in the short run of a domestic détente and in the long run of something akin to a genuinely pluralistic society based on justice. Some advances by minorities are visible to the naked eye and are confirmed by the statistics of political participation, income distribution, and educational attainment. Thus, for example, a report by the United States Bureau of the Census which was released too late for inclusion in the main body of this book indicates that nearly 1.1 million black students were attending college in the fall of 1976, more than twice the number who were enrolled during the same period in 1970.

Even in the crucial instance of housing where the statistics are least impressive, Williams is able to show that the situation is not altogether bleak "and that there exists a set of feasible possibilities for dealing with questions of housing policy in the late twentieth century." He arrives at this conclusion out of the conviction "that the present extent of involuntary ethno-racial segregation in the United States is unnecessary; that the main causes of discriminatory segregation are known (Harrison, Horowitz, von Furstenberg, 1974) —although not their precise operation; that successful residential integration exists on a substantial scale; that practicable social means are available to establish and maintain effective public policies of open access and residential integration." His analysis implies that to the extent that this comes about, it will profoundly alter other aspects of race relations, such as school integration.

The demonstrable improvement of life chances for minorities does not, of course, necessarily portend approaching racial and ethnic equality—the gap between dominant and victimized groups while narrowing in some institutional sectors may be actually widening in others—and in any event a more equitable distribution of social rewards may temporarily exacerbate rather than lessen intergroup tensions. It was Williams, after all, who was among the first to state the once seemingly anomalous proposition that "a militant reaction from a minority group is most likely when the group's position is rapidly improving." It is less paradoxical and equally true that as De Funis and the Bakke cases demonstrate majorities may choose to resist when they discover that one man's benefit may become another man's cost. Conflict, however, is not a synonym for pathology, and Williams's data encourage us to hope that the recognition of necessity, in concert with changing values and attitudes, as well as increased theoretical and applied knowledge, will restrain any latent tendencies toward a war of all against all. Nearly every chapter of this book refers to instances of "successful" intergroup relations, identifies their preconditions and consequences, and offers wise suggestions ranging from fundamental theoretical postulates to practical tips on how the number of such productive transactions might be increased. Robin Williams's entire career stands as testimony against the remotest suspicion of intellectual or moral arrogance, but he is convinced that we are neither as ignorant nor as depraved as we sometimes pretend.

Racial, religious, and nationalist struggles are not a peculiarly American vice. They have been observed throughout history on every continent, in many nations, in all types of societies, under a variety of ideological auspices. Such antagonisms may not be an intrinsic feature of human interaction but their ubiquity rather suggests that they will not yield readily to Utopian solutions. Now and in the predictable future we shall be obliged to measure our successes against aspirations that can be realized this side of paradise.

"Success" is not, of course, a self-evident concept. Williams will not even discuss the matter without first furnishing us with a "tentative and incomplete inventory" of no fewer than thirty-four criteria for assessing intergroup relationships and processes classified under four major headings: "allocations of scarce values among social categories, statuses, and collectivities;" "personality or psychological status;" "intragroup social structures and relationships;" and "intergroup relations." As Williams notes, the "combinations of these criteria produce a large number of radically different kinds of intergroup situations ranging from 'harmonious mutual assimilation' through 'structural integration' and 'symbiotic coexistence' to the most intense mutual hostility and unlimited violent conflict." Whatever else "success" connotes as between "no one human is foreign to me" and "no one foreign is human to me," there is no contest; but all else is open to definitional controversy. The problem of choice is no little complicated by the fact that success in one domain may entail a defeat in another. It is, therefore, difficult to know what to applaud or deplore, to support or oppose.

The reluctance to acknowledge inherent strains among an array of desired outcomes may lead to much conceptual and existential mischief. It is, for example, both inconsistent and futile to seek the eradication of all prejudice and stereotypy if we also support the proper claim of racial and ethnic groups to their distinctive identities, traditions, and cultures. Only yesterday to be enlightened was to believe that social class composition accounts for all variation in the behavior of racial groups. Black people were vastly overrepresented among the poor and powerless, but except for their racial visibility "they were no different from anybody else." If black is merely a shadow category lacking any independently useful descriptive properties, then in a certain sense there is no such group as blacks and it is manifestly perverse to invent prejudices and stereotypes that incorporate false images about a wholly mythical population.

During the past decade the doctrine of color-blindness which never prevailed as a fact lost all credibility even as a concept. The effort by blacks to achieve political, economic, and social equality was accompanied by legitimate claims to a separate group identity. Blackness was transformed from a meaningless physical distinction to a symbol for a proud history, shared traditions, common practices, strong solidarity, and high art which in their totality comprised a distinctive culture worth nurturing and preserving. Not only was it polite, it was mandatory to notice that black people exist. It follows, then, that if blacks and whites are invited to observe that they differ from one another in some respects, unless each judges the other by the standards of an indiscriminate cultural relativism some group characteristics will be admired and others decried. Moreover, although some negative attributions will be distorted and partisan, others will accurately depict general statistical tendencies. Williams is surely correct when he observes that "two opposing views of intergroup stereotyping and prejudice are in error when taken as exclusive claims to valid interpretation: (a) prejudices and stereotypes, on the whole, are accurate, although generalized, reflections of actual differences ('well-deserved reputation'); (b) prejudices and stereotypes simply are expressions of the values, beliefs, and emotional dispositions of the holders (the outgroup functions as a 'living inkblot')."

The concept of success, then, is always equivocal, and inflated expectations must be constrained by the recognition that advances in intergroup relations are invariably partial and uneven. The perception of limits does not imply passive resignation, and no amount of phenomenological sleight of hand can conceal the ineluctable duty of Americans to provide a more equitable "allocation of scarce values among social categories, statuses, and collectivities." But even on that distant day when our lives are governed by perfect distributive justice, citizens in modern societies will be organized in a variety of groups with conflicting interests. Then, as now, we shall need acceptable modes of mutual accommodation. The distinctive merit of the present volume is that Williams is able to demonstrate how much can be achieved within the limits of the possible.

The extravagance of the more apocalyptic view of interracial and interethnic relations is perhaps best conveyed in Charles Mackay's nineteenth-century classic, *Memoirs of Extraordinary Popular Delusions*. His account of the results of an astrological prediction that the Thames would overflow in 1524 may be read as a parable for our times.

At last the morn, big with the fate of London, appeared in the east. The wondering crowds were astir at an early hour to watch the rising of the waters. The inundation, it was predicted, would be gradual, not sudden; so that they expected to have plenty of time to escape as soon as they saw the bosom of old Thames heave beyond the usual mark. But the majority were too much alarmed to trust to this, and thought themselves safer ten or twenty miles off. The Thames, unmindful of the foolish crowds upon its banks, flowed on quietly as of yore. The tide ebbed at its usual hour, flowed to its usual height, and then ebbed again, just as if the twenty astrologers had not pledged their words to the contrary. Blank were their faces as evening approached, and as blank grew the faces of the citizens to think that they had made such fools of themselves. At last night set in, and the obstinate river would not lift its waters to sweep away even one house out of the ten thousand. Still, however, the people were afraid to go to sleep. Many hundreds remained up till dawn of the next day, lest the deluge should come upon them like a thief in the night.

The burden of Robin Williams's message is that although intergroup relations are frequently turbulent there need be no flood next time. He has surely rendered this judgment more probable by teaching us so much about how we might propitiate the gods.

Marvin Bressler
Princeton University

Preface

This is a book about "successful" intergroup relations—a study of how opposing, and often antagonistic, collectivities sometimes are able to reach what can be regarded as reasonable, constructive outcomes. The very title emphasizes two-sided acceptance.

I hope it will be appropriate to begin with a personal note. My "qualifications" for writing about this subject include what must be a fairly run-of-the-mill life for this—the twentieth—century. Observe some of its historical markers: World War I, the League of Nations, the Era of Permanent Prosperity of the 1920s, the Great Depression, World War II, the Korean War, the turbulent 1960s, the war in Vietnam, and the Watergate years. My first full-time job away from the home farm was that of a laborer in a nonunionized cotton mill in North Carolina in the 1930s; I do not have the heart to tell you the rate of pay—and I was regarded by my peers as fortunate to get the job, for otherwise I could not have made my way through college. During World War II, I was in London during the Little Blitz and then with the U.S. Army infantry as a combat observer for rather extended periods during the drive from Normandy into Nazi Germany. Both the earlier and the later experiences were of high educational value for anyone interested in the range of human capacities for good and evil and for the indefinitely large number of mixtures in between. For present purposes we can skip any other details about this sample individual life history. The point I would like to make is that anyone with an IQ of 75 or more who has lived from 1914 to the present with his or her eyes more or less open is unlikely to be an innocent optimist.

Nevertheless, I had the temerity in the first sentence above to speak of "successful" intergroup relations and of "constructive" outcomes. This behavior is all the more remarkable for a sociologist who has been committed for more than thirty-five years to a scientific viewpoint and to an ethic of objectivity in research. Why do these value-laden terms appear at the very beginning of this book? Is it consistent to introduce such explicit value judgments into an analysis of conflict and cooperation in ethnic relations?

All science is relevant to values, including the most abstract theories and esoteric experiments of physical science. Every choice of a scientific rather than an evaluative (moral, aesthetic, expressive) approach involves a value judgment. Every selection of a problem for study, out of all the problems one might have chosen, involves *preferences* and *criteria* of preference, i.e., values. Every study represents an investment of resources, including the individual's scarcest of all resources: allocation of time within the short span of a human life. All this seems clear and does not require argument here.

Yet all science, including of course social science, is by definition committed to objectivity, to "value-neutrality." The objectivity derives from *methodological* commitments aimed at establishing valid knowledge — knowledge that can be communicated, criticized, and accepted by qualified observers. The aim is to follow a process of seeking knowledge in which sheer preferences or ideologies are formally irrelevant to testing hypotheses and arriving at laws and theories.

There is no inherent incompatibility between scientific objectivity in this sense and the unavoidability of value-commitments. In short, while acting as a scientist the student of any field of phenomena makes a value-commitment to the goals of skepticism, methodological objectivity, and public confirmation within a community of peers who are similarly committed. The results then obtained are objective, if the study is successful. But the selection of the subject will have been influenced by values, and there is no scientific dictum that prohibits us from making value judgments about the uses of the findings or about their possible implications for social policy and action. So much for that brier patch.

But why focus on "mutual adjustment" or "conflict resolution" rather than on mutual destruction, chaotic conflict, total war, or unending terrorism? Several considerations were decisive for the present work. First, the author has spent a great deal of time in empirical research, practical action, and synoptic writing dealing with hostility, prejudice, discrimination, competition, conflict, and violence. Accordingly, the present focus does not neglect or ignore these crucially important topics. Second, the social contributions of the social sciences to *praxis* are not limited to *social criticism* on the one hand or *social justification* on the other. There is a third position that appropriately might be called *social assessment*. Sometimes social assessment has to take the form of rectifying a conspicuous imbalance in available public presentations of data and analysis.

As Orlando Patterson has pointed out, modern social science has devoted much effort to explaining disadvantage and failure, perhaps not nearly so much to accounting for success in overcoming constraints and deficiencies. "Indeed, the reluctance of social scientists to take on the latter problem, in continuing preference for the former, which now approaches the level of explanatory overkill, is rather extraordinary" (Patterson, 1973, 47-48).

In the United States during the 1960s and 1970s there had been evident among societal analysts and commentators a pervasive fascination with malintegration, cleavage, and disaster. This preoccupation was not limited to those radical prophets, of Left or Right, who presented apocalyptic visions in secular forms. Rather, the fixation upon problems, crises, alienation, and the like has been common among observers of nearly every political persuasion and life philosophy. In such a climate of opinion, there may be value in raising the question of whether the New Conventional Wisdom of negative appraisal may not have become unrealistic in its preoccupations. Exclusive concentration on weakness, malfunction, failure, and irreconcilable dissension can lead to errors of judgment perhaps as insidious as those that arise from uncritical optimism. To overlook or persistently minimize positively valued outcomes of relationships among ethnic groupings leaves us without models from which to learn practicable methods of constructive action. To use our social and historical experience to focus only on failures and self-criticism leaves us to base our hopes and construct our plans on untested ideas and conceptions. The simple logic of comparison suggests that we must pay greater attention to our successes—recognize them, examine them, and find out why they worked.

Taking stock of successes as well as failures may be needed also to replenish a very important human resource: hope.

At the least, a concern with "positive" outcomes of intergroup opposition may now be unusual enough to elicit curiosity if not agreement. Let us see what refreshment may be found in following a heretical approach. We propose to examine recent and current experience to discover how it is possible that some intergroup conflicts and oppositional relationships seem to lead to mutual accommodation, or even to new relationships of integrated functioning. To avoid feckless self-deception, if for no other reason, we shall also have to be alert continuously to negative findings, contrary instances, and anomalous outcomes.

Understandably enough, many advocates of increased opportunities, rewards, and rights for ethnic minorities reject any special emphasis upon "success" in intergroup relations. A focus of attention on successful outcomes may seem misplaced, when so much remains to be done and when evidences of discrimination and accumulated disadvantages abound. Attention to gains, successes, constructive solutions—or mutual accommodation—may be perceived as implying that enough has been done, that progress has been so great that further social change is not needed. Accordingly, the focus of this book could appear to advocates of substantial and rapid changes as a diversion or "cop-out," distracting us from uncorrected ills, from urgent problems, and from pressing needs for large-scale and persistent collective action.

Such concerns and apprehensions are not without merit, and they deserve thoughtful appraisal. An uncritical assembling of "success stories" conceivably could encourage attitudes of complacency, benign neglect, or political reaction. But a critical study of the conditions under which mutual accommodation *does* or *does not* occur need not have any such effects or implications. It can keep centrally in view the dangers of unintended selectivity. It can be especially vigilant to detect instances in which incremental success may reduce the likelihood of greater long-term attainments. It can search diligently for negative cases that do not fit its hypotheses. It can continually return to the fact that, from the position of involved participants, conflict often is desirable and success through resolution or compromise is regarded as undesirable. Ultimately, it can redefine success to mean not the absence of or cessation of conflict, but a more dynamic and complex phenomenon of effects and outcomes—made up of short-term and long-term goals, achievements, skills, and attitudes.

The aim here is not to justify either social harmony or social conflict, nor to favor either radical change or the *status quo ante*. Rather, we hope to gain a clearer understanding of *how* and *why* intergroup relations have one or another of the sharply differing outcomes that have been observed.

Acknowledgments

My thanks go in the first instance to The Cornerhouse Fund, Inc. and to its Board of Directors. The Fund, established in memory of Sydney S. Spivack of Princeton University, provided both the initial suggestion that led to this book and the financial support to do the needed research and writing during 1972-1976.

But the work would have been impossible had there not been an earlier period of intensive preparation, made possible by the Russell Sage Foundation and its staff, especially the then-president, Orvill G. Brim, Jr. During 1968-1969 as a Visiting Scholar at the Foundation, I began a long-term study of conflict and social order, from which the present work benefited substantially. The work at the Foundation was facilitated by the excellent secretarial assistance of Betty Bonta and Virginia Glickstein. Discussions with Lindsey Churchill, David G. Goslin, and Walter L. Wallace were important in correcting some of my preconceptions and in providing new insights.

After my return to Cornell University the work benefited from discussions with colleagues, especially Henry Alker, Donald P. Hayes, William W. Lambert, and John M. Roberts. As always, the give and take of classroom discussions with students, both graduate and undergraduate, was immensely valuable. Secretarial assistance of high competence was given by Linda Allen and Judith Kapila.

Penultimate work on the manuscript was carried out during 1974-1975 while I was a Visiting Fellow at the Center for Creative Leadership at Greensboro, North Carolina. My thanks go to the Board of the Center, to its President, John W. Red, Jr., and to Vice President for Research and Program, David P. Campbell. Helpful stimulation and criticism were generously provided by Stuart W. Cook, who was also a Visiting Fellow at the Center. Expert secretarial collaboration was provided by Betty Everhart.

Final revisions during 1975-1976 reduced a typescript of some 1200 pages by more than 50 percent. This gain in economy of exposition was greatly helped along by the detailed reading and perceptive criticisms of Marvin Bressler, Allen D. Grimshaw, Everett Hughes, and J. Milton Yinger. Several anonymous reviewers also contributed criticisms and suggestions. My indebtedness to the intensive and thoughtful assistance of Madelyn B. Rhenisch is only partly indicated by listing her on the title page as collaborator.

Robin M. Williams, Jr.
Ithaca, New York

Contents

Mutual Accommodation

Ethnic Conflict and Cooperation

Chapter 1

It Can Be Done: Recovery from
a National Failure of Nerve

Between 1935 and 1970—essentially within a single generation—the United States dismantled a massive system of racial segregation, abolished an elaborate set of restrictions on immigration, swept away discrimination in access to public facilities, reenfranchised millions of black Americans, and enacted one of the most sweeping set of national laws to be found in any nation concerning civil and political rights of minorities. This astounding record has been overshadowed by a later national mood, compounded by Vietnam and Watergate, of self-recrimination and pessimism. The deprecation of the liberating changes just sketched has come from Left, Right, and Center. We shall not attempt here to go into the historical reasons for the curious discrepancy between an unprecedented record of rapid and basic change and a "failure of nerve" among many who might have been expected to rejoice in the accomplishments. But we do believe that it is now time for the record to be made clear, exceptions to be noted, qualifications to be inventoried, and the causes of the changes to be carefully appraised.

The main focus of this book is upon interracial and interethnic relations. Although at other periods of national history it might have been important to give major attention to interreligious relations, our highest priority at this time must go to analysis of ethnic relations, including those formerly called "race relations." Of course, we shall look also at other types of collective relationships—for example, between unions and business firms, or among subgroups within large organizations—but only when the observations seem likely to illuminate our primary concern. Our reconnaissance will be limited largely to

3

the North American case, although comparative materials will be utilized when they are readily accessible and seem promising as an aid to formulating useful propositions applicable to the United States or to its immediate neighbors (if we may be that cosmopolitan without incurring charges of "imperialism").

The main task before us is to critically review and to extract a reasonable synthesis from the significant findings contained in three large and complex bodies of information: (1) published social science research; (2) other published data and commentaries; (3) unpublished studies; administrative, legislative, and judicial records; and interviews with persons having special knowledge and experience. The nature of the evidence used will be indicated as it is brought forward. In a field so charged with strong feelings and preconceptions, it is essential to use every piece of well-tested factual evidence we can find.

When we try to understand the real causes of changes in intergroup relations, it is of great importance just to know the sheer fact that some particular desirable outcome actually does exist or can be produced by appropriate action. What is judged to be desirable is dictated by our values. But we need first to know the facts. If a desired outcome—an event, such as school desegregation, or a relationship, such as enhanced cooperation, among social groups—exists at all, we know it is *possible*, and all we have to do then is to find out what are the necessary and sufficient conditions to bring it to pass. In short, if it can be made to exist, all we have to do is find out how. If social competition, opposition, or conflict between members of ethnic groupings have desirable consequences, we may want to identify those consequences and then search for the conditions that precede their emergence. If antagonisms sometimes are reduced or eliminated, it is important to document that phenomenon. If social conflicts sometimes are resolved sufficiently to permit mutually acceptable relationships, surely we ought to search out such instances—if only to establish their reality.

It seems essential to include as cases of "positive outcomes" not only instances that are mutually satisfying but also some in which the immediate result is one-sided, with one or more parties feeling blocked or deprived—but in which, over a longer period, the outcome is eventually seen by both sides as constructive. Also, we are including cases of conflict, even massive and violent conflict, if we have reason to conclude that the outcomes have represented a resolution of underlying tensions or of incompatible interests, or have led to changes in social organization, knowledge, skills, and values that reduce the likelihood of future recurrence or the escalation of unproductive conflicts. The latter class of cases will represent the judgment of the sociological analyst; such judgments here will be explicitly labeled.

This chapter is limited to an introductory and informal survey of some examples of intergroup relations and of changes in the circumstances of ethnic minorities in the United States. Some of the facts reviewed have not been widely available, and well-informed persons may be surprised by some of the changes we report in this chapter. We hope so.

1. Evidence of Increased Cosmopolitanism

Our first set of examples of significant changes does, in fact, contradict much of the conventional wisdom of those who see the United States as a "reactionary" and "racist" society. For the evidence is overwhelming that over the years since World War II the people of the United States have become not less, but more tolerant of dissent, diversity, and nonconformity in beliefs, values, and behavior. For example, comparisons of responses to identical questions in surveys conducted in 1954 (Stouffer, 1955) and in 1973 show that willingness to respect civil rights for "deviants" has increased substantially (J. A. Williams, Nunn, Crockette, St. Peter, 1974). Underlying the specific changes in attitudes are more basic transformations in social and cultural characteristics, specifically, increased levels of education, larger proportions of the population living in metropolitan areas, high rates of geographic and social mobility, and continued exposure to cultural diversity.

Data concerning tolerant attitudes are available from 4,433 respondents in the 1954 national samples of S. A. Stouffer's study and from 3,310 respondents in a 1973 national survey of coterminous United States. In the 1973 study, J. Allen Williams and associates developed a single-factor, unidimensional scale of tolerance which has as its underlying dimension a willingness to extend civil rights to various kinds of nonconformists. Analysis of the data indicates that major factors associated with high willingness to tolerate nonconformity include: (1) higher levels of formal education (the most important single variable included in the analysis); (2) residence in metropolitan areas (farm residents were the least tolerant of all residence classes); (3) residence in western states (the South is least tolerant, with Midwest and East intermediate); (4) males (more tolerant than females); and (5) white-collar occupations.

Between 1954 and 1973 there was a large change in the proportion of American adults showing high tolerance: the percentage at the highest step on the scale rose from 17 to 41. The average tolerance increased significantly ($p < .001$). Roughly 59 percent of the increase in tolerance was associated with increased education, city residence, changes in regional distribution, and in sex-occupation distributions.

As people have encountered diversity, in the classroom, the city, on the job, in moving from one region to another, in meeting people from other sections of the nation, they have become more willing to respect the civil liberties of others, even when their ideas challenge long-standing traditions and cherished values (J. A. Williams, Nunn, St. Peter, 1976, 405).

The crucial conditions that produce greater cosmopolitanism in this sense seem to be social and psychological security and exposure to social and cultural diversity.

Consistent with the national surveys are the findings of the Detroit Area Study that between 1958 and 1971 there clearly was a trend toward popular tolerance, as indicated by "a greater willingness to interpret free speech liberally" (Duncan, Schuman, Duncan, 1973, 89-90).

In the 1930s many social scientists and concerned citizens in the United States who watched evidences of rising anti-Jewish attitudes, as Hitlerism spread its power in Europe, would have regarded it as an enormous "success" in intergroup relations to find that anti-Semitic attitudes and behaviors had been checked or reduced. From that perspective, a spectacular case of mutual accommodation and acceptance lies in the fact that between 1944 and the 1960s there were steady and large declines in anti-Jewish orientations (Stember, 1966). By the later 1960s, there was no longer any substantial doubt that the more obvious forms of anti-Jewish prejudice and discrimination had been reduced to very low levels. Old-fashioned racialistic anti-Semitism is nearly extinct, except among small and generally politically ineffectual elements of the population. Even the much publicized tensions between blacks and Jews in New York City constitute only a minor countercurrent, and situational antagonisms rather than deep-seated traditionalized hostilities account for most of the observed frictions.

Changes in Educational Levels and Changes in Ethnocentrism

Although some of the positive correlations between educational level and lowered levels of outgroup antipathies and prejudices must be explained away as the result of other factors, some important effects still must be attributed to the intellectual and social experiences of education as such (Williams, Dean, Suchman, 1964; Bettelheim and Janowitz, 1964; Stember, 1966; Selznick and Steinberg, 1969). In the United States, on the whole, higher levels of formal education are associated with lower rates of outgroup prejudice, regardless of authoritarianism. That is, education has an apparent effect over and above its negative correlation with authoritarian attitudes.

Of course, the influence of formal education is complex and is confounded by effects associated with age, historical period, occupation, income, and other factors. Also, the influence may differ across cultures and national societies. To these complexities we shall return later. For now, the point simply is that recent changes in education in the United States have gone along with reduced levels of ethnic prejudice, although most studies indicate that level of formal education and generalized ethnic attitudes are not closely related. Many other sources of information and evaluation (mass media, peer groups, social authorities, personal interactions, etc.) affect attitudes, and the effects of education may differ with its content, setting methods, and its interaction with the individual's characteristics and history (Ehrlich, 1973, 146-47).

The decreasing level of generalized prejudice has occurred along with consistent decreases in specific stereotypes and negative intergroup attitudes. The society has become less provincial, less bigoted, less intolerant of difference and dissent.

Changes in Attitudes of Whites toward Blacks

It also has become less racist. Over the entire period for which comparable national data are available (1942-68) there has been a marked decline in the proportions of white Americans expressing negative opinions about black Americans or supporting racial discrimination and segregation.

Acceptance by white Americans of the equal ability of Negroes and of equality of rights and opportunity increased greatly over the two decades following World War II. Nation-wide data on change in opinions have been analyzed by Hyman and Sheatsley (1956, 1964), by Schwartz (1967), and by Campbell (1971). Other local studies report similar findings. Thus detailed surveys at the University of Texas in 1955, 1958, and 1964 showed only small change between 1955 and 1958 but a considerable shift to a more positive attitude toward Negroes between 1958 and 1964 (Clore, Holtzman, Young, 1967). A survey of both black and white undergraduates at the University of Maryland showed that except in extremely intimate or racially charged situations (parties, blind dates, civil rights discussions) both blacks and whites preferred integrated situations to situations that were racially homogeneous (Brooks, Merritt, Sedlacek, 1974; Sedlacek, Brooks, Mindus, 1973).

Changes from 1958 to 1971 in attitudes of whites surveyed by the Detroit Area Survey show large and consistent trends toward liberalization, or acceptance of racial integration. The proportion favoring separate schools for white and black students dropped from 33 percent to 17 percent. Large changes were found in responses to the question: "Would you be at all disturbed or unhappy if a Negro with the same income and education as you moved into your block?" Between 1958 and 1971, the proportion saying "Not" rose from 40 to 68 percent. As Duncan, Schuman, and Duncan remark (1973, 99): "Since the housing issue is still a vital one, the movement from majority reservations against such integration to two-thirds acceptance of it represents an important change in white sentiments."

In periods of rapid change in attitudes and behavior, when the formerly tabooed becomes accepted and the formerly consensual becomes moot, a condition of *pluralistic ignorance* often veils the mass changes being made, one-by-one, by separate individuals. A new *aggregate opinion* can form long before awareness of it produces the recognition of a new *public consensus*. The Detroit Area Survey's findings suggest that many white people have adopted attitudes more favorable than before to racial integration, but still believe their fellows to hold the older views. As the investigators put it:

> Thus, public opinion on this racial issue [black and white children playing together] is in advance of what the public *believes* to be public opinion. Moreover, while many are aware of their own changes in attitude, as previously noted, there is a lag in recognition of the collective shift in attitudes (Duncan, Schuman, Duncan, 1973, 102).

We recognize, of course, that pluralistic ignorance works both ways—there can be exaggeration of a "liberal" consensus now, just as there was exaggeration of an earlier racialist consensus. A belief that national attitudes now predominantly reject racial and ethnic discrimination can lead prejudiced individuals to testify to liberal views that their behavior belies. Even were this condition more widespread than it actually is, the shift in perceived norms of acceptable attitudes and behavior has had tangible effects in reducing overt public discrimination and segregation (see Ashmore and Del Boca, 1976; Greenberg and Mazingo, 1976; Hirschhorn, 1976; Rothbart, 1976).

Granting that whites' attitudes have become more favorable in general, can we say the same about blacks? In view of the conflict and turmoil of the last decade, would it not seem that the attitudes of black people must have become more hostile, bitter, intransigent, separatist, and favorable to violence? Does this not bespeak a rejection of white America and a deep alienation from the total society?

Again the Detroit Area Survey provides a useful point of departure. The accompanying tabulation shows changes, 1968 and 1971, in opinions of blacks about the political use of violence (Duncan, Schuman, Duncan, 1973, 110). Other findings from these studies show changes toward greater distrust of whites and increased preference for associating with other blacks. Yet the "No" responses to the question, "If our country got into a big World War today, would you personally feel the United States is worth fighting for?" actually dropped from the already small 13 percent in 1968 to 8 percent in 1971. Numerous points of dissatisfaction and grievance exist, but do not summate into anything like total alienation. Similar findings (that also depict complex ambivalence in various attitudes) characterized Black Harlem in 1973 (Bowser, 1975). Some data, from small samples, show that whites predict

Opinions on the Use of Violence (Black Respondents)

	Percentage Distribution	
	1968	*1971*
As you see it, what's the best way for Negroes to try to gain their rights?		
Use laws and persuasion	30	39
Use nonviolent protest	64	49
Be ready to use violence	6	12
(Asked only of those not saying violence to the preceding question)		
If (laws and persuasion/nonviolent protest) don't work, then do you think Negroes should be ready to use violence?		
Yes	22	44
No	78	56

fairly well blacks' responses in ranking fourteen goals of social action, but that the blacks' estimates of whites' ranking corresponded only to those made by the racially prejudiced whites (Wilson, 1970).

The changes in popular attitudes we have reviewed have been accompanied by substantial shifts in the way ethnic and racial minorities have been treated in the mass media.

Changes in Stereotypes and Mass Media Images

As one example of the "small" changes that if multiplied and cumulated can produce a qualitatively new cultural atmosphere, we note that by the early 1970s changes in ethnic emphases in children's textbooks had themselves become newsworthy—for example:

Books for Black Children Increasing

Washington. —To write for children you must think as children do and see things through their eyes. To write for black children living in tenements, well . . . 'You know how it be in the summer, all hot. Everybody be sittin' around in the stoop. We be playin' out in the street. Me and my friends. I gotta lot of friends.'

The passage is from a book for 8- to 12-year-olds by artist-illustrator John Steptoe called 'Train Ride,' published in 1971 by Harper and Row.

Steptoe, 23, is among a growing number of black writers, some new and some established, concentrating on stories about—and for—black children.

As a result of the attention being paid by these authors, librarians, teachers and book buyers report that black children now have a range of books to read that was nonexistent 10 years ago.

In the years immediately after the start of the civil rights movement, a number of books, some of dubious quality, were aimed at black youngsters.

Today the number is not significantly higher, remaining at about 10 percent of the total children's book production. Some even claim there has been a decline. But book buyers generally say that while fewer books are published now, they are better and competition among authors is stiffer. . . .

The gamut of black children's literature includes a book of verse by Pulitzer prizewinning poet Gwendolyn Brooks; a collection of folk tales by Julius Lester called 'Knee High Man and Other Tales'; a group of biographies featuring musicians and political figures; books with African themes, including works by Muriel Feelings and 'All Us Come Cross the Water', written by Baltimore poet Lucille Clifton and illustrated by Steptoe; Virginia Hamilton's fantasies written from a black cultural perspective; stories set in urban neighborhoods; and 'Harriet and the Promised Land', an illustrated narrative about Harriet Tubman by Jacob Lawrence.

There is a mixture of language styles and a definite assertion that those black children who say 'you know how it be' and spend their summer 'in the street' should not feel ashamed of their language or lifestyle; nor, the new writers say, should subjects for children and young adults be limited to the world of Dick and Jane, 'Run, Spot, Run', or the prom date dilemma (Manns, 1973).

As early as 1956 it was suspected that much of the acceptance of racial and ethnic stereotypes reported in various earlier studies had been in part an artifact of the research methods employed, e.g., forced-choice questions and objective checklists that preempted the respondent's freedom to choose a different frame of reference. Above all, the *specific* object of reference often was not clearly designated: rather, white people were asked, for example, to characterize "Negroes." When only the one further characterization of "upper-class" or "lower-class" was added, the apparent stereotyping changed radically. Studies in the mid-1950s showed that whites to some extent stereotyped "lower-class Negroes" as superstitious, ignorant, lazy, and happy-go-lucky — but the same respondents also designated lower-class whites by the same terms. And the white respondents did not attribute stereotypic labels to upper-class blacks—instead such individuals were characterized as intelligent, ambitious, industrious, neat, and the like. Stereotypes, in short, were more closely related to class position than to racial category (Bayton, McAlister, Hamer, 1956).

Marked changes have occurred in the ethnic images conveyed by books, magazines, newspapers, radio, television, motion pictures, and theatre (Cox, 1970). Books of fiction for children today show little negative stereotyping of blacks (Gast, 1967), in contrast to the patterns of a generation ago. In the mass media, black people now appear far more often than in the 1940s and 1950s and the imagery is generally positive (Colle, 1967; Hyman and Reed, 1969). For example, blacks are no longer typically portrayed in unskilled occupations, roles attributed to blacks are more diversified, and black persons are shown as "belonging" in contexts of approval, prestige, and respect. Some of the increasing proportion of favorable images, however, do repeat stereotypes, e.g., of blacks as athletes and entertainers (Karlins, Coffman, Walters, 1969; Maykovitch, 1972; Edwards, 1973, Chapter 7). There is an increased demand for intellectual and artistic productions of black Americans—poetry, drama, music, novels, scholarly works, films (Simpson and Yinger, 1972, Chapter 20).

As the occupational distribution of blacks has changed, a separation of race-linked and class-linked images has become clearer. In television advertising there has been a sharp increase since 1967 in the number of blacks shown, but many still appear in background roles or in "token" numbers. On the other hand, in dramatic offerings the increase in number of blacks has been accompanied by a decrease in token appearances. The giving and receiving of orders between whites and blacks in dramatic roles has equalized at a 50-50 ratio. The record of television shows a remarkable shift toward integrating black persons into both advertising and programming (Greenberg and Mazingo, 1976, 326).

Some stereotypes and prejudicial evaluations are primarily transmitted as taken-for-granted cultural items that are neither heavily invested with emotional commitment nor felt to be essential to the maintenance of vested interests. (An example might be the belief that Italian is a "musical" language or a belief that Eskimos are relatively insensitive to cold.) If such beliefs and evaluations are diffusely disseminated from a few central sources, it may be possible to quickly stop the perpetuation by a focused effort that appeals to or threatens stronger interests. Rapid change in the content of children's textbooks provides a recent fairly important case in point. With a small expenditure of resources, women's organizations have stimulated massive revisions of public school textbooks by major publishing companies, to remove stereotyped treatments of women's roles. Protests and the filing of complaints quickly brought considerable and favorable publicity. Departments of education joined in urging review of instructional materials. Textbook publishers hastened to fall into line. A news story in 1974 noted the similarity between these developments and efforts of a decade earlier to deal with ethnic stereotyping.

Groups Seek Removal of Sexual Stereotypes from Children's Books

Washington.—Prodded by complaints from women's organizations and school systems, the nation's major textbook companies are beginning a massive overhaul of their reading material and illustrations to remove sexual stereotypes from their products.

In scores of studies in school districts from Virginia to California, women's groups have surveyed textbooks and found them to be replete with stories and illustrations depicting women in demeaning and degrading postures.

Many texts, it was found, minimized women's roles by showing females in a limited number of situations—'fairy godmothers, meter maids, housekeepers, teachers and wicked queens' in an Alexandria, Va. study —while others tended to ignore women altogether. . . .

. . . with increasing frequency, the nation's school systems are notifying publishers that their material will not be purchased if nothing is done about stereotypes and biases.

The issue is similar, many publishers say, to demands that arose about 10 years ago for fair treatment of minorities in texts (Raleigh (N.C.) Times, October 18, 1974).

Thus we find that the main changes in attitudes and opinions of the American people and in the messages of the mass media since World War II have reflected greater intergroup acceptance and general cosmopolitanism. But could all these changes be little more than mere lip service? To what extent has actual behavior been consistent with testimony? A first major piece of evidence is the record of national policies and practices concerning immigration. Has the United States become more exclusionist and discriminatory or more accepting and cosmopolitan?

Acceptance of Immigration

Almost unnoticed, apparently, by the general American public during the acrimonious 1960s was the revision of immigration laws of the United States to remove racial and nationality discriminations long embedded in earlier restrictive legislation. As a consequence of the liberalized regulations stemming from the Immigration Act of 1965, the absolute size of immigration was increased and is now the largest of any modern nation. The effects are massive:

... the United States is quietly but rapidly resuming its role as a nation of first- and second-generation immigrants, almost the only one of its kind in the world, incomparably the largest, and for the first time in our history or any other, a nation drawn from the entire world. The Immigration Act of 1965 drastically altered the shape of American immigration and increased its size.... Our immigrants in wholly unprecedented proportions come from Asia, South America, and the Caribbean. (In fiscal year 1973 the ten top visa-issuing posts were Manila, Monterrey, Seoul, Tijuana, Santo Domingo, Mexico City, Naples, Guadalajara, Toronto, Kingston....

In short, by the end of the century, given present trends, the United States will be a multi-ethnic nation the like of which even we have never imagined (Moynihan, 1974, 30).

A Little Quiz Follows

Question: What 44-year-old policy was ended by the Immigration Act of 1965?
Answer: The Act decisively ended the policy of using *national origins* as a major criterion for admitting immigrants. It thereby abolished the *selectively restrictive* policy that started with the Chinese Exclusion Acts of the 1880s (Keeley, 1974, 587).

Question: What proportion of current population growth in the United States is due to immigration? Check one:

    ____ 1-4
    ____ 5-9
    ____ 10-14
    ____ 15-19
    ____ 20-24
    ____ 25 or more

Answer: About 20 percent (as of 1974) (Keeley, 1974, 587-88).

Question: About how many legal, permanent immigrants were admitted to the United States in 1973? Check one:

    ____ Less than 100,000
    ____ 100,000-199,999
    ____ 200,000-299,999
    ____ 300,000-399,999
    ____ 400,000-499,999
    ____ 500,000 or more

Answer: More than 400,000 (Keeley, 1974, 589).

From 1921 to 1965 the United States followed a policy of highly restrictive immigration using national origin as a major criterion for admitting immigrants. The formula heavily favored northern and western Europe and discriminated especially against the Asian-Pacific triangle. The Immigration Act of 1965 abolished quotas based on national origins and ended racialist discriminations. The result has been a dramatic increase in numbers and a change in the composition of immigrants. At the average annual inflow for 1966-73, the total legal permanent immigration will amount to about 3,774,000 for a decade.[1]

Reduced Barriers between Religious and Racial Groupings

In the late 1960s and early 1970s many books and articles pointed to a rising tide of ethnic consciousness, ethnic solidarity, and ethnic militancy in the United States. Meanwhile, the Detroit Area Survey showed that between 1958 and 1971 dependence upon religious membership or background as a basis for friendships and choice of marriage partners decreased, especially among Catholics. Furthermore, for Protestants, Jews, and Catholics the proportion whose friends were actually all drawn from the same faith-grouping decreased significantly (Duncan, Schuman, Duncan, 1973, 63-65).

The acceptance of interracial marriages has increased dramatically since the 1950s, although the numbers of black-white marriages are still very small (around 2 percent of marriages involving black persons as of 1975). Both the favorability of public opinion and the actual frequency of interfaith marriages have increased greatly during the last few decades.

Success in Bilingualism

Many English-speaking North Americans regard learning a second language as a difficult and stressful task, and some feel that bilingualism either is unattainable or represents a threatening and mysterious process. But many Europeans and Asians learn two or more languages as a "natural" part of growing up and do not thereby experience any sense of threat to their cultural identity or social effectiveness.

A program using French as the main language of instruction (from kindergarten through grade 7) for children of English-speaking parents in Quebec, begun in 1965, has demonstrated that bilingual competence can be attained without detriment to cognitive development or academic progress in subject-matter fields. Furthermore, the children consider themselves both English and French and have more understanding and friendly attitudes toward French-speaking people than children in matched control groups. Similar results have been found for ten-year-old French-Canadian monolinguals and bilinguals from comparable socioeconomic and home backgrounds (Lambert and Tucker, 1973).

We have reviewed a small set of examples of the evidence which shows that narrow ethnocentrism and rigid outgroup discrimination is not inevitable and that, in fact, very important changes toward greater universalism-in-diversity have occurred in recent American history. What are the basic conditions that make such changes possible?

2. Shifts in Social Structure

Back of changes in intergroup relations lie changes which initially may have had nothing at all to do with intergroup relations as such—basic changes in technology, in modes of economic production and distribution, in population concentrations and movements, in urban forms, and in characteristics of the main institutions. In the United States, the societal setting for collective harmony or conflict has been basically altered since the turn of the century by massive changes in *social organization, energy utilization, transportation, settlement patterns, migration, economic productivity, patterns of employment*, and related conditions.

Thus changes in economic opportunity created enormous "pushes" and "pulls" which have been primarily responsible for metropolitan concentration and for the movement of millions of immigrants into the nation and of the great shift of black Americans from the rural South to the urban North. Changes in transportation costs which at first had favored the concentration of economic enterprises in central cities later encouraged industrial and commercial location in outer zones.

Many changes in intergroup relations, then, are due not to direct effects of actions intended to influence those relations but to indirect, unintended (and usually unanticipated) effects of actions undertaken for quite different reasons and under the influence of considerations far removed from race and ethnicity.

With regard to any large-scale social change, the only reasonable expectation has to be that some consequences will be desired and some will be undesired by the people who are affected. It would be a limiting case of the most unusual sort were everyone without exception to be benefited or harmed or to experience the same mixture of goods and bads. Heterogeneity of stimuli and diversity of outcomes are normal.

When change is the result of a purposive societal program, accordingly, we can make responsible assessments only by carefully specifying in particular cases what inputs were at work to generate different kinds of outcomes. In the case of the post-1955 racial desegregation of the public schools, the dictum has been repeatedly and vividly illustrated. As Pettigrew says:

No responsible observer ever claimed that *all* interracial schools would be 'good' schools. It takes little imagination to design desegregated schools that are living hells for both black and white pupils. The question, then, is not: Do *all* interracial schools work well? The key questions, neatly skirted by Armor and other political foes of biracial education, are: How do we make interracial schools effective? And what are the discernible differences now between effective interracial schools and ineffective ones?

The racial desegregation of schools is not a static but a complex, dynamic process. One must search for the critical conditions under which the process seems to be most beneficial for all students (Pettigrew, 1974, 381).

With these cautions in mind, let us examine the tangible changes in racial and ethnic relations represented by efforts to do away with categorical segregation and discrimination.

3. Reductions in Segregation and Discrimination

Desegregation of the Public Schools

At the time of the *Brown* decision in 1954, the proportion of black pupils who attended school with whites in the southern states was less than one-tenth

Table 1.1. Changes in Proportions of Black Pupils Attending Public Schools Who Were in Schools with White Pupils, 1954-72.

Year	Percentage in Schools with Whites, 17 Border and Southern States	Percentage in Majority-White Schools	
		11 Southern States	32 Northern and Western States
1954	Less than .001		
1960	6.4		
1961	7.0		
1962	7.6		
1963	8.0		
1964	9.2		
1965	10.9		
1966 (Dec.)	15.9		
1966	25.8[a]		
1968	39.6[b]	32.0 (est.)	
1970	84.3[b]	40.3[c]	27.6[c]
1972	91.3[c]	46.3[c]	28.3[c]

Note: Changes in reporting procedures have made it difficult to construct a continuous series of comparable data (see *Southern Education Report*, Vol. 4, December 1968, pp. 11-13).

[a]Data for 1954 through 1966: Southern Education Reporting Service, 1967. *Statistical Summary* 1967.

[b]*Statistical Abstract of the United States*, 1973, p. 121, Table 186.

[c]*Statistical Abstract of the United States*, 1975, p. 127. Also consulted: *Digest of Educational Statistics*, 1975, p. 186, Table 180.

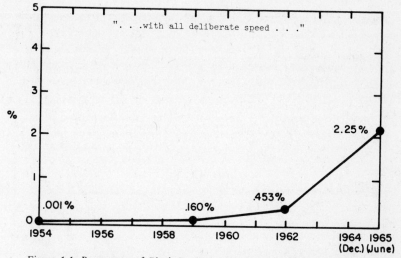

Figure 1.1. Percentage of Black Pupils in Schools with Whites, 11 Southern States, 1954-65. *Source:* Southern Education Reporting Service. 1964. *Statistical Summary*, pp. 67-70.

of 1 percent. Ten years later it had moved with glacial speed to approximately 2 percent (Table 1.1 and Figure 1.1). The Supreme Court's phrase enjoining desegregation "with all deliberate speed" frequently was quoted with bitterness by advocates of "obedience to law" who called for immediate compliance with the 1954 decision and with the implementing decree of May 1955. But then Congress passed the Civil Rights Act in 1964 and the Voting Rights Act in 1965, followed by strong "guidelines" from the Department of Health, Education, and Welfare that tied federal aid to compliance with desegregation programs. Immediately the proportion of black pupils in desegregated schools skyrocketed, from 2 percent in 1964 to 15 percent in 1966. This remarkable rise continued—from 18 percent in 1968 to an astronomical 46 percent in 1973 (Figure 1.2). (Meanwhile, the comparable proportion in the North and West remained at a constant 28 to 29 percent.)

By the fall of 1970 a greater proportion of black children in the South than in the North attended majority-white schools (38 percent versus 28 percent) (Pettigrew, 1974). The magnitude of the social and psychological changes represented by this fact can only be appreciated against the background of more than a decade of massive and strident resistance to desegregation, from the *Brown* decision in 1954 until after the Voting Rights Act of 1965. As Table 1 and Figure 2 suggest, by the 1970s official desegregation in the South was so complete that the proportion of "blacks in schools with whites" (91 percent) was no longer a meaningful figure. Highly meaningful, however, are the data showing the proportion in majority-white schools (Figure 1.3). The

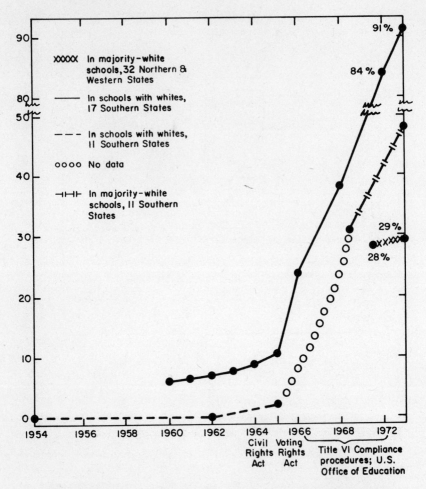

Figure 1.2. Changes in Proportions of Black Pupils Attending Public Schools Who Were in Schools with White Pupils, 1954-72. *Source:* Table 1.1.

very large and rapid changes in the South since 1965 stand out sharply against the nearly static North and West.

Desegregation sometimes resulted in violence, but usually in eventual accommodation. Children who attended genuinely desegregated schools generally did not perform less well and often improved in achievement. The basic findings from the most careful and representative studies of integration and desegregation in the 1950s and 1960s showed that blacks attending school with whites had higher levels of attainment in education, occupational status,

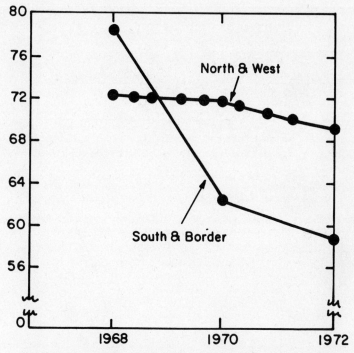

Figure 1.3. Percentage of Black Pupils Who Were in Schools with a Majority of Blacks. *Source:* Levitan, Johnson, and Taggart. 1975. *Still a Dream*, Table 13-1, p. 280.

and income than black pupils in segregated schools (Crain and Weissman, 1972). Blacks who attended nonsegregated schools also had less negative attitudes toward white people. (In Chapter 3 we review the more recent evidence from a large number of studies.)

In lieu of any extensive presentation of data at this early point in our survey, we present the following example of successful change in an initially unpromising setting.

A Vivid Case of the Effects of Desegregation in Higher Education

Analysis of social distance attitudes of white students at the University of Alabama—where highly publicized political resistance to desegregation had been played out in the immediate past—showed that between 1963 and 1969 great increases occurred in acceptance of black students. Each cohort of entering freshmen showed greater acceptance than its predecessor, and each cohort gained even more greatly from year to year while attending the integrated university (Muir, 1971). At the very least, therefore, whatever interpersonal contacts occurred between blacks and whites did not have negative effects. The increased acceptance by incoming freshmen conceivably could be due to pervasive changes in the environing society – changes that merely continued to influence whites while in college, as they had influenced their prior attitudes. But the gains from year to year were greater after entrance to the university than the gain between successive matriculating classes. Within the college setting white students surely were clearly aware of the presence of black students, and there must have been at least casual interactions. It is reasonably safe to infer, therefore, that the net effort of whatever contacts took place must have been more positive than not.

Residential Areas: Evidence of Interracial Accommodation

The most comprehensive nation-wide study of segregation and integration of residential neighborhoods, based on 8,500 field interviews, has concluded that where Negroes had occupational and educational characteristics similar to whites, the hostility or resistance of whites was greatly reduced (Bradburn, Sudman, Gockel, 1970).

A generalized hypothesis that closely corresponds to the particular finding is: "The more similar an outgroup is in customs, values, beliefs, and general culture, the more liked it will be" (LeVine and Campbell, 1972, 177).

A study of relatively high-income black families who have been barrier breakers by moving into previously all-white suburban areas of Los Angeles compared these integrated families with those of similar income and education who were living in the central black ghetto. Although the matching of socio-economic levels was not exact, reasonably well-controlled comparisons show that ghetto-dwellers were significantly more likely than the migrants to express feelings of powerlessness and of "anomia" (hopelessness, distrust, pessimism, sense of unreliability and unresponsiveness of the society). The data suggest that at similar levels of education and income, alienation (sentiments of powerlessness and detached pessimism) tends to restrict movement into integrated residential areas: nonalienated persons more often showed persistence in repeatedly seeking to move out of the segregated area. Thus segregation (Lieberson, 1963; Taeuber and Taeuber, 1965; Kantrowitz, 1973), which tends to produce alienation, is perpetuated by the alienative orientations within ghetto-like areas (Bullough, 1967). A further possibility is that movement of black people out of central-city ghettos into white suburbia will remove primarily not only those of higher income and education, but also the more hopeful and self-confident people – leaving behind the more alienated (and, probably, most hostile).

But to appraise carefully the developments that are affecting the possibilities and limitations of residential racial mixing requires that we try to see a total pattern among the most important facts concerning recent changes in the distribution of blacks and whites in central cities and suburbs (Glazer, 1974). Any single aspect of the situation may give a misleading impression if viewed in isolation (Hawley and Rock, 1973).

(1) The proportion of blacks in the total suburban population declined slightly from 1960 to 1970, while the percentage of whites increased greatly. In the central cities, the percentage of blacks increased greatly.

(2) But the absolute number of blacks living in suburbs has increased greatly: from 2.2 million in 1950 to 3.7 million in 1970.

(3) The total figures conceal enormous diversity from suburb to suburb and from one metropolitan area to another. Between 1960 and 1970, of the twelve metropolitan areas containing the largest numbers of blacks, nine showed a more rapid increase of black than of white suburban population.

(4) Blacks in the suburbs as compared with those residing in central cities have higher incomes and occupational status, more home ownership, and a smaller proportion of female-headed households.

(5) Further, within the large central cities there has been an absolute economic upgrading of the black population and a movement of black households into the areas from which whites are moving. From 1960 to 1970 the index of segregation *declined* in 103 of 109 cities—in contrast to the 1950-60 trend which had shown increases in 45 of those cities.

(6) Surveys of national samples show rapid decreases since the mid-1960s in the proportion of whites and blacks reporting that their neighborhoods are all-white or all-black.

(7) Although racial integration appears to be most easily accomplished when both blacks and whites are of similar and relatively high socioeconomic status (Mussen, O'Hanlon, Winkel, 1974; Zeul, 1976), some low-income housing projects have been successfully introduced into middle-income residential areas.

(8) A substantial minority of the white population—from one-fifth (Bradburn, Gockel, Sudman, Noel, 1971)[2] to one-third (Schwartz, 1967)[3]—live or have lived in close proximity to blacks.

(9) In a tight housing market, both blacks and whites who move into integrated suburbs make their housing choices primarily on financial and other nonracial grounds. Even prejudiced whites report that the racial composition of a (middle-income) suburban area is of secondary importance (Zeul, 1976).

The ensemble of these varied pieces of information indicates that although residential segregation is still massive, it is becoming less rigid. "Black" no

longer automatically means "poor." Legal changes have made overt discrimination illegal in housing rental or sale. Some suburbs are becoming mixed and
some stable integrated neighborhoods have developed (Zeul, 1976). By and
large—with many local exceptions and with fluctuations through time—white
attitudes have changed in the direction of lessened resistance to residential
integration. Between 1964 and 1974 the proportion of whites in a national
sample who described their neighborhood as all-white declined from 80 percent
to about 60 percent (and the proportion who favored "strict segregation" in
all areas of life dropped from about 25 percent to 10 percent). The proportion
of white persons who said that black persons should have the right to move
into any neighborhood they could afford rose from 65 to 87 percent (*Institute
for Social Research Newsletter*, 1975, Fall 4).[4]

Additional evidence and additional complexities will be examined in
Chapter 4. For the moment it is enough to show that residential integration,
although difficult, is by no means an impractical societal objective.

Desegregation of the Armed Services

The Armed Services of the United States moved from total segregation to
substantial integration in less than a decade. Desegregation was accompanied
and followed by improved military performance of blacks, more favorable
attitudes of whites toward integration, and a limited but significant amount
of increased career mobility for blacks. The shift in attitudes toward racial
integration (see accompanying tabulation) was large and rapid (Moskos, 1966,
140). Off-duty association and friendships, however, remained primarily in the
pattern of racial separation, and considerable conflict continues to exist. Integration is most complete and most easily accepted in formalized, functionally
specific, task-oriented settings. Acceptance, especially in the early phases,
was facilitated by the highly patterned, hierarchical system of command and
deference—both because of the strict control exercised through continuous
monitoring and through the threat of negative sanctions, and because of the
impersonal procedures for maintaining fixed social distance between ranks.

*Change, 1943-51, in Percentage Opposed
to Integration in the Army*

	1943	1951	Difference
White soldiers . . .	84	44	– 40
Black soldiers	36	4	– 32

Desegregation of Public Facilities and Amenities

It is easy to forget how rapid and dramatic in their time and place were
some of the changes produced by the Civil Rights movement. On February 1,

1960, four black students sat-in at a lunch counter in a Woolworth store in Greensboro, North Carolina. By March, sit-ins had spread to Alabama, Florida, Georgia, Lousiana, South Carolina, Tennessee, Texas, and Virginia. On March 15, lunch counters were desegregated in San Antonio; Galveston follow-ed on April 5. Segregation at lunch counters was abandoned by many towns and cities during the following three years; included were the major urban centers of Atlanta, Dallas, Durham, Memphis, New Orleans, Oklahoma City, and Savannah. Conflict was frequent. By 1963 a series of court decisions, culminating in the Supreme Court, clearly established that the State laws requiring racial segregation in public accommodations were unconstitutional. In 1964 the Civil Rights Act was passed by Congress; among other major pro-visions it specifically forbade discrimination in most public accommodations (Title II). The constitutionality of Title II was unanimously upheld by the Supreme Court on December 15, 1964.

In this manner a *massive, legally enforced system* of segregation and dis-crimination was dismantled in just under five years.

An often-repeated argument against legal and other restraints on discrimi-natory behavior is that real change can occur only if there is fundamental change "in the hearts and minds of men." We shall return to this contention in some detail later. It is enough for now to observe that situational constraints and incentives no doubt are guided and limited by the beliefs, values, and attitudes of individuals. But numerous instances clearly demonstrate that sub-stantial changes in specific patterns of behavior can and do occur before basic shifts in stereotypes and sentiments. For example, in Washington, D.C. the desegregation of restaurants was carried out suddenly and without any prior efforts to educate the public over a period of time. Nothing was said about changing the hearts and minds of the white population. Rather there simply was a new legal situation in which it was no longer permissible to refuse service to black persons. A massive change in norms and expectations occurred very quickly. Restaurant proprietors and employees were required to change their behaviors; white customers quickly accepted the new order. A deep-seated and pervasive change in attitudes was not mandated, but a highly important change in public behavior occurred with remarkable speed (Martin and Franklin, 1973, 193).

Political Participation

Perhaps even more striking than the desegregation of public facilities have been the changes of the last twenty-five years in political rights and political behavior. In the period just before World War II, blacks throughout the South were almost completely disenfranchised—the minuscule fragment of some 250,000 black persons who were registered as voters constituted about 5 per-

Table 1.2. Black Voter Registration in 11 Southern States

Year	Number Registered	Estimated Percentage of Those of Voting Age
1940 . . .	250,000	5
1944 . . .	(Smith v. Allwright)[a]	NA
1947 . . .	595,000	12
1952 . . .	1,008,614	20
1956 . . .	1,238,038	25
1960 . . .	1,414,052	28
1964 . . .	1,907,279 (Civil Rights Act)	38
1965 . . .	(Voting Rights Act)	NA
1966 . . .	2,657,413	53
1968 . . .	3,112,000	62
1970 . . .	3,357,000	65

Sources: U.S. Commission on Civil Rights, 1968. Political Participation. Washington, D.C.: U.S. Government Printing Office, 256 pp.; U.S. Bureau of the Census, 1975. Statistical Abstract of the United States, 1975, 1050 pp., pp. 449-52.

[a]Decision of U.S. Supreme Court, April 3, ruling that white primaries were unconstitutional when required to follow state procedures.

cent of the adult black population. Gradual gains had brought the level to 38 percent by 1964 (See Table 1.2). With the initial implementation of the Civil Rights Act of 1964 and the Voting Rights Act of 1965, the proportion leaped to 53 in 1966, and 65 by 1970. In the single decade of the 1960s, the proportion of the potential black voters in the South actually registered more than doubled—from less than one-third to two-thirds. This was not a "Revolution" but it was a change so massive and so important in its implications that informed observers in the early 1900s would have thought it very nearly impossible. By 1970 the percentages of blacks in southern states registered to vote were only slightly below the figures for the United States as a whole. And in August 1975 the Voting Rights Act was enlarged in scope and extended for an additional seven years.

The effects of legislated reenfranchisement and subsequent enforcement and political pressures soon were reflected in elective office-holding by blacks (Figure 1.4). It is estimated that in 1964 there were some 70 black elected officials in the entire United States; by 1969 there were just under 1,200 black elected officials; the number then doubled in three years; and by 1975 there were 3,503 such officials. The number is disproportionately small as compared with white office-holders, but the rate of gain is evidence of a rapid change in underlying conditions. By 1973 it was possible for a black candidate to become mayor of a metropolis in the Deep South: Maynard Jackson defeated

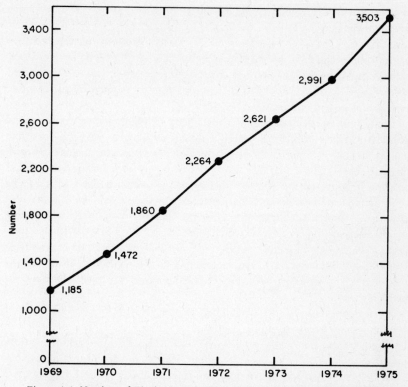

Figure 1.4. Number of Black Elected Officials in the United States, 1969-75.
Source: U.S. Bureau of the Census. 1975. *Statistical Abstract of the United States, 1975.* Washington, D.C.: U.S. Government Printing Office. 1050 pp., Table 725, p. 449.

the white incumbent in Atlanta by receiving 20 percent of the vote in white areas as well as overwhelming support from black areas. In 1974 a total of 94 blacks held office in southern legislatures.

The growth in the number of black elected officials is obvious, but some observers may doubt that the increase in office-holding "makes any real difference." The evidence runs against the pessimists. Intensive research on black and white elected officials in sixteen New Jersey cities concludes that the election of blacks does make a difference in the political and administrative behavior of local communities—including the establishment of the legitimacy of blacks holding office (Cole, 1976, 221-22).

The stereotype of blacks as inactive or "apathetic" in civic and political realms initially found some base of reality in two massive circumstances: (1)

In most parts of the country before the 1960s blacks were *prohibited* from such activities either by legal barriers or by intimidation; (2) Rural residence, low education, and low income are all associated with low political and associational participation among blacks or whites. With growth in education, income, and urbanity – and with decreased discrimination – and with increased ethnic consciousness, solidarity, and pride – it could happen that the stereotype would be demolished. So it has been.

Studies of participation and involvement in voluntary associations and political affairs before 1965 typically found less activity among blacks than among whites, except for church-related activities. But later analysis, controlling for socioeconomic status, showed that at any given status-level blacks were *more* active than whites (Orum, 1966). A more intensive analysis, using information for adults in the Indianapolis metropolitan area, 1967-68, showed that (when properly equated for SES) *participation was consistently higher for blacks than for whites* on some fifteen measures (Olsen, 1970). Furthermore, comparisons with earlier (1957) data from Detroit indicate that activity levels may have increased, even discounting changes in SES. Finally, blacks who identify themselves with the ethnic community are especially likely to be highly active.

The significance of the heightened participation for minorities lies not only in greater access to political influence but also in the increased sense of involvement and efficacy it can bring. The significance for the majority groupings is that the minorities become a more significant element that necessarily must be taken into account in shaping collective decisions. As Representative Yvonne Brathwaite Burke (D., Calif.) has emphasized, the fact that 26 percent of the Democratic votes in the 1972 presidential election were cast by blacks is not something that national political leaders can ignore (Burke, *Focus*, 1976).

The representatives of the dominant majority of the economic and political elites of the nation repeatedly have had their own beliefs and values profoundly shaped by the pressures and claims of aspiring minorities. The processes have been powered by the successive demands of excluded ethnic groups and social strata for political expression and power and for educational and economic attainments and rewards. The result was not simply that an unchanged Establishment eventually opened the doors to successive claimants. Rather, the very concepts, values, and social norms of the Establishment were altered.

Above all, the incorporation of new elements into the middle and upper classes encouraged commitments to standardized universalistic criteria of membership and merit. The crucial principle of citizenship in contrast to "group rights" is that of universalistic rights of individuals (Porter, 1976, 298). Citizenship was linked to knowledge and explicit political commitment. Education increasingly meant passing objective tests and acquiring impersonally attested information. Occupational opportunity, the doctrines held, should be available on the basis of *merit*. But merit often had been defined hitherto in terms of particularistic relations and of intuitive judgments of "character," judgment, promise, and the like. Such judgments were now suspect as contaminated by sheer prejudice and entrenched privilege. More objective indicators of merit, accordingly, were sought: IQ tests, job aptitude tests, merit rating scales, standardized examinations.

What was sought, in short, was a system of universalistic criteria that could be used to justify and legitimate a new meritocracy. So complete was the victory of such nominal criteria that we developed a "certification society"—an elaborate system of test taking and official labeling of types and degrees of formal achievement. The last great breakthrough in the ethnic sector was the opening of the system to Jews, after the 1930s, and to Japanese-Americans after 1945,[5] and to several other ethnic minorities in the 1940s and 1950s. Over the first quarter-century after World War II, the result was to facilitate the upward movement of individuals of diverse social origins into relatively high social locations. Indeed:

> A major, unremarked achievement of the postwar era has been the broadening of the national elite. Instead of a relatively small, white, Eastern-oriented, Anglo-Saxon, Protestant leadership class, a much larger, multiregional and multitribal meritocracy now rules America (Auspitz and Brown, 1974, 59).

The opening up of "the Protestant Establishment" (Baltzell, 1966) was, of course, a long-extended and complex process. The entrance of many new elements into mainstream positions of high income, authority, and prestige was not merely through meritocratic channels—very often it was accomplished through highly particularistic and collectivistic avenues, e.g., ethnic political alliances and economic dealings. But this is a long-standing part of ordinary political life in the United States and is one main avenue to the removal of barriers to individual achievement. The effects of increased opportunities may be well illustrated by the recent changes in the educational and economic status of black Americans.

4. Increased Attainments of Black Americans: Educational and Economic

Between 1950 and 1970, black educational levels as a percentage of white levels rose from 67 to 84 (for males). Figure 1.5 shows the quite substantial reduction in the gap between white and nonwhite males, in terms of median years of school completed.

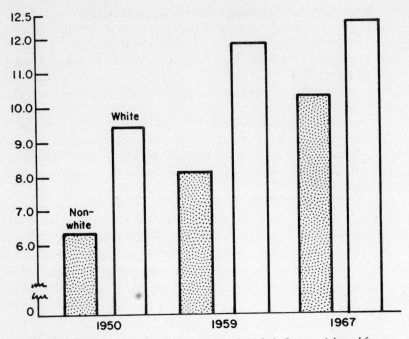

Figure 1.5. Median Years of School Completed (Males). *Source:* Adapted from Szymanski. 1974. Table 6, p. 717.

As a consequence of educational and economic changes and the opening of opportunities, the black "middle classes" are estimated to have increased since 1940 from some 5 percent to about 25 percent of the black population (Pettigrew, 1971; Kronus, 1971). This rather substantial transformation has occurred in the absence of any really widespread residential desegregation in the large cities. A "fundamental restructuring" of American institutions cannot be said to have occurred in the arenas of credit, property, housing, zoning, or other residential and real estate practices. But an expanding economy, rising levels of education among both blacks and whites, increased political participation and influence, increased self-confidence and motivation, and other factors have been sufficient to account for important changes, even without anything like the total abolition of institutional racism or white prejudices.

Although an increase in the economic status of black persons in the United States since World War II clearly has occurred, it is easy for different observers to disagree about the magnitude of the changes, partly because of the different results of the several modes of measured economic positions and changes in them: e.g., median or mean income (the latter is strongly affected by extreme

Table 1.3. Median Family Income in Constant
(1971) Dollars, 1947-71, by Race of Head

Year	Nonwhite Families	White Families	Nonwhite as Percentage of White
1971	$6,714	$10,672	63
1970	6,806	10,674	64
1965	5,160	9,311	55
1960	4,416	7,982	55
1955	3,860	6,976	55
1950	3,142	5,811	54
1947	2,930	5,714	51

Source: Bureau of the Census, U.S. Department of Commerce.
Current Population Reports, Series P-60, No. 85, December 1972,
Table 9, p. 31.

values); family income versus income of families and of "unrelated individuals" (family income is higher); income of all persons who are in the labor force vs. employed workers in the experienced labor force. Statistics on income and occupations of different segments of the population are affected by differences in age distributions in rural-urban and regional location, and by differences in proportions of women employed. If rates of unemployment are based on the size of the labor force, the real extent of unemployment will be underestimated to the extent that discouraged potential workers have withdrawn from the labor market.

All these variations can become highly debatable when data on economic status are used to influence public opinion and public policies. Spokesmen for minorities may regard any talk of "progress" unfavorably, because they fear it may reduce motivation or willingness to carry out reforms. When a large percentage increase in income of blacks is reported, they may point out, correctly, that the absolute size of the base was very small, or that rates of unemployment remain high, or that disproportionate numbers of black wives work to augment family income (Hill, 1973).

Nevertheless, some appraisals of change have to be made. The data presented here are generalized and are intended only to convey a rough first approximation, open to all the qualifications just suggested.[6]

By the criterion of absolute change in real income of family units, the nonwhite population has gained greatly during the quarter-century between the end of World War II and the 1970s: from a median income of $2,900 (in 1971 dollars) in 1947 to just over $6,700 in 1971. Gain was registered also in relative terms: nonwhite income as a percentage of white income went from 51 to 63 during the same period (Table 1.3 and Figures 1.6 and 1.7). One

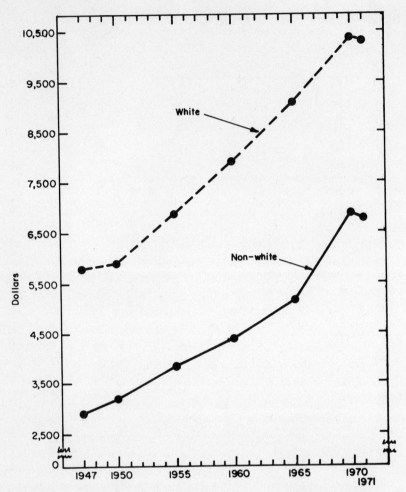

Figure 1.6. Median Income of White and Nonwhite Families, 1947-71, in Constant (1971) Dollars. *Source:* Table 1.3.

may immediately note, however, that 63 percent still is far from 100 percent; also, the absolute difference between white and nonwhite incomes that was $2,784 in 1947 had widened to $3,958 in 1971. But the percentage increase of real income between the beginning and end of the period was 187 for whites and 229 for nonwhites. The combination of depression and inflation, together with the change in national political policies after 1970, resulted in a retrogression in the 1970s—the ratio of nonwhite to white median income was 59 in 1974.

Ratio: Black

White

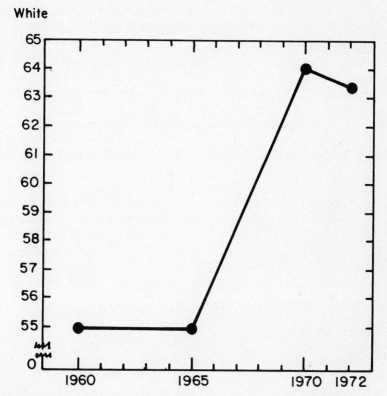

Figure 1.7. Ratio of Median Family Income: Nonwhite to White, 1960-72. *Source:* Table 1.3.

Shifting the comparison to the experienced male labor force, we find that between the late 1940s and 1970 the income (current dollars) of whites just doubled whereas that of nonwhites increased threefold. During the same period, there was a much more radical decrease in the differential between incomes of white and nonwhite females: the income of experienced labor force whites increased by about 20 percent whereas that of nonwhites increased by 300 percent.

Did the economic position of employed nonwhites improve? Obviously the answer is yes for absolute change, for relative change from the baseline, and for position relative to whites. What remains less favorable is relative position and the absolute size of the white-nonwhite differential. We do know that much of the differential grows directly out of past and present racial discrimination.

Thus low incomes of blacks in northern cities are not attributable to in-migration from the South, nor is residential segregation a primary cause of low occupational and income status of black males. Rather, a significant portion of white-black differences in earnings is the result of discrimination in the labor market (Masters, 1975).

By comparison with the facts of the earlier historical situation, there seems no doubt that there was a marked improvement in the ability of nonwhites to command goods and services during the period after 1945 and especially in the later 1960s.[7]

Similar findings and conclusions derive from comparisons of changes in the occupational distributions of whites and nonwhites. For example, taking black and white males only, the years since 1940 have brought a sharp upgrading of blacks' occupations.

Just before World War II, over six in ten black male workers were farmers, farm laborers, or unskilled laborers. In contrast, whites were concentrated in sales, clerical, crafts, and managerial and professional occupations. By 1970, the proportion of black males in farm and unskilled work had decreased to less than 20 percent. During the thirty-year period, discrimination against blacks had decreased in every one of the eleven major occupational groupings reported by the Census. Especially rapid changes occured in the 1940s and again in the 1960s (Szymanski, 1974, 710).

As American society has changed from an agricultural and rural to an industrial, commercial, and services urban economy, major shifts in occupational opportunities necessarily have occurred. During the 1960s, these shifts continued to follow the general pattern of the preceding several decades: from manual to nonmanual occupations and from lower to higher status occupations within both manual and nonmanual categories (Hauser and Featherman, 1973).

As in the case of income, the shifts in occupational differentials were much more marked among females than among males. The last quarter-century brought a wholesale exodus of black women from domestic service, and rapid increases in employment as operatives and in clerical and sales, as well as managerial and professional occupations (Szymanski, 1974, 710-11).

In the decades since the merger of AFL-CIO in 1955, labor unions on the whole have been an economic and political asset for blacks. By 1970 blacks were 11.7 percent of the labor force, 12 percent of union membership, and made up about one-third of all new union members (Levitan, Johnston, Taggart, 1975, 168.

Careful re-examination of the changes in occupational status and income during the decade 1960-70 substantiates our general conclusions (Johnson and Sell, 1976). There was a marked reduction of nonwhite-white differences in occupational distribution, especially among young men. Nonwhite income increased relative to white income. The absolute gap in real income between nonwhites and whites widened, but there was a general reduction of income differentials *within* educational levels. What the last finding means is that the entire labor force has shifted "upward" into educational brackets in which nonwhite-white differentials are especially large (Johnson and Sell, 1976).

Obviously, then, one can view these changes as representing (1) great improvement or (2) no improvement or (3) relative deprivation for nonwhite minorities. However, real income and occupational position did increase both absolutely and relatively — only the absolute gap increased.

Between 1962 and 1973, the occupational socioeconomic status of men in the experienced civilian labor force increased and black workers gained more than whites. Although discrimination continues, both race and class have become less important and schooling has become more important (Featherman and Hauser, 1976, 621).

Of course it is important to remember that the observed economic gains occurred in a period of increasing productivity and affluence. A reminder that such advances are not fully secure is seen in Figure 1.7, reflecting the faltering economy and altered political context that ushered in the 1970s. Decreases in poverty as indexed by both the number and the proportion of persons, both white and nonwhite, below the official poverty line occurred throughout the 1960s but ceased in the early 1970s. "Median black family income as a percent of white family income increased from 51 in 1959 to 61 in 1970, but dropped back to 59 by 1972" (Hill, 1973). In specific parts of the economy, black gains were substantial; in others, slight or absent. The governmental sector represented a favorable set of changes. Thus between 1940 and 1970 black representation in the federal civil service rose from 4.2 to 15 percent. Gross employment of blacks, therefore, is now more than proportionate to the percentage of blacks in the total population. What of actual integration and distribution among grade-levels? For nineteen major agencies, 1967-73, integration increased at all grade levels and in all except one agency. But integration is inversely related to level, and the top civil service grades are not well integrated. Integration was least in the largest agencies and in those with a history of marked discrimination, and greatest in organizations "—where missions involve equality (of) service to disadvantaged groups and where work processes involve factory-type organization or involve tasks not frequently performed by minorities" (Grabosky and Rosenbloom, 1975). On the whole the objective of equality of opportunity for employment is being well served. Integration is proceeding less rapidly in the 1970s than just before, but considerable movement has occurred in recent years.

The economic, educational, and political attainments we have just sketched represent large changes, many of which grew directly out of the mobilization and sustained efforts of minority-group persons. Changes in self-conceptions among ethnic. leaders preceded the objective institutional changes, but the actual progress made, in turn, then aided a collective transformation in self-images and self-evaluations, symbolized by the slogan, "Black is Beautiful."

5. Enhanced Self-Esteem and Collective Morale among Black Americans

An increasingly favorable self-image clearly is becoming more prevalent among black Americans.

Many students of the 1940s and 1950s showed the widespread presence among Negro Americans of white-oriented preferences and of negative evaluations of blackness or the "Negro" identity (Harding et al., 1954). But the studies asked essentially about *group* stereotypes and evaluations, and some respondents may well have reported awareness of such cultural patterns rather than their own *personal* self-evaluations. Self-hate is a difficult attitude to maintain if one is surrounded by family and friends who manifest protection, nurturance, support, guidance, and affection. Centuries of oppression have left many ethnic collectivities with strong self-regard and pride.

But a prevalent view, both in the general population and among scholars familiar with the observational and clinical studies available in the 1950s and early 1960s was that low self-esteem, or even self-hatred, was a "mark of oppression" resulting from racial discrimination and prejudice (Kardiner and Ovesey, 1951; Clark and Clark, 1947; Goodman, 1964). But more recent and more systematic studies of relatively large samples of whites and blacks overwhelmingly either find no important differences in indicators of self-esteem or psychological stress or else show blacks to have more positive self-evaluations. When statistical controls are introduced for sex, urban residence, age, education, marital status, and work-force status, one study finds no evidence of any systematic relation between race and self-esteem (Yancey, Rigsby, McCarthy, 1972). A review of some dozen studies showed higher self-ratings for blacks than for whites in the majority of samples (Rosenberg and Simmons,

1972); see references therein to Baughman and Dahlstrom, 1968; Bachman, 1970; Kohn, 1969; Powell and Fuller, 1970; Gordon, 1969; Hunt and Hardt, 1969. In twelve studies conducted between 1960 and 1968, thirteen comparisons of self-esteem of whites and blacks (children, youths, and adults) showed blacks higher in eight, whites higher in four, no difference in one. In a detailed analysis of public school pupils in Baltimore, as of 1968, Rosenberg and Simmons (1972) indicate that black self-esteem certainly is not lower and may be higher than that of whites. Further research has indicated that on various specific rather than global indicators of self-esteem, whites are higher than blacks in some aspects, lower in others. In general, however, the differences are not large and none of the studies produces evidence to suggest severely lowered self-evaluations among blacks (Heiss and Owens, 1972). A high level of positive self-esteem among black children and youths is reported by additional studies (Greenberg, 1972; Hulbary, 1975) — which show that many blacks "externalize blame" by attributing social and economic deprivation not to individual deficiencies but to social and political arrangements controlled by white people.

These consistent indications of strong self-respect and positive self-conceptions reflect a sense of positive accomplishments, shared fate, and ingroup support against hostile and discriminatory outsiders. The recurrent collective conflicts centering upon segregation and discrimination have accentuated a process of ethnogenesis (Singer, 1962) — the development and elaboration of a sense of positive ethnic identity. Group struggles have provided evidence for black Americans of their collective strength in the face of opposition, of the dependability of their fellows and their allies, and of the strength of collective commitments. Struggles have focused attention upon historical events and outstanding figures in black history. The existence of a relatively distinct Black Culture has been increasingly recognized and emphasized (Bracey, Meier, Rudwick, 1970; Dixon and Foster, 1971; Himes, 1973; Rose, Rothman, Wilson, 1973; Kinloch, 1974, and many others).

Ranking high among the successes of recent years in American intergroup relations is the collective achievement of blacks in establishing new levels and new forms of ethnic solidarity and pride. Thus the moral effects of collective action by black people in recent decades represent enduring accomplishments (Patterson, 1973, 57). The example provided by the Civil Rights Movement and the urban upheavals of the 1960s stimulated other ethnic minorities to reassert similar claims to distinctiveness, respect, and a larger share in political and economic power and rewards. Movements reflecting these characteristics have arisen among Spanish-surname populations (Mexican Americans [Chicanos], Puerto Ricans, and others), Asian Americans, Native Americans, and many "white ethnics" of European origins (Glazer and Moynihan, 1976).

"Black Power" emerged as a nationally known slogan about 1966. Calls for "black nationalism" and "black separatism" received much public attention. But as of 1968, at the height of a period of collective violence Campbell and Schuman (1968, 5 and 19) reported that separatism appealed to only a small minority, from 5 to 18 percent, of black residents in fifteen major cities. The greatest proportions of favorable attitudes concerned black ownership of stores and black administration of schools in black neighborhoods. The smallest percentages were elicited by the question of rejecting whites as friends or in informal contacts. More than three-fourths of those interviewed clearly favored integration—and many expressed the views indicating a commitment to principles of nondiscrimination and racial harmony. Even among young males (16-19)—who are most often separatists—the proportions favoring separation varied between 1 and a maximum of 28 percent.

The data strongly suggest that what *is* wanted is *cultural identity* and *positive black consciousness.* Not secession but autonomy is the main thrust. America's ethnic minorities want a place in the main stream of educational, economic, and political opportunities, and they want these opportunities as a matter of right, not as a favor, and without the loss of their positively valued and distinctive cultural characteristics.

We termed these developments "a success"—but surely there are dangers in ethnic consciousness and ethnic claims? Yes, ethnic assertiveness can have politically divisive effects and can exacerbate domestic conflicts (Porter, 1976, 289-97). The maintenance of a just and viable multiethnic society no doubt requires a flexible and restrained balancing of partisan claims, including the claims and demands of ethnic groupings and organizations. Such "balancing" is possible only if the politically active population shares some minimal core of common values and beliefs.

The growth of ethnic solidarity can have either integrative or disruptive effects upon a national society. Since the end of World War II resurgent ethnicity has aided weak groupings in many parts of the world to attain greater power, participation, income, and self-esteem. It has also helped to produce political instability, ferocious civil warfare, totalitarian movements, mass terror, rigid ascription, and oppression by victorious groups over others (see the exchange of views among Glazer, Greeley, Patterson, and Moynihan, 1974). Like most other all-or-none questions in this field, the question of the effects of enhanced ethnic awareness and solidarity does not allow for any satisfactory simple answer. In very general terms, however, there is a clear difference between ethnic segmentation or separatism and cultural pluralism. The first refers to ascribed and exclusive groupings struggling for "shares" of scarce values, including power; at the extreme, such struggles result in a plural society held together by force. The second, cultural pluralism, implies recognition and respect for distinctive heritages within an economically and politically integrated society that basically requires *universalistic* norms.

6. Common Values and Integrative Institutions

As noted in the beginning of our discussion, many writings on intergroup relations during the last two or three decades have concentrated upon difficulties, evils, recriminations, liabilities, and obstacles. This probably will be generally acknowledged, on net balance, as a salutary state of affairs: social criticism of this kind seems essential to explicate sources of maladjustment and to explore possible remedies. It is a necessary part of social diagnosis—but surely not the whole of the necessities. Essential also in the long run is an appraisal of resources, strengths, workable resolution of problems, and avenues of feasible change.

Among the resources available in the United States today for dealing with conflict among ethnic groupings is one pervasive condition often overlooked or minimized in assessments of future prospects. Without it, the prospects of management of group competition and the resolution of collective conflict would be much less favorable than they actually are. It is a cultural resource: the stock of common beliefs, knowledge, experience, norms, and values that are shared among millions of people from all major ethnic, racial, and religious backgrounds. The importance of shared values has been strongly expressed by Glazer's appraisal of political gains made by minorities in the 1960s.

> If the position of blacks and other minorities is now much better than it was in the early 1960's, it is not only because they and their allies called attention to their situation and organized their political resources. The minorities also made an effective appeal to principles they shared with other Americans—principles demanding equal treatment and concern for the poor—and it is because these principles existed that the minorities were able to make progress, however much some analysts may deceive themselves that it was threat and power alone which improved their position (Glazer, 1975, 29).

Minorities and the poor naturally do not rank all major values in the same way. But it is a crucial fact that *when differences in socioeconomic class are taken into account*, black and white Americans speak the same language of values and beliefs. Without minimizing in the least the uniqueness and integrity and coherence of black cultures in the United States, it is essential for us to understand that most blacks share with most whites a substantial common fund of generalized values. A body of national survey data, collected in 1968, shows that for thirty-six major values—both *instrumental* values such as politeness, cleanliness, and competence and *terminal* values such as freedom, self-respect, pleasure, and salvation—blacks and whites did not differ significantly on most values (Rokeach, 1973). Furthermore, Rokeach's analysis demonstrates, the first-order differences of substantial size turned out to be functions of socioeconomic position rather than ethnic category, i.e., the "racial" difference tended to disappear when socioeconomic status was equated. The *only* value that continued to show a large difference regardless of economic and educational level was—not so surprisingly—equality. It is in the realm of the evaluation of equality that the crucial oppositions develop.

The development of a disproportionately small but still substantial middle stratum among blacks provides considerable evidence that blacks and whites at similar income levels develop very similar patterns of behavior or life-styles (Kronus, 1971). Analysis of family patterns among blacks similarly shows both the prevalence of the ideal of the stable nuclear family and of its actual presence where the economic and social context provide minimal support for it (Billingsley, 1968; Hill, 1972). The "black majority," as Scanzoni (1971) calls the stable-family black population (Willie, 1970), holds nearly all major family values in common with whites of comparable income levels. Data from national samples of both adults and youths reporting on father's and mother's influence and role in family decision-making shows that the "actual white pattern, contrary to expectation, is almost identical to that for Negro [black] families" (Hyman and Reed, 1969, 352). More and more evidence has accumulated to show the high degree of similarity of whites and blacks in family values. As Willie (himself a black sociologist) has shown, black and white families have a common core of values but behave in differing ways when racial discrimination is a factor (Willie, 1976). And the idea that a matriarchy or matrifocal family is a dominant form among blacks turns out to be a stereotyped exaggeration. The same holds for the idea that female-headed families represent a "heritage of slavery." Several recent studies have assembled data that cast doubt on the notion that slavery destroyed the black family (Gutman, 1976). Differences between blacks and whites in the proportion of families headed by females are greatest in central cities of the North and West rather than in traditionalized rural areas of the South (Yancey, 1972). Furthermore, data collected in 1973 as the sixth year of a panel study show that black marriages are not less stable than white marriages of the same general SES; when income, home ownership, and family size are equated, the percentage of black marriages broken by divorce or separation is six percentage points less than for whites (Hampton, 1975).

What the accumulated studies strongly suggest, therefore, is that the conditions associated with low income and unstable unemployment rather than matriarchical traditions primarily account for the high proportion of female-headed black families in central cities. Interracial marriages and adoptions are often considered prime examples of successful ethnic integration, as indicating that mutually accepted intergroup contact has extended all the way to the most intimate interpersonal level. However, the ethnic family may also be considered a success in intergroup relations, if it has arisen in response to intergroup pressures and has provided supportive or adaptive features for survival and competition in dealing with the outside world (Hill, 1972). Thus, as recent studies show, an extensive network of mutual aid and exchange among relatives is a strong feature of low-income black families in the metropolitan setting (Stack, 1974).

The case of family patterns illustrated commonality of values at the level of life-styles and interpersonal relations. On the level of national social structure, at the other extreme, the recent movement toward greater equality of civil and political rights and liberties represents another step in a long sequence of extending universalistic rules to disadvantaged "minority" elements of the society. The process is that of widening inclusion within a core societal community. As we have said elsewhere:

> From the original notion of a political elite made up of white, male, adult, native-born, property-owning and self-chosen guardians of the Republic, we have seen the extension of civil rights and civil participation to non-whites, women, the young, aliens, and the propertyless. The categorical exclusion of anyone on an arbitrary or ascribed basis has come to be regarded more and more as incompatible with the basic tenets of our society. . . .
>
> It was in this context that institutionalized racial discrimination and segregation began to be successfully challenged anew in the 1930's and thereafter (R. M. Williams, 1973, 105).

By the 1970s, *legalized* racial discrimination as it had existed a generation before had been abolished. That result had many causes, but it would not have been possible in the absence of some consensus on values and generalized social norms. Especially significant was the idea of a universalistic rule of law, especially in the doctrine of "equal protection of the laws" and "due process." The basic beliefs and values that were expressed in the original Bill of Rights were for a long time denied application to certain categories of the population —slaves, women, Indians, children, aliens, blacks, exprisoners, and so on. But the potentiality of application always was inherent in the continued adherence to the general principles. In every major instance in which minorities gained so-called new rights, the rights in question already were being exercised by persons who were inside the legitimated political-societal community. The process of successive *extension of rights* was actually one of successive *inclusion of new members of that core "community."* The guarantees of the Fourteenth Amendment were extended step by step as part of a broader movement toward full membership for racial minorities. (Since the 1960s there has been a continuation of the struggle for "equal protection" for younger persons, older persons, women, the mentally ill, prisoners, and others.)

The clashes of values that centered upon categorical discrimination and segregation—whether by race, sex, age, ethnicity, religion, or something else— have produced vast tensions and conflicts. Every new inclusion of formerly excluded persons has been attained only through active collective struggle against resistance. The tensions can be resolved only by "constituting a single societal community with full membership for all" (Parsons, 1966, 740).

The most fundamental contribution of the struggles of minorities for equality and freedom is that such efforts have continually reaffirmed and activated the primary values that are necessary for a democratic political system in the United States.

7. Where Have We Come from and Where Are We Going?

We have tried in this chapter to give illustrations of the fact that in a turbulent period of national history, marked by considerable conflict and pessimism, there have been highly significant changes toward what we regard as more coherent and constructive policies in intergroup relations.[8] We believe also that a great deal has been learned in recent decades about methods, techniques, and organizational arrangements for effecting social change and dealing with collective conflicts. Much of the latter half of this book will be devoted to a critical appraisal of the evidence on these major points.

Because some observers of the national scene are skeptical concerning claims such as we have just made, a preliminary sketch of our own position seems necessary here.

It is our view that systematic understanding of ethnic conflict and conflict resolution has greatly improved during the last several decades. Indeed, the knowledge and the prevalent social practices of the 1930s and 1940s now seem quite undeveloped and crude by comparison. The accumulation of valid and relevant information and, more important, the organization and critical sifting of empirical findings has proceeded to a point at which more systematic and theoretically informed research will produce large increments in knowledge. Rapid progress meanwhile has been made in sharper conceptualization and a clearer organization of propositions and variables (Williams, 1975a, 1975b). Past imbalances and blindspots are being corrected. Thus, there is no longer the excessive preoccupation with the *attitudes and beliefs* of individuals that marked such research on race relations in years before the 1950s. A similar change is the movement away from a preoccupation with *interpersonal relations* that was evident in much research and social commentary during the 1950s and 1960s. Slowly the recognition has grown that decisive influences upon intergroup relations arise from the *structure and dynamics of collectivities* —groups and organizations—as such. Much conflict turns out to hinge upon organizational structures and relationships, rather than directly upon the properties of interpersonal interactions that would exist apart from such organizational constraints and instigations. For example, Thompson hypothesizes: "Racial integration may be more easily introduced into the giant enterprise (for example, the military system) than into the . . . church, whose ideology places all men equal before God, because homogeneity is a necessary defense for the voluntary church but not for the giant enterprise" (Thompson, 1960, 408-9).

Knowledge about intergroup relations, when put together with appropriate value judgments about desirable objectives, has been used increasingly to develop social diagnoses and programs for practical action. Many examples can be cited. Perhaps a good initial example is provided by the set of rules-of-thumb proposed by Pettigrew as necessary for actions to bring about the conditions favorable for effective racial integration of public schools. His proposals obviously are closely linked to his research-based knowledge of experience with widely differing policies and practices. Thus he proposes:

(1) *There must be equal access to the school's resources.* This critical condition means far more than just equal group access to books in the libraries and other physical facilities. More importantly, it refers to equal access to the school's sources of social status as well. . . .

(2) *Classroom—not just school-desegregation is essential if integration is to develop.* . . .

(3) *Strict ability grouping should be avoided.* . . .

(4) *School services and remedial training must be maintained or increased with the onset of desegregation.* Again this condition may appear so obvious as to be unnecessary to mention. Yet it must be listed, for many desegregation programs witness an actual reduction in per student expenditures. . . .

(5) *Desegregation should be initiated in the early grades.* . . .

(6) *The need for interracial staffs is critical.* . . .

(7) *Substantial, rather than token, minority percentages are necessary.* . . .

(8) *Finally, race and social class must not be confounded in the interracial school.* When the white children of a biracial school are overwhelm-

ingly from affluent, middle-class families and the black children are overwhelmingly from poor, working-class families, the opportunities to develop integration are severely limited. . . .

The middle-class black child, then, should be seen as an invaluable resource for lowering the correlation within biracial schools between race and class (Pettigrew, 1974, 381-84).

General principles for identifying effective modes of influencing intergroup relations do, in fact, exist—and continually are being rediscovered. Compare the following two formulations, separated by a quarter-century of experience.

Outside agencies coming into a local community to stimulate, initiate, or otherwise affect programs directed toward intergroup relations will meet minimum resistance when they (a) work through local persons and established local groups, (b) avoid extensive publicity for themselves; (c) adapt techniques and organizations to local circumstances rather than propose a rigid scheme prepared in advance (Williams, 1947, 76).

Major changes in any long-established institution nearly always result from outside pressures rather than purely internal developments. . . . Such relations with 'outside change-agents' usually work better if the outside change agents are locally based. . . . Other parts of the community are more willing to recognize locally originated pressure as legitimate. In fact, the existence of strong locally based pressures for change can provide top-level school officials with useful leverage in accomplishing constructive improvements they want in spite of those who oppose any departures from the *status quo* (Smith, Downs, Lachman, 1973, 22).

Or, observe the congruence among these generalizations.

A general principle of approach is that, except in acute crisis situations, problems of group conflict are usually most readily resolved by indirection rather than by frontal assault (Williams, 1947, 63).

—and:

Conflict is discouraged by providing, through sources of high general prestige, for specific commendation of individuals of the dominant group who work for toleration, minority rights, mutual understanding and the like (Williams, 1947, 67).

—and:

Conflict and hostility are rendered less probable by any activity which leads individuals to *take for granted* the other group (Williams, 1947, 68).

—furthermore:

A general expectation of authoritative intervention and the possibility of punishment for acts of violence . . . will decrease the probability of open conflict (Williams, 1947, 74).

Now note the 1973 generalizations concerning effective school desegregation, as proposed by Smith, Downs, and Lachman (1973, 23).

Community conflict concerning the desirability of school desegregation is greatly reduced if desegregation is regarded as inevitable. This principle has two important corollaries:

a. Strong statements by federal and state leaders—including state education officials—about the inevitability of school desegregation, and clear commitments by them to achieving it effectively, greatly reduce pressures on local school officials to delay or oppose desegregation. . . .

b. School boards and superintendents in *de jure* districts can reduce local controversy about desegregation by taking the position that it is inevitable and must be done, rather than by trying to gain local consensus about whether it is desirable.

Because of a persisting myth that black-white relationships in the South have remained stable over very long periods, it is easy to forget that rapid change in "race relations" in the South is no novelty. During the 1950s and 1960s many white political leaders in the South argued that the system of segregation was deeply embedded in ancient traditions and practices and, therefore, could not be changed to accord with national legal norms. But as Vander Zanden perceptively noted as early as 1963:

The myth persists despite the fact that southerners have probably been more familiar with the shifting fortunes of history than other Americans have been. Their own history has amply demonstrated that an old order and its institutions can perish quite quickly and rather completely (Vander Zanden, 1963, 392).

Later events decisively supported the view that rapid change, indeed, was possible in the South that for so long had seemed so monolithic and rigid.

The later relevance to diagnosis of effects of social policies of historical perspective is further shown by the following observations, made in 1953-54 just before the crucial decision of the Supreme Court in the *Brown* case:

A clear definition of law and policy by legitimate social authorities may reinforce willingness to conform to the requirements of new situations.

Persons coming into an unfamiliar situation, such as that experienced in initial desegregation, will be unusually sensitive to cues as to what is the appropriate and acceptable behavior. Hence the great importance of clarity and decisiveness in early policy and practice in the desegregation process cannot be overemphasized (Williams and Ryan, 1954, 247).

Awareness of an impending social change in intergroup relations, such as school desegregation, produces uncertainty.

Such uncertainty breeds both anxiety and mutually conflicting expectations about behavior; so it can lead to serious trouble. To alleviate this uncertainty, school authorities must take the initiative in establishing clear, explicit policies in writing, and in making sure that all relevant persons both outside and within the school system are well informed about those policies. . . . Clear and explicit policies given wide circulation are absolutely essential to achieving effective desegregation with minimum conflict and disruption (Smith, Downs, Lachman, 1973, 25).

And uncertainty and divided opinions within a community or society signify that *situation-defining* acts by salient authorities can acquire unusual weight. For example:

Where the white community is not strongly opposed or where attitudes are unstructured, confused, and in flux, decisive importance attaches to the policies and actions of school boards and school officials. In such instances these gatekeepers can tip the balance one way or the other in the degree of ease with which the transition is made (Williams and Ryan, 1954, 237).

Individuals in positions of responsibility for organizations or activities in which a major change in intergroup relations is about to occur must decide how widespread their communications with the general public should be. The probable effects differ radically, depending upon (a) whether the change is locally voluntary or constrained by outside forces, and (b) how strongly polarized is the local community on the relevant issue. In the case of public school desegregation, we note the following additional recommendations:

a. Where desegregation is purely voluntary, widespread contacts between school authorities and other community elements are essential right from the start of the issue-resolution period. . . .

b. Where desegregation has been ordered by a court, and intense feelings about it strongly divide the community, school authorities should probably communicate at first mainly with small groups of key leaders. . . .

c. Where desegregation has been ordered by a court but community feelings about it are not strong, school authorities should carry out a much broader initial communications process than the one just described. However, they do not need to engage in the intensive, community wide 'dialogue' required for voluntary desegregation (Smith, Downs, Lachman, 1973, 26).

Desegregating an entire school system simultaneously appears to be more effective than desegregating it a little bit at a time (Smith, Downs, Lachman, 1973, 29).

In general a clear-cut policy, administered with understanding but also with resolution, seems to have been most effective in accomplishing desegregation with a minimum of difficulty. Long-drawn-out efforts and fluctuating policies appear to have maximized confusion and resistance (Williams and Ryan, 1954, 252).

With these examples we end our introductory excursion into hypotheses and possibly useful approaches for purposive social action in dealing with intergroup relations. Much of the main body of the book will be an attempt to arrive at more carefully developed appraisals of these matters. In the interest of conveying a sense of realism we may conclude this chapter's sampling of positive alternatives to destructive action with a case study of how one impending conflict was averted (Shellow and Roemer, 1966).

8. The Riot That Did Not Happen

We hear a great deal about riots that did occur, very little about those that did not: it is difficult to find accounts of nonevents. Nevertheless, it is not nonsensical to think of nonevents — that is, events that seemed at a certain point to be inevitably developing but that failed to occur, because of counterprocesses that prevented the otherwise expectable outcome. In other words, there are instances in which we are on fairly safe ground in formulating a *predicted sequence* of social behavior which is then compared with an outcome different from that which would have occurred had the initial processes been allowed to proceed without alteration or the addition or subtraction of factors.

A useful assessment of this kind concerns the nearconfrontations incident to a national motorcycle race that was to be held at Upper Marlboro, the county seat of Prince Georges County, Maryland, on the Labor Day weekend in 1965. Expectations of violence had been generated by news, earlier in the summer, of a major riot in connection with a similar event elsewhere and by the arrest of three alleged "Hell's Angels" by local police. Collaborative diagnosis and planning by two social scientists and the Prince Georges County

Police Department began six weeks before the projected motorcycle race. The initial diagnosis, based on accounts of disturbances at recreational or sporting events, showed that the outbreaks that had occurred were preceded by a massive and sudden influx of outsiders into a local area, when the outsiders and locals differed in significant and visible ways in interests, age, place of residence, race, or other shared characteristics. The specific conditions that seemed to be predictive of actual rioting included: (1) overtaxing recreational and control facilities by a sudden influx of large numbers of visitors, who thus had no adequate outlets for action; (2) ineffective and inappropriate efforts by police and other local officials to exert control; (3) emergence of a sense of common fate and solidarity among participants in the crowd (Shellow and Roemer, 1966, 222).

The consultants worked with police and local motorcyclists' groups to establish two-way communication and a flow of information. Special efforts were made to ensure that adequate facilities were available (for camping, drag racing, and stunt riding). Police were instructed to avoid harassment or provocative tactics. Limited shows of force and of the presence of substantial organized police groups were made. Authorities did not interfere with camping and drag racing even on private property unless extreme violence was seen to be developing. "Potential troublemakers" were clustered by voluntary action in areas visible to police but separated from spectators—who might have otherwise become both audience and victims of violence.

The purposive measures taken, together with some fortunate unplanned conditions, muted and controlled the conflicts that emerged. Violence was kept at a low level and was sporadic and diffuse rather than organized. Massive confrontations did not develop. What easily could have become a large-scale violent riot was contained and dissipated. The riot did not occur.

Although collective upheavals will continue to appear from time to time in American intergroup relations, much has been learned since the Civil Rights years of the 1950s, by both the partisans and the authorities, about the limits and the means of struggle. Many incidents that would have led to collective violence in the 1960s now are averted by means of negotiation and legal proceedings. And even when hostility has been stirred up and collective conflict has emerged, it is possible under appropriate conditions to reduce hostility, to reduce conflict, and to increase cooperation and interpersonal attraction across lines of prior hostile cleavage (see, for example, Sherif et al., 1961; Sherif, 1966).

Chapter 2

The Problem: Assessing Ethnic and Racial Relations

On the face of it, what with the bewildering array of religious, ethnic, and national groups that make up American society, it would appear that the U.S. is ripe for a massive social upheaval. And yet, except for the Civil War, Americans have managed to hold together as a nation and to extend social and economic opportunities to a succession of groups. The effort is by no means completed, but at a time when attention is focused on the failures of American life, it is important to recognize that by and large this society has succeeded notably in containing ethnic frictions of the sort that are still causing havoc in so many places throughout the world (Friedman, 1974, 98).

1. How Can We Appraise Ethnic Relations?

It is no longer news to report that throughout its history American society has been the scene of many severe conflicts among ethnic, racial, and religious groupings. In this it is not alone. On the recent world scene the emergence of many new nations since World War II, the civil tumults of the 1960s, and the fierce conflicts in the Middle East, Southeast Asia, and Africa—all attest to the enormous importance of ethnicity as a major factor in political events, many of them violent, both at home and elsewhere in the world. Our subject is one of the most crucial in the world today (Glazer and Moynihan, eds., 1975; Williams et al., 1964). When we speak here of "ethnic groupings" or of ethnic relations, we include all those relationships among individuals, groups, or

47

organizations identified by national origin, cultural distinctiveness, so-called racial categories, or religious affiliation.

Within the United States, evaluations of the intergroup relations among ethnic groupings range between radically different extremes. Even while many commentators who put forward analyses of American society apparently despair of finding any integrative solutions to ethnic discrimination, racism, and collective conflict, others regard the extent of mutually acceptable accommodation and political integration thus far attained as remarkably successful, on net balance, in an imperfect world. Indeed, in comparison with some vision of an ideal society, the record of intergroup relations in the U.S. must seem dismal. But in comparison with the fratricide of many actual societies—the tragedy of Nigeria's civil war, the agonies of Lebanon—the record may seem highly encouraging. By what criteria can an explicit and responsible assessment be made?

2. The Problem of Criteria of Judgment

Thus if we are interested in finding instances of beneficial conflict, of successful conflict resolution, or of mutual accommodation, we have to be able to distinguish such outcomes from instances of divergent or contrasting results such as genocide, overwhelming coercive dominance, mutual estrangement, or hostile truce. If we are to compare successful and unsuccessful intergroup relations, therefore, we need criteria to which we can refer to make the crucial distinctions.

Two extreme outcomes perhaps will seem clear enough: (1) everybody wins, (2) everybody loses. There is a wonderful passage in *Alice in Wonderland* that describes how the various creatures dry themselves, after a dunking in the pool of Alice's tears, by racing around and around. At the end of the exercise, Alice asks who has won. The Dodo replies that all have won, and all shall have prizes. Intergroup relations with positive and high outcomes for all—these we shall have no qualms about calling successful. At the other extreme, it is reasonable to consider as unsuccessful the cases of mutual suicide, feuds that continue "to the last man," Pyrrhic victories, and any other self-defeating encounters from which all parties acknowledge themselves to have emerged worse off than before.

It is the in-between sector that requires closer considerations—not only the area of minus-sum or of zero-sum (in which what one party gains, the other loses)—but also the numerous cases of vague or ambiguous outcomes, of mixed motives and unclear goals, of processes of persuasion and of seduction, of co-optation, and of conversion. Human relationships rarely have single, clear unmistakable payoffs that can readily and accurately be calculated in advance, and ill-defined and paradoxical consequences often occur—e.g., "nothing fails like success." Furthermore, short-run and long-term outcomes frequently differ radically. As if all this were not enough complexity, we are forced to recognize also that there is not an agreed-upon scale by which we may appraise the gains and losses of different social actors, either by our standards or in terms of their own diverse interests and values.

And when the prevailing world view of a society comes to be permeated by critical and negative images, disbelief is extended almost automatically to any contrary opinion.

> Are things getting better as most of us would define that term — namely, are we moving away from a past of racism and caste exclusion — or are they getting worse? . . . The fashion of late has been to believe things are getting worse, and I can attest that it is costly to argue otherwise. And yet the data, such as they are, argue that indeed things are *not* getting worse (Moynihan, 1970, 97).

As we saw in Chapter 1, at the very time that a Presidential Commission claimed that the nation was moving toward two sharply separate, black and white, societies, rapid movement toward more nearly equal economic, political, and educational status was occurring. Such sharply divergent evaluations arise in part from differences in the amount, validity, scope, and accuracy of information available to different observers. Divergencies in evaluations derive also from differences in values, interests, and goals of the evaluator, e.g., whether one aims to affect public opinion, to initiate reforms, to resist change, or only to make an accurate diagnosis. But finally, differing evaluations may be drawn from the same facts because various appraisers use different bench marks for making comparisons. Unless we can identify the criteria of evaluation, therefore, we have no stable points of reference for relating social scientific findings to questions of policy and program.

For these reasons it is clear why we need to be sensitive to the contradictory values that are used to judge social outcomes in ethnic relations. Of course, it would be quite easy to judge all intergroup relations if we were to arbitrarily take a single value as that which is to be maximized at any cost. Examples of such unrealistic single-valued appraisals might be:

1. absolute equality of incomes;
2. complete social peace — no violence, no protest, no dissent;
3. banishment or imprisonment of all racial bigots;
4. conversion of everyone to a single religious allegiance and set of beliefs;
5. complete local control of all schools through ethnically homogeneous geographic districts;

6. social placement of individuals strictly on the basis of competitive achievement on standardized tests;

7. social placement of individuals solely on the basis of ascribed membership in ethnic categories, each of which has a definite quota of desirable positions;

8. complete freedom from any kind of legal or other authoritative regulation of education or economic activity.

Sponsors can be found to advocate any one of the positions indicated, but it is doubtful that a viable societal policy for American society could be developed on the basis of any one of the unqualified principles stated.

3. An Approach to Multivalued Appraisals

In short, our society is complex and ethnic problems are multivalued. Simple appraisals are not useful, and often are harmful (Berk, 1974, 764). When challenged, very few thoughtful citizens probably would be willing to advocate judging all intergroup relations by whether or not they maximize some one narrow and partisan interest. Any impoverishment of appraisal is likely to come, rather, when the need for multiple criteria is readily granted but overwhelming emphasis nevertheless actually is given to a single aspect. It is necessary in analyzing intergroup relations, for example, to have considerable attention directed to inequalities of income and occupational position as between whites and blacks — or Appalachian farmers and Michigan industrialists. But if we focus *only* on these outcomes, we eventually may come to implicitly view competitive economic placement as the sole criterion for judging the "quality of life" of the population in question. Or again, it certainly is essential for realistic analysis to pay attention to effectiveness or ineffectiveness of coercion in advancing the interests of disadvantaged minorities or of established elites, but it will not do to reduce all intergroup interaction to a zero-sum power struggle. An important aspect of the total network of relationships among ethnic groupings is the extent to which interactions among individuals are friendly or hostile, but it would be grotesque to judge the total character of the situation from even the most complete evidence about that one characteristic.

The sheer reduction of intergroup tensions or of overt conflict among ethnic collectivities cannot be taken as an acceptable criterion by itself. For people may be fighting less simply because they no longer have any important relationships of any kind. Conflict then has ceased but only because the formerly antagonistic parties now more often ignore one another: social peace has resulted from increasing mutual indifference. Is this outcome to be considered "mutual accommodation"? If two groups have been locked into relationships of chronic opposition and hostility, perhaps punctuated by episodes of collective conflict, it could appear to both parties that a reduction of involvement would be a boon. Such withdrawal of interest and concern is, indeed, neither an unthinkable or even a rare outcome. But at some point of increasing indifference, the parties cease to produce any significant consequences for one another. Such a condition would not be accommodation but rather isolation or fragmentation. Sheer withdrawal or separation represents a failure to sustain a relationship rather than a mutually acceptable basis for continuing interaction, although to be sure some degree of insulation often is a necessary condition for some forms of accommodative interdependence.

A successful relationship, then, is a continuing relationship. This conclusion is, in one sense, a matter of definition, but to state the definition is not trivial for it has significant implications.

When a set of relationships continues between two ethnic collectivities, it is a sign of sustained interdependence. Since they maintain an interdependent relationship, we can infer that at least one of the parties wants or needs to continue the recurrent interaction. Can such a relationship be wholly imposed by one party upon another who would escape it if possible? As a limiting case, yes. But sheer unilateral coercion is rare; almost always some reciprocity creeps into the interaction, some positive exchange, or some commonality of goals and outcomes. In any case, the more nearly a relationship approaches forcible dominance-subordination, the farther it departs from one of our primary criteria of "success"—uncoerced mutual acceptance.

To the extent that a relationship is continued on a voluntary, noncoerced basis, it must be rewarding in some way. A relationship may be rewarding because it directly aids each of the parties to survive in an environment. "Aid in survival" may consist of common defense against external enemies, or of cooperative sustenance activities, or of joint or parallel action to meet environmental hazards, or of market exchanges, or of reciprocity in providing resources. A relationship may be rewarding because it produces gratifications through exchange of goods and services. It may be rewarding because it provides direct satisfactions of communication, expression, and sociopsychological support. (The existence of these consummatory social rewards presupposes some minimal consensus upon values, beliefs, and norms—otherwise there would not be acceptance of a shared conception of what is rewarding.)

All societies, as well as the subcollectivities that constitute them, are open systems—that is, they continuously interchange with their environments, are maintained by complex sets of inflows and outflows of energy and information. All such social units must cope with two sets of tasks: those having to do rather directly with survival in an environment, and those having to do with their "social function" or the contributions they make to other systems, external and internal (Vickers, 1967, Chapter 5). The success of a social unit is a multivalued outcome. The external criteria concern, first, adaptation to an environment such that the unit maintains access to necessary resources for continued functioning, and, second, attainment of particular goals or objectives that provide valued outputs. The internal criteria also are twofold: first, maintaining order and collaboration among subunits, and second, sustaining cultural resources and motivational commitments adequate for boundary-maintenance.[1]

Not all of these desired states can be maximized simultaneously. Scarce resources devoted to immediate goal-attainment, or spent to distribute larger rewards to subunits, may deplete "capital," i.e., the generalized capacities of a group or a society for survival. Similarily, strong needs or demands for conflict resolution may reduce goal attainment. Or, an involuted or "fanatical" emphasis upon maintaining and elaborating a fixed system of beliefs and values can immobilize a society's energies at the expense of flexible and effective adaptation to a changing environment. Excessive concentration on building adaptive capabilities through elaborate technology and economic growth and on attaining tangible political goals can produce great collective achievements —even while disrupting social cohesion, diminishing faith in justice, and destroying commitments to the social system. Because of such unavoidable tradeoffs, any social system must continuously vary its allocations of resources.

Any kind of collective (group or organizational) functioning, accordingly, necessarily involves never-ending processes of ordering priorities, allocating benefits and burdens, assigning rights and duties, monitoring inputs and outputs, locating resources and "customers," sustaining cooperation, and so on. Disparate, and often incompatible, objectives and values continually are involved.

It seems evident, then, that the criteria by which one might attempt to appraise the success of any social unit (or relationship, or process, or event) are

Table 2.1. Main Types of Societal Responses of Ethnic Minorities

Collective Action	Cultural Orientation			
	Assimilation		Retentionism or ethnogenesis	
	Social Orientation			
	Separation	Participation	Separation	Participation
Accommodating	Insulated acceptance	Assimilation	Sectlike withdrawal	Pluralistic acceptance
Militant	. . .	Integration	Ethnic nationalism, or rebellion	Reform pluralism, or revolution

likely to be numerous, complex, variable, interrelated, partly incompatible, and often ambiguous. This generalization holds even for such commonsense gross criteria as "survival," "peace," and "growth." For there are many different degrees and kinds of survival, of peace and of growth, and each may have different implications for the welfare for different groupings even within the same society.

And, as simple as this straightforward lesson may appear to be, it is a view that seems very difficult to keep in mind and to apply appropriately in the real world about us.

4. What Are "Successful" Ethnic Relations?

Thus far we have identified successful social relationships as those that are continuing, interdependent, mutual, and rewarding (either instrumentally or directly). Although these criteria as stated are too abstract to help us very much in assessing particular cases, they do point to broad classes of considerations that crucially enter into valid diagnoses. Let us move progressively toward greater specificity, with particular reference to cases involving relations among ethnic collectivities.

For present purposes we are especially concerned with the relationships maintained by ethnic collectivities of the kinds usually called "minorities." *An ethnic minority is a subpopulation of a political society that is characterized by some kind of cultural distinctiveness, "membership" by birth, an appreciable tendency toward endogamy, and a self-consciousness of an objective condition of relative deprivation or disadvantage in wealth, income, power, authority, prestige, or social respect.*

The main possible types of relationships that a minority can have with the "dominant" or "host" collectivity can be quickly reviewed.

A minority may seek *assimilation* or it may seek to maintain or create a *distinctive culture.*

It may seek to *participate* with or to *withdraw* or to remain socially separate, i.e., to seek or avoid interaction with members of other collectivities in residential areas, work, education, religious groupings, recreation, voluntary associations, informal social life, and family.

It may *engage in collective action aimed at changing the existing distribution of influence, authority, power, and rewards.* Or, it may *accept* the basic institutional structure, accommodating its action to goals attainable within that framework.

Combining these three major orientations gives the main types of responses, listed in Table 2.1. As statistical tendencies, these different kinds of orientations and behaviors are not randomly distributed, but rather appear as out-

Table 2.2. Factors Influencing Collective Responses of Ethnic Minorities

Characteristics of the Minority and Its Situation	Main Patterns of Response			
	Insulated Acceptance	Assimilation	Ethnic Nationalism	Reform Pluralism
Relative size	Moderate to large	Small	Moderate to large	Moderate to large
Settlement pattern	Concentrated	Scattered	Concentrated	Moderate concentration
Within-minority communication	Low	Low	High	High
Socioeconomic status	Low; stable	Low; stable	Low to moderate	Low to moderate, but rising
Political power	Low	Low	Low, but rising	Moderate and rising
Discrimination against minority members	Massive	Massive, but exceptions	Pervasive, but varying	Varying; erratic
Minority organizations and institutions	Intermediate to strong	Weak	Strong	Intermediate
Internal differentiation	Low	High	Moderate	Moderate
Value-similarity with "majority group"	Low	High	Low	High
Economic interdependence with "majority group"	Low	High	Low	High
Personal ties with "majority group"	Few; weak	Many; strong	Few; weak	Intermediate

comes of definite clusters of antecedent conditions. Table 2.2 summarizes a set of major hypotheses, which predict the main tendency that is to be expected under each of several different sets of relevant circumstances. The factors thought to be important determinants are listed in the left-hand column, and their magnitude, frequency, intensity, and the like are characterized in the cells of the table. The predicted patterns of outcome are indicated by the headings of the four columns. Each type of response, thus, may have been characterized by a "profile" of causal antecedents that can be seen by reading down the column.

If we look at the characteristics summarized in the column headed "Insulated Acceptance," we find a geographically concentrated population of substantial size that is poor, has little political power and only weak intra-group communication, and is subject to massive discrimination by a dominant collectivity with which it shares few values and interests. It tends to respond to the hopelessness of its situation under "alien" dominance by reluctant acquiescence and withdrawal from interaction. In contrast, eagerness to become assimilated into a dominant ethnic grouping is likely when the aspiring minority is small, geographically dispersed, experiences discrimination but also the possibility of escape by adopting the culture of the dominant grouping — with which it has active relations of economic interdependence and positive personal interactions. The other patterns can be similarly inferred.

5. Examples of Complex Appraisals

The outcomes of relationships between ethnic groupings depend in part upon the *prior position of each grouping*; changes in position, in turn, depend in part on the character of the prior relationships. Therefore, to appraise relationships it is helpful, first, to have information about position, e.g., measures of wealth, income, education, political participation, occupations, access to housing, access to public services and facilities, stereotypes and social evaluations, participation in voluntary associations, informal social interaction.

Many specific indicators may be needed to describe even one aspect of "position," such as income, or occupation, or education. Composite indexes can be developed. For example, a standard index of equality (EI) has been developed to measure trends in diverse characteristics of populations. According to this index, black Americans made substantial movement toward equality between 1940 and the late 1960s in income, education, occupational status, and quality of housing (Palmore and Whittington, 1970).

A second category for which criteria and descriptive indicators are needed is the *actual character of the relationships between ethnic groupings*, e.g., hostility or friendliness, extent of interaction, segregation, participation in cooperative activities, equality or inequality of status, open or blocked communication, degree of trust or distrust.

Given a description of *position* and of *relationship*, a third set of criteria has to do with the *goals*, implicit or explicit, of *assimilation or convergence* versus *cultural distinctiveness*. What will be rated as "successful" or "unsuccessful" in this regard will depend upon how we take into account (a) the desires of the members of the ethnic groupings themselves, (b) the effects on some larger encompassing social system and (c) second-order effects upon each of the collectivities.

These generalities need anchorage in concrete examples. Take the case of Central European skilled workers who emigrated to large cities in the United

States in the 1890s. By the second generation, their collective economic, political, and social position was good and improving; their relations with the "core majority" were moderately friendly and participative; their basic orientation was assimilationist; their values and social skills were isomorphic with the occupations and urban social structures in which they participated. "Successful intergroup relations" in this instance clearly meant gradual assimilation and the substantial reduction of ethnic cohesiveness in favor of individual upward mobility. In contrast, the secession of the Confederate States from the Union might well have resulted in an autonomous nation with a viable economic system, based on slavery. It then would have been successful from the viewpoint of its own political elite—but a disaster from the stand-point of the Union or of the black population.

We have chosen to speak of *mutual accommodation* as a signal that in our diagnosis *the interests of both (all) parties will be in view, not just those of one participant*.

The particular indicators that will serve to stand for the main variables we have inventoried may be specific to the situation being studied. Each type of collectivity and set of relationships may require different indicators for the same conceptual variables. For example, suppose we want indicators of conflict for industrial labor-management relations and for urban black-white relations, and that our conceptual variables are *conflict-proneness*, *extensity*, and *volume* of conflict (see Britt and Galle, 1972). Our indicators could well be those given in the accompanying tabulation.

Let us look at a second important example of the problem of indexing outcomes. A major societal effort to alter intergroup relations had been under-way since 1954 in the school systems of the United States. It is not simple to define what is meant by "effective desegregation"—the crucial phrase used by the Supreme Court (*Davis v. Board of School Commissioners of Mobile County*, No. 436, April 20, 1971). What is probably the most comprehensive attempt to state a definition reads as follows:

Effective desegregation is a process of educational change which elimi-nates any inequalities in the educational opportunities provided by the state in a public school system which are caused by race, color, or nationality. This process involves three separate elements, all of which are essential to its success. They are (1) meeting specific desegregation requirements established by the Supreme Court, (2) avoiding any undue disruptions in school and community life, and (3) achieving the positive goal of quality unified education for all students (Smith, Downs, Lach-man, 1973, 1).

The authors of this description specify several more detailed criteria, e.g.,

Variables	"Industrial relations"	"Racial relations"
1. Proneness to conflict	Number of work stoppages from lockouts, strikes, and walkouts	Number of riots, demonstrations, protest marches
2. Extensity of conflict	Ratio of mean number of workers involved in stoppages to total employed X 1,000	(1) Ratio of number of participants to total potential participants X 1,000 (2) Total arrests per 1,000 participants
3. Intensity of conflict	Number man-days idle ÷ number of workers involved in stoppage	(1) Number person-days involvement ÷ total number of participants (2) Number injured and killed
4. Volume of conflict	Number man-days idle ÷ number of workers employed X 1,000	(1) Total days involvement ÷ number of participants X 1,000 (2) Total property damage

equal resources devoted to education per pupil regardless of race, adaptation of resources equally to the particular needs of each student, treating children with respect and dignity and with positive expectations about their ability and worth, desegregation at the level of the classroom, an atmosphere conducive to self-confidence and mutual respect, avoiding "undue" violence or hostility, maintenance (or improvement) in academic performance.

When we come to our own analysis of desegregation (Chapter 3), we shall find ourselves drawn to all of these criteria. We shall want to look for information concerning academic performance, aspirations and expectations of pupils, integration among pupils and teachers, self-evaluations, intergroup attitudes, conflict, and cooperation. For each of these categories, specific indexes can be devised. Given the data on such points, any community, organization, or social system can be described in enough specific features to permit realistic assessment in terms of whatever values an observer chooses to apply. But perhaps the more important implication is that major societal programs always have *multiple* outcomes, each of which is likely to be judged by several different criteria. Thus, there typically will be a profile of outcomes, ranging from "successful" to "catastrophic" as evaluated by different individuals and groups. We could arrange schools that would produce high academic performance by a few and poor performance by the great majority. An educational program can be imagined that would produce happy peer-group interaction and almost no subject-matter learning. It is commonplace to find unintended results that are also undesired from well-intentioned activities. Not surprisingly, for instance, any procedure that publicly identifies and stigmatizes individuals as members of a "bad" or "inferior" category will tend to undo rehabilitative efforts. Thus a work-study program for inner-city high school boys that seemed on its face to have many possibilities for rehabilitating "problem" youths turned out to have unanticipated negative effects.

For example, a more permissive school program was accompanied by much unruly behavior and fighting. The boys themselves felt so strongly that they would lie on the floor of the school bus on the way to work projects rather than be seen by their friends. Their teachers similarly felt that their peers looked down on them because they were working with "failures" (Robins, 1973, 237).

In general, our evaluations of the internal functioning of those collectivities that have specifiable goals tend to fall into three broad categories (Caplow, 1953):

1. Performance in attaining explicit objectives, e.g., votes, profits, victories, election of candidates, growth in membership, competitive placement of graduates, contributions taken in, patients returned to work. The performance always costs something. Therefore, the outcomes typically are assessed as to whether they were attained at minimal cost, at acceptable cost, or at a maximum cost-benefit ratio.
2. Minimization or acceptable resolution of internal conflicts.
3. Maximizing or optimizing the satisfactions of members.

These are aspects of internal effectiveness or efficiency. When we look at organizations or other collectivities from the standpoint of the whole society of which each is a part, we have to judge how much the subunit contributes to other parts of the system—no matter how difficult it may be to estimate that contribution.

For a total society an important criterion of intergroup relations is the extent of value consensus among its ethnic constituents. In Chapter 1, we noted briefly that in the United States, there is much evidence of important similarities of opinions, attitudes, beliefs, values, and overt behavior as between whites and blacks (see the extensive compilation in Miller and Dreger, 1973). Agreement often is remarkably specific: in a Baltimore sample Rossi et al.

(1974) find that blacks and whites agree quite closely ($r = .89$) in their rankings of the seriousness of 140 crimes. A complex configuration of similarities and differences between white and black workers has been described for St. Louis as of 1968 (Kahl and Goering, 1971). In samples of stable working- and middle-class men, blacks and whites had similar job aspirations and satisfactions. Both segments of the population shared economic ambition, high hopes for their children, satisfacton with job and advancement, and had a sense of personal security in employment. Blacks and whites differed appreciably, however, in political orientations: blacks were more critical, more favorable to protest, and more likely to see a need for group militancy. In short, personal satisfaction among blacks did not imply political conservatism. A 1973 survey of a state-wide sample of adult heads of households in North Carolina found that when income levels were controlled, there were no significant differences at all between blacks and whites on seven personal values (such as personal freedom, achievement, material comfort); of seven social values, whites ranked higher on "patriotism" and "political democracy" whereas blacks gave high ratings to "humanitarianism" and "racial equality" (Christenson and Yang, 1976).

For a national sample of adults surveyed in 1968, the rankings of 18 instru-mental values and 18 terminal values were highly similar for blacks and whites. When roughly matched for income and education, most first-order differences disappeared (Rokeach, 1973). Only one really large and pervasive difference in value-rankings remained after controlling for socioeconomic status: black Americans gave very high rank to the value of equality whereas whites gave it much lower priority. This highly important difference does not come from some vague subcultural ethos but from the specific experience of a disadvan-taged minority struggling against discrimination.

It is clear that any appraisal of ethnic relations depends both upon our *values* and upon our knowledge *and beliefs about social realities*, their causes and consequences. The effects of any given social process—including strategies, tactics, or procedures—upon intergroup relations may be assessed in terms of ingroup attitudes and outgroup attitudes, of the overt behavior of each of the parties, and of various kinds of psychological changes. Any assessment that is not to be seriously incomplete or partisan must consider all these aspects, expecially since the active parties are more likely than not to have different evaluations of the situation and its outcomes (Levy, 1968; Ford, 1973; Bullock and Braxton, 1973).

But suppose we have an excellent causal analysis based upon incontrovert-ible evidence and that we also have a clear set of generalized value-standards for judging what social conditions are desirable. There will remain a crucial step. We still have to select specific empirical or ideal points of reference for making value-judgments.

Such reference points can have decisive influence on evaluations. For example, historical memory often is defective with regard to the period just before the most recent past. A gap in perspective thus may arise. By the end of the 1960s advocates of changes that would be both more rapid and more far-reaching than those of the preceding decade could deprecate the outcomes of the Civil Rights Movement as "merely cosmetic." The abolition of legally enforced segregation, for example, sometimes was discounted as of benefit only to blacks of higher education and income ("the right to be overcharged at the Vesterbilt Hotel").

But the actual changes could be called trivial only against some very high ideal standard, not one of historical comparison of the specific details of racial segregation before World War II. A vivid account of the *status quo ante* has been given by Chief Justice Earl Warren in this account of how black citizens then fared in the public life of various southern states.

They could not live where they desired; they could not work where white people worked, except in menial positions. They were prosecuted for breaking peonage contracts that kept them in a state of subjection. They could not use the same restrooms, drinking fountains, or telephone booths. They could not eat in the same restaurants, sleep in the same hotels, be treated in the same hospitals, or be transported to a hospital in an ambulance which on other occasions was used for whites. They could not enter by the same entrance that whites used, or sit in the same section with them in theaters or other public accommodations. They could not use the same public parks, playgrounds, beaches, golf courses or athletic stadiums, even though the facilities were supported by public funds. They could not use the same reading rooms or even the same books in a public library. They could not compete with or against whites in the same athletic event, or in some states, even in close proximity to one.

They could not attend the same public schools, but were relegated to substandard school facilities and inferior teaching provided at grossly less cost than at white schools. They were bused for hours each day to inferior and crowded schools when there were underoccupied white school rooms in proximity to where they lived. They were denied admission to any university or college attended by whites, whether public or private.

They were denied the right to sit on juries even when their own lives, freedom, or property rights were involved. In court, they were all addressed as Joe or Willie or "boy," as Jennie or Gertie, regardless of age. They were segregated in the court rooms, sworn to testify truthfully on different Bibles. And because of the poverty of the overwhelming majority of them, they were denied the right to be represented by counsel, except in capital cases, and in many such cases, as illustrated by the Scottsboro cases, the representation accorded them there was a travesty on justice. They were segregated in prison and were often permitted to be lynched while in custody without a trial of any kind.

They were segregated on buses, street cars, trains, ships, and airplanes and at terminals of all kinds. They were not allowed to vote. . . .

Going hand-in-hand with all this was an aggravated condition of mal-apportionment in State Legislatures, County Boards of Education, and City Councils, designed in some instances, through gerrymandering, to place them in segregated districts where they could not participate meaningfully in any way in their government. . . .

All of this and much more, either through statutes or customs enforced by vagrancy statutes or others called "breach of the peace," "unlawful assembly," were used oppressively to prevent the blacks from asserting their constitutional rights. All of this was done under the umbrella of the benign-sounding phrase "separate but equal." Separate it was in all its implications, but each and every law, practice, or sentiment it spawned was the very essence of inequality.

About the time these conditions reached the height of pervasiveness, we entered World War II, and President Roosevelt announced the Four Freedoms. They were incorporated into the Atlantic Charter as "Freedom of speech and expression; Freedom of worship; and Freedom from want and fear." This, with the statement of our Allies and ourselves that the freedoms we were fighting for were pledged to both our own people and to those in other countries we were seeking to liberate, ignited a spark that awakened the hopes of oppressed people throughout the world. These statements and our victory in that war broke up the colonial systems of the world that were based on the subjection of people of color as inferior races, and struck a responsive chord in the racial minority groups in this country—the blacks, the American Indians, the Chicanos, and the Asiatics of which there are 34 million in our country at this time. A flood of litigation challenging discriminatory laws and practices started, and much of it found its way to the Supreme Court (Warren, 1973, 20-22).

As we reviewed in Chapter 1, the eventual outcome of the civil rights actions was legal abolition of state-supported segregation and discrimination. Actual segregation and discrimination were greatly reduced, but not eliminated.

The actual implementation of Supreme Court decisions and Congressional legislation required a long and painful struggle against the "massive resistance" of white segregationists. Massive resistance was the mobilization during the 1950s and 1960s of white southern segregationists against court decisions and legislation that threatened the old system of white supremacy and of forced inequalitarian segregation. Massive resistance took the forms of hundreds of legislative acts, numerous court battles, widespread propaganda campaigns, economic threats and deprivations, filibusters and parliamentary maneuvers, lobbying, censorship, administrative evasions, fiscal sanctions, and so on. By the end of the 1960s, however, it was plain that massive resistance had been a massive failure in its announced aim of preventing change (Wilhoit, 1973). But it delayed public school desegregation for a full decade, mobilized and hardened prejudices in many people, and aborted many promising moves toward racial integration by transforming them into tokenism. As a rearguard action, therefore, it could not be termed wholly unsuccessful from the viewpoint of segregationists. It certainly was able to impose very high social costs upon millions of people.

Perhaps the examples already reviewed are enough to permit us to formulate a general framework that will help us to locate any particular instance of assessment. We have seen that comprehensive assessments require:

1. an agreed-upon set of values;
2. a valid causal analysis, based on valid empirical evidence;
3. a specification of short-run versus long-term evaluations;
4. a specification of the similar and differing evaluations of the immediately involved parties;
5. some method of deriving a profile of evaluated outcomes, or else of aggregating qualitatively diverse values.

So stringent are these conditions that any appraisals currently possible fall far short of adequacy. But failure to pay attention to any of these intrinsic characteristics would only make matters worse. An inventory of needed types of assessment criteria will help us to guard against unwitting omissions and distortions.

The tentative and incomplete inventory in the accompanying tabulation will be our first guide to analysis of ethnic relations today.

The combinations of these criteria produce a large number of radically different kinds of intergroup situations, ranging from "harmonious mutual assimilation," through "structural integration" and "symbiotic coexistence," to the most intense mutual hostility and unlimited violent conflict.

One other implication seems evident from this brief review of the tasks of social appraisal. Various characterizations of intergroup relations that may be

Types of Criteria for Assessment of Ethnic
Intergroup Relationships and Processes

I. How equal or unequal are existing distributions and allocations of scarce values among social categories, statuses, and collectivities, e.g.:

1. Income
2. Wealth
3. Prestige
4. Power
5. Authority
6. Influence
7. Safety (health; violence)
8. Education ("enlightenment")
9. Access to facilities (housing, medical care, public accommodations, recreation)
10. Privacy
11. Respect
12. Protection from environmental assaults (noise, heat, cold, noxious smells, interference with activity, exposure to morally repellent stimuli)

II. To what extent are the members of the various ethnic collectivities characterized by such personality or psychological characteristics as:

1. Sense of fate-control
2. Self-conception (general self-esteem; specific evaluations of abilities; sense of potency; sense of integration or integrity)
3. Anxiety; fear; guilt
4. Intrapunitive or extrapunitive dispositions
5. Hostility
6. Dogmatism; rigidity; authoritarianism
7. Alienation; anomia

III. What conditions exist among the social structures and relationships internal to each ethnic collectivity, e.g.:

1. Stability and integration of families, communities, associations
2. Mutual liking
3. Cooperative activity; mutual aid
4. Cohesion or solidarity of the collectivity
5. Degree of consensus
6. Consensual evaluation of the collectivity

IV. What are the main features of intergroup relations with regard to:

1. Extent of interactions
2. Equalitiarian or inequalitarian
3. Hostile or friendly
4. Degree of interdependence
5. Degree of rigid stereotyping vs. flexible situational realism
6. Mutual and asymmetrical group evaluations (competence, moral qualities)
7. Degree of sharing of values, beliefs, norms
8. Extent of development of representative and mediating organization and procedures
9. Extent of joint enterprises, common goals, collaborative activity

highly suitable for purposes of persuasion, propaganda, and political planning and action, no matter how laudable, are not the same as the formulations most useful for comprehension and analysis. For political purposes it often is desired that diagnoses be simple, that facts be aggregated, that alternatives be sharp, that solutions be definite, that ambiguities be ignored. For responsible sociological analysis, it is equally essential that complexity and ambiguity be faced, uncertainties acknowledged, and missing data noted.

The subtitle of this book, "Ethnic Conflict and Cooperation," points to the inherently dual and complex nature of the collective relationships we shall examine; the simple case of pure cooperation or pure conflict is rarely found.

6. Conflict or Cooperation; Which Is the More Important Social Reality?

The story has it that when Margaret Fuller finally announced she accepted the Universe, Carlyle opined, "Gad, she'd better." That was a case of deciding whether to stay with the Only Show in Town. Our present choice is rather more open, but in one respect it is parallel: we either decide to pay attention to both conflict and harmony, both opposition and cooperation, or else we cut ourselves off from a major part of the human social world.

First of all, it is a fantasy to suppose that any society can be devised that will have no conflict. So long as people have wants, needs, and desires, they will sometimes encroach upon other people, and they will sometimes have to defend themselves or be encroached upon by others. Resistance or opposition to the demands of others is essential for that separateness without which neither individuals nor collectivities can have integrity—i.e., boundaries. Then, given that there will be opposition, it is inevitable in any considerable sample of oppositional occasions that some "assertions" will be met by efforts to injure, obstruct, or deprive the encroacher, and that some assertions, in turn, will have damaging consequences for anyone who stands in the way of the outreaching social actor.

Conflict is not the same as assertiveness but does grow out of it. Social conflict is two-sided: it consists of interaction in which one party intends and acts to control, deprive, injure, or eliminate another, against the will of that other. Pure conflict is a *fight*; both its goal and its effect is to immobilize, neutralize, destroy, or otherwise harm an opponent. In the world of real events, some overt struggles are conducted according to rules and for limited goals; oppositional behavior may then have the primary goal of winning rather than of injuring the opponent; we usually call the encounter a *game* (Rapoport, 1960). Although an interest in winning is common to games and *debates*, the latter are characterized by the fact that the actor's primary aim is to persuade opponents or others of the rightness or correctness or attractiveness of one's views or claims.[2]

Social conflicts arise from three great classes of opposition: (1) from incompatibilities of claims to scarce loci of value, whether transferable or not transferable; (2) from incompatibilities of beliefs, norms, and value standards; (3) from the expression in behavior of affective dispositions and impulses. An important subtype of (2) consists of contradictions or incompatibilities of obligations, allegiances, or loyalties to different individuals and collectivities.

Not opposition of interests, nor incompatibilities of beliefs and evaluations, nor expressions of dispositions such as "aggressiveness" necessarily lead to social conflict. Claims to scarce, divisible, and transferable values such as money may be directly incompatible as first presented, but may be open to settlement through exchange, compromise, adjudication by third parties, and in many other nonconflictual ways. Similarly, particular incompatibilities of beliefs and evaluations may be resolved by debate and persuasion, by mutual withdrawal from interaction, by agreement to disagree, and the like. Even the direct acting out of aggressive dispositions or the direct expression of hostile sentiments may not lead to conflict, for the person who is the target may treat the behavior in question as accidental, or mistaken, or neurotic (or psychotic) or simply as natural and inevitable expressiveness—thereby refusing to impute a valid intent to injure and refusing to respond in kind.

Contrary to some impressions, some highly conflictful groups are quite orderly; some peaceful groups are filled with confusion and lack commitment. We do not assume here, therefore, that "order" and "conflict" necessarily are opposing social conditions. In any event, both social order and social conflict always are continuing, simultaneous aspects of interaction among individuals and groupings in every society. There is no society without some conflict. Without some order, there is no society.

If one can adequately explain conflict, one will also have advanced our knowledge of order; if one can adequately explain social order, one will have helped us to understand conflict. The evidence is clear beyond dispute that conflicts of various kinds are frequent in every human society. The evidence is equally decisive in showing that stable systems of interaction are marked by the development of substantial consensus concerning goals and norms (Williams, 1966).

Thus, just as in the opposite instance, it is a fantasy to suppose that any society can be devised that will represent a pure system of conflict. Fully recognizing the prevalence of conflict, we must acknowledge at the same time that people often do find that they have common goals, convergent or complementary interests, and similar norms and values and beliefs. Social harmony and cooperation are facts of life, along with disagreement, opposition, domination, and conflict.

7. The Basic Characteristics of Ethnic Relations

Why are we concentrating our attention upon ethnic relations? Partly because of the present importance in the United States of racial, religious, and nationality-origin groupings. But partly also because of the permanent and basic significance of a better understanding of what the study of ethnic relations has to teach us about conflict and cooperation as basic features of the human situation. What is distinctive about such relations?

As usual, the first lesson is to recognize that the evident complexity of relationships among ethnic collectivities stems from the diversity of ethnicity itself. Ethnic relations vary greatly in *psychological* aspects such as salience, clarity, importance, hostility or positive affect, ambivalence, commitment, or identification. In the *cultural* system, ethnicity may involve language, religious beliefs and practices, institutional norms and values (family, stratification, education, etc.), expressive styles, food preferences, and so on. Ethnic collectivities vary in such *social* properties as size, interconnectedness, definiteness and strength of boundaries, degree of closure, centralization, stratification, control of resources, relationships with allies and enemies, internal interdependence, or degree and kind of control of members.

Ethnicity in the U.S. has diminished greatly during this century, as indicated by decreased rates of ingroup marriage, lessened interethnic hostility and exclusion, lessened participation in ethnic voluntary associations, and lessened sharing of a non-American nationality culture. What remains is a sense of ethnic membership that may be intensified by a sense of frustration, by fraternal deprivation, and by perceived threat from newly militant racial minorities (Goering, 1971); what remains also are diffuse networks of social relationships linked both to a sense of identity and solidarity and to tangible economic and political interests. Because of these linkages, ethnic identities do not quickly or easily disappear even under the conditions most highly favorable to acculturation and assimilation.

A large amount of historical evidence seems to support the following conclusions:

1. Both complete assimilation ("melting-pot") and ethnic nationalism are unrealistic in a multicultural national society of complex interdependence.
2. The balance between ethnic retentionism and separatism versus partial assimilation and social integration is delicate and variable, changing over time and from situation to situation.

3. Both positive and negative stereotyping of ethnic groupings inevitably occur to some extent.

4. In the absence of interactions that are both close and situationally diverse, stereotyping is especially likely to be sharp, unrealistic, and hostile.

5. Competition is most likely to lead to ethnic conflict when: (a) cultural differences are great, (b) social segregation is prevalent, (c) economic conditions are severe, (d) social change is rapid. Also the greater the number of interests and values that differ as between any ethnic collectivities, the more salient will be ethnicity and the more likely that conflicts will emerge.

6. Two opposing views of intergroup stereotyping and prejudice are in error when taken as exclusive claims to valid interpretation: (a) prejudices and stereotypes, on the whole, are accurate, although generalized, reflections of actual differences ("well-deserved reputation"); (b) prejudices and stereotypes simply are expressions of the values, beliefs, and emotional dispositions of the holders (the outgroup functions as a "living inkblot").

7. Although negative prejudices toward outgroups are intercorrelated, the tendency toward generalized outgroup rejection is only moderate in most cases, and is highly variable in the general population over time. Intergroup relations are not wholly "blind."

8. A durable situation of mutually acceptable cultural pluralism seems to require the development of: (a) a common core of agreement on norms of public interaction and modes of settling disagreements and conflicts, (b) relatively slow change in size of ethnic fractions in the population, (c) a substantial amount of equal-status collaborative interaction across ethnic lines, and (d) effective protection of basic political and civil rights for all members of the societal community (Williams, 1974).

In our view, intergroup relations (racial, ethnic, religious) constitute a recurrent or permanent and distinctive sector of all continuing total social systems (Parsons, 1951; Williams, 1965). All persisting societies have kinship and family systems within which ascribed statuses are assigned in terms of particularistic, diffuse, and collectivity-oriented norms. There is always a minimal geographic community, imposed by the necessities of regulating interaction within an area of residential proximity. Universally also, there develops some institutionalized system of ranking individuals and kinship units in scales of privilege and esteem. To the degree that subcultural differences arise and are transmitted between generations through kinship groupings, a fourth basic set of groupings develops: ethnic "communities."

Upon the base of these four structures, further differentiation produces economic institutions, i.e., systems of production and allocation of scarce resources. Stabilization of power relationships leads to specialization in the acquisition and use of power, giving the system a set of political institutions. Religious institutions, probably present "from the beginning," often stand in close relation to the political structures. Finally, with the loss of exclusiveness of the kinship institutions, education arises as a special subsystem.

Thus ethnic relations in the broadest sense are deeply embedded in the ascribed, particularistic, diffuse substructures of societies. The strength and ubiquity of these relationships clearly derive in part from their close connections with kinship, community, and social stratification. For subcultures and economic and political positions are transmitted by kinship groups and relationships (Zeitlin, Ewen, Ratcliff, 1974); occupational groupings often represent ecological clusterings of kinship units; and any given cultural distinctiveness of a segment of the population tends to become a part of institutionalized social ranking.

But if ethnic groupings are "primary," as they surely are in the special sense just indicated, they are also "derivative": that is, they may be created or reinforced by economic and political processes, as when the political power established by conquest is used to assign menial occupations exclusively to a subordinate population. Similarly, occupational specialization (arising, for example, from religious orientations) may create an objective basis for social strata that have distinctive cultural characteristics.

Evidently an enormous part is played in intergroup relations by *power*—in allocating rewards and penalties and in establishing subcollectivity boundaries. Major changes in racial and ethnic relations require changes in the balance of social power. Hence, the character of particular political institutions and political movements is of central interest in our effort to analyze both conflict and mutual accommodation.

8. Ethnic Categories and Collectivities

Racial and ethnic relations refer to two very different types of social formations: (1) social categories and (2) collectivities. A social category represents a classification of people on the basis of a common attribute, or attributes, real or imagined. Categories may be based on age (infants, old people, teen-agers), sex, height and weight, ancestry, nationality, IQ, length of residence (oldtimers and newcomers), and so on. But the individuals in a given social category need not form a collectivity—there is no collectivity of day-old infants. We do not speak of a collectivity unless four characteristics are present: (a) social interaction among the members, (b) a sense of common membership (e.g., "shared fate"), (c) norms governing interaction, both within the collectivity and with outsiders, (d) some effective sense of obligation to support and defend the collectivity and its symbols. (Specific *groups* are highly organized and well-bounded collectivities.) The extent to which ethnic classifications represent real collectivities varies greatly from very weak distinctions based on a single characteristic to a totally exclusive, nonoverlapping boundary defined by many variables (Moxley, 1973; Barth and Noel, 1972; LeVine and Campbell, 1972). In the weak sense, all socialized members of human societies have an ethnic identity. This means that everyone is a member of "a collectivity within a larger society having real or putative common ancestry; memories of a shared historical past, and a cultural focus on one or more symbolic elements defined as the epitome of their peoplehood" (Schermerhorn, 1970, 12). Yet as nearly universal as ethnicity in this sense clearly is, it is also a condition that often is ambiguous, multidimensional, vague, and changeable (Gould, 1971; Greeley and McCready, 1974). So-called racial groupings are ethnic collectivities and often have such changeable and ambiguous or vague boundaries—a fact that may be of considerable importance in analyzing the outlook for mutual accommodation among blacks and whites in the United States.

9. Racism

When we accept the task of analyzing possibilities for mutual accommodation among ethnic collectivities, therefore, we cannot avoid a basic consideration of both white and black "racism." How important is such racism and how rigid and fixed or flexible and subject to change is it? The first point that requires attention is to clarify what racism means. Above all, it is essential to distinguish racism in the sense of ordinary *prejudice* (or in the sense of diffuse expressive discrimination by separate individuals) from racism as an *institutionalized, interindividual system* of practices, rules, vested interests, and interconnected social structures (Greenstone and Peterson, 1973, 312). In this work, when we wish to refer to prejudice, we shall use that word instead of racism. When we refer to a specific type of prejudice that invokes belief in unchanging, innate biological characteristics, we shall speak of "racial prejudice." When we refer to an institutionalized system that results in persistent racial discrimination, we may occasionally speak of "institutional racism." But we want especially to avoid the misleading popular use of "white racism" as a global characterization for an undefined mélange of prejudice, racialist beliefs, segregation, discrimination, and institutional structures that have discriminatory side effects. Such a term has no clear or definite referent, and its widespread use already has contributed too much to public confusion and misdiagnosis even since the 1968 Kerner Commission popularized the expression.

"Racism," like "prejudice," is a label; it explains nothing. When taken as a surrogate for diagnosis, it leads to the false conclusion that discrimination is merely an emanation of prejudice. It easily degenerates into name-calling. To avoid falling back into the very modes of thinking that have impeded clarity in the past, we must move beyond the easy formulas of racism (Dixon and Foster, 1971). The more difficult but essential job is to analyze the specific sources and outcomes of different kinds of ethnic relations. For example, to understand the initial development of cooperation or conflict between any two ethnic groupings we must know the extent of their interdependence, their equality or inequality in power, the importance of their interdependence (relative to their involvements with third parties), their autonomy in decision-making, and the initial and continuing incompatibilities and complementarities in their interests, beliefs, and values. Social units will neither cooperate nor come into conflict if they are mutually inaccessible or irrelevant. High accessibility and high relevance, on the other hand, means that the units *must* take one another into account. Whether interaction will continue and, if so, whether cooperative, competitive, or conflictful relationships will result, depends upon the balance of congruity and reward as over against incompatibility and threat or blockage in the concrete situation at hand.

10. Why Does Collective Conflict Occur?

Essentially, conflict develops out of two primary sets of conditions: (1) social opposition based on incompatibility of interests or of beliefs and values, and (2) processes that are then occasioned by the opposition itself, such as deception, expressing derogatory judgments, blocking goal-directed activity, or inflicting injury (Walton, Dutton, Fitch, 1966, 458).

For the preliminary purposes of this chapter, we propose the following very general sketch of the basic elements of conflict and cooperation that must be kept in view in later and more specific discussions.

1. Preferences typically outrun opportunities, desires outrun opportunities for gratifications.
2. Hence, more often than not, resources for the satisfaction of needs and wants are in short supply.
3. Accordingly, given that there is motivation among a plurality of actors to strive for scarce resources, the short-run game is zero-sum.
4. A zero-sum game implies competition, rivalry, or conflict.
5. Consensus on norms is required for *competition* and *rivalry*.
6. But there are inherent sources of diversity of interests, beliefs, and values among social persons and collectivities.

7. The diversity cannot be eliminated without occasioning overt conflict; some social units, persons, or collectivities will resist the efforts of others to control the necessary components for reducing diversity —whether these be genetic, cultural, social.
8. People tend, no matter how slightly, to favor their own interests and those of the collectivities to which they belong over the interests of other persons and their collectivities.
9. Hence, the irreducible diversity will produce from time to time occasions in which overt conflict will arise.

It follows from these assumptions that the likelihood of conflict will be increased, all other things being held constant, by:

1. a decrease in resources for attaining gratifications;
2. an increase in expectations or aspirations for control of scarce resources;
3. an increase in differentiation of divergent interests among individuals;
4. an increase in differentiation of divergent interests among collectivities;
5. a decrease in consensus concerning *regulative* norms;
6. a decrease in consensus concerning *values constitutive of a system of relationships* among social units;
7. an increase in communication among similar units and a decrease in communication across units having incompatible interests;
8. a decrease in the salience and effectiveness of social agents capable of imposing negative sanctions for conflict-behavior;
9. a decrease in advantageous interdependence with parties having some incompatible interests.

If the social system is highly differentiated by industries and occupations, and by regional and local economies, any important technological change or shift in demand will have a very uneven impact in altering economic advantages and disadvantages and, consequently, social esteem, prestige, and power. If such changes are frequent and massive, the effects will include (1) high awareness of differentials in control of scarce values and (2) widespread experience of frustrations and deprivations that are perceived as arbitrary. Accordingly, it is to be expected that rapidly changing societies will experience frequent conflicts. The conflicts may be mild or severe, depending upon other conditions. They may or may not have an ethnic focus.

Many of the lines of social cleavage in our industrial, commercial, urbanized society are expressed in economic competition. As Blalock (1967) has shown, competitive threats more than power-threats tend to produce gradual rather than abrupt mobilization of resources. Because competitive threats most often concern divisible and transferable values, they are relatively open to negotiation and compromise. Also, to the extent that competition initally involves a tacit acceptance of some restraining rules, the competitors are thereby informed that the threat is less than total and that their potential opponents are not wholly without scruples. On the other hand, power-threats more often are perceived as "total" or, at least, as leading to undefined and indefinite possibilities.

Collective conflict, then, arises directly out of very ordinary, recurrent, and specific conditions of social systems. Because of inherent territorial restrictions on social interaction and the necessities for the temporal ordering of interactions, persisting clusters of recurring interaction will (must) arise. Social behavior is time-bound and space-bound; it must concentrate at particular points. Because these clusters also involve interdependence in vital activities, there emerge enduring solidarities and cleavages—for example, local communities, kinship groupings, ethnic groupings. Among social units there then will develop; (1) *complementary activities*, expressed in both collaboration and exchange; (2) *divergencies* of interests, beliefs, and values, resulting both from specialization and from cultural diversification; and (3) *oppositions*, due to incompatibilities or contradictions of interests, values, and beliefs. To the extent that oppositions develop, there will be increased potentialities for conflict. However, some oppositions will be embedded in relationships that also contain advantages. To the extent that more attractive alternatives are not available, or are not perceived, the result will be competition, rivalry, or peaceful bargaining within mixed-motive interactions.

Low rates of social conflict are resultants of greatly varied combinations of consensus, interdependence, insulation, and balance of power. Many situations of stable peace are those that integrate power and consensus in definite patterns of roles (deVos, 1966, 62). Low rates of conflict also may occur when social complexity is low, groupings are small, organization is loose, social differentiation is slight, and power is evenly distributed.

To assume that objectively deprivational or oppressive conditions inevitably lead to discontent is unwarranted. And widespread discontent, in turn, does not necessarily result in collective protest or rebellion. For discontent may be diffuse and unorganized and the discontented often are faced with overwhelming coercive capacity in the hands of committed supporters of an existing regime. Especially clear is the crucial importance of the willingness of police and armed services to put down protests and uprisings. Without substantial disaffection within the agencies of political authority, effective rebellion is highly unlikely, and even large-scale attempts will be rare (Russell, 1974).

It is not consistent with experience to assume that all intergroup struggles and their accompanying antagonisms are open to peaceable resolution. Some are not. At a particular time and in a particular conjunction of circumstances, some conflict is unavoidable and some of the conflict will be violent. Nevertheless, the *ex post facto* appearance of inevitability of many conflicts may conceal large components of uncertainty, imperfect information, and cumulative misapprehension, and the processes of conflict themselves are similarly affected by bias, ambiguity, vagueness, and lack of accurate information. The *extent* and *kind* of threats and coercive acts vary greatly even in massive overt struggles. The variations, in turn, have significant consequences for the character of any eventual accommodations that may emerge from a particular episode of conflict.

11. Realistic and Utopian Visions

We must reject the assumption that every social problem must have a solution. Many problems arise that are never solved, and for some of them it has not been possible even to imagine a "solution." No one yet has found a way to abolish those two proverbial certainties of life—death and taxes. Thus if anyone thinks that the only "successful" intergroup relations have to be those in which no problems remain unsolved, then there are not now and never will be any successful intergroup relations.

A second illusion, only slightly less pervasive and stubborn than the first, is that real remedies—for social dislocations, malfunctionings, and excessively costly functions and conflicts—have to be permanent. But there are *no* really permanent solutions to any problem in society. All things change. What is "permanent" depends entirely upon the time-scale in which we are interested. Practitioners who devise social remedies typically learn that permanent solutions are mirages and that pragmatic wisdom dictates a less cosmic time-perspective.

> Somehow when we are prescribing for a mechanism like collective bargaining, we ought to keep in mind that a mechanism that works for as much as five years before it becomes obsolete is a good remedy. We are in the same position as the medical profession which in its search for a cancer cure, defines a cancer cure as a five-year freedom from symptoms. If any mechanism to resolve the kind of conflict we have in collective bargaining works for five years, then I would say that it has been a success. When new problems present themselves, new mechanisms will have to be invented (Gomberg, 1974, 413).

There are real solutions that can be devised for many conditions that we may regard as social problems. But no solution ever will be found that does not in its turn create *new* problems, and no one has been given either the ability or the right to bind the future irrevocably for those who will live in it. To expect permanent perfection is to ensure inevitable disillusionment, as one rejects the only workable solutions. Often enough that road ends in apocalyptic visions and ferocious utopias.

Utopias do have crucial uses (Moore, 1966) and we cannot and should not dispense with visions of some kind. But a realistic agenda for social policy and action for the immediate future of intergroup relations calls, in addition, for causal diagnosis and detailed consideration of actual limitations and opportunities.

If we do not learn from past experience, we shall continue in each generation to repeat avoidable mistakes. If we desire to manage or resolve at least some of the disruptive conflicts that inevitably will arise in the future, we may find lessons in the study of how such conflicts sometimes have been regulated, managed, or resolved in the past. For instance, ambiguity of power-relations and misestimations of likely outcomes often lead to conflicts in which all parties lose heavily. Any less costly means of improving the accuracy of forecasts presumably would be generally welcomed. (Test cases, advisory opinions straw votes, opinion surveys, and simulated contests are examples of means of checking appraisals in advance of full-scale conflicts.)

The relatively unorganized, diffuse, multicentered character of ethnic and racial conflicts in American society suggests that there may be value in looking at other collective conflicts having similar structural characteristics. One may immediately think of the struggles of economic interest groups and social classes. But even quite small and inconspicuous cases also may have much to teach us. Thus, among the numerous localized conflicts will be found useful examples of the spontaneous development of tacit bargains, informal regulation, third-party intervention, and the like.

12. Requirements for Effective Social Action

We spoke of learning from experience—but of course we recognize that the effectiveness of particular actions or programs is rarely obvious or easy to appraise. Effectiveness often is masked by counteraction. In a very large number of instances, the effects of actions taken by some social unit—a local community, a union, a voluntary association, a corporation, a church, a court, a legislature, a governmental agency—are neutralized or reversed by other actions. In a stubborn world of a plurality of values and interests that often are opposed or incompatible, the strength of interests and the astuteness of strategies—not just the virtue of our cause—are pitted against other interests, strategies, and virtues.

And these considerations point to the fact that programs may be ineffective not only because they are explicitly counteracted but also because the new incentives and powers they command do not match the strength of established incentives. For it must be evident that any existing set of social arrangements that is thought to have undesirable consequences will not owe its existence to sheer perversity or whim or accident. Social relationships and structures persist in large part because someone "profits" from them; if no one gains, the status quo can be toppled with a push, but when the old order strongly benefits its supporters, resistance to change will be great.

Many purposive attempts to change intergroup relations work with weak incentives applied to groups that have low power. To paraphrase Alfred Marshall, such efforts fail to make the necessary appeal to the "stronger rather than merely the higher motives of men." The crude measures available for large-scale social intervention usually do not permit overly delicate work. Rather, the workable incentives are those that appeal to widely held and strong interests—such as the status and security of one's family, the esteem and prestige enjoyed in a community of peers, the desire for revenge, the fear of loss of power, or the hope of economic gain.

Now, much valid social analysis quite properly aims only to describe and to find causal connections—why discrimination exists, how intergroup bargaining occurs, and so on. This may be called contemplative analysis. A quite different way of proceeding is to ask what conditions are potentially open to purposive change. Social science that hopes to aid purposive action must not only seek to describe and predict, but also to identify key points of intervention. There is no need here to argue about the extent to which conflict is "ultimately controllable"; the intention rather is merely to search for an understanding of the dynamics of conflict that will aid those individuals and groups who wish to deal with conflict to maximize its positive outcomes.

An analysis of "positive" and "negative" aspects of conflict processes and methods of conflict resolution must be carried out in each of various major sectors of the social system—e.g., housing, labor, education, politics, religion, the judicial system, and other social institutions. Although conflict is often handled similarly in each of these social systems, it is likely that each social sphere has unique features. Hence the more useful analyses are likely to be those that specify how conflict and conflict resolution are affected by institutional setting and organizational context—school, union, church, local community, political party, or whatever. Each main social sector has its own norms and value emphasis. Thus, the energetic and relatively unrestrained competition that is highly valued in the political system often is regarded as an impropriety in religious affairs. Dramatic public confrontations of collective representatives usually are less disruptive in a labor dispute than in a school system. Similarly, issues of concern vary by sector: although housing conflicts center upon property values, patterns of social mobility, and neighboring, many political conflicts deal with highly regulated competition and with issues of representation. An analysis of the distinctions between social sectors, accordingly, helps to locate unique constraints and opportunities which a given conflict situation will contain.

All social life involves influence and influencing. Each person is affected by the presence and activities of others and in turn affects those others. The effects may be intended or unintended; most often, both. When we speak here of purposive attempts to maintain or change ethnic relations, we are merely focusing upon one of the many areas of life in which influence *will* be exerted, whether intended or not. The question, then, is not one of "playing God" or, less dramatically, whether or not we shall influence others. We do and we shall, inevitably, even if only by inaction or by sheer presence. The relevant questions for anyone who seeks to understand how human groupings cooperate, compete, or come into conflict are much more specific than the usual global query, "Can we influence social events?" We have to ask:

Who is seeking to influence *whom* by *what means* for *what purposes or goals*, under what circumstances of *constraints and opportunities*?

The first question always is: Who are "we"? Suppose someone says, "We can do little to influence the character of racial and ethnic relations in the United States." Who is "we"? The president of the United States—or of General Motors—or of Exxon? The president of the AFL-CIO? A college professor? The secretary of defense? A local minister? A news commentator? Personnel director of a small factory? The referent of "we" may be any one of millions of individuals or thousands of collectivities. Someone or some grouping certainly *will* influence intergroup relations. To think clearly about such influence it is essential to specify the actor we have in mind.

The second question is: Who or what is the object of influence or attempted influence? An audience of sixty million television viewers? Real estate dealers in Rochester, New York? School administrators and teachers in Atlanta, Georgia? Union labor leaders in Detroit? Parents of school children in South Boston? Commanders of U.S. Navy submarines? Children in a newly integrated kindergarten?

What are the means used? Do the attempts represent primarily persuasion, inducement, or coercion?

What is it that is being changed or maintained—what goals or purposes, if any, can be discerned in the activities under observation? Are there multiple goals? If so, to what extent are they compatible or incompatible?

What are the resources available to those who seek to influence and to those who are the objects of attempts to influence? How are strategies and tactics affected by specific constraints and opportunities?

These brief considerations are sufficient to show that the possibility of influencing social change in ethnic relations is always open to someone. Any existing state of affairs is the outcome of constancies in the balance of forces in a given set of relationships. Social change represents a shift in the pattern of influences. Both stability and change always are present. Understanding change requires the same concepts as understanding stability. When one seeks to think about purposive change in, or maintenance of, collectivities and relationships, the first step has to be a clear conception of possible modes, means, and objects of social influence.

For the foreseeable future, many of the world's political societies will contain two or more major ethnic groupings that will not assimilate or merge and that will constitute relatively self-conscious collectivities, each providing a complete communal life from cradle to grave for its members. Interethnic relations, therefore, will be a central fact of societal functioning for a long time to come. The viable functioning of such "communal pluralism" depends to a high degree upon structural or institutional resources and procedures for resolving excessively costly conflicts and for regulating conflicts that cannot, or should not, be resolved. Our task in the chapters that follow is to explore the possibilities for mutual accommodation and useful conflict among ethnic groupings in a pluralistic society.

Chapter 3

Conflict Resolution and Mutual Accommodation: The Case of the Schools

In the preceding chapters we have reviewed in a general way the overall direction of recent changes in American racial-ethnic relations and have surveyed some of the main criteria for appraising the significance of such changes. The next step is to apply the conclusions of this introductory survey of the field to particular sectors of national life. Originally we had written four lengthy chapters for this part of the book dealing with residence and housing, education, the economic sector, and political institutions (including the military and the legal system). But this treatment turned out to be too detailed and too massive for the present volume. Instead we shall try to describe briefly the central processes that appear to be most important in both social change and resistance to change in ethnic and racial aspects of education and in the institutions and practices that determine ethnic residential patterns. Only passing attention will be given to the most salient economic and political changes already mentioned in Chapter 1.

First, we turn to the arena of education, which is by far America's largest "industry," occupying the primary time and attention of nearly one-third of the population. Then, in Chapter 4 we shall deal with ethnic relations in housing and residence.

1. Where Have We Come from? Equality, Consensus, and Local Control in Education

The study of social behavior continually reveals the importance of paying close attention to familiar facts. In the case of the American public schools, the most impressive, simple, and obvious facts often are ignored in controversies concerning public policy.

The various local public school systems have several distinctive and important characteristics. In the aggregate they are *massive*, occupying the primary time and attention for most of every year of over 62 million persons (Grant and Lind, 1976, 6 and 11). They are enormously *varied* — in size, amount and source of funding, ethnic and socioeconomic composition, organizational structure, political significance, and other important characteristics. There are fifty state systems of education and some 20,000 school districts. There are competing and complementary systems of private and parochial schools.

This enormous diversity means that quick and simple diagnoses are practically certain to be wrong. If one seeks simple and sovereign generalizations concerning the effects of desegregation and integration, for example, in a "nonsystem" of this character, one must be prepared for substantial frustration. Valid diagnoses can indeed be made, but valid generalizations concerning the conditions that promote conflict and separation or lead to acceptance and cooperation require analysis that *specifies* those conditions in an actual social setting. For example, aggregative national analysis of information about large metropolitan centers may lead to conclusions inappropriate for medium and small cities, especially those in the South. Again, it is known that certain specific arrangements within schools and within classrooms can be used either to increase intergroup polarization and competition or to increase intergroup cooperation. Both social science and social practice now urgently need research findings that show causal relations among manipulable conditions in specified settings.

Our first point, then, is a reminder of the stubborn variety and complexity of the social context - a reminder that implies the great hazard of global aggregate analyses that are not qualified by a precise knowledge of *situational variation* and of the *specific processes* through which various outcomes are produced.

Basic to the character of American public school education until well into the twentieth century has been the dominance of local financing and control. Even today, centralized control is far less than in most industrialized nations. The Constitution left education among the powers reserved to the states, since it was not specified as belonging to the federal government. Even as late as the 1960s the total federal contribution to public schools was less than 10 percent of the costs.

Three issues of educational policy have been of dominant importance for intergroup relations: (1) the question of whether the schools should seek national unity through consensus upon a "core culture," as over against cultural separatism and autonomy; (2) the question of segregation or integration of social categories or collectivities in the schools—religious, sex, ethnic, racial, "ability," and socioeconomic strata; (3) the question of the actual effects of education—upon skills, knowledge, values, beliefs, income, citizenship, and so on.

The various state and local public school systems of the United States were born in struggle and acrimonious disputes and have developed through a long series of conflicts (Ravitz, 1974). It is no new thing to have militant groups demanding "community control": New York City had such a system in the nineteenth century and eventually abolished it on the ground that it was an acknowledged disaster. The southern system of enforced racial segregation, circa 1896-1965, rested firmly on community control (white) of separate and highly unequal systems of public schools for blacks and whites.

The long history of struggles over racial segregation and integration in northern schools probably is not widely known to the general American public. In 1854 legislation calling for separate schools for black and white children was passed by the legislature of the state of Pennsylvania. After the Civil War, when a section requiring desegregation of public schools seemed about to be passed by the Congress in the pending Civil Rights Act, the Pennsylvania State Senate passed a measure to repeal school segregation—but the matter was dropped after the bill failed to come to a vote in the lower house. When the Civil Rights Act of 1875 was passed by the Congress, it did not mandate public school desegregation, and northern states often maintained segregation. But continuing struggles were waged by black parents and their allies to do away with segregation, for example, in Pennsylvania in 1881 (Franklin, 1974) and in Chicago in the 1850s and '60s (Homel, 1974).

Laws permitting or requiring separate public schools for whites and blacks were widespread in the North during the nineteenth and twentieth centuries (Homel, 1974) in Delaware, New Jersey, New York, Pennsylvania, Massachusetts (ended in 1857), Missouri, Illinois, Indiana, Ohio, and other states. Indeed, a century after the struggles of blacks against segregation in the post-Civil War period, it is easy to conclude that the more things change, the more they remain the same. But this pessimistic conclusion cannot be generalized to all settings nor to all aspects of education. For, as already noted in Chapter 1, formal desegregation has proceeded rapidly since 1967-68 in the southern states, and we shall review below the data showing rapid advances in educational levels among black Americans and other ethnic minorities.

In general, it has been possible to transcend particularism and ascribed or assigned status in the schools only by setting standards and giving direction to local systems from external sources—professional, economic, or governmental (Simms in Mack, ed., 1968). For the local systems typically have been governed by lay boards made up for the most part of persons who were highly sensitive to local values and to the interests of powerful elements of the local community.

A basic question of policy is whether the schools are to aim for sharing a common culture, for cultural separateness for each ethnic grouping, or for some combination of common culture and ethnic distinctiveness (*Commentary*, 1972, 54:10-24, on Novak, 1971). There clearly are alternatives to making a Hobson's choice between having everyone become facsimile British-Americans or else developing closed ethnic communities, each with its own educational system.

A crucial historical decision was that English would be a common language for the nation in the public schools. Recent reexamination and criticism of the policy, coupled with demands for use of other languages (e.g., Spanish in New York City) as the media of instruction, have revived old issues in new forms. A special form of the controversy centers upon the claim that "Black English" is a distinct mode of communication, that black children are disadvantaged and damaged by being taught "Standard American English," and that black teachers must be used to teach black children in this distinctive language of instruction.

A related question concerns the extent to which public education should emphasize the separate cultures, histories, and accomplishments of various ethnic and racial groupings. If the curriculum is to contain Black Studies, shall it also include Native American, Italian, Polish, German, Irish, Puerto Rican, Swedish, Chicano, Japanese, Chinese? How far should formal education be different for children of different ethnic origins? Is it necessary to highlight separateness in order for children to develop a clear sense of personal identity and historical connectedness within a cherished collective heritage which elicits respect and pride?

Clearly there are substantial practical problems that limit the possibilities of full development of ethnicity in education. In a mobile, highly interdependent, technologically demanding social system, some kind of substantial "common culture" is required if the system is to function effectively. It does not have to insist that everyone learn *only* English—indeed, it may well need in the future to insist that everyone learn at least a modicum of one or more other languages. But, given the factual dominance of English, the nation cannot hope to act collectively in a unitary way if a Tower of Babel is allowed to develop. All the real arguments come in deciding policies that fall between these extremes. Similarly, there is no simple formula for balancing "common" vs. "ethnic" emphasis throughout the curriculum. Not everyone can "get equal time"—there is not that much time. There is likewise a delicate balance between recognizing and positively appreciating ethnic and other collective differences, and teaching invidious stereotypes and narrow provincial perspectives (*Carnegie Quarterly*, 1974, 22:1-4). Where does ethnic identity shade over into ingroup exclusiveness and outgroup prejudice?

Then there is the central issue of equality of access to education. Note this striking pair of observations:

(1) On the increase in black enrollment in colleges and universities:

In 1973, the U.S. Census Bureau reported one of the most significant statistics in American history. For the first time, the percent of black Americans of college age entering an institution of higher education is identical with the proportion of comparably aged white youth (Lipset, 1974, 59).

The total number of black students enrolled full-time in college in 1968 was 209,000; by 1974 the number was 508,000, constituting 9.3 percent of the total enrollment of 5.6 million. By October 1974, blacks were 12.3 percent of entering college freshmen, whereas blacks were 11.4 percent of the total population.

(2) On segregation in the late 1960s:

As of 1967-68 to achieve full desegregation in urban public elementary schools would have required a shift of schools by 32 percent of children in Southern, and 26 percent in Northern cities. At that time, teachers typically were assigned to pupils of the same racial category (Farley and Taeuber, 1974).

Among persons of college-completion age in 1970 (ages 22-24), there were no large differences in median years of education between whites and blacks or Native Americans. Median years of schooling completed for native population of native parentage were as follows: white males, 12.8; black males, 12.2; Native American males, 12.2; white females, 12.7; black females, 12.3; Native American females, 12.2 (Borgatta, 1976, 71).

The history of education in the United States shows a consistent long-term trend toward greater and greater inclusiveness—from an ideal of "education for gentlemen," restricted to a tiny minority of white, Anglo-Saxon, upper-class males, to the ideal of equal educational opportunity (or outcomes) for all (R. M. Williams, 1970, Chapter 8). The step-by-step extension of elementary, secondary, and postsecondary education to the less affluent, to both sexes, to younger and older ages, to the handicapped, to rural as well as urban areas, and to all ethnic and racial categories certainly is on its face a societal success story of epic proportions. To focus only on the tensions and struggles that accompanied these massive transformations is to see the half-full glass as wholly empty. To find the results unimpressive would seem to require a truly dedicated pessimism.

Observe these facts. In 1920 nearly one-half of nonwhite adults were functionally "illiterate"—having completed less than five years of elementary school; by 1973 the proportion had dropped to one-eighth. From generation to generation, since the middle of the nineteenth century, schools have multiplied, enrollment has grown, curricula have broadened and diversified, higher education has vastly expanded. The total result is something new under the sun. As of the late 1960s, the proportion of the *total* population that was in some kind of "school" has increased to nearly 3 out of 10. Elementary and secondary school enrollment amounted to 59 million persons by fall 1975. The United States has the most comprehensive system of mass education in the world (Williams, 1970, 315-16).

To the degree that formal educational certification becomes a requirement for occupational entrance and promotion in the more desirable occupations, open access to education becomes crucial for anything approaching "equality of opportunity." As shown by Tables 3.1 - 3.3, rapidly rising levels of formal education mark the recent history of the United States, and the attainments of nonwhites are rapidly converging with those of whites.

Table 3.1. Median School Years Completed by
Persons Age 25 Years and Over, and 25-29
Years, by Color: United States, 1940-75

Years	Persons 25 Years and Over		Persons Ages 25-29 Years	
	White	Nonwhite	White	Nonwhite
1940 . . .	8.7	5.7	10.7	7.1
1950 . . .	9.7	6.9	12.2	8.7
1960 . . .	10.8	8.2	12.3	10.8
1970 . . .	12.2	10.1	12.6	12.2
1974 . . .	12.4	11.1	12.8	12.5
1975 . . .	12.4	11.4	12.8	12.6

Source: W. V. Grant, and C. G. Lind. 1976. *Digest of Educational Statistics, 1975 Edition.* Washington, D.C.: U.S. Government Printing Office, p. 14, Table 11.

At all levels of the educational system, widened access did not "just happen" by diffuse historical accidents but rather developed as the outcome of definite social decisions. For example, the rising college enrollments that apparently were long regarded as inevitable and inexorable have resulted from particular public policies in conjunction with other favorable historical conditions. Enrollments are powerfully affected by quite specific policies. For example, the presence of a local public junior college has been shown to raise the college-enrollment proportion among lower-class males from 15 percent to about 50 percent, and the presence of a four-year college with more selective admission policies raised enrollment rates by one-third (Trow, 1962, 255).

Table 3.2. Percentage of Population Ages 25-29
Completing Four Years of High School or
More, by Color, United States, 1920-75

Years	White	Nonwhite
1920	22.0	6.3
1940	41.2	12.1
1950	55.2	23.4
1960	63.7	38.6
1970	77.8	58.4
1974	83.4	71.3
1975	84.5	73.8

Source: Digest of Educational Statistics. 1976,
p. 14, Table 11.

As these examples suggest, our present appraisal of whether or not mutual accommodation among ethnic groupings has been successful in education requires very careful attention to factors that facilitate or work against equality of opportunities and equality or differentials in outcomes.

Table 3.3. Percentage of Population Ages 25-29
Completing Four or More Years of College,
by Color, United States, 1920-75

Years	White	Nonwhite
1920	4.5	1.2
1940	6.4	1.6
1950	8.1	2.8
1960	11.8	5.4
1970	17.3	10.0
1974	22.0	11.0
1975	22.9	15.2

Source: Digest of Educational Statistics. 1976,
p. 14, Table 11.

2. Does Education Make a Difference? The Question of Effects

Much public debate during the years since 1965 has centered upon the question of what effects could be validly imputed to: (1) formal education in general, (2) additional expenditures for support of education, including special or "compensatory" programs, (3) desegregation and integration. Widespread disagreement, considerable confusion, and not a little mistaken and ill-proportioned inferences marked these debates. Let us make the necessary heroic attempt to extract a set of dependable conclusions from the complex data and arguments.

Two major documents constitute the set-pieces of the controversies: (1)

the multiauthored "Coleman Report," *Equality of Educational Opportunity*, (Coleman et al., 1965) and (2) the multiauthored *Inequality* (Jencks et al., 1972). Around these works as centers has developed a large literature of analysis, criticism, and advocacy (e.g., Cain and Watts, 1970; O'Reilly, 1970; Mosteller and Moynihan, eds., 1972; Keyfitz, 1973; Herrnstein, 1973; Miller and Dreger, eds., 1973).

The findings of the Coleman study are limited by the sampling problems of the survey (some of the largest urban systems refused to supply data), by the crudeness of the measures of outcomes (e.g., summary scores on standardized tests), by the high levels of aggregation of the data (e.g., by schools rather than "tracks," classrooms, or individual teachers and classes). Nevertheless none of its problems of data or analysis destroy its main findings. The findings are limited in a much more sweeping sense by the historical period in which the study was conducted. It dipped into the stream of history at a time when educational expenditures were higher than ever before and after a period in which special efforts had been made to improve physical plants and other formal inputs in black schools. The "marginal gains" from added expenditures surely were then less than when really gross disparities were common. There does not appear to be much doubt that public schools earlier did make a decisive difference in the socioeconomic fate of the children of poor immigrants in large cities, of poor rural whites in the South, and of blacks lucky enough to be located near "good" schools.

The study showed that gross average attainments on standardized tests were less for blacks than for whites at the time of *entering* school and that the differences widened at higher grades. Most of the variation in student attainments was within-school rather than across-schools. Not measured characteristics of teachers (e.g., length of training) nor of curricula, nor of schools' physical facilities were highly correlated with pupils' test scores, when family backgrounds and the socioeconomic status of the school's student population were held constant; the two sets of factors associated with the largest proportions of the "explained variance" were (1) indicators of family socioeconomic position and educational orientation, and (2) the socioeconomic status of classmates in the school.

A widespread popular interpretation of commentaries on these results was that "differences in schools make no difference," or "adding money won't help." Both inferences are false as stated. There is abundant evidence that educational level attained is a major determinant of later occupational position (especially among blacks). (See Jencks et al., 1972; Pettigrew, 1971; Duncan, Featherman, Duncan, 1972; Weinberg, 1970; Miller and Dreger, 1973; Sewell, Haller, Ohlendorf, 1970; Sewell and Hauser, 1975.) Lack of schooling penalizes poor children more than children of affluent families. Hence, access to schooling is crucial. (Of course, if easy access is available to nearly everyone, then access as such ceases to predict later careers). Differences in financial support do make a difference—but only when the facilities or other resources are essential. One cannot train students well in physical sciences without laboratories or hold pupils' attention in snowy weather in a school without a roof. Once one has laboratories or roofs, as the case may be, additional facilities may matter much less. Thus it is evident that if expenditures per pupil were to rise continuously for an indefinite period, there would come a time at which additional increments produced decreasing returns per unit. But this is not to say that at lower levels different inputs do not have significantly different effects (Ravitz, 1973a).

Of course, it is true that the sheer correlation between educational level attained and later occupation and income is partly spurious, because both educational aspirations and attainments and later occupational positions are also correlated with economic origins. But the more important counterconsideration is that minimum literacy is essential for most occupations and that high levels of training are required for many well-paying and desirable occupations. An M.D. degree is not inconsequential, and a person who cannot read above a third-grade level has a serious problem in metropolitan society.

The pervasiveness of effects on educational and occupational attainment of whatever it is that "race" implicates in American society is strikingly evidenced in Porter's analysis in which no other factor showed such a marked pattern of differences: data for blacks show at least ten departures from expected path correlations that were observed among whites (Porter, 1974). Although the specific social processes through which education may contribute to occupational and income position of blacks are not known in detail, it is certain that not knowledge and skills gained nor formal certification nor both together can fully account for outcomes. Additional factors may include access to "contacts" and information about economic opportunities (Crain, 1970), sponsorship (Porter, 1974), and aspirations and motivation (Gurin et al., 1969).

Analysis of socioeconomic characteristics of men in the experienced civilian labor force, 1962-73, has shown that blacks at each educational level were able to attain higher occupational status in 1973 than in 1962. And each increment of education brought larger returns in 1973 than in 1962 (Featherman and Hauser, 1976, 649).

3. Factors Affecting Desegregation and Integration

Insufficient attention has been given to the extent of successful resolution of community oppositions and disagreements related to school desegregation.

Both social science research and the mass media have highlighted conspicuous tensions and conflicts. A side-effect is that widespread processes of mutual accommodation receive little public attention.

A critical review of research since 1954 permits us to identify several social mechanisms of accommodation and of integrative resolutions of conflicts. The evidence shows that effective strategies have been developed for coping with "realistic" issues and that much resistance to specific modes of desegregation is rooted in processes of "symbolic politics."

Many current debates concerning public policy are being couched in terms of outmoded and simplistic appraisals of demographic and social trends. Available data and analyses provide a basis for less volatile opinions. Effective school programs represent specific local applications of composite strategies of persuasion, inducement, and constraint. Useful rules-of-thumb have been formulated from critical reviews of experience in many episodes of community conflict. Let us review the relevant materials, briefly.

First, contrary to some impressions, *desegregation has been effective.* Certainly it has not been wholly effective, nor wholly accepted, nor fully applauded. But massive desegregation has occurred, since the firm actions of the Congress, the federal courts, and some of the federal executive agencies in the late 1960s. As already noted in Chapter 1, the very rapid desegregation has been almost wholly in the South and has occurred mainly since *administrative* implementation of legislation and court rulings began (1966-67 and after).

Desegregation of the public schools did not occur on any really substantial scale so long as only weak legal sanctions and moral persuasion were invoked for failures to comply with court rulings. When economic penalties loomed, in the form of possible withdrawal of federal aid, and when the courts began to insist upon definite and prompt compliance to court-ordered plans, a remarkable movement occurred.

> *Proposition 1:* Our conclusion is that a *primary immediate factor in bringing about desegregation is the presence of clear and authoritative policies, national and state and local, that can be enforced by strong sanctions.*

Actually, this diagnosis of policy was evident in the very beginning of the period of struggle and transition that began in 1954. Note this statement, written just before the Brown decision:

> Public school desegregation or integration is only loosely correlated with the attitudes or prejudices of the population. . . . In general a clear-cut policy, administered with understanding but also with resolution, seems to have been most effective in accomplishing desegregation with

a minimum of difficulty. Long-drawn-out efforts and fluctuating policies appear to have maximized confusion and resistance (Williams and Ryan, 1954, 251-52).

In the 1950s and early 1960s the *most* important single variable in explaining intercommunity differences in rates of desegregation (as well as rates of black voter registration) in the South was simply the state in which the communities were located. For state policies and state political institutions decisively set the boundaries for possible local actions (cf. Pettigrew and Cramer, 1959; Matthews and Prothro, 1963a, 1963b) — until federal authority intervened.

The importance of federal (or state) requirements and incentives lies partly in the sense of universality they can convey ("we are not guinea pigs — everybody else is having to do it"), and partly in the remoteness of the impersonal authority. These features are helpful to local officials in "taking them off the hook" of personalized responsibility: the external requirements can be invoked as unavoidable necessities, divorced from personal preferences and local obligations (Aiken and Demerath, 1968, 103). Formal requirements, universally applied according to categorical rules, also help to ward off charges of favoritism or of class discrimination (Williams and Ryan, 1954, 243-44; Anson, 1974).

The effectiveness of tangible sanctions extended into higher education as well. The Civil Rights Act of 1964 provided that any business firm, state, municipality, college, or university that receives grants or has a contract with the federal government is prohibited from practicing any form of discrimination on grounds of race, color, sex, or national origin. (Title IX of the 1972 Education Act additionally lays down specific prohibitions against sex discrimination, e.g., in sports, in university-supported student associations.) Because federal support has become an important part of the necessary income of nearly all major universities and colleges, these legal regulations can have large effects. Indeed, marked effects have occurred — in admissions of students, in hiring and promotion of personnel, in granting of financial aid in residential accommodations and assignments, in use of facilities. The regulation of policies and practices through federal monitoring and threat of withdrawal of funding has raised new questions and problems.

Proposition 2: Another important generalization is that *even when there are external inducements and constraints, local communities will vary greatly in their responses* (Williams and Ryan, 1954, 233-34).

To identify causes, we always have to be able to observe variance in outcomes. The great variations in resistances to change in intergroup relations are well illustrated by the fact that in 1965, eleven years after the Supreme Court decision that had declared racial segregation in public schools to be unconstitutional, one-half of the southern states had extensive desegregation while the other half had practically none. Very great local differences existed in the speed of desegregation, its completeness, its acceptance, and the amount and kind of controversy surrounding the process.

A correlation analysis of the seventeen southern and border states (Vanfossen, 1968) showed that the single variable most closely related to the extent of desegregation was simply the proportion of the state's population that was nonwhite: the higher the proportion nonwhite, the less the desegregation $(r = -.78)$. Variables also negatively, but only slightly, related to desegregation include median education of white adults $(-.10)$, percentage of whites age 25 and over having some college education $(-.18)$, and proportion of the white male labor force in professional, managerial, clerical, and sales occupations $(r = -.14)$. On the other hand, the higher the income in a state, the greater the extent of desegregation $(r = +.44)$.

When nonwhite income is expressed as a percentage of white income, the correlation with desegregation is positive and very high: $r = +.75$. When this proportion is controlled, the first-order correlation of $-.71$ between desegregation and the proportion nonwhite is reduced to $-.42$, suggesting that a substantial part of the original association was due to factors associated with low socioeconomic position of the nonwhites in the states having high concentrations of black population.

There are moderate positive correlations between desegregation and several indicators of urbanism and industrialization. However, these associations may be spurious: for example, the $r = +.45$ between desegregation and proportion of the labor force in white-collar occupations drops to zero when the proportion of nonwhites in the population is controlled.

Thus not education, nor urbanization, nor industrialization, nor occupational status of the white population is unambiguously predictive of desegregation. But affluence, high SES of nonwhites, and low proportion of nonwhites *are* predictive. The total pattern of relationships is consistent and strongly suggests a basic generalization:

> *Proposition 3:* The *resistance of whites to desegregation is lowered by conditions that minimize a sense of potential threat of economic competition or of a major shift in the existing distribution of social power* (Pettigrew and Riley, 1972).

Other factors that partly determine local variations have been described by detailed case studies of communities. Thus the complex processes that led to peaceful desegregation in Newark, Delaware, centered around a concern by local decision-makers to avoid high-cost disruption by means of low-cost modes of desegregation (Barringer, 1968; Jones and Long, 1965, 37).

Looking back on the 1950s and 1960s an important observation is that, in a very direct sense, a proximate cause of desegregation was the fact that segregated black schools had long been inferior in resources and that attendance of blacks at segregated schools was perceived by both blacks and whites as a badge of inferiority. The pressure to desegregate resulted in upgrading of resources, even before the Brown decision and much more after it. Where desegregation has occurred, parents quickly translate their concerns into demands for "quality education." Even when the call from white parents for quality education is a code for resistance to desegregation, it tends to focus attention upon what both white and black children are getting in the schools.

The legal and moral bases for ending racial segregation and discrimination in education constitute an additional set of factors. These legal and moral constraints and inducements have been clear for a long time: ethical universalism, equality of opportunity, and respect for individual personality and individual achievement. Support for educational integration has come from the elements of the white population most strongly committed to those values, as well as from other persons whose commitments were more narrowly focused upon the rule of law and the support of "due process" and "public order." The *active* pressure for desegregation has come mainly from organized efforts of black people and other minorities. Once the initial legal victories had been won, further movement depended upon the conjunction of highly motivated and organized action by blacks and the support and acceptance of white allies and sympathizers. Indeed, both active pressure and the support of the various third parties (the courts, federal executive agencies, educators, voluntary associations) have been—and still are—essential, for the sources of resistance to desegregation are numerous and complex.

4. Sources of Resistance to Desegregation

It is entirely possible for extensive school segregation to be maintained without any specific overt support. If there were no gerrymandering of school district lines, and if schools were fully integrated within districts, there would still be a great amount of racial separation. Over 80 percent of blacks in metropolitan areas live in central cities, over 50 percent of the whites in such areas live in suburbs—and in almost all cases the city and suburbs have separate school districts. The effects of residential de facto segregation are accentuated wherever a large proportion of white children attend parochial schools—for only about 6 percent of black Americans are Catholic, and a large parochial system necessarily reduces the number of whites available to attend public schools (Pettigrew, 1971, 56-57).

Proposition 4: Residential segregation alone is the single most crucial source of school segregation, where attendance areas are based on geographic proximity.

Given any substantial segregation, whether intended or not, the passive resistance of simply not acting is the most effective veto imaginable, in the absence of any organized action to bring change (see Simms, 1968, 136). Passive resistance is, literally, totally effective when a community or an organization that is called upon to act simply refuses or ignores the demand or request and when no external inducement or constraint is brought into play. The demand disappears into silence. Nothing happens.

But the days of veto-by-inaction were already numbered by the time of the Brown decision and were further shortened by Congressional actions of 1964 and 1965 and by increasingly specific court-ordered plans and other measures. Faced with an inescapable decision, local officials and community residents must act. Why do some accept desegregation as necessary, while others overtly or covertly resist?

Let us examine a few illustrative instances in a preliminary search for clues.

First, consider the very instructive case of Jackson Heights-Corona in New York City. By a plan put into effect in September 1964, two elementary schools located five blocks apart were to be paired. One was 87 percent white, the other was 99.5 percent black and Puerto Rican. Exchanges of pupils would require almost no busing, class sizes would be reduced, and both schools would have improved facilities. The black community of Corona and the white community of Jackson Heights did not differ in average educational level of the adult population. The whites were about 75 percent Jewish and 20 percent Catholic in religious background. Some 40 percent of the Jewish residents had moved into Jackson Heights as a "respectable refuge" from deteriorating areas of Brooklyn and the Bronx. Resistance to desegregation through pairing of the two schools was greatest among these in-migrants, especially among those who had friends in the area before moving in and had more of their current social circle in the local area. Those opposed to desegregation less often envisaged any further upward social mobility or additional geographic mobility. The resisters more often than the integrationists regularly attended religious services. Compared with the resisters, the supporters of the desegregation plan had more often been active in PTA, more often were continuing their own education, more often expressed concern for the quality of their children's education, and less often were concerned about the market value of homes in the area (Lang and Lang, 1965; cf. Cuomo, 1974). Thus within a traditionally "liberal" and prointegration population, substantial resistance developed among those who were most completely embedded in religious and personal localism and most completely blocked from further social mobility.

A case in which a desegregation proposal was blocked and a "liberal" school board was replaced by a "conservative" board has been described in some detail for the community of Richmond, California (Rubin, 1972). In the beginning there was the objective possibility of instituting an immediate and comprehensive desegregation program on the initiative of the school board, presenting the rationale concurrently with the action itself. But the board was ambivalent and divided in its own commitment. It developed a plan that was perceived locally as favoring the white upper-middle class, while placing the "burden of desegregation" on the white working class and the black population. It appeared to take equivocal stands concerning busing of children, and it delayed carrying out a desegregation plan. These tactics gave time and opportunity for opponents of desegregation to mobilize, to organize, and finally to defeat effective desegregation. The delay, unclarity, and weak quality of the board's exercise of authority opened the way for opposition to mobilize. But the mobilization itself was favored by a plan that would have left most white pupils from upper-income families in schools with few black pupils or none and schools attended by working and lower middle-class families would have experienced desegregation.

Thus the approach used to initiate a desegregation plan maximized threat and a sense of inequity, without seeming to provide clear advantages or to give a realistic show of firm authority. The resulting activation of the voters was impressive—from 16 percent of the eligible electorate voting in 1965, to 37 percent in 1967, and to more than 80 percent in 1969, when a new school board was elected. Participation then declined in the 1971 election, after the new board had instituted a system of open enrollment with free transportation. Yet after three years under the new system, the number of black pupils in the ghetto schools had decreased from about 6,000 to about 4,800, and some 1,500 children were being bused. Thus even with the "weaker" plan, a considerable amount of desegregation did occur.

In South Boston, Massachusetts, the court-ordered desegregation plan in 1974 was met by mass turbulence and violence (formerly attributed stereotypically to the "Little Rock" syndrome of the Deep South) among Irish Catholic whites. The area, containing 38,000 people, is a geographically and socially separate section of Boston, inhabited largely by working-class people and characterized by cultural homogeneity, low social mobility, strong particularistic and ascribed social ties, considerable interpersonal violence, social authoritarianism, and aversive attitudes toward "outsiders." In short, it exhibits *the characteristics that cultural isolation and social segregation typically produce, including rigid ingroup-outgroup distinctions, closed social horizons, extreme exclusiveness, and hostility toward social change and extralocal groups.* Not all of the characteristics together, however, are enough to explain the attempted mass defiance of the courts. Local political leaders for years have encouraged resistance to desegregation; the President of the United States (incredibly enough) lent implied sympathy to defiance of the law, and the Boston School Committee (by a 3-2 vote) refused to comply with a U.S. District Court order.[1] Without authoritative support from local leaders for compliance, a community of this kind always is easily incited into violent resistance.

Many other local cases could be described, but enough material is at hand to permit us to identify the recurrent clusters of conditions that make desegregation either difficult and conflictful or straightforward and cooperative.

At the most general level, the local factors that facilitate or hinder movement from segregation to desegregation to integration in schools fall into five main categories.

1. Cultural coding of the population, that is the extent to which ethnocentrism, racism, localism, and related beliefs and values dominate over commitments to universalism, equalitarianism, individual-personality values, achievement, and related orientations.
2. Demographic and technical factors, e.g., extent of concentration of various ethnic populations; geographic conformations; transportation facilities; organizational structure of the schools or of local government.
3. Vested interests in a segregated system, e.g., job security and future prospects of white and nonwhite teachers and administrators; personal advantages and public commitments of school board members, elected officials, political leaders, business groups, unions, and religious groupings.
4. Prospects for social disruption and economic loss if desegregation is or is not carried out.
5. Apprehensions concerning possible objective consequences, e.g., sensed threat of loss of position on the part of black or white teachers; fear of violence in the school; apprehensiveness of black or white children and their parents concerning possible hostility and harassment.

More specific factors will be identified below. But from available research we can conclude, on the basis of first-order correlations alone, that successful desegregation would be most likely in communities with the following characteristics:

—large size (holding residential segregation constant); small to medium size, when segregation in large cities is massive and rigid.

—low proportion of minority children.
—ethnic and religious diversity.
—moderate rates of geographic mobility.
—moderate rates of upward occupational mobility.
—moderate to high average per capita or per family incomes.
—moderately high political participation, including minorities.
--competitive political elections.
—appointed or district-elected school board members (rather than area-wide at-large elected); concentrated decision-making authority.
—moderately high levels of participation in voluntary associations.
—relatively high average education, small gap between white and black populations in educational levels.
—relatively high proportion of black workers in nonmanual occupations.
—"cosmopolitan" leadership in government, education, religion, and economic enterprises.
—low degree of racial segregation in residential areas.
—active minority and intergroup organizations.
—a community history of low levels of rancorous intergroup conflict and of substantial cooperation in common causes among leaders from each major racial or ethnic segment of the community.

Proposition 5: The one basic characteristic that is common to most local communities that have shown greatest rigidity and violent resistance to educational desegregation is *local social closure or ingroup-embeddedness.*

Outgroup intolerance is most salient among populations characterized by limited experience with cultural and social diversity, by closed social networks, by few options for gratification of basic interests, and by dependence upon a fixed set of local relationships for status and security.

Proposition 6: For example, the more nearly individuals in a given community or area have had their past social contacts limited to ethnically homogeneous settings and relationships, the less they will understand or initally accept changes in patterns of interaction with ethnic outgroups (cf. Williams et al., 1964, 355-66).

It is in large part through the effects of past social separation that *both* localistic cultural ethnocentrism *and* ethnically linked vested interests become rigid and emotionally dominant (cf. Roof, 1974, 643).

But some of the conditions listed above are locally pervasive outcomes of long-continued social processes, and thus are not easily accessible to purposive control by local individuals or community groups. Since our primary interest here is in diagnosis as an aid to policy, decision, and social action, we must pay special attention to conditions that can be manipulated.

Factors that are relatively accessible to purposive control by local action include:

1. orientation and training of teachers and other staff to function in an integrated program;
2. integrated staff;
3. location of school district lines; pairing of schools; location of new schools; busing;
4. intergroup-relations content in teaching and in extracurricular activities;
5. information and orientation for parents and the general public;
6. disciplinary policies and practices in the schools; counseling; grievances procedures; provisions for security;
7. development of cooperative and joint activities involving integration.

But let us not overdo such sheer listing. More important is an effort to grasp how the several processes that are lumped together under the terms "desegregation" and "integration" actually operate in real-life circumstances.

5. Processes of Desegregation and of Integration

It is obvious enough that formal desegregation and actual integration within schools are two different things. Desegregation is the process of removing barriers and bringing together in the same schools persons of different ethnic, racial, or religious backgrounds who formerly were separated. But sheer proximity is not integration; integration occurs only if there then develops joint participation and mutual acceptance in all activities normally associated with school attendance, from classroom to extracurricular activities. From this level of mutual accommodation, a fuller measure of integration may develop in the forms of mutual respect and liking, interpersonal friendships, cooperation in attaining superordinate goals, and a shared sense of common membership and solidarity. Between sheer mechanical desegregation and the most highly developed integration are many intermediate gradations.

Because desegregation is not a single brief event but a set of diverse processes, necessarily continuing over a substantial and often quite long period, it involves numerous decision points concerning pace, sequence, changes in emphasis, and the like. The same characterization holds for the more subtle processes of integration, should these develop subsequently.

In those instances in which black parents have seen desegregation as their only hope of getting better quality education for their children (as in some

Deep South areas in the late 1960s), freedom-of-choice plans may be regarded as an acceptable point of leverage. Thus in "River City," Mississippi, black leaders viewed any desegregation as a way to force the hand of school officials —because the presence of any white students in a particular school would lead to improved facilities and instructional resources (Aiken and Demerath, 1968, 104). But freedom-of-choice plans are most likely to be attractive to black parents only when no other alternative to segregation exists; such plans put the burden of initiative on the black parent, place the child in the position of supplicant or intruder, and result in minimal desegregation. There also are disadvantages for school authorities, especially in localities where many blacks wish to transfer to formerly all-white schools (Aiken and Demerath, 1968, 104).

Desegregation in the 1950s and early 1960s occurred in a historical context quite different from desegregation in the late 1960s and the early 1970s. In the early phases, black parents often saw desegregation as a moral issue and as the only route to well-supported education for their children. Desegregation occurred in three sharply contrasting types of situations: (1) massive white resistance followed by reluctant capitulation; (2) "token integration" that was polite, quiet, and highly limited in effects; (3) "liberal" communities in which middle-class whites and blacks were able to attain mutually acceptable integration (Weinberg, 1970, 347).

In the absence of strong incentives originating outside of segregated local communities, movements to desegregate generally have developed only after some conspicuous public events that have stimulated collective action among dissatisfied elements of the minority population. In the case of Riverside, California, in the period immediately following the civil disorders in Watts, it was only after the burning of a building housing a segregated black school that the black community was mobilized by fears that moving children to other segregated schools would result in overcrowding and poor instruction.

> This issue awakened an otherwise indifferent Negro citizenry to a level of participation in civic matters unheard of up to that time. A school boycott was called. Freedom Schools were established under private auspices. . . . Negro and Mexican-American parents . . . achieved an effective one-day boycott of the public schools.

> It was during this period that the board of education began considering various possibilities, conducting informal inquiries on the problem, and most especially, listening to the sentiments of articulate members of both the minority community and the university (Duster, 1968, 5).

Riverside was one of only three cities in California that had instituted plans for school integration at the time of Duster's study. The unanimous decision of the school board was announced in terms of moral principle, but the decision was made at a time when an implicit threat of collective violence was understood.

School boards and administrators are not, of course, simply "free agents." Even when the individual incumbents may desire change, vast resistance often inheres in interlocking interests, beliefs, values, commitments, investments, relationships, and established procedures and routines among teachers, parents, publishers, unions, auxiliary school staffs, business concerns, municipal governments, and so on. Not surprising, therefore, is the fact that civil rights groups in dealings with the educational hierarchies of the large cities may come to believe "that important changes result from displays of power rather than from programs of persuasion" (Lauders, 1967, 291).

Understandably, school boards and school administrations rarely are eager to respond decisively and positively to requests and demands from ethnic minorities for changes in policies and practices (Stelzer, 1974). Typically, a decisive move for desegregation, for example, comes only after strong pressure —a boycott, a court order, a mass protest, a threat of withdrawal of funds, or the incipient defeat of a bond issue. Usually desegregation occurs as an accommodation of opposing views and interests. For the accommodation to occur, concentrated pressure typically is necessary to start the movement. Members of school boards characteristically seek to avoid open and acrimonious controversy. The more they perceive conflict, the more likely they are to be receptive to public participation and communication with the board. The more competitive the process of electing board members, the more the receptivity.

Thus far we have summarized illustrative case studies. But these localized findings have been validated by the striking results of a national study of all cities outside the South having at least 3,000 blacks in the National Opinion Research Center's Permanent Community Sample. The 91 cities that were included omit only four northern cities of over 250,000 population (Kirby et al., 1973; Kirby and Crain, 1974).

The findings are strikingly consistent with the various case studies already citied. First of all, militant or conflict-increasing tactics seem to have been necessary to make desegregation of the schools an issue that would be seriously considered. In small cities with a small proportion of minorities and with a relatively affluent and well-educated population, the black community tended to be relatively passive and did not develop a strong civil rights movement. In cities that *did* develop a demand for desegregation, school authorities initally made minimal responses, e.g., by appointing a committee to study the problem. A typical next step was for desegregation forces to mobilize nonviolent demonstrations. Eventually, about 60 percent of the cities took some action (often "token" or symbolic), but only one-fourth adopted a major desegregation plan.

What factors favored desegregation? Desegregation was most likely to occur in cities in which there was disagreement and conflict within the school board, when militant protest made the matter salient. However, civil rights demonstrations were more nearly a response to the authorities' failure to desegregate rather than an effective cause of desegregation. Similarly, whites' mass movements generally were ineffective in preventing desegregation. The findings seem to imply that decisions were made by an elite that was either insensitive to or alienated by mass pressure, whether pro or con school desegregation.

On the basis of the total pattern of findings Kirby and Crain (1974, 480-92) propose these hypotheses:

Proposition 7: A nonissue can be made salient by a powerless group that uses conflict-raising methods—tactics that create public controversy.

Proposition 8: A history of conflict within a decision-making body encourages the raising of issues and the advocacy of change.

Proposition 9: "Grass-roots" activity that does not involve local elite members who have exerted influence in the past tends to be dismissed or treated lightly by persons in authority.

Proposition 10: When decisions typically are made by an informal rule that in effect requires consensus as well as the backing of some recognized leaders, nonviolent protest and mass demonstrations are relatively ineffective in producing desegregation.

Proposition 11: Confrontational and conflictful tactics are most likely to be effective when the decision-making body has continuing membership and compulsory attendance and reaches decisions by majority vote or other nonunanimous action.

We do not have definite evidence—such as would come from clear-cut controlled experiments—concerning the detailed effects of different processes and sequences of actions in attempted desegregation. But some lessons come from many years of experience in hundreds of communities. As already mentioned above, clear decisions and firm policies discourage confusion and lower the likelihood of mass resistance. School-of-choice plans are *not* highly effective.

Proposition 12: Clear policies of geographic districting or of universalistic, nonvoluntary transfers minimize particularistic accusations and attempted evasions. Partial desegregation opens the doors to many resistances; desegregation is most effective when it is across-the-board, prompt and simultaneous (Williams and Ryan, 1954, 241-43).

Before desegregation, advance planning within the schools is necessary if (1) appropriate reassurances are to be given to parents, children, teachers, and other school staff; (2) needed instructional procedures and materials are to be available, and (3) provisions are to be made to cope with inevitable problems. Integration of school staffs helps to allay fears of displacement among teachers and facilitates movement toward integration among pupils.

We cannot emphasize too strongly that *extensive successful desegregation already has taken place* in all regions of the United States. Such successful experience shows that the technical knowledge and resources are available if the effective desire and will can be found.

Substantial information is available for the following communities, among the many local instances of effective school desegregation that illustrate unusual or especially useful techniques and policies, (Smith, Downs, Lachman, 1973): Chapel Hill, N.C.; Clarke County, Ga.; Cleveland, Ohio; Colorado Springs, Colo.; Gainesville, Fla.; Muskogee, Okla.; New Albany, Miss.; Portland, Ore.; Providence, R.I.; Sacramento, Calif. A detailed review of these cases has led to the formulation of over 100 specific techniques that seem to be helpful. A recapitulation here would be inappropriate. The important thing is that a body of codified and partly tested "rules of thumb" is now available, and that successful applications do exist and have been documented.

Although we cannot here review the numerous specific techniques, it does seem essential to note the main assumptions and empirical generalizations upon which they are founded.

In the first place, since desegregation stems from consistently reiterated rulings of the Supreme Court and other courts and of the executive branch of the federal government, and since the basic national policy that forced segregation is unconstitutional will not be reversed, school desegregation will be facilitated *when local leaders clearly inform their constituents that it is inevitable.* At the same time, desegregation is in fact a major change and usually comes about because of some direct or indirect pressure upon local authorities. Hence, not only clear policies but effective communication to those affected is needed, and detailed advance planning is essential. Specific plans should be drafted *locally*, and that fact should be made known to the community at large. Further, the development of informal channels of communication and working relationships among all major community agencies facilitates effectiveness.

Within the school system itself, policies that seem to facilitate effective desegregation include the following:

1. "representation," informal or formal, at all levels of the educational system of the main ethnic groupings of the community;
2. maintenance of an extensive informal network of communication with parents, police, social service workers, communications media, and other relevant community agencies and groups;[2]
3. arranging for participation in the planning of school policies and programs by teachers, students, and parents;
4. establishing a diversified curriculum;
5. providing extensive and diversified nonacademic activities;
6. publicizing and implementing clear rules for the expected and permissible behavior of students and school personnel, and ensuring that parents know of the rules;
7. taking prompt, regularized, and predictable disciplinary actions;
8. providing for immediate access to administrative authorities by both students and teachers;
9. maintaining preventive planning to cope with controversies and possible outbreaks of violence (Smith, Downs, Lachman, 1973, 30-37).

Proposition 13: Each of the principles and techniques here reviewed is only illustrative of useful possible approaches to coping with problems. None is a fixed prescription to be applied without close diagnosis of *specific* settings (cf. Guttentag, 1972). This caution must be strongly emphasized.

For example, more widespread and active participation of local citizens in decision-making concerning school policies and practices may appear to be obviously desirable as a means of facilitating racial integration. But such participation is likely to have the opposite effect if it occurs in a population already apprehensive or hostile toward integration, especially if mass meetings are used to "air the issues." When desegregation is being initiated, or new measures are to be taken to increase mixing, the appropriate model of democratic processes typically is not the town meeting but rather extensive informal consultation among representatives and leaders, together with carefully designed programs of information and of training for all types of school personnel. Extensive interest-group mobilization, especially if public polarization already has begun, is likely at best to result in inconclusive compromises and failure to find decisive resolution of the problems (see Bonacich and Goodman, 1972).

Each community is unique. But each community has basic similarities to others. As experience accumulates and research-testing proceeds, practical guides become increasingly useful for constructive collective action in efforts to achieve racial and ethnic integration. Thus a study of desegregation in three urban settings — in Charlottesville, Virginia, Providence, Rhode Island, and Sacramento, California — has been able to develop thirty fairly specific recommendations for planning comprehensive desegregation, equalizing the desegregation process, dealing with special characteristics of multiethnic and multilingual school districts, gaining acceptance for and adjusting the schools to desegregation, improving local administration and state and federal policies (Holden, 1974).

Viewing the rich accumulation of information, evaluation, and diagnoses, we close this section with a final proposition.

Proposition 14: Substantial specific knowledge is now available for guiding diagnosis and action in any effort to establish and maintain ethnically integrated education.

Finally, an intensive review of the controversies related to racial and ethnic relations of the decades since the Great Depression will make vivid to any student of the matter the salience and importance of labels and symbols: equal opportunity, all deliberate speed, massive resistance, civil rights, desegregation, integration, backlash, white flight, black power, forced busing, welfare mothers, workfare. It is conventional in studies of intergroup relations to talk about stereotyping. But the language that *defines public issues* itself *sets the terms* of debate — it is far more than a mere matter of derogatory images of collectivities. Labeling or classification is a primary *political* act. The terms in which issues have been formulated have prefigured the lines of battle and, often, the outcomes. Image-making often is myth-making, and myth-making is a form of mystification.

6. The New Yellow Peril? The Strange Case of Busing

I was bused to school — after elementary grades. During my attendance in the first seven grades, I walked — two miles each way, frequently through that remarkably deep red mud characteristic of my native Orange County, North Carolina. When I started to high school, fortune smiled: by walking only about one mile, I could (if on time) catch the fine yellow bus for the remaining two miles to the county seat town of Hillsborough. Busing was to me a great privilege, especially on cold days and in rainy weather. (There was another advantage. When I walked, I usually had several fights a week, being "jumped" by gangs of white youths whose idea of sport was to beat up a lone victim.)

That is what "busing" once meant to one school child. In the late 1960s and early 1970s, the term became richly endowed with surplus meanings, as acrimonious debate swirled around the use of busing to achieve "racial balance" under court-ordered desegregation plans. The earlier history has been forgotten.

The mass media in the late 1960s and in the 1970s came to use as a standard label the phrase *"forced* busing." But why the word, *forced*? Most public busing from the beginning has been forced: children have been required to attend school, their parents have been required to send them, the location of schools precluded walking, busing was provided. There is nothing new about busing being compulsory, anymore than of school attendance being compulsory. Why, then, the careful and conspicuous inclusion of the word "forced"? Clearly this is a way of editorializing. Regardless of intent, this mode of labeling imposes a negative judgment on busing, which then becomes a popular symbol of desegregation.

The sheer frequency of public references to busing creates an impression that a vast change has occurred and that great numbers of children are suddenly being required to ride school buses for long distances. The impression is false, but the image has done its work.

Compulsory school attendance and public school bus transportation had become firmly linked as established and legalized systems before the 1920s. Once school consolidation had overcome initial resistances, controversy subsided, and at no time before the 1970s had busing itself been a major issue. Agitation against "busing" arose only after it became linked, in public controversies, with racial desegregation. Indeed, by 1972, well over 40 percent of all public school pupils regularly rode tax-supported buses to school. At most, Barron estimates, some 3 percent of the bused pupils or 1.3 percent of all pupils were being transported for purposes of achieving desegregated schools, in areas where residential segregation had prevented local-area school integration by other methods (Barron, 1975, 160-61).

The obvious question, how extensive is busing for purposes of desegregation, apparently almost never is raised in public debates. Yet it surely is an important question. Let us look at the available facts.

In 1963-64 prior to any extensive desegregation of public schools, some 39 percent of pupils were bused. Two years later the proportion was 40; at this slow rate of increase, the percentage bused should have risen by 1971-72 to about 43. The actual 1971-72 figure was 46.1. At maximum, therefore, the increase attributable to busing for purposes of desegregation could not have been more than 3 percent. The true figure probably is lower, because both school consolidation and the growth of special training programs must have required some additional busing. (Data from the Reference Department of the National Center for Educational Statistics; see also: U.S. Commission on Civil Rights. 1973. *School*

Desegregation in Ten Communities. Clearinghouse Publication #43. Washington D.C.)

Why, then, such a remarkable furor—involving even the attention of President Gerald Ford—over such a minor addition to the large population of pupils being transported at public expense? If the 97 percent of busing that is unconnected with desegregation elicits no public controversy—as, indeed, it generally does not—how could the familiar yellow bus become the symbolic focus of so much disagreement and political debate?

This question becomes particularly puzzling when one observes the frequent contrasts between communities in which busing has been accepted and those in which it has the appearance of a stimulus to collective violence. There are many such contrasts. Thus in Niagara Falls, New York, busing becomes an accepted and normal practice, while in South Boston it becomes the occasion for local violence and for national political controversy and manipulation. As we noted earlier, in the latter case the local disorders occurred in an inwardly oriented, ethnically homogeneous area in which a relatively immobile population, feeling economic pressures (inflation and underemployment) and social-status threats, interpreted desegregation as an outside imposition. For political reasons, various officials, both local and national, encouraged the local white population to resist legal orders; the predictable effect was to exacerbate hostility and encourage diffuse violence.

In many instances the implicit strategy of opposition to school desegregation, and especially to busing as a means of desegregation, has been to disclaim opposition to integration but to claim that the proposed plans would lower standards or impair the quality of schooling or be dangerous or fatiguing and inconvenient (cf. Duster, 1968, 9; Rubin, 1972). Of course, there is no reason to doubt that parents whose children formerly have attended a school within walking distance over a safe route would have real concern over an impending prospect of a long bus ride to an unknown school over heavily trafficked routes. Such concern would exist whether or not desegregation were involved. Similarly there is no reason to doubt that where there is strong local identification with a neighborhood or community school, parents and children tend to resist either transfer to a school outside the community or a marked change in the "historic" character of the local school. Indeed, resistance to this kind did occur in thousands of American communities between, say, 1920 and 1970. No issue of desegregation was present; rather the controversies were set off by consolidation of districts and schools—a process that reduced the total number of school districts in the United States from *127,000* in 1932 to *49,000* in 1958, and then to about *20,000* in the 1970s. Eventually, consolidation was accepted along with the necessary accompaniment of extensive busing. Often forgotten or somehow not apparent to many white persons is the fact that much busing—often very lengthy and inconvenient—was used in the service of maintaining racial segregation before the 1970s.

One approach for achieving racially balanced schools and countering problems of "white flight" and consolidation in urban districts is to create "magnet schools," schools with attractive often unique programs which will attract students from various ethnic groupings, avoiding the feeling of "coercion" that some see implied by busing plans. This use of such new schools may bypass resistance to change seen as enforced or external. Its promise is supported by findings of research that show that integration of public facilities and residential areas seems easiest when prior segregation does not have to be overcome (e.g., Hunt, 1960).

Actually, busing to achieve desegregation was initiated by court order only after all other methods had been ineffective. As we discuss in more detail below, by the late 1960s the chief remaining source of large-scale *school* segregation was *residential* segregation. It was only when the courts began to require that children be assigned and transported to schools outside their immediate neighborhoods that further substantial desegregation could be attained. It was partly through rerouting of busing in the South that the percentage of black students attending majority white schools increased from 18.4 in 1968 to 44.4 in 1972 (Giles, Gatlin, Cataldo, 1974, 493). Concurrently however there was some increase in transfers of white pupils to newly organized private schools. Although the total percentage of pupils transferred is small, we must ask whether busing itself has any substantial effect upon white enrollment in the public school system.

One useful set of data on the question (for 1971-72 and 1972-73) comes from 1,386 interviews with white "rejecters" and 2,112 white compliers in eight county-wide desegregated districts in Florida. *No statistically significant relation existed between the prospect of busing and attendance in or withdrawal from public schools.* On the other hand, compliers more often than rejecters already had experienced busing in the previous year: 74 percent of the compliers were experienced and among rejecters only 57 percent had children who were bused in the preceding year (Giles, Gatlin, Cataldo, 1974, 496). The findings indicate that *prior* apprehensiveness about busing is more influential in parents' decisions than the actual experience with busing; also, such apprehensiveness seems to be more potent when an increase in distance bused is in prospect or when the onset of busing is combined with relatively long prospective bus rides. Very striking, on the other hand, is the fact that parental decisions to continue or discontinue their children's enrollment in public schools are *not related* to whether the school of assignment has a majority of black pupils. An increased distance bused was associated with rejections of busing only when assignment was to a majority-black school (Giles, Gatlin, Cataldo, 1974, 500).

This case study illustrates in a local area a crucial point that holds true nationally — but that seems to be persistently ignored or misinterpreted. The evidence concerning actual behavior — not merely "attitudes" — conclusively shows that *neither busing alone nor the broader and more important total process of racial desegregation has significantly hastened the long-term movement of white population from most central cities*. Indeed, for all except a few very large cities, "school desegregation causes little or no significant white flight, even when it is court ordered and implemented in large cities" (Rossell, 1975-76, 688).

Acceptance of busing presumably will be favored to the extent that cumulation of apprehensiveness can be avoided — e.g., when the first prospect of busing involves a short distance and a majority-white school. Once a year's experience has been gained, increased distance does not seem to be a deterrent (Giles, Gatlin, Cataldo, 1974, 495-501; Rossell, 1975-76, 688-89).

Busing of children to school is a long-established and generally noncontroversial part of common practice. It has become controversial only when it appears as a part of school desegregation. Were school systems to cease the practice of busing and cross-busing *the effect clearly would be to perpetuate segregation and educational inequality*. Is opposition to busing, correspondingly, simply an expression of anti-black or anti-minority prejudices?

Prejudice (or "racism") clearly does contribute to anti-busing attitudes but does not seem to be the primary factor (Kelley, 1974). Resistance to busing is highly situational, especially as a reaction to anticipated changes of unknown negative potential.

Nowhere is the confounding of "race" with "class" more evident than in the controversies concerning cross-busing. White parents who justify their opposition on grounds of fears of violence and harassment often simply express a stereotype. But disorder is, indeed, a serious problem in many schools in metropolitan areas (as also are extortion among students, fighting, intimidation, theft, and drug use). Clearly, however, most of the objectionable behaviors are linked to low income and educational backgrounds rather than to racial composition of schools. Other feared behaviors (e.g., drug use) occur frequently in white middle-class schools, "even" in the suburbs. Furthermore, in the central cities, black parents of middle-class and "respectable working class" status often have to contend with severe problems when their children are, note, *forced* to attend de facto segregated schools, dominated by lower-class ghetto conditions.

Almost wholly neglected in mass media presentations are the dimensions of compassion, empathy, and moral and aesthetic appreciation of the positive experiences of black and white children and parents who have made busing successful in many instances. For a sensitive portrayal in photographs and text see Underhill, Coles, Baldwin, Whitney, 1974.

Several points of clarification, therefore, seem within easy reach. If segregation is an unconstitutional and socially undesirable policy, means must be found to avoid segregation. If residential segregation is marked, there will be some situations in which busing is one of the necessary means of desegregation. It is reasonable to make every attempt to have busing as safe, convenient, short, and nonstressful as possible. If cross-busing involves schools in which disorder is a problem, public policy must provide resources to control and prevent disorder.

In short, where there is a serious problem — from the standpoint of the parents and children involved — the problem is not busing as such, but other conditions for which specific remedies must be sought.

7. The Question of Consequences: Outcomes of Desegregation

The decision of the Supreme Court in the Brown case (and in prior and subsequent cases concerning segregation) was a *legal*, not a "social," decision (Warren, 1973). It established a *superordinate norm* for social policy, on the ground of constitutional law. The primary values to which the norm refers are those of *universalism* and of *equality of procedural rights* within the societal community. The ethical and legal grounds do not depend upon whether or not ensuing desegregation in any particular instance or series of instances results in faster or slower learning, greater intergroup harmony, or greater opposition, and so on.

Nevertheless, the question of actual consequences obviously is important, for any social norm or value always will be judged by how its apparent results relate to other norms and values. Moreover, desegregation and integration can occur in myriads of forms at differing tempos and in diverse settings. No abstract rule can fully encompass all the practical consequences of compliance or defiance in these endlessly varying circumstances. Hence, we want to know as much as possible about the effects of the various kinds of actions that occur when desegregation is attempted. Only when the specific characteristics of clearly defined *kinds* of desegregation are identified can we discover what "outcomes" reasonably can be imputed to desegregation as such.

When these cautions have been taken into account as fully as possible, is racial desegregation of public schools successful on net balance? Nancy St. John (1973, 1975) has provided a useful answer: the results have been positive, but these results will be found only when certain specified conditions have been met. For example, effective desegregation will increase black

Americans' sense of participation and control only if desegregation is both desired and achieved. Black children will find rewarding experiences to the extent that they are accorded equal status, do not feel deprived relative to white pupils, feel that expectations of teachers and white pupils are fair, do not experience overly severe competition, and are not segregated within the school. Negative effects of anxiety, discouragement, confusion, and resentment can be avoided to the extent that peer group relations are friendly, teachers and other authority figures emphasize pluralism and give individualized attention (see St. John, 1973, 45).

Of course, we know that "education" has yet to usher in an ultimate utopia anywhere, and desegregated education has never promised anyone a rose garden. Every serious piece of research on the subject is consistent with the conclusion that school desegregation is no panacea for all "problems"— and that it certainly cannot overnight undo the vast consequences of past segregation and discrimination. Also, it is clearly not realistic to expect large-scale, complex social changes in a diverse society to have uniform results. Nevertheless, such questions arise as, "Has desegregation of schools been successful?" The obvious answer is, "Yes and No." To garner a more sensible answer, a more sensible question has to be asked. For desegregation necessarily involves diverse social settings, characteristics of students and teachers, school organizations, pace, timing, methods, scope, objectives. Further, what outcomes are to be classified as "successful" may be defined in terms of academic achievement, personality development, self-esteem, group solidarity, individual satisfaction, character of peer-group relationships, and so on.[3] A besetting hazard in appraisal is overgeneralization.

Overgeneralization (stereotyping) often occurs with regard to both "majority" and "minority" children, perhaps especially the latter. Children from minority racial groupings are, of course, highly diverse in motivation, attitudes toward school, personality dynamics, social skills, work disciplines, measured academic abilities, and many other characteristics (Weinberg, 1970, 10-24).

Total appraisals, therefore, represent summaries of main tendencies that are accompanied by diverse side-effects. Thus a review of a great many studies, leading to a positive appraisal of main effects of desegregation in elementary and secondary schools, has been presented in the following terms:

> At the elementary level, desegregation has positive effects, on the whole, for minority children. . . . Good teaching and superior facilities seem to be more important than desegregation or integration per se. One earlier fear has been found to have no basis, and that is that the academic achievement of white American children would suffer under integration. . . . Busing seems not to affect academic achievement adversely. . . . At

the secondary level also, desegregation appears to be beneficial, but there may be problems concerning cocurricular activities and social participation (Roberts and Horton, 1973, 318-19).

Adding to the agreement on positive outcomes shown by the major research reviews just summarized are the findings of a large-scale survey of some 1,500 black adults who attended school before 1966. Those who had early experience in integrated schools are less likely to fear white people and more likely to attain higher levels of education. Although self-selection undoubtedly was a favorable factor, the experience of integrated schooling was positively associated with total educational attainment, adult occupational status, and adult income (Crain, 1970; Crain and Weisman, 1972). Findings congruent with these conclusions come from many independent studies (e.g., Lewis and St. John, 1975; Beers and Reardon, 1974; St. John, 1975; Katz, ed., 1976).

Pupils have higher academic achievements and higher educational aspirations when they attend schools in which a substantial proportion of other pupils are from middle-class backgrounds. In spite of many efforts to attack the data and methods of the studies that support this conclusion, the evidence remains convincing (Pettigrew, 1971, 57-64).

Further, studies that trace changes through time give corroborative evidence. For example, under a comprehensive reorganization program in 1970 the Harrisburg, Pennsylvania, schools were integrated through recombination, busing, hiring of minority staff, and other measures. Comparisons of pupils as they moved from the 5th to the 7th grade showed that Stanford Achievement Test scores for blacks were higher than past performance predicted for five out of seven areas; SAT scores for whites were maintained for five areas and fell below predictions for two areas. Attitude changes were positive: beginning below the state average in self-esteem, degree of understanding of others, and interest in school, the pupils in two years equaled the state norm.

In spite of the great diversity—of initial backgrounds of pupils and teachers, of school procedures, of facilities, of community attitudes—the net effect of desegregation on academic attainment of black children, on the whole, has been positive and little evidence has been found of any significant unfavorable effects for white children.

Race and ethnicity almost always are confounded with average differences in education, occupational status, and income. Accordingly, the outcomes of segregation and desegregation must be analyzed in relation to both socioeconomic status and ethnicity, if we are to avoid mistaking the consequences of one for those of the other. It is striking to find, for example, that the forms and the consequences of school segregation in Sweden based on socioeconomic status strongly resemble those of racial segregation in schools of northern cities in the U.S. (Swedner, 1971).

Both Coleman (1966) and Jencks et al. (1972) cite data showing that *blacks in integrated schools have higher scores than blacks in segregated schools and that the higher scores are associated less with racial composition than with other socioeconomic characteristics of other students in the school.* Both show that variance within the white and the black populations is greater than variance between group averages.

The need to disaggregate such diverse conglomerations as "white population" or "black population" is evident to sociological common sense but often ignored in practice. An illustration of its importance is provided by evidence that *interethnic differences in educational attainment in New York City are greater than white-nonwhite differences* (Rosenwaike, 1973). Another instance in point is that educational attainments of children of southern and northern blacks in the North are substantially different; statistical controls for generation (and rural-urban background) appear essential for locating sources of variance within the black population (Lieberson, 1973).

Effects of desegregated and integrated schooling upon self-conceptions, aspirations, and self-evaluations are complex. Space limits forbid a detailed review of the evidence here. In general, however, the aspirations of black students (as well as self-acceptance) are higher in desegregated settings; these findings seem to hold but less certainly for Mexican American and Native American pupils (Weinberg, 1970). Coleman et al. (1966) found that blacks in integrated schools more often than those in segregated schools felt that they had control over their school success. It is also true, however, that among elementary students in predominantly black and predominantly white schools the black students' sense of control is decidedly lower than that of the whites (Brookover et al., 1975). Although many other aspects of the school affect self-appraisals, the data at hand suggest that segregated schools have unfavorable effects on black students' sense of control of their environment.

On the whole, the effects of self-evaluations thus far found to follow desegregation fail to support either the higher hopes or the most negative forebodings (Christmas, 1973).

Community solidarity and family support protect black children against negative effects of white hostility and invidious comparisons (Meketon, 1966; Coles, 1967; Rosenberg and Simmons, 1971). In general, the self-esteem of black children and youths who have entered school since the early 1960s appears at least equal to—and may excel—the self-appraisals of whites of comparable socioeconomic levels (Rosenberg and Simmons, 1971). As J. D. R. Porter (1971) has insisted, the evidence is overwhelming that group identity and individual identity are by no means coterminous and that negative out-group evaluations do not always (or even typically) override positive ingroup evaluations of either the individual or his collectivity-of-membership.

Effects of cross-ethnic interactions in the schools also are variable and diverse. Without going into the qualifications and complexities, it is safe to summarize the main trends. The essential conclusions are two: (1) many American children and youths today attend substantially integrated schools; (2) the weight of evidence is that the greater the opportunity for interethnic contacts, the less the prejudice and the more frequent the development of cross-ethnic acceptance and friendship (Coleman et al., 1966; Weinberg, 1970; Pettigrew, 1971; Muir, 1971; Miller and Dreger, eds., 1973; Lewis and St. John, 1974; Katz, ed., 1976). There are many local exceptions (Weinberg, 1970), but the aggregate effect clearly is positive in the long run. This effect often is obscured by the salience in popular reporting of incidents of conflict. But behavior in such situations is a poor basis for predicting later conduct under more nearly routine circumstances. Once desegregation had been established as the inevitable and normal situation, the basic factors governing interpersonal relationships elsewhere reassert their determining influence, e.g., interpersonal liking is favored by equal-status interaction, mutual interdependence, positive social norms, counterstereotypic characteristics of others, and ease of personalized association.

In the interests of brevity we pass over the large literature of analysis and evaluation of the desegregation of higher education.[4] The broad trends, however, must be mentioned.

In the year 1910, it is estimated, there were between 3,000 and 4,000 black college students in the entire nation. As late as 1950, there were only 100,000. The spectacular growth occurred in the 1950s and 1960s. Most of the increase represents enrollment in predominantly white colleges and universities. In these terms, desegregation of higher education is a resounding success. Actual outcomes are less easy to ascertain.

One fundamental problem is reconciling "affirmative action," aimed at redressing categorical disadvantages experienced by minority youths in the past, with maintenance of universalistic tests of achievement as the basis for competitive placement and reward (cf. Glazer, 1976). The other basic question is separate residential clustering and separate educational programs for minorities within the college or university.

The actual outcomes of college education, whether of minority or nonminority students, have been little studied (for a notable exception, see Althauser and Spivack, 1975). However, data from Project TALENT, based on a stratified random sample of male seniors in American high schools, show that socioeconomic origin is *less* closely related to educational attainment among blacks than among whites, whereas attitudes of social conformity tend to predict attainment among blacks. Additionally, educational attainment has a strong effect on black occupational success. These findings imply that once a black youth acquires a higher education, the opportunities for advancement are relatively good (Porter, 1974). Negative effects of discrimination tend to take effect before college graduation, and high educational attainments appear to serve as a basis for "sponsored" entry into desirable occupations (Wilburn, 1974). It is clear, at any rate, that prestigeful black models and "success stories" are increasingly available to black youths.

8. Policy Reexamined

The Supreme Court, the Congress, and the federal executive during the 1950s and 1960s finally launched American society on a comprehensive program of educational desegregation. The Brown decision, originally designed for an overt system of legislated segregation with what seemed at the time to be clear regional boundaries, is now being used to effect change in a broad pattern of segregation, which is neither clearly overt nor regionally contained. The original action destroyed the legal basis for a dual system. Now the "dual system" involves such issues as the ghettoization of northern cities, employment discrimination, and housing barriers. It has become increasingly evident how difficult it is to resolve social inequities in education apart from the larger social framework in which it is set (Cohen, 1974).

Does experience indicate that educational integration through mutual accommodation is feasible? And are the consequences grounds for pessimism or optimism?

Where residential separation is not overwhelmingly massive—that is in the "small ghetto" situations of many small and medium-sized towns and cities—technically feasible and relatively simple administrative means are available to effectively produce desegregation. Redistricting can help to reduce white or black preponderance in any one district. Princeton-plan pairing of white and black schools along margins of areas of residential concentration can supplement this procedure. Any new schools can be located so as to minimize the possibilities of de facto separation. District-wide specialized schools may be instituted. And the flows of pupils from elementary to intermediate to senior level schools can be arranged to facilitate mixing at the higher grades.

For the areas of very large cities that are almost wholly populated by blacks, on the other hand, very little desegregation can be accomplished, in the short run, without extensive busing or without major alterations in location and organization of schools. The metropolitan educational parks, described by Pettigrew (1971, 69-70) and others, are technically feasible, although not yet politically possible.

In terms of the feasibility of desegregation, all the major lines of interpretation we have followed in this chapter converge in one case study of highly successful school desegregation in a small, "conservative" southern city in which more than half of the school-age population was black in 1970 (Mayer, King, Borders-Patterson, McCullough, 1974). The city is in a semirural region that voted for George Wallace in 1968; a billboard a few miles ouside the city limit recently read, "Welcome to Ku Klux Klan country." Yet Goldsboro, North Carolina, desegregated its schools rapidly, effectively, and peaceably. The city won a national award in 1970 for having one of the eight "most progressive" desegregation plans in the United States. As we shall see below, desegregation had generally positive academic and social results.

How was all this possible? Some factors were specific to the city and its particular history—such as the "liberal" political inclinations of a leading family, the personality of the school superintendent, or the unique character of local civic pride—but the most important variables are of general significance across a wide range of types of communities.

The decision to move ahead with a comprehensive desegregation program came in response to strong external pressure. But limited desegregation had been in process for several years, under a "freedom-of-choice" plan, and the major decision to accelerate desegregation was made in advance of specific external compulsion. In a general and "token" way, the Board of Education earlier was responsive to the Supreme Court decision of 1954 and to Title VI of the Civil Rights Act of 1964. But it acted in 1968 to merge the two racially separate high schools, before the October 1969 decision of the Supreme Court that called for the immediate elimination of dual school systems.

Substantial desegregation already had been achieved, under the freedom-of-choice plan, in two schools. The others were desegregated by a combination of other methods—redrawing boundaries of attendance areas, pairing of schools, and busing. Administrative and teaching staffs were immediately desegregated. Teachers were impartially reassigned to different schools, so that all started anew. Innovations in organization and teaching were encouraged. Buildings and facilities were improved. Top administrative leadership defined the change as necessary and encouraged staff to regard it as an exciting educational challenge.

Thus the plan for full desegregation was authoritative, comprehensive, and technically well-designed. It was built upon much prior experience and analysis, both local and elsewhere (Williams and Ryan, 1954, Chapter 12). Community leaders foresaw the possibility that continued resistance to desegregation would be costly and disruptive. They wished to preserve an excellent public school system. In effect they said, "if we have to do it to preserve our public schools, let's do it right."

The program was conceived and carried into effect by an appointed Board of Education whose members may serve two six-year terms. The Board is made up of well-educated and influential persons with multiple relations to persons in law, the churches, industry, and business. They are oriented to issues of the public interest, are not exposed to popular pressure, are pragmatic, legal-minded, prudent, and committed to "working within the system." Within the community the Board was active, not merely reactive, and it acted quickly and decisively.

Thus the leadership of the community generally, and the Board of Education in particular, is "a classical case of elitism" (Mayer et al., 1974, 25). Because of its high prestige, stability, continuity, homogeneity, expertise, and established authority, it could treat the whole problem as an *educational* matter in which its own authority was paramount. It did not need a plebiscite and it did not confront any opposing elite.

The rapid and detailed implementation of the plan bypassed overt resistance, and the educational results were remarkably positive. In particular, academic achievement improved on the average among blacks and remained stable among whites. Curriculum and teaching changes appeared to have effects favorable to integration. Extracurricular activities tended to be avoided. Relationships among white and black pupils in the high school often were tense and abrasive, partly reflecting tensions among teachers. Yet the students tended to be optimistic about their own ability to resolve the problems "if given a chance."

The study of Goldsboro gives a picture of many fascinating details that must be left aside in our summary. Obviously the outcomes are mixed; utopia is not at hand. But the program on the whole must be judged as an impressive achievement by any reasonable contemporary standards. As the authors conclude:

> This case clearly indicates that racial balance can be instrumental in creating changes in the educational process toward greater equality of opportunity. . . . This study has important implications for educators. In contrast to dire predictions, desegregation can be accompanied by an increase in the quality of educational programs (Mayer et al. 1974, 110).

Of course, no one solution is universally applicable. In many instances, mutual accommodation will occur only through prolonged controversy, conflict, and bargaining. But what can be done once is a possible thing. It can be done again under the appropriate conditions—as shown by the impressive documentation of conditions that have led to successful desegregation in a national sample of ninety-one cities (Kirby, Harris, Crain, Rossell, 1973). And sufficient knowledge now exists to make successful educational integration a realistic goal in thousands of school systems throughout the United States. If we want to do it, we have the knowledge and the tools to do it well.

Contrary to much popular skepticism, we now have had enough practical experience, research findings, and reflective consideration of questions of racial and ethnic integration in educational settings to provide workable answers to many if not most of the difficult questions that are entailed. Specifically, integration need *not* result in lowered standards or performance, in "loss of identity," or in unmanageable conflict. There are definite conditions and procedures, as we have seen, that can ensure good academic quality, mutual respect for group identities, and the gradual building of realistic interpersonal relations within a common community of experience.

In briefest possible summary, leaving aside all details and qualifications, we conclude that:

1. Schools do make differences. They affect both individual attainments and social welfare and unity.
2. Desegregation and integration in schools are feasible, given the necessary agreement to take authoritative action.
3. Under specifiable and realistically possible conditions, educational desegregation can lead to integrated accommodation and effective education.
4. Specific techniques that have proved effective in practice are available for critically selective use in public schools and in higher education.

Of the hundreds of particular suggestions that could be drawn from considerations reviewed in this chapter, we propose four modest normative pronouncements as worthy of adoption by educators, parents, and taxpayers.

Dictum 1. Every child should be made welcome.

Dictum 2. No one should be powerless.
   Implications:
   a. No minority category (including white pupils) should be present in merely token numbers in a school.
   b. Every pupil should have several like-group associates in every classroom or major activity.
   c. Teachers, administrators, and auxiliary staff members should be selected and trained for observing and dealing skillfully with situations of isolation and of ganging-up.

    d. Any child should have easy and prompt access to both nonpublic and public channels for expressing grievances and apprehensions and for receiving counseling and effective protection and redress.

    e. Staff should be fully integrated.

Dictum 3. Authority figures should be firm, impartial, and compassionate.
    Implications:

    a. Universalistic policies should be clearly and explicitly communicated to staff, pupils, parents, and the larger community.

    b. Sanctions should be explicit.

    c. Disciplinary actions should be taken in the context of the study of motivation and other causal circumstances.

    d. Students should have effective access to some person or group acting in an ombudsmanlike capacity, as well as to psychological and social counseling.

Dictum 4. Cooperative interdependence should be fostered.

Finally, for the reader who prefers skeptical and cautious hope over despair, we offer a quotation from Ann Holden's sympathetic interpretation.

Although . . . many members of minority groups have become increasingly disenchanted with the kind of desegregation they are experiencing in the schools, most minority leaders in these communities were still amenable to the *right kind* of desegregated schools. Most of the newer, more "militant" demands . . . represent attempts to equalize the desegregation process and improve racial conditions in the schools and are in no way hostile to desegregation. Willingness on the part of school districts and communities to meet these demands, to correct existing racial problems in the schools, and to fully incorporate minorities into the intellectual and social life of the schools offers the best and probably the only hope of offsetting further disillusionment and a stronger movement in the direction of separatism. Not just desegregation, but desegregation and racial balance combined with racial justice must be the goal for the public schools (Holden, 1974, 453-54).

Chapter 4

The Fluid Mosaic: Ethnicity
and Residence in American Communities

"Where do you come from?" said the Red Queen (to Alice). "And where are you going? Look up, speak nicely and don't twiddle your fingers."

Lewis Carroll. Through the Looking Glass.

1. Facts and Fiction: Where Have We Come from? and Where Are We Going?

Repeated efforts have been made in many urban areas to stabilize segregated neighborhoods, to stabilize integrated neighborhoods, to break up segregated areas, or to integrate previously segregated localities. And an elaborate ideology developed during the last decade around the various demands for "community control" of local schools and other organizations and institutions.

These developments need to be seen in historical depth. In the 1970s, some black educators favor local control. But for a half-century, community control in the South meant forced racial segregation. Again, contemporary emphasis on neighborhood schools often is linked with an assumption of stable neighborhoods. But stable urban neighborhoods never have been very common in the United States. For example, analysis of trends in Omaha (Chudacoff, 1972) shows that mobility and change dominated over neighborhood stability from 1880 on. Shifts in the ethnic and racial composition of the population in various parts of metropolitan areas—"ecological succession" —appear to be more nearly consequences than causes of other social and economic changes (Molotch, 1972a, 1972b; Hunter, 1974a, 1974b). Higher

116

income among blacks, taken by itself, has done little to reduce concentration of blacks in central cities, and further improvements in income will not alter the pattern unless barriers to an open market in housing are substantially reduced, or white preferences are changed, or both developments take place (Farley, 1970).

Housing remains, as it long has been, the one major commodity that is essential for normal living in our society but is not freely available for a price in an open market. The restrictions still enforced on sales and rentals of dwellings would be thought outrageous, no doubt, for automobiles or household furnishings. Racial separation in residential areas is not primarily the result of differences in income; as the Taeubers showed, for 1960, some 80 percent of the racial segregation in Chicago cannot be accounted for on the basis of income differentials (Taebuber and Taeuber, 1965). Nor is segregation primarily due to the preferences of black people (Campbell and Schuman, 1968, 15-16; Timms, 1971; Hermalin and Farley, 1973; Hawley and Rock, eds., 1973; Zeul, 1976).

Mobility, of course, does not necessarily lessen ethnic segregation. The persistence of urban residential clustering over the last thirty years has been well-documented for the New York metropolitan area, not only for blacks and whites but also for whites of different national origin stocks (Kantrowitz, 1973). For the nation as a whole, however, as many as one-fifth of all white households live in racially integrated neighborhoods. Nor is newness a necessary condition for racial integration of residential areas—a 1967 nation-wide survey showed that the typical integrated neighborhood has been well established for some time—it is not a new development (Bradburn, Sudman, Gockel, with Noel, 1970).

Fact: One of every five Americans lives in an integrated or nonsegregated neighborhood—one in which both blacks and whites now live and into which both are moving (Bradburn, Sudman, Gockel, Noel, 1970).

Proposition 1: Most studies of racially mixed suburban neighborhoods have agreed in reporting that housing costs and the characteristics of housing services and physical surroundings are more important to both blacks and whites than whether the area is or is not racially integrated (e.g., Hawley and Rock, 1973; Zeul, 1976).

Even explicitly prejudiced white persons in suburban areas adjacent to Washington, D.C. chose to live in racially mixed areas when attractive housing was available there (Zeul, 1976). And among blacks in the North, relatively easy adjustment and high satisfaction have been found among young, well-educated, middle-income families moving into suburbs in which whites were in the great majority and in which the white residents did not react to incoming blacks as a threat (Mussen, O'Halon, Winkel, 1974).

The future prospects are being shaped not by a single type of change but by several diverse trends that are occurring at the same time. In areas that are now exclusively inhabited by whites, the likelihood is high that there will be a small but continuous in-movement of black residents especially in the higher rent areas of northern cities and suburbs. In neighborhoods that are now open to residents of both racial categories and that are integrating, there are likely to be moderate increases in the proportion of black families. Neighborhoods that already are substantially integrated often will experience increased in-movement of black families, and many such areas eventually will become predominantly black. Solidly segregated black ghetto areas are likely to remain for some considerable time almost wholly black; low to moderate rent areas that are all-white, that are resistant to integration, and that are located a substantial distance from concentrations of black population are likely to remain segregated (Bradburn et al., 1970; Ryan et al., 1974).

It is true, of course, that both black and white individuals and families find housing choices sharply constricted by low income.

Proposition 2: Furthermore, it is well established that poor people generally have not benefited from the types of governmental subsidies of housing that have been used in the past.

Instances in point include federal credit agencies, housing assistance programs and assistance to rural homeowners, mortgage insurance guarantees, and Internal Revenue Service regulations that implicitly subsidize homeowners. Except for public housing for low-income families, nearly all the major federal programs have primarily favored middle- and upper-income groupings, home-owners, large investors, and building and construction industries (Aaron, 1972).

The introductory considerations just sketched are enough to suggest two main conclusions:

Proposition 3: The residential areas of American cities and suburbs are highly segregated by race and ethnicity. But integration definitely does exist on a substantial scale.

Proposition 4: Segregation partly results from income differentials, partly from preferences, but primarily from economic, political, and social constraints (Hermalin and Farley, 1973).

Let us more closely examine the structure of some determinants of residential patterning.

2. Preferences, Choices, and Constraints in Residential Location

Even without any exclusionary discrimination, a consistent (even if only slight) preference for same-ethnic neighbors can lead over time to a surprisingly high degree of residential segregation (Schelling, 1971). This kind of ethnic clustering is greatly accentuated by a discriminatory real estate market and high mobility. The result is a *dual housing market* in which, for example, blacks are forced to pay higher prices. To the extent that the price differential widens, the incentive grows for real estate dealers and individual sellers to sell or rent to blacks, who are willing to pay a premium because of discriminatory barriers elsewhere. The primary factor is the institutionalized system of market discrimination that generates surges of black population into the limited "open" areas. Local efforts to halt or reverse these processes will be nullified unless two conditions are created: (1) marked reduction of discrimination in the housing market, (2) availability of substantial supplies of new housing (Marris, 1968; Molotch, 1972a; Hecht, 1974).

The evidence is clear that as separate individuals freely choosing in an unrestricted market, both blacks and whites in metropolitan areas tend to select residential locations primarily on the basis of nonracial criteria (J. A. Williams, 1971; Hawley and Rock, 1973; Zeul, 1976, and many others). However, as already noted, housing markets are not free but are partitioned and constricted in various ways. What are some of the most important restraints upon choices, other than income? The major barriers are: multiple autonomous local governments, public and private policies and practices in credit arrangements, discriminatory use of zoning and inspection regulations, private collusion among sellers and renters and their agents, limited information and secretive practices among real estate agencies, manipulation of local markets by dealers (Hawley and Rock, 1973, 19). Furthermore, the sheer existence of ethno-racial discrimination may be enough in itself to deter sensitive members of minority groupings from attempting to rent or buy in areas that are understood to be exclusionary (Kitano, 1960, 193-96).

> *Proposition 5:* Taking all other conditions into account, the one most crucial factor in ethnic residential segregation is the *institutionalization of diffuse prejudices and preferences into systems of selective information, referral, access, financing and restricted occupancy.*

This analysis does not discount the influence of preferences, nor does it overlook the fact that some preferences are based on local familiarity and social trust—both of which often are linked with ethnic ingroup sentiments and patterns of association (Suttles, 1972; 1974). But fully autonomous and self-sufficient neighborhoods do not exist in metropolitan areas, nor did they in the past. Local social organization consists of differentiated and interpenetrating activities that flow across any precise territorial boundaries. Various levels of centralization and specialization are required for effective provision of goods and services. Every neighborhood or community is a differentiated part of a larger system, and most territorial "units" are to some degree internally heterogeneous. Solidary territorial communities of high consensus on values, beliefs, sentiments, and attachments are rare in modern urban settings.

The effects of residential clusterings upon the potentialities of interracial or interethnic contacts vary greatly with different *patterns* of separation (Bennet, 1973). For example, the smaller and more densely packed the homogeneous clusters, the greater the potential for intergroup contact. Changes in size of clusters will have greatest effects upon groupings that constitute a small proportion of the total population. Even with a constant "segregation rate," there are large differences in interaction potentials, as between persons living in residences across-street and those who are same-side neighbors.

These considerations are crucial for development of realistic policies concerning residential patterning in urbanized areas. Existing ethnic and racial concentrations unquestionably generate sentiments of localistic exclusiveness and outgroup antipathy — as in South Boston. But the concentrations did not develop in the first place simply because of diffuse individual preferences. Rather the "ethnic mosaic" developed from political and economic arrangements that originally had little to do with social sentiments. Particularly important were employment opportunities, transportation costs, and public policies on taxation, zoning, and credit (Kain and Persky, 1969, 75).

Proposition 6: Contrary to some popular beliefs, *suburbanization is not a new trend, nor did white people go to the suburbs because of migration of ethnic minorities into the cities.*

Movement of central-city residents to suburbs was noted in the late nineteenth and early twentieth century and was well advanced by the 1920s. Although the mid-century decades brought explosive growth in outlying areas, the movement to suburbia was not primarily a "white flight" — the suburbs simply continued to attract those whites who had good incomes — because of better housing, more living space and recreational territory, better schools and other facilities, cleaner air, and access to decentralizing employment opportunities. These same features, of course, are appealing to many black people. Given open access, suburban intermingling of "ethnics" is certain to occur as income and transportation facilities permit (Miller, 1973; Zehner, Chapin, Howell, 1974; Zeul, 1976).

3. Causes of Segregation and Integration

Each major wave of immigration to American cities resulted in concentrated areas of ethnic settlement—the classic Little Italies, Little Norways, and Little Polands of the rapidly growing central cities. With succeeding generations, rising socioeconomic levels and increasing cultural assimilation led to greater or less dispersal. Although some ethnic groupings remained highly clustered, most became residentially dispersed to a substantial degree. Since World War II, the dense concentrations of black Americans in metropolitan centers have grown rapidly and the classic sequences of dispersal have been only weakly manifest or have not appeared at all (Meade, 1972). Thus the historical record provides clear contrasts between gradual ethnic dispersal and residential inter-mingling versus sharply segregated ghettos that persist over long periods. What are the factors causing these contrasting patterns?

We already reviewed most of the determinants: income, ingroup prefer-ences, governmental policies of discrimination or antidiscrimination, discrimi-nation by business, prejudice. Let us try to make these "factors" somewhat more concrete. Both residential segregation and very sharp contrasts of wealth and poverty in central areas of great cities have been accentuated by these roughly simultaneous developments:

1. segregated residential clustering of black people, typically in areas adjacent to low-income white areas;
2. relatively slow growth, or actual decrease, in manufacturing employ-ment in central cities;
3. concentration of managerial, communicative, clerical, and technical activities in central sites of the largest metropolitan areas;
4. growth of middle-class suburbs and fringe areas, drawing large num-bers of white persons of higher income away from residence in the central city.

The growth of upper- and middle-class suburbs was made possible not merely by the widespread ownership of private automobiles, but also by public policies of subsidizing highways, providing financial incentives for building detached single-family homes, zoning, low support for public housing for low-income families, not providing cheap public transit facilities for low-income workers to live in suburban areas. De facto segregation thus occurs through socioeconomic sorting in private real estate and housing markets. It also may occur or be prevented by the action of public authorities that provide housing. In Great Britain, for example, in some urban areas up to one-half of the housing spaces are controlled by local authorities who have scope to make allocations that will avoid dense contiguous clusterings of distinctive racial and ethnic populations (Patterson, 1969).

In the United States, the nominally private market is a dominant influence —but it is by no means "private" either in its effects or in its modes of operation. For example, for many years restrictive covenants were legally enforceable compacts that were ethnically discriminatory; political authority thus directly supported segregation. Although restrictive covenants were voided by the Supreme Court,[1] other governmental policies have favored de facto segregation. Early examples of federal programs that benefited middle classes and whites rather than blacks or low-income strata included the Federal Home Loan Bank system (1932), the Home Owner's Loan Corporation (1933), and the National Housing Act (1934) that established the Federal Housing Administration. In the 1960s, there appeared the countersegregation laws illustrated by the Civil Rights Acts of 1964 and 1968, the Demonstration Cities and Metropolitan Development Act of 1966, and the Intergovernmental Cooperation Act of 1968. Partly based on such legislation, a series of executive orders and regulations further extended the potential federal role in checking the segregation that earlier policies had helped to create.

One of the great forces for suburbanization of whites, initally leaving blacks and other minorities in the central cities, has been the federal Interstate and Defense Highway Program, coupled with lack of adequate support for public, urban mass transit. Even the little-known federal program of assistance for sewage systems and treatment plants accelerated suburbanization (Walter and Wirt, 1971).

After 1969, the Department of Housing and Urban Development attempted to provide some low-income housing in suburban areas. Dispersal was achieved in some cases without meeting serious resistance; in others, conflict was intense. But the program was abruptly constrained in 1971 when a Supreme Court decision held that a local jurisdiction could decide by vote whether to accept public housing within its territory. Local referendums typically go against public housing in suburban areas. At the same time, efforts to disperse public housing were discouraged by the explicit opposition of then-President Nixon (Walter and Wirt, 1971). Future years will bring continuing struggles to achieve equal access in housing through actions in legislative bodies, in various executive and administrative agencies, in business firms and labor unions, and in the courts (see sections 6 and 7 of this chapter.).

The weight of the evidence clearly shows that it is incorrect to accept the notion of "white flight" from inner cities to suburbs because of anticipated movement of blacks into previously white residential areas. The several lines of evidence consistent with this conclusion are as follows (Grier and Grier, 1960; Glazer and McEntire, 1960; Wolf and Lebeaux, 1969; Molotch, 1969,

1972a, 1972b; Guest and Zuiches, 1971; Hawley and Rock, 1973; Zeul, 1976; Rossell, 1975-76):

1. Substantial movement of whites to suburbs antedated any large in-migration of blacks to the areas of departure.
2. Both observational studies and correlational analyses show that only a small proportion of the total amount of variance in white out-migration from inner-city areas is associated with racial factors (e.g., amount of racial change, proportion of blacks in adjacent areas).
3. Both whites and blacks explain their moving and staying behavior primarily by nonracial considerations—price, quality of housing, access to good schools, and the like.

Mobility from residence to residence is quite high in urban areas. About one-fifth of all households move each year and mobility is especially high in areas of shifting economic use. Accordingly, substantial socioeconomic and ethnic de facto segregation easily can come about even in the total absence of *negative* discrimination. The very high degree of residential separation of whites and blacks in central cities in the United States, however, can occur only through some form of systematic blockage (Taeuber and Taeuber, 1965; Molotch, 1972a, 1972b). To remove monolithic residential segregation, there-fore, it is necessary to greatly reduce or eliminate discrimination against blacks and to eliminate informal inhibitory barriers that prevent blacks or whites from exercising free choice in the housing market (Hermalin and Farley, 1973, 608; Darden, 1973). Since neither differences in income nor individual prefer-ences explain the segregation of black people, the only condition that could account for the extensive ghettoization is constraint; in short, segregation is primarily the result of the past and present actions of business firms, private associations, governments at all levels, and individuals and groups of white people (Hermalin and Farley, 1973).

Analysis of longitudinal data is needed to show what effects come from *change* in racial or ethnic composition of residential areas. Fortunately, some studies are becoming available that do make observations at two or more points in time. Thus a study of two residential areas in suburbs of St. Louis shows that inmigration of black families was not followed by an exodus of whites. No definite "tipping point" was discernible, i.e., no specific level of increases in black population led to the accelerated movement of white families, nor did racial transition result in racial succession. Changes in housing values were less affected by the racial composition of the incoming population than by deliberate actions of business firms and local government, e.g., discrimination by realtors, "red-lining" by mortgage companies, and unusual enforcement of housing codes (Sutker and Sutker, 1974).

Some of the restrictive actions have been diffuse responses by unorganized individuals and small informal groupings. Far more important have been, and are, the *organized* actions of federal, state, and local governments; of business organizations such as credit-granting agencies, brokerage companies, banks, life insurance firms, real estate dealers and associations, and local associations of suburban homeowners.

Another hoary belief—held with great tenacity in many instances in the face of overwhelming evidence to the contrary—is the myth of "declining property values." In the myth, the movement of ethno-racial minority families into an all-white residential area is believed to cause declines in housing prices. The accumulated evidence of many studies is that the myth is a myth. Prices indeed will decline for a time—*if* whites "panic" and by selling their houses or moving away, create a self-fulfilling prophecy.

Proposition 7: But unless the area already is in a state of economic decline for other reasons, the in-movement of high-demand black or other minority families soon results in maintenance or actual increase in sales prices and rentals (see, for example, Phares, 1971).

We can efficiently summarize our own review of the available information by quoting from the comprehensive appraisal by the Advisory Committee to the Department of Housing and Urban Development, as follows:

Discrimination in the sale of housing is evident in concern about property values and in the behavior of owners, brokers, and some developers.

· The weight of evidence is that, in comparison with similar all-white neighborhoods, property values in areas entered by nonwhites do not generally fall.

· Real estate brokers, despite fair-housing laws and policies, continue to screen home seekers on the basis of race.

· Policies of large firms of home builders toward racial mixing have become more affirmative. Changes in the policies of large developers can be very significant.

· However, progress in other sectors of the market is also essential to open up opportunities for minority families along the chain of moves resulting from the occupancy of new housing (Advisory Committee to HUD, *Freedom of Choice in Housing*, 1972, 61).

4. Effects of Population Concentration and Segregation

Residential segregation of densely concentrated ethnic populations in urban areas has massive social effects including political and economic consequences.

To the extent that ethnic homogeneity exists in a residential area, a general effect is to enhance ingroup versus outgroup distinctions.

Proposition 8: Segregation tends to increase social segmentation and cleavage. Restricted local interaction promotes similarity of outlook and increases the likelihood of a sense of alienation and hostility in relations to outsiders.

Consensus and understanding across ethnic lines are not promoted by residential segregation (Williams, Dean, Suchman, 1964, Chapters 6, 7, 8, 10). Segregation encourages and strengthens a sense of territorial closure. Economic and political struggles acquire a cumulative importance to local residents as part of a total opposition. Thus much evidence indicates that conflicts involving black populations in metropolitan centers during the late 1960s were accentuated by critical massing in particular settings. In the case of political disorders in the New York City schools during 1968-69, no measured characteristic of the schools as such was significantly related to disorders (Ritterband and Silberstein, 1973). Rather, protest and tumult were directly related only to the sheer number of black pupils and of black teachers in the several schools. One reason for the frequency of such overt conflicts is that the territorial concentration of distinctive ethnic populations tends to turn limited intergovernmental oppositions into struggles for control. This tendency is especially important because of fragmentation of governing authority in metropolitan areas. For example: "Local government autonomy in metropolitan areas results in an uneven distribution of public sector costs; some government units are forced to assume the costs of decisions and policies adopted by other units" (Hawley and Rock, 1973, 20). Thus where segregation prevails within units, struggles for security and advantage become "communal" fights.

During a period of rapid expansion of the suburbs and of job opportunities therein, it has seemed plausible that the concentration of blacks in central cities (partly because of discriminatory exclusion from suburbs) would restrict economic opportunity for black workers. But the case is not self-evident or factually simple. Central-city job opportunities do continue to expand—in periods of prosperity, at least—even if slowly. The costs of commuting are sufficiently high to make central-city jobs preferable to suburban jobs for many black workers. Because of poor mass transportation facilities, black families without automobiles may even find suburban residence a severe handicap in locating and keeping suitable jobs, especially jobs for youths and housewives.

Once more, we must be alert to the possibility that some commonly accepted beliefs may not be well founded. In response to the changes in U.S. urban centers from the end of World War II into the 1970s, many analyses and commentaries have converged upon a limited set of assumptions and diagnoses, e.g., the cities are stagnating or dying, there is a massive "white flight," job opportunities are moving into the suburbs, blacks in central cities need to move to suburbs to follow the opportunities. None of these can be accepted without critical inspection. During the period of greatest pessimism, say 1965-75, there is evidence that all of them were and are incorrect, at least in part (B. Harrison, 1974). For example, much of the growth in new jobs in recent years has been in the public sector and most of this growth is in the cities. Also, blacks who live in the central city do not have markedly lower incomes or occupational status than those who live in the suburbs. In addition, the economic troubles of the cities are not automatic, or "their own fault," or somehow inherent in the nature of cities; rather, the difficulties are due in large part to the shrinking of the tax base as a result of deliberate actions by politically independent suburbs (B. Harrison, 1974; Danielson, 1976).

Concentration of a self-conscious minority in separate residential areas has several different kinds of political implications, under different circumstances. Most obviously, under a system of territorial representation, segregation can create a base for ethnic political power. But the "power" will have an important effect only if the ethnic representation is large enough *and* well enough articulated with collective interests to make a difference at the level of controlling important allocations and rule-making and adjudicative decisions. (To control a single ward in Chicago or New York City may have some patronage payoff and "symbolic" value; little else.)

Proposition 9: Residential segregation contributes to inequality of access to public goods and services, to political fragmentation, and to social conflict.

How do these consequences develop? Income, wealth and social prestige, and respect are unequally distributed among the various distinguishable ethnic populations within cities and metropolitan regions. Residential segregation concentrates and separates these unequal segments. Separate municipal governments for suburbs, cities, towns, and other areas serve to put highest affluence in some areas and the highest needs for governmental services in different areas. In this way, inequality is accentuated and perpetuated through the political structure of local communities. A further consequence is that resources are not made available to deal with region-wide or metropolitan area-wide problems; and still another result is that differences in the immediate self-interests of individuals are aggregated and polarized in the form of inter-organizational oppositions and conflicts.

5. Changing Neighborhoods: the Dilemmas
of Transition and Integration

Ours is a society of high geographic mobility and rapid social and economic changes. It is not surprising, accordingly, that residential areas change over time: in types of buildings, ethnic and socioeconomic composition of the population, location of services, and in patterns of public behavior. All neighborhoods eventually change their character. Our special interest here is change in ethnic, including racial, composition of the indwelling population. Regardless of its causes, segregation exists as a fact whenever a defined local area contains only one ethnic grouping or excludes one or more such categories. An integrated neighborhood may be defined in terms of *process*; for example, a racially integrated neighborhood is one into which both whites and blacks currently are moving into housing of comparable value (Bradburn, Sudman, Gockel, Noel, 1970, 7). Integration in this sense is a matter of degree, ranging from merely "open" ("token" representation of one racial category) to substantially integrated.

Given a predominantly private market in housing and given substantial differentials and rapid changes in income of individuals and families, there is a large and incessant reshuffling of people and residences. Under these conditions, marked segregation by income is typical and inevitable. Given that there are changes in numbers of persons black and white desiring housing and given a high correlation of racial category and income, apparent de facto segregation will result. If prior patterns of discrimination result in dual housing markets, special pressures for movement of blacks will develop in areas adjacent to ghettoized areas. Therefore:

> *Proposition 10:* Normal mobility makes neighborhood racial change
> *possible*; when markets are structured so that blacks continuously
> constitute the bulk of those who move into the resulting vacancies,
> racial change is *inevitable* (Molotch, 1972a).

Many of the processes of segregation, integration, and ecological change are counterintuitive—i.e., they are paradoxical from the standpoint of common sense or everyday assumptions. For example, some white people who have believed that the in-movement of black families foreshadowed rapid change to an all-black area have reacted in hostile and disruptive ways. But such reactions, far from slowing turnover,

> appear to have the effect of reducing white demand for housing in the
> area and thus bringing about a more rapid increase in Negro in-migration

and white out-migration. The hostile and panicked white response has all of the characteristics of a "self-fulfilling prophecy" in which the white residents act in such a way that they create a situation which brings about the very state of affairs they are afraid is going to happen (Bradburn, Sudman, Gockel, Noel, 1970, 16).

Again, it seems only obvious common sense that attitudes of racial prejudice will strongly affect whether a person does or does not live in an integrated neighborhood. But in fact even attitudes specifically favoring integration of residential areas have very little relationship to actual choice of housing and play little part in processes of integration or segregation (Hawley and Rock, 1973, 19; Bradburn, Sudman, Gockel, Noel, 1970, 16). Collective processes do involve preexisting attitudes, of course, but it is in the social process that the crucial causes of neighborhood stability and change are to be found.

Marked disparities between talk and action, expressed attitudes and other behavior, are common in situations in which residential integration or "succession" is a salient issue. In Chicago's South Shore dramatic expressions of intentions to move followed a violent incident in the high school, and many residents had the conviction that whites in large numbers were fleeing from the area. But counts of "For Sale" signs actually showed a slight decrease rather than an increase (Molotch, 1972a, 167). Another study (of a racially changing, predominantly middle-class Jewish area in Detroit) showed a high correlation between anti-black prejudice and stated *intention* to move but no correlation with *actual movement* over a two-year period. Several other studies in other localities document the same tendencies (see Fulton, 1960; Rapkin and Grigsby, 1960; Grier and Grier, 1960; Aurbach, Coleman, Mausner, 1960; Gans, 1967).

Pessimistic appraisals of the future possibilities for integrated residential areas often ignore the extent to which past segregation has been due to specific constraining and instigating policies and practices of business and government. Instead, attention has been focused on the microprocesses of "panic" and "flight"—which are themselves largely products of such policies and practices. Thus a study of Beverly, a white suburb of Chicago, stresses the fact that resistance to in-movement is not primarily based on prejudice but derives essentially from fear of change and fear of loss (Greeley, 1972, 232). Once an exodus of whites has begun, apprehensions that earlier were based on stereotypes or erroneous beliefs may become increasingly realistic as the self-fulfilling prophecy operates. The processes are those that underlie outcomes variously called social costs, economic externalities, the "tragedy of the commons" (Hardin, 1968), aggregative consequences of "micromotives," (Schelling, 1971) and the like. The prototypical conditions are that it is to someone's advantage to pursue a private interest that has an undesirable side-effect, so long or insofar as others do not behave in the same way; but as more and more individuals join in the process a collective condition will be created that is disadvantageous, noxious, or lethal to most or all. The overwhelming force of a shift in perceived individual advantages is shown in stabilized areas of residential mixing: there individual familes do not anticipate "flight"—hence the area is stable.

Proposition 11: Where residents do not see themselves as being displaced or economically threatened by the presence of "outgroup" migrants, overt conflict does not develop.

6. Intergroup Relations within Local Areas

Interracial living is feasible. Evidence to confirm this proposition is both varied and compelling (Advisory Committee to the Department of Housing and Urban Development, 1972, 6).

Relations among neighbors, regardless of ethnic memberships, are not always close or always cordial. We should not expect that harmony will reign in ethnically mixed areas if it does not in ethnically homogeneous areas. But mutually accepting and accommodative relations are possible and do exist among co-dwellers of different ethnic, racial, and religious backgrounds. What are the favorable factors?

The main findings reported by research before the 1970s concerning the relationships between intergroup contact or interaction and intergroup attitudes are the following:

Proposition 12: Among white persons, acceptance or other favorable attitudes toward black persons is directly and positively related to the frequency of prior extended interracial contact (Deutsch and Collins, 1951; Cook, Walkley, Wilner, 1952, 1955; Kelley, Ferson, Holtzman, 1958; Hunt, 1960; Greenfield, 1961; Williams, Dean, Suchman, 1964; Morris and Jeffries, 1968).

Proposition 13: Neighboring is greater the closer the residential proximity among persons of similar socioeconomic characteristics (Festinger, Schachter, Bach, 1950; Caplow and Forman, 1950). This generalization holds for interactions both among whites and between whites and blacks (Rose, Atelsek, McDonald, 1953; Hunt, 1960; Williams, Dean, Suchman, 1964; Meer and Freeman, 1966).

Although the more recent studies of interracial contact still have only partially specified the effects of fine-grained processes and of specific social contexts, indirect evidence comes from such findings as Ford's (1973) study—that "neighboring" in public housing projects is significantly related to lower prejudice among whites, but not among blacks. In earlier periods there was a time when sheer acceptance by whites of co-dwelling in a nonsegregated housing development was regarded by many blacks as a favorable sign of change. Today, in contrast, any remaining indications of discrimination or prejudice may increase negative attitudes of blacks toward whites. Of course it is to be expected that outcomes of interethnic association in residential areas will vary in the many clearly different sets of conditions that actually occur in our society.

An excellent example of the specificity of effects of co-residence comes from a study of ethnically diverse Honolulu. There the so-called Caucasian Americans who had been long-term residents of integrated neighborhoods felt less social distance from Japanese Americans than from other "non-Caucasian" residents (whereas Caucasians with little integrated residential or informal social experience felt closer to Chinese Americans). Samuels reports that working class Haoles (whites) living in an integrated neighborhood with both Chinese and Japanese neighbors prefer Japanese over Chinese. But in an all-white upper middle-class area, the Chinese are preferred to Japanese. These differences in evaluations are said to develop from local interactions with different social types of persons in the contrasting neighborhoods. In the working class area (Makiki) the Chinese residents are operators of small grocery stores, factory workers, or landlords; they are not in high economic or social positions. Thus when white residents compare Chinese and Japanese in this locality, they necessarily compare working-class Chinese with the highly disciplined and tidy working-class Japanese (Samuels, 1970, 79). But among the upper-class whites in an all-Haole neighborhood, interaction with Chinese involves only the upper business and social strata, whereas the Japanese with whom the whites interact are more often of a lower socioeconomic level (Samuels, 1970, 86).

A frequently reported finding from studies of public housing is that when equal-status interaction took place between blacks and whites, intergroup attitudes became more favorable, especially when there were not strong initial barriers to interracial contact (Ford, 1973).

Further, Ford finds in comparing attitudes of whites and blacks in an integrated housing project that blacks were significantly more likely than whites to have racially tolerant or accepting attitudes (Ford, 1973, 1436). Although blacks more frequently showed "tolerant" attitudes, the data indicate that among whites more favorable intergroup orientations develop from equal-status contact in the residential environment. But the generalization is, at most, inconclusive for blacks. Apparently many of the black housewives entered the desegregated situation with substantial reserve and suspicion. Furthermore, both blacks and whites experienced complex sequences of reactions as the extent of desegregation increased. The "contact hypothesis" was not disproved, but was shown, once more, to depend upon the specific character of the situation—in this case, the lack of a prior set of established norms, together with the mutual apprehensiveness of residents concerning a new and "unpredictable" set of relationships (Ford, 1973, 1440-43). In another study, Zeul and Humphrey (1971) find that the attitudes of whites in suburban neighborhoods are largely unaffected by contact with black co-residents. Negative effects have been directly observed in some instances, as in the movement of white families, about 1960, from a New Jersey suburb into which blacks were moving (Fishman, 1961).

Prior socioeconomic status of white residents affects outcomes of codwelling experience.

Proposition 14: In general, the higher the SES (as indexed by occupation, education, and income) the higher the frequency of "cosmopolitan" rather than "localistic" attitudes and values. And the greater the cosmopolitanism, the greater the acceptance of racial integration in the residential area.

As Zeul and Humphrey suggest (1971, 470):

The positive relationships between cosmopolitanism and social class, and cosmopolitanism and tolerance suggest *cosmopolitanism is the crucial variable in explaining why racial attitudes in a particular neighborhood are initially positive or negative.*

In a poll of housing attitudes, Kitano found striking differences among Japanese Americans in the San Francisco area according to education. Education had the effect of both raising the level of expectation and encouraging the development of an assertive attitude "in the search for one's rights and a better life" (Kitano, 1960, 194).

On the whole, a set of varied studies in residential areas seem consistent with experimental data in showing that favorable intergroup orientations are the more frequent (a) the greater the current amount of equal-status intergroup interaction; (b) the greater the amount of prior contacts; (c) the greater the length of residence in a desegregated residential area; (d) the less the perceived status threat from desegregated residence.

Analyses of successful desegregation of residential areas consistently find that an important factor in nonconflictful and stable outcomes is the disconfirmation of negative expectations. In eighteen suburbs of New Haven, a comparison of areas receiving black families with those receiving white families showed initial resistance to in-migration of blacks. But after a period of one year, the suburbs that had received new black arrivals showed *decreased* symbolic racism in areas of prior high concern. Minimal interaction between white and black families had occurred—but the absence of apprehensiveness seemed to reduce racialistic attitudes (Hamilton and Bishop, 1976).

One of the peculiar assumptions implicit in some objections to residential intermingling of populations is that neighborhood co-residence implies informal social intimacy. But urban patterns of interaction clearly show that the assumption can only be stereotypic in origin. It has long been known that routine neighboring patterns typically stabilize at a level of limited mutual acceptance. In ordinary "ingroup" neighborhood interaction, one does not assume that there is a choice only between enmity and close friendship. Similarly, interethnic neighborhoods may be highly acceptable to many persons who never develop close friendships with their co-residents (Hunt, 1960, 205).

We have much evidence of good social relations between blacks and whites in interracial neighborhoods. [Good relations imply] . . . access to important networks of information (as to jobs, housing, education), as well as a reduction of interracial conflict (Glazer, 1974, 101).

Summarizing a large body of information, a National Research Council study points out three important generalizations:

1. Most whites who "experience" racial mixing by living in a neighborhood containing nonwhites are in overwhelmingly white neighborhoods. They may have no contact with nonwhite neighbors and in some cases may not acknowledge their neighborhood as mixed. Very few whites live in neighborhoods containing more than 10 percent nonwhites.

2. Most nonwhites who experience racial mixing do so in neighborhoods with substantial, often predominantly, nonwhite occupancy.

3. Token integration is probably more widely accepted than the troubles of some pioneers would suggest, but it cannot provide racially mixed residence for many nonwhites. This would require that many more white households be willing to enter and remain in neighborhoods where 10 percent or more of the residents are nonwhite. This is particularly true of those metropolitan areas where much of the nonwhite population now lives (Miller, 1973, 154).

Since the emergence in the 1960s of Black Power movements and other manifestations of ethnic self-consciousness, solidarity, and cultural autonomy, many ethnic spokesmen resist any implication that desegregation must mean being absorbed into a dominant majority-culture. Some members of ethnic-racial minorities argue for maintaining ethnic residential concentrations in metropolitan areas in the hope that territorial separation will provide political leverage, local control, and cultural autonomy. But advocates of open housing and residential integration question the realism of these hopes, and further suggest that even complete territorial intermingling under urban conditions today would still permit the existence of distinct ethnic "communities" in the form of networks of both formal organization and informal networks. Some community activities could be integrated, others separate or autonomous, e.g., integrated labor unions and Parent-Teacher Associations coexisting with separate church groups and sociability networks.

From the standpoint of public policy concerning housing and residential patterns, the primary questions concern equal opportunity of access and use of satisfactory living space. Questions of harmony, interethnic friendships, and other aspects of neighborhood social life are secondary. (They must be secondary so long as privacy and freedom with regard to sociability are respected in such public policy.) The extent of mutual acceptance is relevant primarily insofar as it affects stability of integrated areas, i.e., the maintenance of multiethnic in-movement as normal residential turnover occurs. Finally:

> Hitherto, the formal and informal operations of the housing market have restricted freedom of choice for minority group members. To enlarge their freedom is to permit greater diversity, not to seek a new uniformity in interracial living patterns (Miller, 1973, 149).

7. Organized Actions and Social Control

As with public schools, the short-run difficulties in the way of desegregation of residential areas are obvious, massive, and persistent.

Faced with the dense and tangled thicket of obstacles, many observers are attracted to short-run programs that tacitly accept segregation "as a fact" and aim only to improve conditions in low-income ghettos. But, obviously, such programs to the extent that they are effective will serve to reinforce dual-society trends and will foreshadow continuation and intensification of many of the very conditions that have led to condemnation of racial segregation in the past. Under present institutions of property and government, substantial and stable residential integration requires a supply of new housing and a genuinely open market for housing.

Current problems of ghettoization exist because earlier social decisions were made—for example, decisions that located subsidized housing for low- and moderate-income families mainly in concentrated clusters within the inner city. These decisions necessarily perpetuated and speeded up the processes of social and economic cleavage between central cities and their encircling suburban areas. Once such segmentation of metropolitan areas had become established

> the thinking of those seeking to reverse this trend was logically directed toward housing a balanced proportion of low and moderate income households in the outer growth areas, including racial minorities, and infusing central city populations with more affluent households and its economic base with expanding enterprises (Erber and Prior, 1974, 4).

But such proposed remedies clearly required the use of political power and authority, and consideration of the fragmented governmental structure quickly led to the idea that a necessary step would be the development of "more comprehensive metropolitan planning" and "intergovernmental coordination." Behind such brave phrases lay enormous political complexities. As many well-intentioned and technically impeccable plans went awry in the face of vested interests, complex organizational problems, scanty resources, and other difficulties, efforts to "save the cities" turned in the 1960s to the Congress, the Courts, and the Federal Executive. Only at the national level, it seemed, could be found the necessary political responsiveness to the perceived problem of urban decay, inner-city poverty, and racial segregation.

As early as the late 1950s, astute observers of suburban developments were reminding readers of sociological journals of two crucial points: (a) suburbs were highly diverse, both internally and from one type of development to another (upper-class vs. "Levittown") (Dobriner, 1958; Gans, 1967); (b) white resistance to racial integration could reach nearly incredible heights of acrimony. A third point was clearly illustrated by Bressler's detailed account of the prolonged turmoil surrounding a lone black middle-class family who moved into all-white Levittown, Pennsylvania: persuasion was wholly ineffective in controling violence and harassment of the family by local whites, in contrast to the decisive impact of statements and actions by the courts (an injunction), by the governor and the attorney-general of the state, including the use of the state police and the prosecution of violations of the injunction. Harassment of the black family ceased when high political authorities made it unmistakably clear that violence would be promptly punished (Bressler, 1960).

A significant indication of how rapidly norms and policies have changed since 1960 is that four years later Congress passed the Civil Rights Act and that in the 1970s it is not the local or state governments but the federal courts that represent the effective level of jurisdiction. By 1968, the new Civil Rights Act contained in Title VIII prohibitions against discrimination in the sale, rental, financing, and advertising of dwelling units or vacant land for residential purposes, and directed federal governmental agencies to undertake affirmative action in accordance with fair housing legislation. Title VIII generally has been interpreted by the courts to render illegal the use of federal funds or authority in such ways to sustain or increase racial concentration (Erber and Prior, 1974, 22-23).

As legal provisions against segregation finally began to have some substantial importance, local communities that formerly might have maintained an all-white front recognized that black migration would be inevitable. Some such communities then turned toward policies intended to preserve a stable integrated area, including measures to forestall resegregation by limiting the number of incoming minority families—e.g. as in Oak Park, Illinois (National Committee against Discrimination, 1974). Although maximum quotas obviously can be held to be unconstitutional as discriminatory on their face (see exception in *Otero v. New York City Housing Authority*), informal quotas often have been tolerated by local and municipal governments who claim them necessary to stabilize a community (Brown, 1973; Molotch, 1973; Downs, 1973; Erber, 1974).

Over against such efforts to manage a more or less fixed degree of integration, there are recent evidences of movements to reintegrate central-city sections by the return of whites to areas that have become all-black. In some instances, white families and individuals have been buying homes in formerly prestigeful areas that had been "taken over" by black settlement after the white exodus, with the explicit intention of physical improvement and establishment of a cosmopolitan community, e.g., the case of the prominent Church Hill section of Richmond, Virginia, site of Patrick Henry's famous speech ("Give me liberty . . ."). Recognizing its historic appeal and traditional charm, whites, mostly young couples with financial resources, are moving in and renovating the old homes. Although the whites clearly desire an integrated neighborhood, and blacks with enough financial resources to remain will do so, many blacks fear they will be pushed out and economically excluded as rents, housing values, and property taxes increase (Hall, 1973).

Both the sale and rental of existing dwelling spaces and the construction of new residential properties increasingly are carried out as a large-scale enterprise by a single firm or consortium. The possibility thereby grows of more and more centralized control over the ethnic composition of residential neighborhoods.

New, large-scale developments of residential properties for sale have been more amenable to racial mixing than have been older housing units widely scattered in established neighborhoods. Factors of importance in this respect appear to be (a) the central control of sales policy, (b) the strong market orientation of the home building industry, and (c) the absence of precedent in the newly created development (Hawley and Rock, 1973, 19).

We may recall that the founder and builder of the mass-produced Levittown long maintained a policy of total exclusion of black persons (Bressler, 1960, 127)—whereas some of the Eichler developments in California early became multiracial and multiethnic. As in all other fields, centralized authority can make a big difference, but—which way? The answer to the question depends largely upon the external structure of constraints and incentives which decision-makers must take into account.

Exclusionary land-use litigation has only recently developed as a strategy in the attempt to overcome the barriers to equal housing opportunity. It is only since the "adoption of strong legal safeguards against housing discrimination, and the enactment of massive housing subsidy programs," that the more subtle barriers to equal housing opportunity, such as zoning and other land-use controls, have become evident (National Committee against Discrimination in Housing and Urban Land Institute, 1974, 7).

Increasingly, advocates of antidiscrimination policies argue that the "right of local control" is giving way to a more inclusive view—that the "general public interest" outweighs that specific to the municipality (National Committee against Discrimination in Housing, 1974, 59). And the advocacy of authoritative guidelines and allocations of housing resources have become increasingly explicit and detailed.

Yet the idea of authoritatively established guidelines, limits, zones, or quotas clearly contradicts the individualized, universalistic "color-blind" orientations that pervaded the antidiscrimination, antisegregation movements of the 1950s and 1960s. The fact that those orientations were the avowed bases of court decisions and of the legislation that abolished legally enforced housing segregation has made the emerging dilemmas of strategy especially acute. Thus it sometimes is suggested that residential integration of major urbanized areas can be attained only through the "diffusion of minority groups throughout the whole metropolitan region by a system of subsidized quota integrations" (Greeley, 1972, 216). But the author soon adds that there are "immense legal, political, social, and moral obstacles to subsidized quota integrations in a metropolitan area" (Greeley, 1972, 243).

In the areas of both housing and education, executive, legislative, and judicial attention to civil rights has moved from the outlawing of specific legislated discriminatory practice (such as the segregation of schools and housing) to affirmative action and social policy formulation (ensuring equality of opportunity). This evolution has occurred along with the growing acceptance of the belief that discrimination results from deep-rooted social forces.

Eventually some of the initially separate issues of education and housing opportunity are likely to merge. An example already is at hand in the case of *Hart et al. v. Community School Board, et al.* (1974) in which not only the schools but also the Housing Authority and recreational and other social agencies were designated as responsible parties in acting to prevent the racial segregation of the community, and thus of the schools.

In the United States the history of governmental regulation of economic activity has had three major phases: (1) an early period of reliance upon common-law and private law suits to regulate any aspects not controlled directly through the market; (2) increased reliance on legislation and upon that type of administrative regulation that was responsive, primarily, only to specific complaints; (3) development of public agencies that take the initiative in enforcing categorical rules and in seeking out and remedying violations or inequities.

In the field of allocations and of access to residential housing, similar sequences can be detected. Starting with a system that thoroughly supported enforced segregation, changes have moved toward open access and affirmative action to promote voluntary integration. In decisions by the courts, for example, these tendencies seem apparent: (a) a movement from *purely local* to *metropolitan-regional* scope, going beyond the boundaries of an offending local jurisdiction, e.g., *Crow v. Brown* (1971); (b) from the *prohibition of exclusionary practices* to requiring *provision of affirmative programs of access or inclusion;*[2] (c) from *redress of grievances* arising from violations of civil rights of individuals to emphasis upon municipal responsibilities, e.g., *SASSO* (1970), *Southern Burlington County NAACP v. Township of Mt. Laurel* (1972); (d) from *particular remedies* to *comprehensive programs* of opportunity and equalization, e.g., *Crow v. Brown* (1972), *Brookhaven* (1972), *Mahaley v. CMHA* (1972).

In every field in which over a period of some length private actions increasingly come to be regarded as having socially unacceptable results, a similar sequence can be observed in the dominant means of social control that are used. With regard to judicial actions, at first the only remedy for grievances is a private suit brought at the initiative of an individual plaintiff in a civil or criminal suit. Later there may develop "class" suits, brought by organizations on behalf of properly situated prototype individuals. Still later there comes legislation that permits or requires public officials to initiate court actions. In the area of regulation by statute, the initial policies are likely to specify only *forbidden actions*. More effective laws will be those that lay down *positive, enforceable obligations and duties*. In the area of enforcement, the weaker remedies require an adversary court proceeding. Stronger effects are gained when *administrative* agencies are given authority and resources to promulgate and enforce particular *regulations*, subject only to court review when challenged.

8. Social Change and Effective Public Policies

The landscape of America is covered with examples of the effects of past public policies upon land-use and settlement patterns. The associated social arrangements, therefore, also have been shaped by those same policies. The territorial patterns of living have not originated in mysterious invisible forces that have to remain forever faceless and nameless. The chains of causes and effects are, of course, complex and many are nonobvious. But the most pervasive effects have come from a few really massive factors. Even a haphazard listing is enough to make the simple and basic point:

1. fee-simple ownership of land.
2. property taxes on buildings and improvements.
3. use of property tax as the main source of revenue for the local government, including public schools.
4. use of tax revenues to build highways and associated structures.
5. subsidization of airports and airlines—relative lack of subsidization for low-fare, convenient mass transit facilities in metropolitan areas.
6. restrictive covenants.
7. credit and mortgage policies of federal agencies.
8. zoning, e.g., in suburbs to bar multifamily housing and low- and moderate-income housing.
9. building codes and inspection practices.
10. provisions in legislation for public housing that permit localities to veto location of developments within their borders.

Whether or not access to and control of residential land use and housing are directly allocated by central social authorities, patterns of residence are socially determined to a high degree. Apparent are both the legal framework of markets and the guiding influences of governmental policies concerning taxes, credit, financing, housing and land-use regulations, location of transportation routes, provision of public services and facilities. There is no such thing as a completely impersonal free market in this field.

The most permanent part of any urban settlement is its physical layout, primarily the location of streets and fixed facilities.

It follows that the most straightforward procedure for planning urban growth is to establish streets and locations of major fixed facilities in advance of settlement. Unless this is done, urban sprawl will result. If it is done, much of the remainder of the ecological pattern will be shaped around the skeletal arrangement by "natural" economic and other social processes.

But the layout cannot be guaranteed without a minimal central control. Adequate control cannot be obtained if an unregulated private market is allowed to dispose of land as an exploitable commodity, without regard to the social costs.

Hence it is inescapable that orderly development of urbanized and urbanizing areas can be attained only through some system of regulative incentives and constraints—or else through public ownership of the land. If public control could be clearly established through outright public ownership, various methods then could be used to return a portion of the land to private developers and users—through joint public-private corporations, cooperatives, long-term leasing, or conditional resale with only minimal regulation of use. Short of the currently "unthinkable" policy of public ownership, equality of access for minorities now being subjected to discrimination must be sought by a complex assortment of partial measures.

In the field of housing and residential distribution, we are confronted by a gigantic institutional sector of highly consequential social allocations and of institutionalized power and exchange. When our criteria of success include universalistic norms of equal access under impartial rules, the American system of housing and residential land use perforce exhibits numerous failures. It fares no differently when the criteria are those of nonutilitarian justice, or of social harmony (cf. Rainwater, 1967; Moore, Livermore, Galland, 1973).

Consider, for instance, urban renewal. As it actually developed in the 1960s, it rapidly became a program for central-city builders and other business interests. A case in point was Newark's remarkably thriving urban renewal program that was an object of envy in the early 1960s. Newark ranked very high in the nation both in total and per capita dollars spent for urban renewal, and was a favorite of national development corporations and of the Urban Renewal Agency and the Federal Housing Agency (Kaplan, 1963). The Newark Housing Authority emphasized clearance and redevelopment, it vigorously pressed the building of public housing, but summarily relocated low-income populations and eliminated whole areas of small business. It was in no sense responsive to democratic decision-making in the local community, nor to the desires of the people most directly affected. It surely did not act primarily to increase supplies of low-cost housing nor to facilitate desegregation. In a similar way, Atlanta shows the great power of business interests to shape the character of urban renewal programs. City officials chose actions in line with business preferences in the face of active resistance by neighborhood and low-income groups. Organized and articulate opposition and a high level of conflict were insufficient to prevent political authorities from following the dictates of business interests (Stone, 1976).

Many of the so-called urban renewal and slum clearance programs of the recent past have drastically reduced the total supply of residential housing, especially in the low-rent brackets (Greer, 1965). Most public housing has been built within central cities and has reinforced "ghetto" patterns of con-centration. Alternative programs could expand the supply of housing and provide incentives for dispersal. Conceivably useful measures include federal and state funds, in lieu of urban renewal, to be used for residential construc-tion anywhere within a metropolitan area—thus favoring use of lower-cost land in outlying areas. If large supplies of lower-cost housing could thus be created in suburbia, real-estate developers and landlords possibly would lose much of their resistance to residential integration (Kain and Persky, 1969, 79-80).

Without substantial new supplies of housing, residential intermingling is minimized. The generalized but important policy-goal has been stated by the Advisory Committee to HUD:

Recommendation 8

Federal policy should continue to emphasize the expansion of the supply of good-quality housing for all economic groups conveniently located in relation to where job opportunities exist or can be created, whether in the suburbs or the central city (Advisory Committee to HUD, *Freedom of Choice in Housing*, 1972, 60).

The distribution of persons among dwelling spaces in urbanized areas constitutes the *fluid mosaic* of this chapter's title. The facts of population mobility and social change, which render all public policies in some sense temporary or provisional, also point to opportunities for purposive social action—for no particular historical pattern of residence has to be accepted as immutable. Hence, if present-day segregation has been so strongly developed by public policies, as we know it has, it is responsible to consider which policies could be rescinded and what new policies may be feasible that would tend to reduce involuntary segregation.

Not all the technically effective and economically feasible policies and programs that we can imagine would be politically possible under present conditions (Foley, 1973). But this consideration is not a valid ground for failure to note such potential policies. For what is politically unthinkable at one time often becomes the conventional wisdom of institutionalized practice at a later date.

Things do not have to be exotic to be useful. Some measures that are quite evident to common sense are likewise sound in terms of current social science knowledge. Thus improved transit between ghetto areas and places offering relevant job opportunities would, other things being equal, encourage desegregation, especially if joined with improved information about job opportunities and improved training and job placement programs (Kain and Persky, 1969, 79). But the impact of such programs is not likely to be great.

Measures that improve the absolute and relative level of income of black and other ethnic families will facilitate desegregation. (Special leverage could be developed through rent subsidies to be used anywhere within a metropolitan area.) Black and white populations are becoming more alike in education, occupations, and public life-styles. All other things being equal, such convergences make desegregation easier.

Other relatively noncontroversial developments will be useful to some degree. For example, the sheer diffusion of accurate information about housing and residential areas can have gradual but appreciable influences. In the very short run, research, fact-finding, and dissemination of information can do little to alter patterns of discrimination and segregation. Over a longer span of time, the diffusion of valid information through appropriate and credible channels to the general public and to key types of decision-makers in government and business can appreciably alter expectations and beliefs and thereby facilitate changes in behavior and in values. Since adequate information concerning some aspects of the housing-and-residence sector does not now exist, future polices may benefit from deliberate efforts to generate knowledge. For example:

Recommendation 2

Carefully planned experiments on a number of different scales and patterns from the neighborhood to the new town should be undertaken to determine the conditions under which residential mixing of families or individuals of different racial and economic categories may be most feasible (Advisory Committee to HUD, *Freedom of Choice in Housing*, 1972, 56).

Recommendation 4

To provide a better basis for policy formulation and implementation, the federal government should support survey research on attitudes toward racial and economic residential diversity on a regular and comparable basis (Advisory Committee to HUD, p. 57).

Integration occurs more easily in rental properties than in areas of homeowners. Policies encouraging construction of such properties rather than, e.g., loans to homeowners and to those who wish to build and own would therefore facilitate desegregation.

When housing is to be offered for sale, it is the new, large developments that are more open to equal access than older housing units scattered through established neighborhoods (Advisory Committee to HUD, p. 9). On this basis, minority and civil-rights groups and relevant business and governmental agencies will find that managers of large-scale rental properties are especially suitable candidates for inducement, pressure, and persuasion.

Governmental actions can facilitate the possibilities of "fair shopping" and "freedom of consumer choices" in housing markets. Among the recommendations of the Advisory Committee to the Department of HUD, note these:

Recommendation 3

Barriers to stable interracial neighborhoods and housing are numerous and pervasive. . . . It is essential that HUD pursue a multiple strategy that takes account of the interplay of all the factors in the market as they are modified by prejudice. Undergirding the strategy must be enforcement of the law to a single standard—the attainment of one open housing market, not two (or more) segregated markets (Advisory Committee to HUD, p. 57).

Recommendation 9

Comprehensive government action is required to strengthen the processes and facilities necessary to achieve a single open market in housing and to ensure "fair shopping" conditions. Action required includes:

(a) Positive assistance for minority home seekers;

(b) Positive incentives for housing middlemen to operate in a manner that encourages stable racial mixing;

and

(c) Measures to ensure equal access to real estate board listings throughout the metropolitan area. This may involve the creation of new marketing institutions (Advisory Committee to HUD, 60).

There is a general recognition among analysts of the urban housing scene that continuous pressure from interested groups having some political influence or capacity to mobilize threats is necessary to maintain a system of limits upon discriminatory and dual-market behavior. The desired goal is even-handed enforcement of a nondiscriminatory set of rules concerning sale, rental, and credit-granting. Actually, the firm enforcement of existing open-housing laws often could create a more effective market that would work to the economic benefit of real estate businesses themselves (Kain and Persky, 1969, 80).

Enforcement of such rules obviously has political limits. It is not a panacea for eliminating discriminatory segregation (Foley, 1973, 137). But the continuing existence of effective enforcement of some minimal rules of fair practice gradually results in increased acceptance. A major difficulty, however, is that acceptance may mean highly restricted tokenism, while really large-scale open markets are prevented by zoning—which is at the heart of land-use control— and by other crucial forms of control.

The growing role of federal action has had indirect effects. For example the number of full-time, staffed "housing opportunity centers" operating multiservice programs over large geographic areas in all regions of the nation increased from 36 in 1970 to 54 in 1974 (National Committee against Discrimination in Housing, 1974, 1). Initially, housing centers devoted their efforts to the pursuit of discriminatory incidents and subsequent litigation, to the resolution of landlord-tenant incidents, to minority group support, and to information dissemination. Many centers later turned to contractual arrangements with businesses, which either need housing consultants or wish to hire an agency that will arrange "fair housing opportunities" for their incoming employees. The fact that any employer in order to secure a federal contract must comply, at least on paper, with equal opportunity guidelines, including provisions for housing,[3] has created the need for agencies that can assist employers in assuring nondiscriminatory, equal-opportunity housing.

A relatively new major strategy for resisting further segregation and for opening up equal opportunity in housing purchases and rentals is litigation challenging exclusionary land use, including zoning provisions in suburbs (NCDH and ULI, 1974, 7). The background basis for such litigation begins with the largely symbolic Executive Order 11063 (Equal Opportunity in Housing) in 1962. The 1964 Civil Rights Act included Title IV, already noted above, as a provision against discrimination in housing. Judicial decisions already noted as well as *Jones v. Mayer* (1968), and additional Executive Orders further established nondiscrimination as policy and provided examples of affirmative action, as in the requirement of Executive Order 11512 (1970) that availability of low- and moderate-income housing be considered in selection of sites for federal installations.

The 1968 Housing and Urban Development Act eased the requirement for local governmental approval in building subsidized housing out of urban areas. As fair housing laws and lower-income programs thus reduced traditional obstacles to equal access in housing,

> other barriers to minority access to non-ghetto housing then emerged; chief among them were exclusionary land use controls. The principal forum for the attacks on these barriers was not Congress, but the courts

—and the principal means was not legislative lobbying, but litigation (National Committee against Discrimination in Housing and Urban Land Institute, ULI Research Report 23, 1974, 9).

Administrative changes proposed for HUD proved difficult to implement. The absence of strong executive support for open housing or civil rights directives in the 1970s led proponents of open housing to turn toward the processes of litigation (National Committee against Discrimination, pp. 10-11).

As the last example suggests, there is no reason to suppose that social invention has come to an end or that new knowledge and new ideas will not influence the social world created by housing policies in the future. New forms of local organization may be developed. Existing institutional arrangements undoubtedly will be altered by extra-local developments that may range from gasoline shortages (making long-distance commuting by automobile much less feasible) to revenue-sharing to basic change in structures of authority.

Since 1968 discrimination based on race, color, religion or national origin has been prohibited in the sale, rental, financing, and advertising of dwelling units and land.[4] The struggle for open housing has been protracted, extending well back of the 1948 outlawing of restrictive covenants by the Supreme Court, and each legal victory has required additional difficult struggles to secure effective use and enforcement. Measured by the ideal of full compliance with the law, open housing still is largely a myth. Measured by change from the rigid and legally buttressed discrimination and segregation of the 1940s, substantial movement is observable, e.g., the rapid growth of black population in formerly all-white suburban areas.[5] Substantial practical experience and good research data show that enforcement of new laws can bring about substantial changes even in long-entrenched patterns of discrimination (Williams, Dean, Suchman, 1964; Rothbart, 1976). But legislation without enforcement is an empty gesture. Given the intricate network of interlocking interests and prejudices that were linked to racial discrimination in housing, it is to be expected that the legislation and court decisions of the 1960s would be nullified in practice unless interested agencies and groups pressed incessantly for implementation.

A few studies have produced analyses of responses to the new legal requirements. Saltman s research in Akron, Ohio (1975) showed that:

1. executives of real estate firms were highly conscious of the antidiscrimination laws;
2. but nearly all of the surveyed companies engaged in racial discrimination "in terms of types of locations offered, price differentials, access to units, access to listings, forms required, and courtesy" (Saltman, 1975, 43);

3. and two-thirds of apartment complexes audited revealed clear indications of discrimination. Although black persons often were shown
available housing, complex tactics were used to "steer" whites into
different residential areas and types of accommodations. Although
there was strong resistance to the pressures for open housing arising
from the Akron audits, prolonged efforts by the local Fair Housing
Contact Service resulted in some changes in practices, in emphasis on
open housing by several planning agencies, and in greatly increased
local awareness. The existence of continuous monitoring by a local
"watchdog" organization has been a major factor in such changes.

This example of imaginative and persistent local effort once more shows
that effective methods of organized change do exist. In this chapter a great
deal of our discussion of policy questions has been couched within the Conventional Wisdom and has looked for possibilities "within the System." As we
conclude, it may be stimulating to consider a few examples of less conventional, even if still not radical ideas. We call attention to two exhibits.

Policy Exhibit #1: Why Have Any Suburbs At All?

It is possible to think about the unthinkable by considering how the lines
between suburbs and cities could be obliterated or at least rendered much more
permeable. Present governmental policies usually accept local jurisdictions as
fixed and inevitable. But is is conceivable that the federal government could
be brought to regard local boundaries as open to change as group interests
and statuses change. Federal grants and tax rebates and various administrative
regulations could be used to encourage relocation of city and suburban boundaries. Translocal areas could be encouraged for purposes of taxation and
delivery of governmental services. Policies could be designed to shift the
emphasis from relatively small closed geographic units to larger areas, based
on socioeconomic characteristics (Walter and Wirt, 1971, 766).

An example of a quite different kind of unconventionality is found in the
suggestion that "tokenism" in the context of residential desegregation need
not always be a dirty word.

Policy Exhibit #2: An Expansion of Block-Busting and Tokenism:

Opinion A:

Efforts to integrate suburban areas sometimes are guided by deliberate
policies aiming at a gradual introduction of small numbers of black
families. The rationale is that rapid in-migration could reach a tipping
point, beyond which the area would quickly become all-black. But
restrictive policies seem self-defeating as a general rule. If all suburban

areas are opened to the maximum amount of free migration, the creation
of new ghettos would be less likely (see Kain and Persky, 1969, 81).

Opinion B:

> Token integration is a necessary stage in the enlargement of minority
> group opportunities. Although token integration appears to have made
> considerable progress, it is not an adequate solution and does not assure
> swift or smooth advance to more substantial integration. Racial mixing
> in neighborhoods with 50 percent or more non-white occupancy but
> including a substantial and stable white minority offers considerable
> potential for integration (Millen, 1973, 154).

In all transitions from zero representation to some, a first step is likely to
be "token." That movement can then be arrested or frozen, when a small
change is used to prevent further change. This is the Achilles' heel of incre-
mentalism or gradualism. But there are circumstances in which the other
possibility can be developed: the movement is continued, gaining acceptance
as unrealistic apprehensiveness is dissolved, advantages are perceived, routines
established, and new norms and vested interests are created.

But if gradualism is to be prevented from slowing into glacial immobility,
continuous inputs of "energy" and "information" are necessary—such as
money and legislation, respectively. Advocates and analysts of open housing
often remind us, for instance, that litigation is not enough; new legislation
is called for as experience reveals inadequacies, loopholes, and undesired
side-effects. Neither legislation nor litigation is sufficient to change entrenched
patterns of vested interests; required also are continuous monitoring, persuasion, inducements, and organized social action (cf. Rothbart, 1976; Hirschhorn,
1976).

Are the policy suggestions we have reviewed enough for now? Probably
not, but our own "space" has been used, and the discussion must end.[6] At the
least, we have seen a set of feasible possibilities for dealing with questions of
housing policy in the late twentieth century. A summary would be redundant.
We believe that the crucial points of this chapter's survey are:

1. that the present extent of involuntary ethno-racial segregation in the
   United States is unnecessary;
2. that the main causes of discriminatory segregation are known (Harrison, Horowitz, von Furstenberg, 1974)—although not their precise
   operation;
3. that successful residential integration exists on a substantial scale;
4. that practicable social means are available to establish and maintain
   effective public policies of open access and residential integration.

Chapter 5

Processes of Change and Stability:
Basic Modes of Influence

It is surprising, considering the very long span of the world's history
and the prevalence of pluralistic societies, how little is known about the
ways minority and majority communites can live together harmoniously
and with respect for the autonomy of each other's cultures within the
requirements imposed by the maintenance of viable nation states. Now
that the United States has rejected oppression as a solution to this
problem and is also beginning to reject an assumption of automatic
conformity by minorities to the majority culture as the price of equality,
the search for this knowledge will, I believe, be one of our major
preoccupations for the balance of this century, not only in regard to
blacks but with respect to other minorities as well (Pifer, 1973, 46).

We turn now to social processes and strategies that have to do with influence
and power as seen in efforts to maintain or to change various kinds of ethnic
relationships.

Chapter 1 carried us through a quick reconnaissance of recent changes in
intergroup relations in American society. We found that many significant
alterations in those relations have occurred since mid-century. We then
attempted to identify criteria by which to appraise such changes, and we
accepted the challenge to analyze successful as well as unsuccessful intergroup
encounters and relationships (Chapter 2).

In Chapters 3 and 4 we examined in considerable detail two great sectors
of social life in which ethnic identities and collective relationships are of out-

147

standing importance: education, and housing and residential patterns. In both cases we found many changes, substantial controversies, and conflicts, and evidence of some large-scale and successful accommodations and settlements. In each area there were important examples of entrenched resistance to change and many instances of discrimination, of clashing values, and of unproductive and rancorous controversies and unresolved oppositions. Interspersed throughout the descriptions and examples were hypotheses, empirical generalizations and tentative causal diagnoses.

We hope that what has gone before has been worthwhile in its own right. But in a larger sense the preceding chapters have been primarily a prologue to the "real business" of this book. For it has been our intention all along to use successive sets of data and interpretations as steps toward more specific and penetrating analyses of what kinds of purposive social actions can decrease the destructive outcomes of intergroup opposition and increase the likelihood of mutually advantageous outcomes.

It is now time to look more systematically at two questions that have continually reappeared as we have tried to see how and why such widely different outcomes could occur within the same society during a relatively short historical span. The first question is: what combinations of social and cultural conditions are necessary and sufficient to produce each of the radically different results? This is the difficult problem of social causation. The second question is even more challenging: which of the causal factors that we can identify seem to be beyond the possibilities of purposive control at this time and which can be changed to some important extent by purposive intervention of individuals and social collectivities?

Recognizing how limited is the reliable knowledge in this field and how remarkably complex are the problems, skepticism must be our close and faithful companion in the search. But skepticism is a monitor, not a guide—and certainly not a leader. Skepticism does not mean blind hopelessness. For we already have found an impressive accumulation of useful knowledge, and we know in any case that in the real world of practical affairs, many successful purposive actions are being carried out in this field. If nothing at all were known about social causation, the world would be in much worse shape than it is. Some policies do have empirically based and well-reasoned foundations. Some decision-makers are able to develop correct diagnoses and to take appropriate action. There are causal regularities in the social world—it is not completely different from the rest of the universe—if we have the wit and good fortune to discover them.

So we shall use the old-fashioned words "cause" and "causation." And we shall look for those causes that are open to *some* kind of control by *someone*. We cannot abolish mortality, but we can successfully treat many biological malfunctions. We cannot abolish scarcity, but there are better and worse ways of allocating resources. We cannot produce a blissful utopia, but we do not always have to settle for a chaotic and inhumane society. Our present aims are limited. We hope only to find a few dependable insights to add to the heritage of cultural resources for dealing with problems of adaptation and social integration.

Intergroup relations are not separate from the other basic types of relationships that make up the endless web of social life. The same kinds of influences exist in ethnic-racial relationships as in other major spheres of society. Accordingly, before we examine the specific problems of policies, strategies, and tactics for changing or stabilizing intergroup relations, we shall do well to briefly review facts and theories concerning the basic modes in which social influences can be exerted. "It is a startling fact that almost the last area to be investigated empirically by the social sciences is the area of the constructive forces in human nature and society which makes for the reduction of intergroup conflict" (Janis and Katz, 1971, 219).

1. The Varieties of Influence

It is easy to slip into thinking of society as a thing apart from the relationships that make up its structure. But "society" is merely the name we apply to one type of human collectivity. Societies are the most inclusive social systems that are relatively clearly bounded. The networks of relationships that occur within a society's limits and that determine the character of its internal organization consist of repeated, patterned interactions, especially those that are regularly expected and regarded by the participants as obligatory. No matter how stable, extensive, and complex the various types of relationships may become, we always can trace them back to one individual affecting another's behavior.

The process by which individuals reciprocally affect one another we call interaction. Interactions consist of transfers of information (communication) and movements of valuables (transactions). Communciation consists of the conveying of meanings. Transactions result in the transfer of the control of valued rights of possession or use from one person or collective unit to another. These interactions do not occur in isolation but rather in definite social settings. The ensemble of networks of such social settings makes up a society. Each interaction has effects, large or small, on the social environment, on the participants, and on concurrent and future interactions. Behavior affects behavior.

Thus if we want to know how to change intergroup relations, to maintain them as they are, or even how to avoid having any effect whatsoever upon them, we have to know something about how one piece of behavior affects another. We must find out, that is, whatever we can about modes of *influence* in human affairs.

The ancient mystery of influence is not, of course, wholly inscrutable; indeed, the fact of influence is in many ways the most commonplace of everyday experiences. Nor are the main forms of influence too difficult to identify (Gamson, 1968, especially Chapter 4).

Persons influence others in five, and only five, major ways.

1. *By physical presence and activity*, directly affecting the organism of another person or the surrounding environment of that person: e.g., by touching, colliding, hitting, supporting; by removing or adding or altering biologically relevant aspects of the situation; by being a part of the stimulus-field of the other. Note, for example, that the human face is universally one of the most powerful stimulus-fields, under a great variety of circumstances. Even the sheer presence of another person can rarely be totally ignored.

2. *Modeling.* We influence others by providing examples of behavior, by becoming models for emulation or imitation or for rejection and negative exemplification. The cultural bases and psychological processes involved in "taking someone as a model" are exceedingly subtle, complex, and only very imperfectly known. But the fact that modeling, positive and negative, does occur in indisputable and important. These processes include taking the role of another person, as well as several different kinds of psychological "identification." Taking another person as a model, however, may be primarily a process of searching for clues to what behavior one should perform to attain goals—how to do a task, how to avoid danger, how to win approval, and so on.

3. *Persuasion.* In speaking of processes of persuasion, some element of intentionality seems to be implied. The varieties of persuasion are numerous; our understanding of how they work is primitive. Basically, persuasion is attempted when a given person appeals to others by communicating information that is intended to have effects upon attitudes, beliefs, and values. In purest form, persuasion itself consists of changing another's beliefs about reality or of changing another's evaluations of something.

4. *Inducement* is the "addition of new advantages in the situation at hand, or the promise to do so" (Gamson, 1968, 77). When inducement occurs there is an actual transfer of resources or a credible promise to transfer resources, e.g., "You will be granted immunity if you

cooperate," or "If you land this deal, you will get a promotion," or "Information leading to the apprehension of this individual will result in a reward." Inducements can also be subtle, or implicit—the transfer of valued somethings is understood rather than explicit.

Relationships of presence, modeling, persuasion, and inducement account for a large proportion of social influence. But another universal mode of influence usually is not welcomed by those who receive its impact—influence by the imposition of constraint.

5. *Constraints* include both the actual imposition of barriers or disadvantages and the threat to produce negative consequences for the other party. To influence another by means of constraint is possible only if one has sufficient control of the situation to make a threat credible or to impose an actual injury or deprivation when threat is not effective.

Note that if one party can maintain a high level of coercive control, the promise of removal of the disadvantages may be used as an inducement. The mode of influence is constraint if and only if a negative feature is to be *added* to the situation unless compliant action is forthcoming.

In brief, then, social influence occurs in the form of presence and activity, modeling, persuasion, inducement, and constraint. Of course, the distinctions between various forms of influence (Gamson, 1968, Chapter 4) are often not as clear in practice as in the pure types we have presented here. For instance, persuasion often shades over into inducement. "Do it because you like me" is persuasion that implies a diffuse social inducement, because it holds out an exchange of social values. But strictly speaking: "Any exchange in which the influencer retains control of the resource being used is . . . persuasion" (Gamson, 1968, 78).

Influence may be purposive or nonpurposive; it may occur without intention or even awareness but often is intentional and sometimes highly calculated. Of course, it is always true that many factors affecting the possibilities of influencing another person will not be under the control of a would-be influencer in a given situation. Such fixed factors must be regarded, for that situation, as conditions or contexts. Of special interest, however, are those factors which can be manipulated, for these represent resources or opportunities for the involved parties to whom they are accessible.

No doubt the easiest way to think about influence is to take the case of one individual influencing one other individual, and then to generalize our findings to *all* collective behavior. But, unfortunately, the easiest way is also the most misleading. Direct generalization from individual behavior to complex large-scale social systems will almost always lead to serious errors. The reasons are simple but profound and inescapable: (1) interactions in complex social systems always have unintended consequences in the aggregate; (2) actions advantageous for separate individuals often create collective disadvantages; (3) actions essential for the welfare of a collectivity often entail sacrifices and deprivations for some individual members. Intergroup relations provide numerous examples.

One of the basic problems is that some of the preferences of individuals or of groups and other subunits of a total system lead to actions that have the following properties: (1) they are highly advantageous in the short run to the initiating party; (2) but there are effects disadvantageous to other parties; (3) the disadvantageous effects upon the initiating party are small relative to the advantages; (4) the degree of accountability, if any, is low; (5) the advantages are widely desired and can be widely secured; (6) in the long run the cumulative disadvantageous effects will become noxious to the larger society or collectivity (Williams, 1971).[1] Obvious examples include traffic congestion, environmental pollution, and energy conservation. Indeed, a more basic case may be population growth itself.

What we just described is the Tragedy of the Commons, so called after the prototype of the village grazing lands that were freely available to all: When herds are small relative to grazing land, everyone can enjoy the use of the commons without interfering with his or her neighbor's use. But if the number of cattle increases, eventually the commons becomes overused. Then, if each individual pursues his or her own short-term advantage he or she will seek maximum use before others can use the grass. The result will be destruction of the commons and the ruin of all.

The Problem of the Commons—also discussed as "social costs" or "externalities"—is the first of the two basic problems of relating individual or subgroup welfare to the welfare of a larger collectivity. Collaboration for the "public good" always is problematic—no matter how advantageous cooperation would be "if everyone would cooperate." For the whole nub of the matter is just in the word "if." This is so because many decisions that are best for individuals deciding for themselves, one by one, are not optimal and may be disastrous for the collectivity as a whole and hence, in the last instance, for the individuals as an aggregate. Thus "others" will *not* "cooperate," and accordingly "I" will not cooperate, when there is contradiction between those actions that will maximize my interests (or minimize my risks) as an individual here and now, and those actions necessary to advance the collective interests of all of us taken together.

The second of the two problems is the Problem of Collective Action, which is the mirror-image of the Tragedy of the Commons. The problem of collective action is present in all the numerous cases in which numbers of individuals who have interests in common are not able to organize to defend or advance those interests or to provide themselves with goods and services of benefit to the collectivity. Some individuals are reluctant to act, out of fear, uncertainty, or considerations of propriety. In a defensive or challenging situation, those who do initiate action, hoping to inspire others to join them, are the easy targets of quick and often harsh sanctions. This confirms the fears of those unwilling to "lay themselves on the line." In situations where new activities or services are proposed, the failures of the few who are motivated to create something out of insufficient resources confirm the "hopelessness of attempting anything."

The often tragic dilemmas or paradoxes of social costs and of collective action can be resolved only through some form of *collective* influence that alters the individual's perceptions and preferences. The two main types of influence are: (1) development of norms and group sanctions for cooperative versus competitive behavior, (2) development of knowledge and concern for the welfare of others and of coordination through mutually understood expectations (Buckley, Burns, Meeker, 1974). The two types might be called, respectively, *normative control* and *social solidarity*. Examples of sanctions used for normative control include social approval and disapproval, fines, imprisonment, taxes, fees, denial of access or membership, deductions from wages or salaries, promotion and demotion, guarantees. Social solidarity, including trust, is sought through socialization, propaganda, mutually known expectations, common standards, frequent communication. The greater the reliability of normative control, all other things being equal, the greater will be social trust. The greater the trust and other solidarity, the easier it is to establish institutional norms and effective enforcement of consensually adopted rules.

If we assume that individuals act separately without regard to the interests of others, that each seeks his or her own immediate advantage, and that the pursuit of self-interest is not socially constrained, then there is no solution whatsoever to these collectively self-destructive processes. If individuals are simultaneously striving for scarce values under the joint conditions of *interdependence, pure self-interest*, and *lack of enforced norms of distributive justice*, their actions always will lead to competitive escalation, e.g., "crazes" and "panics." Collective needs remain unmet when each separate individual sees that his or her efforts and sacrifices will be disproportionate to any benefits he or she will receive *unless a substantial number of others also contribute*.

In all the cases just reviewed, there is a maximum welfare outcome that requires cooperative action, but each individual's short-run welfare is best served by noncooperative action that eventually and in the aggregate reduces the collective payoff: the aggregate of all individuals "rationally pursuing their individual interests obtain payoffs less than those obtainable through irrational coooperative behavior" (Buckley, Burns, Meeker, 1974, 287). The Tragedy of the Commons is strictly inevitable if individual short-term gain determines conduct. And the advantages of collective action always will be lost unless the parallel problem of "free riders" can be solved. (Everyone gains if everyone contributes, but if a minority does not contribute, it shares in the collective gain and pays nothing.)

Both the Tragedy of the Commons and the Problem of Collective Action are everywhere conspicuous in intergroup relations. Under a discriminatory economic system, for example, the existence of a split labor market results in immediate advantages to workers of the dominant ethnic grouping—but the total society not only loses in economic productivity, it may also incur severe social costs in the longer term. The minority against which discrimination is directed will be able to improve its situation only, if at all, through bargaining power based on collective solidarity. But members of the minority confront the Problem of Collective Action in its sharpest form: effort and sacrifice are required to achieve collective gains; however, if the gains are achieved, all those shirkers who did not contribute do benefit.

Both problems can be solved *only* by somehow attaining a social solidarity in which commitment and loyalty can be relied upon to override the immediate short-run advantages that would accrue to individuals from breaking ranks. How to achieve this remarkable condition is the central question for all social movements that aim to strengthen the position of weak collectivities.

2. Adaptation, Order, and the Prevalence of Intrasocial Conflict

Groups and societies survive only by adapting to their external environments, and the successful adaptations, greatly varied as they are, also require some minimal solutions to the internal problems of dissensus, opposition, and conflict. As we have just seen, only if these problems are kept within limits can a collectivity mobilize resources and coordinate its efforts sufficiently to master the problems and threats of its changing physical, biological, and social environments.

The highly disruptive and destructive effects of many intrasocietal oppositions and conflicts need not be detailed. But a reminder of their prevalence may be useful. Where, during the period from 1945 to 1974 (from the end of World War II to the withdrawal of the U.S. forces from South Vietnam), have ethnic and racial oppositions and conflicts been most conspicuous? Observe this impressive but incomplete roll call.

Northern Ireland: Catholics and Protestants
Quebec: French-speaking and English-speaking Canadians
Belgium: Flemings and Walloons
Spain: Basque separatists vs. governmental authorities
Portugal: Military conflict and eventual independence of African territories
  (Angola)
U.S.A.: Blacks and whites; Chicanos; Native Americans; white "ethnics"
Fiji: East Indians and native Fijians
Middle East: Arab nations and Israel
Uganda: East Indians and the Ugandian government
United Kingdom: Commonwealth immigrants and native Britishers; Scottish
  and Welsh nationalists
Netherlands: Indonesian and other overseas immigrants and native
  Hollanders
Sudan: Muslim Northerners and Christian and "animistic" Southerners
Nigeria: Secessionistic Biafra vs. a coalition of coalition of central
  government supporters
Rwanda:
        Watusi and Hutu
Burundi:
Switzerland: French-speaking separatists of Jura vs. others; immigrant
  workers
U.S.S.R.: Eastern Europe; Jews; various non-Russian minorities
Kenya: East Indians and the Kenyan government after independence
Phillipines: Collective actions against Chinese, East Indians
Republic of South Africa: opposition and tensions among Blacks,
  Coloured, Whites
Egypt: Coptic Christians and Muslims
France: Algerians; immigrant workers from southern Europe
Yugoslavia: Serbs, Croats, Albanians, Macedonians
Burma: Indians
Thailand: Thai-Lue
Laos: Meos
Malaysia: Chinese and Malays
Israel: European-origin and Oriental-origin
India-Pakistan separation
Pakistan: Bangladesh
India: various so-called linguistic groupings
Ceylon: Singhalese and Tamils
Lebanon: Palestinian refugees; Muslims; Christians
Bulgaria: Dobrudjian Turks
Cyprus: Greeks and Turks

Iran:
Iraq: } Kurds

Ethiopia: central military government vs. rebels in Eritrea

The list could be extended. These examples, however, are sufficiently numerous and varied to show that many conventional ideas about collective conflict are simplistic and inaccurate. First, ethnic conflicts are not merely disguised forms of "capitalistic class struggle." Second, many of the conflicts listed clearly do not fit into the category of the struggle between imperial powers and exploited subject peoples, nor do they represent rebellions against "colonialism." Third, the world-wide prevalence of intrasocietal struggles between ethnic collectivities should free us of any illusion that "race" alone is the one central factor or that ethnic conflict is restricted to Western or industrial or capitalistic countries. Fourth, ethnic mobilizations and struggles are not merely symptoms of economic and political underdevelopment. If anything, the contrary is more nearly the valid view, for the spread of modern methods of communication, of education, of urbanization, and of some degree of industrialization, and commercialization has given ethnic aggregates new self-consciousness, new aspirations, and new political resources (Enloe, 1973). Furthermore, neither highly centralized one-party states nor federal decentralized democracies have found any magic formulas to prevent ethnic divisiveness and struggle (Amalrik, 1970).[2]

In the years after the 1970s, in a world of economic and political instability, where struggles for scarce resources between and within nations are sure to be intense and continual, both the international and the domestic problems of conflict management and resolution will be highly salient for those who are responsible for maintaining the social order. Our attention here must focus upon the way in which modes of influence are used and can be used in intergroup relations within the United States.

Before we can see what the possibilities are for dealing with conflict, we must have some idea of what generic kinds of collective situations we may confront. The following are types that are both important and frequent:

1. Unregulated diffuse community conflict, e.g., rancorous disputes, factional cleavages, communal violence.
2. Social movements of dissent and protest directed against established institutions and decision-making elites, e.g., fundamentalists protesting courses in biology vs. school boards; integrationist blacks and white sympathizers vs. a housing authority.
3. Confrontations of highly organized opposing social movements, e.g., civil rights organizations vs. white citizens' councils in the 1960s.

4. Organized conflict between centralized agencies, e.g., unions and business firms; interest groups; religious bodies.
5. Continuous individualized protest and discontent within an authoritatively regulated social organization—a school, a corporation, a labor union, a military unit.

The social arrangements that are feasible for regulating or resolving disputes and fights typically differ from one type of conflict to another. This conclusion holds because different social structures strongly affect the results of different attempted modes of influence.

3. Influencing Social Actions within and between Collectivities

Few social actions are isolated events; most (if not, indeed, all) are part of a complex set of interrelated reactions. In general, positive (rewarding, cooperative) behavior toward a person tends to elicit cooperative responses. Similarly, aggressive (depriving, frustrating) behavior tends to elicit negative responses. The most likely response is a response in kind.

Another way to say this is: the rule is reciprocity, or "pass it on." If these "rules" are followed, quarrels or disputes escalate, friendships grow.

Obviously the key questions are two:

1. What starts the process in a mostly competitive or a mostly cooperative sequence?
2. What checks a sequence once it is well underway?

We take it as given that social actors are energized, have needs, wants, and desires, and evaluate themselves and others. What we want to understand is how, *given* that they are socially active, they influence one another in the collective life we have been calling intergroup relations.

Individuals or groups are unrelated when their actions have no consequences for the other. They are positively interdependent when goal attainment by each facilitates goal attainment by another; and negatively interdependent when one's gain reduces the attainment by others (Deutsch, 1973, 20-21). Their communications are consensual when what is communicated by one actor is consistent or congruent with the values and beliefs of the other, dissensual when the result is disagreement, contradiction, dissonance, or incongruence. Positive or negative interdependence and consensus or dissensus determine whether relationships are either of positive attraction or of repulsion, aversion, or hostility. These relationships form the social structures and arrangements through which cooperation, competition, and conflict are enacted.

Evidence from small-group experiments shows that mutually rewarding behavior is most likely when (1) the parties see their separate interests as compatible; (2) they have similar or compatible attitudes, beliefs, and values; (3) they engage in frequent communication; (4) they make relatively little use of threats, insults, or recriminations. To find all of these conditions strongly present in ethnic relations must be a rare explorer's experience.

When various small groups with diverse interests are held together in a larger collectivity that to an important extent *must act as an entity*—such as political parties, nations, large bureaucracies—the very processes that transform diverse interests into unified action tend to blur cleavages and to moderate demands. These processes involve successive sets of bargains and compromises, each of which may be renegotiated and modified as it proceeds from one more-inclusive stage or level of negotiations to the next (Katz, 1971, 209).

But bargains and compromises are often hard to come by and only sometimes are achieved in a smooth and orderly fashion. Usually, various types of conflicts play an important role in the working out of diverse interests. The high costs of destructive effects provide incentives for restoring order through resolving or limiting conflicts. It is, therefore, valuable to identify the dynamics which make certain conflicts difficult to resolve as well as those which are more amenable to resolution.

Very difficult to resolve, without the authoritative intervention of an overwhelmingly powerful third party, are diffuse community conflicts. The lack of clear or dependable structures of communication and authority, the lack of prior ground rules, and the diversity of interests and aims that generally prevails—all these conditions militate against regularized procedures or stable compromises.

In contrast, when social interests are articulated by stable elites that interact as representatives of formal organizations or as elected representatives within governing bodies, the resolution of disputes is most likely to take the form of "secret agreements privately arrived at," which are then formalized as public compromise agreements (Lijphart, 1968). Such authoritative and formalized modes of dealing with disagreements and conflicts are illustrated in two-party legislative bodies (especially in the continuing committees that in effect serve as sublegislatures), as well as in administrative councils and hierarchical grievance procedures in bureaucratic organizations.

When diffuse dissent and protests against authorities reach high levels or become focalized in definite collective movements, the most common form of response by authorities apparently is to attempt to bring "representatives" of the dissent or opposition into the decision-making structure (Coleman, 1957). This process replaces diffuse, unorganized heterogeneous and often "erratic" demands with organized and simplified demands and claims. It replaces a multitude of protestors with a few claimants or representatives. It thus reduces diversity, organizes communication, and centralizes responsibility. It is, of course, a form of cooptation—which may or may not involve a genuine sharing of authority:

> The moment the decision of the local group is carried by its representatives to a higher level, we are dealing with a political process of compromise and majority rule. . . . The representatives are no longer free to work through to a full agreement as individuals. . . . They must take something back to their constituents and hence they bargain and trade and finally reach some compromise rather than the integrated solution of group process. The dynamics differ from small group process and the outcomes differ (Katz, 1971, 209).

Convergence toward mutual agreement through persuasion is relatively effective in certain kinds of small groups. When repeated interactions occur among the same persons over an extended period, the relationships tend to become diffuse and particularistic. Because of high interdependence and relatively strong emotional attachments, interpersonal persuasion can become powerful. On the other hand, in relationships between representatives of collectivities, persuasion typically is a weak process, requiring supplementation by inducements or constraints (Katz, 1971, 208-9). When mass persuasion is used, the conditions needed for effectiveness are quite special: effectiveness is greatest when the objects of persuasion are peripheral stereotypes, opinions and preferences, when countermessages are minimal, knowledge is low, and prestigeful figures and charismatic leaders monopolize attention.

The complex interplay of persuasion, inducement, and constraint that is mediated through changing group structures can best be appreciated by an examination of concrete examples. For this purpose let us examine more thoroughly a case of community struggle already noted in Chapter 3.

4. Complex Situations Are Real: a Case-Study[3]

Almost continuous acrimonious controversy and occasional violent conflicts characterized the years 1963-73 in the city of Newark, New Jersey. Three principal groups were prominent in the disputes, which involved a teachers' strike, black power and community control, and major political changes. At almost all times two of these three groups were at odds with each other, with the third either allied to one or the other, or acting as a third party in the dispute by disagreeing with both of the others.

The decade of turmoil began in 1964 when a jurisdictional dispute arose in Newark between two teachers' unions, the Newark Teachers' Union and the

Newark Teachers' Association. This prolonged and disruptive dispute resulted in a representational election. Although NTA won the representation, a 1965 contract negotiation with the Board of Education resulted in only token gestures to the teachers. When the NTA thus proved ineffectual, the two unions continued to vie for power in making demands on the Board, becoming involved at times in competing strike actions.

As early as 1960 the proportion of black students in the school population had reached 50 percent, but the staff included few black administrators, even at the lowest levels of administration. Pressure mounted from the black community to have greater black participation in school affairs. Charges of discrimination were brought against the Board before the State Department of Education but were dismissed. When the Board criticized the superintendent for personnel discrimination, the NTA and the NTU rose to his defense. This issue created a three-way dispute between the teachers' unions, the black community, and the Board of Education. In addition, many of the demands of the teachers, such as a need for increased numbers of teachers' aides and reduced responsibilities, became heated issues of "quality education" to the black community.

By 1967, the proportion of nonwhites in the school system had climbed to 74 percent, an increase of 24 percent in only seven years. Although white teachers were changing residence by moving out to the suburbs of Newark, they were not giving up their jobs; the result was a resident population increasingly black, but an educational system staffed and administered primarily by whites. Some if not all members of the black community felt that the city's "black-majority population and larger black-majority student body should be reflected in the composition of the school system's personnel at all levels" (Conforti, 1974, 24).

The conflict began to appear to blacks as one of outsiders versus insiders — of "suburbanites exploiting the city. . . . That most of the teachers did live in the suburbs (blacks as well as white) reflected the extent to which contention between the teachers and the black community was also a class conflict" (Conforti, 1974, 26). To white teachers, the principal issue was job security. To the School Board it was the maintenance of power.

The outcome of the initial struggles was a triangular set of relationships in which the Board was the target of efforts to induce change on the part of the teachers' organization and of spokespersons for "the black community." The black community and the teachers' organization had different goals and often were in indirect opposition through their separate and incompatible demands on the Board. Yet each regarded the other as sharing a view of change. The effect was to create a series of shifting alignments in relation to successive issues and confrontations — of city vs. suburbs, labor vs. management, black vs.

white, professionals vs. laypersons, and centralized vs. decentralized control of the school system.

Both the teachers' unions and black community groups tended to adopt strategies that would promote their own particular goals. For whites, who sought to maintain their jobs, this meant an emphasis on particularism. Since whites had historically been successful in overturning residency requirements for employment, blacks devised other strategies: they argued that a basic requirement for providing education and other social services to black populations was a kind of "community sensitivity" for which only black persons are qualified. This demand was coupled with claims to territorial jurisdiction. The combination of particularistic and ascribed claims was difficult for whites to resist in cities that were rapidly becoming predominantly black (Conforti, 1974, 32-33).

In 1967, ONE (Organization of Negro Educators) was formed. They took political stands on various racial issues which arose. The responses of the Board and mayor to black demands only increased the tension in an already polarized situation. In the summer of 1967, a severe riot followed close on the heels of a disruptive school incident. In the post-riot period, whites continued to leave the city, the proportion of black students in the schools formed an ever-increasing majority, and various black activist groups emerged. Blacks continued to press for greater inclusion, while white teachers went on strike to ensure their own job security. The more white teachers gained in grievance rights and benefits, the more blacks felt that teachers were being relieved of their accountability to the community.

When a black person, Kenneth Gibson, was elected mayor, he immediately changed the racial composition of the Board by appointing two blacks and a Puerto Rican to the five-member Board, leaving only two whites. Now disputes raged not only at a local level, but within the Board as well. When another strike occurred by teachers in 1970, it quickly escalated into a racial crisis, and set a record as the longest teachers' strike in American history. Gibson finally managed to effect a compromise. When contract negotiations came again in 1972, the predominant NTU was deeply in debt, out of favor with its national affiliation, and could ill afford another strike. It contented itself with maintaining the advantages it had gleaned in the 1970 compromise regarding salary and teachers' duties and acceded to many black demands regarding teacher transfers, grievance procedures, and accountability.

The Newark situation shows that a school system is only one of several transition sectors that almost certainly will change when a city goes through a massive shift in ethnic composition. Residential ethnic transformation is only the beginning of a long process of economic change, which will affect schools, employment, and local government. Any one of the major on-going processes inevitably becomes a factor in other processes. The change from majority-white to majority-black in large cities tends to create interracial oppositions, as the residential transition generates changing economic and political opportunities and claims. A resident population often can make a strong political case for access to economic opportunities within the territory it occupies. Claims are likely to be especially strong and effective in the case of jobs in local government, including the schools (Conforti, 1974, 32).

The school system may be the first to be affected, because of the fluidity of its population, and the "accessibility of its governing board." But the same basic questions confront all the principal institutionalized organizations of the community. The basic dilemma in local government is how to incorporate rapidly increasing numbers of black persons in public sector jobs without arbitrarily displacing whites who have legitimate claims based on prior service and technical qualifications.

The two main processes that facilitated Newark's "racial transition" were *attrition* and *expansion*: the gradual attrition of white workers opened places for blacks, while additional openings developed in "temporary" parallel structures in various antipoverty efforts and other governmental programs. In the teachers' strikes, teachers' demands for more aides could accommodate black demands for inclusion and employment by creating a paraprofessional corps, "a means of sharing teaching jobs in the schools without displacing the regular teachers."

The case study ends with a comment that assumes the inevitability of the major changes described:

> There are many large cities in the United States approaching the compositional changes that Newark experienced over the past decade. . . . There is at least the opportunity to learn from Newark's experiences that what appears to be chaotic conflict need not be prolonged nor indefinite (Conforti, 1974, 33).

Our own review of the materials suggests that a fuller appraisal over a longer period needs to seek answers to a set of additional questions about the relation of social policies and the political processes that were exemplified in Newark of the 1960s. For example: Are there marked inequities that result? Do these, if there are any, lead to resentments that have longer-term consequences?

To what extent did the struggles themselves and their political outcomes result in new forms of occupational selection? What were the effects upon performance?

To what extent are the new social structures likely to facilitate intergroup accommodation and cooperation or to what extent will they accentuate intergroup competition and opposition?

In Newark, a decade began in a situation of quiet inequality, moved into a period of opposition, disruption, and violence, and ended in a new phase of acquiescence to a new alignment of power in the community. The turbulent years show a sequence of events in which the opposing segments of the community developed, through conflict, a collective response to the political problems produced by major demographic and ethnic changes. The period was marked by disruption and sharply felt successes and failures by different groups on specific issues. The outcome was that political power and representation passed from one segment of the "community" to another. The process involved violence and other social costs. In the end, all major elements of the city's population had been included in a complicated new set of interactions and relationships of power and influence.

The crucial question raised by cases of this kind will be in the background of all our discussions during the next several chapters: When such collective oppositions develop, are there any practically useful policies and strategies that could produce mutually acceptable settlement at less social cost? To move toward a fuller understanding of the problem we need to examine further the interplay of common and divergent values, of competitive and cooperative interdependence, and of the exercise of power and authority.

5. Relations of Partisans to Authorities

No matter how complicated the processes by which a consensual social order comes to be established or how diverse the values that are agreed upon in different societies, once such an order has become dominant and has been maintained for two or more generations, strong forces are generated that support continued stability (Mousnier, 1973). The vested interests of the dominant strata and groupings lead them to create conditions that reinforce the original order. Beliefs and values are organized into a pervasive set of ideologies justifying the status quo. The predictability and security and continuing gratifications that are widely experienced create strong incentives for maintaining the current system. It is unlikely that the mere fact of a history of successful collaboration or the sharing of a residue of common values is itself sufficient to maintain the coalition's solidarity beyond the context that gave rise to it. But when the factors of security, rewards, ideology, and strong constraints have worked in concert over an extended period, many of the participants in the system are incapable of conceptualizing a radically different order.

These considerations make highly plausible the proposition that "advantaged" interests tend to form interlocking systems that will not initiate major changes. As Alford has put it, "When institutions and laws continuously serve the interest of dominant interest groups, challenge must come from elsewhere"

(1972, 9). This generalization may appear simple, but its implications are not obvious. Surely it is not meant as a mere tautology—as it would be if dominant groups were *defined* as those and only those whose main interests are served by the prevailing social norms and organizations. If the proposition simply questions whether well-satisfied groups whose major values, beliefs, and interests are clearly protected, supported, and advanced by the existing social order will turn against that order to radically change it, the question has an easy answer. Such mass insanity is rare.

This principle put forward by Alford is neither vacuous nor trivial. Part of its significance lies in the fact that it can be valid even when there is pervasive and intense opposition among the so-called dominant groupings themselves. Severe struggles among different business-interest groupings do not prevent such groups from mounting a united front to resist higher taxes or national-ization of corporate property. Even more striking is the fact that struggle between dominant groups may be "symbiotic," actually advantageous to each of the parties and contributory to the unchanging persistence of the total system. Thus in Alford's example of the health-medical system in the United States, the struggles between the medical professionals and "reformers," (hospital administrators and advocates from government agencies, insurance organizations, and other nonmedical sectors) serve to bolster, expand, and elaborate the existing inequalitarian and costly modes of providing health services.

In this instance, as in many intergroup situations, the sheer complexity of interrelations among the interests of varied groups and organizations represents a major barrier to significant social changes.

The implications, for strategies of collective action, of understanding the total system within which oppositions and conflicts occur are real and specific. For basic strategies—as distinct from tactical choices in particular struggles— will depend upon whether a situation of conflict is interpreted in terms of specific issues or is regarded as an aspect of a total system of power and authority.

What makes conflict revolutionary? Why is it not a mere dispute among men [and women] over specific grievances? . . . Increasingly in our own country [1969] we have conflict where one side of the confrontation sees it as an eruption of specific grievances and the other sees it as some-thing so deep that only a great transformation can resolve it (Schurmann, 1971, 263).

Revolutionaries generalize all particular conflicts in terms of a struggle against a ruling class, or elite, or other dominant social formation. Sharp disagreements exist among revolutionary ideologists about the definition of the target— Marxian (capitalists, bourgeoisie), Maoist (concrete and particular "classes"), Fanon (oppressors of the "wretched"), and so on—but all seek a comprehensive and unitary foe whose defeat will transform the location and use of power.

From observations of many community conflicts, Cormick and Laue (1977) have suggested that stability or equilibrium depends upon two conditions: (1) that local power—the control over allocations of resources—is regarded as legitimate by a large enough proportion of the population, and (2) that such resources as goods, land, facilities, jobs, and public services are regarded as adequate in quantity and equitably distributed. What is implied in this statement is an equilibrium based on consensus. But the sheer fact of social peace does not imply consensus. Acquiescence may occur simply because power based on control of resources is so great that resistance is hopeless and very nearly unthinkable—yet that power is not necessarily considered legitimate. Moreover, resources may be inadequate and their distribution considered inequitable, but so long as the little that one does have would be totally at risk in the act of opposition, then little competition or conflict is likely to occur over the issues of illegitimate power or inequitable resources. Peace or stability (lack of conflict) need not imply equity or satisfaction.

It is difficult to overemphasize the actual importance of the *sense of inevitability* in accounting for the acceptance of inequality and discrimination. We might perhaps make the point clearer by a crucial question: in the search for causal explanations of human social behavior, what is the single most important question one can ask? Many possibilities can be given, but there is much to recommend this one: *How could it possibly be otherwise?*

To ask how the outcome could be any other than that observed is to ask: *Are there any alternatives?* If there is some other behavior that is objectively possible, why is it not selected: Is knowledge of it lacking? Are necessary resources unavailable? Is access blocked by physical barriers or limitations? Does any alternative involve net costs highter than those incurred in the existent conduct? Pertaining to our current example, we can ask these questions of every concrete case of intergroup relations, whether in employment, schools, housing, politics and government, or other sectors of the society.

6. Special Characteristics of Influence in Intergroup Relations

To understand intergroup relations for purposes of practical diagnosis and action we need to practice the art of taking into account at all times both

(1) the micro-level of person-to-person relations in small groups and relatively unstructured collectivities, and (2) the macro-level of large-scale social movements, associations, and formal organization. The reasons for continuous attention to both levels have been suggested at several points already, but a more systematic account may now be useful.

Informal personalized relationships allow for great ambiguity and vagueness, for much tacit coordination, for rapid change as well as subsequent resumption of previous modes of interaction. The *immediate situations* and the *particular histories* of individuals and their past interactions often are overriding influences. But interactions between various leaders and representatives of large collectivities are radically different.

The tasks of the leader or representative are fourfold. He or she must seek to build and retain support within his or her constituency. At the same time, there is the imperative to negotiate, bargain, fight, or otherwise deal purposively with the representatives of an opposing collectivity. Actions undertaken to cope with either one of these tasks may be counterproductive for other types of action. Furthermore, third parties must be taken into account as actual or potential allies, enemies, or neutral bystanders. In negotiating and bargaining, there are many zero-sum problems in which one who seeks advantage for his or her own side may seek to weaken the bargaining power of an opponent, e.g., by limiting the opponent's options for repression, denying access to resources, seeking to convert or detach the opponent's followers and allies, or confusing the opponent through deceptive tactics. But one may also anticipate future dealings with the opponent once the present episode is past, and thus may desire to maintain or promote positive attitudes of trust, respect, and approval. Finally, in negotiations, bargains, and other forms of dealing with an adversary there is likely to be a problem-solving aspect—a need to seek mutually advantageous procedures and outcomes that will enhance the likelihood of stability and reward for all parties (Walton and McKersie, 1965).

A simple illustration is the role of a leader of an ethnic grouping engaged in a boycott of employers who have refused to end obvious discriminatory practices. The specialized organization that the leader represents is likely to contain active supporters of two or more divergent positions on the issue. The organization itself depends upon a larger, more diffuse ethnic collectivity that contains passive supporters of the boycott, those who are indifferent or apathetic, and those who are opposed to the boycott. Representatives of the employers similarly may be answerable to a divided constituency of active supporters of resistance, passive supporters, indifferent, and alienated or unpersuaded. On the sidelines in the beginning may be civil officials, police, news media, military organizations, various voluntary associations, and a large unorganized "general public." Any one or all of the subgroupings and opinion-publics may be mobilized by events and become important in the outcome of the struggle. And within each of the contending collectivities a similar situation may exist. Therefore, each individual in each set of negotiators may need for some purposes to deal with parts of his or her own constituency as third parties, even while he or she attempts to appraise the effects of the ongoing actions upon a similarly differentiated opponent and upon an even more diverse and unpredictable set of third parties.

The nature of most ethnic relations in our society is affected by the diffuse, amorphous nature and internal heterogeneity of these collectivities. Both these features increase the difficulty of united action as well as the probability of "unreliability" (instability) in settlements. Conceivably, however, these same characteristics allow for flexibility in many local situations by maximizing the opportunities for use of a wide range and combination of tactics and modes of influence on both sides.

But flexibility of approaches and diversity of tactics are reduced by another prominent feature of "ethnic" relations. Because membership is primarily ascribed, although not exclusively so—one can lose membership, and an occasional "token" or "honorary" member is created by consent—and tends to be highly salient, ethnic relations tend to be seen as involving quite high stakes and long-term implications. Hence, bargaining over specific localized issues often "escalates" into intense struggles over symbolic issues and global power.

Observations of many cases show that when racial collectivities or groups are involved in local community disputes, and when the anticipated or proposed outcomes will change the relative power of whites and nonwhites, the salience of group membership is increased. The central issue becomes power—as a goal and as a central element in tactics and strategy. And the more salient "race" becomes, the more likely it is that the stakes of the contest will increase and that the struggle will be intense, prolonged, and uncertain in results (Cormick and Laue, 1974, unpublished).

A third feature of ethnic relations is that a large number of peripheral and highly diverse issues can easily be brought into any given instance of disagreement or conflict. A dispute over the location of a school or a housing project can lead rather quickly to a proliferation of issues involving jobs, union membership, police behavior, political representation, municipal services, and so on indefinitely.

Fourth, ethnic relations always involve a historical dimension. This means that people are aware of old wrongs and past glories—and no "statute of limitations" seems to hold for recriminations based on the behavior of long-past ancestors.

Thus ethnic relations put together the characteristics of *large size, vague boundaries, loose and unstable organization, internal diversity, diffuse relationships, ascribed membership, high stakes, multiple and symbolic issues, and historical embeddedness (including rigid stereotypes).* Small wonder that ethnic conflicts are volatile, easily subject to runaway escalation, and often difficult to resolve by conventional bargaining and mediation tactics.

Chapter 6

Persuasion and Inducement

1. First Considerations

Observe this scene. At rush hour in Grand Central Station a tired businessman boards the Lexington Avenue subway. As he struggles to a hand strap in the crowded car, a heavy weight suddenly and painfully descends upon his already aching foot. Another passenger owns the foot that does the damage. The injured party, normally the soul of courtesy, prepares a vigorous insult as he glares furiously at the offender—who contritely says, "I'm sorry. Did I hurt you? I couldn't help it." Suddenly the symptoms of righteous rage disappear; the victim says, "Oh, that's okay. No problem."

Does not the outcome seem magical? How could mere words make such a difference? The immediately prior events included invasion of personal space, pain, moral indignation. All seem to foretell acrimonious personal conflict. But, not so—a few words, a facial expression, and a gesture somehow seem enough to avert a potentially violent confrontation. Civility won, even if it may have been by a narrow margin.

How are such events possible?

Successful persuasion often does have about it an aura of the uncanny or magical, especially in instances of sudden conversion. The bigot becomes a defender of the oppressed. Ferocious pursuit of vengeance seems inexplicably transmuted into gentle forgiveness. Dispirited and disunited masses find a charismatic leader and then display unprecedented discipline, enthusiasm, self-sacrifice, and courage against powerful opponents.

Less dramatic but quite impressive in the aggregate are the day-by-day out-comes of socialization of children, induction of individuals into occupations, effective advertising, various interpersonal interactions, and long-term changes in beliefs, attitudes, and values.

And persuasion appears to have low costs in resources and in risks.

Why, then, does persuasion not become a preferred approach in ethnic relations? Evidently because the results are not always so impressive as in the hypothetical outcomes just sketched. There is much evidence of advertising campaigns that fail (the Edsel automobile never did well at all), and of pro-paganda that has boomerang effects. Valuable information that is vital to health and well-being is ignored or resisted and rejected (cigarette smoking). Furthermore, experimental findings on short-term exposure to persuasive communication indicate that the effects diminish with the passing of time (Abelson and Karlins, 1970, 70). Such failures and reverses are familiar in efforts to reduce prejudice and discrimination by information, exhortation, and numerous specific forms of persuasion. But, as we noted in Chapter 1, it seems reasonable to conclude that many ethnic and racial stereotypes and hostile beliefs have been eroded and reduced in intensity by the long-term influences of information, propaganda, and education.

What is known about the factors associated with effective as over against ineffective efforts to change intergroup attitudes or behavior[1] through persua-sion? And what additional inferences—more or less in the nature of the informed folklore of experience—seem plausible enough for us to accept at least tentative formulation, pending additional evidence?

2. Persuasion through Information

Let us begin with the simplest approach: give the people the facts and they will change their attitudes and behavior. Fantastic as it may seem, this boldly stated piece of common sense has been the implicit basis of enormous efforts and large expenditures of resources in the field of "public education"—concerning tobacco, dental hygiene, venereal disease, alcohol and other addictive drugs, as well as ethnic and racial ethnic prejudice. What do the data of systematic psychological and sociological research suggest about the usefulness of supply-ing factual information as a means of persuasion? (We exclude cases in which recipients are totally ignorant of the matter at hand and the purveyors of information enjoy a monopoly.)

The weight of the extensive research findings, over a period of at least a half-century, is that sheer information alone typically has little short-run effect upon already established beliefs and attitudes (or upon behavior, unless a pre-existing strong motivation is thereby released, e.g., by information that the expression of a given belief certainly will be punished by death). Compare these independently formulated conclusions taken from works published over two decades apart (1947 and 1970).

> (1) The mere giving of objective general information in print or by lecture about a group which is the object of hostility has only a slight effect, or no effect, in reducing hostility—at least in the short run (Williams, 1947, 64-65; cf. also 27-34).
>
> (2) Information by itself almost never changes attitudes (Abelson and Karlins, 1970, 33).

Unless reinforced by social reward or other inducements, individuals when free to choose tend to select those communications "that are favorable or congenial to their predispositions; they are more likely to see and hear congenial communications than neutral or hostile ones. And the more interested they are in the subject, the more likely is such selective attention" (Berelson and Steiner, 1964, 529). In short, those persons "you may want most in your audience are often least likely to be there" (Abelson and Karlins, 1970, 84). Both through actual absence of exposure and through selective attention even if exposed, persons ward off potential effects of uncongenial or unwanted information. Furthermore, even if the message is received it may be neutralized or reversed by psychological processes. "People tend to misperceive and misinterpret persuasive communications in accordance with their own predisposition, by evading the message or by distorting it in a favorable direction" (Berelson and Steiner, 1964, 536).

Attitude change after exposure to a message instigating change often tends to be "minimal," viz.

> People whose predispositions are close to a particular communication are more likely to be changed—small discrepancies rather than large ones are most likely to be followed by change.
>
> Communications are most likely to reinforce existing positions, than to activate latent positions, and least likely to change or counter existing or latent positions (i.e., to convert) (Berelson and Steiner, 1964, 541).

But these plausible propositions do not always hold. There are circumstances under which it is more effective to ask for a large change rather than a small one. The effects seem to vary with the credibility of the persuader and with the degree of involvement or commitment of the recipients. The generalization has been advanced that "the more extreme the opinion change that the high credibility communicator asks for, the more actual change he is likely to get." (Abelson and Karlins, 1970, 126-27). Most of the opinions regarding ethnic relations that one may wish to change are likely to be held with considerable conviction and are often bolstered by group support. Sharply divergent views presented by an outsider may in themselves diminish his or her credibility. On the other hand, when the desired changes are regarded by the persuader as justified by basic moral considerations, he or she can hardly ask for a "little" change. A possible approach is to ask for specific behavioral changes that can be defined as relatively nonthreatening and then to make sure that any subsequent changes among recipients are strongly reinforced. This guideline for persuasion is important not only in efforts to bring about initial changes but also in subsequent development of changes. It is clear that when persuasion runs counter to continuing social influences persons often will "use their own changes of opinion, however recent or immediate, as blocks against further modification of opinion under the pressure of communications" (Abelson and Karlins, 1970, 127). The tendency to backslide or to reach a premature stabilization is so frequent that a reasonable rule of thumb is to assume that frequent and continuing reinforcement is needed to ensure that major reorientations actually can be maintained.

This series of generalizations from surveys and experiments consistently indicates that supplying information is not an effective way to influence important attitudes and beliefs. But it is unrealistic to expect information to act by itself. Information can result in massive changes in behavior when the information *directly concerns strong interests* of the individual, including the interests and values of collectivities to which he or she belongs. For example, both the incidence of conflict and the difficulty of resolving those conflicts that do break out will be lessened to the extent that the parties receive information leading them to believe that their opponents have limited aims, especially aims primarily related to defense and security.

It is plausible that information per se would most often affect behavior when an individual already is highly motivated to act but does not know how. A fairly common example in intergroup relations is the "person of good will" who wants to behave appropriately in a newly desegregated situation. Very large programs of "race relations training" (for example, in the U.S. Armed Forces) include much information concerning *how* to act, as well as materials addressed to awareness and motivation.[2]

Conflict, therefore, involves information—knowledge and beliefs about social norms, limits of various types of actions; about strategies, tactics, techniques, resources, precedents; about alternatives of persuasion, inducement, cooperation, withdrawal, capitulation, bargaining, migration; about allies and possible allies; about the intentions and resources of opponents. Collective conflict is *never* a sheerly mindless expression of feeling. Orientations and actions in situations of conflict are profoundly shaped by beliefs and knowledge—that is, by cognitive factors. In this sense, if in no other, the extent and kind of information that people possess is of crucial importance.

What we have just said has a reverse side: misinformation and ignorance are important. Information often is inaccurate, misleading, or lacking. Ethnic and racial relations often combine scanty communication, inaccurate and unreliable information, many stereotypic beliefs, strong affects, and low levels of trust. An inevitable side-effect is that in times of tension or of large-scale conflict there will be a proliferation of rumors. Plausible rules of thumb for attempting to reduce the conflict-inciting effects of rumor have been known for a long while.

For example:

> The effects of public refutation of hostile rumors vary with the nature of the refutation and with the type of rumor and attendant situation, e.g.:
>
> (a) *In chronic but relatively stable and mild intergroup* tensions, rumors are probably best ignored, or refuted, only by indirection and propaganda of the deed.
>
> (b) *Rumors of unusual character, intensity, or prevalence* (e.g., role of minorities in the armed forces in war) probably should be met by "official" propaganda. However, publicizing the rumors themselves should be avoided; the refutation should be as indirect (nonmanifest) as is consistent with the necessity of gaining attention.
>
> (c) *In crisis situations* (pre-riot, etc.) refutation of rumors of hostile intentions or of hostile actions of opposing groups, weakness of control forces, and the like tends to check conflict.
>
> . *Note:* Contrary assumptions are also advanced by experienced authorities. Almost nothing is definitely established on these propositions (Williams, 1947, 68).

Unfortunately we still await the definitive research needed to resolve the contradictory views.

The presumption that information about widespread aggressive acts by others like oneself may tend to elicit collective tumult may underlie release of information by mass media. For example, by the early 1970s riots and confrontations were being "played down" by news media. The riot in St. Albans, Long Island in July 1974, which almost certainly would have received major national media reporting a few years earlier, actually received almost no attention outside the New York City metropolitan area. This limitation of publicity, in conjunction with many relatively quick piecemeal responses to local grievances (Bowser, 1975), apparently has been one factor in reducing the occurrence of large-scale confrontations.

The long-continued and widespread dissemination of information concerning the changing characteristics and aspirations of black people in the United
States almost certainly affected the attitudes of educated white Americans.
From the early 1940s to the 1970s, the recorded changes among whites
included a large decrease in the belief that some "races" are inferior in intelligence, the rejection of many invidious stereotypes, greater acceptance of
equality of political and civil rights and liberties, and greater acceptance
of integration in a variety of social settings. (For the evidence see: Hyman
and Sheatsley, 1964; Sheatsley, 1966; Schwartz, 1967; Greeley and Sheatsley,
1971; Pettigrew, 1971.) A comparison of reasonably comparable data for a
single city—Detroit—for the 1950s and for 1969-71 concludes that

> all evidence reviewed here on white attitudes points to a large and
> continuing shift toward acceptance of principles of equal treatment and
> equal status for black Americans. . . . (But) . . . black Americans reading
> these pages today may be struck as much by the distance still to travel
> as by the distance already traversed (Duncan, Schuman, and Duncan,
> 1973).

Yet we must be careful not to equate "information" with formal education
and the mass media, for the vivid experiences of everyday life often overpower
other channels of influence. Thus the data for Detroit showed that during
the period of great civil turmoil, 1968-71, there was an increase among black
persons of distrust of whites, an increase in preference for interaction with
blacks, and greater acceptance of violent means of achieving social change
(but not a greater total rejection of the United States) (Duncan, Schuman,
and Duncan, 1973, 104-111).

Rising levels of knowledge about ethnic and racial groupings seem to be
indicated by other evidence of reductions in gross stereotyping. Thus studies
that have used comparable methods enable us to trace changes between the
1930s and the 1960s in attitudes of college students. There has been a marked
decrease in uncritical acceptance of traditional stereotypes. Also in the later
period there more frequently was active resistance to stereotyping and a
greater frequency of attributing "favorable" traits to minority groups that
formerly were stigmatized. (For evidence, see: Braly and Katz, 1933; Bayton,
1941; Gilbert, 1951; Jensen and Prothro, 1952; Coffman, Karlins, Walters,
1969).

It has become somewhat fashionable in recent times to be skeptical of
the effectiveness of information and persuasion. This is no doubt a healthy
skepticism, but we must not allow it to blind us to the fact that *some* issues
under some circumstances can be redefined to permit agreements and compro-

mises that avoid mutually destructive, minus-sum confrontations. Thus Doob makes persuasive use of what he calls "an oversimplified analogy I borrowed from a forgotten source":

> If one person wants a window in this room open and another person wants it shut, and if they keep phrasing their desires in terms of the window, one of them must win and the other must lose, or there will be some sort of only partially satisfactory compromise. But if it can be discovered that the first person really wants fresh air and the second seeks only to avoid a draft, a creative solution may be possible: opening the door or a window in another room could provide fresh air without a draft (Doob, 1970, 2).

Similarly, the presentation of convincing evidence of impending violent conflict may aid in stimulating efforts to find solutions to ethnic confrontations. Thus, "appeals to local pride are sometimes useful in motivating leaders to prevent open conflict. Mass violence is widely regarded . . . as bringing discredit upon the community in which it occurs" (Williams, 1947, 67).[3]

3. Effects of Approval, Models, and Examples

That group agreement and approval or disagreement and disapproval typically have marked effects upon both overt behavior and psychological processes certainly is one of the social science generalizations most strongly confirmed by numerous and varied evidences (Abelson and Karlins, 1970, 49-56). It follows that changing the attitudes and beliefs of an individual will be more difficult and harder to maintain when external pressures and social groups important to that individual do not support and perhaps even oppose the new attitudes. Because people are strongly influenced by the significant others in groups to which they belong, it is difficult to induce change that is opposed to group norms and opinions (Abelson and Karlins, 1970, 57-61). However, if change can be produced in a group as a whole, the effects tend to persist and to become stabilized. "Changing the attitudes of *groups* rather than isolated individuals is the more effective approach for breaking up intergroup stereotypes and prejudices" (Williams, 1947, 66).

The presence of other persons who are regarded as making *evaluations of one's behavior* is in itself a source of arousal that affects performance. Nearly everyone has learned to regard the evaluations of other people as a significant form of reward and deprivation and as gratifying or disgratifying in themselves. Glass and Henchy have shown that task performance was higher for persons who thought their responses were being evaluated than for persons who worked alone or in the presence of a nonevaluating audience. "Social facilitation," therefore, appears to depend primarily upon arousal through the expectation of evaluation (Glass and Henchy, 1968).

The powerful effects of personal relationships and group atmosphere have been abundantly documented; there are many practical implications.[4]

> In intergroup relations, as in many others, word-of-mouth propaganda, especially that which appears (or, is) spontaneous and informal, is more effective than visual or formal propaganda in influencing attitudes and behavior (Williams, 1947, 66).

> When opinions do shift under the impact of communications, they tend to regress to the pre-existing position unless they are reinforced by events, other communications, or group pressures (Berelson and Steiner, 1964, 543).

The influence of behavior-examples and of social models is particularly accentuated in "unstructured" situations, i.e., those characterized by little information, ambiguous cues, inconsistent and vague norms, uncertain goals and outcomes. When there is strong instigation to act, but when there is also a high degree of uncertainty regarding options and norms, people are alert to any cues that will help to define appropriate behavior. Detailed study of many such unstructured situations of interracial contact has demonstrated how a single act can be decisive in redefining acceptable behavior or shaping a new pattern of conduct. The Cornell Studies in Intergroup Relations showed that behavior often could be swung toward either discrimination or nondiscrimination by what superficially appeared to be trivial initiatives (Williams et al., 1964, 311-51).

To induce some minimum of trust and a disposition to regard other persons favorably, it is helpful to show valid evidence of similarities between members of different social categories. In general, persons tend to like others and to cooperate with them more often when the others are perceived to have similar attitudes, beliefs, and values. It is therefore important to note that when socioeconomic status (income and education) is matched, blacks and whites in the contemporary United States differ in very few generalized values (Rokeach, 1973, 66-72; Triandis, 1972, 134). Although there are, of course, many specific differences attributable to effects of past segregation and discrimination, at comparable occupational and income levels, there is a great amount of common culture upon which mutual influence can be based (Goering and Kahl, 1971, 306-18).

Effects of modeling and social approval are very strong *in the absence of countervailing influences*. But the effects of similarity of models are small in the face of felt inequalities and inequities in control of scarce resources. Nevertheless, under conditions of a common threat or crisis, as in war or natural disaster, vivid reminders of shared destinies and commitments often are effective. For example, at a time when national unity and pride were highly valued in the United States, it was a valid precept that an effective persuasive approach in intergroup relations was to emphasize "national symbols and common American achievements, sacrifices, destinies, etc., while unobtrusively indicating the common participation of minority group members" (Williams, 1947, 67).

The influence of social example is best seen in direct interpersonal relations. Thus the mere act of observing other persons violate a social rule that prohibits an easily performed and rewarding action (for example, jaywalking) increases the rate of violation, especially if the violator is of "high" or "respectable" status and is seen to go unpunished. Conversely, a high degree of conformity strongly influences would-be deviants toward compliance with norms. "In intergroup relations, as in many others, the 'propaganda of the deed' is especially likely to have effects upon attitudes and behavior" (Williams, 1947, 67).

Several studies have shown that whether or not bystanders or passersby will help a person in need is affected by modeling behavior. For instance, Wagner and Wheeler conclude: "In summary, helping behavior was negatively affected by a selfish model as well as positively affected by a generous model. Both model effects were facilitated by low costs of helping but inhibited by high costs" (Wagner and Wheeler, 1969, 15).

The technique of eliciting opinions in a group first from those members most likely to favor one's own position uses the leverage of social example and approval; it is a cumulative appeal to conformity to induce any negatively inclined members to join the "rolling" sequence of acceptance and approval. Zimbardo and Ebbesen (1969, 115-21) review instances of dramatic effects from this approach.

When sufficient commonality of values exists, reduction of a sense of threat and correlative reduction of intergroup hostility can be facilitated by showing concrete exemplars of common culture, shared fate, or shared collective aspirations.

> Hostility is reduced by any activity which leads members of conflicting groups to identify their own values and life-activities in individuals of the other group. To be most effective this requires devices for inducing *personal* identification before the introduction of group labels.
>
> *Dictum:* Personalize, personalize, personalize (Williams, 1947, 68).

Both *differences* and *changes* in the public behavior and typical social positions of members of visible ethnic groupings are likely to influence the members of other collectivities. Hence it is plausible to suppose that:

> Conflict and hostility are rendered less probable by any activity which leads individuals to *take for granted* the other group (e.g., . . . films which show Negroes as members of various kinds of groups, where the emphasis of presentation is upon what the group is doing) (Williams, 1947, 68).

On the other hand, when sense of group position is strong and attitudes are highly competitive, an inevitable hazard in persuasive communication is that signals of common fate, similarity, and shared values will be interpreted as indicators of threat. For example:

> Propaganda which appeals for minority rights on the basis of the group's achievements tends beyond a certain point to arouse insecurity-hostility in the dominant group by stressing group differences and competitive success.

> This hypothesis implies that appeals which suggest a status-threat to prejudiced groups are to be avoided (Williams, 1947, 67).

(The implication of avoidance does not necessarily follow: members of the "defensive" grouping simply may have to become accustomed to the new and legitimately higher status of a rising minority.)

An old and plausible notion is that observation of or vicarious participation in competitive or aggressive activity will reduce hostility, through some kind of "catharsis" or "expressive release." Recent speculation, as well as some experimental findings, may seem to have lent support to the idea (See for example: Feshbach, 1956, 1961; Lorenz, 1966; Ardrey, 1966; Storr, 1968).

However, the weight of the experimental evidence suggests that hostility (or aggressive behavior, as the case may be) increases after observation of violence (or of objects associated with violence) (Berkowitz, Corwin, Hieronimus, 1963; Bandura, Ross, Ross, 1963; Geen and O'Neal, 1969). Further, additional findings from nonexperimental settings indicate the hostility-stimulating effects of viewing competitive and aggressive sports events. For example, spectators become more hostile after viewing a football game; the increase apparently is not attributable to effects of frustration, for those whose preferred team won were as likely as those who identified with the defeated team to show heightened hostility. No such increase in hostility was found in a "control" group consisting of persons who observed a competitive but not aggressive event—a gymnastics meet (Goldstein and Arms, 1971, 83-90).

4. Successful Persuasion? Some Interpretations

The difficulties of inducing change in ethnic attitudes are well attested and well recognized (Zimbardo and Ebbesen, 1969, 101-8). We know that the typical experience is that success rarely occurs through direct attack on the views of a recipient, through sheer exhortation, through unadorned "facts," or through abstract ideological appeals. For example: "The appeal once made by the Red Cross to the patriotism of potential donors proved to be a dismal failure. This was because abstract, ideological principles rarely motivate immediate, concrete action" (Zimbardo and Ebbesen, 1969, 109). A large accumulation of evidence consistently shows that unsupported individual opinions on transitory and peripheral topics can and do change; on the other hand there is great resistance to change of value-commitments that are normatively approved and enforced in social groups. We suggest that only a *combination* of persuasion and institutional change can be most effective in producing intergroup attitudes that will be conducive to conflict-resolution (Triandis, 1972, 127-36).

In general the attitudes and opinions that are easiest to change are those of least importance to the person to whom communication is to be addressed. This is one of many "paradoxes" of efforts to alter behavior and attitudes. Opinions that are accessible to relatively simple and easily managed appeals tend to be those that are lightly held, not salient, peripheral to central values and self-conceptions, or concerned with unfamiliar events or objects. Persons change most easily, other things being equal, when they have little information about the issue; do not perceive their vital personal interests to be endangered; and are not reinforced in incongruous or incompatible attitudes by their reference and membership groups. Persons who are most fully informed about an issue and who are supported in a prior opposing opinion by high-consensus social groups are most resistant to change (Berelson and Steiner, 1964, 541-42).

In this brief glance at some evidence on the effects of social approval and social modeling we have seen strong connections between intragroup processes and intergroup attitudes and behavior. Influence of ingroup members upon one another often is the dominant factor in determining whether relations with members of another group will be cooperative or conflictful. Note this fact implies that the specific objective characteristics of the outgroup sometimes will have little to do with the outcomes.

Evidently there are many barriers to successful persuasion when one seeks to change group-supported attitudes and behavior. Are there any circumstances in which tactics of persuasion can be successful?

To persuade, one must be credible. To be credible, one must above all be accepted as *socially* trustworthy — not lying, distorting, misrepresenting, deceiving, tricking, suppressing information, and the like. One must be seen as willing to accept valid information and as motivated to communicate truthfully. Second, credibility rests also upon a belief in *competence* — one must be regarded as having the ability or technical training to understand the issues and the situation at hand.

Both credibility and the intrinsic appeals of a persuader are increased if his or her initial messages indicate that she or he shares important beliefs, preferences, opinions, or values with the audience. Low credibility, however, has less negative effects if the persuader seems to argue against his or her own interests, or is identified in terms of his or her interests only after his or her views have been presented (Abelson and Karlins, 1970, 120-21).

Given high credibility and an initial sense among the audience that persuader and hearers share important values, a persuader is likely to induce maximum changes in attitudes of those addressed when he or she asks for great rather than small changes (Zimbardo and Ebbesen, 1969, 20-21).

The effects of "emotional" versus "factual" appeals vary: sometimes one is more effective, sometimes the other, depending on type of audience, content of message, and other contextual factors (Abelson and Karlins, 1970, 35-38).

Any attempt to influence people to do something other than what they have learned to do or to want in the past will be less effective when it communicates only a generalized negative injunction and more effective when it adds a positive suggestion for alternative behavior. The most effective combinations seem to link a specific prohibition or warning with a feasible alternative. Thus to activate feelings of guilt among white Americans about racial discrimination by emphasizing the injustices and deprivations suffered by blacks or Native Americans in the past, without indicating any tangible action that the concerned individual can take now, will tend to motivate the individual to simply withdraw from an uncomfortable situation in which there is no obvious opportunity for relief. If both positive action and escape are difficult, persons experiencing guilt may seek communications which rationalize or support their previous position (Berelson and Steiner, 1964, 531).

Other consequences that are still more hazardous for positive attitude-change may be set off through the use of extremely strong appeals that neither aid the individual to take nondiscriminatory and nonprejudicial actions nor support those actions. There still has not appeared any convincing evidence to refute these long-standing hypotheses:

It is dangerous technique to employ *mass* propaganda emphasizing "rising tides of prejudice" as a means intended to mobilize defenders of minority rights and good intergroup relations. Such propaganda is likely to have a boomerang effect upon slightly prejudiced or wavering elements: it creates the presumption of group support for hostile actions.

Appeals to conscience or ethics must be carefully handled, if they are to diminish rather than intensify hostility. In general, such appeals are probably most effective in reinforcing the sentiments of persons who are already convinced; they are probably not effective (immediately, at least) with militant anti-ethnics, and may even result in increased hostility as a reaction to guilt-feelings. That is, where individuals are utilizing prejudice to satisfy strong emotional urges, activation of the conscience-functions may tend to heighten psychological conflict and thus to result in increasingly devious or irrational hostilities (Williams, 1947, 67).

Research on responses to persuasive attempts certainly shows the necessity of taking into account the personality "needs" that are being served by beliefs and attitudes toward outgroups, as well as the value-commitments and self-protective or ego-defensive beliefs that may be threatened by instigations to change.

The suspicion of being manipulated, of being secretly used through devious techniques, is frequent in our mass-communication society. In this context the following generalization seems valid: "Cues which forewarn the audience of the manipulative intent of the communication increase resistance to it, while the presence of distractors simultaneously presented with the message decreases resistance" (Zimbardo and Ebbesen, 1969, 22).

Resistance is also manifested through *reactance*, the negative response to the feeling that one's options are being reduced, one's freedom to choose is being restricted (Brehm, 1966): "Awareness of someone's intention to manipulate your behavior is often sufficient to render the influence attempt ineffectual — even when its goal is to your benefit" (Zimbardo and Ebbesen, 1969, 19). When the threat of loss of freedom to choose is strongly present, individuals will seek to regain the lost option rather than to be guided by the specific content of the persuasive attempt. (Reactance-based behavior, of course, will be influenced also by the risks and costs involved in the particular situation.) Thus persuasion generally will be more effective under these conditions when it avoids explicit and strict prohibitions or advice, and offers incentives leading toward the choice of certain options without abridging the right to choose. To counteract reactance, one practical dictum is to make sure there is something in the situation that the recipients can control.

In persuasion aimed at ethnic prejudices, one frequently encounters reactance combined with unresolved psychological dissonance — that is, tensions aroused by inconsistencies of beliefs, evaluations, feelings, self-conceptions, and actions. At the same time it is usually also true that the individuals in question are being subjected to social influences that favor conformity to ingroup prejudices. Such situations pose a special communicative trap for outsiders who attempt to induce change in ethnic prejudices. Compare this long-standing observation:

> Where strong prejudice is present in a group which is highly self-conscious, and strongly bound together, outside criticism of its prejudice is likely to be taken as an attack on the group; and *one* immediate effect is to strengthen the prejudice, which by virtue of the attack becomes a symbol of in-group membership and solidarity.

Furthermore:

> A general principle of approach is that, except in acute crisis situations, problems of group conflict are usually most readily resolved by indirection rather than by frontal assault. In propaganda, for example, direct arguments tend to present a sharp issue which arouses maximum resistance; a more effective procedure is to emphasize common aims and suggest group integration as a means for their attainment.

> Insofar as possible, if it is desired to avoid defensive hostility, guided changes in intergroup relations must be made in such a way as to avoid or minimize the interpretation that they threaten security with regard to those things in which the groups have important emotional commitments. (It should be clear, however, that various gradualistic ameliorative proposals for reducing hostility or conflict do not directly reach the problem of "interested", calculated discrimination or the conscious use of group visibility as a means for perpetuating a privileged social and economic position) (Williams, 1947, 63).

A related generalization continues to be supported by much practical experience as well as by more systematic research findings.

> Attempts to reduce intergroup hostility by education will be the more effective, (a) the more the learners are convinced in the beginning that they themselves are not under attack for their opinions; and (b) the more the learners are allowed initially to express freely their verbal hostilities to instructors who maintain an atmosphere of calm objectivity (Williams, 1947, 65).

Through persuasion one hopes primarily to convince those already favoring the orientation being promoted (activation) and to increase the favorability of the noncommitted, inconsistent, dissonant, wavering, or confused.

One aims persuasion not only at opponents, bystanders, and potential allies but also at members of the ingroup, co-believers, and fellow participants in a collective consensus. For even the faithful need support, reassurance, protective information — and inoculation against counterpersuasion. Especially vulnerable to counterattack are beliefs, attitudes, and values that the individual takes for granted and has not had to defend. For example,

"cultural truisms" — widely shared beliefs that are seldom, if ever, questioned, such as the belief that one ought to brush one's teeth often — are extremely vulnerable to counterargument, probably because they never had to be defended. Two ways have been found to produce resistance to counterarguments. The first method involves provision of support for belief. The second method, similar to biological inoculation, involves exposing the persons to weakened or refuted versions of the attacking arguments. Repeated experiments have demonstrated the superiority of the later method, even when the inoculating arguments are quite different from the arguments contained in subsequent attacks (Clark and Miller, 1970, 101).

Protection against subsequent counterpersuasion seems to be enhanced by the early arousal of favorable predispositions, e.g., by initially congenial messages followed by preparation against counterargument (Berelson and Steiner, 1964, 551).

On the whole, the somewhat complex evidence seems to favor the policy of giving "both sides" of the arguments on an issue if those one hopes to persuade will be exposed later to counterpersuasion and propaganda. Having been persuaded by a two-sided argument seems to render individuals less vulnerable to later counterappeals (Berelson and Steiner, 1964, 553). The two-sided presentation may enhance the credibility of the persuader by inspiring confidence in his or her honesty or openness or fairness, and by exposing the subjects of persuasion to the probably weakened forms of the opposing case, thus providing "inoculation" through rehearsal and rejection.

Some experimental studies showed that under conditions in which people are likely to be exposed to competing messages about an issue (as usually is the case in ethnic issues in the United States), using a strongly threatening appeal is less effective than a minimally threatening (fear-producing) communication in changing behavior or attitudes. But some other studies have found that strong fear appears to be more effective than milder persuasive attempts. Strong appeals seem most effective when they come from a highly credible source, deal with unknown or problematic events or effects, indicate danger to an individual's family or other loved ones, and are presented to persons who have high self-esteem or low perceived vulnerability to the threatening condition. In short, a person receives information indicating strong hazards to highly valued social objects but is not overwhelmed by fear to the point of avoidance or denial. Appeals that invoke fear or anxiety-inducing conditions are most likely to be followed by changes in relevant behavior when clearly understood and specific action can be taken immediately and when the persuasive communication provides definite instructions about how to take the recommended action (Abelson and Karlins, 1970, 6-10).

Although complex and varied findings have come from studies of the effects of concurrent stimuli—of surroundings, food or drink, visual or auditory distractions—in general, persuasion is not enhanced by strong distractions or noxious stimuli. (Lest this statement seem banal we must point out that irrelevant fear-inducing stimuli can increase persuasive impact under some conditions.) Persuasion usually—not always—is facilitated by a context that provides a moderate level of rewarding stimuli (Abelson and Karlins, 1970, 15-18).

If we wish to persuade people toward a view we regard as valid and important, and see an ethical obligation to make an effort, should we present facts and value implications and let our hearers (viewers) draw their own conclusions? Or should we explicitly state our conclusions?

No sweeping answer is realistic. Drawing explicit conclusions seems more effective whenever the source of persuasion is not rejected and the recipients find the message difficult to comprehend, either because it is unfamiliar (or complex, or ambiguous, or poorly organized) or because they do not have the concepts and skills to formulate the desired conclusions. Drawing explicit conclusions may have negative effects if the audience finds the materials simple and the implications obvious; stating conclusions may be perceived as boring, insulting, stupid, or insensitive. Negative consequences are likely also when the audience is initially highly suspicious or hostile (Ableson and Karlins, 1970, 11-14) and fears that it is being manipulated or "brainwashed," or when explicitness commits the persuader to conclusions that are uncertain and that may be seen to be making excessive demands upon the participants ("to reduce residential segregation you must be prepared to risk death").

More generally, an active rather than a passive role by the listener seems to facilitate change in opinions and attitudes, perhaps owing to the investment of self. Thus, "evidence points to the 'exertion of effort' (within reasonable limits) as helpful in enhancing the power of persuasive appeals" (Abelson and Karlins, 1970, 19). For example, discussion often is found more effective than lectures in changing attitudes and behavior. The element of participation makes it impossible for the listener to remain uninvolved. Given a minimal level of interest, however, sheer information may be equally well communicated by use of either method (Berelson and Steiner, 1964, 547).

On the whole, then, two-sided rather than one-sided presentations seem more effective in changing attitudes (and in stabilizing the change against later counterpersuasion) when the recipients are well-informed or well-educated, are later exposed to counterarguments, initially have some disagreement with the message or have some doubt about the objectivity of the persuader.

Firm conclusions are not available for assessing which argument to advance first in a two-sided presentation. It seems likely that the side presented first will be the most effective when the controversial topic is not crucial but is nevertheless interesting to the audience and when the issue is quite familiar. When the audience is uncertain of its position but is interested in a decisive resolution of the question or issue, and when the debates and presentations are skillful and subtle, the last position presented will tend to have the greater impact.

Information, suggestions, and arguments are recalled best when presented either at the beginning or at the end of a presentation or discussion. The most effective order depends upon the initial interest of the recipients. If the audience is uninterested, the most impressive items should come early; for a highly interested group, the major arguments or most important information may be more effective toward the end (Abelson and Karlins, 1970, 27).

5. Attitude Change through Induced Behavior

Research evidence and accumulated observations have shown that changes in beliefs and attitudes often follow, rather than precede, changed behavior (Zimbardo and Ebbesen, 1969, 13; Berelson and Steiner, 1964, 211, 213).

> It is implicit in the thinking of many social scientists and laymen that attitudes are among the "causes" of social behavior. Yet the evidence that has been accumulating during the past 15 years of social psychological research suggests that the reverse direction of causality is more powerful. . . . People do something first, then bring their attitudes in line with their behavior. Actually, it is best to think of attitudes and behavior as interacting in reciprocal process, but the more powerful influence involves that from behavior to attitude, the less powerful, that from attitudes to behavior (Triandis, 1972, 127).

> In the particular instance of race relations in the United States, many studies have shown that attitudes of whites toward blacks usually have changed most rapidly after, rather than before, major changes in institutionalized rules and social arrangements (Pettigrew and Riley, 1971, 184.)

As the examples already reviewed clearly show, basic knowledge about processes of persuasion has many practical applications in intergroup relations. Another case in point is the well-established finding that learning through active participation has more powerful effects than the passive reception of stimuli. For instance:

> Active participation in the communicating itself—e.g., passing on the message to someone else, making a speech about it, or simply putting it in one's own words—is more effective for retaining information and for persuading than is passive reception of the communication, especially for people who are low in ability or motivation and for difficult or complex material (Berelson and Steiner, 1964, 548).

Similarly, if a person anticipates having to use the information of a message in a future social situation, this will tend to foster the retention of facts, arguments, and appeals—even when the remembered materials were initially uncongenial. Thus one study showed that white college students who favored racial segregation remembered antisegregation arguments when they anticipated being involved in later debate but did not remember the materials when they did not expect to use them further.

Other findings consistent with the principles of active involvement include the following.

> Opinions which people make known to others are harder to change than opinions which people hold privately (Abelson and Karlins, 1970, 59).

> Audience participation (group discussion and decision making) helps to overcome resistance (Abelson and Karlins, 1970, 62).

> Opinion change is more persistent over a period of time if the persuasive appeal is: (1) repeated and/or (2) requires active (rather than passive) listener participation (Abelson and Karlins, 1970, 78).

Several major theoretical formulations in social psychology lead to the idea that changes in attitudes and behavior may be induced by creating some kind of psychological discrepancy in a person—some kind of incongruency or contradiction. This psychological effect has been called *dissonance*. Great variation exists in what is considered to be dissonant and in what specific processes are thought to produce various outcomes (Zimbardo and Ebbesen, 1969, 67ff.). If a person is experiencing dissonance, a crucial factor in the behavioral result is how strongly motivated the individual is to reduce the inconsistency or incongruity among beliefs, values, and feelings. If the possible behaviors are limited (either by threat of sanctions or lack of resources, or by the inducements of rewards), a state of dissonance produced by behavior that is "inconsistent" with attitudes often leads to change in the attitudes. There is considerable evidence that both attitudes and behavior can be changed when persons are led to act in ways felt to be discrepant with their initial values, or to perceive that certain attitudes or behaviors are inconsistent with values that are basic to their own self-conception and self-evaluation (Rokeach, 1973, Chapters 8-13). In a series of experiments—some in "natural" settings—Rokeach was able to produce marked changes in both attitudes and behavior related to racial discrimination and civil rights by revealing to students that their professed values were inconsistent (in a manner presumably contradicting the self-conception they wished to hold). The changes were not fleeting but persisted over substantial periods of time (up to twenty-one months).

6. A Composite Program

The most effective program of persuasion in intergroup relations would require conditions that, to be sure, are rarely found in the everyday real world. Nevertheless, it is worthwhile to know what conditions we need. The only trick then is to get them. We shall be most likely to be persuaded or to persuade others, as the case may be, when:

- the communicator is trustworthy and competent and shares important beliefs and values with the recipients of communication;
- the communicator shows empathy with the recipients, reveals his or her own beliefs and feelings and accepts criticism;
- communication is recurrent over a substantial period;
- communication is personalized and usually face-to-face;
- the recipients sense that they are basically accepted and respected as persons;
- suitable opportunities and inducements are provided for active learning and the subsequent expression of changes in knowledge, beliefs, and values in concrete behaviors;
- psychologically significant discrepancies are induced between behavior and values, or between behavior and self-conceptions, and feasible modes of resolution are provided, with rewarding outcomes;
- social reinforcement is provided in supportive groups;
- the person is exposed to counterarguments against the persuasive communication and is simultaneously given refutations of these counterarguments to increase the capacity to resist subsequent counterappeals.

7. Persuasion, Inducement, Helping and Exchange

We have seen how persuasion imperceptibly can merge into inducement. For instance, there is the intrinsic possibility in any person-to-person persuasive attempt that the favorable responses and judgments of the communicator will come to be a form of contingent reward. In other words, the giving of social approval may itself be a major form of inducement—often available at relatively low cost. Public signals of approval, for example, appear to have considerable long-range usefulness in producing a social climate relatively favorable to mutual accommodation among ethnic groups. Thus, "conflict is discouraged by providing, through sources of high general prestige, for specific public commendation of individuals of the dominant group [sic: or of 'subordinate' groups] who work for toleration, minority rights, mutual understanding" (Williams, 1947, 67).

Note that when we spoke of persuasion it seemed somehow natural to think of the persuader either as a spokesperson for disadvantaged minorities or as someone specially positioned and motivated who is seeking to bring about change in others similar to himself or herself. Yet when we shift attention to inducement as a mode of influence, it is interesting to observe how easily the examples come to mind of authorities seeking to induce compliance from potential partisans.

Persuasion is a preferred mode of attempting to influence others with whom we have relations of substantial solidarity (trust, affection, consensus). It is often used when highly asymmetrical relationships result in one party having few resources for inducement or constraint. Such relationships may be those of superordination and dependence, or those of lesser positive interdependence in which one party is capable of very drastic retaliation for any attempt by the other to use constraint. Persuasion is a favored approach of weaker parties to the stronger. This is easy to understand.

By definition, parties possessing few transferable resources have only limited possibilities for successfully using inducement. They must persuade, or somehow mount a credible threat, or present inducements in the form of cooperation and social approval. Dominant groups having large resources are unlikely to place a high value upon social approval of economically and politically weaker minorities. So long, however, as the labor of minorities is valuable and negotiable, it constitutes an inducement, and cooperation in maintaining social peace may be valued also. In periods of social stability, however, both these forms of cooperation become routinized and tend to be taken for granted by the economic and political authorities. The reward-value of cooperation then becomes slight. It seems that an appreciable rate of nonconformity and threat may be a necessary condition for maintaining the inducement-potential of cooperative activity by members of disadvantaged groups.

The essential feature of relationships in which the cooperative behavior of one party is an inducement for compliance or cooperation by another is simply that the cooperative behavior of another is *contingent* upon one's own behavior and cannot be assumed to occur "no matter what." We note that in two-person competitive experimental interactions, Deutsch (1973) finds that the strategy most successful in inducing an adversary to cooperate is reciprocal, nonpunitive, and equalitarian — that is, to reward the other party for cooperation but to retaliate in kind for the other's efforts to gain competitive advantage, without escalating the negative sanctions. A firm tit-for-tat policy that is clearly defensive rather than punitive, coupled with rewards for fair exchange, seems to check escalation and to make for rewarding exchanges.

Helping

What shall we make of the behavior of *giving* and *helping*? When one person gives to or helps another, are the consequences those of influence, and if so, of persuasion, inducement, or constraint? The so-called altruistic behaviors of giving and helping are very frequent within solidary groups and less frequent but still quite important across group lines.

Under conditions of very high social solidarity, some helping and giving is done without either compulsion or any specific inducement: it approximates a "pure gift." Such behavior is very rare outside of intimate relations of love, friendship, and kinship. In less solidary relations, as noted in Section 3 above, both *examples* and *cost* become important. Does the apparent need of the potential recipient influence helping? One study shows how complex the main effects are. The self-defined need of the person seeking help did not strongly affect helping behavior. But the donor's perception of need does have a strong effect. That perception, in turn, is influenced by the generous or selfish behavior of a model (Wagner and Wheeler, 1970, 115). It thus appears that if we see someone being helpful to a person we are likely to regard the recipient as having a real or valid need. If the help is not given, we may suspect that the need is less genuine or less urgent.

Factors affecting the likelihood that helping behavior will occur have been identified in various experiments.[5] Included are:

1. competence to help;
2. the immediate costs to the donor of giving help;
3. the presence of other persons; especially those: (a) judged able to help; (b) having an assigned social responsibility to help;
4. anticipated obligations that will be or may be incurred by helping;

5. anticipated risks or threats that may arise as a consequence of helping;
6. social norms of altruism versus rules against "interfering" with others.

Among the costs of helping, there always is the cost of the time forgone from other activities. Apparently the claim of a competing activity can sharply reduce helping behavior even among persons nominally committed to a religiously related altruism. Students at a theological seminary who were in a hurry to go to a building to give a talk on the parable of the Good Samaritan were no more likely to help than those going to talk on a nonrelevant topic. Only the degree of hurry, not religiosity, significantly predicted likelihood of helping. Since the subject's hurry was induced by the experimenter, whom the subject was helping, the persons in the high-hurry condition seem to have been caught between two sets of implicit obligations.

Helping is more likely when the potential donor:

1. has recently received help—which may mean that a norm of helping or of reciprocity is salient;
2. sees someone else helping;
3. perceives only low cost in helping;
4. perceives the need for help as owing to external factors beyond the control of the person who is in need;
5. has very recently experienced success or gratification rather than failure or deprivation;
6. believes that the recipient will know of the help and the identity of the helper;
7. expects that the person helped will be seen again (Berkowitz and Macaulay, 1970).

Observe: the person who receives help has either persuaded or induced the donor to help—no matter how slight the influence may appear. Once again we see the striking fact that a properly socialized, sensitized, and motivated actor may be strongly moved by the sheer presence of another person—in these cases, a person perceived as "needing help." The effectiveness of the person-in-need as a *persuasive* stimulus depends *upon a relationship of social solidarity*. Effectiveness in terms of inducement depends upon apparent costs, rewards, and future interdependence.

It is apparent, then, that sheer appeals to need from a disadvantaged ethnic minority to authorities in a different and advantaged ethnic grouping are unlikely to be highly persuasive. Somewhat more effective, it seems to us, are the inducements that may become built into systems of giving-dependence-reciprocity. For a flow of "gifts" from the economically and politically advantaged necessarily creates implicit or explicit claims to reciprocity, e.g., of future service, of compliance with norms, or deference.

Exchange

For intergroup relations in which asymmetrical dependence is undesired, the one remaining type of inducement that may be acceptable is exchange. In exchange, the transfer is not regarded as establishing relations of dependence but at most of *inter*dependence. Hence when both parties have resources desired by the other, trading is advantageous; and self-respecting systems of exchange are a common mode of intergroup accommodation. Exchange systems, unlike threat systems, can be easily expanded into complex networks of mutual advantage. Therefore the search for appropriate exchanges is an important part of efforts to build peaceable and productive relations in pluralistic societies.

The growth of solidarity and organization within minorities can enhance possibilities for inducement/exchange. That high levels of mutual intergroup trust are assets for individuals in terms of emotional and social security seems self-evident. But the significance of trust as a social resource is not easy to grasp in its full particularity and widely ramifying effects. Modern systems of economic exchange are networks of *promises*. What changes hands in millions of transactions is a piece of paper or an entry in a computer. Observe how many kinds of promises we accept and exchange: currency, checks, credit cards, stocks, bonds, certificates of deposit, letters of credit, mortgages, bank deposit slips, notes, tickets of admission, warranty certificates and guarantees, bank drafts, postal money orders, bills of exchange, vouchers, "numbers" slips, lottery tickets. Loss of trust in such promises can be economically disastrous. Low levels of trust in economic promises among individuals in low-income urban areas lead to heavy costs through reliance on loan-sharks, the numbers racket, and high-interest buying on credit. Under conditions of high trust in stable communities, mutual aid can serve in lieu of money capital in establishing economic enterprises, can reduce or obviate dependence on external sources for family support and child care, can reduce and regulate social deviance. To the extent that *other* resources are present—skill, tradition, information, capital, access to markets (or to supplies, credit, sources of economic and political information, etc.)—the higher the level of social trust, the greater the possibilities for sharing among members of the relevant community.[6] As Coleman summarizes the point:

> In short it appears that the provision of any community asset requires
> two elements: some set of individual resources that *can* be shared . . .
> and the cohesion, institutions, and system of trust that allows these

resources to serve the whole community. . . . The community cohesion and trust act as a multiplier, multiplying the assets of individuals by the number of individuals to make the assets of all available to each (Coleman, 1971, 41-42).

It would be an obvious and therefore almost willful error to regard ethnic-racial minorities in the United States as devoid of resources for effective inducement vis-à-vis political and economic authorities. But the error is prevalent. To assume, for example, that black Americans have only a Hobson's Choice between the weak effects of persuasion and the strong but costly tactics of threat is to ignore completely the enormous resources actually commanded by the more than 22 million people who are black. There is a vast "black market," represented by a total purchasing power of over 40 billion dollars as of the early 1970s. The growth of a substantial, black middle class has created strong incentives for producers and distributors of consumer goods to avoid obvious discrimination and to make special positive appeals. Reenfranchisement and concentrated voting power in many important urbanized areas makes the potential "black vote" a mighty inducement for many political aspirants. Increasing numbers of skilled and well-educated black persons are desired as employees in business and government. Increasingly, inducements are two-way flows.

But inducements are generated within a set of overarching institutional arrangements. Structural conditions of power, authority, and the distribution of scarce rewards and facilities in a society establish the primary inducements to and constraints upon social conflict. When there are dominant and subordinate groups and strata, the subordinates will receive many demands and will be expected to give much deference to members of dominant social formations. When relations of accommodation to these inequalities begin to break down, the typical accompaniment is an increase in open conflict (Grimshaw, 1971).

To these matters we now turn in Chapter 7.

The Uses of Constraint: Power, Authority, and Threat Systems in Intergroup Relations

Relations among ethnic, racial, and religious collectivities frequently involve overt conflict and even more often entail inequalities of power and social rewards. Because such collectivities in the United States are subordinate segments of a large and complex nation-state, relations among them inevitably have a strong political aspect. If continuous strife is to be avoided, or even somewhat controlled, some societal rules concerning intergroup struggles must be established—and then changed when relative power and other basic conditions change. For other reasons to be explored in this chapter, any realistic consideration of intergroup relations must pay close attention to power, authority, and the varying ways in which coercive means are used to change or to maintain particular states of those relations.

1. Limits and Constraint: Problems of Power and Control

Accordingly, we now leave the relatively benign world of the last two chapters— the realms of persuasion, conversion, convergence, inducement, and exchange. No society operates solely on the basis of the happy circumstances of achieved consensus and mutually advantageous exchange—not even if we allow for the use of persuasion its many and varied guises. In addition to the influences of social approval or sociability systems, of consensus systems, and of exchange systems, every society contains systems of threat and constraint. Such systems of attempted coercive influence by partisans and of attempted social control of challengers by the authorities are very prominent indeed in racial and

193

ethnic relations. This central prominence is easy to understand when we recall that ethnic and racial relations the world over have originated primarily in processes of conquest, enslavement, expulsion, or migration—processes that usually signify fate-control by members of one collectivity over the members of another.

Recall from earlier chapters that authority is here conceived as the right to make binding decisions for a collectivity; this right is based on legitimated coercion, and that coercion (as effective threat) rests on control of resources and especially on control of the means of violence. Remember also that the power of authorities is "social control," but the power of partisans (those who are subject to authorities) is influence, especially in the form of threat, i.e., the power to produce disadvantages for authorities (Gamson, 1968). The numerous ways in which constraints may be imposed upon the behavior of other persons or collectivities range from directly inflicting injury or deprivation, to blocking access or exit, to overt threats, and to indirect intimidation and subtle hints.

The uses made of constraints, i.e., in terms of the *goals* to which constraint is directed or the *consequences* of constraining another actor in specific ways, may differ depending on whether the user is an authority seeking social control of the actions of a partisan, or a partisan seeking to affect the binding decisions of an authority, or—a case not identical with either of the others—two parties who have a partisan-to-partisan relationship.[1] Within each of the three types of relationship, we may again subdivide the types of constraint according to whether the aim seems to be primarily to prevent immediate actions, to deter the recipient from certain potential future actions, to elicit compliance with social norms, or to instigate new behavior. For example, the leaders of an ethnic organization may use their ability to organize an effective work stoppage to demonstrate to city officials that it is to their advantage to change a social control, e.g., a civil service rule, rather than to enforce it.

Constraints can be implicit. The sheer presence of military forces, police in uniform, a silent crowd waiting outside the legislative hall, a revolver on the desk—all symbolize the potential for coercive restraint in the situations in which they occur. The effects, however, are not always self-evident. For example, although some studies have found that the sheer presence of a weapon is associated with increased aggressive behavior (Berkowitz, 1968), in some other populations and in other contexts the physical presence of a firearm was followed by decreased aggression, thus making its presence a form of constraint (Ellis, Weinir, Miller, 1971).[2]

When coercion, whether of physical threat or restraint or of symbolic manipulation, is used by *authorities*, it can be regarded as social control. Social control is always control *for* someone or something. Thus the prevention and minimization of conflict may advantage some individuals and collectivities more than others, even though such control may be advantageous in the long run and in varying degrees to all parties. The principle is manifested most clearly when two or more potential authorities claim exclusive legitimacy of political control. When such contradictory claims force potential subjects to choose between those who claim exclusive power, then the relative capabilities for coercion of the rival potential authorities become crucial. The weight of historical experience seems to be on the side of the hypothesis advanced by Leites and Wolfe (1970): as between a choice of obeying one or another of two or more potential authorities, the behavior of target persons will be primarily controlled by perceptions of which of the authorities is most *able and willing to inflict negative sanctions*. This belief in the relative coercive capabilities usually will be a more powerful determinant of compliant behavior than the perceived ability of one of the potential authorities to deliver current or future rewards, if the potentially rewarding party lacks the primary coercive resources and the resolution to apply them in the immediate situation. This principle holds, of course, only under conditions in which extreme polarization is coupled with extreme threat of drastic sanctions. But these are just the conditions that are crucial in situations of severe political struggle. In less stressful circumstances of peaceful exercise of generally accepted authority, the importance of rewards increases relative to threat and punishment.[3]

The exercise of social constraint by authorities tends to produce greater conflict when social groupings are segmental and are arranged in hierarchical order ("pyramidal-segmentary") than when the social structure consists of cross-cutting, overlapping groupings. When each successively smaller group is included in a larger structure, any conflict between the larger collectivities necessarily ties together all subordinate groupings and thereby raises the stakes to include all the interests of the individuals who are dependent on these group memberships. Furthermore, it seems that oppression is likely to be more deeply resented than exploitation; that is, coercive subjugation seems to be more humiliating and damaging than economic disadvantage. To be denigrated is experienced as more obnoxious than to be deprived. It is partly for this reason that the exercise of political authority usually is more crucial for social conflict than the exercise of economic power alone.

The interaction between social structure and the use of constraint in inter-group relations is illustrated in the important case of external threat. When the members of a solidary collectivity—a group, a community, a nation—sense a threat or criticism from outside, the most common effect is an increase in ethnocentric prejudice toward the threatening or critical outsider. Indeed, negative evaluations of the outgroup typically become symbolic of ingroup unity. Any constraint imposed by external authority upon a collectivity—

for example, enforcing regulations that prohibit ethnic discrimination—may produce these effects, and successful accommodation requires countering such undesired consequences (Williams, 1947, 58). Of course, there are many situations in which one may decide to criticize or threaten a collectivity even when a "backlash" is expected; in such cases the defensive mobilization of the target-grouping simply has to be accepted as an inevitable cost when one advances criticism or applies coercion to express predominant values or to carry out some essential part of a larger or longer-range strategy.

Constraint as a basic method of influence is primarily used by powerful groups, ruling strata, governing elites, established social authorities. When a polity is stable, the pervasive constraint is not conspicuous to those who have access to the authorities. But the excluded partisans feel its weight, especially when they seek change. Although it is true that conflict often occurs among collectivities of approximately equal power, the more widespread and chronic conflicts are those between dominant and subordinant groupings (Deutsch, 1973, 93). But, as we noted earlier, the have-nots, precisely because they are have-nots, usually lack the capability to persuade or induce the authorities to alter the basic distribution of resources or the institutionalized rules. Hence, if and when the initially powerless finally gain prominence in the political arena, it usually is because they have been able to pose a realistic threat to the decision-makers.

Examples of Coercion by Authorities

In a society in which a superordinate grouping imposes discrimination upon a racial or ethnic minority, any highly visible increase in the relative numbers of the minority is likely to be perceived as potentially dangerous by the dominant grouping. The power-threat curve should go up with an increasing slope with higher proportions of the minority in the total population. For example, this prediction was specified by Blalock (1967, 159) to mean that the historical occurrence of lynching in southern areas would be disproportionately greater with higher proportions of black population. Using improved methods of calculating rates, Reed (1972, 356) shows that the prediction fits the case of Mississippi counties during the period 1889-1930.

A remarkable example of the use of constraints is found in the case of South Africa where four million whites seem to have nearly complete economic and political dominance over fifteen million nonwhites. How is this possible? Control in this instance has been characterized as rule by a "pragmatic race oligarchy" which totally excludes nonwhites from all crucial areas of power, uses extensive and detailed surveillance and police control, fragments potential nonwhite power by curtailing mobility and communication, and allows a selective trickle-down of economic rewards. The government has attempted also to neutralize political dissent by a policy of developing geographically segregated but not politically autonomous ethnic-racial enclaves (Bantustans). The initial effects were to institutionalize and compartmentalize the expression of intergroup struggle, in the interest of weakening and containing dissent. The dominant regime has had large resources, a high degree of unity on the general directions to be followed in basic governmental policies, effective organization — and considerable flexibility in particular tactics (Adam, 1971). The latter feature has been underestimated by observers who concentrated attention upon the rigidity of the whites' ideology. But the "pragmatic oligarchy" when faced with new power relationships resulting from the collapse of the power of metropolitan Portugal in neighboring territories (Southwest Africa, Mozambique, Angola) immediately initiated communication with the new black governments and set up a banking organization to extend credit and promote trade. For present purposes, we do not need to follow the continuing political struggles and changes in that part of the world.

Coercive Tactics of Partisans

Any social actor may be an authority in one situation and a potential partisan in another, and the two positions may be interchanged from one time to the next. When seeking to exert influence upon the decisions of authorities, partisans may exercise constraints in two primary ways: (1) through existing political institutions and arrangements, (2) through extrainstitutional mobilization, usually in some form of direct collective action. For minorities with unsatisfied political demands that cannot be effectively presented through the institutionalized electoral, legislative, and judicial channels, the only means of gaining strength is through the development of a cohesive organization. Once organized, the group can then "multiply resources" to be used for inducement and, especially, for pressure (Coleman, 1971, 74-78).

Rarely can the imposition of constraints by partisans against authorities proceed without cost. The tactics of threat lead toward polarization and politicization. A weak minority can afford a program of threat, without high risk of self-defeating action, only if it has powerful allies or can count on relatively great flexibility in the threatened group (Blalock, 1967, 180)[4] — either because the latter's abundant resources give scope for relatively easy concessions or because the dominant collectivity actually lacks cohesion or effective organization. Otherwise, a challenge to dominance reliably produces mobilization of the authorities. For example in the early phases (1945-60) of the movement for civil and political rights for black Americans in the South, white mobilization against black demands for increased political participation resulted in sharply *decreased* black registration in areas where the proportion of blacks in the total population was between 30 and 60 percent. Below and above these percentages the registration rates did not change so sharply, reflecting a more stable power situation (Matthews and Prothro, 1963, 28-29).

2. Characteristics of Constraint in Intergroup Relations

Social control is greatly dependent upon the presumption among those subject to it that noncompliance or defiance will be met by the imposition of negative sanctions, with the support or acquiescence of relevant others. Thus all political regimes, from tribes to world powers, rely upon negative sanctions, loyal enforcers, and massive acquiescence in what has been called the grand bluff of authority. Because disadvantaged partisans tend to be collectively weak, there is a negative relationship, on the whole, between dissatisfaction based on disadvantage and hope of success in a potential conflict with a regime. It is quite understandable, therefore, that collective conflict against incumbent authorities is most likely when a disadvantaged collectivity's sense of potential power is increasing. Accordingly, "great power inequalities increase dissatisfaction at the individual level but for this to be collectively recognized, some power and some expectation of improvement by one's own efforts in opposition to an adversary is necessary" (Kriesberg, 1973, 92). When used by partisans, the constraints (of threat, withdrawal, nonco-operation, disruption, injury, etc.) are effective only if the authorities make binding decisions that are desired by the partisans (including the authorities' retreat or abdication). How are constraints actually used, and with what effects?

Because disadvantaged racial and ethnic minorities necessarily must start from a position of relative lack of power, special attention must be given to the probable reactions of authorities to attempted use of constraint. In Chapter 6, we noted the frequent appearance of reactance—a sociopsycholog-ical process that, by hypothesis, may seem to imply that all attempts to use constraints will arouse a specific form of resistance, elicited by any sense of loss of freedom to choose (Brehm, 1966, 2). Is it therefore impossible for minorities to effectively reduce the power of dominant authorities?

Obviously, behavioral freedom may be threatened or reduced in many ways, ranging from a specific personal prohibition by another individual to obstruction through impersonal events or chance. Even though the object eliminated may be the least desired of a set of choices, when it is withdrawn the freedom *not* to choose it has also been withdrawn, and behavioral freedom is correspondingly reduced. Similarly, an attempt to influence another person supports the acting individual's own position. Even a favor, if it is seen as forcing something upon the recipient, can produce reactance.

But the response is thought to occur only when a person believes he or she has the *right* to choose. When choices are made under conditions of subordination to a recognized authority, reactance may be absent or slight, depending upon the attractiveness of the desired alternative (low), the degree of perceived legitimacy of the subordinate role (high), and the realistic appraisal of the likelihood of regaining options (low).

Experiencing reactance tends to produce one or more of the following effects upon the person: (1) an increased desire for the behavior that has been eliminated or threatened, and an increased feeling of being able to have what was eliminated or threatened; (2) a tendency to engage in the threatened behavior; (3) a tendency to engage in any behavior that implies he or she could also engage in the threatened or eliminated behavior; (4) a tendency to encourage an "equivalent person to engage in the threatened or eliminated behavior or in a behavior that implies he could so engage" (Brehm, 1966, 118-19).

To the extent that these reactions are typical outcomes of a sense of illegitimate restriction of choice by other persons, organizations, regimes, or institutions, it is clear that the use of unusual constraints is a two-edged weapon in intergroup relations. In dominant-subordinate relationships between collectivities, for instance, it often happens that the members of a dominant grouping regard any increase of the subordinate's power as a threat to their "freedom"—their freedom to feel superior to and to control subordinate persons. Under these conditions, even a small increase in power or rewards among subordinates is likely to be perceived as a step leading toward greater and greater threats. The pattern has been caricatured in such clichés as, "If we let them get away with this now, there is no telling what they will want next," and "If you let black children into the schools, you would better be prepared to have your daughter marry one."[5] One common element in many such responses is the leap from a sense that there is a threat to freedom in one area to the fear that it will be lost in another.

Yet much free behavior eventually is successfully controlled and ceases to be regarded as a right, e.g., acceptance of compulsory vaccination and health quarantine or acceptance of prohibitions against enforced segregation in public facilities. In many such cases, what were originally regarded as arbitrary threats have come to be defined as routine enforcement of legitimate rules. As Deutsch (1973, 124) has pointed out, although threats often are interpreted as signals of ill-will, persons being threatened do not always react with resistance or hostility.

Reactance is lessened by legitimation or justification—by giving normatively accepted grounds for the imposed loss of options. Where authority is acknowledged, there will be tendencies to seek restoration of freedom in indirect or substitute ways rather than by direct attempts to exercise the precluded options (Brehm, 1966, 8).

Especially noteworthy is the effectiveness of threat, supported by sanctions, in producing changed behavior in situations in which each individual suffers loss if he or she alone changes but no one loses if everyone else conforms to a new requirement. This mechanism for avoiding "innovation loss" is highly important in eliminating discrimination and segregation, e.g., in restaurants, hotels, and other commercial facilities (Coleman, 1971, 59). Furthermore, under conditions of constraint, attempts to resume blocked activities apparently are drastically reduced in situations in which recovery of the eliminated freedom is perceived as impossible: "the effects may be minimized when they clearly fly in the face of reality." Under extreme constraint, indeed, there may be a sour grapes effect, i.e., individuals in a high-pressure/low-reactance situation actually minimize the value of the eliminated behavior (Brehm, 1966, 119).

Experimental findings indicate that limitations of free behavior seem to be followed by reactance even when the restriction is perceived as unintended or as occurring purely by chance. However, it seems plausible to bet on the (untested) hypothesis that reactance will be greater when a restriction appears to be intentional and personally directed. Agents of social control who exhibit vindictive and sadistic behavior under the cover of enforcing institutional rules arouse especially strong feelings of reactance to unjust constraint. Such reactions are common among members of low-income, low-power minorities who encounter the police as the front-line instruments of violent social control by ruling strata and groupings. There is abundant evidence in the United States that programs of so-called human relations by police departments often fail to mask the punitive (not "fraternal") orientations of the police. For example, a detailed case study of the Police-Community Relations Unit in predominantly black Richmond, Virginia, depicts a program of this kind that failed to arouse enthusiasm among the people most directly familiar with the actual conduct of police (Norris, 1973).

When many persons thus experience a common fate of being repeatedly subjected to capricious coercive control, they are likely to regard the holders of power as unfair and illegitimate. If the subordinated population then acquires a sense that collective resistance is feasible, one of its first acts will be to challenge the legitimacy of the incumbent authorities or of the entire regime they represent.

In rejection of authority, a group refuses to recognize claims to legitimacy, e.g., it is asserted that the courts have no right to try a black defendant because the entire legal system allegedly is "racist."

Reactance, then, is one of the bases of the many forms of political noncooperation, including public rejection of governmental authority, noncompliance with requests and orders, refusal to accept release on bail, suspension of publication of restricted or censored newspapers and magazines, noncompliance with cease and desist orders and refusal to pay taxes or post bonds (Sharp, 1973, 281).

If the use of punitive sanctions by authorities is intended to deter specific types of actions, what little evidence we can find suggests that effectiveness is greatest when most offenses are promptly detected and punished by moderate sanctions, those sanctions regarded as "proportionate" to the seriousness of the offense. But an entirely different set of possibilities appears if we examine situations in which authorities attempt to totally suppress dissent through the use of terror. "Terror" in this special sense is a complex condition. The population is allowed to learn of mysterious deaths, disappearances, and torture. It is made known that secret police and informers are at work, and that eavesdropping, spying, wiretapping, and the like are being carried out. Rumors are encouraged. Arrests, detentions, confiscations, beatings, killings, imprisonments occur without warning and without public explanation. Sanctions seem to be arbitrarily applied. Some apparently exemplary conformists are punished. The pattern of *inexplicable capriciousness* is superimposed upon overtly legalistic processes. The impression that may be sought, if these practices derive from deliberate policies, is that no one is safe, that surveillance is omnipresent, that the most innocent-seeming deviance can be fatal — in short, one cannot be too careful. The aim often is not deterrence at all but rather the inculcation of obedience in a radically changed social system.

Under conditions of control by terror, all private, voluntary social formations are permeated by distrust, and friends and family members are encouraged by authorities to inform against those closest to them. A pervasive sense of insecurity and continuous exposure is created. A sense of pseudoreality is created by staged events and by pronouncements made by the authorities, which nearly all members of the population know to be false. The disorienting effects of such forced acquiescence in false images and assertions is reinforced by the apparent senselessness of the terror. The world of actual events is made to appear as phantasmagoric; manipulation of events and reports creates continually shifting sets of mixed illusions and realities, of falsehoods and valid perceptions that merge into complex successions of blurred images, creating diffuse anxieties and continual apprehensions.

If immobilization of dissent is achieved by terror, the outcome may *not* be apathy — for the authorities may insist upon continuous, strenuous public participation and the intimidated populace then throws itself into activity as an escape from apprehensiveness and impotence.

On the other hand, severely coercive regimes become highly vulnerable to countercoercion when they lose both their monopoly of violent means and the unified social organization that formerly sustained an atmosphere of invincible repression. As we noted, a major factor in violent collective bids for political power is the appearance of weakness and disunity in the dominant grouping. Cues that will create an appearance of weakness may take many forms: public dissension among authorities, lack of negative sanctions for defiance, ill-timed concessions ("too little and too late"), signs of fright or timidity among those who normally exercise coercive authority, support for protesters or rebels from police or military forces, threats that are not carried out, known lack of resources, or quick capitulation to extreme demands.

In general, therefore, we can expect that the use of coercion by a weaker party against a strong set of authorities will be most frequent as well as most successful when the partisans are gaining in relative power. The sense of growing strength can emerge from greater collective awareness and consensus, greater control of resources, increased aid from third parties, and increased belief in the weakness of the dominant party. If a rapidly increasing sense of potential efficacy coincides with increased grievances that are attributed to the incumbent authorities, the stage is set for attempts to coerce the latter. The incompetence of the leaders of the grouping "not only weakens their legitimacy but makes them weak and vulnerable. Assuming that there are always grounds for dissatisfaction, the weakness of the formerly stronger party invites rebellion" (Kriesberg, 1973, 131).

Thus far, in reviewing how dominant collectivities use constraint, we have seen that the outcomes can range from nearly total dominance by means of political terror to situations in which attempted coercion elicits revolution. We have seen that it is the *interplay* between the strengths and weaknesses of partisans and authorities that shapes the actual character of intergroup relationships. Let us now look more closely at the possible uses of constraint by partisans against authorities.

3. Concerted Action: Mobilization and Organization

Let us first remind outselves of a few basic considerations that appear almost self-evident but that are often overlooked in diagnosis and in action.

—By definition, partisans are not those who make the binding decisions but are the individuals and collectivities who are subject to binding decisions made by others (the authorities). To the large extent that disadvantaged strata and ethnic collectivities in the United States have been outside the main decision-making positions, they have been continually placed in the position of partisans. To attain their goals, accordingly, they must seek to bring influence to bear upon persons and organizations that are successfully claiming the right to make collectively binding decisions.

—Unorganized masses of individuals cannot effectively influence authorities.

—Nor can "The People" as a total aggregate act directly to produce collective decisions for large and heterogeneous social groups.

—Neither diffuse action based on popular convictions nor the efforts of a few concerned individuals acting independently of one another can produce effective national political initiative. What is required is that individuals and subgroupings be definitely *organized* in order to aggregate and to articulate interests and to produce actionable demands. Compare this conclusion with Steiner's analysis of the use of the formal mechanism of the popular initiative in Switzerland: "The rule is that the popular initiative is used by well-organized groups such as political parties and economic interest groups" (Steiner, 1974, 203).

—Actionable demands are those for which a definite decision for or against a proposed line of action can be taken. The demand to "do something" is not actionable. (It is even less helpful in reaching decisions than the classic telegraphed message allegedly received by a Congressman urging him to "use your own judgment.")

—We are considering only the cases in which authorities will not spontaneously act to always favor a deprived partisan group, obviating any need for influence.

It follows directly from these assumptions and conclusions that members of disadvantaged groupings must create special organizations for unified action and must concentrate their resources if they are to carry out actions that will produce desired decisions from authorities. The mobilization of uncommitted resources is particularly necessary and problematic for groupings having less initial power and public standing than the established authorities they are opposing. Therefore, disaffected and dissenting collectivities are likely to carry out many actions aimed at *developing resources* rather than *directly exerting immediate influence* upon authorities (Gamson, 1968, 108).

Mobilization and concerted action are facilitated by territorial concentration, easy communication, high visibility of common interests and grievances, high education, substantial control of income, politically experienced leadership, high intragroup trust. Many aggrieved groups lack most of these strategic assets. Unless the organizational focus can be created to bring together the scattered aspirations and grievances of the potential partisans, even widespread discontent cannot acquire "hands and feet." Furthermore, objective deprivation and oppression will have produced in many members of disadvantaged minorities the conviction that they are faced with overwhelming coercive capacity in the hands of committed supporters of an existing regime. Concerted action is necessary to demonstrate that the authorities are not omnipotent.[6]

Under less extreme conditions, when only limited reforms rather than a major transfer of authority are sought, individuals frequently lack adequate information concerning their condition and means of changing it, and do not have social cohesion or the organization required to solve the fundamental dilemma that is called the Problem of Collective Action. This basic problem arises because *collective* welfare and *individual* welfare do not coincide, in the absence of a mediating social organization. Specifically, especially in large and complex social systems, there are many cases in which any hypothetical self-interested individual who is not being coerced and who is fully rational in the pursuit of his or her interests nevertheless will not join with others to attain even a greatly desired common or group interest unless induced by some external incentive. The fact that all will gain if all invest effort and resources will not suffice. Collective action in heterogeneous and large collectivities must rely heavily upon external incentives and coercion (Olson, 1965; Buckley, Burns, Meeker, 1974). The essential reason already mentioned is that each must sacrifice to gain collective ends, but if the collective effort succeeds, all will benefit, including the dissidents, the laggards, and others who did not do their part. This is the "free-rider" dilemma. Only through organization can it be solved, when organization means that universally binding rules are enforced upon all members. When sufficient solidarity can be generated through mutual identification, recognition of common values, recognition of shared fate, and group sentiments—one can mobilize individuals to establish "mutual coercion, mutually agreed upon." The Black Revolt of the 1950s and 1960s is a remarkable case in point.

The difficulties that lie in the way of those who would mobilize weak potential partisans may seem insuperable. Is it actually possible for a less powerful segment or subcollectivity to cause a dominant collectivity to increase the rewards, opportunities, and power of the less powerful? The answer is yes. The evidence of the unqualified positive answer is that, in fact, such success has been attained on many occasions—as in the rise of trade unionism in industrial countries, the extension of the franchise, the protection of children, the rights of women, the independence of colonies, and the status of ethnic minorities.

Can success be gained through the use of constraint? Again, the answer is yes, but the necessary conditions and strategies are complex. One central variable is the intensity of pressure and threat and conflict. Extreme measures invite retaliation and repression. But continuous, "moderate" protests, demands, claims, and threats can create an incessant pressure without at any point setting off an irreversible buildup of counterthreats and of resort by the authorities to increasingly drastic means.

But if the less powerful grouping has little to offer as inducement and is unable to persuade by sheer appeal to values and beliefs, it will have to resort to threats and conflict.[7] Resort to conflict encourages escalation of means in a rising spiral of injury and counterattack. Can the escalation be avoided without giving up the possibility of gains?

Violence does not create an effective political threat when it appears to be sheerly expressive and when no organized group appears to make focused demands. A striking case is the massive riot in Winston-Salem, North Carolina, in 1967 that was set off by the death of a black man who had been beaten by a white city policeman. That act of police brutality resulted in turmoil that necessitated a force of 1,000 National Guard troops being sent to the city, in property damage of more than one million dollars and in 200 arrests (mostly of black persons, of course). It was a costly police action. But there was at that time no organized partisan collectivity and no militant black leadership to put forward tangible demands for redress of grievances and for a larger share in allocative decisions, nor was the riot publicly defined as a political action. The collective violence remained as an isolated expression of moral outrage, while the white elite continued for the time being to control the same repressive local system that had produced that outrage in the first place (Moore, 1970). Political passivity and lack of organization thus made it impossible for the riot to become a point of leverage for effective action on behalf of the disadvantaged racial minority.

Individuals or collectivities which do not have positive values to offer in exchange nevertheless may and often do desire greater income, wealth, prestige, influence, power, or authority. If they cannot otherwise elicit the desired responses, the only remaining recourse is to attempt bargaining through deprivational, punishing, and threatening actions. Members of disadvantaged collectivities that lack skills and knowledge or resources of high value in exchange must confront authorities from a position of weak bargaining power. If they are to gain influence, they will find it necessary, sooner or later, to resort to threat and violence. Such attempts are "unconventional politics." "In an important way both violence and politics are outside the formal and legal processes of conflict resolution. Both represent the dynamic factors by which social consensus is itself reinforced and modified" (Nieburg, 1969, 9).

A well-justified recognition of the limited effectiveness of coercion alone when used by partisans as a means of influence should not lead us into the serious error of underestimating the social control effects of highly organized coercive systems when used by authorities in conjunction with positive incentives for compliance with authoritative decisions. For ethnic partisans facing such systems of control a flexible strategy of unceasing pressure but varying specific means seems to have greatest average chances of success. A strategy of unceasing pressure is likely, of course, to make members of the dominant grouping more or less uncomfortable, defensive, and often resentful. But these responses are consequential only if they instigate undesired actions. To minimize and to contain any countermobilization that these responses may produce, it will be helpful if the assertive minorities use tactics and put forward requests, claims, and demands that are defensible in terms of their opponents' own high-ranked values and beliefs. In situations of conflict, persons who have long experienced racial discrimination may use violence and justify it as a response to alleged conspiratorial actions by the authorities of the dominant ethnic group. Such charges tend to escalate the conflict. Successful negotiations may require a tempering of the rhetoric of uncompromising righteous indignation: "To hold out for total victory, and believe that nothing short of total humiliation for the other party merits consideration, is but to adopt a futile path in conflict situations" (Tunteng, 1973, 240).

On the other hand, we must hasten to add that weak minorities struggling against discrimination need not be unduly sensitive to the discomfort of their opponents nor unduly apprehensive about the effects of their actions upon the safety of the larger polity. For one thing, situations of very severe mutual threat are not necessarily unstable. Contrary to some impressions, even the classic escalation represented by an "arms race" between nations does not necessarily lead to increasing instability; stable standoffs are possible under the extreme condition of a balance of terror, which "amounts to a tacit understanding backed by a total exchange of all conceivable hostages" (Schelling, 1960, 239). And often the defensive mobilization of authority groups may be alleviated to some extent by frequent reminders of shared goals and values and of common and complementary interests. Useful also are expressions of willingness to consider alternative means to effect necessary changes, especially when actual flexibility in tactics can indeed be manifested along with firm commitment to major goals. The likelihood of unwanted escalation can be reduced also by concentrating the effort of the less powerful grouping more upon increasing its own resources and cohesion than upon destroying the resources of its adversary (Deutsch, 1973).

Thus for understanding intergroup relations within our own society there may be important lessons to be learned from analyses of international uses of constraints. It often has been assumed that mutual deterrence policies lead to unlimited arms races. But stable mutual deterrence sometimes is achieved when each party maintains protected retaliatory capabilities sufficient to destroy or inflict unacceptable damage upon an aggressor after receiving an all-out attack. In such cases, the basic limit on escalation is the "diminishing returns" of additional threat posed by additional offensive capacity of the opponent, when there is a mutual attempt to maintain deterrence. As the number of parties involved increases, however, the size of the necessary retaliatory forces increases so rapidly that it may be prohibitively costly for more than two "parties" (units or coalitions) to maintain mutual deterrence (Kupperman and Smith, 1972). Although a large number of other conditions—e.g., technological vulnerability, accuracy of intelligence (in relation to deception), alternative weapons systems—affect the stability of mutual deterrence, the principle of diminishing incremental threat tends to produce stability, although at high levels of armed readiness.

A radically different outcome is likely if policies are directed not toward retaliatory capacity for assured destruction but toward ensuring capacity to continue offensive action after absorbing attack. There is the so-called war-fighting strategy, i.e., a multistage series of offensive exchanges in which an attacker would reserve some forces as a counterthreat to retaliation. The attacked party thus would need to have a surviving counterforce to meet the threat of the reserved weapons of the attacker. Somewhat analogous situations in domestic intergroup struggles tend to produce extended sequences of conflicts that rarely produce mutually satisfactory settlements.

One crucial difference between international and domestic relationships of collectivities is that in most intranational struggles both parties operate under some common rules within the same polity. This implies that legal means have an important place in domestic intergroup relations.

4. Law and Authority; Partisans and Claims to Rights

Controversies are numerous among persons who attempt to make strategic judgments concerning the effectiveness of law and legal action in maintaining or changing ethnic relations. Obviously legal means often are used by dominant economic and political groupings to maintain their advantages and power. Legal means may be used by dissidents and by disadvantaged aspiring groups to gain rights and advantages and power. Is law, then, primarily a mechanism for domination, or is it more nearly a mechanism for attaining redress of grievances and access to opportunity? Or, more specifically, what is the extent to which both characterizations fit the reality of American intergroup relations? The negative appraisal holds that unpopular laws are unenforceable, that folkways always defeat statutory laws opposed to them, that change is effective only "in the hearts and minds of men." The positive evaluation "is that social change can be effectively brought about through legal statutes aimed at prohibiting certain actions, enforcing others, or allowing still others" (Coleman, 1971, 55).

Law represents a special form of organized social control and conflict resolution. The diverse kinds of social organization used in the settlement of disputes and other forms of conflict in various societies range from unspecialized and diffuse arrangements to those that are specialized, relatively autonomous, and complex. Some societies lack any specialized organization at all. When agencies for enforcement of norms and regulation of conflict do appear, they seem to emerge in a definite order (Schwartz and Miller, 1964). First comes mediation in which non-kin third parties intervene to settle disputes. Next courts emerge, initially weak in authority and operating with such techniques as oaths, ordeals, and divination. Later appear specialized armed forces (i.e., police) used at least in part for enforcement of norms and penalties. Finally there develops a system of specialized counsel—non-kin advocates who are regularly used in settlement of disputes (Wimberley, 1973). It is a striking indication of underlying regularity in social processes that the occurrence of these types of organization in a sample of 51 preliterate societies forms a precise ordering, as indicated by a Guttman scale with a coefficient of reproducibility of 0.984. There is thus a nearly universal tendency for societies that have courts but not police to have strong corporate kin groups and to use oaths or ordeals (Roberts, 1965). Use of impersonal devices such as ordeals may have made it possible for courts to be effective in dealing with conflicts between strong kinship groupings, even when no police power was available. Such courts could function in situations in which mediation could not secure the necessary voluntary acceptance of recommendations (Wimberley, 1973, 79).

Through long trial and error, legal formalism developed out of efforts to control conflict arising in the very process of attempted settlement of disputes. The bizarre-appearing formalities of medieval courts served to channel and control aggression. The lessons of that development are relevant today:

> *The formal speech and the theatrical gestures of medieval law had a profound significance.* When parties engage in litigation, they are as a rule full of ill-will towards each other; indeed, they may be on the brink of a brawl. It is absolutely vital that their aggressiveness should be curbed. . . . The temper of the litigants had to be cooled down, and it was an excellent thing to force them to pay attention to points of formality. A man who must watch his tongue because a slip of the tongue might make him lose his case is not likely . . . to go into invectives . . . which in their turn might lead to blows. [With similar effect, a rule develops] . . . never to address the other party but always to address the judge. By this trick a direct confrontation of the litigants is avoided (Stark, 1965, 4-5).

"Fully developed" systems of law—those that are most complex—have four major components: rules, agents, judiciary, legislatures. The rules either are written or are relatively explicit norms, customarily and widely recognized. The agents are incumbents of specially designated statuses enpowered to enforce compliance by monitoring, detecting, apprehending, or punishing violators. There is a judiciary, some type of court that mediates or adjudicates disputes or alleged violations of rules, in accordance with some set of procedural and substantive norms. There is a legislature, some social position or collective body that claims and regularly exercises the right to change old rules or to establish new ones (Hoebel, 1954).

Systems of this kind constitute vast networks of relationships for managing, resolving, and, ironically, creating conflicts.

Law defines rights—what belongs to or is due each person or other social unit. To the extent that it thus reduces uncertainty and at the same time is able to obtain adherence to its rules, it *prevents* conflicts. But some conflicts do still emerge, and their legal character often makes them especially intense: every opposition of interests then takes on an ideological quality as a struggle between the just and the unjust (Roling, 1966). Further, the enforcement of law often, perhaps usually, involves substantial bias, arbitrariness, and both willful and inadvertent injustice. Moral indignation and unrequited desires for revenge are two of the usual by-products of "Law"—at least as now observable in the United States.

Some portions of the legal order have been especially productive of felt injustice and accumulated grievances, e.g., the segregation laws of circa 1896-1964 or sex bias in many laws still extant in the 1970s. Other laws and legal procedures directly encourage high rates of institutionalized conflict, e.g., adversary rules in divorce or in provisions of workmen's compensation laws and administrative regulations. In the latter case:

> Although workmen's compensation was meant to overcome the litigious-
> ness that had prevailed under common law employers' liability, it
> actually perpetuated the confrontation of "claimants" and "defendants"
> it had sought to avoid. This it did mainly by preserving the idea that
> benefits would be assessed as a personal liability of the employer toward
> his employee. The system gave the employer an immediate stake in
> each particular claim any of his employees would make. Each claim
> involved a threat of new liabilities, and therefore invited challenge and
> resistance (Nonet, 1969, 67).

In this work we are making a special effort to examine both desired and undesired outcomes of different types of actions and programs. Therefore, we have not presented a great number of "success stories"—only enough examples to indicate what is meant by success and failure, and to suggest hypotheses concerning the conditions that strongly affect outcomes. For illustrating the use of legal challenges in the courts as a method of bringing about change in intergroup relations, a prototype of successful action is supplied by the NAACP Legal Defense and Educational Fund.

To challenge segregation, the National Association for the Advancement of Colored People (established in 1910) set up the Legal Redress Committee, which in 1940 became the Legal Defense and Educational Fund. As Pifer says:

> The achievements of this organization, operating with limited financial support and often in the face of severe public hostility, have become legendary. . . . *Between 1940 and 1963 the Legal Defense Fund argued successfully 43 of the 47 cases it brought before the Supreme Court.* However, it is in the field of education that the most impressive record of legal achievement is to be found. Indeed, it was a case involving segregation in education, *Brown vs. Board of Education*, in 1954, which finally led to the overturn of the "separate but equal" doctrine established by *Plessy v. Ferguson* in 1896 and thereby invalidated the entire framework of legalized or *de jure* segregation (Pifer, 1973, 21-22).

Gains made since the 1930s in black participation, prestige, prosperity, and power, even if very short of achieving equality, have been made possible to a very large extent by *political and legal means*, based on the norms, values, and interests vested in the American constitutional order. It was primarily through the Supreme Court, the Congress, and the federal executive that decisive steps were taken to reinstitute *the rights of blacks as citizens* and to somewhat widen economic and social opportunity. The leverage for such changes basically rests upon the "reserved rights" of the constitutional system. As Greenstone and Peterson note:

> Of the four American regime structures, constitutionalism presents the fewest obstacles to black demands. Of course, constitutionalism has been used to protect the freedom of White Power advocates . . .—but it has been appealed to far more often to protect the rights . . . of blacks seeking to criticize and agitate against white domination. In general, then, blacks will benefit to the extent that official behavior conforms to constitutionalism as a patterning orientation (Greenstone and Peterson, 1973, 313).

How effective are legislative measures and law enforcement in reducing ethnic and racial discrimination? After a detailed review of experience, up to 1952, with legal measures against discrimination Berger concluded:

All this evidence indicates that law in our society is a formidable means for the elimination of group discrimination and for the establishment of conditions which discourage prejudicial attitudes. . . . In summary, law can affect our acts and, through them, our beliefs.

Proper legal controls fortify the unprejudiced and the believers in fair play (Berger, 1952, 192-93).

Many subsequent appraisals of later experience and research essentially support these conclusions (Williams et al., 1964; Simpson and Yinger, 1972; Williams, 1975a). After a period of intensive pressure by civil rights groups, furthermore, it was observed that when discriminatory patterns are not privately supported by some of those who publicly conform to local segregationist demands, antidiscrimination rules often are welcomed because they provide a legitimate alibi for not continuing practices that are distasteful or that have become inexpedient. For example, in the early days of desegregation of public accommodations in the South, "Florida hotel owners were reported needful of federal coercion to integrate, to avoid being accused of doing it voluntarily and subjecting themselves to reprisal" (Schelling, 1965, 367).

We see, then, that enforcement of antidiscrimination statutes can reinforce the convinced, support the waverers and the expedient conformists, and make noncompliance costly to the would-be violators. On the basis of these considerations alone, reforms through legal measures would seem self-evidently advantageous to disadvantaged and aggrieved elements of the polity.

Can legislation and law-enforcement produce major changes in widely shared, long-established and consensually supported patterns of categorical segregation and discrimination? Actually, there is no doubt that on the whole the answer to the question as posed is affirmative. Not affirmative under all circumstances, of course, but definitely true under some conditions. What kinds of conditions? Let us examine an example.

By many different criteria, the state of Mississippi over a long period was one of the most extreme cases of *institutionalized* white supremacy in the United States. It was characterized by legally mandated and enforced segregation in public facilities and services; by large white-black differentials in income and education; by disenfranchisement of the black electorate; and by a history of systemic terrorism (e.g., lynchings) (Silver, 1966). Yet since the late 1950s massive and dramatic changes in race relations have occurred, under the direct influence of law and law-enforcement stemming from Congressional statutes and Supreme Court decisions. These changes have permeated local social systems. A detailed study of Panola County shows how civil rights laws and court decisions have effectively increased voting rights, educational opportunity, and nondiscriminatory employment possibilities (Wirt, 1970).

How are such results possible? For changes of this character to occur, a politically dispossessed minority must have found some ways to avoid disastrous suppression. First of all, the crucial problem of vulnerability to coercion had to be solved (Schelling, 1965). Enforcement of voting rights, for example, could not depend exclusively or primarily upon black persons being willing to testify that their rights had been infringed by political authorities: secrecy of testimony was impossible; for public evidence, not private transmittal of information, was essential (Ross and Wheeler, 1967, 583-85). Two types of solutions have appeared: (1) the intervention of a powerful third party, (2) the inability or unwillingness of a dominant group to take drastic steps. Both processes were apparent in the southern case.

But the fear of reprisals, the lack of knowledge of the law, and the economic costs of using a system that requires adversary proceedings always will deter many aggrieved persons from filing complaints or charges. A study of the 1958 Fair Housing Practices Law of New York City showed very low rates of filing cases. Furthermore, the complainants were disproportionately well-educated, young persons in middle-class occupations. Persons most likely to experience extreme segregation were unlikely to file charges: "44 percent of the complainants already resided in areas 90 percent or more white. . . . The protection of the Fair Housing Practices Law is made use of to a surprising extent by Negroes already resident outside the major ghetto establishments of the city" (Goldblatt and Cromien, 1962, 369).

In general, any law prohibiting segregation or discrimination that relies solely upon individual complaints, especially from a population that is economically and politically vulnerable, will be difficult to enforce and hence will be of limited effectiveness. Even when laws and administrative rulings do not require initiative from disadvantaged and vulnerable victims, they are unlikely to be effective unless enforcement is lodged firmly in responsible parties. As Coleman puts it: "the more nearly a legal action requires implementation by a set of actors who owe no responsibility, direct or indirect, to the lawmakers, the less likely will it be that the action will have an effect" (Coleman, 1971, 57).

When vulnerability can be reduced to low levels, legal measures are likely to have marked effects when there is at least one set of strongly interested parties that is mobilized to seek protection or advantage through the legal channels. A clear example is the immediate use by organized labor of the redefined mechanisms of bargaining established by the National Labor Relations Act of 1935. Although the situation of action was less highly structured, many organizations and groups of black Americans made effective use of the Civil Rights Act of 1964 and the Voting Rights Act of 1965.

It is apparent that the capacity to utilize the law effectively is not equally distributed in the population. A crucial factor is the degree of autonomy a claimant enjoys.

> Legal competence requires a certain degree of autonomy, a detachment of the person from the system of social relations that determine his position and interests. . . . Dependence makes the person insecure and captive of his social situation; it encourages passive acceptance and accommodating compromises, rather than moral assertion (Nonet, 1969, 87).

The analysis we have presented here implies that an extremely important mode of action for establishing and strengthening the power of a disadvantaged ethnic minority in our society is to increase the participation of its members in law-making, law-enforcing, and law-interpreting. Among the crucial points at which the process of empowerment must occur, if it is to be real, are: election to public office, election and appointment to judgeships, selection for jury service, employment in law enforcement positions, training and employment as lawyers (advocates, defenders, solicitors, district attorneys, attorneys-general, and other barristers), appointment to quasijudicial commissions and boards. Recent efforts to increase the number of well-qualified black lawyers in the South show one more facet of the complex uses of resources in strategies of constraint (Spearman and Stevens, 1974).

Given that there is sufficient influence to establish laws useful in protecting rights and opportunities of individuals or ethnic minorities as collectivities, what conditions favor effective enforcement and acceptance of the norms?

A law or rule that prohibits or requires certain actions is most likely to be followed by high rates of conforming behavior when its enforcement occurs under the following conditions:

1. A governmental bureaucracy, with accountable and administratively removable officials, is directly charged with carrying out particular policies.
2. Individuals and organized groupings that have strong interests in implementation also have resources for monitoring violations and bringing sanctions to bear upon violators.
3. Potential complainants have job security or legal resources to defend themselves against potential negative sanctions of those against whom complaints will be directed.
4. Third parties either support enforcement or do not interfere.
5. The actions prohibited or enjoined are overt and public (observable).

6. The actions prohibited or required are clearly identifiable.

7. Potential offenders occupy economic and residential statuses that repeatedly require their presence in the same observable contexts and that involve legally defined responsibilities and duties.

8. The sanctions that are legally enforceable include payments of damages or costs; fines; or withdrawal of contracts, grants, subsidies, exemptions, or compensation; or imprisonment; or liability of being sued, with the attendant possibility of incurring such definite penalties.

9. Positive actions required or permitted by the law, rule, or decisions are capable of being carried out either by definite officials or by individuals who are the directly interested parties.

Chapter 8

Strategy and Tactics
in Collective Action

Dictum: *Whatever the context, there is a good chance that one is better off confronting a skillful and effective recourse to nonviolent action than a savagely ineffectual resort to violence.*[1]

Question: *Perhaps so, but what do we do if our opponent chooses a "savagely* effective*" resort to violence?*

1. The Meanings and Limits of Strategy and Tactics

Particular efforts to alter the behavior of other persons (even apart from unintended or accidental influences) occur in such endless variety as to appear incomprehensible in all their details. But as we have seen, most of the patterns of influence nevertheless can be identified under the three broad headings of persuasion, inducement, or constraint (Gamson, 1968, 74-81). Between the unlimited particularity of concrete instances and the abstractness of such generalized categories are middle-range generalizations about strategies and tactics in purposive collective action.

The central idea of strategy developed historically from military experience, as indicated by the dictionary meanings given to *stratagem*, i.e., "1. a plan, scheme, or trick for surprising or deceiving an enemy. 2. any artifice, ruse, or trick to attain a goal or to gain an advantage over an adversary." By extension a *strategy*, then, means "a plan, method, or series of maneuvers or stratagems for obtaining a specific goal or result." Indeed, it is possible to speak of "a strategy of cooperation" when no element of guile or trickery whatsoever is

215

involved. But the aura of a deadly game of ruse and deception lingers around the word, and we must be aware of these connotations. Things are no more aseptic in the companion term *tactics*, which we find defined as "the art or science of disposing military forces for battle and maneuvering them in battle" or, in a tertiary meaning, "any maneuvers for gaining advantage or success."[2] In short, strategy and tactics are names for instrumental types of actions— those definitely intended to have effect, to defend or to seek some interest or advantage.

Strategies and tactics fascinate us, it seems, by the promise they appear to hold that proper understanding of the appropriate calculations will lead us to—or, at any rate, nearer to—our goals. But, of course, strategies and tactics cannot tell us what our objectives should be in the first place or what moral, aesthetic, and conventional restraints should be respected. An exclusive preoccupation with instrumental rules, calculations of losses and payoffs, options, and "game-plans" often erodes commitments both to goals and to social and moral norms (Tullock, 1969; Firey, 1969). Steadiness of purpose and of loyalties may be incompatible with some strategies for gaining and using power and may preclude the use of otherwise attractive tactics. Especially in the case of leaders of weak minorities, evidences of opportunistic "immoral" tactics can quickly destroy the fragile trust upon which united action depends. More broadly, exclusive stress upon whatever means will bring power can erode the tacit understandings and rules of the game that are essential for any stable political order. In a political democracy, the institutions that regulate the striving for power and the settlement of conflicts must also limit the strategies that are permissible. There are occasions when technically effective instrumental means must be subordinated to other values and norms, *if* a given social order is to be maintained. A "pure strategy" approach does not itself generate any societal objectives, save "victory" or "power," nor does it provide shared moral guidelines.

There are, after all, two basic dimensions to the use of strategic thinking in politics. The first is the use of strategy within a framework of morals and tradition to *attain* objectives; this is strategy as used under the representative ideal. The second is the use of strategy outside such a framework to prescribe objectives, notably winning as an end in itself (Auspitz and Brown, 1974, 52).

To these two dimensions we must add a third. Many of the struggles that are carried on by ethnic minorities within our society represent attempts to alter the dominant values and norms, or at least some of the particular applications of those values and norms. The central problem in these cases is not the effects of purely instrumental political action versus "moral" politics but rather a struggle over *which* norms are to be followed. The main question then is not what strategies and tactics are most effective but which are most effective when questions of values and goals have been settled.

All strategies, of course, involve at least some implicit trading off of actual and predicted costs and benefits. To decide what strategies are possible and what the costs and benefits may be cannot be done exclusively by general rule, but always requires close appraisal of *specific* situations. Decisions necessarily require frequent reappraisals in the shifting circumstances of particular courses of action. The use of particular tactics often reinforces the conditions that encouraged the choice of these tactics in the first place. For example, emphasis on strategy and tactics aimed at seizing and holding power, rather than at the attainment of substantive goals of social policy, thrives upon a fluid electorate, confused ideological contentions, weak party organization and commitments, short-range issues, and strong pressures from diverse interest groupings. Tactical politics, in turn, encourages the very conditions, just named, that initially gave it preeminence, making the continued control of power that much more difficult.

We have seen, thus far, that strategies both affect goals and norms and are shaped and limited by purposes and values. Considerations of costs and benefits involve, further, beliefs about the actual consequences of alternative lines of action. The prominence of nonviolent strategy in the early Civil Rights movement of the 1960s makes that approach an especially useful example. In a major examination of the political uses of nonviolent action Sharp conceives of such action as based on "the belief that the exercise of power depends on the consent of the ruled who, by withdrawing that consent, can control and even destroy the power of their opponent. In other words, nonviolent action is a technique used to control, combat and destroy the opponents' power by nonviolent means of wielding power" (Sharp, 1973, 4). This is a quite special meaning of "nonviolent," which clearly does not deal with all types of actions in which violence is absent. Much persuasion, social example, providing information, exchange, offers of inducement, and the like are not included even though they are nonviolent and contain no hint of threat to use violence. As Sharp's formulation makes clear, those who advocate nonviolent action typically are talking about a subtype of *constraint* — attempts to develop counterpower against the exercise of constraining power. It employs a basic strategy of *withdrawal and noncompliance*. To the extent that this strategy is effectively credible, it becomes a strategy of threat, i.e., of coercion.

The strategies of withdrawal and noncompliance described by advocates of nonviolent action will have the effects, if successful, of *depriving* opponents (of labor, customers, votes, tax revenue, etc.), or *disrupting* normal activities through blockage or other interference, or of *damaging* reputation, prestige, rewarding relationships, and so on. Many of the specific tactics necessitate direct confrontations and physical interpositions in which large numbers of persons are involved. Under these conditions, the likelihood of violence is so great that every leader of nonviolent movements must know (1) that the actions he or she asks of his or her followers probably will expose them to violence on some occasions, and (2) that the initially nonviolent resolves of the followers sometimes are likely to be broken under the pressures of great provocation by opponents. This is not to say that violent and nonviolent coercion are the same; they are not—nonviolent tactics, for one thing, often allow the opponent a larger measure of perceived choice and are on the whole less likely to produce irreversible consequences (death, destruction, etc.). But part of the total cost-benefit appraisal must be a responsible appraisal of the likelihood that nonviolent action will be answered by an opponent with violence.

2. Social Movements and Organizations

Our concern here is with *collective* action. The acting collective unit may be small or large, highly organized or diffuse, enduring or ephemeral. Social movements of ethnic, racial, and religious groupings frequently are both large and diffuse. Out of such movements may come formal organizations, interest groupings, political parties, and lobbies. Social movements of dissent and reform may accept most of the values and norms of the larger society in which they arise and confine their activities to those modes of opposition and advocacy that are institutionalized, e.g., electoral politics, legislative change, judicial proceedings. Often, however, a movement for social change does not initially have acceptance as a legitimate claimant within the established political arena (Gamson, 1975). It then may both advocate and act in terms of alternative or new standards and modes of behavior—civil disobedience, noncompliance, mass agitation, noncooperation, violent opposition, subversion, revolution.

The tactics used by a new social movement obviously depend not only upon the character of the opposition and the institutional setting but also upon the objectives and internal characteristics of the movement. For example, whether it will choose tactics solely to "win" or reflecting broader considerations will be affected by (1) the internal politics of the group—is there a strong indigenous leadership structure, do these leaders make the decisions, what decisions are consensual, how well does the group work together toward the achievement of certain goals?; (2) the characteristics of the group—its homogeneity, size, resources, sense of community, ability to suffer hardship; (3) its past experiences—cultural heritage, experience with other groups, familiarity with certain tactics and strategies; (4) its motivations—immediate needs, desire for power or recognition.

Although outstanding individuals have strongly influenced particular movements on behalf of American ethnic minorities, the enduring effects have come from the movements and organizations that pressed for change and defended positions won over the long-pull. In the case of black people in the United States, no account of major changes during the 1950s and 1960s toward greater participation, power, and social unity could overlook the essential instrumental role of the National Association for the Advancement of Colored People, the Congress of Racial Equality, the Student Nonviolent Coordinating Committee, the Southern Christian Leadership Conference, and many ad hoc groupings and temporary coalitions (e.g., the March on Washington, various Black Liberation Fronts).

Certain events, such as protests, riots, and rebellions have often been regarded in the past as disorganized, "irrational" outbursts among disoriented and uprooted elements of the population. But there is now a growing awareness that such events are often effective in mobilizing support, establishing collective identity and organization, and attaining goals. Conflict increasingly is seen in research analyses as less "irrational" and more instrumental and selective than was the case in some traditional "collective behavior" interpretations (Williams, 1975a). Collective violence, for example, often is a direct extension of conventional political processes, not an aberrant contradiction of normal politics. Much behavior in protests, demonstrations, and rebellions is highly purposive, selective, organized, instrumental, and effective in attaining goals.

These revisions of older views of collective behavior do not deny that much of what happens in social movements is not deliberately chosen as strategy but arises out of uncontrollable circumstances. The useful question is: *under what conditions* do particular types of collective behavior manifest one or another set of processes and consequences? For example, while an almost "gladiatorial" escalation of militancy occurred among black spokesmen during the northern urban upheavals of 1964-68, the leadership of the southern civil rights movement developed from a reliance upon charismatic figures to a specialized cadre, as long-range objectives became more central (Nelson, 1971). Similarly, grievances among blacks in fifteen large cities have been shown to be positively related to objective conditions—in some cases the expressions of grievances arise spontaneously, in others they are the result of calculated strategy. Responses to police behavior, for example, depended not only upon police practices but also upon the reputation of the local chief of police; however, objectional behavior by ghetto merchants apparently became an issue only when made salient by black leaders (Rossi and Berk, 1972).

When social movements of protest and dissent arise in a diffuse and spontaneous form—without centralized leadership or highly structured organization—their significance, meaning, and intentions typically will be amorphous, variable, and multifaceted. Thus the collective upheavals among urban black populations in the 1960s were interpreted in a great variety of ways—from "rioting for fun and profit" to "principled revolution." Intense controversies arose over the political significance to be attributed to them. Were the events civil disorders, riots, criminal conspiracies, spontaneous political rebellions, hostile outbursts, or organized revolt? Or something else? The very labeling of the events thus comes to be in itself an important political act. In terms of tactics, the public interpretation of protest is an uncertain tool. To interpret public disorders as political protests rather than as unfocused expressions of discontent may strengthen efforts to bring about social reforms. But to be effective, such efforts must be carried through quickly, before receptivity vanishes as memory of the crisis fades (see Turner, 1969, 829). For the most part, however, the effectiveness of group strategy will depend less on the definition of events than upon the degree of group unity and the ability to use organization toward the achievement of power and resources. A detailed description of how a small organization of Puerto Rican migrants in a northeastern city attempted to bring pressure to bear upon local government shows how the failure was made unavoidable by disunity and lack of a power base (Rogler, 1972). That consolidation and institutionalized organization of a diffuse set of local social movements does not necessarily reduce militancy or effectiveness is suggested by analysis of open housing movements of the 1960s (Saltman, 1975).

By now we have enough evidence to show that the unity of large-scale social movements is to a high degree constructed symbolically upon a base of great heterogeneity—of goals, motivations, interests, and social positions. The Black Revolt in the United States has been no exception. Polls of black opinions repeatedly have shown great diversity of values, beliefs, and preferences regarding both goals and strategies of collective action. For example, only a small segment (5 to 6 percent) of the black population agreed with the proponents of black separatist nationalism at a time (1968) when the latter were featured in the mass media. Nevertheless, a definite sense of a unified movement and of an agreed-upon strategy often is superimposed upon the diversity through focus upon leaders who control resources and speak for the entire constituency.

Thus the strategies and tactics of social movements depend not only upon issues, resources, and other social and cultural conditions but also to some extent upon the values and personality characteristics of individuals. Studies of student activists in the United States during the 1960s and 1970s found that different types or levels of moral judgments were strikingly related to participation. Block, Haan, and Smith (1968) found that students arrested in the 1964 sit-in at Berkeley were disproportionately either *very high* or *extremely low* according to the Kohlberg Moral Judgment Interview. Students with conventional moral views were greatly underrepresented. A 1970 study found that conventional (or "law and order") moral reasoning was linked to political conservatism; "preconventional" moral levels were associated with violent radicalism; students with "principled morality" or postconventional orientations rejected political conservatism but did not accept radical ideology. Alker and Poppen utilize the prior research to develop the idea of *resonances* between personality structure (including moral style) and preferred ideologies. They propose that "there is an attraction or resonance of persons with closed belief systems to ideologies with content advocating an authoritarian structure in the society" (Alker and Poppen, 1973). A dogmatist can reject logical consistency and apply ad hoc and ad hominum arguments. The principled moralist is committed both to normative rules and to consistency between rules and behavior and between one's own behavior and that of other people. Alker and Poppen found, in a sample of 192 students at Cornell University, that ideological .preferences were linked to three factors: (1) consistency with external standards *or* with one's own emotions and experience; (2) with external attribution of causality *or* with self-efficacy; (3) with acceptance of consequences as a self-responsibility. The results show that *either* humanism *or* normative morality can be compatible with dogmatism, while both "principled morality" and "Machiavellianism" share a lack of constriction by conventional moral rules.

Because social movements necessarily develop and change over time, longitudinal studies are needed to understand them. Such studies are rare, but we do have an analysis covering the period 1965-69 of civil rights activists in the 1965 Summer Community Organization and Political Education (SCOPE) program, which shows in detail the greatly varied responses (radical, reformist, drop-out, disengaged) of these volunteers some four years after their intense experiences in the South at the peak of the black-white civil rights coalition (Demerath, Marwell, Aiken, 1971). And one of the most illuminating studies of change within a developing movement is the striking documented case of limited collaboration under conditions of radically asymmetrical trust represented by the participation of whites in the southern civil rights movements, in which they only gradually learned of the pervasive and deep mistrust with which they were regarded by their black co-participants (Levy, 1968).

Worthy of special emphasis is the historical evidence that those social movements among disadvantaged minorities that emphasize separatism and withdrawal always contain the possibility of subsequent development of more active confrontation, as collective consciousness grows and political demands are articulated. Initial withdrawal often is followed by active return. This potential exists even in movements that initially are strongly millenarian and other-worldly (Watson, 1973).

In the following section we examine the methods of collective action that conceivably may be available to a social movement or an organization. Given the objective possibilities, then, what approaches are likely to be effective? What undesired consequences may come along with the desired ones?

3. Selecting Modes of Action: Possibilities and Plans

In the midst of intense social controversies and struggles, it is often unclear, either to the participants or to outside observers, whether particular collective actions have been deliberately selected or whether they represent largely unforeseen results of many originally uncoordinated impulses, needs, and aspirations. Nevertheless there always are some occasions and situations in which alternatives can be reviewed and choices made. Accordingly, an essential part of developing effective collective action is to bring together a set of persons who have or will develop the particular knowledge, skills, and channels of communication needed to define goals and tactics and to carry out coordinated actions needed to move toward goals. The importance of *specific* or *particular* knowledge must be emphasized—for example, knowing where to direct protests within a local community (Bailey, 1974), which of the many laws and administrative regulations are applicable to a particular kind of job discrimination, which members of a legislative committee are open to persuasion.

The selection of methods to be used in a given instance will be affected in the first instance by appraisals of the relative merits of persuasion, inducement, or constraint. "Where conversion of the opponent is sought, such methods as the general strike, mutiny and parallel government are obviously not appropriate. But where nonviolent coercion is intended these may be precisely the methods needed. . . . In most cases more than one method will be used" (Sharp, 1973, 502-3). Given that several different methods are to be used, numerous questions must be resolved concerning the order in which the methods are applied, the pace and timing of action, the specific combinations of tactics at each phase, and the observable effects of each combination both upon the immediate situation and upon the long-range development of the total collective effort.

Although such ongoing appraisals and decisions are necessarily situation-specific, it is useful that decision-makers have a grasp of the wider range of possible tactics and of practical lessons that may be drawn from the experience of others. Thus it is important to realize that both direct persuasion and nonviolent protest actions may be undertaken *either* primarily to express and reinforce certain values and beliefs among members of the ingroup *or* primarily as a means of attempting to influence opponents or third parties to accept certain views or to take certain actions. By themselves such demonstrations and protests and persuasive appeals do not hold out definite inducements, nor do they have the constraining influences that can be exerted through noncooperation and active intervention.

The effort to produce change through use of constraint may take the "mild" form of social noncooperation rather than the strong form of active threat. The various modes of noncooperation include ostracism of individuals or groups of persons (social boycott), withdrawal from social ceremonies and public observances, refusal to comply with norms or follow customs, nonparticipation in obligatory or expected activities, and more or less complete withdrawal from a given social system (Sharp, 1973, 183ff.). Tactics of noncooperation are most effective when used in small, solidary groups, or under conditions of extraordinary mass mobilization in highly interdependent systems. Small groups with scanty resources will not find these tactics generally very rewarding to use against powerful opponents in the economic and political sectors of complex state-societies such as the contemporary United States.

Withdrawal of cooperation, noncompliance, disobedience, and obstruction have many different effects in differing contexts. What these tactics have in common is that they do not directly attack the person or property of an opponent and, hence, are *generally* less likely to provoke the more extreme forms of counterassault. As Coleman argues: "*The principal virtue of nonviolence as a strategy is that it does not serve the opponent by unifying his force and intensifying his anger, as does an aggressive or violent act*" (Coleman, 1971, 77; italics in original text). Although this generalization seems valid under many conditions, we must add the rather evident cautionary note that nonviolent action does not always avoid unifying and angering an opponent; as noted below, such action often has strongly polarizing consequences.

Ethnic organizations and movements in the United States have used many different forms of political noncooperation, with greatly varying outcomes. Such noncooperation encompasses a large array of diverse collective actions: for example, Sharp (1973, Chapter 7) has noted some thirty-eight methods of withholding the normal, expected, and desired obedience to or cooperation with political officials, organizations, and regimes.

Economic boycotts likewise occur in many specific forms. They may be primary or secondary, i.e., either direct withdrawal from economic dealing with an adversary or a secondary boycott of third parties in an attempt to move them to take part in the primary boycott against the main opponent.

Withdrawal of cooperation appears in a highly active or focused way in the strike—a widely used form of nonviolent coercion. It consists of a deliberate collective cessation of work, intended to bring about a change in the relationships between employers or managers and workers or unions—or to induce some other type of change in the behavior of social authorities. A strike may arise as a protest against actions of political or religious authorities as well as against economic authorities. The wide range of noneconomic issues that have been invoked in strikes is suggested by the frequent appearance of symbolic strikes, e.g., those undertaken as public protests or as expressions of shared feelings rather than as direct efforts to present specific demands. Such token or symbolic work stoppages have several possible effects, not all of which are immediately obvious. The demonstration strike that shows massive solidarity of large numbers of workers gives a signal to authorities that more serious noncooperation lies ahead unless remedial action is forthcoming. When a social movement is in its early phases or lacks adequate support and solidarity, the symbolic strike is a low-cost method of testing sentiment and developing organizational strength. It focuses attention and increases the commitment of those who participate, when they see many others join in the collective action. There seems little doubt that such effects occur in successful sympathy strikes and mass sick-calls.

In an ascending scale of active rather than passive emphasis, intervention is the fourth and most active form of nonviolent collective action, following upon persuasion, protest, and noncooperation. Nonviolent intervention as described by Sharp (1973, 357-58) consists of some forty-one subtypes of collective action. Their common characteristic is active intervention, either to disrupt or destroy established social patterns or to initiate new relationships or behavior patterns. This active character implies that success may come quickly —but so may severe repression. Because the intervention when successful usually changes the opponent's behavior with minimal change in values, any weakening in the bargaining power of the challengers is likely to be followed by renewed attempts of the dominant grouping to undo the recent social change. In any case, the tactics of intervention almost always ensure an intensification of struggle, a sharpening of group boundaries, and an increased degree of polarization within the community or society in which the struggle takes place. Noncommitted persons and collectivities come under increasing pressure to take sides.

4. Choices of Strategies: the Special Place of "Nonviolent Action"

We have seen repeatedly throughout this work that in all selections of strategies and tactics the choice of particular modes of action always entails an explicit or implicit weighing of multiple values, some of which may be incompatible or contradictory. One appraises risks against stakes—shall we seek to minimize loss or to maximize gain, by going for a low-risk, low-yield option or by taking the gamble of high risk for high stakes? One looks at likely cost-benefit ratios: aside from risk, is the most probable gain worth the anticipated costs? And, to repeat once more, one attends to expected effects not only upon adversaries and upon the members of one's own collectivity but also upon some third party or parties. Actions that are highly effective in relation to one of these sets of actors often have undesired impacts upon another.

All these considerations are sharply salient in controversies concerning the doctrines and practices that have come to be called "nonviolent action." The term is heavily laden with historical connotations because of its associations with pacifist movements and with the civil disobedience campaigns successfully led by Gandhi in India against British rule. As formulated by Gandhi and his interpreters the system eventually included eight main social norms or ethical dicta (see the details in Janis and Katz, 1971, 219-32).

1. Refrain from any form of verbal assault or overt violence toward rival groups.
2. Admit plans and intentions to rival groups, including the considerations that are determining one's tactics and long-range objectives.
3. Refrain from humiliating actions toward rival groups.
4. Make visible sacrifices for one's cause.
5. Carry out a consistent set of positive activities that are explicit realizations of the group's objectives.
6. Try to start direct personal interaction, oriented toward friendly verbal discussions concerning issues.
7. Maintain a consistent attitude of trust toward the opposing party, and manifest it in appropriate actions.
8. Maintain a high degree of empathy to motives, affects, expectations, and attitudes of rival groups.

Advocates of nonviolent resistance to violent repression hold out the possibility that the ability or will of the violent adversary to continue violent repression will be reduced by the demonstration that the target group refuses to be cowed. But the main argument centers upon a hoped-for withdrawal of support by members of the constituency of the aggressor and loss of support by third parties. The possible and hoped-for effects of continuing nonviolent resistance to repressive force include the following: increased sympathy and support from third parties, increased uneasiness and doubt among the opponent's own people, development of dissent and eventual internal opposition within the repressing group. The "theory" is that overreaction of the repressor increasingly will weaken the capacity to deal with resistance and will augment the dissenting forces—thus creating a kind of political *jiujitsu* (Sharp, 1973, 113).

Such hopes were more or less well-fulfilled in the Gandhian movement against the British in India—but nonviolent action failed catastrophically against the Nazis in Germany. Nonviolent protest was effective in the Civil Rights struggle in the South, 1960-65, but could not be maintained in northern cities after 1965 or so.

It seems clear enough that strategies of nonviolence, openness (trust), nonhostility, and empathy have greater potentialities for gaining objectives and reducing conflict when one's opponent holds values and beliefs congruent with one's own. Appeals to humanitarian values and universalistic ethics could have some effect when used by Gandhi against the British; they had no observable efficacy against the German Nazis' slaughter of European Jews. If one appeals to another's conscience, the effect depends upon whether the other, indeed, has a conscience of the kind to which appeal is made.

What effects we can expect from passive resistance or from active but nonviolent methods of struggle thus hinge first of all upon the reactions of an opponent. For example, it is a central doctrine of nonviolent strategy that one should design actions against more powerful opponents that will cause them to react in ways that will weaken their own position, e.g., provoking a powerful adversary to a disproportionate use of force, which weakens the needed support of third parties. Thus violent actions that effectively disrupt protests of an aggrieved ethnic minority may bring support to the dissidents from third parties; a case in point was the widespread reaction of sympathetic white people to the use of police dogs, fire hoses, and cattle prods against black participants in civil rights demonstrations of the 1960s in Birmingham, Alabama, and elsewhere in the Deep South. "In 1965, the American public witnessed on television the beating of demonstrators in Selma, Alabama, who were seeking to achieve for Negroes the right to vote without discrimination. Congress thereupon [took] a more direct approach to dealing with these problems" (U.S. Commission on Civil Rights, 1968, 10).

But much nonviolent strategy concerns active collective struggle rather than passive resistance to an opponent. Violent actions are a small subset of all social behavior; hence, most behavior is nonviolent. The particular reference of nonviolent action is, first, to collective efforts intended to persuade or convert others by observable actions, e.g., by (1) exemplary behavior or by (2) mass protests. An element of coercive threat that is implicit in protests bulks larger in the second group of actions: (3) withdrawals of cooperation and (4) nonviolent but obstructive or disruptive intervention. Thus nonviolent action in the special sense used by its strategists is oppositional behavior that does not employ violent force against persons or material objects but rather seeks to develop a coercive potential through protest, nonsupport, withdrawal, obstruction, and intervention. Its users may seek only to persuade, but the very nature of the techniques implies the possibility of threat, whether moral or physical. Persuasive and expressive forms include such actions as marches, parades, gatherings, and vigils. Noncooperation consists of withdrawal or withholding — of taxes, labor, purchases, voting, registering, and so on. Intervention includes sit-ins, obstruction, invasion, and development of parallel organizations (including government) (Sharp, 1973, 65-69).

Inspection of the strategic commentaries presented by advocates of nonviolent action suggests that little is said about the question of central importance: why should we expect that the necessary numbers of individuals will make the sometimes very great sacrifices that must be made for the benefit of a movement or an organization? Of course the question is also crucial for the case of violent action, but there seem to be quite special strains when the person is under the severe restraints of nonviolent discipline and cannot retaliate in kind for assaults and torments. It seems evident that nonviolent strategies are peculiarly dependent upon solidarity or "trust" among the participants. If intragroup discipline is to be maintained, when only nonviolent sanctions may be employed, members must be sensitive and responsive to social disapproval — and vulnerable to noncooperation and withdrawal of support. The nonviolent sanctions will be ineffective within the weaker collectivity unless there is near unanimity in willingness — or perceived willingness — to use them against errant colleagues. Further, a great many of the most important techniques for action against opponents (e.g., boycotts, strikes) will be effective only if there is mass support and participation, often over extended periods and under severe circumstances.

Thus solidarity within the weaker collectivity is an essential ingredient if it is to succeed against an opponent initially having greater resources for coercive retaliation. In addition, as we have indicated, some minimum bonds of solidarity must exist between the challenging collectivity and its more powerful opponent. An implication is that strategies of the Gandhian kind are more likely to be effective when many members of each of the contending collectivities are psychologically close to members of the other grouping, i.e., have vivid and concrete appreciations, know the others in many social situations, understand their "common humanity" at the level of basic needs, fears, and hopes. All stereotyping and dehumanizing processes lessen the likelihood of positive response by one's adversaries to nonhostile, self-revealing tactics.

Futher, positive nonviolent approaches to an adversary are most likely to be advantageous when both parties are committed to institutionalized modes of competition, conflict, and conflict-resolution. Such institutionalization facilitates mutual restraint and the development of reciprocities in two main ways: (1) implicitly or explicitly, it sets boundaries upon the scope and intensity of conflict; (2) it increases realistic trust in the intentions of one's opponent or rival.

Additional plausible hypotheses, as formulated by Coleman (1971, 77-78), concern the characteristics of the collective opponent against which nonviolent tactics are used. Coleman suggests that:

1. The less internally mobilized the enemy, the more effective the nonviolence will be, and the more quickly it will have an effect.
2. The more divergence there is in strength of commitment between the central core of the enemy and its potential supporters, the more effective the nonviolence will be.

It is further implied that:

3. The larger is the uncommitted public, and the more influence it can have on the central core of the opposition, the more effective the nonviolence.
4. The more violent and brutal the tactics that are publicly used by the opponent against a nonviolent movement, the greater the likelihood that third parties will support the nonviolent parties; this result is especially favored when third parties already hold humanitarian values.

Although one can think of historical circumstances in which these generalizations seem to have been contravened by factors not here taken into account, these hypotheses appear useful as rules of thumb and worthy of further research under conditions prevailing in our own society.

The outcome of a particular strategy may depend upon *who* exercises it. For instance, the standard doctrines of nonviolence seem to assume that violence carries different symbolic weight depending on whether it is the superordinate or subordinate group that is employing it. Thus when a protest group is committed to nonviolent demonstration: "the nonviolent resisters . . . consciously assumed the burden of nonviolence. That is, they had made a commitment to the public not to have recourse to violence. When violence was used against them, this hence came to be seen as a breach of tacit reciprocal commitment on the part of those they oppose" (Coser, 1967, 90). Because of the moral significance of nonviolence, it is asserted, an act of violence on the part of officials or keepers of the status quo will often appear repressive to the third parties and win sympathy from onlookers. The hope for this outcome often is the basis for a conscious decision to use nonviolent tactics. Partisan groups who are challenging the status quo, typically from an initially weak position, often have a need to discredit the representatives of the status quo; one possible way to do this is to maneuver officials or representatives into situations in which they violate accepted norms or principles—in this case, disturbing the public order and using violence against those who will not fight back.

How realistic is it to expect positive gains from opposing violence with nonviolence? Although the answer, as usual, has to recognize much complexity and uncertainty, it seems that in American intergroup relations violence by authorities and established groupings only rarely alienates any strategically important third parties. We have cited some of the few cases in which the long-run outcomes from the challengers were positive and important. But both historical studies (Graham and Gurr, 1969; Lane, 1976) and analyses of contemporary public responses agree upon two crucial facts: (1) relatively high levels of violence, including illegal violence, have been tolerated and widely approved throughout American history; (2) the general public gives a strong presumption of legitimacy to force used by authorities and tends to disapprove of force used by dissenters and other partisans (Turner, 1969; Gamson and McEvoy, 1970; Graham, 1970; Blumenthal et al., 1972; Rothbart, 1976, 355-58). The authorities can use a great deal of violence before they seriously undercut the support and acquiescence of the bystander public. Even peaceful protests, on the other hand, tend to be defined initially as nonlegitimate. Not suprisingly, when the protesters themselves use violence, the situation changes drastically. Violent tactics then run the high risk of being labeled as lawless and destructive rather than as a form of legitimate protest. It requires exceptional political and social insight to attribute rioting or other collective violence to deep-seated grievances and legitimate needs, and quite apart from sympathetic attitudes, this political sophistication cannot always be depended upon. Furthermore, as Mueller points out, violence against property and symbols of authority lacks the cultural legitimacy and moral superiority of the nonviolent tradition of civil disobedience and other nonviolent direct action tactics. Thus violence as a protest tactic tends to legitimize the use of force as an official response to protest (Mueller, 1971, 9). Because the group in power has the advantages of both a presumption of legitimacy and a mandate to maintain the status quo, in the name of safety and order it can enforce already existing rules and laws, and institute new and even more stringent forms of social control. Any action out of the ordinary can be considered abnormal and therefore warranting correction. Thus "in any class-differentiated society, the upper classes tend to have internalized more strongly the guiding normative standards, for these are, to a significant extent, their standards" (Coser, 1967, 65).

Another limitation upon the effectiveness of nonviolent political *jiujitsu* is that the authorities may not be stupid and they may refuse to be enticed into an unacceptable display of unnecessary brutality. All in all, one must agree with Kriesberg's (1973, 194) dryly understated observation: "Clearly, making things worse for the people by provoking the government to harsh measures is an inadequate revolutionary program or course of action." Characteristically any sophisticated polity or group will already have provided for the eventuality of civil disorders with measures such as martial law or curfews. The official use of violence is all the more likely to be considered legitimate since it will have been built into the existing social order.

Although the tolerance for violence is one-sided, strongly favoring the authorities over the dissidents, the challenging partisans do not always pay for violence by failing to gain their objectives. For a diverse sample of American protest movements, Gamson (1975) finds that "unruly" groups (many of which used violent means) benefited more than peaceful groups under many circumstances.

5. The Major Choices

As over against the great variety of nonviolent modes of struggle there stands the great variety of violent modes. Very familiar to everyone is the ancient doctrine of violence as a last resort, a final instrumentality. But in modern times special emphasis has come to bear upon violence as a means of self-definition and of the development of collective identity and cohesion (Coser, 1967, 81). The choice of strategy cannot ignore the likelihood that there are other forces at work which may exist in opposition to a given mode of action. A particular strategy such as nonviolent action may itself unleash radically different forces as time and sentiments change. In many social movements and protest activities that are far short of violence, the very example of overt struggle has a symbolic meaning that goes much beyond the immediate practical or instrumental effects. By arousing hope, demonstrating defiance, and showing the character of the opposition, such actions can increase support and give confidence to potential partisans. Thus when student organizers went out to work for black voter registration in the South in the 1960s, their presence and activity had effects much beyond their explicit intentions. Even though they restricted their actions to persuasion, simply urging black persons to register to vote, they tended to stimulate direct action. When local people then became aroused, they often seemed to feel that although the problems were overwhelming, the need for action was compelling. Many risked injury and even death to symbolically defy the system of segregation—for example, by sitting at lunch counters (Braden, 1965). Therefore, in this case, what might have tactically led to more direct power, i.e., the political power of the vote, was bypassed because of the more immediate symbolic needs to confront an adversary—in situations where violence was likely and often did occur. Similarly, a great deal of esteem and prestige-status among student radicals was determined by the frequency and severity of arrest. "The act of violence, in other words, commits a man symbolically to the revolutionary movement and breaks his ties with his previous life and commitments" (Coser, 1967, 81). In these ways participation in acts of violence, protest, and confrontation often becomes both a personal and a social *rite of passage*.

Likely to be met with force are the tactics of intervention by physical presence in "forbidden" areas and activities, occupancy, use, or obstruction. Such tactics, often thought to be new in the 1950s and 1960s, were already familiar in the various sit-ins, stand-ins, and the like used by antislavery and antisegregation movements as early as the 1830s. These methods were widely used by blacks at several later periods in the nineteenth and early twentieth centuries. The most recent wave of activity extended from the 1940s through the 1960s.

The sit-in has been widely used in the United States to break down racial discrimination in restaurants and lunch counters. In this method the actionists progressively occupy a large number or all of the available seats and refuse to leave until the Afro-American members of the group are served, the restaurant closes, the group [is] arrested, or a certain predetermined period of time elapses.

The Congress of Racial Equality used this method in Northern and border states during the 1940s and 1950s. It first became widely practiced on a large scale in the South in early 1960, with sit-ins in Woolworth's in Greensboro, North Carolina, conducted by students of North Carolina Agricultural and Technical College. Shortly thereafter, high school and college students all over the South began to stage similar sit-ins at lunch counters, and a movement of major proportions developed. The Southern Regional Council reported that within seven months at least 70,000 Negroes and whites had actively participated and 3,600 had been arrested. A U.S. Supreme Court decision on December 11, 1961, outlawed the use of disorderly conduct statutes as grounds for arresting Negroes sitting in to obtain equal service (Sharp, 1973, 373).

In some programs of direct action, if negotiations have been developed but are failing to lead toward desired outcomes, a next major step is to issue an ultimatum, that is, to threaten drastic action of some kind unless stated demands are met by a specified time, and to offer to desist if the demands are met. If the threat is credible, it serves to indicate to the opponent the likelihood of increasingly costly struggle, and a willingness to settle on the terms stated. It may also serve to unify a constituency behind a commitment to act. If preceded by publicly visible efforts to negotiate what third parties have come to regard as a reasonable settlement, the ultimatum puts the opponent in a position either of having to admit capitulation or of escalating the struggle. The latter is always a distinct possibility unless the opponent is predisposed to grant the demands.

And, of course, there are many instances in which an ultimatum is intended to escalate the conflict—for example, by stating demands that the opponent cannot possibly meet or issuing demands in an insulting or provocative manner. On the other hand, efforts may be made to give the opponent information and assurances to reduce fears and hostility, e.g., reminders of nonviolent intentions, continuation of negotiations in good faith.

Established political groupings do not need to use violent means to obtain considerate responses from authorities. If such groupings, on the other hand, wish to suppress dissident partisans, they typically have ready access to call upon police and armed forces to use "legitimate" violence.

> The central difference among political actors is captured by the idea of being inside or outside of the polity. Those who are inside are *members* whose interest is vested—that is, recognized as valid by other members. Those who are outside are challengers. They lack the basic prerogative of members—routine access to decisions that affect them (Gamson, 1975, 140).

The outsiders cannot count upon having their interests taken into account, much less favored. Far from being able to call upon institutionalized agents of violence for protection, they are likely to be the objects of political repression.

Strategies require consideration of the resources of one's own group in relation to those of opponents, the dispositions and resources of third parties, the issues under contention, the strength of commitments, the probable responses of opponents to different tactics, the values and beliefs to be served, and many other factors, only some of which we have reviewed here. Hence, particular strategies are endlessly varied. But metastrategies—the strategies for choosing strategies—are more limited in number. It is at this level that we find little decisive empirical evidence but a number of plausible rules of thumb that seem sensible in the light of what knowledge we have. In this category fall Sharp's suggestions that

> the methods of non-violent protest and persuasion . . . are largely symbolic in their effect and produce an awareness of the existence of

dissent. . . . Depending on the numbers involved, the methods of non-cooperation . . . are likely to cause difficulties in maintaining the normal operation and efficiency of the system. . . . The methods of nonviolent intervention . . . possess qualities of both groups, but in addition usually constitute a more direct challenge to the regime. . . . Moving from . . . nonviolent protest and persuasion to . . . noncooperation and thence to nonviolent intervention generally involves a progressive increase in the degree of sacrifice required of the nonviolent actionists, in the risk of disturbing the public peace and order, and in effectiveness (Sharp, 1973, 501).

The larger the stakes—the more important the issues initially are or the more crucial they become during the conflict—the more likely it is (a) that the conflict will be severe and (b) that it will escalate from low to high levels of intensity and magnitude. For example, in the resistance to or defiance of authorities that constitutes a campaign of nonviolent struggle, "the severity of repression frequently tends to increase significantly as the campaign continues and as earlier forms of repression prove ineffective" (Sharp, 1973, 540).

Escalation is favored by: (1) competition among leaders, especially in early stages or when hope of success is high; (2) increased anxiety concerning the opponent's threat, while hope of success is still retained; (3) increased hostility toward the foe, induced by injuries and threats (Tunteng, 1973) or by selective communication and perception; (4) centralization of control; (5) decreased tolerance of internal dissent; (6) increased participation of individuals and subcollectivities who have no positive ties with the opponent and who have little knowledge or appreciation of long-range complexities of relationships with the opponent and with implicated third parties; (7) polarization in which supporters of the conflict are visibly predominant, driving opponents into extreme intransigence and neutralizing all "moderates"; (8) widening of the issues and increase in magnitude of the stakes—from specific interests to wider interests, beliefs, and values; from distributive interests to struggles over power and revenge, to a struggle for survival; (9) reduction in common ties to friendly third parties; (10) increasing involvement of allies on each side, thus increasing the resources of each for additional struggle, and widening the scope of the conflict.

Sparing use of coercion during the course of a struggle facilitates later development of mutually acceptable outcomes and relationships. Insofar as threats are necessary to arrive at a mutually acceptable balance of gains and losses or advantages and disadvantages, future reciprocally satisfactory accommodation will be most likely if use of threats has been minimal in frequency and intensity. A few well-timed threats that the opponent can perceive as having been intended to be as mild as possible while still being effective are, therefore, preferable to many threats and to extremes of rhetoric and instrumental gestures.

Mutual accommodation becomes more likely the more steeply net costs rise for both parties with successive increments of time or with successive increases in "involvement" or "effort" (e.g., proportion of the time spent in conflict). During the urban disorders of the 1960s it was both the *articulation* of grievances and the critical "smoke signal" of rioting itself that combined to encourage a bargaining response by city officials. But it is clear that other constraints and inducements affected the likelihood of negotiations. It is plausible to suggest that a bargaining response is favored when (1) officials believe that because the basic conditions producing discontent will not change quickly, further disturbances will be likely; (2) humanitarian values are important in the politically relevant portions of the community; and (3) public support for suppressive and punitive measures is wavering or uncertain. Both prudence and "civic pride" may thus favor bargaining rather than toughness.

If in each of the conflicting parties there are subgroupings that favor compromise, or convergence, the escalation of conflict at the behest of the more militant members eventually will bring about a counterreaction within each party. Intragroup cross-purposes reduce bellicosity. De-escalation and mutual accommodation will be facilitated by such internal divergences of interests, when each party contains substantial opposition to continuing the conflict. It may then be possible for leaders to propose feasible means for reducing the level of conflict (Kriesberg, 1973, 163-65).

From the standpoint of degree of success in attaining collective goals, the evidence to be reviewed in more detail in Chapter 11 shows that "unruly" tactics generally are superior to conciliatory tactics (Gamson, 1975). For collectivities whose members previously have been excluded from an effective voice in the political system, an active threat may be the only means that will bring serious attention from authorities. But unruly tactics are successful only under a narrow range of conditions. The threat or prediction must be credible, realistic — and measured. It does little good to bluster or make empty or exaggerated threats. It is a sure invitation to disaster when a weak movement loudly proclaims its intention of totally displacing or destroying anyone who does not forthwith accept all its demands. In general, a strategy of measured coercion is safest when the social movement representing a disadvantaged minority is well disciplined and has a strong central organization, and when the goals sought are limited (rather than total). Demands are most likely to be met when the minority can maintain a sustained campaign through a continuing organization — which is able to press hardest when its bargaining power is greatest (e.g., in wartime) and to be conciliatory when intransigence would be counterproductive.

A centrally important factor influencing whether settlement of issues will be sought through large-scale and intense public conflict or through low-intensity persuasion and bargaining is the degree to which leaders of relevant collectivities perceive clear boundaries defining a *zone of possible settlements*. Clear mutual expectations concerning limits of possible changes in policy encourage a concentration on bargaining concerning those particular interests which can be divided. In contrast, a lack of recognized limits encourages collective mobilization, debate couched in terms of broader ideologies, public confrontations, and a politics of threat. For instance, these generalizations seem to be implied by the analysis by Greenstone and Peterson of differing outcomes and styles of policy-making concerning OEO programs in five major cities (New York, Philadelphia, Detroit, Chicago, Los Angeles). (Greenstone and Peterson, 1973, 281-85).

Aside from descriptive case studies we have found only one major empirical analysis of the negotiation and bargaining outcomes of the urban civil disturbances of the 1960s: *Riot Negotiations, Conditions of Successful Bargaining in the Urban Riots of 1967 and 1968* (Mueller, 1971). Mueller showed that by 1967 city officials were engaged in negotiations with black leaders or spokesmen in response to over one-half of the riots. "Success" in such negotiations was indexed by a Guttman-type scale, ranging from the fact of simply gaining access to city officials or to other targets of protest, to formal negotiations, to public commitments to take some or all of the positive actions demanded by black leaders. It was found that the amount and intensity of violence had been greater in communities having successful outcomes. However, the apparent effect was produced by an intervening variable—the articulate militancy of the black community as reflected in the number and scope of demands presented by spokesmen. The greater the militancy, the greater was the success of bargaining. When level of militancy was statistically controlled, the effect of violence turned out to be negative rather than positive. That is, militance tended to go along with successful outcomes, but if militance was low, a high level of violence not only did not produce successful negotiation but it tended to lead to hardened resistance and to forcible repression.

The negative effects upon third parties of the constraining tactics of protest, intervention, obstruction, and the like used against one's opponent can be minimized when: (1) less coercive means can be shown to be unavailable or ineffective in attaining legitimate goals; (2) the objectives are clearly identifiable and reasonably connected with the tactics used (e.g., a sit-in to desegregate a restaurant); (3) any disruption of third-party activities is short;

(4) the tactics do not appear to be a sheerly provocative breaking of commonly accepted taboos or social norms; (5) the active organization seems representative of its claimed constituency; (6) the bystanders are reassured that future disruptions will be minimal. The strength of the Civil Rights Movement of 1960-64 derived in part from these characteristics (Walton and McKersie, 1965, 402ff.).

The initial characteristics of the persons who directly carry out negotiations, apart from the issues and other conditions, may influence styles of bargaining and outcomes. Negotiators of desegregation in ten southern cities tended to have had an unusual amount of interracial experience in cooperative or co-worker relationships:[3] many had lived outside the South: nearly all were college-educated, engaged in business or professional occupations, and were active in voluntary organizations and civic affairs. Their expertise, flexibility, and personal self-control facilitated pragmatic but firm bargaining styles.

The specific conditions surrounding the actual conduct of negotiations can be quite consequential. Thus if confidentiality of preliminary discussions can be assured, the likelihood is greater that exploratory discussions of a given issue actually will precede any negotiations, debates, or public representations on the part of interested parties. Confidentiality of exploratory efforts increases, in turn, the likelihood of compromises among the parties (Steiner, 1974, 269-74).

More basic changes also can occur. Because negotiations necessarily entail reciprocal adjustments of each participant to the other, any negotiative process of near-equality of power will bring convergence of styles of behavior. In recurrent bargaining between representatives of large-scale unions and of large corporations, it has been frequently observed that both parties tend over time to become more alike in their beliefs, values, and practices with regard to issues and procedures in bargaining (Kuhn, 1968, 286-96).

Low-keyed bargaining and infrequent collective conflicts characterize oppositions between interests and values represented in groupings or strata that already have been accorded access and other rights within an established system of authority. This means that the interests are not merely "vested" (i.e., recognized in bargaining processes) but also "institutionalized" (i.e., represented by *enforced norms* defining *definite statuses*).

If institutionalized negotiation is to be fully accepted as a method for reaching binding settlements of collective oppositions and disagreements, the settlements must not only represent "tolerable" levels of reward to the parties in particular instances but must also elicit from the less advantaged parties an attribution of legitimacy. In short, both the processes and the outcomes must be accepted as, on the whole, binding because rightfully valid (Dahl, 1970, 8ff.). The bases of such attributed validity are complex. Here we need only note in passing that full acceptance is found when each party agrees that the total process serves its interests, is effective (competent), is efficient (economical), and is fair (follows norms of justice) (Gamson, 1968, 39-58).

A strategy of confrontation and threat is likely at some point to result in violence—if only because one's opponents resort to force in an attempt to repress the challenge. Many groupings in the past have been willing to accept that hazard as a necessary cost. A key factor, always, is the degree of consensus in the society about the legitimacy of the claims.

We shall return to these considerations in Chapters 13-15. For the moment, we have sought only to outline methods of collective action that sometimes do lead to mutual accommodation or even to cooperation and integration. This brief review is not intended to be at all complete but only to remind us of the range of procedures conceivably open to groups or movements that seek change in an existing social system. Out of all the theoretically possible modes of action, which will be used? In large-scale social movements, events often move beyond the control of any one set of decision-makers. One cannot precisely manipulate a Mississippi flood, guide a hurricane, or "orchestrate" a war. *Conditions* arise that are not controllable by anyone. This much we can infer from history: in complex collective events, *purposes* often are submerged in a flood of unanticipated *consequences*. Yet, short of these overwhelming magnitudes, many collective actions do permit an important amount of guidance by facts, reasoned strategies, and informed appraisals of likely consequences.

Chapter 9

Composite Strategies in
Social Policies and Programs

We have now examined in succession the important kinds of attempted influence and social control that shape intergroup relations. We have seen some of the uses and limitations of several types of persuasion, inducement, and constraint. A diverse array of tactics and strategies has been examined from the standpoint of aspiring partisans and from the perspective of social authorities. It is time now to pause in order to emphasize the interconnections among the separable components of strategies of collective action that already have been described one by one. In the everyday world of practical action one deals with concrete situations, not with abstract modes or techniques; the situations *always* are multidimensional, requiring the skills of social diagnosis as well as the ability to adapt general principles to particular conditions of imperfect information and rapid change.

In this chapter we shall try to depict some of the problems of conflict and accommodation in particular types of situations by taking the point of view of a low-power party seeking to bring about changes in the social system of which it is a part. We do this for purposes of illustration — assuming, as it were, that the Authorities can look out for themselves for the time being.

1. Why "Composite Strategies"? a Matter of Context

If social situations always are complex and particular, it is easy to see why actual strategies must be composite rather than simple. Pure cases are, understandably, rare — it is unusual, for example, to rely only upon persuasion,

238

only upon inducement, or only upon constraint. Most intergroup relations combine cooperation, competition, and conflict. They involve both positive and negative interdependence. These characteristics alone, even were there no other considerations, dictate that negotiation will be an art and that strategies will be complex both in their aims and in their methods.

And what is true of intergroup relations in these respects is only a special case of a universal feature of our understanding of the environments of action. Long ago Galileo, it is said, observed that iron sometimes is molten, sometimes a hard greyish metal, sometimes a substance covered with a reddish rust; he noted that water sometimes is a fluid, sometimes a solid, sometimes a vapor. Reflecting upon these and other instances in which a "thing" is radically transformed under different conditions, he came upon a remarkable generalization: things are what they are *in the situations in which they occur* — not otherwise. We may call this statement the Situational Axiom.

The Situational Axiom is indispensable·for understanding human social behavior. It implies that the specific context is crucial for knowing how to act. We have said early in this book that when we consider the interests of all parties rather than only one party's interests, a successful instance of intergroup relations is one in which the joint returns (payoffs) are greater than some other actual or conceivable outcome — greater than in the past, than in a comparative current situation, and so on. But — just *who* are "the parties" and what kinds of interests are of concern to them? Only knowledge of context will tell us.

One can create in imagination social interactions in which motives are unmixed, information is perfect, goals are definite, and good and bad actions are unambiguous and clear. To generate even a rough approximation to these conditions in controlled experiments in the laboratory requires enormous effort and care — including much preliminary intellectual work. In the concrete events of social life that occur outside of such laboratory constraints, complexity, ambiguity, and uncertainty are normal conditions (Yinger, 1965).

For a first example, note the remarkable scope of ambiguity that can exist even in apparently well-known collective events. To many citizens whose impressions were formed by quick encounters with the mass media, the recurrent drama of civil tumults in large cities during the period 1965-1972 must have been experienced as events in which implacable representatives of racial or ethnic minorities presented nonnegotiable demands to frightened leaders of an Establishment that seemed to be forever placating militant demands. Such citizens might well have imagined that the wealthy and politically powerful authorities acceded to demands by "extremist" leaders who altruistically gained advantages for their oppressed constituencies. Closer inspection would have revealed complexities and, perhaps, some perplexing anomalies. Our hypothetical John Q. Citizen might have noted that funds necessary for the first national conference of self-styled black nationalists (Newark, 1967) were supplied by Big Business—by "socially concerned" national corporations. This fact violates commonsense stereotypes of implacable opposition. It could lead one, then, to wonder whether there could be merit in the provocative thesis that it was in the interests of large corporate businesses to form an implicit alliance with militant ethnic spokespersons for black people and other disadvantaged ethnic minorities (Milstein, 1970). In what must at first have appeared to be an outrageous suggestion, Milstein proposed that business leaders who then supported the Republican party already had anticipated the possibility that a successful black political movement as of the late 1960s could so strengthen the Democratic party as to threaten a conservative balance of power. Hence, the conservatives could visualize the threat of new governmental programs intended to increase both economic equality and the political influence of low-income strata and of dissident social formations of various kinds. It is certainly conceivable, then, that some corporate leaders might conclude that an effective tactic to counter this threat would be to strengthen separatist and nationalistic movements among ethnic minorities. Properly supported and encouraged, such movements conceivably could widen cleavages within low-income groups over various concrete issues concerning housing, community control, taxation, minimum wage, and income-maintenance plans, and so on. Corporate-supported financing meanwhile could provide militant nationalist leaders with resources to disburse and with accompanying claims to legitimacy as leaders. Furthermore, even if it should happen that the tactics of militant leaders resulted in collective violence or threats of violence, this very development could become a basis for legitimizing use of repressive force by existing authorities.

This lengthy scenario may seem precariously based on a tiny foundation of well-attested facts. Indeed so, and in the nature of the case the intentions and motives hypothesized would be very difficult to pin down empirically. Hence, the account just sketched is of uncertain applicability to real events; at most it probably could have characterized only a small fragment of black movements and their leaders or of large corporations and philanthropic foundations. Nevertheless, it usefully highlights the kind of complexity and ambiguity to which realistic social analysis must be continually alert.

A not very profound but very useful example of situational complexity is implied by the apparently simple tactical question of whether or not leaders of partisan movements should meet with the authorities they seek to influence. Groups in conflict, particularly political groups, may be reluctant to engage in "goodwill talks" with authorities if they believe that such talks are only "window-dressing for political advantage" (Rangel, 1974, 4-5). To avoid being trapped in pseudonegotiations, the partisans may seek guarantees or explicit assurances that substantive issues actually will be addressed in a serious way. Thus in advance of a proposed meeting between newly installed President Ford and some sixteen members of the Congressional Black Caucus, representatives of the caucus sought to gain assurance that participation would bring discussion of substantive issues, rather than a pro forma meeting useful primarily to a new president seeking to create a good public image. In this particular case, the invited participants reserved their judgment and open political support pending action by the president which would indicate that he had taken their concerns and recommendations seriously. One of the ways in which the caucus hoped to see such a response was through the "institutionalization of the communication between the executive branch and the Caucus symbolized by the meeting with President Ford," i.e., a regularly scheduled series of conferences (Rangel, 1974, 5).

These topical examples—dated and localized—are deliberately chosen to suggest the high concreteness of real situations of action. With this anchorage in particularity, perhaps we can move safely to less specific but more fundamental examples. Note how often in preceding chapters we have seen that for conflicts that occur in direct interactions between the individuals whose own interests and values are at stake in the opposition, it is almost always important for adequate diagnosis to distinguish between the effects of short-term and long-term interactions and expectations. Long-term interpersonal relationships typically—although not inevitably—become cognitively and affectively complex in the orientations of the actors. Relations become particularistic—strongly affected by *who* is involved; and through this development of strong particularism it usually happens that each individual's position comes to be quasiascribed, i.e., accepted as given, not subject to retesting on each separate occasion. Such strong and stable relationships typically also generate strong sentiments and develop acceptance of relatively open expression of feelings. Finally, each member of the collectivity will be expected to put the group's interest above his or her own immediate desires, in at least some important situations. And all these characteristics will be important for diagnosing the qualities of any intragroup conflicts that may develop. To the extent that the suggested psychological involvement and social structures do develop, conflicts will tend to be diffuse and value-centered rather than specific and instrumental. Each particular occasion of conflict will be affected by the character of past conflicts and their resolutions. The strategies that are effective in impersonal transitory relationships are likely to be inappropriate and may be disastrous in these conditions.

How can a social movement develop dependable long-run commitments and the sense of time-perspective needed to avoid catastrophic loss of morale and will when "things go wrong"? We shall return to this question. Perhaps the most important thing to say at this point is that both long-range perspective and enduring commitment require a continuing *organization*. To have an organization means division of labor, assignment of responsibilities, regularized allocation of resources. It means group support for individuals in positions that make the incumbents' self-interest dependent upon maintaining the organization, and planning and working for collective goals. To develop reliable and effective organization is rendered easier when there is a nucleus of persons already linked together by multiple solidarities.

Such solidarities are most likely when the members of the potential organization have extensive knowledge of one another, based on frequent interaction, and have already successfully accomplished some joint tasks. The more these conditions are present, the more likely it is that the members will have important identities and interests in common, will know what to expect from one another (especially in situations of threat and stress), and will trust one another. If, then, a collective action is successful, it tends to produce a greater sense of collective identity, confidence, and pride. On this basis, in turn, there can develop increased participation and greater support from a mass constituency. Note, for example, this conclusion from a study of a black militant organization:

> In order for black militant organizations to gain a reasonable chance for survival, they must have, at the very least, the support of the black community. Such support must in turn be the result of these organizations' attempts to stress positive and meaningful aspects of the black experience, rather than focusing simply on the negative aspects of the larger society (Helmreich, 1973, 167).

A period of conflict and opposition may be crucial in helping a group to get a sense of its own identity — its strength in the face of outside opponents, the makeup of its membership, who are and are not dependable members, and the strength of commitment to each other. Joseph Fichter describes these aspects of an educational campaign intended to promote integration of colleges and schools within the New Orleans Catholic community: "We were able to distinguish between the friends and the foes of integration, between the fearful and the courageous, both within the Catholic Church and the New Orleans population. . . . Strong opposition came from some Catholics; strong support came from some non-Catholics" (Fichter, 1973, 109).

Similarly, individuals involved in various programs of "non-violent direct action for social change,"[1] place high stock in knowing each other well, developing a sense of community and commitment; and they often undergo "stress trials" and exercises in order to be prepared for coping with the ways in which individuals and the group will react under conditions of stress. Such shared preparatory experiences themselves often increase group commitment and loyalty.

Obviously then, a group does not have to "go blind" into situations or operate on faith alone—it can take stock of its makeup, strengths, and weaknesses, and can plan accordingly. Ignorance of its own capabilities and limitations may be a new movement's greatest weakness.

A good case can be made for regarding the following as the first crucial questions to be answered by leaders of an emerging partisan collectivity: What are our resources for concerted action? What may they become? Given that our collectivity in the beginning has little power, how can it maximize its influence to gain more resources? What kinds and amounts of the resources we do have can be used in what ways to be both effective and efficient in (1) blocking undesired actions of our opponents, (2) attaining positive common goals. The ways in which ethnic group partisans will react to authorities are strongly shaped by three kinds of evaluations of expected political outputs (Gamson, 1968, Chapter 3).

1. *Interests:* do their actions serve my interests or the interests of others similar to me or others with whom I identify or sympathize?
2. *Fairness:* do their actions correspond to norms that I regard as valid?
3. *Competence or efficiency:* do they do well whatever it is they do?

Judged in these terms, trust in the outcomes to be expected from authorities may be high or low—when authorities are simply left alone without any direct attempt to influence them. But potential partisans also judge their own capability to influence the decisions; this is the "efficacy" or "input" aspect of relations to authorities. Combining the two sets of judgments gives us four main types of appraisals of a political system (see accompanying tabulation

Judgments of Output (i.e., of Need to Attempt Influence)	Judgments of Ability to Influence the Authorities (Input)	
	High Efficacy	Low Efficacy
High trust	Responsive and in my interests (identification)	Unresponsive but will serve my interests anyway (benevolent elite, etc.)
Low trust	Responsive but requires continuous pressure	Unresponsive and opposed to my interests (hostile dictatorship)

[Gamson, 1968, 42-57]). When authorities are "benevolent"—no matter why —members of a low-power minority sometimes find they can gain sufficient response from the decision-makers simply by using persuasion and implicit inducements (such as voting for incumbents in the next election); the partisans thus receive adequate rewards without having to resort to special pressures. A somewhat marginal case in point appears to be the rapid rise in opportunities and social status opened to Japanese-Americans immediately following World War II, as facilitated by their military service records. Widespread and favorable publicity had been given to the "most decorated" Go-for-Broke battalion that fought in Italy, and the meritorious record of service in the Pacific had a quieter but appreciable influence. Furthermore, the military experience itself caused them to develop skills, motivations, and expectancies that aided in rapid upward social mobility. Returning Japanese-American servicemen had a self-image of heroism and social worth (Samuels, 1970). Black servicemen also returned with new reputation, self-image, and expectations, but unlike the Nisei confronted a rigid castelike system that initially was not responsive to the new claims. When authorities do not respond positively to persuasive claims of this kind, low-power minorities must turn, as we have seen in Chapter 8, to some form of pressure or constraint if they are to effect substantial gains in political outputs received.

Influence on political processes can take three quite different forms. In the interest-group mode, definite organizations are developed that present requests, claims, and demands through institutionalized channels to decision-makers, e.g., to key committees in a legislature. In the second form, attempted influence is informal through particularistic relationships and tends to focus upon administration and enforcement. In the third case, coercive means are used in nonconventional political action.

For any set of potential partisans in a society, the influence that can be brought to bear upon authorities depends upon the base values or resources that the partisans can mobilize for attempts to influence. Examples of such values and resources include: the ability to elect, hire, fire, promote; authority to make decisions about public demonstrations; ability to allocate corporation funds to civic projects; possession of a reputation for wisdom in public affairs; ability to enhance or damage reputation through communication media; ability to influence voters to withdraw support from individuals or projects. Control of "movable" resources means that one can hold out inducements, offer to withdraw inducements, threaten disadvantage.

A grouping that has relatively low power in the society as a whole nevertheless may be able to develop substantial power within local areas or particular organizations and institutions. For white merchants located within black ghettos, a boycott can be a decisive threat. Observe how many formerly all-white colleges and universities that admitted considerable numbers of black and other minority students under a liberal-universalistic ideology were unable or unwilling to resist subsequent internal pressures for separate racial programs, including residential segregation. Concentration in large cities in swing states may give a well-disciplined small grouping special political bargaining power in a close election. If an ethnic minority can become the predominant work force in a strong union in a key "bottle-neck" industry, it can use the strike as a major resource to build both its resources and its long-term political influence.

Appraisals of political strategies and subsequent outcomes make sense only if we distinguish between insiders and outsiders in the institutionalized order of power and authority.

> Pluralist theory is a portrait of the inside of the political arena. There one sees a more or less orderly contest, carried out by the classic pluralist rules of bargaining, lobbying, coalition formation, negotiation, and compromise. The issue of how one gets into the pressure system is not treated as a central problem (Gamson, 1975, 141).

What we have called conventional politics occurs inside the arena. Outside are not only the challengers — who *must* be "unconventional" if they are to be listened to — but also the inarticulate, the unorganized, the disconnected people who do not appear at all in the collective struggles of the day. If one wishes to see the powerless and unrepresented elements of the polity effectively taken into account, one may count as successful social change only developments that mobilize discontent and precipitate conflict until the authorities must attend to a new partisan component as a legitimate contender.

An excellent example of the multiple resources involved in any successful movement to increase the influence of a low-power minority is found in the changing political position of black Americans. The increased influence was not established by any single and simple line of action, but rather was built through many prosaic, interrelated processes such as fund-raising, campaigning, propagandizing, registering, voting, petitioning, bringing suit in the courts, protesting, and so on.

Back of these specific activities were the changing political resources that developed from five main sources: (1) concentration of black population in large northern cities, with resulting political organization and representation; (2) the development of greater economic strength; (3) the rise of an articulate and sophisticated leadership, skilled in organization and legal action; (4) activation of white allies especially among college students, religious groups, unions, and mass media; (5) demonstrated capacities for both organized nonviolent coercion and collective violence.

We are trying to understand the practical implications of situational specificity by inspecting a series of diverse examples. Let us try another case. One of the major built-in dilemmas of collective social action on behalf of disadvantaged people lies in the *inevitable* differences between aspirations and consequences. To evoke involvement and commitment of the necessary participants, there must be strong motivation, which requires a mixture of discontent and hope. Unless there is an expectation of gain, motivation will flag. But no approach, ideology, strategy, technique, or device ever brings instant realization of all goals or gratification of all desires. Therefore, when mobilization for action does occur, almost always both the aspirations and the expectations of the rank and file will exceed the gains possible in the moment at hand. The tactics of direct collective action on a large scale are especially likely to produce an extreme rhetoric that encourages inflation of expectations. When the outcomes then inevitably fall short of claims, the results are intensification of frustration and generalized cynicism (Meier, 1973, Introduction).

Still more generally, it is important to see that the very character of conflicts always results from a particular social context. The situation producing conflict will influence the program of means used in carrying on and in ending the struggle, whether in small groups or great collective movements. As Bendix (1963, 538) has pointed out, different kinds of social structures produce different types of protest movements among those who feel aggrieved. Medieval European societies, for example, produced social banditry and religiously influenced millenarian movements. By the nineteenth century the typical forms of protest had shifted to movements demanding rights of citizenship. To see the relevance of this observation for contemporary intergroup relations one need only contrast the change in types of organizations and in the purposes of social movements among black Americans between the beginnings of desegregation in the 1940s and the Black Caucuses of the 1970s.

Even in what outside observers often see as a monolithic and unchanging system of racial domination, complex and subtle strategic possibilities may exist. Thus in South Africa

focus on the static nature of entrenched White rule and Black subordination easily overlooks the latent dynamics of the contradictions of apartheid. . . . Racial supremacy, at the very least, has to legitimize itself at the end of the colonial era and cannot afford to rely on the brute and cynical use of force alone. This interplay between legitimizing ideology and contradictory reality opens one avenue of challenge to the existing power. Its necessary interconnection with outside forces, and its reliance on external economic and political support, constitutes a lever of influence absent in an isolated fortress. Finally, the internal economic scene with its own dictates would seem to lead to an alternative setting in favour of the subordinates. Not that economic expansion will automatically or necessarily lead to different race relations, as the old liberal illusion asserts; but the inclusion of better skilled Blacks into a diversified economy will change the constellation of power whereby the powerless are able to act with more likely success in a strike situation (Adam, 1973, 149).

The large-scale historical cases will illustrate — not surprisingly — greatly varying combinations of the basic conditions to which partisans must adapt strategies. At the opposite end of the scale, however, one still finds complex strategic possibilities even in small ad hoc situations. Thus over an extensive series of experimental trials in which persons played the Prisoners' Dilemma game, Deutsch, Epstein, and Canavan studied the outcomes of strategies of altruistic benevolence, reactive defense, reactive threat, and of threat or attack followed by altruistic or cooperative responses. The investigators concluded that mutually rewarding cooperation was not maximized either by a punitive or by a rewarding reaction to noncooperative behavior. Meeting noncooperation with reward leads to exploitation of the benevolent party, unless the latter already has demonstrated aggression capabilities. Punitive responses effectively conceal any cooperative intent. The third possibility is to respond generously to cooperative behavior while not allowing the other party to gain rewards by noncooperation. This policy of being firm in defending one's own interest, but reciprocating altruism and cooperation, brings high joint rewards (Deutsch, 1973, 54).

These few examples obviously are inadequate to even suggest the richness of the diverse elements and combinations of elements that necessarily affect selection and execution of strategies in actual situations. But perhaps all we need to do at this point is to make explicit the Situational Axiom and to state its corollary: all effective strategies are complex composites of different tactics, variously phased and paced. We already have seen numerous particular examples, expecially in Chapter 1, Chapters 4-5, and Chapter 8.

A main task of planning and leadership in collective efforts to influence intergroup relations, therefore, is to *diagnose the basic strategic problems and to devise appropriate sequences of action* — in short, to fit the remedy to the problem.

2. How May Conflicts Be Resolved? a Preliminary Example

In Chapter 12 we shall deal in depth with the problems of conflict resolution. Here we note that composite strategies are required. Before we can see what the possibilities are for "dealing with" conflict, let us identify some of the generic kinds of collective conflict situations we may confront. The following are types that are both important and frequent:

1. Unregulated diffuse conflict, e.g., rancorous community disputes, factional cleavages, communal violence.
2. Individualized rather than organized protest and discontent within an authoritatively regulated social organization—a school, a corporation, a labor union, a military unit.
3. Social movements of dissent and protest directed against established institutions and decision-making elites, e.g., fundamentalist protesters versus school boards; integrationist blacks and white sympathizers versus a housing authority.
4. Confrontations of highly organized opposing social movements, e.g., civil rights organizations versus white citizens councils in the 1960s.
5. Organized conflict between centralized agencies, e.g., unions and business firms; interest groups; religious bodies.

Some generalizations apply to all these types. Many sequences of increasingly intense conflict are checked by the rising costs in (a) direct outlays of resources and (b) deprivations and damage suffered. Such direct costs lend strong credibility to threats of further dire consequences; in this way, the use of threat may serve as a conflict-limiting and conflict-reducing means. The effectiveness of threat apparently is enhanced in most instances if threat is coupled with positive inducement, e.g., an offer of cooperation or exchange and indications of willingness to reciprocate friendly behavior from the other side (Deutsch, 1973, 52-54).[2]

Often noted by analysts of large-scale and continuing oppositions between collectivities is the fact that any two major contenders will use conflicts between still other parties as vehicles for negotiation, threat, mutual cooperation, and symbolization through tacit maneuvers of changes in the primary relationship. For example, two super-powers use disputes between other countries as a means of communication and as a tactic in their own conflictual relationship. A restricted conflict, for instance, in a peripheral region allows them (1) to compete, by supporting various countries with arms and military supplies; (2) to negotiate in the context of a mutual threat of escalation regarding "what to do about the Middle East situation"; (3) to cooperate in putting forward a joint proposal or even in simply agreeing upon a common goal of finding a settlement to a current crisis; (4) to reinforce the image of themselves as "peace-loving" or "uncompromising"; and (5) to use the situation as an opportunity to approach each other, to negotiate and establish a channel of communications without losing face in a situation in which it might otherwise appear that one or both were making a concession indicative of weakness.

The social arrangements that can be instituted for regulating or resolving disputes and fights typically differ from one main type of conflict to another.

Very difficult to resolve, without authoritative intervention of an overwhelming powerful third party, are diffuse community conflicts. The lack of clear or dependable structures of communication and authority, the lack of prior development of ground rules, and the diversity of interests and aims that generally prevails—all these militate against regularized procedures or stable compromises.

In contrast, when social interests are articulated by stable elites that interact as representatives of formal organizations or as elected representatives within governing bodies, the resolution of disputes is most likely to take the form of "secret agreements privately arrived at," which are then formalized as public compromise agreements (Steiner, 1974). Such authoritative and formalized modes of dealing with disagreements and conflicts are illustrated in two-party legislative bodies, especially in the continuing committees that in effect serve as sublegislatures, as well as in administrative councils and in the hierarchical grievance procedures often found in bureaucratic organizations.

When diffuse dissent and protests against authorities reach high levels or become focalized in definite collective movements, the most common form of response by authorities apparently is to attempt some form of co-optation, that is, bringing into the decision-making structure some persons who are regarded as representatives of the population from which dissent or opposition is emerging. When co-optation is successful—from the standpoint of the authorities—it replaces diffuse, unorganized, heterogeneous, and often erratic demands with a coherent set of organized and simplified demands and claims. It replaces a multitude of protestors with a few claimants or representatives (Coleman, 1957). It thus reduces diversity, organizes communication, and centralizes responsibility. For an organization representing a low-power collectivity, there always is a dilemma when its growing influence leads to offers by the formerly intractable authorities to accept members of the minority as part of the decision-making structure. Great potential advantages may come from participation in authoritative allocations of scarce resources and in establishing basic social norms. The dangers are those of token acceptance, unduly limited concessions, and subsequent constriction of growth in influence.

3. Conditions Appropriate for Different Programs and Styles of Collective Action

As over against established organizations and highly institutionalized groups, social movements are structurally loose, changeable, and internally fluid. As such movements pass beyond initial agitation and mobilization, and begin to engage in concerted actions, pressures develop for changes in structure, leadership, and patterns of participation. The demands of instrumental goal-oriented collective action are different from those of actions of expressing sentiments and developing solidarity. At a very simple level, just the pressures created by the internal logistics of collective action tend to turn the movement in the direction of becoming an organization with a differentiated structure. For in collective expressive processes, the time required is a direct function of the number of persons involved: if everyone in a large collectivity were to express himself or herself with regard to an issue, it is unlikely that a decision could be reached at all—for the issue would have changed before the expressive processes could be completed. The real time required is not reducible. In instrumental processes, therefore, the alternatives must be simplified and participation curtailed in some manner if decisions are to be made that will direct some future collective actions (Kolaja, 1968).

For conflict to become genuinely *collective*, rather than individualistic, particularistic, or relational, some process of depersonalization of the opponents must occur. Collective conflict involves some definition of characteristics that are common to all or most members of an aggregate or category, rather than the unique characteristics of an interpersonal relationship or the idiosyncratic qualities of a particular individual (Howard, 1974, 140-41). Collective conflict implies—and helps to generate—a conceptualization of the Others as some kind of a social system or social grouping. A collective-systemic conception rather than a personalized view of the sources of discrimination and blockage of opportunity also works toward dissolving both psychological and social barriers to the acknowledgment and expression of grievances and of claims and demands. The two related developments—attributing difficulties to collective rather than individualized sources, and articulation of grievances and demands—seems to grow with participation in group action. Social movements arising in disadvantaged collectivities often generate their programs by improvisation through mass action.

In every particular historical struggle, collective goals and appropriate strategies will change as a movement begins to attain some of its initial objectives. Thus a disadvantaged minority that strives for equality will face a moral dilemma if and when it begins to move into a position of greater autonomy and responsibility. For example, in the initial struggles, there are great tactical advantages in espousing a doctrine of social determinism.

If we can say that we are victims of a social system we did not make, we can claim to be victims of conditions. And by the same social determinism, we can explain away any failures or deficiencies in our own behavior (Patterson, 1973, 52-54). But to fully accept social determinism as a working philosophy[3] involves the victim in a relation of dependency upon the victimizer, reduces his or her social role to that of an object, and ultimately provides moral exculpation for members of the collectivity that has been identified as the oppressor—who, after all, must have been so determined by social and cultural factors that they could not have acted otherwise. To completely attribute one's undesired condition to a determining environment while at the same time taking pride in the positively valued characteristics that have been developed in that self-same environment is to fall into inconsistency, and to attribute all responsibility to the dominant group is, as Patterson says, to grant it the moral autonomy one thereby denies for the oppressed. This valid and useful insight, however, can easily lend itself to misunderstanding. It does not imply that "social determinism" is equally compelling upon politically dominant and subordinate collectivities. For just to the extent that an ethnic minority has experienced coercive deprivation, it actually will not have had the objective freedom for autonomous moral action that has been open to its more powerful opponents.

Finally, the need for persistent probing and skeptical analysis to identify and anticipate the possible consequences of all major aspects of a concrete situation often is not obvious. It is especially difficult to stay alert to this need in cases in which immediate advantages obscure more fundamental realities. A generic case in point is the "strategies of diversion," whereby more powerful groups may reduce the political threat of minority discontent.

"Diversions" may be subtle. Thus it is no surprise to note that one way of reducing and managing protest and dissent with reference to central issues of political power and economic distribution is for the authorities to demonstrate full acceptance of complaints and prompt correction of difficulties in those matters that are of less importance to the authorities. When small grievances thus can be freely expressed, and are speedily redressed by authorities, the attention of the partisans often will become centered upon securing small changes that are immediately rewarding but are marginal to more crucial long-term questions. A striking example is reported for the highly segregated society of southern Africa. In spite of rigid racial segregation in most activities, there is very active joint black-white concern for the beer halls that are major centers of social life for African male workers. There is rapid communication of shortcomings as perceived by blacks, and prompt remedial action by white authorities. This active communication and collaboration in one area of life seems to shunt attention and communication from other issues (Walcott, 1974).

Quite often in human affairs the features of situations that appear most obvious in retrospect turn out to have been ignored at crucial earlier points in diagnosis and subsequent strategies and tactics. It is for this reason that we have so strongly emphasized the need for making every application of scientific principles (and generalized lore of experience) contingent upon *particular, detailed attention to the characteristics of each situation.* In making such diagnoses clear, initial conceptualization and general analyses are highly useful but never enough, and must always be appraised carefully and skeptically in view of the peculiarities of immediate tasks and problems.

We believe there is value, for example, in making explicit the way styles of negotiation probably will vary under the different possible combinations of three generic factors: (1) the extent to which we have important and continuing relations of positive interdependence with an opponent, (2) the degree of immediate opposition or disagreement, and (3) the degree of confidence (or "trust") we have that our opponent will subsequently carry through any negotiated agreement we make.

Put in tabular summary, what seem to be the more likely—and more appropriate—modes of negotiation and settlement are noted in the eight cells of Table 9.1. These possibilities are greatly changed if one party is overwhelmingly powerful either (a) because of extreme control of penalties or (b) because the other is greatly dependent on the first party for essential security and gratification. It is instructive to think through the probable effects of various other modifying conditions that are likely to be encountered. The generalizations indicated by Table 9.1 seem to us broadly valid. They can be of substantial heuristic value for purposes of action by leaders of partisan organizations. But they will be useful only if applied with the vigilance and skepticism implied by our understanding of the Situational Axiom.

4. Main Conclusions

In this chapter, we have taken the point of view of a low-power party seeking to bring about changes in the social system of which it is a part. We note these generalizations.

1. All efforts to maintain an existing state of affairs or to change it are made by particular people in specific contexts.

2. Some factors at a given time are manipulable and others are not. Which are and which are not partly depends upon who is acting and what the issues are.

3. The interests of individuals or collectivities must be made politically visible if they are to be taken into account by authorities. This means that interests must be articulated and grievances made explicit, and these views must be communicated to focal centers of influence and decision-making. Authorities must be shown that incorrect decisions or failure to take necessary actions will have negative consequences for them or to values they hold, or authorities must be convinced that positive consequences will ensue from an attentive and appropriate decision.

Table 9.1. Negotiative Styles Appropriate to Types of Relationships between the Principal Parties

Degree of Confidence in Commitments of Opponent	Positive, Continuing Advantages in Interdependence			
	High		Low	
	Immediate Opposition of Interests			
	High	Low	High	Low
High	(1) Fully formal, conventionalized negotiation. Reliance on "Rules of Accommodation."	(2) Informal negotiations; agreements "in principle."	(3) As in (1) but more likely to seek finished 'ad hoc agreement.	(4) Informal understandings.
Low	(5) Tacit bargaining; use of intermediaries; "hard line"—amenities secondary.	(6) Informal negotiations; but explicit bargains, with third-party sanctioning power.	(7) Formal procedure; maximum explicit safeguards.	(8) Minimal contact or commitment.

4. Strategies may primarily emphasize direct attempts to influence decision-makers or may emphasize the developing of resources and of organization within the low-power grouping as a basis for increasing the grouping's capabilities for autonomous persuasion, inducement, and constraint.

5. Persuasion is the most obviously appropriate first approach for a lower-power collectivity seeking decisions from authorities. But low-power groups that have not effectively exerted influence in the past usually will not receive much attention for their efforts to persuade. The more effective means of offering inducements will be limited by the scanty resources controlled by the low-power groups.

6. If neither persuasion nor inducement is effective, constraints may be invoked, i.e., some form of threat. To be effective, threats must be credible. The most credible threat is continuing a noxious or destructive activity already underway or recently demonstrated. Once a threat has become credible and important to authorities, the most effective tactic for partisans is to present the cessation of the threat as a positive inducement for action desired by the partisans. Spokesmen for the partisans often can truly say that both parties desire an end to the unpleasantness. A conciliatory attitude harmonizes well with a highly credible threat, making an agreement more likely without loss of face. In general, with many exceptions, threat is more effective in getting attention and in opening access to negotiation than in producing desired actions.

7. Whatever the tactics used, minimal costs will be incurred if inducements and threats and other constraints are those that will be regarded by third parties and opponents as *proportionate* to the objectives, *appropriate* to the situation, and *legitimate* in terms of major relevant beliefs and values.

8. One's opponents rarely constitute a completely solidary formation. A diversified strategy generally is more effective than a single mode of approach.

9. Because we are less powerful, in some sense, than our opponents, we rarely can do without allies. Hence our strategies should pay special attention to effects upon potential allies.

10. Effective, comprehensive, and enduring change in intergroup relations requires a combination of five classes of factors: (1) legitimating values and beliefs that are specified in (2) a localized and current ideology, (3) economic resources, (4) organization, (5) political power (in the broadest sense). These factors then have to be combined to generate crises through challenges to established patterns of control and privilege. Only after a crisis has been experienced can substantial change be instituted and maintained. (Whether or not there are exceptions to this generalization depends upon one's definition of "crisis.")

If we were in the business of supplying cookbook rules for low-power minorities striving to change the behavior of authorities, we probably would start by restating the points just reviewed in the form of such crude dicta as the following:

Illustrative Prescriptions: Handle with Care

1. If you can persuade, do.
2. If you cannot persuade, try inducement. If selective incentives are not too costly, use them. Fair exchange is no robbery.
3. If neither persuasion nor inducement brings satisfactory outcomes, test the available modes of noncooperation. If these procedures are not effective, consider the likely costs and gains of nonviolent intervention.
4. If intervention is used and opens opportunities for negotiation, use them.
5. If negotiations fail, responsible individuals must use their best ethical judgment to help decide whether more drastic means are justified or can be tolerated.
6. If one decides not to acquiesce in stalemates or to accept the status quo and if it is ethically acceptable to use violence as a last resort, the risks of escalation and the probable costs may require careful estimation and difficult strategic decisions. Forethought may be needed to anticipate eventual possibilities for settlement.

Implicit in all such dicta for action or in "proverbs" concerning intergroup strategies are ethical judgments. Also implicit (as all our readers fully know by now) are estimates of the characteristics of our own group and of the responsiveness and efficiency of the authorities with which we must cope. As Gamson and McEvoy (1970, 164-72) have shown, our *basic* choices of strategies depend upon whether our group's relation to the authorities is *confident, neutral,* or *alienated.* If we are confident, we believe that the regime and the incumbent authorities generally will favor our interests if they know what those interests are. Our preferred strategy, then, evidently ought to be the low-cost program of *persuasion.* If we believe the authorities to be essentially neutral, we shall use whatever resources we can bring to bear as *inducements.* But if we believe that decisions opposed to our interests are the typical outcomes of the existing institutions, of the decision-making structure ("the regime") and of the particular incumbents who are making binding decisions, then we shall have only a strategy of *constraint* to protect us.

Actual instances of collective social actions manifestly often are so complex in detail and imperfectly known as to be impenetrable to real-time analysis. In the abstract, a freely choosing leader could select from literally hundreds of *major* techniques. A Manual of Techniques could not list in less space than this entire book the specific techniques known to have been used on some actual occasion. It is easy to see why the preparation of such a manual could not be our objective here. Enough has been said, perhaps, to suggest how a student of strategy and tactics can go about the job of becoming adequately informed (Shellow and Roemer, 1966). He or she must count upon the necessity for experiencing many mistakes of practice and many sometimes unpalatable personal discoveries before *information* becomes assimilated into a set of personal capabilities for quickly making sophisticated *judgments* in practical situations.

It makes no sense to talk of strategies unless we can refer to centers of decision-making, and there are no centers of decision-making unless there is some definite social organization. To say "organization," in turn implies continuity, control of resources, and commitments and loyalties on the part of participants. Sustained purposive action is implied. Thus we are once more reminded that the possibilities for attaining collective goals of any kind always are shaped by the degree and kind of organization, authority, and control of resources available in any particular situation. No matter how intense the diffuse aspiration of even large aggregates of potential partisans who have been excluded from primary political influence, successful claims to greater access and efficacy are unlikely unless such definite social structures can be developed.

A second fundamental basis for thinking about strategy is that no partisan movement or organization deals with an opponent on a one-to-one basis in a social vacuum. Always there are other potential adversaries and other potential allies. Always the decision-makers must consider whether coalitions are feasible and advisable.

A third fundamental point is that, practically speaking, nearly all important intergroup relations represent mixed-motive games, i.e., varying mixtures of interests that are common, complementary, divergent, opposed, and incompatible. Both effortless cooperation and pure conflict are fictions.

Further, in intergroup strategies one must take into account the real-world fact that in nearly all instances one's opponent and one's allies will still be there tomorrow. Interactions and transactions are rarely if ever purely immediate and ad hoc: they represent relationships rather than mere occasions or isolated events. Hence realistic strategies must somehow balance or tradeoff short-range and longer-term interests.

For all these reasons, the actual strategies employed in this field are likely to be mixed or composite programs that are used in varied situations, which change over time. Only in rare and extreme cases, therefore, is it possible to give an unequivocal answer to such broad questions as "Should coalitions be sought?" or "Should we choose threats or inducements?" or "Is it better to negotiate now or take direct action first?"

Chapter 10

Effects of Persuasion, Inducement, and Participation

PART I. PERSUASION AND INDUCEMENT

The pen is mightier than the sword.
Edward Bulwer Lytton

Power grows out of the barrel of a gun.
Chairman Mao

Every man has his price.
Proverb

1. The Importance of Context

We have noted that persuasion is a relatively low-cost process that is effective under quite specific conditions, many of which were reviewed in Chapters 5 and 6.

In general, the successful short-run uses of persuasion are found in relationships of trust in which the persons to be persuaded are either neutral or already favorably disposed. On the other hand, persuasion often has almost no short-run efficacy against the opposition of solidary groups that are defending strong interests and rigidly held values and beliefs that are supported by high ingroup consensus.

The attempt to persuade or convert one's opponent often depends less upon sheer exhortation or offering of factual information than upon the complex impacts of "propaganda of the deed." Thus advocates of a policy of nonviolent and nonhostile behavior toward opponents claim that a "conversion

257

mechanism" may operate among individuals in the opposing group and among third-party witnesses which will make repression or acts of violent opposition by authorities appear less justifiable when exercised against people who are nonviolent and personally friendly (Sharp, 1973, 634). But this outcome depends upon so many specific conditions being favorable (Sharp, 1973, 727)[1] that it is not really very useful to ask the bald question, "Can one persuade or convert a hostile opponent?" The answer has to be yes and no: the effectiveness of attempted persuasion always depends not only upon the nature of the issues and the characteristics of the communicating parties but also upon the inducements and constraints that are present.

2. Persuasion and Inducement in Organized Religion

No thorough examination of the varieties of influence can overlook the tremendous role of organized religion in the attempt to persuade, induce, and constrain individuals to behave and think according to a particular set of social values. Yet the absence of uniform results shows that here, as in other sectors, the outcomes are strongly affected by complex differences between social contexts.

Over and over again, studies of attempts to produce changes in ethnic relations and in directly relevant governmental and other institutional policies (in corporations, churches, unions, etc.) show the inherent tradeoffs between maintaining amicable relationships and actually getting tangible results. Exclusive reliance upon persuasion often means that one must not press too hard for immediate change in economic and political relationships. To challenge and to confront in the interest of exerting pressure for change means accepting controversy and resistance. The familiar pattern is clearly shown by comparison of church groups in the United States that have engaged in direct action to correct what they held to be racial injustices, with those that have elected to inform, interpret, and persuade, and with those that have supported the status quo and strongly resisted change in racial-ethnic relations (Hadden and Longino, 1974; Quinley, 1974).

What meager evidence there is suggests that, on the whole, persons from dominant ethnic communities who are active participants in organized religion are not thereby persuaded to act in more equalitarian or cooperative ways toward the economic, political, educational, or other claims of aspiring minorities (Osborne, 1967; Bouma, 1970; Stark et al., 1971; Smith, 1972). And studies that have tried to find specific causal relationships between religious beliefs or participation in religious groups and ethnic attitudes and behavior have been fully convincing in only a few instances (Williams, 1947, 68; Bouma, 1970).

One well-established finding is that ethnic prejudice is lowest among persons who either do not participate in organized religion at all or participate very intensively. Those who participate, but only infrequently, are highest in prejudice. This curvilinear relationship is found consistently in many different populations, suggesting that the social conformity of conventional religiosity supports ethnic prejudice, whereas "intrinsic" religious commitments to an ethic of universalism discourages prejudice (Allport and Ross, 1967). Also there is evidence that, on the whole, high participation in church by black Americans in the 1960s was associated with low militancy with regard to civil rights activities (Marx, 1967; cf. Nelsen et al., eds. 1971).

A minority of high-participators and religious leaders, however, drew upon religious beliefs and commitments to support the struggle for equal rights. And multiple regression analysis of historical data indicates that nineteenth-century revivalism in Ohio had tangible effects on attitudes and beliefs that directly led to increased antislavery voting (Hammond, 1974). The manifest effects of revivalism are not removed by controls for rurality, population growth, denomination, prior political party tradition, or ethnicity. Thus "the revivals transformed the religious orientations of those who experienced them, and this transformation affected their voting behavior" (Hammond, 1974, 175). Among black people, furthermore, a common element in the very diverse types of religious movements and organizations has been a concern with social power on the part of a powerless people; cults, sects, and denominations frequently were the context from which political leadership emerged (Washington, 1972).

It is plain that there are, indeed, some situations in which religious values and beliefs can become powerful means of persuasion (Yinger, 1957). And it is equally evident that religious persuasion often arouses intense psychological dissonance and ambivalence. For example, appeals to religious values and norms may arouse feelings of guilt or pangs of conscience about ethnically discriminatory behavior—even while the individual also has contradictory motivations. Thus appeals to conscience in intergroup relations, as elsewhere, are double-edged and often produce dissonant or counterreactive outcomes: e.g., *either* intensified prejudice *or* strong "conversion" (Williams, 1947, 67-68, 73-74; Williams et al., 1964, 94-96, 108-10, 202-22). Indeed, ambivalence seems to act as an *amplifier*, intensifying prior orientations whether unfriendly or friendly, depending upon which way the balance tips in behavior (Katz, 1970). The contradictory outcomes in behavior have been observed repeatedly. Individuals who have been exposed to strongly religious training, or who participate in organized religious activities, do not necessarily manifest less hostility or greater tolerance than individuals not having these characteristics. Only certain types of religious training are effective in lessening intergroup hostility.

Early sociological studies were quick to note the "double-faced" role of organized religion—acting sometimes as "opiate," sometimes as "awakener." These differing orientations are more closely related to such factors as regional, rural-urban, and class differences than to particular religious orientations (Francis, 1954; Rogg, 1974). Although there is some evidence that white Protestant ministers are more liberal than their congregations on racial issues, regional differences (South vs. non-South) continue, possibly because of selective migration and of decentralized organization (Rymph and Hadden, 1970). Equivalent complexity is evident among southern white Protestant groupings, where rural-urban and class factors seem more predictive than religious beliefs of racial attitudes (Harrell, 1971).

Lack of consensus often severely limits the persuasive influence of religious groupings. It has been shown, for example, how the unanticipated involvement of a complex and heterogeneous religious organization with a social movement for civil rights can place substantial strains upon initial commitments, which did not include civil rights; maintenance of the organizational commitments is then possible only through multiple processes of reassessment (Wood, 1972). Evident in many studies of orientations of religious collectivities to ethnic and racial relations are instabilities arising both from incompatibilities between religious values and the values and interests of the social settings in which organized religion is embedded, and from incompatibilities within sets of religious beliefs and values themselves (Smith, 1972; Stark et al., 1971).

3. "Symbolic Interaction": the Interplay of Persuasion, Inducement, Constraint

In almost every conflict, processes of persuasion and inducement are going on *within* groups at the same time they are operating *between* groups. Persuasion toward a stand on particular issues may be directed to followers or other fellow members as well as to opponents; the inducements of enhanced peer evaluation or increased self-determination may motivate a group toward mobilization and direct action, whereas opponents may be induced to grant certain demands by an offer of future cooperation that, in turn, has been rendered especially desirable by evidences of one's own growing strength. Thus in a single situation, the leaders of a challenging group may be involved simultaneously in all of the following processes: (1) falsifying claims of the dominant ideologies; (2) exposing inconsistencies and illegitimate elements in beliefs that formerly justified conditions or behavior now regarded as unjust; (3) holding out to disadvantaged persons new images, self-conceptions, and possibilities for social change; (4) stimulating hope; (5) reducing fear. These processes, if successful, will enhance the sense of injustice already present in the challenging group and will increase mobilization for collective effort (Deutsch, 1973, 66).

Persuasion without substantial effectiveness is sometimes institutionalized —as a kind of gesture or ritual. A prominent example is provided by arrangements for the conciliation of disputes that rely entirely upon the initiation of complaints by weak parties who are vulnerable to retaliatory actions. When the power of the parties is grossly unequal and the stronger party has strong interests that would be adversely affected by a bilateral settlement, to have efforts at conciliation depend upon complaints initiated by aggrieved individuals is to ensure ineffectiveness (Lawrence, 1974, 204). Careful assessment by a governor's committee in New York State, for example, led to an eloquent statement of the severe limitations of a conciliatory-legalistic approach to entrenched practices of ethnic and racial discrimination (Debevoise, 1968, 7-9).

But if there are, indeed, many contexts in which persuasion fails in the face of counteracting constraints and inducements, there are other instances in which prior persuasion is essential to successful tradeoffs. Every compromise involves not only relative power (control of constraints) and capability to offer inducements but also some agreement on values and norms.

For compromise to occur between parties who disagree over the distribution or allocation of benefits and advantages, it is not sufficient to "divide up the differences." An additional requirement is some shared conception of what is fair and appropriate. A stable settlement, in other words, is one that can be defended to other concerned persons as a just compromise (Wilson, 1975, 93).

Similarly, the interplay of structural constraints with the use of inducements often is close and subtle. Negotiators may be willing to negotiate, for example, because their own interests are thereby served, and they may then be effective just because their very position of involvement enables them to hold out implicit inducements and threats or warnings. For example, Jones and Long report that white negotiators in desegregation of public schools in southern cities often were branch executives of large companies. These persons were able to make bargains acceptable to white segregationists because of their unquestioned legitimacy, their economic control, and their self-interest in the resolution of community conflicts.

Management of such enterprises is tuned to "company policy" rather than to local vagaries of custom. Centrally controlled industries and business enterprises are operated under rules determined by top management and recognized as unchallengeable directives by widely dispersed branches. This convincing fact fitted local managers of big business enterprises for the negotiator role. The success of their immediate concern depended upon volume of business for which order and equanimity are essential. The prominence of bankers among the negotiators suggests another expression of the same over-riding interest. Since they control capital they are concerned about the general economic welfare that depends upon the productive use of capital by varied enterprises. Regardless of the personal predilections of the small entrepreneur he is accustomed to hear and heed the banker (Jones and Long, 1965, 37).

Persuasion involves an exchange of meanings between persons—it is a special kind of symbolic interaction. And offers of inducements and the presentation of threats likewise depend upon communication of complex symbolic materials. In interactions that involve struggle or opposition, the actions of each party usually will communicate to the other multiple meanings, including implicit signals concerning resources, intentions, and probable future actions. For example, the choice of options always is an indicator which may be used to infer a group's or an individual's values, sincerity, desperation, resources, and constraints. These expressive indications may be intended or unintended, overt or implicit.

The choice of options can either limit or open up possibilities for action by other involved parties, or do both simultaneously. When an opponent, party (A), secures an injunction or holds a strike or begins to carry out a publicity campaign, the responding party, (B), is forced to deal directly with the new conditions which have been imposed on the situation—by resistance, counterrestraints, matching opposition, withdrawal, or other options. At the same time, new militant actions by (A) may break precedents or exceed the "rules" and thereby open the conflict to escalation by both parties. Or the opponent, (A), may show weakness or reveal a previously undisclosed willingness to exercise restraint, thus allowing more aggressive action by (B).

The *symbolic* importance of such interchanges, i.e., their *persuasive* effects, should not be underestimated. As in strategic games such as chess, the shows of strength, fair play, foul play, and manipulation all take place. If a group is issued a challenge, its behavior may be considered a display of weakness if it does not respond to the "dare." Or the refusal to act may symbolize a fervent belief in moral principle. And, of course, the same action often is seen by different social participants in different ways. Most crucial, however, is not the variety of reactions a group receives but the significance of its actions in relation to certain strategic groups, such as authorities or possible sources of support.

The correct interpretation of cues often is the key to the type of influence that will be most successful. Valid diagnosis requires continuous attention to the changing admixtures of signals of uncompromising resistance as well as signs of willingness to accept limits and possible compromises. Indeed, it is not uncommon that a dispute will entail a highly emotional stance of principled opposition which tremendously raises the stakes, including the risks of violence and disturbance, while at the same time the leaders of the opposition may be using this emotional atmosphere to gain strategic advantage and are, in fact, actively working toward a situation in which compromise will yield favorable results. Thus, contrary to surface appearances, it might still be worthwhile to attempt persuasion with negatively inclined targets. In contrast, one will *not* wish to use constraints against friendly or neutral actors. The effects of the successful use of given means of influence on political trust, for example, are shown in the accompanying tabulation (Gamson, 1968, 173):

Trust Orientation	Means of Influence		
	Persuasion	Inducements	Constraints
Confidence . . .	Reinforces	—	—
Neutrality	+	Reinforces	—
Alienation	+	+	Reinforces

+ = increased trust (confidence).
— = decreased trust (confidence).

Accordingly, the choice of the type of influence depends upon the *situation*, the *audience* addressed, and the type of *outcome* desired. Up to this point we have dealt with the purposive attempts to exert influence by means of persuasion, inducement, and constraint. But there is no basis for assuming that influence must always be intentional. As we noted earlier, one of the most basic forms of influence is sheer presence. Any interaction with others as individuals or as groups has its effects on our experience and attitudes, and thus on our future conduct. Interaction often *is*, in itself, a primary form of persuasion.

We turn next, then, to the variety of effects that our coexistence with other groups in the social system may produce. It is immediately apparent that unplanned social contacts have extremely widespread and important effects that have not been specifically intended. But it will be seen also that intergroup contacts *may* be consciously planned and directed. In the latter instances, social interaction may be deliberately used as a primary means of persuasion.

PART II: INTERGROUP CONTACT, INTERACTION, PARTICIPATION

Proverbs

Absence makes the heart grow fonder.

The more we get together, the happier we are.

Birds of a feather flock together.

Variety is the spice of life.

Familiarity breeds contempt.

The enemy of my enemy is my friend.

4. "Context" Revisited

What sense can we make of common sense when it produces such ill-assorted dicta as these listed above? Very little. For the effects of social interaction are almost as varied as the contents of a total inventory of social behavior. Accordingly, if we are asked what effects to expect from social contacts between individual members of different ethnic categories, we can give no responsible answer until the *conditions* of the interaction are further specified. We said that water sometimes is a liquid, sometimes a solid, sometimes a gas. It even flows uphill if properly assisted. So, how does water behave? It depends upon the context. Much is known about water, and about social interaction, and the more we know, the more we become aware of the need to specify the conditions under which any description or generalization may be expected to hold. To repeat, things are what they are in the situations in which they occur —not otherwise.

We definitely know that there are circumstances under which even quite strongly prejudiced individuals will develop respect and liking for persons from an initially disliked and stereotyped outgroup category. Thus Cook (1969, 1971) has demonstrated experimentally that prejudiced whites can be brought to like and positively evaluate black co-workers in a cooperative task.

If it *can* be done, the only problem is to find out *how*. Once we know that intergroup interaction has positive outcomes under some conditions, the only additional step needed is to distill from experience just exactly what those circumstances are.

One can imagine an indefinitely large number of complex conditions that conceivably could influence the outcomes of group interactions. Many of these conditions will be trivial or specific to rare situations. What we really need to know is what are the really powerful clusters of recurring conditions that predictably result in clearly negative or clearly positive outcomes. The weak effects of extraordinary variables and exotic situations can be left aside for study at a later day of less social urgency.

Studies have shown that decreases in stereotyping, social distance, or other negative attitudes have often followed intergroup contact and interaction in the following situations:

Merchant Marine service (Brophy, 1945).

Co-workers (Harding and Hogrefe, 1952; MacKenzie, 1948; Minard, 1952; Palmore, 1955; Williams et al., 1964).

Customers and clerks (Saenger and Gilbert, 1950).

Residential proximity (Irish, 1952; Wilner, Price, Cook, 1952; Deutsch and Collins, 1958; Works, 1961; Shuval, 1962; Meer and Freedman, 1966; Morris, 1970).

Military service (see references in Chapter 1 above).

Attendance at a desegregated university (Muir, 1971).

Public schools in the United States (see studies listed in Amir, 1976, 259).

Summer camps (Amir, 1976, 259).

Church groups and religious settings (Leacock, Deutsch, Fishman, 1959; Parker, 1968; Irvine, 1973; Amir, 1976).

"Experimental" interactions (Sherif, 1966; Aellen and Lambert, 1969; Amir, 1976).

On the other hand, instances in which studies have reported that interracial contacts were followed by no change in attitudes or by increased social distance or animosity have included white and black women in a residence for unmarried mothers (Wertzer, 1971), white and black prisoners in a short-term penal institution (Bugansky, 1959), black and white patients in a hospital for chronic illness (tuberculosis) (Brown and Albee, 1966), desegregated schools under conditions of extreme threat or intergroup competition (Katz, 1958), residential areas being "invaded" by members of a racial grouping (Winder, 1952; Star, 1967; Kawwa, 1968; Orbell and Sherrill, 1969), and Israeli and Arab co-workers in Israel (Amir, 1976, 269).

What the negative cases show is that interaction, even if frequent and informal, is not a *sufficient* condition for increased tolerance, acceptance, or positive attraction. Nor is the sharing of common condition or fate, nor a nominal policy of nonsegregation on the part of social authorities. These conclusions should be in no sense surprising: the limitations of sheer "contact" have long been recognized (Williams, 1947, 69-73). We must welcome evidence of sharp differences in outcomes—for the variations give us our only chance of identifying the conditions that lie behind failure or success in reaching intended outcomes. We turn, accordingly, to our next central question.

5. What Conditions Affect Outcomes of Interaction?

In a concise review of studies of "behavior toward members of disliked groups," Cook (1970) cites the following as the main variables relating to the outcomes of intergroup interaction:

1. *Proximity*; opportunities for interaction.
2. Social *norms*, e.g., approval of persons in positions of authority or prestige; attitudes of peers.
3. *Equality* or inequality of status within the situation of interaction.
4. Degree of mutual *interdependence*.
5. *Similarity* or *divergence* between stereotypes and actual characteristics of persons with whom interaction occurs.
6. *Personal-intimate* versus impersonal-distant character of the situation.
7. *Valued traits* of outgroup persons.
8. *Similarity* (actual and perceived) of outgroup persons to the subject-person in beliefs, attitudes, and values.
9. *Relative socioeconomic-educational status* of the members of the disliked group.
10. *Proportion* of outgroup members in the population present in the situation.
11. *Outgroup attitudes* of the participants (perceived and actual).
12. *Norms of the peer group* regarding association with members of the outgroup.
13. Extent to which ingroup *peers are similar to one another* in beliefs, attitudes, and values.
14. *Sources of reward* and gratification and of deprivation and punishment: (a) social approval or disapproval; (b) other rewards and punishments.
15. *Norms* stated by accepted authorities regarding actions which should or should not be taken toward outgroup persons.
16. *Observed relationships* between particular behaviors toward outgroup persons and subsequent pleasant and unpleasant events; cues concerning probable consequences of various courses of action.
17. Acquaintance potential: *opportunities* provided by the situation for personal acquaintance with particular outgroup persons.
18. *Motivational* and *personality-system* factors, e.g., needs for approval, achievement, affiliation, economic return; self-esteem, ego-defense, anxiety, cognitive complexity, and flexibility.
19. *Values*.
20. *Competitive* versus *cooperative* structure of situational interdependence.
21. *Situational intimacy*.

This is a very long list, but long as it is, it surely is incomplete. Not surprising, therefore, is the complexity of outcomes — and the consequent necessity to be highly specific in our diagnoses of probable outcomes of interactions. Some useful evidence, for instance, comes from what might appear to be an unlikely source, that is, studies of "experimenter effects" in sociopsychological research. Among the many studies of this kind, some deal with differences in responses of subjects that are elicited by white as compared with black experimenters. There is solid evidence that the racial membership of the experimenter affects responses of subjects. But the data also show that the effects are exceedingly varied and depend in very elaborate ways upon the tasks, the reinforcements provided, the instructions given, and the sociocultural characteristics and attitudes of subjects and of experimenters or interviewers (Sattler, 1973).

The complex pattern of results is partly due also to variations in experimental or interview situations and to individual differences among experimenters and interviewers. Certainly *the lack of clear and overriding effects of racial category per se* is an important finding—contradicting the easy assumption that "race" will always have a substantial and unambiguous influence. The more specific findings that seem reasonably well supported have been summarized in a long passage, worth quoting in full:

> General trends emerge from the studies cited in the review, even though, as noted above, there are difficulties in making generalizations. (a) Though the experimenters' race in general may not affect physiological reactivity, high-prejudiced subjects have greater physiological reactivity to black experimenters than low-prejudiced subjects. (b) The experimenters' race at times affects black children's and black college students' performance on motor, cognitive, and decision-making tasks; the direction of the effect is by no means consistent. (c) Intelligence test data, based on global scores, suggest that white examiners do not adversely affect black children's performance. (d) On paper-and-pencil measures of personality, black college students express more hostility but less test anxiety to black examiners than to white examiners. (e) Doll preference studies with children do not show a significant racial experimenter effect. (f) A black discussant is more likely to bring about favorable replies toward programs involving blacks from white college students than a white discussant. (g) The interviewers' racial membership is not a significant factor when the interviewers occupy a high-status role. (h) The limited psychotherapeutic research data suggest that black clients prefer and work better with black counselors than with white counselors (Sattler, 1973, 26).

The actual diversity of outcomes here noted indicates that "race" per se has ceased to be an unambiguous cue for a fixed set of expectations and claims.

This inference alone suggests that present-day interracial interaction is not necessarily dominated by group stereotypes or racial prejudgments.

It is quite possible, of course, for severe intergroup conflict to develop even if the opposing groupings share extensively in a common culture and have developed pervasive relationships of accommodation and friendship. A striking case in point is the prolonged violence between Catholics and Protestants in Northern Ireland (Ulster). Yet even in that situation of chronic collective violence, many Protestant and Catholic neighbors continue to maintain relationships of interdependence and civility (Harris, 1972). Such interpersonal ties are powerful. An extensive web of interpersonal relationships can reduce the scale of conflict, moderate its destructiveness, and provide a residual basis for negotiation, resolution, and new accommodations and solidarities. But it would be too much to expect that individuals in separate relationships with one another would be able to prevent or reduce conflict that is sustained by encouragement and resources (e.g., weapons) that come from outside the local communities and their long-standing accommodative relationships. Nor will interethnic friendships be enough to stop or resolve communal conflict once it has developed into large-scale violence.

6. Some Illustrative Cases

If the circumstances of intergroup contact are clearly defined and prescribed, an inegalitarian relationship between ethnic groupings may be peaceful and orderly; such interactions often occur within the context of a superordinate/subordinate relationship, based upon prejudice and discrimination. If it is *not* a relationship based on established norms of superior-inferior status and if members of each group initially appear to be of equal status in the immediate situation, they will nevertheless interact in such a highly restricted fashion as to foster the development of outgroup prejudices and discriminating attitudes. In this case, the relationship is formally equal only in the sense of acceptance within situations where rigid social conventions prevail. Although conventionalization may reduce violent conflict, when members of a local social unit are actively seeking the same scarce, distributive values, the very fact of similarity of status and equality of rank, combined with frequent interaction, can lead to intense competition or rivalry (Orenstein, 1965, 307).

We may recall from Chapter 4 that a study of interracial contact in desegregated public housing showed complex relations between the social characteristics of the individuals, the type of contact experienced, and the extent and kind of changes in racial attitudes that seemed to result (Ford, 1973). Among white housewives, the greater the interracial experience, the more favorable were attitudes toward black people and toward interracial contacts.

Among black respondents, personal equal-status contacts with whites were not significantly associated with favorable attitudes. Length of residence in a desegregated public housing project was not significantly related to interracial attitudes among whites and was associated with relatively unfavorable attitudes among blacks. In this case, the attitudes in question apparently were influenced by dissatisfaction with housing conditions and by some unpleasant interchanges among residents during initial phases of desegregation.

The study hypothesized that "the longer one resides in a desegregated housing project, the greater will be the opportunity for this environment to affect one's racial perspective" (Ford, 1973, 1429). The hypothesis was not supported. Although the reasons are not entirely clear, a possibly important factor is whether greater quantity of interaction also means greater variety of experience that could be persuasive. Effects may depend not only upon frequency of contact but also upon the extent to which individuals have the opportunity to evaluate others in diverse social situations. Further, we already know that in many situations there is an initial period during which changes in attitudes and behavior occur rapidly, followed by periods when there is little additional change. Old patterns of behavior, new information, status-threats, and new forms of contact are all vital inputs during this first stage. Once an attitude or pattern of behavior is established, however, if no radically new events occur, the attitude will stabilize and is not likely to change further unless confronted by a challenge. Once a white woman has decided that black neighbors are tolerable to live with, she will not be surprised if they continue to be tolerable to live with, but that does not mean she will find them desirable to live with.

We can say, however, that on the whole, the longer individuals from clearly designated groups interact over a period of time and across a variety of situations, the more evaluative standards shift from those *specific* to the status, position, or social category of the group to those applicable to *a total person*, including the *particular* personality characteristics of the individuals involved. Every day millions of Americans interact with ethnic others as co-workers, co-residents, fellow students, members of associations, or participants in congeniality groupings. Through the pursuit of compatible and complementary interests and after collaborative attainment of individual and group goals, they often establish mutual acceptance, respect, and liking. Numerous positive interpersonal relationships inhibit stereotyping, aid genuine communication, and facilitate the resolution of group conflicts.

In a new and undefined situation, major social cues for behavior generally are taken from peer groups. Therefore, it is an incomplete account to explain differing levels of prejudice through duration of residence, or previous contact experience, or even extensive neighboring with outgroup residents, without also analyzing peer-group interaction. How blacks relate to whites and whites to blacks will be determined in part by what they see their racial peers doing, and how they feel their actions and attitudes will be viewed by their peer group. Thus if a newly arrived white housewife, who is also prejudiced, sees her white neighbors engaging in many acts of neighboring with black residents, she is more likely to feel pressure to redefine her norms, and the legitimacy of her attitudes will encounter a greater challenge than if she had arrived to find whites socially isolated from black neighbors.

Evidently the term "equal-status contact" is ambiguous. It is often used to refer to the interaction of members of traditionally unequal groups under conditions where both receive equal treatment, e.g., in schools or work situations. But as Cohen and Roper (1972) point out, objective standards of equal status cannot be divorced from the perceptions of the participants. There is research evidence showing that initial differences in social status are followed by the development of a power and prestige ordering that resembles the rankings given to individuals on new group tasks—even though competence in performing the task has no rational relationship to the original status characteristics (Bergen, Cohen, Zelditch, 1966).

Both blacks and whites often enter a new task situation with a preconceived determination of competence. This results in a self-fulfilling prophecy: for example, blacks not only are reticent at initiation and participation but also underrate their own performance, both objectively and in relation to the performances of whites (Cohen and Roper, 1972). In experiments in which black subjects were trained to perform more competently than whites in the group, they nevertheless underrated their own competence and rated whites higher than themselves.

Even when blacks perceived their own success, its saliency was nevertheless weakened in the interaction with whites if white subjects were not equally conditioned to recognize blacks' competence. The study thus implies that the efficacy of programs of education designed to strengthen the self-confidence of blacks is likely to be greater when the expectations of whites in the interaction also are changed.

Cohen and Roper conclude that equal-status contact is an interaction process directly dependent on the expectations which members of both groups bring to it. Such a phenomenon is not confined to race—it occurs whenever members of different status groups come together for some activity; status ranking will be the means by which individuals will rank their expectations of competency.

One way to create an equal-status situation is to enhance the competence of the lower-status group in a highly visible manner to both groups; the aim is to override the effects that expectations made on the basis of status have created. An experiment designed to raise *both* black and white expectations for black performance of certain tasks resulted in an equality of interaction that heightened the task initiation rate of blacks and lowered it for whites (Cohen and Roper, 1972, 654). Such "expectation training" often can be helpful in developing equal-status interaction in any task or learning experience in which participants initially have predetermined status evaluations.

The experimental evidence that both whites and blacks in some situations bring with them expectations that result in misevaluation of competence and performance-based status is important. Explicit training to alter such expectations undoubtedly is needed for equal-status acceptance to occur in many settings and types of task. It is not necessary to assume, however, that purposive manipulation always will be necessary to produce recognition and appropriate evaluation of competent performance. When members of a social category that formerly was stereotyped as less competent do show superior performance in highly visible activities over successive occasions, it is likely that expectations will change—as they have in many fields, from music to athletics, to politics, to mathematics.

Programs to develop intergroup interaction intended to promote coopera-tion or to render attitudes more positive often have concentrated upon changing members of the "majority" and have paid little attention to the possibility of resistances and prejudices among members of minorities. In an intensive training institute on school desegregation in Houston, Texas, white teachers showed decreases in prejudice, but no significant changes occurred among black teachers. Most of the materials used in the training dealt only with whites' stereotypes and prejudices toward blacks (Preston and Robinson, 1974). The most effective programs are likely to be those that deal with both majority and minority attitudes.

Surely we need few reminders that people do not get along better merely because they interact frequently: family quarrels, ingroup homicides, and bureaucratic infighting immediately leap to mind. Not surprisingly, interac-tion across ethnic-group lines does not invariably produce greater liking or enhanced cooperation. Many intergroup contacts lead to an increase in negative feelings and to a perpetuation of unfavorable orientations. Among many other examples we find that studies in the Israeli army showed lack of change in ethnic attitudes even after long and continued interethnic contact in that setting. Other examples cited earlier include intergroup contacts between patients in a hospital for the chronically ill and contacts between black and white prisoners in a penal institution. A lack of favorable change or a worsening of intergroup attitudes is most likely in (a) competitive contacts, (b) under unpleasant conditions, (c) when there are marked differences in status and rewards, (d) when the interaction is frustrating or damaging, and (e) when the participants hold incompatible beliefs and values.

On the other hand, the fact that interaction sometimes either has no effect upon or actually intensifies prejudice and conflict does not signify that *reduced* interaction would facilitate nonconflictful coexistence.

Care is required in interpreting the results of studies reporting a positive association between intergroup contact and favorable attitudes (Amir, 1969; 1976). The situation or population studied may have been selected partly because favorable attitudes or change toward more positive orientations was of special interest. Respondents may have sensed "the right answers" and given the investigators the socially desirable answers. When change has been estimated through retrospective accounts, there is the possibility of selective recall or modification of reports of earlier attitudes. In many cases, finally, it is not clear whether favorable attitudes led to contact or whether contact led to favorable attitudes.

It is unlikely that we shall ever find real-life behavior that is a function only of "predispositions" (attitudes, values, motives, etc.) or only of immediate situations (specific contexts and sequences of events). First of all, behavior does not come alone from attitude-toward-object but also from attitude-toward-situation and from the interplay between the two (Rokeach and Kleijunas, 1972). Going a step farther toward a situational view, Cook (1970) gives an excellent illustration of how different combinations of the same variables produce different effects. For example, negative racial attitudes of whites toward blacks when combined with high anxiety would be expected to produce avoidance of interracial interaction. But when the white person perceives that his or her own peer group approves of interracial interaction and disapproves of discrimination, high anxiety would tend to increase such interaction. Another example of a different kind is the well-attested finding that high rates of interaction *within* a collectivity when coupled with low rates of interaction with an opposing collectivity lead to an increased likelihood of intergroup conflict and increased severity of any conflicts that do develop (Kerr and Siegel, 1954; Williams et al., 1964; Gamson, 1968; Kriesberg, 1973).

In view of all the negative forces and confounding factors that can influence intergroup relations, it is all the more striking to note that the many studies of intergroup contact carried out from the 1930s into the 1950s—the period in which the ground was prepared for the civil rights movements of the 1960s —were practically unanimous in showing a positive association between amount of black-white interaction and favorability of whites' attitudes toward blacks or toward some form of integration.

Change in interaction and continuing relationships between persons from formerly distant or antagonistic collectivities seems most easily achieved in new social settings and new kinds of activities, especially when an expansion of opportunity for acquiring desired goals is simultaneously afforded.

Observation of many situations of racial desegregation suggests that new rather than old social settings provide a greater likelihood of acceptance, accommodation, or other favorable responses. An important factor is that new settings are less likely to involve displacement of previously advantaged persons from their positions—for example, if all the workers are hired at the same time in a new factory. Lesser competitive threat will be perceived if *vested* interests are not challenged. In short, new settings are less likely to be perceived in terms of constriction of reward opportunity. Examples of successful integration into new settings include: workforce integration of whites and blacks in a new factory (Hope, 1952); augmentation of combat effectiveness by the addition of platoons of black soldiers to white infantry companies (Stouffer et al., 1949, Chapter 10); integration of waiting rooms in new southern airports before 1965; entry into new housing or residential areas (Hunt, 1960, 204). Of course some new settings do represent constriction and threat; in such cases we would anticipate negative rather than positive effects of new intergroup contacts, e.g., in prisons, "relocation" or "concentration" camps, "native reservations," and the like.

A second factor in new settings that may favor positive effects is the absence of fixed rules or customary understandings. In situations of ambiguity and weak normative structure, new rules of the game may be developed through pressures and inducements specific to the particular situation. The lack of preestablished norms provides opportunities for individuals to develop adaptive rather than stereotypic solutions.

An experiment by Cook assigned highly prejudiced white college students to tasks where they unexpectedly found themselves working with black co-workers (Cook et al., 1971). Significant in itself, all the prejudiced whites remained to complete all the series of twenty sessions. The positive incentives and conforming tendencies outweighed generalized negative predispositions. Further, in the work situation the whites exhibited dominantly friendly behavior—unfriendly deportment toward blacks was very rare—although persons whose initial attitudes were most negative showed less frequent friendly behavior. Although the large proportion of the participants in the experiment who did not change indicates that an important factor or set of factors remains to be accounted for, the study does demonstrate that the positive effects can be produced even against marked initial resistance.

7. A Review of Research and Interpretations

It is difficult to arrive at a conclusion more heavily documented in history than this: A breakdown of social interaction and communication between one individual or social group and another, instead of bringing the development of either group to a halt, usually only insures that the lines of growth will diverge progressively from one another to engender misunderstanding, hostility, and conflict (Jacobson, 1960, 394).

Thus far in this discussion we have been careful to stay close to findings of research. But evidence for the conflict-reducing effectiveness of intergroup interaction comes also from direct observation of the extensive networks of collaboration, cooperation, and close personal relationships among persons of different ethnic origins. We already have noted that both commonsense observations and a very large accumulation of research findings demonstrate that interaction between persons from different ethnic categories may have either positive or negative effects upon attitudes and behavior relevant to cooperation. What are the main differentiating factors in these contrasting outcomes?

Earlier in this chapter we reviewed a lengthy listing of possibly important factors. A more concise summary, reflecting the main findings of many studies, identifies five groups of conditions as most important in producing positive (favorable) change in attitudes as an outcome of intergroup contacts: (1) equality of status in the immediate situation; (2) a situation of contact encouraging or requiring mutually interdependent relationships; (3) social norms favoring intergroup association and equalitarian attitudes; (4) characteristics of participants contradictory to negative stereotypes; (5) a setting that tends to promote intimate rather than distant or casual association (Cook, 1970). A few additional examples of the empirical evidence behind these conclusions may be useful in visualizing the real-life meaning of "intergroup contact."

Conspicuous among the factors that have been found to be associated with important differences in outcomes of intergroup contacts is the extent and kind of cooperation in the attainment of group goals or the accomplishment of group tasks. Studies showing varying effects or correlates of cooperative interaction (in addition to those listed above) include Deutsch, 1949, 1973; Thomas, 1957; Wilson and Miller, 1961; Raven and Eachus, 1963; Crombag, 1966.

Many studies have dealt with cooperation in school settings. An early study of white elementary school pupils compared an all-white and an integrated school that emphasized interracial cooperative activities. White children in the integrated settings were more favorable toward blacks and toward further interracial interaction (Singer, 1966). Within-school separation of white and black students is a pervasive pattern in "desegregated" schools. DeVries and Edwards (1975) report that rewarding racially mixed student teams as a learning-teaching procedure "created significantly greater" cross-race helping and friendship; a similar result occurred for cross-sex helping and friendship (DeVries and Edwards, 1975). Team success did not increase these outcomes. Instructional game-playing had only slight effects, but a combined team-game procedure did increase cross-race and cross-sex interaction. The heterogeneous teams received team-rewards, thus confounding interdependence and heterogeneity. Because performance was individually judged, within-team interaction was not required, but considerable helping developed nevertheless because of the group-reward incentive.

Several studies, scattered over the years, have found increases in interpersonal liking, or reduction in stereotyping, or increases in favorability of generalized ethnic attitudes subsequent to cooperative interracial activity in groups, ranging from such early work as Smith (1943) and Brophy (1946), to the research of Katz (1964), Kephart (1957), Williams et al. (1964), Cook (1970; Cook et al., 1971), Cohen (1973), and Amir (1976). The study by Katz suggested that cooperation in pursuit of common goals reduced prejudice; competition for status and leadership increased prejudice (Weissbach, 1976; Amir, 1976). Compatible findings have come from studies of intraracial competition and cooperation, e.g., Sherif et al. (1961).

Our understanding of favorable outcomes has been increased also by research on interaction that has reinforced stereotypes, intensified or aroused animosity, and increased the amount of conflict. What are the conditions most likely to facilitate such negative outcomes?

First, interaction which occurs in conformity with an established system of status- and group-differentiation typically perpetuates the values, beliefs, and interests already dominant.

> [Where] . . . there is no opportunity for anyone to observe and react to out-of-status behavior, new status-role combinations, or other forms of innovative behavior, . . . the "consequence" is an incessant verification or reinforcement of traditional stereotypes, norms, and evolutions. . . . Intergroup contacts in which behavior follows traditional norms of super-subordination and/or social distance will, on the whole, perpetuate and reinforce patterns of prejudice and discrimination (Williams, Dean, Suchman, 1964, 219).

Second, competition or negative interdependence promotes hostile or rejecting attitudes (see summaries of evidence in Weissbach, 1976). This is an extensively documented principle. Third, even if neither prior prejudice nor negative interdependence is present, just dividing individuals into separate groupings that are distinctively labeled can produce ingroup-outgroup discrimination (Weissbach, 1976, 90-91).

Preferential evaluation of the "ingroup"—even an ad hoc, arbitrarily created grouping—quickly develops over a considerable range of diverse circumstances. Anthropological, historical, and sociological evidence depicts some kind of ethnocentrism in most, although not all, identifiable collectivities, large and small (Williams, Dean, Suchman, 1964, Chapter 3; LeVine and Campbell, 1972). Experimental findings regarding traits of ethnically homogeneous groupings include the following: high evaluation of ingroup performance (Ferguson and Kelley, 1964); unbalanced allocations of money (Tajfel, 1970); favorable ratings of ingroup characteristics (Rabbie and Horwitz, 1969; Rabbie and deBrey, 1971; Rabbie and Wilkins, 1971); and punitive or aggressive behavior toward outgroup members (Schulman, 1974). Furthermore, there is a strong tendency for individuals who are free to do so to move into groups that are similar to the individual's values for the given activity or situation (e.g., religious, recreational); within such groups, perceived consensus tends to be greater than actual consensus; this leads over time to greater actual consensus.

In general, the evidence indicates that within wide limits positive interdependence is more important than sheer social or cultural similarity in producing positive attitudes among individuals and groups.

Some of the more important factors that have been shown to affect interpersonal relations within social groups are summarized below.

Participation in discussion and in decision-making. Participation in small groups has been found to go along with liking for group members and satisfaction with the group (Bavelas and Barrett, 1951; Hare, 1952). Studies of workers have shown that participation in decision-making seemed to be followed by positive attitudes toward management and toward co-workers (Coch and French, 1948; Likert, 1961). Attraction among members of cooperating interracial groups is higher when there is high rather than low participation in group decision-making (Weigel, Wiser, Cook, 1975). Across a series of experiments, the latter finding has been further specified: participation in decision-making seems to have a positive effect upon intragroup respect and liking when the reward associated with group success is small, and little or no effect when the reward is large (Blanchard, Adelman, Cook, 1975).

Individual differences in competence and perceived competence. In cooperating interracial groups, whites showed less liking (attraction) to a black groupmate when he or she performed less competently than when he or she performed more competently relative to a white groupmate. No such effect appeared in attraction of white subjects to white groupmates' competent or less competent performance, suggesting that racial stereotyping mediated responses (Blanchard, Weigel, Cook, 1975).

Type and intensity of competition. It seems prudent, at the least, to clearly distinguish among the following quite different kinds of "competitive" situations: (1) impersonal and anonymous *indirect competition* in which outcomes are rewarded either by "market" processes or by judges presumably using universalistic criteria; (2) *contest-rivalry* against known competitors in performance assessed against known and fixed standards (e.g., height of pole vaulting); (3) *confrontation-rivalry*[2] in team efforts in which the other group's performance interacts with the success-failure of one's own group's performance. Attributions of responsibility for outcomes are likely to be more heavily weighted toward the opponent in the third case.

Changes in appraisals of other persons during and after interactive competition are not necessarily global or diffuse — for example, negative evaluations need not be total. Experiments give examples of specific or focused evaluations that could have been inferred directly from the competitive interaction itself (e.g., greediness, aggressiveness, coldness) (Wilson, Chum, Kayatani, 1965; Wilson and Kayatani, 1968). Even in confrontational rivalry the losing party may emerge with some attitudes more favorable to the adversary than before the encounter, e.g., esteem for skill or acknowledgment of fairness. Because, however, competition and rivalry so frequently do produce alienative or hostile attitudes, efforts to induce interethnic solidarity through group competition presumably would do well to pit one ethnically mixed group against another similarly mixed, as was the case in the experiments reported by Weigel, Wiser, and Cook (1975).

When individuals of different ethnic groupings are competitors, increased interaction across ethnic lines typically increases tension and antipathy. When individuals of different ethnic groupings are placed in relationships of positive interdependence in which successful performance requires cooperation, there will be an increase in helping, in mutual liking, in self-esteem, and in satisfaction (Aronson, Blaney, Stephan, 1975).[3] Team competition in mixed black-white classrooms significantly increased cross-race helping and friendship choices within each team (DeVries and Slavin, 1975).

Degree of group, or individual, success or failure in task-accomplishment. Positive effects of success upon interpersonal attraction in groups have been reported in many studies (Lott and Lott, 1965; Collins and Raven, 1969). Task-success was shown to go along with attraction in studies by Shelly (1954), Deutsch (1959), and Wilson and Miller (1961). Contradictory or qualified and complex findings have come from other research (Shelly, 1954; Deutsch, 1959; Wilson and Miller, 1961). On net balance, however, we must conclude that unless strong contravening factors are present, successful task-accomplishment does increase intragroup cohesion and liking (Blanchard, Adelman, and Cook, 1975).

An investigation of the effects of three independent variables of level of participation, race (black or white), and degree of group success showed that neither race nor level of participation affected outcomes directly, nor were there interactions among the three variables. But group success or failure significantly affected interpersonal liking, and the effects were similar for blacks and whites. Also, success increased individuals' perceptions of the extent of their own participation in decision-making in the group. The *combination* of group success plus a relatively high reward produced significantly greater liking and respect for group members than did group failure (Blanchard, Adelman, Cook, 1975).

One might think that a scapegoating reaction would develop among whites toward their black workmates under conditions of group failure on a task. But such a response apparently is inhibited, if it does arise at all, under conditions of cooperation in attaining mutually accepted goals (Weigel and Cook, 1975).

Level of difficulty of a group task or environmental challenge, as related to success or failure. When group success or failure (in an experimental setting) is held constant, the more difficult tasks are associated with more favorable feelings about the group (Zander, 1971).

Homogeneity or heterogeneity of the group. One study showed that task-success increases interpersonal attraction only in groups made up of persons having similar *personality* traits (Hoffman, 1958). But opposite effects are shown for *social* heterogeneity that increases functional complementarity (ability to help one another) among members of aircraft crews (Gross, 1956). Differences among individuals in prior level of liking or degree of popularity affect outcomes, e.g., success or failure in group tasks affected the liking felt by unpopular members for their associates but did not so influence the popular members (Thibaut, 1950).

Amount of reward. It is plausible, of course, to suppose that intergroup and interindividual attitudes may be affected by the intensity of the frustrations and deprivations that individuals experience within the situation or as a consequence of their participation in it. Conversely, we would expect the results of interaction to be affected by the importance ("size") of the extrinsic rewards that accompany or follow the interaction. If participation in joint activities (or even in mere association) with members of a previously disvalued social category results in high rewards or removal of frustrations, a resulting state of generalized satisfaction becomes linked to the co-participants. Thus, satisfaction can act as a mediating variable between the participation and change in attitudes and behavior toward outgroup members (Blanchard, Adelman, Cook 1975).

8. Some Implications

From these and the many other available experimental studies we infer a synoptic picture: the greatest effects upon social solidarity between persons of different ethnic categories will occur in cooperating groups that are successful in task-performance, highly rewarded as a group, low in intragroup competition, function with relatively high rates of participation in decision-making, and encourage development of competence in all members.

The total pattern of research findings is consistent with conclusions drawn from observations of real-life communities. As noted in Chapters 6 and 7 above, the qualities of social interaction within an ethnic community can appreciably affect that community's capacities for developing economic and political resources. A high level of interpersonal trust, for example, allows for the development of autonomous credit institutions and capacities for capital accumulation, and the sharing of other resources. Mutual trust also provides a base for the development of collective political action, for the sharing of information, and for social support in dealing with external authorities (Coleman, 1971). Rewarding interdependence, positive attitudes, social trust, successful coping—these conditions reinforce one another to create social solidarity and effective functioning, both within and between ethnic categories.

Both experimental and observational studies also consistently highlight the importance of ensuring equal-status interactions if social solidarity is to be enhanced. Although intergroup contact may be orderly and peaceful when two groups exist in a subordinate/superordinate relationship, the underlying premises of superiority-inferiority, prejudice, and discrimination make the success of such arrangements problematic, if no other steps are taken to ensure it. Any challenge to this status quo threatens the security, advantages, and basic social assumptions of those who are committed to the social system as it exists (Williams, Dean, Suchman, 1964, 216).

Once the barrier of a superordinate/subordinate structure has been overcome, however, relations between two groups may open up *positive* equal-status experiences that would not have been possible within the old structure. It is only then that "lessened hostility will result from . . . intergroup collaboration, on the basis of personal association accepted as worthwhile" (Williams, 1947, 69).

Finally, a factor that can have important and complex consequences is the extent and kind of interpersonal *helping* in cooperative groups. Helping can arouse resentment on the part of the helper if he or she feels imposed upon, manipulated, or exploited. The person helped may resent unwanted help or aid that implies undue dependence or social inferiority. But help that both parties feel to be a spontaneous response to a functional problem typically has strongly positive results.

9. Conclusion

Our main conclusion from this close examination of persuasion, inducement, and participation is that definitely positive and important outcomes have been demonstrated in intergroup attitudes and behavior. The necessary conditions are, of course, complex and not always easy to arrange or to find. But the requisite settings and influences often do exist or can be created (Katz, 1976). There are no grounds for nihilism or defeatism among persons who hope for lessening hostility and greater constructiveness in American ethnic relations. In particular it is important to continually recall that *mutual participation* is an essential condition for eliminating racism (Pettigrew, 1971, 298)—of any color—and for aiding the growth of problem-solving oppositions, realistic accommodations, and relationships of mutual appreciation within a common social order.

Chapter 11

Consequences of the Use of Constraint

*Ever since men climbed down from the trees and found it necessary
to establish ground rules, they have fought over what those rules shall be.
They have fought longest, and perhaps most bitterly, over the most
fundamental rule of all—the rule by which the ground rules themselves
shall be determined. For he who controls the ground rules is in a position
to control the game (Spitz, 1974, 259).*

1. Can We Safely Use Constraint? How and When?

The various appraisals by intelligent and knowledgeable observers of the
effects of strategies of constraint in our society show surprising divergences.
At one extreme, we are told in effect that all forms of noncooperation and
coercion are self-defeating. Other views seem to say that nonviolent coercion
sometimes is effective, but that violence is counterproductive (Sharp, 1973).
And at the other extreme, an impressive roster of societal analysts and advocates see the effective threat of violence as indispensable for the attainment of
justice by partisans or for the maintenance of legitimate order by authorities.

Here, clearly, we confront once again the fallacies of overgeneralization.
For it is not true that strategies of constraint always are ineffective, and it is
not true that they always are effective. As usual, it depends. Upon what?

First one must analyze separately the consequences of constraint when used
by partisans against authorities and when used by authorities against partisans.
In general, authorities are freer to use constraints, including force and violence,

281

without incurring adverse consequences. They command the symbols of legitimacy and often control the means of communication through which the meanings of public events are defined. Thus to consider only the instigations toward conflict experienced by restive partisans—rising discontent, increasing aspirations and claims—is to leave out half of the equation by neglecting the counteractions of their opponents. In Gamson's terms, such an approach deals only with *potential partisans* (the "influence perspective") and does not consider the actions of *authorities* (the "social control" perspective). Such an approach resembles an effort to measure water pressure without taking into account the strength of the container.

When the members of a social collectivity feel themselves disadvantaged or oppressed in relation to a powerful and unresponsive set of authorities (or to a whole system or regime), often they can gain even minimal attention only by dramatic acts of constraint. But if mass media are receptive to the "news value" of events of protest and confrontation, even very small and weak groups sometimes may attain substantial influence, at least for a time, by such acts of constraint. During the 1960s and well into the 1970s, for example, mass media in the United States carried continuous message about intense public criticism of the acts of authorities in all major institutions. Relatively small organizations such as Students for a Democratic Society, the Black Panther party, Nader's Raiders, Public Interest Research Groups, and Common Cause were able to attract enormous attention (Levitt, 1973). The capacity to enact newsworthy events has become an increasingly important political tactic.

But in the American setting the use of constraints, even in nonviolent forms, by relatively weak partisans has to contend with the disadvantages imposed by widespread attitudes that favor the authorities over the aggrieved minorities.

Only a very small proportion of the adult population is willing to agree that persons who feel they are being treated unfairly have the right to engage in civil disobedience, mass demonstrations, and sit-ins and walk-outs (Baden and Olsen, 1974). In contrast, there are a great many people who question the legitimacy of boycotts or picketing, public marches, or even public meetings. We have noted that it is the less powerful who most need to resort to protest activities if their grievances and aspirations are to be heeded by the authorities. And it is the relatively powerless who most need to engage in protests and demonstrations if they are to gain the attention and sympathy and attract the support of third parties. Attitudes of doubt and disapproval, among potential allies, therefore, may become an important factor affecting the outcomes of attempted constraint against authorities. To find the widespread disapproval that exists among the general American public toward properly legal modes of protest and pressure might lead us to wonder whether mass protests ever could be effective—if their aims include the goal of inducing third parties to enter the bargaining scene as allies, or at least as nonadversaries of the dissatisfied protestors (Lipsky, 1968). Indeed, the data on responses to mass protests do seem to show that an immediate effect of even slightly disruptive collective demonstrations or other public protests is to arouse annoyance and attitudes of rejection in the uninvolved "bystander" publics. But the finding is not very surprising—for presumably protests *have* to have somewhat aversive or negative effects in order to elicit changes in the behavior of the opponents to whom they are directly addressed. If protests are to have a bargaining value, they must present detriments that can be removed by granting redress to the aggrieved. And often these constraints are likely to have some aversive effects on some third parities as well as upon adversaries. If protests are effective in directly inducing the desired concessions, of course, such temporary negative responses from relatively unorganized and peripheral publics often will be a small cost to incur. But if negative reactions are strong in bystander groupings, whose authority to grant claims or demands is also great, then the use of mass protest tactics will be counterproductive by definition.

One major effect of the exclusion from decision-making of a disadvantaged minority is to put a premium upon the use by that minority of tactics of constraint. We have shown how rarely it is that dominant groups spontaneously give up control and we have noted that, in the nature of the relationship, subordinated groups have little to offer as inducements. It follows that if low-power groups wish to change their disadvantaged position, the most effective tactics often are those that disrupt or threaten existing relationships. Essentially the challenger with few positive resources has to make effective threats to reduce the gains of the dominant party (Deutsch, 1973, 11). Yet there is an apparent dilemma, because the compliance resulting from coercion is typically minimal and may be gained only at high cost; voluntary cooperation is preferable (Deutsch, 1973, 119).

Again, both sets of claims are valid under some circumstances, but we need to specify what the favorable conditions are. We have seen abundant evidence that some tactics of constraint are more likely than others to arouse strong resistances. Thus when partisans are considering how and when to attempt to constrain opponents, it is both reasonable and necessary to analyze as well as possible which actions will reduce the unavoidable disadvantages.

A first step in such an analysis is to ask, What are the main conceivable classes of effects to be anticipated from the use of constraints? Some of the more important possible effects are:

1. attainment of desired positive objectives, e.g., legislation, jobs, representation;
2. blocking or deterring undesired behavior;
3. winning support of third parties;
4. increasing the unity, morale, cohesion, or mobilization within one's own group or movement;
5. opening opportunities for negotiation;
6. achieving domination over an opponent;
7. eliciting undesired "backlash" effects, e.g., alienating third parties, mobilizing new opponents, activating increased hostility, escalating conflict beyond suitable levels;
8. creating conditions for new learning, adaptations, and changes in the total set of relationships.

Let us, then, examine some of these possibilities. The discussion can be brief, for much of the relevant material already has been reviewed in Chapters 7-9.

2. Attainment of Positive Objectives

As we saw repeatedly in earlier chapters, in the fields of employment, housing, schools, and political affairs, there is abundant evidence that law and legal processes, as one form of constraint can be effective in protecting and advancing the interests and rights of disadvantaged partisans. But we also noted that gains are achieved and preserved only under specific types of conditions; that gains often are piecemeal, limited, and precarious; that undesired side-effects often appear. Let us examine the diverse consequences further, in an effort to strike some balance in the assessment of net effects.

During the past forty years and especially since 1954, a vast range of diverse modes of action have been tried out in the real world in efforts to reduce prejudice, to reduce discrimination, to increase the economic welfare and political efficacy of disadvantaged minorities, and to strengthen the personal and sociocultural resources of individuals, families, communities, and ethnic collectivities and organizations. The result is a remarkable stock of techniques, methods, tactics, strategies, programs, policies, philosophies, and ideologies. From a long and diverse historical experience, we now know that many methods and programs are at least feasible, and that some probably can be depended upon to produce reasonably definite outcomes that many thoughtful persons consider valuable. We also know that many plausible approaches and techniques simply do not work—they will not produce the results originally hoped or claimed for them.

We have reviewed numerous cases in which partisans have used constraints effectively. We have seen that gains made in the United States since the 1930s in black participation, prestige, prosperity, and power have been made possible to a very large extent by *political and legal means*, based on the norms, values, and interests vested in the American constitutional order. It was primarily through the Supreme Court, the Congress, and the federal executive that decisive steps were taken to reinstitute *the rights of blacks as citizens* and to somewhat widen economic and social opportunity. The leverage for such changes basically rests upon the "reserved rights" of the constitutional system (Greenstone and Peterson, 1973, 100ff.). Thus when the constraint exerted by partisans comes through *persuading* one set of authorities (the courts) to *constrain* others (state and local governments, business concerns, unions, etc.), effectiveness is likely to be high.

Legal avenues were successfully used in most instances only after collective pressures had been developed through noncooperation, disobedience, and mass intervention. These results are not peculiar to the United States. In two major historical cases in Britain collective violence rather clearly was successful—as a proximate cause of the Reform Bills and of guarantees of rights of free speech. In other instances, violence seems to have been on the whole ineffectual or, as in the General Strike of 1911, counterproductive (Critchley, 1970). And nonviolent actions that impose constraints on authorities have succeeded, in a great many very important historical cases, in winning crucial gains for aggrieved collectivities. Particularly impressive is the effectiveness under some conditions of large-scale disobedience by a unified population. The indispensibility of economic constraint as a tactic of challenger groupings appears over and over again. In contemporary South Africa:

> For if there is any realistic hope of gradual change inside South Africa in the absence of external intervention, it would seem to result from the combined pressures, operating from within the system. Above all, what would appear decisive is the only weapon which Blacks share, their withdrawal of labour and its potential effects (Adam, 1973, 163).

Of course, potential effectiveness can become actual only if two prerequisites can be developed: mobilization of partisans and access to decision-makers. A substantial accumulation of case studies of efforts in large urban centers by poor people and ethnic minorities to gain greater influence in political processes shows the great difficulty of mobilizing the needed numbers of active participants for sustained struggles. The basic problem is that of exclusion from city-wide centers of decision-making. Where influence has been successfully attained, it has required intensive organizing efforts to create enough protest and disturbance to generate some modicum of bargaining power (Fainstein and Fainstein, 1974).

One useful way to define power is to say that it is control over sources of uncertainty. If all the benefits and detriments that a social unit produces for others are completely noncontingent and predictable, we do not think of that unit as having power. But just as soon as its outputs are shown to be purposively variable, we can identify it as a source of power. It "confers" benefits—because it also can withhold them, and does so on occasion. It can produce disadvantages for others, and it can make both benefits and detriments contingent upon what other social units do or do not do. To be able to create a new source of uncertainty is not enough to acquire power—one must also be able to demonstrate a capacity to reduce the new uncertainty—to turn on and to turn off the contingent events. Thus if leaders of aspiring groups can manifest such control, they thereby acquire a credible capability to reward or to deprive, hence to promise and to threaten.

This capability is essential for effectiveness in the political arena. For example, the effectiveness of legislation is strongly enhanced when it places a means of constraint at the disposal of a party that is able and willing to use the new leverage (Coleman, 1971, 57). But ability and willingness depend upon other specific circumstances. Thus a civil rights law may be effective in a city where urban minorities can bring complaints to court without facing overwhelming social pressure but not in a closely knit rural community.

Four strategies of eliciting cooperation have been described as (1) turn-the-other-cheek, (2) deterrent, (3) nonpunitive, and (4) reformed-sinner. Some include constraints, others do not.

> The turn-the-other-cheek strategy seeks to elicit cooperation by appealing to the social conscience and goodwill of the subject; such an approach has characterized many religious groups and the advocates of nonviolence. The deterrent strategy attempts to elicit cooperation by use of the carrot and the stick—i.e., by rewarding cooperation and punishing noncooperation; . . . The nonpunitive strategy places its emphasis on rewarding cooperation and on neutralizing or nonrewarding aggressive behavior; it appeals to the self-interests of the subject through positive rather than negative incentives and thus attempts to avoid the misunderstanding and hostility that may result from the subject's experience of punishment (Deutsch, 1973, 315).

(The "reformed sinner" uses a constraining, followed by a more cooperative, strategy.) In two-person experiments designed to produce high risk for cooperation and strong incentive for aggressive action, only the nonpunitive-equal power actor was able to reduce aggressive responses to less than one-half of the total. The turn-the-other-cheek strategy resulted in massive exploitation by the other party. Only the nonpunitive strategy was consistently successful (Deutsch, 1973, 347).

Exclusive concentration upon the hazards of using coercion against author-ities would blind us to the everyday fact of effective use of coercive authority in situations of *high legitimacy* and *strong hierarchy*. It is a striking fact that the most rapid and well-accepted racial desegregation in the United States, circa 1945-75, occurred under those conditions, e.g., in the military services, in industry, in schools. Striking differences in outcomes have been observed between authoritative, unequivocal desegregation programs and programs that have attempted to follow a less decisive, consultative approach. A concrete illustration is found in the instance of two southern industrial plants under the same national company acting on orders to implement a policy of deseg-regation and nondiscrimination.

> One Southern plant was headed by an authoritarian Southern gentleman who received his orders and carried them out. He called his plant super-intendents together and said, "Gentlemen, we have these instructions to integrate and we are going to do it. There will be no difficulty, it will just be done." A superintendent spoke up and remarked that he was a Southerner and just did not think he could work in such a situation. "That's fine," said the plant manager, "we will give you two weeks' pay." The superintendent changed his mind. Another superintendent said, "What will happen if some of the men get in a fight with these new colored recruits?" "I'll fire the people who are fighting, I'll fire the foreman, and I'll fire the superintendent of the group."

> Integration took place speedily and without incident. "We don't like it, but we are living with it," one superintendent told the writer.

> In another plant of the same company, the man in charge was a well-trained graduate of a human relations-oriented business school. He saw the integration task as a fine case study for his alma mater and invited a team of professors to observe and to advise him. He began a long education process, hired local sociologists, consulted with the branches of the Urban League and the NAACP, and carefully indoctrinated all his people. The result was a walkout, much difficulty, problems of supervision, and general turmoil. The job of integration still remained to be accomplished six months later, but the manager had by then been replaced (Northrup, 1967: cited in Burkey, 1971, 89).

When the workers are initially prejudiced and see desegregation as a threat, it seems obvious that "polling" them simply gives them the opportunity to define the situation in these terms, rather than to respond to terms of legal requirements and possible long-term advantages. In contrast, authority which is clear, explicit, demands accountability, and provides legitimacy for obedience provides strong motivation for compliance as well as sanctions for noncompliance. As Gamson points out:

> Perhaps the most powerful and common means of social control is simply the conveying of expectations with clarity and explicitness coupled with clear and direct accountability for the performance of such expectations. As long as legitimacy is accorded in such situations, individuals will regard their noncompliance as a failure and any interaction which makes such a personal failure salient is embarrassing, unpleasant and something to be avoided (Gamson, 1968, 134).

The more direct the lines of responsibility from the highest positions in a hierarchy to the lowest, the more effective is implementation of the policy. Although such established hierarchical authority is present only in limited sectors of a pluralistic society, there are many extremely important instances in which it can be used – legitimately and reasonably – to effect agreed-upon policies of ethnic integration and universalistic criteria of social access.

Antidiscrimination laws and regulations have led to varied extensive experience with different forms of organization and methods of enforcement. Some approaches have had substantial results, others have been ineffective. Comparisons of the contrasting outcomes suggest that effectiveness has been greatest in instances in which a regulatory or quasijudicial body emphasized affirmative compliance, prompt and universal applications of sanctions, extensive monitoring of compliance, as well as sufficient resources to carry out such measures in full (Burkey, 1971, 65-72). The crucial importance of clear explicit policies and of firm positions by authorities who are invested with the responsibility for making binding decisions and ensuring enforcement was recognized in studies of antidiscriminatory actions as early as World War II (Watson, 1946; Fleming and Haas, 1946; Williams, 1947, 72-75). Initial observations and research on school desegregation in the 1950s supported this assessment in a different series of contexts. Clear policies and forthright decisions minimized mass confusion and conflict (Williams and Ryan, 1954; Dean and Rosen, 1955; Suchman et al., 1958). And appraisals by jurists, action leaders, and social scientists of the legal developments of the 1960s further corroborate the basic point (Warren, Jordan, Wilkins, Williams in Rooney, 1973).

3. Constraints as Negative Sanctions

Exhibit A:

Treat 'em rough and make 'em like it.

Traditional slogan

Exhibit B:

If sheep and dogs can be immobilized by random, senseless punishment, think of what political terror can do to people.

Authorities often resort to threats and punishment in avowed efforts to deter undesired behavior. Although it is clear that such efforts represent high-cost control, there is little reliable knowledge of the exact consequences of attempted deterrence through imposing negative social sanctions on offenders. Yet to understand the significance of constraint as a strategy, either of social control or of influence, in intergroup relations we necessarily have to make judgments about the effects of "punishment" and threat.

Quite apart from particular applications to intergroup relations, the appraisal of effects of punishment is made difficult by prevalent dogmas, myths, and sentiments. Only a few spots of light generated from careful studies have penetrated this murky atmosphere. Some things we do know. At the moment we are sure that the effects are enormously complex. Also, it is likely that the magnitude of stable changes in behavior produced by punishment has generally been underestimated rather than overestimated. And it is a reasonable guess that severe psychological disturbances are produced in individuals who are punished in arbitrary, random, or otherwise nondiscriminating ways for consummatory behavior (e.g., behavior related to sex, food, self-expression, social respect) (Solomon, 1964, 251). Much of the environment of persons of low income and low power is randomly punishing — that is, the person is deprived and blocked relatively regardless of his or her own particular behavior at a particular time. The effects probably include the seeming apathy and fatalism often noted among such persons.

On the other hand, a great deal of social punishment is deliberately imposed. Let us refer to punishments and deprivations of this kind as negative social sanctions. Such sanctions, when applied for alleged violations of social norms, may be justified or rationalized in terms of four main arguments: (1) punishment is regarded as obligatory on the basis of absolute moral or religious dicta; (2) punishment is said to be necessary as an expression and reinforcement of the moral sentiments of a society or of unavoidable demands for revenge; (3) punishment deters undesired or forbidden behavior; (4) punishment reforms, rehabilitates, or converts offenders. It is by no means clear that these four classes of negative sanctions are comparable or have similar effects. Indeed, there has been very little systematic study of the deterrent effects, if any, of punishment even in the field of ordinary crime (Tullock, 1974, 103-11). It is freely admitted by many students of the matter that the data available for analysis are very bad—unreliable, seriously biased (but to an unknown extent), variable in validity through time and in different jurisdictions. Nevertheless, attempts to use the appallingly poor information generally have produced the conclusion that punishment on the average does act as a deterrent for many, but not all, crimes (Zimring, 1971, 57-85). In addition, it has been shown that ignorance of the severity of penalities for violations of laws is widespread among convicted lawbreakers.

In the field of intergroup relations, negative social sanctions historically have been manifested as (1) responses to ordinary social offenses, not specific to any particular ethnic group, nor discriminatory in application; (2) discriminatory responses to ordinary social offenses when allegedly committed by members of a particular ethnic category, e.g., crimes of blacks against whites; (3) responses to attempts by subordinated groups to gain rights or advantages; these may be sanctions (a) against the claimants or (b) against authorities who deny rights or withhold due benefits; (4) actions by claimants against dominant groupings.

Coercive sanctions often are applied by dominant ethnic groups to those who challenge that dominance. The costs of these uses of constraint often include reactive effects upon the dominant grouping.

As we saw in Chapter 3, the efforts of whites and blacks acting together to challenge discrimination and segregation in the Civil Rights Movement of the 1960s were met by coercive, often violent, resistance. The net effects of southern "Massive Resistance" upon the white majority included a long series of legal defeats, much disruption of community life, substantial economic losses, curtailment of freedom of speech, restriction of political and religious liberties, and educational censorship. (Its "success" lay in delaying desegregation and re-enfranchisement for more than a decade, and in perpetuating a pattern of tokenism into a longer future [Wilhoit, 1973].)

It may be well in this connection to once more restate the obvious: coercive action does not necessarily produce a clear outcome in any particular struggle. Instead, as we have seen, an indefinitely oscillating sequence of conflict can develop. For instance, the decision-makers of one collectivity estimate that the costs of conflict are likely to be less than those of a continuation of the status quo, and so they mobilize the collectivity for threat or actual attack. The opposing collectivity reacts by countermobilization. If the ensuing conflict is indecisive and costly, both sides may reduce the level of conflict in an attempt to create a basis for later success. Surges of conflict then may recur many times. More extreme oscillations will occur when high levels of mobilization result in a severe defeat for one party but not the effective removal of its potential power. Periods of suppression may then be followed by regrouping and rebuilding—and subsequent massive tests of strength (Blalock, 1967, 179).

But let us further examine the general case of effects of penalties upon behavior before going into the particulars of the use of constraints in intergroup relations. First, there is no one universal generalization, rather, very great variation is to be expected in the effects of penalties, of negative sanctions generally, upon rates of violation of social norms. For many practical affairs (e.g., parking in cities), in which gain through violation is slight and penalties are small but high relative to gain, penalties have a clear deterrent effect if detection rates are high (Chambliss, 1966, 70-75). There is some evidence that threat of penalties is more effective than moral appeals in controlling cheating among college students (Rowe and Tittle, 1973). In general, the deterrent effect is likely to be greatest under the following conditions:

1. Offenses are extremely difficult to conceal and actually are detected in a high proportion of instances; these facts are widely known in the relevant population.
2. Detection results in prompt action by social authorities to ascertain culpability.
3. Where a judgment of guilt and culpability is rendered, imposition of negative sanctions follows promptly in almost all instances.
4. Penalties are such as to generally remove any advantage from detected nonconformity, as judged by local norms and values, but they are not so severe as to seem absurd, inhumane, or atrocious. Very severe penalties have little detectable deterrent effects when the probability of punishment is quite low (e.g., less than 4 percent of homicides in years of maximum enforcement in the United States were punished by execution).[1]

Pending further evidence, the most plausible conclusion is that in the case of punishment of individuals for alleged violations of ordinary (as distinct from political) crimes some deterrent effect exists varying with time, place, and offense, but that certainty of punishment may be more important than severity of sanctions in producing whatever effects there are (Tittle, 1969; Zimring, 1971, 89).

When behavior that is being punished by authorities is regarded by the victims and by substantial proportions of third parties as having a high positive moral value, harsh penalties typically *increase polarization and recruit new sympathizers.* This lesson was illustrated abundantly by the history of the Civil Rights Movement, as well as by some protests on university campuses (Barton, 1968).

Whenever people feel that their external social world has become severely threatening—as in war, depression, or civil disorder—they tend to become more accepting of authoritarianism. Police in America were brought into a position of increased power during the 1960s as part of a reaction to protests and dissent. National political authorities provided large new sums of money: The Law Enforcement Assistance Administration in 1963 sent about $800 million into various "law and order" agencies. Given the strong feelings of many policemen that they are an underpaid minority in a hostile society, the new resources together with increased levels of education and "professionalization" helped to create tendencies toward political activism (Ruchelman, 1974). Marked tendencies have appeared to defy superior authorities by "police riots" (unauthorized and lawless use of force as in 1968 in Chicago), lobbying, unionization, slowdowns, summonses campaigns, and refusals to obey orders (Bopp, 1971).

Spokesmen for "police power" often stress the dangerous or heroic nature of the police officer's duties as a justification for frequent use of violent means. In fact, being a police officer is not a particularly dangerous occupation in comparison with many others: death rates per 100,000 persons in various groups of occupations show mining with a rate of 94 as most dangerous, followed by construction work (76), agriculture (55), transportation (44), and finally police (33) (see President's Commission on Law Enforcement and the Administration of Justice, 1967). Even at that, the hazards of police duties might be substantially less were police less inclined to use deadly force against persons who present no physical threat. In New York City shootings of suspects by officers in 1964, a significant proportion of the targets were fleeing, presented no threat, and were not suspected of a serious crime. The number of injuries to police in Detroit in 1964 was a tiny fraction, per capita, of the number of injuries inflicted by police. Of the civilians injured by police, two-thirds received injuries to face, scalp, eyes, nose, head, or jaw; police injuries concerned hands, knuckles, and fingers.

Police enjoy a "societal delegated privilege to exercise nonnegotiable coercive force," but arrest data show that citizens are most likely to be arrested if they are conspicuous, powerless, and unwilling to show deference to the interrogating officer. If capricious behavior in making or not making arrests is an abuse of authority, these data indicate that police abuse their delegated privilege (Lundman, 1974). More generally, the practice of police in making field interrogations without explaining their intrusion upon the person produces widespread anger and feelings of being capriciously and unjustly treated. Only 14 percent of such interrogations result in arrests: the other cases presumably are adjudged innocent by the interrogating officer. Negative reactions of citizens to these encounters are found in at least half of the instances (Hudik and Wiley, 1974).

These considerations suggest why relationships of police to persons in disadvantaged social strata and ethnic groupings so often have generated conflict and precipitated civil disorders. Given the widespread doubts in the United States among minorities about the legitimacy of past and current police practices with regard to minority groups—and, indeed, with regard to any dissenting or "unconventional" behavior—the use of police in attempts to harass and intimidate partisan exercises of free speech and assembly sometimes produced increased support for the dissenters. This process was illustrated during the 1960s in responses of third-party public opinion to police attacks on black and white civil rights demonstrators in the South, to repressive actions by police and National Guard against college students, and to the massive police riot of 1968 in Chicago. In the aftermath of these events, some efforts were made to increase police discipline and to protect citizens from the most conspicuous forms of abuse, but it is a safe judgment that the basic problems remain. As Mayhew points out:

> The variety of forms of police organization and control makes it difficult to generalize adequately, but it is probably fair to say that formal guarantees of protection from the police have little chance of implementation within current procedures. Apart from the fact that reliance on individual complaints is an ineffective way of attacking *patterns* of abuse, the protective devices and the political power of the police is overpowering in most individual instances. Legal responses that rely upon specification and elaboration of the official limits on police activity, though they may decrease the policeman's sense of official support for his work, do not alter the day-to-day pressures and constraints on police conduct (Mayhew, 1971, 205).

The effects noted in cases of violent repression by collective police action are similar to those observed when the National Guard has been used. Thus the killing of four students by the National Guard at Kent State University in 1970 served not to intimidate but to further activate and radicalize the students who were present at the scene of the fatal shootings (Adamek and Lewis, 1975). Students at Kent State who were less immediately involved were neither repressed nor radicalized in their subsequent behavior. Judging from less direct evidence, the effects upon the larger society were primarily to "polarize" opinion. The sharpening of divisions, however, was not a simple accentuation of pro and con groupings but a more complex process. A substantial segment of "Middle American" opinion was reinforced in an attitude of authoritarian punitiveness. Another substantial segment of the population was embittered and alienated and took the killings as evidence of the unjust and repressive character of the political order. A third aggregate interpreted the event as evidence that tactics of confrontation had become dangerous and unproductive. There were other types of responses in various other "publics," but the essential lesson was that the main immediate effect of violent repression is to sharpen lines of social cleavage.

The immediate effects of collective violence often differ from the longer-term effects. Immediate political objectives may be attained by revolutionary partisans who seek a freer and more equalitarian social order—and who later find that the revolution has produced a New Leviathan.

> It has been widely recognized that violent revolutions and wars have been accompanied and followed by an increase both in the absolute power of the State and in the relative centralization of power in its hands. . . . Political violence, therefore, even when used against a particular tyrant, may contribute to increased difficulties in controlling the power of future rulers of that society and in preventing or combating future tyranny (Sharp, 1973, 800-801).

On the other hand, negative immediate responses to efforts of challenging groups may not prevent eventual victories. In the long history of struggles of labor against employers in the United States, the authorities repeatedly and violently repressed strikes with the acquiescence of third-party publics. In the long run, however, there was public revulsion against the repression, and the unions eventually won rights which probably could not have been attained without the prior struggles.

Analysis of a random sample of social protest organizations that were active in the United States at some time during the period 1800-1945 shows clearly that the movements of protest and challenge in the United States which have used violence have been more successful than movements which were nonviolent. Of course, this finding simply states a correlation, not a proof of the efficacy of violence. Especially significant is the fact that tactics involving violence generally are used by relatively strong and hopeful groups against weak or indecisive opponents (Gamson, 1975). Impatience and confidence, rather than desperate frustration, seem characteristic of violent movements. Gamson says: "It is not the weakness of the user, but the weakness of the target that accounts for violence. . . . Violence is associated with successful change or successful repression; it grows out of confidence and strength and their attendant impatience with the pace of change. It is, in this sense, as much a symptom of success as a cause" (Gamson, 1975, 82). Consistent with our earlier discussion of composite strategies is the additional finding that the successful protest movements did not use violence as a primary tactic; typically violence was incidental or supplementary to the main nonviolent efforts. For example, it has been the strike, not violence, that has been effective for labor unions in gaining rights vis-à-vis employers. And it must be re-emphasized that the great preponderance of purposive violence has come from dominant groups, not from partisans, and has been inflicted upon the weaker parties.

Gamson's analysis shows that successful partisan challenges to the authorities to gain acceptance or advantages have come from social movements having distinctive characteristics. Successful movements tend to be large; to seek goals other than total displacement of their antagonists; to have sufficient resources to offer members special inducements or to impose special constraints; to use violence or other coercive means under conditions that make such tactics at least partially acceptable to third parties; to be centrally directed or to have a "bureaucratic" form of organization. When a challenging group has already established itself, it fares best in times of economic crisis and, especially, in wartime (Gamson, 1975, Chapters 4-8).

4. Development of Ingroup Solidarity

It is easy but potentially misleading to point to the many instances in which external threat heightens the cohesion or integration of collectivities. Both the internal properties of collectivities and the character of the external threat must be specified if useful predictions are to be made. Such specification needs to take into account, among the most important internal properties affecting response to threat: the degree of centralization of decision-making; the extent of reserved capacities for decentralization in case of need; the effectiveness of communication systems; potentials for mobilization, e.g., fluidity of resources relevant to coping with the threat; the homogeneity or heterogeneity of interests and values; and pluralism or polarization of internal conflicts and contradictions. Among the most important characteristics of external threat are: severity and duration; whether the threat comes from physical environment or from other social collectivities (e.g., an earthquake versus a military invasion); concentration or dispersal of threats in place and time; and the homogeneous or diverse character of the threats.

Maximum positive effect upon cohesion is likely when the threat is from another collectivity; is sudden and severe; originates in a single clearly identified source; threatens interests and values of all important segments of the collectivity; is homogeneous in nature, e.g., contains no possible rewards or avenues of escape.

A sense of a common fate or goal has a strong effect on the nature of conflict groups; where it results in the search for a common, cooperative solution to a problem, it plays a positive role (as in labor unions, military units in combat, some cases of school integration). But where cooperation and the achievement of a positive goal offer no hope in alleviating or eliminating a threatening common future—as in a tuberculosis hospital or a prison—a sense of common fate is not a positive attribute.

Where cooperation offers some hope of benefit or success, however, a sense of sharing may contribute to a cohesion of effort and thought which may temporarily or permanently suppress areas of disagreement between groups and individuals. A remarkable and little-known example is the three-way collaboration among whites, blacks, and Indians in guerrilla actions by the Lowry Band against the Ku Klux Klan and the white political establishment in North Carolina during the first decade after the Civil War (McKee, 1971). In a much larger and more recent instance, a sense of common fate in the face of external threat and of the need for coordinated efforts in wartime allowed policies of racial integration to be implemented in the armed forces immediately after World War II with less social resistance than was later encountered in other sectors of our society.

Coalitions and other heterogeneous groupings often are formed in response to a common threat and tend to disintegrate once the threat is past. The likelihood of continuance is greater to the extent that the ad hoc solidarity has produced advantageous interdependence, a history of successful cooperative accomplishments, and reasonably promising prospects for future attainments. If the threat is no longer immediate and the sense of common purpose or fate is ambiguous and unclear, the group, organization, or collectivity will begin to suffer from the effects of its heterogeneity, even in areas with which it has dealt successfully in the past.

Consensus may be necessary to, and expressed in, the limited conflicts of rivalries and contests. Political opposition and struggle may be the means of modifying and thereby maintaining a national consensus, through developing "day-to-day agreements and compromises which may eventually modify and reshape the slowly developing habits and attitudes that compose a consensus" (Rozwenc and Schultz, 1964, 3). For example, in instances of rebellions or guerrilla operations against colonial powers, if a rebel movement has been able to firmly establish its own network of government, services, and communication, even while it is fighting a superordinate power (e.g., as an underground movement) then when it does achieve self-determination, less turmoil and restructuring are likely to occur because alternative structures, norms and values, already have been accepted. For example, during the 1960s and early 1970s the Guinea-Bissau underground was able to achieve a certain amount of political power, authority, and acceptance among the population, developing clinics, schools, and outposts even while it was fighting the colonial power of Portugal. With the granting of independence, little restructuring was necessary: the government already had established its effective power and its legitimacy locally.

5. "Backlash" and Other Undesired Consequences: Can They Be Avoided?

To speak of collective actions as producing backlash means that an undesired outcome is produced: the mobilization of opposition, the creation of new opposition, and eventual loss rather than gain.

At the micro-level, an observation frequently made by students of conflict is that personal attacks on an opponent increase the difficulty of a settlement and intensify resistance. When an opponent feels under personal attack, the struggle is made more intense than when only differences in interests are at stake. Perceiving personal hostility and denigration, the opponent resists change in outlook and policy and becomes less open to persuasion or inducements, whether from the challenger or from third parites (Sharp, 1973, 727). Thus responses to a sense of being personally attacked or of being made to appear lowered in position or social value—as stupid, mean, immoral, incompetent, and so on—can destroy otherwise promising negotiations or original inclinations toward mutual accommodation (Brown, 1971, 86).

Special importance, we believe, must be attached to personal *humiliation*—a condition and a process difficult to define but indubitably real and powerful. Humiliation involves a public process of derogation and exposure in which the actor's *persona* is successfully labeled as inferior, shameful, disgraceful. The social person is exhibited in a literally degraded condition—as foolish, weak, stupid, naive, contemptible, morally reprehensible. It must be a rare case indeed in which a person exposed to such social evaluation will be able to insulate self-conception from its impact, especially if one knows that other persons with whom one has positive affective ties share the relevant social standards. Then if the humiliation is believed to have been inflicted *purposively* and *needlessly*, reactions of rage and desires for revenge are likely to be exceedingly strong. To forgive a person who has been the active author of one's humiliation may be more difficult than to forgive physical harm.

Numerous examples can be readily adduced of actions of constraint—both by authorities and by partisans—which produced undesired consequences (Friedman, 1973). From the standpoint of the objectives of the authorities who wish to control partisan violence, some types of violence by control-agents are definitely counterproductive. For example, escalation of violence as a result of inept or undisciplined actions by police and National Guard forces was observed frequently in the urban civil disorders of the 1960s. Especially instructive were reactions of the control forces to scattered sniper fire. Most law enforcement units had never before experienced envelopment firing and felt themselves surrounded. In the absence of special training and of effective command systems, they often returned fire indiscriminately, e.g., by spraying an apartment building with bullets. They thus killed and wounded some innocent persons and endangered many others. The uncontrolled firing sometimes mobilized new participants who attacked police and firemen (Janowitz, 1968, 14-16).

Study of these problems suggests some highly specific implications. For instance, if in efforts to control riots or other mass violence, the police and paramilitary personnel are supplied only with weapons of deadly force (rifles, bayonets, armored vehicles) they are incapable of avoiding escalated violence once their threat is challenged. As Janowitz has observed, if the control forces are instead equipped with instrumentalities of protective use and of minimal rather than maximal destructiveness (helmets, water-base equipment, batons, wicker shields, etc.), then "the emphasis is on a selective response and a concern with the minimum application of force" (Janowitz, 1968, p. 26). Just as experienced negotiators sometimes suggest that "if you must lose your temper, do it deliberately," so a maxim for social control through force may be, "use it quickly, decisively, briefly — and minimally."

The overuse of coercion is not confined to the employment of violent means. When a more powerful party decides to press hard bargaining (e.g., final offer first), its victory in a test of strength will have certain costs. One may decide to use a "no quarter given" approach, but one must be prepared to accept the resulting costs and consequences.

For example: "The more (management's) commitments approximate the final-offer-first strategy, the less problem-solving activity will occur during negotiations, and the more negative will be the sentiments relating the parties" (Walton and McKersie, 1965, 10).

Potential for constraint may itself be a source of conflict. When a powerful third party has the authority and ability to intervene (or not intervene) in a conflict, and it has made such choices in the past, its discretion in doing or not doing so may itself become a cause for contention. We may think of the role of the United States in disputes between Greece and Turkey as an illustrative case. The essential point is that the use of constraint by a powerful authority is not only highly important in its immediate effects on interests, but also sets up and alters crucial expectations. Indeed, in appraising the effects of purposive social action, one fact of human behavior of great and frequently overriding importance is often left out of account. The fact is the extreme sensitivity of collective social processes to *changes in expectations* that in turn are set off by salient events affecting individual and group interests.

When changes in expectations have undesired consequences, such as run-away increases of intergroup hostility or uncontrollable economic inflation, control may be rendered very difficult by the sheer costliness and inaccessibility of corrective information. In the economic sector, for example, many events have their main effects through *expectations* that affect both production and consumption decisions in the face of the nonexistence of real markets for future goods. Because of the costs of information and the irreducible elements of uncertainty about the future, only rarely can there be effective markets for future goods—insurance contracts, equity markets, and cost-plus contracts provide only rough approximations. In an economic world of uncertainty, current policies then can act as gigantic generators of *signals* that can initiate run-away processes of deflation and inflation (Arrow, 1974).

Economic expectations, of course, constitute only one case among many. The shell of anxiety extending forward into the future from the head of the human being is one aspect of a generalized vigilance toward external threats. Political events often have collective effects that are far more massive and intense than would occur were not apprehension raised about future events. Thus the Community Action Programs of the Office of Economic Opportunity in the 1960s had only minor actual effects upon power and authority in American municipalities. But the programs stirred substantial uneasiness, fear, and resentment among many local officials and political party leaders who anticipated greater effects in the future. At the same time, the presence of the programs seemed initially to have stimulated the claims of the poor—and then to have produced increased disillusionment when hopes were dashed (Kershaw, 1970).

The high importance of an immediate sense of personally relevant threat in producing negative evaluations of identified racial-ethnic groupings is shown by all studies we have found that bear on the matter. A study of over 1,200 white students at Washington State University in 1969 showed that perception of threat was the strongest predictor of negative evaluations of the Black Student Union, in comparison with either generalized prejudice or the credibility and legitimacy of the protest against discrimination. The authors of the study suggest that "the emergence of threat in the situation has the effect of altering or reversing the perceived credibility of the activities of protest-oriented organizations, and reduces the likelihood of a favorable evaluation by members of the majority group in the community" (Wilson and Day, 1974, 701).

Undesired consequences of constraint occur both in macro- and in micro-processes. The use of nonviolent constraint by weak groups against authorities often gets out of hand. We have noted elsewhere that in the macrocases very few social movements of nonviolent intervention by a protesting ethnic minority can develop the enormous discipline required to avoid massive violence, especially if the movement becomes large and meets with increasing success against its opponents (Williams, 1965). On the other hand, the less purposive, instrumental, and planned an instance of collective violence (e.g., rioting) appears to outsiders, the less likely it is to arouse counterconstraint, i.e., the less will be the apprehension among those not immediately involved that the disorder will recur, and the less likely it is that strong sanctions will be invoked in the period immediately following the outbreak (Hubbard, 1968, 16).

The more overtly threatening the behavior of the original group, the more active subsequent groups will be in eliciting support, enlisting membership, and developing goals, tactics, and strategies in pursuit or defense of their own interests. These processes can be observed in specific local events. For example, blacks in the educational system in Philadelphia responded to the model of successful political machines within the Italian and Irish communities by trying to apply such ethnic tactics to the schools (Berson, 1974). Subsequently black educators and other leaders actively pressed for proportional representation on commissions and boards and in teaching positions. Similar issues arose concerning cultural facilities and courses. Other ethnic groups were quick to perceive a threat to political power, white jobs, and cultural cohesion. As older modes of achieving ethnic mobility were becoming obsolete, ethnic groups began to develop new forms and styles of competition with other groups. In 1967 Italian-Americans formed a lobbying organization called the Columbus Forum. Through later alliances with the Sons of Italy and local Italian-American politicians, it developed considerable influence. Soon the Jewish Community Relations Council began to participate actively in educational issues. Small organizations formed in response to being "caught between the black thrust on one side and the Italian consolidation on the other," but they were the weakest of the three groups, partly because many Jewish persons already were teachers or administrators in the school system. And the Irish, whose system of parochial schools had been a response to their own earlier experience of discrimination, were strongly represented in the Philadelphia Federation of Teachers.

The efforts of black leaders were focused on the attainment of increased representation, cultural responsiveness, and political representation. Other ethnics—Italian, Irish, Jewish, WASP—seem to use cultural solidarity and political power in defense of established positions and in competing for the scarce resources of the educational system. Thus in this small-scale example one sees in attentuated form the interplay of mobilization and countermobilization among visible collectivities in response to indicators of changing positions and inferred changes in intentions and future prospects.

These few widely varied examples indicate the great range in forms and intensity of "backlash" responses to attempted constraints. Are there any reliable generalizations that can be found concerning counterreactions to constraint? We believe that the following rough rules of thumb are generally valid.

Mutual accommodation is more likely when opponents have restrained themselves from inflicting extreme injuries. Extreme injuries are those that inflict large amounts of damage to important values.

Damage is greater if it is *irreversible* than if it is easily reversible. In general, damage of property not immediately essential to life is less extreme than damage to persons, with mutilation and death at the extreme.

Damage is judged by whether it exceeds *expectations*. When expectations are for highly restrained behavior, even mild verbal threats may be regarded as extreme.

Damage is appraised also by its *functional appropriateness*, i.e., the extent to which it is judged as necessary or greater than needed to accomplish an objective. Needless damage will be interpreted as provocative, sadistic, or insane, or as a symptom of excessive hostility and of unrealistic aims of the opponent.

Perhaps because of seeming obviousness, one easily can underestimate the extent to which reactions to constraints are determined by the acting parties' *appraisals of realistic possibilities*. When authorities use coercive means to enforce rules and exactions, resistance tends to occur when persons subject to the constraint feel there is a definite possibility of reversing the decision or changing the circumstances. They then tend to move to regain the freedom they lost and to seek additional power as "insurance" to make it more difficult for them to again be robbed, forced, or deprived of this freedom or possession. Sometimes the sheer physical accessibility of a person in authority who can be threatened, bribed, or entreated is enough to suggest the possibility of reversal or retribution. For this reason, authorities sometimes may either present themselves or be deliberately placed in the position of officials who lack authority within a "hopeless bureaucracy." This is the classic bureaucratic "run-around." The supplicant may be confronted at the end of the line with a computer, the universal scapegoat, merciless in its inability to be flexibly responsive. Such denial of responsibility is an effective means of diffusing grievances only if the complainant either accepts the legitimacy of the structure or is convinced of the hopelessness of the attempt.

If from the beginning the partisans see resistance as hopeless, those who are being coerced are more likely to "make the best of it," and by cooperating, obtain the few advantages they might have lost by resisting.

"Gradualism" *versus* "immediate and total" enforcement of change can be appraised in the light of these processes. So long as the opportunity for effective resistance exists, opposition will be undertaken by those who demand a return to the status quo. If it is demonstrated to all factions that the change is both irreversible and unopposable, little opposition will occur and efforts will turn toward acceptance and coping with a new and unpleasant status quo. Gradualism because of its very structure would seem to offer many possibilities for change, reversal, or compromise. It is likely to be slow, passing through several stages, each of which may be resisted, and its gradualistic label signals the assumption that it is open to change. Such institutions as the military, however, deal with change such as racial and sexual integration in an across-the-board way. In the racial desegregation of the armed forces, any outright opposition to authorized change would be opposition to military authority, and all sectors are affected at once, from social life to KP, and from commander to foot soldier. Once the change is set in motion, it is swift, complete, and in appearance unopposable (Bradford and Brown, 1973).

As we know, then, "backlash" does not always occur. Perhaps the most striking illustration—also showing that mass media and ensuing popular beliefs were greatly in error—was that the civil rights protests and demonstrations of the 1950s and 1960s did *not* produce any appreciable long-term negative effects upon attitudes of whites. Quite the contrary. Although there were, of course, hundreds of local incidents of white violence and flare-ups of hostility, the basic trend *throughout the period of frequent civil disturbances* was one of growing acceptance by whites of equality of rights for black people (Hyman and Sheatsley, 1964; Schwartz, 1967; Campbell and Schuman, 1970). As this case implies, backlash is minimized when the cause of the partisans is backed not only with increasingly effective political power but also by prima facie moral validity within the society or community in question.

6. Escalation of Conflict, and Goal-Displacement

An obvious possible consequence of the use of violent means is an undesired mobilization of opposition and the development of increased violent conflict. The best single predictor of rates of recruitment to guerrilla forces in some very important modern instances is the rate of casualties inflicted by the counterguerrilla forces: the greater the violence used by the authorities, the greater the mobilization of insurgents (Zawodny, 1962, viii). This result can be avoided but only under quite specific conditions—e.g., by native regimes of high legitimacy, using limited and selective coercion coupled with persuasion and strong inducements (Bohannon, 1962). But violent constraint obviously is often a dangerous instrument for its wielder.

Conflicts occur in clusters in time and space. There are escalating and de-escalating series of conflicts. Studies of conflict sometimes seem to imply that any outbreak of conflict tends to lead to further conflict (Kriesberg, 1973, 153; also, Tanter, 1966). If this generalization were to hold universally, it would do so because: (1) the conditions producing small conflicts are sufficient, if continued, to produce larger conflicts; or (2) the initial conditions themselves inevitably increase over time in conflict-generating efficacy or lead to additional conditions that have this effect; or (3) each event of conflict tends to produce a response that increases the level of conflict.

But if each small conflict were followed always (or more often than not) by a larger conflict, it is obvious that the entire world would long since have been engulfed in continually escalating conflict, increasing asymptotically to Armageddon. Since the logically entailed escalation does not occur, the claimed predictability is not universal but is an empirical generalization, applicable only to some times, places, and circumstances. Prior conflict is a good predictor of escalation only when the "circumstances" are suitable. It is this necessary configuration that must be specified for genuine prediction rather than mere empirical extrapolation. In general, escalation is likely when the opponents struggle for high stakes, are closely matched in apparent coercive potentials, have few positive interdependencies, and have early resort to violent tactics regarded by the other party as disproportionate and unfair (Timasheff, 1965).

As a conflict intensifies, less effort is spent in the direct pursuit of prior desired goals or gains, and more energy in various forms is directed toward blocking or damaging the other group. This process entails main subprocesses: (1) As conflict increases, the amount of effort devoted to hindering the opponent increases; (2) As conflict increases, the act of impeding, eliminating, or breaking the resistance of the opponent comes to be seen as an increasingly essential temporary goal, the necessary means to pursue the original goal unhindered. A fully escalated conflict may become essentially uncontrolled. Any doubt one may have on this point can be dispelled by noting that near-genocide occurs even in so-called conventional warfare. Thus it appears likely that in the Lopez War of 1865-70, Paraguay may have suffered the loss of 80 percent of the adult population and up to 90 percent of the adult males (see Klinberg, 1966).

Little is known of exactly how other subprocesses interact to produce escalation, but suggestive hypotheses are available. Thus among the possible effects of the use of violence in collective conflicts, the following may contribute to heightened violence (Janis and Katz, 1971, 219-32).

1. The use of violent means may alter the actual goals of the violent user, e.g., transforming an initially limited objective into a goal of dominance.

2. Violence tends to evoke counterviolence.

3. Even when the use of violent means is publicly endorsed or accepted by legitimate authorities, both the users of violence and those associated with them by being members of the same group or society may feel doubt, guilt, and fear. Such ambivalent or aversive reactions may include: (a) apprehension concerning possible retaliation, or other punishment by the target group or by third parties; (b) preoccupation with questions of whether the violent actions were justified or excusable; (c) reduction of conscious guilt by mechanisms of denial and projection and displacement, e.g., convincing oneself that the target population is evil.

4. Ambivalence and dissonant beliefs may increase dislike for the adversary, leading to increased violence, decreased willingness to consider compromises, and increased alienation from humanitarian values.

5. Participation in violence—including passive acceptance and vicarious involvement—may weaken psychological restraints against further use of violence and eventually may incorporate violence into self-conceptions.

6. Continued use of violence may shift the limits of respectable, normal, acceptable behavior, e.g., as legitimized leaders and representatives use and accept violence, their followers or constituencies become less inhibited about using similar violence and extending the use to additional contexts.

When collective violence is frequently repeated, or becomes continuous, a frequent accompaniment is the development of specialization in violence and the establishment of social positions whose incumbents are committed to violent roles will be under strong psychological imperatives to make their linked to self-interest and self-esteem, e.g., the police who advocate maximum discretion in use of firearms and other deadly means. Persons committed to violent roles will be under strong psychological imperatives to make their violent behavior congruent with positive self-esteem, hence to find justifications. A possible solution is the acceptance and advocacy of an ideology stressing the inevitability of conflict, the intrinsic evil of the outgroup ("criminals," "the enemy"), the social virtues of aggression (bravery, manliness, obedience to orders), or the necessity of strategic defense. Persons who specialize in obedient aggression easily find in their social roles opportunities to vent hostilities and satisfy sadistic needs under the guise of "enforcing norms," "doing one's duty," "just following orders." A further extension may occur in the form of passive acceptance of any dictum or example emanating from higher authority. In addition, social roles involving violence and brutality

—police, executioners, torturers, prison guards, and the like—may be selective of personality types, by attracting those with appropriate psychological predispositions.

7. Learning and System-Adaptations

Social systems can be said to *learn*—and this in a double sense. The individuals whose behavior constitutes the system learn new skills, perceptions, knowledge, beliefs, values. And new norms, relationships, and cultural resources become built into the changed system, into its institutions and its social organization.

For new norms and procedures to become institutionalized in a complex social system, it is necessary not only that beliefs and values change but also that a great deal of both individual and system learning occur. The learning typically is protracted. No exception is found in responses of established organizations to protest and violence. Nevertheless it does appear that there has been some learning, not only of techniques and tactics but also of "an etiquette of [dealing with] disruption and protest, as part of a more general pattern of new etiquettes toward previously labeled antisocial activity" (Coates, 1973, 35; Janowitz, 1968).

Out of the protracted struggles of recent decades, for ethnic rights and economic and political advancement of minorities, have come complex changes in American culture and social structure.

One set of effects has been the mobilization of "social control" or repressive social formations, as represented in the "beefing-up" of police forces, especially through the Law Enforcement Assistance Administration and in the attempts to institute "preventive detention" and other measures that abrogate the nominal protection of the Bill of Rights (especially of the Fourth Amendment). On the other hand, as we have reiterated, a great deal of long-established forced segregation and discrimination has been swept away, and political rights and liberties and civil rights of racial minorities have been greatly strengthened, often as a result of actions of collective constraint. Clearly a group or social movement may achieve some of its goals and fail to attain others. Its leaders may gain great rewards; its followers, nothing. It may lose many battles but gain decisive advantage in the long pull. It may win every contest but find the total set of outcomes useless or actually disadvantageous. It may gain power, only to find unanticipated burdens and constraints. One must heartily agree with Gamson (1975, 29): "Success is an elusive idea."

But no matter how difficult it may be to determine whether collective actions have been successful, political movements and organizations do set forth objectives, work for other goals that are implicit, make plans, devise strategies and tactics. Their actions have consequences, some desired, some undesired. Those actions are judged by the members of the collectivity and by others to have been more or less successful. The outcomes of the actions of a "challenging group"—a set of potential partisans who seek to influence or overthrow an authority—fall into two categories: (1) whether the partisan organization is accepted by its opponent as a valid spokesman for its claimed constituency; (2) whether the movement or group gained the objectives it sought. The four possible outcomes accordingly are (see accompanying tabulation [Gamson, 1975, 28-29]):

Objectives: New Advantages Gained?	Acceptance Gained? Yes	No
Yes	Full response	Preemption
No	Co-optation	Collapse

Acceptance of an organization or movement as representative of an acknowleged constituency may take the form of consultation, negotiations, formal recognition, or inclusion in positions of authority or prestige within its opponent's own organizational structure. For fifty-three challenging groups in American history, 1800-1945, Gamson finds this distribution of outcomes: full response, 38 percent; preemption, 6 percent; co-optation, 9 percent; collapse, 42 percent (Gamson, 1975, 37).

In the context of the 1960s black political pressures, aided by white allies, often produced clear outcomes, as in the Congressional acts of 1964 and 1965. In other instances, the effects were greatly attenuated by subsequent processes. A minor example will illustrate the general point: between 1966 and 1970, under pressure of legal actions and adverse publicity, the Selective Service system of local boards moved from having 1.3 percent black members to 6.7 percent. And by 1970, with little overt opposition, black members had been appointed in many strongholds of white supremacy. But primarily because national regulations narrowly constrained local boards, the change in composition was not related to any obvious change in local practices, e.g., the rules and practices were differentially used by white youths to secure deferments or exemptions (Murray, 1971).

Participation does not necessarily lead to power—no matter how attractive the idea of participatory democracy may appear. A conspicuous example is the fact that popular elections of low-income representatives or urban poor people in the Community Action Programs of the 1960s did not result in effective representation of the collective interests of the poor (Greenstone and Peterson, 1973). But there is a marked positive relationship by states between the percentage of black population and the proportion of elected officials who are black. In short, the effects of participation depend upon whether it provides access to influence through constraint.

A national social system is an incredibly complicated thing. Because of numerous interconnected interests and the interactions among them, effects of collective actions typically are less than hoped for by advocates. A good case in point is the establishment of organizations to deal with complaints and grievances of partisans. Grievance procedures that work well for resolving discontent typically are those that operate within complex formal organizations where aggrieved persons are well-informed and are represented by a relatively powerful group, e.g., a labor union. But racial and ethnic discrimination typically affects most severely a population that is relatively uneducated, relatively poor, unorganized, and lacking in relevant information. *Where these conditions are prevalent, grievance procedures are ineffective when they rely upon the aggrieved individuals to initiate a complaint to a court or to an agency of government.*

The evidence that supports this generalization is consistent, although drawn from diverse settings. The New York City Commission on Human Rights grew out of responses to the Harlem riot of 1943. It was supposed to ameliorate ethnic and racial hostilities and to reduce discrimination in housing and in employment. A detailed study of its long experience shows that its nominally substantial authority has not been effective in any major way in reducing discrimination. Although its limited impact is due to political and administrative factors other than its procedural structure, it illustrates the weakness of a "nonadvocate" agency as an antidiscrimination instrument (Benjamin, 1974).

System-adaptation to diffuse collective violence may include public policies that reduce immediate sources of discontent without changing the structure of decision-making. During the later 1960s, there was a rapid increase in welfare expenditures and in the number of urban families receiving assistance. One major interpretation was that the "welfare explosion" was a political response to urban riots and that it had the effect of reducing the momentum of civil disturbance (Piven and Cloward, 1971). Subsequent analysis showed great difficulties in securing appropriate evidence to test these suppositions but found data consistent with the presumption that riots were followed by disproportionately large increases in welfare expenditures (Betz, 1974). Although alternative interpretations cannot be ruled out, it is likely that officials who could control decisions would favor increased aid to poor black families in riot cities. An expansion in welfare expenditures was the one direction of change least likely to directly threaten the prerogatives of established interest groups. In the second place, welfare payments would be distributed to individuals, not to a publicly salient dissident group as such. And the partial relief of individualized distress and grievances, as well as some co-optation of leaders, may have reduced the impetus for organized partisan action.

Of course, it is equally plausible to suppose that any regularized means for redress of diverse grievances *may* have similar effects. Since redress is often costly, time-consuming, and frustrating, it is far easier for the individual to settle his or her own grievance than to altruistically pursue what may be a collective problem, solely on principle. Were a procedure of individual redress in equity to apply to all, it would provide a measure of "collective justice." But in many cases, it is only "the squeaky wheel that gets greased," while the community or organization continues to say, in effect, "it is the responsibility of each person to speak up." To the extent that individual concessions satisfy articulate dissidents, individualized grievance procedures may also reduce the development of potential leadership.

We infer that accommodations to the demands of individuals and small groups, even when fairly costly, may be made by an organization when its decision-makers foresee the concessions as a means of averting more threatening collective mobilization. For the authorities are likely to believe that once the discontented have developed organizational discipline and leadership, there is always a better than even chance that aspirations and demands will increase. And collective mobilization increases the likelihood of disruption— always of concern to authorities. Hence decision-makers often will prefer to avoid the collective mobilization of aggrieved parties by accommodating to individual grievances rather than responding to a general condition which may be affecting all.

Because of complex adaptative pressures that operate incessantly, all "victories in matters of principle" won by minorities are vulnerable to retrogression. In the field of civil rights since the 1960s, extremely complex legal developments have emerged. Wavering and ambiguous policies and decisions found in governmental regulation and enforcement of antidiscrimination laws reflect the tension between a *strictly universalistic* ("color-blind") emphasis and a doctrine of *retributive or "affirmative" action*. A classic court case that brought these tensions to a focus was *DeFunis v. Odegaard*. DeFunis, a white college graduate, was denied admission to the University of Washington Law School in 1971 although his college grades and Law School Aptitude Test scores were above those of some minority students who were admitted. DeFunis sued, claiming racial discrimination that violated his constitutional rights to equal protection of the laws. The case eventually went to the Supreme Court. In the meantime DeFunis had been accepted and had attended the law school in question. On April 23, 1974, the Supreme Court avoided the constitutional issue by declaring the case moot, on the grounds that DeFunis would graduate in June 1974. A clear decision to end all affirmative action of the type represented by the University of Washington Law School's policies conceivably would have endangered a great deal of the rectification of past discrimination that has been occurring since 1964. A clear decision to permit categorical "reverse discrimination" conceivably would have opened the gates for development of quota systems that would grow into new systems of rigid vested interests and group discrimination (cf. Totenberg, 1974; Himmelfarb, 1974).

If an organization or institution appears unresponsive to a minority group's needs, one possible adaptation is to set up an alternate institution, patterned after the unresponsive one, but which meets those needs. Following the urban civil turbulence of the 1960s, for example, separate voluntary funding agencies for social services emerged in some metropolitan centers, e.g., the United Black Fund of Washington, D.C. and the United Fund for Social Change in San Francisco. Advocates and organizers of these agencies contend that the established funding agencies are unwilling or unable to initiate new and controversial programs needed and desired by minority groups. They believe that the established agencies, such as the typical United Way, will fail to initiate anything other than token or ineffectual programs to meet special needs of minority communities. A composite diagnosis based on this view would run as follows:

> The established fund has no representational status and thus little accountability outside its own structure; it is often beyond the jurisdiction of legislative authority; any regulatory control is largely internal.

> It is likely to be operating in accord with the majority population's priorities and views of acceptable behavior.

> Its power is likely to be derived from a strong network of vested interests, whose values determine policy decisions and oppose an altered focus.

> Established alliances tend to exert pressure against any effort to have their own allocations reduced.

> The inclusion of marginal groups in the allocation of resources would symbolize a change in traditional power relationships.

> The policies of the institutionalized agency itself would be challenged by having to recognize the special needs and problems of marginal groups.

> The failure to include certain groups will be "forgivable" in the public view because of the agency's good works and the belief that it is the minority group that is employing the "wrong" strategy.

Decisions concerning allocations of funds are less likely to be made on the basis of need than on the basis of political compromise and previous commitments.

On the basis of these assessments, certain black and other minority leaders have organized alternative funding organizations to support groups and activities that have not received aid from the United Fund. In San Francisco, the United Fund for Social Change provides funding for fourteen member organizations, representing ethnic minority and low-income white constituencies. In the case of the United Black Fund, Inc. of Washington, D.C., funds are allocated only to groups or agencies that are not receiving support from other fund-raising organizations.

Such "alternate institutions" have an uncertain future. But their very presence introduces an implicit threat of a more thoroughgoing separatism that conceivably may become part of the bargaining pattern in urban resource allocations.

The continuing struggles within the arenas of judicial and administrative processes abundantly show how incessant is the interplay of pressures and constraints that shape emerging intergroup relations. Observe two court cases decided in 1974. A sharp potential restriction on metropolitan school desegregation was implied by the ruling in a Detroit case that held that the Fourteenth Amendment does not obligate states to desegregate schools by crossing school district lines within metropolitan areas. Even while this decision restricted the scope of actions that may be taken to reduce racial segregation, another case pointed to the possibility of greatly increased scope: the decision regarding the Mark Twain Junior High School in Coney Island, New York (*Hart et al. v. Community School Board of Brooklyn*, 1/28/74; 72 C1041; U.S. District Court for Eastern District of New York). In the area in question, low-income housing developments increased the number of black children attending area schools. In response to this change the school board redistricted and established busing policies that reduced the white preponderance in the schools. In 1973, court action was brought against the schools, charging discrimination because of the change in racial composition of school attendance. In the legal processes the issues were broadened to include consideration of the effects of housing policies on school integration. In the end, the court ruled that not the schools alone but all public services were responsible for preventing discrimination and for maintaining racial balance.

Having thus squarely asserted authority to require *the state* to take part in *remedial action*, the court proceeded to lay down specific dicta addressed to local, state, and federal authorities. Although the detailed intervention of the court in this case almost certainly will not become a general practice, the frequency of activism of the courts in recent decades is a response to the opposition or neglect of other arms of government in the field of civil and political rights. Obviously also, in relation to the complicated patterns of organizations and interests involved in residential segregation in metropolitan areas, the simple formulas that initially worked well in the South against clear and rigid patterns are being slowly and painfully revised. Learning will continue, as will struggle.

8. Back to Strategies Again

And thus we are brought around once more to the necessity for continuous reexamination and analysis of strategic problems in endlessly changing social circumstances. Eternal vigilance is the price not only of liberty but of fraternity and equality as well. It is essential to hold any gains made by a minority in the political arena.

Thus many of the apparent victories at the national level in the 1960s' War against Poverty were largely illusory — by reason of underfunding in relation to overpromising, by organizational ineffectiveness, by fierce resistance of entrenched local political and economic interests, and by what appear to be willfully "suicidal" policies of administration. From this history, one observer has noted "lessons" for any future efforts by central governmental authorities:

> Establish simple, direct channels for program execution; avoid implementation schemes that require cooperation of a multiplicity of organizations, some of which may be indifferent or negative; more fundamentally, consider implementation as part of making policy and do not assign program initiation to one group of people (especially fly-by-night governmental amateurs, one might add) and implementation to others (Sundquist, 1973; reviewing Pressman and Wildavsky, 1973).

But we must also continually reexamine what it takes to win acceptance or advantage in the first place. Advocates of expressive politics might well take seriously the evidence that sheer confrontation can be consistently self-defeating. Among protest movements in the United States, one particular set of tactics and strategies has proved, time and again, remarkably unsuccessful. The prototype is an organization that makes drastic threats and demands total change but is not unified, has only a loose structure, and does not command large resources. One may say that it manages to be provocative without being potent. "This group seeks to displace its antagonist and relies on ideological appeals without selective incentives, it lacks bureaucratic organization, and although not itself a user of constraints as a means of influence, it experiences attack by hostile authorities" (Gamson, 1975, 128-29). Initially weak movements seem to ensure their own destruction when they drastically threaten opponents and create fear and alienation among potentially sympathetic third parties (Chiles, 1971). It seems obvious that movements which avowedly seek to wholly displace their opponents give the latter no choice but to resist or "cooperate in their own demise." In Gamson's study, regardless of how limited or ambitious their other goals and regardless of the means of struggle they used, less than one in ten of such challenging movements, 1800-1945, in the United States were successful (Gamson, 1975, 49).

Selection of strategies within any collectivity inevitably entails controversy; if it were perfectly clear what to do, we probably would not even think of the concept of strategy. It is not a necessary part of our task in this book to offer gratuitous comments on the strategic questions faced by various groupings within the American body politic. But, resolutely undeterred by these considerations, we think it appropriate to close this chapter's assessment of the varying consequences of constraint by reflecting briefly on a chronic practical question in the political strategies oriented to class and ethnicity in the United States. In terms of sheer numbers of persons this is a working-class society (Levison, 1974). In terms of central lines of authority and power, it is a strongly inequalitarian system in which a quite small elite stratum of great wealth and high income effectively influences the most important binding decisions that affect the entire population. It is also a society in which the ethnic minorities that currently regard themselves as disadvantaged partisans constitute perhaps a third of the electorate.[2] On the whole, the middle-income "nonethnic" strata have tended to act, contrary to fact, as if their interests coincided with those of the corporate managers and wealthy elites.

Ethnic minorities have made considerable recent gains in civil and political rights. Future gains, however, increasingly will involve changes in employment, income distribution, and distribution of authority. In the forthcoming struggles, it seems plain that partisan minorities are unlikely to profit greatly from alliances with upper-class groupings. On the other hand, there is a historical record since the 1930s of reasonably clear support by organized labor of developments favorable to minorities. Labor groups have been "anti-ethnic" in politics primarily only when ethnic partisans and union groupings have been maneuvered into confrontations, e.g., by the old divide-and-rule tactics of employers who for long succeeded in setting whites against blacks by using nonunionized work-desperate blacks to break strikes (Levison, 1974).

Our own judgment is that *in central matters of economic and political power*, strategies of ethnic organizations should include a strong component of coalition action with organized labor. For many less central issues (and for many predominantly local economic and political questions) there is considerable utility in common action with middle-class liberals and some conservatives. When the interests of an ethnic bloc diverge sharply from those of coalition parties, some ethnic organizations will be prepared to go it alone. But neither separatist politics nor reliance upon elite benevolence or "trickle-down" benefits will be effective as main thrusts in a total strategy for reducing discrimination and severe poverty in an affluent but inequalitarian republic.

We conclude that for all its sometimes quite high immediate costs, a strategy of selective and considered use of constraints is indispensable for minority partisans. It is essential not only to gain recognition and advantages but also to restrain the venality, arrogance, and insensitivity that are symptoms of the occupational disease of those who exercise unchecked power in any society.

Chapter 12

An End to Conflict? Terminations, Settlements, and Resolutions

1. The Problem: How Can Conflicts End, or Be Resolved?

Given that a particular conflict exists, we may wish to know several important things about that conflict. Such additional desirable knowledge may include: what the possible *outcomes* are; what conceivable *modes of termination* exist; what conditions affect the selection of strategies and methods of *attempted settlement*; what factors favor or militate against the *institutionalization* of arrangements for regulating or settling conflicts. And, of course, we shall want to learn anything we can about the factors that are important in accounting for *the success or failure of attempted resolutions*. These are the concerns of this chapter.

In any sustained review of individual empirical propositions taken one-by-one in an extended series, it is almost impossible to keep continuously in view that each will be true only if "other relevant conditions are of no effect in *this* instance." Each of the propositions put forward in this chapter is embedded in an invisible context of assumptions about the meaning of the terms used, the concrete reality to which variables refer, and the constancy of the environment within which each proposition is thought to hold. These qualifications apply to all the propositions already stated concerning the sources and outcomes of collective social conflicts. Even with their many limitations, these generalizations, hypotheses, and guesses do provide the basis for a firmer grasp of the causes and consequences of this complex field of behavior than we could have had without such an inventory and appraisal. But we now ask, in addition,

314

not just how conflicts begin and what effects they have, but also how they are terminated (Coser, 1967, 37-51).

Ordinary observation shows that one common outcome of conflict is continued conflict. That is, some conflicts never are actually settled: they either run on indefinitely (Harris, 1972) or until the parties are exhausted or are diverted by other issues and interests. If such conflicts ever are managed, their domestication, so to say, comes when individuals and collectivities learn ways of continuing to live with the conflict rather than to end it. Unresolved conflicts are common in everyday affairs. Many conflicts end only with the disappearance of the original actors or of the original values and interests at issue. Cessation of conflict, ironically, sometimes occurs as a result of the development of a new conflict, which allows the old one to recede into relative peace.

The processes of conflict do not leave participants unchanged. The contenders themselves are altered by their own activities and by the activities of their opponents and allies. The main consequences of conflict for the participants include:

1. *learning*—of tactics, strategies, norms; capabilities of self and opponents; consequences of types of action; how to assess costs and benefits;
2. *changes in organization within each collectivity*—for example, in communication networks, subgroupings, hierarchies, or centralization;
3. *changes in goals and values*—in their specific content, scope, ordering of importance, or urgency.

The probabilities of future conflicts and of their outcomes are affected by each of these changes and by the interactions among them.

Sequences of outcomes depend also upon the specific social setting. For example, within complex formal organizations frequently two or more subunits (departments, divisions, etc.) have relationships that are partly cooperative but also competitive, and that require the two units to engage in some joint decision-making. Under these conditions, the more competitive the decision process,

1. the less frequent will be the interaction concerning the decisions;
2. the smaller will be the number of persons who participate in the joint decisions;
3. the larger the number of explicit regulations governing interunit interactions;

4. the more frequently will third parties be brought into the decision process, and the greater the proportions of such interventions that represent appeals to authority (coercive capacities);

5. the more the rules that will be developed will be formal, strictly applied, and infrequently revised;

6. the less frequent will be changes in organization, procedures or practices for making joint decisions (Walton, Dutton, Fitch, 1966, 453-58).

It is not always clear in advance whether a given opposition will lead to overt conflict or whether a conflict is or is not resolvable. But some reasonable judgments can be made. In extreme cases we find opposition marked by intense and fixed commitments, high stakes, total ideological incompatibility, mutually exclusive goals, and complete lack of common values or convergent interests. No resolution of the initial opposition is to be expected under these conditions, although subsequent conflict conceivably may prove so costly to both sides that some settlement may be achieved, out of a common interest in avoiding further loss.

The likelihood of early resolution of a conflict depends also upon the extent of intragroup consensus or dissensus on issues related to the conflict. When both parties have high internal consensus, their will and ability to continue the struggle will be high. When both are afflicted by a chaos of disagreements, their representatives are likely to be unable to make reliable bargains. But when each of the collectivities retains substantial consensus but also is stressed by domestic disagreement, moderate elements on both sides are likely to seek outcomes more or less on the basis of "rational" estimates of gains and losses.

Outcomes will vary, however, with different combinations of consensus-dissensus between the parties. When one collectivity is strongly consensual and the other is not, the latter will lack the capacity for continuing struggle and will be compelled to enter into negotiations in a weak bargaining position.

In general, resolutions of conflicts realistically can be sought in those cases in which the parties have both opposing and common (convergent or complementary) interests; that is, they have both "cooperative" and "competitive" interests.

In fact, most intergroup relations probably are mixed-motive games: they contain possibilities for pure conflict but also for mixed conflict and cooperation (Deutsch, 1973, 18). As we have seen repeatedly in prior chapters, many difficulties stand in the way of the regulation of conflict and of the institutionalization of the norms or social structures actually used for settlement of conflicts. Once conflict has begun, there is a self-developing cycle of threat-fear-counterthreat-fear which is likely to be rapidly augmented by new incentives for aggressive action. Although the processes of conflict also contain such countervailing possibilities as exhaustion of resources, "disproportionate" losses, or loss of intragroup solidarity, the tendency of conflict toward escalation is sufficiently frequent to suggest that effective regulation must depend upon special conditions—and that the conditions required for the *mutual* acceptance of *rules* for terminating conflicts must be especially stringent.

Control of conflict is a universal problem in human groups. Take, for example, the commonplace everyday aggressions that occur in school settings among children and youths. Behavior of this kind has been subjected to intensive study. Research by Olweus (1973) on aggression of the type called "mobbing" in Sweden shows that among males age 7 to 16, about 5 percent are classified as highly aggressive ("bullies") and about 5 percent as consistent targets ("whipping boys"). The behavior patterns in question are stable over time—e.g., there is a high correlation between being aggressive in one year and being aggressive in the following year.

The bully-whipping boy pattern is not primarily created by any obvious external forces. Its sources seem to lie within social processes that develop within the school setting. No systematic relationship appears between the aggression pattern and either size of class or size of school, nor is the pattern importantly associated with particular types of relations of the participants to their teachers or to their school work. Furthermore, the "whipping boys" showed only small and insignificant deviations from their classmates in looks, language, clothing, physical handicaps, or hygiene. However, the "bullies" were stronger than average and markedly stronger than the whipping boys. But how did this sheer fact of potential physical advantage become a *permitted* and *effective* source of social dominance?

The whipping boys, we note first, were not protected by peers—rather they were very unpopular among the boys as well as, perhaps more significantly, among the girls. The bullies were almost up to the average in popularity among the boys—somewhat more popular than the "control" (well-adjusted) boys and clearly much more popular than the whipping boys. The whipping boys were generally anxious and insecure, isolated, and had low self-esteem. The whipping boys were not markedly different from bullies in school achievement —both were average or slightly less than average—nor in socioeconomic background. Whipping boys resembled the well-adjusted boys in having relatively close and strong relationships with parents, although teachers felt that the parents of whipping boys were somewhat overanxious and overprotective. In short, the whipping boys were not *initially* stigmatized or vulnerable in any very obvious way.

These results suggested that *the crucial factor in mobbing was the appear-*

ance in a class of one or more persistently aggressive "bullies"—the whipping boys were less crucial because they simply were the passive targets. (Only a few were judged to be "provocative.") When a bully appears there are two major effects: (1) social contagion and (2) a weakening of control or inhibitions against aggression. The "contagion" factor refers to the effects of viewing the behavior of an aggressive model, and second factor operates because the bully typically is *not* punished, and, in addition, is directly rewarded both by victory and by the gratification of aggressive or destructive tendencies.

The findings of this study are consistent with other evidence which indicates that aggressive acts may be encouraged by diffusion of responsibility for control, as well as by those cognitive changes whereby onlookers may come to define the abused person as deserving of punishment. Through these mechanisms it is likely that guilt is reduced and a sense of personal responsibility is attenuated. It is the acquiescence and partial approval of the bystanders, the peer group, that continuously regenerates the social pattern and perpetuates it within each school cohort.

This account of a self-perpetuating process of social aggression is consistent both with numerous direct observations in diverse social settings and with experimental findings. Thus Deutsch shows that under conditions that make rewards (payoffs) depend upon competitive behavior, an individual who acts cooperatively ("altruistically") will be exploited. On the other hand, a punitive strategy invites retaliation, even when joint payoffs are lowered by the use of retaliation. *A nonpunitive tit-for-tat policy deters exploitation and tends to reduce aggressiveness of an opponent* (Deutsch, 1973, Chapter 12).

2. The Character of the Conflict as a Factor in Its Possible Outcomes

Why, indeed, should the parties facing a conflict or already actively involved accept any rules or limits, and why should they ever agree to conditions for terminating the struggle? These are crucial questions; for we know that in many instances the parties do not accept rules and do not agree upon procedures for termination, even when the conflict is extremely damaging to all parties. Often the relevant interests, beliefs, and values of the parties are so incompatible that "one cannot seek a true meeting of the minds—only ways of doing business between fundamentally different viewpoints" (Wedge, 1968, 27). Let us further examine conditions that may determine outcomes, including resolutions of conflict.

In analyzing conditions favoring continuation or termination of conflicts, a central fact already emphasized must never be overlooked: conflict itself changes the situation. Modes of resolution that might have been effective in the very early phases may be impossible later on; others that were at first "unthinkable" may later be readily accepted.

Thus the *sequences* of social processes have important effects. This is true for the processes that *constitute* conflict and for the other processes that usually *accompany* acts of conflict. Both continuously change the possibilities for different kinds of terminations. Among the more important effects intrinsic to conflict are: (1) frustration and deprivation of some members of one or more of the parties; (2) threats, producing fear, anxiety, anger, rage, hostility; (3) changes in relative power; (4) changes in expectations of gain or loss; (5) social approval, within each solidary unit, of externally directed aggression by its members; (6) lowered psychological barriers to aggressive acts against members of opposing collectivities; (7) enhanced authority of functionally salient leaders.

In the initial phases of large-scale conflict between more or less well-organized collectivities, the main effects constitute *mobilization* (Blalock, 1967, 126-39). In mobilization, many individuals are psychologically prepared for combative action—attention is focused, information gained, motivation elicited. Physical and cultural resources are allocated and organized. Social organization is revised and tightened. Values, norms, and collective symbols are emphasized and reinterpreted. A sense of solidarity, obligation, and collective confidence typically is enhanced. Each of these developments increases the thrust toward conflict and reduces the likelihood of early termination. In the absence of apprehension of early defeat or overly severe loss, any kind of resolution of conflict is most unlikely during the period between first major acts of mobilization and the crescendo of subsequent exchanges of attempts to damage the opponent.

The second phase may be called *full engagement*. Each side commits its resources and exerts whatever constraints, including force, it can muster or regards as prudent to use against the adversary. All elements of striking power and defense are tested. Since defense rarely, if ever, is completely effective, all principals suffer some injury and loss. Each collectivity begins to experience internal strain.

If the period of full engagement does not produce a clear indication of dominant power, the conflict may enter into a *struggle of attrition and strategic maneuver*. All parties are likely to suffer heavy losses, commit many resources, endure severe internal tensions. Both the leaders and many of the other members of each collectivity are likely to have a sense of having made a very great investment in the outcome. Provided that each collectivity begins with high internal consensus that the struggle is necessary, the widespread mobilization of sentiments of ingroup solidarity and of outgroup rejection and hostility, as well as the increase in negative evaluations of the opponent occasioned by the injuries received, results in a hardening of resistance to capitulation or compromise. Resolution of the conflict short of marked weakening of one party is correspondingly difficult.

The effects of social context on the character of conflict and thereby on possibilities of resolution or settlement are further illustrated in the tendency of bipolar conflicts within hierarchical organizations to produce a characteristic pattern of tactics including "increase in formality, fixing of obligations, appeal to superiors, and selective circumvention of procedures." On the other hand, when the struggles are multicentered, involving many diverse groups and individuals, the tactics are more likely to center upon coalitions, development of cliques, cultivation of allies through distributing favors, and the like (Dutton and Walton, 1966, 215).

Another generalization concerning situational effects rests on the fact that in organized bargaining between representatives of collectivities, each party tends to follow the "principle of unanimity"— to present a united front and to regard intragroup dissent as a weakness. On the other hand, it is conceivable that if *both* parties followed a rule of permitting public expression of intragroup differences, the likelihood of compromise or integrative solutions often would be increased. Some limited experimental evidence suggests that such bilateral dissensus, when it can be expressed, does favor agreement between the parties and may encourage "mediation" by members of the negotiating teams (Evan and MacDougall, 1967). Although most highly structured bargaining encounters definitely do not favor this "open" type of behavior, a two-party political system often produces approximations to bilateral-dissensus negotiations. Scattered observations suggest that this mode of bargaining appears also in local community disputes and in racial-ethnic relations, primarily as an unintended result of intragroup diversity and the lack of centralized hierarchical control (Jones and Long, 1965; Killian, 1968). (Further notes on the effects of these latter factors will be found in our discussion of intragroup processes in section 6 later in this chapter.)

3. Types of Outcomes and Modes of Termination

When a conflict ends, it has certain results; these are the *outcomes*. It is ended through certain kinds of major social processes; these we call *modes of termination*. Such modes of termination consist of relatively specific subprocesses —of procedures or techniques that are used in bringing the conflict to a halt.

First, although the outcomes of conflict may be classified in many different ways, the principal aspects to be taken into account should include the parties' *attainment of goals*, the degree of their *acceptance of the end-state*, and the degree of *acceptance of norms* for a continuing future relationship. Combining these variables for a simplified two-party conflict we have the types of outcomes shown in Table 12.1.

The labeling of the cells in the table is intended only to be suggestive; the working assumption is that when both parties fail in goal-attainment and both reject settlement, there is a high likelihood that future conflicts will have minus-sum outcomes. Clearly the mere fact that an episode of conflict has ended does not necessarily imply a satisfactory *settlement* or a *resolution* of opposition, nor does termination necessarily signify any decrease in the likelihood of future conflicts. Only if there is positive acceptance by both parties of both the immediate outcome of the present episode and of basic norms and procedures for resolving future oppositions can we say that there has been a full settlement.

The modes by which the various outcomes may be reached are likewise diverse. They can be reduced, however, to four basic types: (1) complete dominance, (2) withdrawal or stalemate, (3) compromise, (4) value-change. In the case of dominance (or "obliteration"), one collectivity removes the other as an effective force in the situation by literally destroying the other (genocide, extermination), or by expulsion (exile, excommunication, deportation), or by destroying the other's resources and capacities for opposition. Short of these drastic outcomes, conflicts may be terminated by the withdrawal of some or all of the principals—by unilateral or mutual physical separation (emigration, segregation), by cessation of communication (suspending diplomatic relations, refusing to accept messages, jamming radio broadcasts, committing suicide), and by social separation or insulation (resigning, quitting, divorcing, deserting, seceding).

In both dominance and withdrawal, the conflict ends because one side is no longer an effective actor in the conflict. In compromise and in value-change, in contrast, both sides remain active; the termination comes about through changes in their relationships to one another and in their orientations to the issues which are in contention. Intermediate between full withdrawal and compromise is adjustment through a reduction in direct interpersonal relations between members of the collectivities, either by separation in space or by social insulation through sparse and formalized communication. A combination of partial withdrawal and positive compromise can be called *pluralistic linkage*: in this case there is mutual acceptance between culturally distinct and partly separate collectivities, and the joint acceptance of a system of intergroup interactions and procedures whereby conflicts are limited and resolved from time to time.

A *compromise* is any kind of settlement in which one or more of the parties agrees to accept something less than or different from the goal originally held to be indispensable for a termination of the struggle. The compromise may be

Table 12.1. Main Types of Outcomes of a Particular Conflict

Goal-Attainments of the Principals

Acceptance of Immediate Outcome (Acquiescence)

Acceptance of Norms for Future Peaceable Resolution of Opposition	Both fail			A succeeds; B fails			Both succeed
	Both accept	A accepts; B rejects	Both reject	Both accept	A accepts; B rejects	Both reject	Both accept
Both accept	"Anti-disaster pact"	"Good loser" pattern	(—)[a]	Institutionalized "contest," "game," "compromise"	Stable dominance; intractable loser	(—)[a]	Positive-sum; consensus
A accepts; B rejects	(—)[a]	Intractable loser	(—)[a]	Continuance of conflict	Continuance of conflict hope of gain	(—)[a]	(—)[a]
Both reject	Intransigent, self-defeating opposition	"Suicide pact"	(—)[a]	Continuance of conflict hope of gain	Continuance of conflict hope of gain	Continuance of conflict hope of gain	(—)[a]

[a] (—) indicates extremely rare or nonexistent outcome.

322

worked out between the parties or arrived at through third parties. It is not necessarily symmetrical nor necessarily confined to the issues present at the beginning of the conflict.

Finally, one or more of the parties may change goals, values, beliefs, and interests in such a way that the opponents come to *converge upon a common formulation* that is mutually acceptable. In these cases the processes of conversion and persuasion are prominently involved (Boulding, 1962, 308-28; Holsti, 1966). Convergence may be symmetrical or one-sided. When complete it is called assimilation—the outcome of a complex set of processes that result in the disappearance of boundaries between formerly distinct parties. Two main types of assimilation are possible. In *convergent assimilation* the separate parties interweave their cultures and social relationships into new forms in such a complete and mutually acceptable way that a new sociocultural unit replaces the two prior collectivities. In *incorporative assimilation*, one collectivity takes on the culture of another and merges with it, culturally and socially.

Complete assimilation of either type is very rare as a large-scale phenomenon during short historical periods (e.g., less than a century of close and continuous cross-cultural interaction). Partial assimilation in a pluralistic society, however, can greatly reduce the incidence and severity of ethnic conflict, as shown by the history of most national-origin collectivities in the United States.

For the foreseeable future, many of the world's political societies will contain two or more major ethnic groupings that will not assimilate or merge but rather will constitute relatively self-conscious collectivities, each providing a complete communal life from cradle to grave for its members. Interethnic relations, therefore, will be a central fact of societal functioning for a long time to come. The viable functioning of such "communal pluralism" depends to a high degree upon the development of institutional resources and procedures for regulation and resolution of ethnic conflicts (cf. Blalock, 1967; Rabushka and Shepsle, 1972; Enloe, 1973; Esman, 1973; Steiner, 1974).

4. Social Structures and Processes Affecting the Avoidance and Termination of Conflicts

Much of the regulation of conflict occurs through avoidance, evasion, diversion, and other tacit solutions. Let us first survey these built-in and largely nonintentional structures and procedures that help either to avert impending conflicts or to reduce their frequency or severity. These modes of avoidance and regulation overlap with but still are partly distinct from the explicitly purposive processes of conflict resolution we shall discuss later.

Some conflicts are never resolved because they never happen. This counterfactual statement is a device to focus our attention to the fact that on many occasions when an incipient conflict is at the point of breaking out, the event does not occur. It is "nipped in the bud." These are cases of the almost-war, the riot that did not erupt, the rebellion averted, the confrontation avoided, the issue evaded, the retort courteous, the turning of the other cheek, the saving grace of humor, the providential distraction, the unexpected peace-maker, the disarming admission, the outrageous joke—examples race to mind by the dozens. Although such cases lack the apparent certainty of events that did happen, they often permit fairly acceptable versions of the Weberian "mental experiment," i.e., what would have happened can be projected with reasonable confidence.

Even apart from the lessons to be seen in large and dramatic events, the ways in which microconflicts are avoided or aborted may have much to teach us. In small-scale conflicts we find many examples of spontaneous development of tacit bargains, informal regulations, third-party interventions, and the like. Street gangs appear as likely candidates for study, as do recurrent situations of diffuse public disorder. Studies of teenage beach resort riots during the 1960s, for example, showed the rapid development of anticipated and patterned sequences of behavior by the crowds, the police, and third-party publics. These patterns foreshadowed similar developments during the urban disorders of 1965-70. Observation of the early disturbances involving teen-age crowds showed a typical pattern of behavior: members of the crowd shout insults and exhibit defiant and hostile actions; in return the police accept the expressive behavior but enforce some return to orderly conduct. Both police and their opponents accept what amount to mutual degradation ceremonies. The outcome is a new informal system of authority. Meanwhile the bystander public shows indulgence for the "riot," which serves as a kind of public entertainment (Smith, 1968).

Among other instances, we note that "hot rodding" and drag racing at one time appeared to contain substantial possibilities for social conflict. Early experiences involving the use of snowmobiles similarly seemed to presage rancorous controversies and conflicts between rural landholders and the participants in a new and noisy invasion. Much of the disruptive potential in both instances was avoided by the rapid growth of voluntary associations with self-enforced regulations, by provision of special facilities, and by extensive public regulation.

For a quite different type of potential conflict, analysis of budgeting in United Way organizations in four cities in upstate New York showed little evidence of overt and direct conflict among agencies (Chirayath, 1974). Although the various agencies were active rivals for shares of a fixed sum of scarce resources, it turned out to be strangely difficult to find instances of direct confrontation or public controversy. Detailed study showed that a whole set of United Way practices acted as devices that avoided or reduced overt conflict. The following procedures were found:

1. Budgeting was incremental; little year-to-year change occurred; the best predictor was last year's budget.
2. Representatives of agencies met with UW separately, not in direct rivalry.
3. Changes tended to be categorical.
4. Agencies were "cooled out" by successive failures to raise budgets.
5. Expectations were regulated by informal preliminary negotiations as well as by anticipatory publicity.

The crucial common elements in these behaviors are: (1) that principals never confront one another directly; (2) decisions typically occur in stages that foreshadow outcomes; (3) allocations almost never occur as open options but as minor modifications of standing bargains.

Much conflict is avoided or minimized by stylized or conventionalized rankings of individuals and groups and by conventionalized restrictions on expression of hostilities (Gluckman, 1954; Chance, 1967; Berk, 1972; Langness, 1972). Conventionalized patterns of behavior tend to cluster at points of recurrent tension in interpersonal and intergroup dealings. Particularly conducive to formalized and restricted modes of conduct is the coincidence of three crucial conditions: (1) the continuance of the interaction is highly important to the participants; (2) apart from the need to continue the relationship, however, the parties have relatively few common interests and congruent values; (3) the relationship involves some strong incompatibilities and oppositions (Woodard, 1944). In short, the relationship is aversive but valuable and unavoidable. Being unable to avoid unwanted tensions, the parties tend to develop means of minimizing additional conflicts within the recurrent situations. Examples include: diplomatic protocol, military courtesy, high-status etiquette, ceremonies of retirement and succession, interracial etiquette, rituals of sportsmanship, conventionalized deference. In all these cases, the conventional patterns serve to maintain a high degree of role-distance, thus minimizing personal involvement and reducing the likelihood of status-injury.

Although *any* contradiction or incompatibility of interests conceivably can become the basis for overt collective conflict, very few such potential conflicts actually develop on a mass scale. How can this striking fact be explained?

First, many potential oppositions simply never are directly encountered because geographic and social separation and insulation prevent the conflictful interactions from occurring.

Second, in much the same way, many oppositions that are potentially society-wide in scope actually remain localized or encapsulated by particular-istic structures of interaction and allegiance—especially by kinship groupings, ethnic relationships, and territorial communities. For example, social classes in the Marxian sense are so crisscrossed and subdivided by other lines of attachment and cleavage in our society that class solidarity on a national basis is comparatively rare. Similarly, separations among status groupings fragment ethnic minorities.

Third, the polarization of large collectivities is retarded and limited by the fragmentation produced by many gradations of rank and reward within the major structural divisions, e.g., by thousands of occupations and many socially recognized differences in income, prestige, security, and so on within each major stratum of industrialized societies (cf. Bendix, 1974, 160). Both class solidarity and ethnic solidarity are reduced by these gradations.

Fourth, in many situations opposition and subsequent conflicts do not arise because the actors do not actually know that their interests are being contra-vened; do not have access to the resources required for collective resistance; or are unable or unwilling to oppose because of low trust in associates or because of deficiencies in motivation, confidence, energy, and decision-making skills (Buckley, Burns, Meeker, 1974). This is to say that ignorance, deprivation, and anomie are formidable barriers to collective action.

Other social mechanisms include interpersonal avoidance. Under conditions of high interdependence and asymmetrical power, patterns of avoidance are developed along with mutually necessary "quasi-impersonal cooperation" (Himes, 1973, 11). Furthermore, some oppositions, disputes, and physical conflicts are avoided by appeals to chance. Randomization is an ancient technique used in many societies for allocating privileges or duties, rewards or deprivations, and sacrifices, e.g., in distribution of lands, selection of leaders, assignment of tasks, selection of jurors, military conscription, and settlement of civil disputes (Fienberg, 1971). Randomization reduces conflict by diffusing and depersonalizing responsibility. In the case of disadvantaged minorities or social classes, much the same effects can be produced by a widespread belief that social positions and rewards are due to luck. Belief in luck is a highly conservative social ideology (Jencks, et al., 1972).

Many conflicts are reduced or settled by tacit or implicit processes. Tacit agreements are indispensable for social peace. If peaceable relationships de-pended upon explicit and full consensus, there would be far fewer peaceable relations than actually exist in everyday life. All social transactions represent implicit bargains. Very frequently an explicit bargain cannot be struck, but tacit coordination produces convergent actions that maintain the peace. A striking large-scale case is the 1958 nuclear test moratorium arrived at by the United States and the Soviet Union, in the absence of any kind of formal agreement. Having had assurance from a conference of experts form the U.S., the U.S.S.R., and the United Kingdom that supervision and enforcement of a test ban would be technically feasible, the two superpowers ceased nuclear testing during a political conference convened to debate whether or not to even consider the matter. The resulting moratorium "was not a treaty; it was not even an agreement; it was merely a matched set of unilateral actions" (York, 1972, 14).

Tacit agreements are very common in ethnic relations within our present-day society. It is easy to see that we have a quite remarkable variety of implicit as well as explicit social mechanisms that serve to avoid or regulate conflicts. These mechanisms arise by trial and error out of numerous experiences of collective oppositions and confrontations. When collective disruption and violence occur, third parties often suffer substantial inconvenience, depriva-tion, and destruction. Their frustration and loss is a basic source of demands for societal regulation of the use of the most drastic means of coercion—force and violence. Given that a polity exists, i.e., that there is a concentration of control of force which commands effective legitimacy—political institutions can provide for the *setting of limits* to domestic intergroup conflicts. Within some authoritatively stabilized limits, all the other processes of conflict-settlement may then occur. *The crucial implication of all this is that it is the political system in complex state-societies that is the central and primary mechanism for regulation and termination of the more serious conflicts.* (Of course, it also is the source of many actions leading to conflict.)

In general, the following rules of thumb seem to summarize *main tendencies* in social systems that affect the structure of conflict and its regulation.

Proposition 1: On the whole, members of the groupings that make and enforce the basic rules concerning power and property will seek to preserve the existing institutions and organizations.

Proposition 2: Norms of procedural conformity ("following the rules" or "going through the proper channels") will often be invoked by those in power toward those seeking redress or change; such rules and procedures will operate, on the whole, to the advantage of those in power.

Within a well-established political system, the management of the great majority of collective conflicts occurs through the daily activities of police, lawyers, courts, prosecutors, judges; of commissions, boards, tribunals; of administrative and executive agencies. The legal system is built in large part on the problems of coping with opposition and conflict (Fuller, 1964, 64). In a society with a democratic political system, the active members and leaders of political parties constitute large aggregates of specialists in conciliation, negotiation, mediation, and compromise. The old aphorism has its point: politics is the art of the possible, in conflict resolution as well as in other fields of collective action.

Proposition 3: The greatest likelihood of rigidity in resisting change in response to the discontent of strata or groupings low in income and power may be expected in polylithic structures.

A monolithic power structure has a few decision-makers who make binding decisions on collective issues. A polylithic structure is one in which there are many separate sets of decision-makers, but only a few decide on any particular issue. Contrary to a popular view, the polylithic structure may be the less responsive to minority needs and claims. For, although a monolithic structure will be slow to respond to pressures, its leaders must keep in view the full range of interests and values in the collectivity; furthermore, when such leaders do act, they will be able to carry out changes consistently and decisively (Clark, 1968, 37-39). On the other hand, a polylithic structure means that on any particular issue a few decision-makers are in control, just as in a mono-lithic structure. But in the polylithic case, the decision-makers are "specialists" —in education, real estate, hospitals, religion, industrial development, and so on—who are likely to render decisions in terms of a relatively narrow range of interests and values, with minimal attention to possible repercussions in other areas. Furthermore, even if a given specialized elite does acquiesce to demands from discontented elements of the collectivity, the same battle may have to be waged all over again for *each* issue or institutional sector, e.g., when desegregation or antidiscrimination policies have been won in governmental employment, these policies may have to be renegotiated in succession in education, religion, unions, and so on.

Collectivities that are trying to change an established order or to alter allocations often confront defenders who are committed to the status quo and who benefit most by its continuance rather than its alteration. Whenever this is the situation, the party advocating change usually is not in a position to offer positive value in exchange. Therefore, the challenging party "always needs a threat (or warning) to make the defensive party fear that it would lose more by not reaching an agreement than by agreeing to accept the detrimental change" (Ikle, 1968, 118). In the case of American ethnic minorities, those groups that seek to change an existing set of arrangements (of political power, allocation of income, distribution of social honor, and so on) typically will initially be the weaker of the parties.

Proposition 4: Usually, therefore, the weaker or the disadvantaged party will be inclined to resort to the use of threat as a major strategy—note the cases of labor unionization, peasant rebellions, anticolonial revolts, the civil rights and Black Power movements in the United States, and student movements.

In such instances:

Proposition 5: Successful negotiations are most likely to occur when an increase in the weaker party's external opportunities gives greater credibility to possible implementation of its threats and its ability to withdraw from negotiations. When a strategy of threat is used, the following generalization holds.

Proposition 6: Where there is no fear of increased risk, the likelihood of escalation increases. On the other hand, the presence of real danger for all tends to enforce restraints and thereby to facilitate the movement of confrontation away from warfare and back to strategies of resolution (Nieburg, 1969, 80-81).

Aggressive actions and expressions of hostility may be used in the challengers' efforts to create a belief in the threats they direct against an existing set of arrangements. Such strategies always carry the possibility of instigating a counterstrategy of threat. It therefore frequently turns out that what initially had been intended as a move to initiate negotiations may lead to a new conflict or an increased magnitude or intensity of a conflict already in process. The most desperate conflicts are the most difficult to regulate. The desperate quality arises from high stakes and the conviction that one's opponent intends to inflict utter defeat.

Proposition 7: Conflict is more likely to be regulated effectively when neither of the parties in conflict sees the contest between them as a single contest in which defeat, if it occurs, would be total and irreversible with respect to a central value.

The anticipation of a total loss if one is defeated, such that nothing of value is preserved, makes the effective regulation of conflict less likely (Deutsch, 1971).

Antagonists can be affected by sanctions. It is a mistake to suppose that collective violence is primarily irrational or nonrational; rarely does it occur without some appraisal of at least the immediate risks and losses. If no external party opposes a principal who aims to attain goals by violent force, the violence typically will occur. Given a sufficiently deep incompatibility of values or interests, violence will occur if and when "established authority is unwilling (or unable) to use force to make the costs of violence prohibitively great for any minority unwilling to resign itself to losing in a nonviolent struggle for power" (Wilson, 1968, 119).

5. Conditions Favoring or Hindering Development of Explicit Procedures of Regulating Conflict

What are the conditions required if explicit and purposive conflict regulation is to be developed effectively?

Proposition 8: The more often that conflict occurs between given parties or within a given social structure, the more likely it is that regularized modes of dealing with conflict will arise.

Recurrence of conflicts with unsatisfactory outcomes for one party or more seems to be a necessary condition for development of explicit regulation. (The unsatisfactory character may consist of high costs even for the victor.) Particularly likely to be candidates for regulation are those recurring conflicts between two parties that have destructive and deprivational effects upon well-organized third parties. Recurrence plus costliness provides *incentives* for management or regulation, either by the opposing parties themselves or by others.

Proposition 9: Previous experiences with conflict, its regulation and resolution, tend to predetermine the nature of subsequent conflict —precedents are set, values are developed, modes of conduct and procedure evolve, and knowledge is limited to the familiar.

Proposition 9a: Early experiences with conflict resolution that have in a high proportion of instances resulted in successful resolutions will tend to set valuable precedents and encourage the development of conditions and practices favorable to future conflict resolution.

Recurrence of conflict tends to produce knowledge and skills and the development through trial and error of "procedures, institutions, facilities, and social roles for limiting its destructiveness" (Deutsch, 1973, 378).

Any effective *purposive* control of a large-scale differentiated organization or social system requires not just an approximate knowledge of general tendencies or kinds and directions of influence, but an organized and *highly specific* knowledge of both structures and processes. Therefore, information is a primary resource for those who may wish to avoid or resolve unnecessary or excessively costly conflicts. This is true in several different ways. Knowledge about one's self, one's opponent, and the common situation of action can aid in finding suitable solutions. In the processes of maneuver and negotiation, either principal in a dispute or a third party may be able to present valid information concerning available resources and probable outcomes that, if accepted, will reduce unrealistic expectations, lower the stakes, and encourage efforts to make objective appraisals. When one party supplies the other with information that subsequently proves correct, credibility may be enhanced; over time, a series of exchanges of correct information helps to create or maintain the valuable resource of justified social trust. Provision of accurate information, furthermore, obviously is essential for coordination of purposive acts, reducing interference and frustration. Appropriate information may prevent competitive panics and crazes—e.g., the theater actually is not on fire (the smoke was only from a wastebasket in the foyer).

Deliberate efforts to avoid or resolve conflicts involve exchanges of information whereby possible settlements are explored in terms of commitments, inducements, and constraints.

Conflicts will be most likely to be resolved by persuasion, inducement, and nonviolent coercion within a process of bargaining when:

a. both parties are subject to a common legitimate authority that possesses superior resources;
b. other powerful third parties are or would be adversely affected by protracted and violent conflict;
c. the parties share important exchange relationships or superordinate goals that both regard as essential for the future;
d. the parties have a common set of central values and beliefs (including important social norms);
e. the parties have partly overlapping memberships or important positive relationships to some third parties;
f. the members have somewhat diverse interests and values, so that the issues or objects of the immediate contention are not exclusively or overwhelmingly important to most members in the long run.

Procedures that facilitate the resolution of conflicts generally develop only over a period of experience with the consequences of unregulated conflicts. Of course there is no guarantee that experiencing highly negative consequences will by itself lead to establishment of regularized means for managing and resolving a particular kind of conflict. The negative effects may not come back to the crucial decision-makers. The social system in question may have a very poor "memory"—by reason of rapid turnover of personnel, or of systemic distortion of the past by ruling groups, or of fixed beliefs and values that are insulated from practical exigencies. The situations of opposition and conflict may change too rapidly and drastically to permit the development of stable norms or reliable procedures. Regulation is likely to be of low effectiveness until the parties develop a coherent organization that can provide for binding decisions, i.e., for reliability of agreements and commitments. Some stabilization of expectations must occur before institutionalized regulation can hold much promise. (Of course, any effective regulation makes subsequent stabilization more likely.)

Institutionalized regulation thrives upon successful past experience.

Proposition 10: Conditions of social organization, procedures, and supporting skills, knowledge, beliefs, values, and motivations that are favorable for negotiation and other regularized modes of conflict-resolution are most likely to become established if the given collectivity has had an early experience of relatively small conflicts which were successfully resolved through collective action in a high proportion of the instances (cf. Coleman, 1957, 1).

Proposition 11: In the long run, *recurrent low-level* conflicts between parties that have at the same time an *important continuing relationship of advantageous interdependence* will create strong pressures for regulation and institutionalized procedures of settlement (Deutsch, 1971, 51).

The likelihood of successful regulation is greater if: (1) there is a prior history of successful compromise and other types of peaceable resolution of opposition between the parties; (2) norms for peaceable solutions are strongly supported (taught, publicized, approved, enforced). A past record of successful resolutions of opposition and conflict tends to increase mutual confidence in dependability of response and to produce consensus on norms. Consensus on norms increases predictability, thus enhancing confidence. Of course, opposition is not thereby abolished; indeed, severe conflict still may occur. But the likelihood of violence is greatly reduced, and the conflicts are less likely to be protracted under the conditions stated.

Proposition 12: The institutionalization and regulation of conflict increases the number of values, norms, and procedures relating to conflict which contending parties will come to hold in common, thus increasing the likelihood of a cooperative process of conflict resolution.

Where two opposing parties within a traditional setting have been able to balance strategies and resources of opposition such that each dispute becomes an acceptable test of wills and pitted resources, and both sides perceive a fair chance of acceptable outcomes, rules and traditions regarding such opposition will become institutionalized in both a social and legal sense. Definable limits regarding strategies and resources become acceptable.

Proposition 13: The larger the number of procedural rules that the parties can agree to in early stages of discussion, the greater is the likelihood of mutually acceptable resolution of substantive issues.

As dispute settlement moves out of the realm of the more institutionalized arenas such as collective bargaining and the courts into community issues and intergroup relations, the lack of institutionalized resources for regulation and settlement makes for less predictable and more volatile situations. Although a certain amount of custom and strategy may be borrowed from the more formalized procedures of law and labor management relations, they are only possible guidelines and often are not directly applicable.

In fact, the development of particular modes for the attempted settlement of a conflict is itself an aspect of the very struggle that a settlement would modify or terminate. When the parties are fairly evenly matched in power and when they visualize a long-term necessity for their interdependence, but the initial level of trust is low, a mode of regulation may be for each party to permit a drift into passive settlement by gradual acceptance of limiting rules. Thus, in some cases, conflicts that are never clearly resolved or decisively terminated may be controlled by becoming "encapsulated" within a set of rules that limits recourse to drastic means of conflict (Etzioni, 1966, 115-35). The rules of greatest interest in such cases are not those imposed by an authoritative third party but rather self-generated limitations that develop directly out of the interaction. Etzioni cites three large-scale cases that approximate the self-encapsulating processes: the struggle of *Colorado* and *Blanco* opponents in Uruguay, of labor and management in the United States, and of the transition in Europe from the religious wars of the sixteenth and seventeenth centuries to the modern peaceable rivalry among churches.

Proposition 14: Structures of regulation are most likely to develop when the parties are convinced that unrestrained struggle (1) will not defeat the opponent, and (2) will be highly dangerous or deprivational, whereas (3) a set of rules can be found which retains substantial advantages for each party. Regulation through encapsulation requires a clear mutual understanding—which seems to require *explicit* rules as well as definite social organization for validating, enforcing, and changing the rules.

So far we have focused on the conditions that affect the likelihood that *any* structure of regulation will develop. The next important question is, *if* institutionalization does occur, what forms will it take under varying conditions? Different types of conflicts have radically varying implications for the subsequent character of institutionalization. Mack and Snyder (1957, 244) hypothesize:

Proposition 15: Conflict which is organized, realistic, characterized by only a few modes of resolution, by focused and stable power relations, and by consequences that are perceived on net balance as positive in value will be institutionalized in relatively decentralized, autonomous and specialized agencies or groups. (Example: U.S. labor-management relations since the 1930s.)

Conflict which is disorganized, unrealistic, diversely resolved, marked by diffuse and unstable power relations and by consequences that powerful third parties regard as undesirable will be institutionalized — if at all — in relatively centralized and authoritative (usually coercive) bodies. (Example: many ethnic and racial conflicts.)

As the preceding propositions indicate, the possibilities for control, management, or purposive resolution of conflicts depend in specific ways upon the degree of *closure* and of *structure* of the particular social system in which conflict occurs. In a diffuse and fragmented society or community that lacks any clear central leadership or authority, no one may be in a position to exert significant influence or control. In a clearly bounded formal organization having a strong hierarchy of authority, on the other hand, great leverage will exist for dealing with opposition and conflict among subordinate units. The varying types of conflict arise from different sources and call for different types of regulation. As shown by Thompson's analysis (1960, 389-409), oppositions within business organizations arise in *technology*, in divisions or cleavages (e.g., age, sex, ethnic or racial membership) among *personnel* ("labor force"), and in the *task-environments* confronted by the organization. To each of these sources corresponds a particular of struggle or conflict. In the technological sector, conflicts arise over administrative allocations of statuses and of facilities and rewards (inducements). From the composition of the labor force emerge latent social identities of sex, age, ethnic collectivity, educational level, and the like; these identities then can become the basis of latent role-conflicts. From the constraints and opportunities of differing enviornments for goal-attainment, or task-activity, arise competing pressures upon members of the organization, e.g., external loyalties and inducements, threats, and strains.

To answer each type of opposition or conflict, an organization may develop a certain kind of defense device or coping mechanism. Struggles, actual or anticipated, over allocations of scarce values within the organization lead to formal or informal defenses, such as: (1) restriction of size, maintaining informal modes of conflict-resolution; (2) reliance upon volunteers for unde-sirable assignments, or systems of rotation; (3) reduction in emphasis on norms of technical or economic efficiency; (4) reliance on consensus among the members of the organization to legitimize allocations of prestigeful or otherwise especially rewarding responsibilities.

Given that there are rules specifying allowable limits and modes of behavior in conflicts, what are the main conditions that favor compliance? Many hypotheses can be found. The main generalizations are summarized in Proposition 16.

Proposition 16: Parties in conflict will be more likely to adhere to any existing rules when:
  — the rules are known, unambiguous, consistent, and not biased;
  — the other party adheres to the rules;
  — violations are quickly known by significant others;
  — there is significant social approval for adherence and significant social disapproval for violation;
  — adherence to the rule has been rewarding in the past;
  — one would like to be able to employ the rules in the future;
  — the rules are flexible enough to allow for necessary change (Deutsch, 1973, 379-80).

Intergroup Conflict and Intragroup Processes: Relations to Conflict Resolution

We have noted at various points in earlier chapters that all types of conflict and of modes of termination are affected by the internal heterogeneity of the parties, both in modes of organization and in the content of interests and values represented. Thus in any instance of negotiation, mediation, or arbitration, the outcomes will be affected by the bargaining that goes on within each of the contending parties — within labor union and management groups respectively, between diplomatic representatives and the nations for which they stand, among party leaders and their constituencies, between ethnic spokespersons and their followers.

Proposition 17: As a general tendency we find that the less definite or enduring the internal structure and membership of one or more parties in a given conflict, the more difficult it will be to resolve the conflict, and the less reliable will be any agreements that are reached.

For example, when leader-representatives have little control over members, they will be unable to guarantee compliance with agreements. Hence, mutual trust will be (realistically) low between the adversaries in the negotiative process. Both the uncertainty of members' reactions and the mutual lack of confidence will increase the likelihood of miscalculations and of the intrusion of diffuse apprehensions into the relationships between the representatives.

If one is a leader or planner of a collective movement that is organizing protests, demonstrations, or interventions, it often will be difficult to prevent participants from engaging in unwanted and tactically disadvantageous violence. (Opponents often will seek to provoke violence in order to discredit the movement and to justify repression.) Reduction in the severity of conflict sometimes is attainable without strategic loss, by systematic safeguards against undesired violence from one's own group. The procedures that are available to develop such protections (Sharp, 1973, 628 ff.) include:

1. screening and selection of participants;
2. training in nonviolent behavior, in advance of confrontations;
3. clear and repeated messages in advance, plus on-the-spot appeals;
4. clear and detailed instructions;
5. designation of persons to speak for the group;
6. requiring pledges from participants;
7. promulgating codes of discipline;
8. use of marshals;
9. establishing committees or courts to enforce discipline by nonviolent sanctions;
10. active intervention, such as night patrols.

If both parties find it advantageous to have some relationship continue, i.e., their interests are positively interdependent, and if instability and uncertainty of agreements and of processes of conflict resolution are quite costly to both parties, the repetition of conflicts over time will generate pressures to develop increased centralization of authority in both collectivities. A high degree of internal structure with relatively stable central leadership or representation will enable each party to make reliable bargains with opponents. Both the clear structure and the security of the leadership (Kriesberg, 1973, 67) reduce the likelihood of "induced" conflict, derived from intragroup processes, and encourage the restriction of conflict to realistic issues. To the extent that these conditions prevail, repeated episodes of collective confrontation between two such collectivities, each of which can deliver important gratifications and punishments to the other, will result in the establishment of norms and procedures for institutionalized rivalry and conflict.

Proposition 18: In stable, organized groups, to the extent that both parties find it mutually advantageous to continue their relationship, and when instability and uncertainty of agreements and of the process of conflict resolution are quite costly to both parties, the repetition of conflicts over time will lead to:

a) increased centralization of authority in both collectivities;
b) a proliferation of detailed, explicit rules (defining rights and obligations of the parties and specifying procedures for regulations of oppositions and conflicts); and
c) the development of specialized positions charged with the implementation and enforcement of conflict-related norms and rules.

Proposition 19: The more rapid the turnover in the leadership or representation of one or more conflicting collectivities, the less important become informal social relations and personality characteristics, and the more important become formal rules and power strategies.

Proposition 20: Regularized negotiations are most likely to be entered upon and to result in eventual agreements when each of the parties makes a formal allocation of bargaining (decision-making) power to designated representatives and when the normal continuing interaction between the parties before the immediate conflict has had a representative-centralized form.

The likelihood that organizations representing interests of ethnic minorities will develop stable internal structures depends partly upon the diversity and compatibility of the interests and values of their constituencies.

Proposition 21: The more homogeneous the constituency represented —in beliefs, interests, and values directly implicated in the issues of contention—the less flexibility and scope will the negotiator be able to bring to the bargaining.

However, the more homogeneous the constituency, the more likely it is that if they do accept a settlement the agreement will remain firm.

As this proposition illustrates, there are ironies in the implications of our analysis. What is desirable from the standpoint of social peace may not be desirable from the standpoint of disadvantaged minority partisans. Observe the following realistically possible scenario.

Short of actual political rebellion or revolution, as oppositions of claims and demands in a complex, large-scale society increasingly involve (a) large collectivities and (b) the regulatory or judicial agencies of the polity, the contending units must place increased reliance upon expert legal and other technical specialists who command the skills and knowledge necessary for effective struggle within the system.

Therefore, increased scale of organization in conjunction with opposition of interests leads directly to a secondary institutionalization in which processes of conflict become normatively controlled. Because of the complex character of such regulated opposition, the main developments favor the collectivities that control large resources and can use sophisticated techniques of struggle.

The more extensive the scope of such regulated opposition, accordingly, the less likely it is that loosely organized collectivities that have few resources will be successful in pressing their claims.

Under these conditions, members of collectivities that are weak in skills, knowledge, and economic resources are likely to come to believe that established institutions will not respond to demands advanced through use of institutionalized means. Hence it will sometimes happen that the very development of well-organized procedures for peaceful settlement of disputes will generate new disadvantages and grievances among the weaker claimants in the society.

It follows that the acceptability of the several possible strategies and procedures for continuing or for terminating conflicts depends not only upon immediate outcomes but also upon the parties' appraisals of longer-term consequences. Contrast the two following cases. In industrial relations it often happens that both employers and workers wish to avoid loss of wages and profits in strikes—both hoping to gain an acceptable settlement without a protracted strike. A large strike quickly has adverse effects on widening sections of the general public and, if continued, sooner or later will have political significance, nationally and internationally. Therefore, both the mutually advantageous relationship of workers and employers and the presence of third-party power will favor the establishment of organization, norms, and procedures for negotiation and settlement of industrial disputes. On the other hand, the ethnic-racial conflicts of the 1950s in the South produced an effort by whites to reduce turmoil through the establishment of local biracial committees; the arrangements failed when it became apparent to blacks that their most important claims could not be met by this means (Killian and Grigg, 1964).

Granted, then, that interest in conflict resolution will vary from highly negative to highly positive among different parties in different situations, we nevertheless do observe that in many important instances both parties are willing to use available means for seeking settlements. What procedures can they possibly use?

7. Main Procedures of Purposive Conflict Resolution

The principal classes of procedures include conciliation, mediation, arbitration, investigation, adjudication, and administrative decisions. In their pure forms, (1) mediation or conciliation, (2) arbitration or adjudication, and (3) administrative decisions represent sharply different approaches (Eckhoff, 1966). In practice, of course, mixtures are frequent. Conciliation and mediation are diplomatic processes in which a mutually acceptable third party attempts to aid the contending principals to find a solution that both will accept voluntarily. In partial contrast, arbitration is a process of adjudication the results of which are legally binding upon the parties. (Although entrance into the process may be voluntary, the resulting judgment is supposed to be compulsory.) "Investigations" may be formally voluntary or required by law. Reports and recommendations of fact-finding or investigating bodies may generate public pressures for settlement; the effects are perhaps somewhat more binding than those of mediation, less than those of arbitration or adjudication. The distinction between the latter two procedures often cannot be drawn with precision. Adjudication refers to binding decisions by courts or public administrative bodies having particular jurisdiction in such disputes— which generally means that adjudication requires authority to interpret legal rights of the terms of agreements (Ross, 1968, 507-9). Arbitration may best be regarded as simply a special form of adjudication.

It is typical rather than unusual that the formal procedures do not completely dictate the actual processes through which settlements are reached. Certainly the term "adjudication" suggests a highly formalized social mechanism, but it is common knowledge that something more than deduction from fixed and clear rules is involved. An especially useful illustration is provided by the international legal cases in which two or more sets of national laws are applicable and are in contradiction or opposition. The courts that have jurisdiction in such cases have developed tacit strategies for extracting judgments of fairness or equity from this unpromising situation. The analysis of a specialist warrants quotation:

> Furthermore, courts are less inclined to follow the dogmatic solutions proposed by scholars than to seek to do substantial justice to the parties in dispute. Therefore, a court will tend to manipulate the criteria governing the choice of laws to fulfill its view of what justice demands. A good illustration is the basic idea that a court will always apply domestic *procedure* even if it defers to foreign *substance*. This allows it to characterize as "procedure" any device that will produce the desired result (Falk, 1968, 251).

Anyone who is familiar with our own civil courts will find this description quite familiar. As this example suggests, the agents who attempt to terminate a conflict have not a single choice of alternatives but rather a series of objective options, in descending order of generality, in which each successive selection affects the next. Given a commitment to a mode of termination other than complete dominance or withdrawal, there are then the strategic choices of whether or not third parties are to intervene and in what way. The option of third-party participation, in turn, allows for several different methods or techniques, as just reviewed. Within the limits of a particular method or technique, again, the distinction which has been drawn between tactical and strategic mediation (Kerr, 1954, 230-45) is applicable to all the other forms of action designed to reduce a particular conflict, to resolve it, or to put it in abeyance. That is, any type of procedure may focus on resolving immediate and particular items of contention or on readjusting the basic interests and rules of the game for subsequent interaction of the parties.

What conditions will be most important in affecting the selection from among the major procedures for exploring possibilities of terminating a conflict in some regularized way?

8. Negotiation and Bargaining: Conditions Affecting Selection of Main Procedures

A major condition that strongly preselects modes and strategies of terminating or regulating processes of conflict is the degree to which the community or society is organized around direct social reciprocities or around a system of indirect and impersonal relationships. In highly differentiated and segregated metropolitan society, reciprocal social controls based on long-term relationships between persons from different ethnic categories cease to be highly effective in the economic and political sectors. Thus, in the case of black-white relationships, fewer interactions involve repeated contact with the same concrete individuals over a long period and in many areas of life.

> Shared experiences decrease; mutuality of role-taking diminishes; interdependence of particular persons across the color line becomes less prevalent and less crucial. Withdrawal of reciprocity on the part of a specific person becomes less effective as a sanction.
>
> To the extent that person-to-person reciprocal social control breaks down, the regulation of intergroup interaction either fails altogether or is shifted into the area of collective and formalized controls—above all, administrative and legal action. Hence, the greater the diminution of informal control, the greater the likelihood that intergroup relations will come to have an important political aspect (Williams, Dean, Suchman, 1964, 308).

In all collectivities two sources of conflict are found: (1) competing or otherwise incompatible immediate interests, (2) disagreement concerning facts, norms, or values considered relevant for resolution of competing interests (Eckhoff, 1966, 148-49). Typically both competition and dissensus are involved. Several implications follow:

Proposition 22: The more complete the agreement between contending parties concerning the *social norms and values* that they regard as relevant to resolving their opposition, the more likely it is that they will arrive at a settlement without having third-party intervention.

Proposition 23: To the extent that the parties have *shared interests* in a settlement (e.g., both see advantages in terminating the conflict) the more likely they are to arrive at a voluntary resolution, either by their own efforts or by seeking the aid of a third party.

Proposition 24: To the extent that the parties are divided by *incompatible or competing interests* and by *disagreement concerning norms and values*, the likelihood will be lessened that they can resolve their struggle without the intervention of a third party.

Proposition 25: A conflict between two parties may have negative consequences for other persons or collectivities; even the sheer existence of hostile relations may be viewed as undesirable by other parties. Further, there may be third parties who have a direct interest in having the conflict resolved. As third parties show their concerns, the opposing parties may come to have a greater interest in finding ways to settle their differences (see Eckhoff, 1966, 156).

Whether or not a third party enters into the processes of attempted settlement, the principals may carry out activities to which we apply the term "negotiation." Negotiation is an explicit process of real or pretended rearrangement of common and conflicting interests; if successful, its outcome is a mutually endorsed or accepted agreement of some kind. Negotiation differs from tacit bargaining; in the latter, the parties attempt to find a new arrangement "through hints and guesswork, without explicitly proposing terms for agreement" (Ikle, 1968, 117). Tacit bargaining often occurs when public negotiation is not acceptable—by reason of internal conditions in one or more of the bargaining collectivities, or of the desire to prevent third-party involvement, or because of fear of premature commitments, and for many other reasons. Such bargaining can serve to limit or restrain conflict and to prepare a situation conducive to later negotiation. It is, however, a highly uncertain and gross mode of communication—more suitable for setting limits and indicating possible avenues to agreement than for establishing firm and detailed understandings and commitments.

Proposition 26: Accordingly, negotiation is more likely than tacit bargaining to be used for transactions of exchange,[1] for complex forms of collaboration, for highly technical agreements, and in general for any arrangements of long duration and high specificity (Ikle, 1968, 117).

Proposition 27: Tacit rather than explicit public bargaining or negotiation tends to be used when a complex set of conditions makes explicit bargaining appear dangerous to the principals, e.g., there is a likelihood of undesired third-party intervention; it is feared that public negotiation will force the revelation of information to one's opponent; there is a fear that public agreement to bargain may alienate allies, reduce one's own group's mobilization, be taken as a signal of weakness, and the like (Walton and McKersie, 1965, 14-15).

Whenever one party has some control over events or conditions desired by another, the control can be expressed as a threat or as a promise. Every threat contains an implicit promise and every promise carries an implicit threat, but the form makes a difference in the effects. A "positive" message is in the form "I'll do X or give you X; next time [or later] you can do Y or give me Y." A negative message says, "If you don't do Y, I won't do X" [or "I'll do Z" (an undesired thing).] Messages that offer inducements-in-exchange for a given behavior are more likely to be favorably received than those that threaten to withdraw the inducement in case of noncompliance. Evidence from laboratory experiments consistently shows that "threats are much more likely to be viewed negatively than are promises" (Deutsch, 1973, 129). Outside of the laboratory where stakes often are much higher, there are many situations, of course, in which negative evaluations from an opponent are readily accepted when it is judged that threats are far more effective than promises, even though the threats are disliked. However, unless there is a very substantial gain to be derived from it, it is a hazardous tactic to heap criticism on a group or organization whose cooperation may soon be needed.

Two major propositions summarize the general prospects for use of bargaining between contenders.

Proposition 28: Bargaining and negotiation occur most easily when they are least needed, that is when there is no severe opposition of interests between the parties. When each can make some concession to the other without serious loss, it is relatively simple for the parties to develop agreements, rules of procedure, standards of equity, and sentiments of trust.

Proposition 29: Where there are substantial differences in values and goals between contending parties, compromise occurs only when (a) the parties are positively interdependent to such an extent that neither can find in the situation at hand better bargains in any other relationship *or* (b) neither party can be protected adequately from negative sanctions within the control of the other.

In the most general terms, the settlement of conflict through bargaining and negotiation is possible and likely when:

(a) the negative consequences of conflict outweigh any possible gains for all parties;

(b) the negative consequences of conflict outweigh the negative aspects of compromise;

(c) there is some objective basis for agreement and compromise (i.e., negotiable goods or problems, as opposed to issues of fixed and absolute principle or belief);

(d) there are no serious barriers to a cooperative relationship (such as a third-party interest in maintaining the conflict);

(e) there are precedents, procedures, and incentives for a negotiated settlement;

(f) the structure and stability of the groups are such that agreements are likely to be kept and carried out;

(g) norms of procedure are supported by a third party or parties to whom each of the protagonists has relations of confidence or trust;

(h) concessions do not result in a loss of face, stature, credibility, or legitimacy.

In the following pages we shall examine in more detail the grounds for these generalizations.

Hypotheses concerning the effectiveness of different specific procedures in facilitating negotiated settlements are still largely at the level of commonsense plausibility but appear open to formulation in testable terms. Examples of such "informed folklore" follow.

Provided that each of the parties seeks a peaceable settlement and has scope for bargaining, and that the negotiators are not vulnerable to damaging charges of unwarranted secrecy, exploratory negotiations are facilitated by minimum public exposure of the detailed process. Minimal dissemination of the details of early informal interaction between the parties: (1) encourages disclosure of information that is useful in reality-testing but which would be embarrassing, or provocative, confusing or otherwise disadvantageous if prematurely or widely made known; (2) reduces the likelihood of activating the third parties whose intervention would complicate and retard the search for a resolution; (3) creates a presumption of some serious mutual commitment to seek a solution within the negotiative framework at hand—not always justified, but other evidence would be required to demonstrate to the parties that the implication is not warranted; (4) creates a presumption of some minimal initial solidarity between the contending parties because of their mutual willingness to close a boundary against potential allies and enemies; (5) because of the effects of (2), (3), and (4), limits the scope of additional issues that are likely to be injected later into the initial set that has been explored off the record.

Responsible and careful preliminary negotiations carried on informally in the manner indicated are favorable to later successful formal negotiations. But, of course, there are other kinds of secrecy that can destroy the negotiative process. Some kinds of nondisclosure constitute deceptions that reduce the likelihood of any mutual agreement—for example, the failure of one party, at a point of crucial choice to the other, to indicate that its own constituency is certain to reject a proposed set of terms for settlement. Also, extreme difficulties are likely to be created if informal understandings and agreements are accepted in the negotiations but then used as a basis for secretly recruiting new allies or other resources to be used for further conflict, or seeking to enlist third parties, contrary to prior understandings, to counter one's opponent.

Negotiators' decisions may be classified under three basic choices: "(1) to accept agreement at the terms he expects the opponent would settle for (the 'available' terms), (2) to discontinue negotiating without the agreement and with no intention of resuming them, and (3) to try to improve the 'available' terms through further bargaining" (Ikle, 1968, 118).

Major components in negotiation are *commitments*, *threats*, *warnings*, and offers of *values-in-exchange*. In the strategy of commitment, Party A attempts to influence Party B by showing that he or she has fixed commitments that make it impossible for him or her to retreat from a certain position or to reduce his or her claims below some particular point. In the strategy of threat, Party A attempts to make credible an intention and a capability to cause special loss to B should the latter not accept A's proffered terms. In using warnings, Party A predicts that B's actions will result in high costs, e.g., "we can't control our people's reaction—they will take to the streets again." In the strategy of value-in-exchange, A offers B a certain positive value in return for another. Both the exchange and the threat strategies may be (and almost always are) coupled with the communication of commitment.

Bargaining positions may be changed by *commitments*—one party by committing itself or its resources may alter its opponent's expectations—or by *warnings* and *threats* (either of which may or may not be bluffs). In a warning, one party points out to the other natural consequences of its failure to heed the warning. In a threat, the assertive party indicates that it intends to cause the opponent to experience a predicted loss or damage. To threaten is to make a prediction and to commit oneself to a special effort to make the prediction come true if the opponent does not comply. Both commitments and threats are risky: if the opponent does not accept the proffered terms, one may have to choose between costly action and loss of credibility.

Minimal rather than larger threats or promises are more effective in eliciting sustained performance of conforming behavior after the immediate threat or promise has been removed. The psychological processes that lead to this result are, no doubt, quite complex (Deutsch, 1973, 130-32). But the social result is dependable, *if* one can estimate in advance what level of threat or inducement is sufficient to elicit the desired behavior. A "restrained" threat or a "reasonable" promise maximizes credibility and legitimacy, and probably encourages a high degree of attention and involvement. Certain imprecise but helpful empirical generalizations concerning effective procedures have developed on the basis of repeated experiences in more or less formalized negotiations.

Proposition 30: For instance, successful bilateral negotiation depends upon bypassing generalized opposition and diffuse hostility by isolating particular areas of common concern, and beginning negotiations in any of them in which potential mutual advantage is clearly present.[2] Any agreement thus achieved is used as a basis for improved confidence in moving systematically to other such areas of common interest that may be found or developed.

Proposition 31: Bargaining is a process which occurs most easily when it is least needed, that is when there is no severe opposition of interests between the parties. When each can make some concession to the other without serious loss, it is relatively simple for the parties to develop agreements, rules of procedure, standards of equity, and sentiments of trust.

When, however, the situation contains such opposition of interests that what one party gains is a serious loss to the other, the likelihood of unmediated bargaining based on mutual trust decreases sharply. Under these conditions, some third-party intervention seems to be necessary if a resolution through bargaining is to occur. The problem becomes one of finding the conditions under which formal agreements can be reached to terminate or control conflict and to prevent the resort to more and more drastic means.

The conditions which will lead the parties to favor one rather than another of the possible procedures for seeking a settlement are likely to be both specific and complex. For example:

Proposition 32: Arbitration will be a feasible and attractive possibility when the parties foresee that an impasse in bargaining (a) is very likely, (b) will be extremely costly, and when (c) neither party wishes to have to defend to its constituency the settlement it realistically expects (Contini, 1967, 456).

The available research evidence suggests that two main conditions are usually found whenever conflict is successfully resolved or controlled through direct bargaining between the opponents themselves. The first is the active presence of a third party having no clash of interests with either of the adversaries and able to act as a disinterested participant in the immediate situation. The second facilitating factor is that the weaker party gains improved external opportunities, so that a threat to withdraw from the negotiations becomes a credible threat.

Proposition 33: Given an impartial third party[3] and the capability of effective threat by the weaker of the contestants to withdraw from bargaining in favor of external alternatives there is "a good chance of reaching a formal agreement in which each party, in return for protection from the other, is required to inhibit its power to damage and disrupt" (Clark and Miller, 1970, 103).

The contenders in conflict often seek to create the impression that their "rightful claims" are definite, fixed, unalterable, and that what constitutes victory or defeat, a gain or a loss, is similarly definite and unequivocal. Rarely, however, are all the issues or stakes really so clear and exactly ascertainable. Over the course of a conflict, each party's conceptions and evaluations may change many times, sometimes radically altering the cutting point between gain and loss and changing the relative weight of the components of victory or defeat. The experience of the conflict not only changes *expectations* about outcomes but may transform *evaluations* of the stakes and of what is an acceptable or desirable outcome. In most cases of complex negotiations, "the notion of fixed minimum positions for each party is realistic only for short time periods and very simple issues . . . a view that the payoffs between the parties are equal, or 'fairly' distributed, is in itself an outcome of the negotiating process" (Ikle, 1968, 120).

Indeed, negotiations are not likely to be entered upon unless at least one of the parties is uncertain what the outcome will be. It follows that at the time of beginning negotiations, the final settlement usually is somewhat indeterminate. (In rare cases, both sets of negotiators know rather well what the outcome will be but appeal to a third party essentially as a way of validating the settlement to make it acceptable to their respective constituencies.)

Proposition 34: Expressive conflicts are especially likely to show this indeterminate quality; more exactly, the greater the importance, salience, or proportion of expressive or symbolic issues in a controversy, the less likely is it that a mutually accepted settlement will be found, or if found, that it can be developed quickly.

The degree and kind of consensus necessary for social peace—without which conflicts will develop—differ in instrumental and expressive conflicts. Expressive conflicts are more volatile, far more sensitive to a consensus that can exist only by being both detailed and diffuse. A society can more easily contain, and function effectively with, a high incidence of instrumental than of expressive conflicts. Given proper conditions of social organization, it is possible to avoid severe disruptions from frequent or large-scale instrumental conflicts by establishing (1) even a very loose or vague agreement on the boundaries of a wide range of permissible or tolerated actions, plus (2) consensus on a set of procedural norms for establishing allocations, enforcing bargains, and settling disputes. In contrast, the avoidance of expressive (symbolic, "nonrealistic") conflict may require the "matching" of entire styles of life across a population—from political beliefs to speech habits and recreational preferences—with the consequence that any one of a large number of specific issues may be seized upon as indicative of basic group allegiances or of basic differences in values, beliefs, and interests. Reactivity to symbolic differences, therefore, gives to each opposition or controversy an indefinite, amorphous quality—which, in its turn, facilitates a kind of irradiation or spread of controversy to a variety of originally unrelated matters.

Avoidance of symbolic irradiation is made easier if bargaining can be restricted in its earliest phases to instrumental or allocative issues.

Proposition 35: In particular, the greater the number of qualitatively different issues (each of which either exists in divisible degrees or parts, or else is small enough to be conceivably subject to a tradeoff), the greater is the likelihood of a mutually acceptable resolution of opposition.

Unsuccessful attempts to reach agreement tax the patience of strongly interested contenders. To avoid escalation of conflict is not easy and may require a procedure of withdrawal-and-return.

Proposition 36: If early phases of bargaining result in successive failures, an impasse may be reached in which the opponents' discussions focus on acrimonious exchanges of charges, countercharges, and recriminations. Under these conditions, eventual resolution may be ill-served by continuing a heated argument, and it often will be more effective to temporarily adjourn the encounter. A party with a greater interest in eventual settlement may be well advised to refuse to go beyond some point of escalation of rhetoric or tactics—to refuse to be seduced into the "entrapment of the fight." Escalation of differences or of the drastic character of the means used often will be reduced if negotiators refrain from reciprocating personal attacks.[4]

Whether to enter into negotiations at all obviously is a crucial decision. The complexity of that decision is well illustrated by situations in which one must decide whether to enter into discussions with an adversary who presents a "nonnegotiable" demand as a first move. This is a special form of the well-known tactic of making a "final offer first." Originally most commonly used by employers in negotiations with workers, this mode of bargaining was widely adopted in the 1960s by student protesters and leaders of some black organizations. On the surface, this approach seems to transform all issues into a single claim for power. Its real character, however, is multifaceted. It may be used, indeed, when the user is in fact very sure of possessing overwhelming coercive power. But it may also represent one or all of the following conditions: (1) The user wishes to make sure that his or her initial demand will *not* be met, because he or she wishes to make a later demand, more important to him or her than the first, after his or her opponent's fairness or credibility has been discredited in the eyes of the partisans or of third parties. (2) The partisan's primary aim is only to humiliate or irritate or otherwise inflict social and psychological damage on the other party, or to "throw him or her off balance" through distraction. (3) The user wants to convince his or her constituency—the ingroup—that he or she is carrying out a hard fight, is not being co-opted, and the like. (4) The partisan leader advances what he or she knows to be an extreme claim in order to solidify his or her following by convincing them of the intransigence or hostility of the opposition, or he or she wishes to identify and weed out those adherents who are unwilling to support the leadership in its hard-bargaining tactics.

Even when both parties proclaim a willingness to seek a settlement, actual aims may differ from stated intentions. Thus the opponents may enter into negotiations "in bad faith"—not actually intending to conclude an agreement but claiming or implying a serious desire for a negotiated settlement. Such behavior may arise out of a need to use negotiation as a delaying tactic. During the time gained by negotiation, the delaying party hopes to gain resources, find allies, build unity in his or her own constituency or increase dissension in his or her opponent's following. Pseudonegotiation is rendered likely when at least one party foresees the possibility that negotiations may win the support of third parties or may neutralize those who otherwise would be likely to intervene or to bring pressure to bear for an undesired settlement. Another factor encouraging "fake" bargaining is the prospect that Party A sees of inducing Party B eventually to bear the onus of breaking off negotiations and thereby increasing third-party pressures on B, leading to eventual resumption of negotiations in which Party A will have enhanced bargaining power.

Both "bad faith" and "hard bargaining" are likely to arouse strongly negative feelings in opponents. In addition to other bases of such reactions, the "loss of face" is important (Brown, 1971). Experimental findings show that loss of face tends to increase subsequent recalcitrance or aggressiveness. For example, experiments show that bargainers who suffer public loss of face (by being made to appear weak or gullible) are especially prone to retaliate against their opponents (Deutsch, 1973, 267). In long-term relationships, a wise negotiator will *not* make maximum use of coercive power on every possible occasion.

In addition to the relative power of the conflicting parties, the following factors will have important influences on the selection of modes of attempted settlement:

1. Scarcity of the transferable objects of value which may be allocated between the parties:
   (a) scarcity relative to each party's separate standard of an acceptable outcome;
   (b) scarcity relative to the summed claims of all parties.
2. A preference-ordering by each party of the four main desiderata in negotiative processes:
   (a) distributive bargaining over allocations;
   (b) integrative bargaining, consisting of problem-solving efforts which benefit all parties;
   (c) approval of the other parties; achievement of agreement with other parties;
   (d) maintaining or building intragroup solidarity (adapted from Walton and McKersie, 1965).
3. Extent to which a superordinate authority or power-holder sets limits or imposes norms upon the conflicting parties.
4. Given an order of preference among outcomes, the degree of objective interdependence of the parties.
5. Degree to which the parties share social norms concerning both appropriate goals and permissive means of contention; such sharing is facilitated by prior experience in resolving opposition and conflict between the parties.
6. Expectations of duration and character of future interdependence with the opposing party in the immediate conflict.

Various combinations of the factors mentioned result in several major syndromes of attempted settlements. For example, we may anticipate both the most severe conflict and the hardest bargaining when these conditions are present:

1. Allocative values are extremely scarce.
2. Both parties give highest rank to distributive values, second rank to intragroup solidarity, and lowest rank to consensus.
3. No superordinate authority can enforce norms.
4. Interdependence is very great for the values currently at stake in the conflict; low otherwise.
5. The parties share few norms and have not successfully resolved any prior conflicts.
6. Both parties expect that their future interdependence either
   (a) will be slight, or
   (b) will be essentially an interdependence of mutual threat rather than rewarding exchange.

On the other hand, the processes of negotiation generally will proceed most smoothly and reliably:

(a) the more stable the leadership structure;
(b) the more centralized the decision-making systems of the respective collectivities;
(c) the greater the control of authorities over members to guarantee compliance with agreements;
(d) the greater the similarity between present negotiations and other successful resolution of the same type of conflict in past encounters of the same collectivities;
(e) the greater the extent that each party makes a formal allocation of bargaining (decision-making) power to designated representatives;
(f) the more frequent the interaction between leaders, representatives, or prominent spokespeople of the respective groups.

And, finally, successful negotiations tend to produce conditions conducive to future success.

Proposition 37: The more often a continuing bargaining relationship results in mutually acceptable resolutions of opposing interests, the greater becomes the likelihood of future joint acceptance of bargaining norms and of other values, and the greater will be the growth of reciprocal positive sentiments between the parties.

Although we have paid attention thus far primarily to the direct relationships between the contenders, we have been aware that there usually are other parties who may be involved. We turn now to the important additional considerations that arise when third parties are active.

9. The Roles of Third Parties

Any very extended study of actual cases of conflict resolution is bound to impress the observer with the ubiquity and great importance of the benign third party. The third party appears in a thousand different guises — the mutual friend, the government as referee, the mediator, the arbitrator, the regulatory commission, the judicial board, the court, the lawyer, the administrative adjudicator, the ombudsman, public opinion, the appeals board, the neutral nation, the public representative — even figuratively, "the contract," "the marriage" — the parent who intervenes between quarreling siblings, the world court, and so on. As we have said already, it is in the nature of the situation that parties in conflict will find it difficult to terminate their own conflict short of substantial injury to one or both, and the desire to avoid unacceptably high costs is one powerful instigation for the frequent turning to the third party.

Clearly the presence of the third party can be a vast resource for conflict resolution. But note that the potential usefulness for conciliation and mediation is wholly dependent upon the extent to which the third party is thought to be trustworthy for the purposes at hand. To be trustworthy, he or she must not be identified with biases and interests of only one of the parties, nor suspect because of having special interests at stake on the outcome of the struggle. The third party must not be unreliable because of a demonstrated incapacity to avoid partisanship.

Modes of benign intervention by third parties include the following: "(1) to reduce or eliminate the conflict potential in a situation; (2) to resolve directly a substantive issue in dispute; (3) to facilitate the parties' efforts to manage a particular conflict; and (4) to help the parties change their conflict-prone relationship" (Walton, 1967, 24-30). These several kinds of intervention obviously will have widely varying degrees of acceptability in different situations or social settings. Most important, voluntary resort to third-party solutions is widely practicable only if there is a relatively high level of social trust within a social system. Anything that greatly reduces the general level of social trust, therefore, is likely to increase the difficulty of conflict resolution through third-party channels and, correspondingly, is likely to raise the costs of conflict.

How may a third party aid parties who are engaged in struggle to arrive at mutually acceptable procedures and outcomes? Deutsch proposes the following as possible contributions of a (suitably qualified and motivated) third party:

1. helping the parties identify and confront the issues;
2. aiding in creating favorable conditions and procedures for confronting issues;
3. stimulating and interpreting interparty communication to remove blockages and distortions;
4. attempting to establish and maintain rules and emphases that encourage persuasion rather than coercion, open communication, mutual respect, and the desirability of a mutually acceptable settlement.

Proposition 38: Agreement will be facilitated if a third party, without being considered obstructive or offensive, is able to remind the parties of any prior agreements or common understandings upon facts, procedures, rules, objectives, or substantive matters.

Proposition 38a: Whenever the parties in dispute or conflict have a larger and longer-term set of common or complementary interests and values, a third party may be able to facilitate agreements by finding ways of reminding the contestants of this larger context (Deutsch, 1971, 494).

It is an important fact that arbitration, now used as a final resort in grievance procedures in more than 90 percent of labor-management agreements, was initially strongly resisted by employers and was finally accepted in large part in exchange for a no-strike clause in union agreements (Livernash, 1968, 494).

5. searching out possible solutions and making suggestions about them;
6. finding ways in which a practicable agreement can be made acceptable to the contending parties (Deutsch, 1973, 386);
7. helping to make the agreements reached seem fair, reasonable, or otherwise meritorious to third parties and to the constituencies represented by the negotiators.

In *any* controversy or conflict, the principals always will be acting within *some* structure of interests and relationships involving third parties.

Proposition 39: Regularized modes of managing conflicts generally are favored by the presence of those otherwise disinterested third parties who will be adversely affected by a continuation or recurrence of unregulated conflict.

We have already noted instances in which some of the very conditions that favor the emergence of conflict tend to restrain its severity (e.g., identification with the larger collectivity within which conflict occurs). Another case of the same kind is the hypothesis that "high organizational density in a community tends to draw the community into controversy, but it also acts to regulate the controversy and contain it" (Coleman, 1957, 21). The point is that third parties are most likely to act to regulate or contain the conflict when (1) their own interests are adversely affected and (2) they believe they have some means of bringing influence to bear upon the contending principals. (Of course, they sometimes may be mistaken in these appraisals, or they may be rejected as "busybodies.")

Similarly, a desire to use third-party assistance may be stimulated either by the parties' high degree of common interest in reaching agreement or by their fear that common interests will not be enough to ensure an appropriate resolution. Hence:

Proposition 40: The greater the common interest between conflicting parties in having a dispute resolved, and the greater the agreement between parties concerning norms and values relating to resolution, then

  (a) the greater is the probability of their being able to resolve the conflict on their own without a third party; and
  (b) the greater is the probability of their voluntarily calling in a third party, if needed.

And, on the other hand:

Proposition 40a: The stronger the competing or incompatible interests the parties have in the outcome, and the more they disagree on normative factors they consider relevant, the less probable is it that they will be able to resolve the conflict on their own, and the greater need they have for bringing in a third party, presuming that they have a common interest in having the conflict resolved.

We have dealt with impartially benign third parties. A great many third parties are not benign or impartial. Very commonly they aid one of the parties in the attempt to defeat the other, or they act to instigate or escalate conflict. Since this chapter deals with resolution or settlement, we shall not discuss these cases here.

Benign third parties may attempt (a) to persuade the contestants to cease their conflict, or (b) to force a resolution by the threat of overriding sanctions, or (c) to offer to act as unbiased mediators.

10. Mediation

Within the broad category of "collective and formalized controls" there are, of course, a great many particular forms through which processes of conflict resolution may operate. One of these is formal mediation.

The basic character of mediation is that it favors compromise, lacks strong coercive capacity, depends heavily upon actual convergence of interests between the parties. Because mediators must retain impartiality to be effective, they can make only sparing use of rewards or threats. Mediation often appeals to norms and tends to be a weak technique in strong disagreements over norms and values (Deutsch, 1973, 387). Where severe oppositions of interests appear, as in the generic Problem of the Commons, constraint through some kind of consensual authority is likely to be required for a solution.

The reliance upon a balance of compatible interests favors mediation; reliance upon consensual rules favors adjudication. Adjudication focuses on rules and principles: the questions are, who is correct? what rules apply? who is at fault? Mediation does not try to arrive at judgments of rightness or conformity to norms; rather it focuses on compromise of interests and reconciliation of perceptions and feelings. The mediator is primarily interested in what effects will be produced by this or that potential settlement. The judge, in contrast, tends to emphasize rules, precedents, and the past behavior of the parties. Adjudication does not depend upon the agreement of the parties; mediation must attempt to find mutually acceptable outcomes (Eckhoff, 1966, 161). Third parties are most likely to be trusted in the role of mediator when they have:

(a) a high stake in the successful resolution of the conflict;
(b) either no interdependent or equally interdependent ties with the conflicting parties; and
(c) no biased or self-serving interest in the nature of the outcome.

A reasonable hypothesis concerning conditions that favor development of mediation as an accepted mode for seeking settlements follows.

Proposition 41: Formal mediation as a means of resolving conflict is most likely to develop and to be accepted when recurrent opposition and conflict between collectivities results in:
(a) severe damage or annoyance to powerful third parties, or
(b) resolutions of very high cost to the contending parties, who, at the same time, are strongly dependent upon one another for long-term advantageous outcomes.

Mediation has only a very limited efficacy in situations in which the parties are struggling for possession and use of extremely valuable and scarce items, and in which each party claims the right to impose its own values and norms on the other, against the similar counterclaim of the other. On the other hand, the widespread acceptance in our society of mediation as a legitimate and desirable procedure often commends it to newcomers to the political arena. Thus in the field of community dispute settlement for racial and ethnic issues, it seems likely that many of the forms of labor-management relations, including mediation, will be adapted for use in the community-relations sphere. The availability of these well-known, legitimized, and procedurally well-developed techniques already has been recognized as a potential resource for minority ethnic groups in their efforts to establish their legitimacy as negotiating parties. Mediation, as well as other formal processes of negotiation, may be an effective means of securing appropriate settlements from the opposition. And mediation also may be effective both as a means of legitimation with the established authorities and as a way of established regularized direct communication in what would otherwise be a chaotic or noncommunicative situation.

> *Proposition 42:* Mediation, however, is not a procedure that will maximize the opportunity of challengers to bring pressure to bear upon dominant groups. It is better suited to negotiations with fairly restricted scope, in which there is substantial need for technical expertise in dealing with the issues.

In general:

> *Proposition 43:* Mediation is likely to have greatest effects in reducing conflict and facilitating acceptance of a settlement (or other resolution) when:
> (a) all of the parties have relatively stable internal structures;
> (b) all of the parties have clear delegation of authority to spokesmen or representatives to make agreements binding upon the collectivity;
> (c) the contention of the parties involves considerable misunderstanding and lack of knowledge of potential points of agreement, commonalities of interests, and "reasonable" intentions;
> (d) the parties have made public demands or claims substantially stronger than those upon which they are willing to settle in private.

11. The Significance of Social Norms

Bargaining can go on between two parties. Conciliation and mediation requires in addition, at the least, one trusted third party. Arbitration and adjudication further require the acceptance of binding authority. Before we discuss these authoritative procedures, accordingly, we need to note the general significance of social norms for processes of conflict resolution.

One cannot have a genuine game without having rules. And rules are not merely the expression of the immediate self-interest of a party that happens to be dominant at a particular time. Norms make a difference in their own right; they have an independent *causal* significance (Thibaut and Kelley, 1959, Chapters 8 and 13).

Unless there is some understanding of and agreement on the legitimate procedures to be followed in resolving conflict within any particular collectivity, the processes of conflict and termination will require numerous improvisations. In such cases, since no initial agreements have been established, each question of developing an ad hoc procedure will open up a further possibility of disagreement and conflict in addition to the substantive issues that are in dispute. Without any mutual advance orientation to limiting and guiding norms, each shift in the modes of attempting to resolve conflict will constitute a new crisis. Accordingly, a primary factor affecting modes and strategies of conflict termination is just the extent and kind of procedural consensus existing (a) among the principals who have any substantive disagreement and (b) among any third parties that have actual or potential influence or power in the situation.

One immediately may ask, why is there procedural consensus in some instances and no such consensus in others? The statement that a norm exists does not tell us why the norm has developed, nor why it is followed, if it is. But if we assume, as usually is the case, that some *technically* effective norms already exist (i.e., norms that *if* followed will limit conflict or aid in settlement), a prior question is what conditions will favor procedural limitation and settlement of conflicts when suitable norms are available.

Acceptance by the parties who are in opposition or conflict of norms for bargaining and for carrying out agreements aids in the resolution of conflicts.[5] Although at first glance this assertion may seem self-evident, it is not trivial nor is it to be taken for granted. Procedural agreement often is highly consequential; and often the available norms are not accepted. Accordingly *normative consensus itself already represents a substantial base of seeking further areas of agreement or for eliminating areas of disagreement.*

Proposition 44: The larger the number of procedural rules that the parties can agree to in early stages of discussion, the greater is the likelihood of mutually acceptable resolution of substantive issues.

Proposition 45: In general, acceptance of procedures for regulation and resolution of conflict heightens the likelihood that the contending parties will each experience settlements as fair or just in their substance.

Proposition 46: Procedure affects substance. It is sometimes argued, on the contrary, that there can be impartial application of rules of justice in the service of an unjust system of laws or other norms. But it is more likely that proper procedure will tend to alter improper rules. As Cahn has said:

In actual fact, procedural injustice not only accompanies substantive injustice; it also aggravates its cruelty. Procedural justice has the opposite influence; sooner or later it prompts and promotes advances in substantive justice. Thus, whereas unfair trials have aggravated the laws that discriminate against Negroes in certain American communities, fair trials and impartial tribunals have committed other American communities to the full vindication of equality and human dignity (Cahn, 1968, 344).

It is worth explicit note that in adjudication a relatively high degree of impartiality can be achieved in independent tribunals with a strong commitment to procedural norms. The judges of the International Court of Justice at the Hague, in 24 of 103 votes involving their countries, have declared against their own nations. In the *Interhandel* case, the Soviet judge voted in favor of the United States on 3 of 5 issues; the United States judge voted against the U.S. in one of these (Larson, 1962, 337-38).

12. Adjudication and Authoritative Conflict Settlement

Conflicts vary from highly regulated, limited, and ritualized encounters to total wars of mass extermination with few clear normative boundaries and without definite prospects for termination. The latter obviously are not easily resolved, the former are open to effective settlement. And some conflicts have positive outcomes—so no one wishes to regulate them.

Control of anything is costly. Its costs include the resources expended or immobilized and time and energy spent in monitoring activities or processes, recording results, instructing and educating. Control activities have opportunity costs because the resources used (or immobilized) by control-needs have other possible productive uses. And the more complete and detailed the attempted control, the more the costs per unit: it is more expensive to control the "last x percent"—which is likely to be the more ambiguous, complex, far-away, difficult, and so on. It follows that the *total* prevention of *all* conflict would be so very costly that few, if any, collectivities would accept the full burden required to ensure that no one even attempted to injure another against his or her resistance.

Yet social control is always required to some degree if conflict is to be held to manageable levels whenever different collectivities strive for scarce values. For example, recording and monitoring performance and adherence to rules are continuous processes essential to the operation of organizations, especially those that deal with highly prized and scarce desiderata (Drucker, 1969, 15).

Stable processes of authoritative social control ultimately rest upon an effective social agreement or acquiescence that permits imposition of constraints, that is, of negative social sanctions.

As a means of controlling behavior, negative sanctions—whether of threat or of actual deprivation, frustration, or injury—are most effective when the recipients have few alternative courses of behavior available to them. Effectiveness will be manifest in three main ways: (1) lowered rates of violations of norms; (2) lowered rates of escaping the field by selecting alternatives outside the range of the available sanctions: (3) fewer side-effects in behavioral deviance or violation of norms other than those directly supported by the sanctions. Note these points:

> The wider the range of a man's alternative means, the more difficult it is to control his behavior through the use of the punishment power alone. It will ordinarily be easier to control behavior, in this instance, by rewarding the use of a single particular means than by punishing him for selecting one of the larger number of alternatives (Blalock, 1967, 216).

When the contending parties themselves attempt to use constraints, the availability of a *range* of negative potential sanctions against a rival or opponent probably is more conducive to use of threat than is the availability of *only* quite severe sanctions. A threat to impose a mild sanction tends to be credible, and the cost of imposing the sanction is relatively low—thus allowing easy reinforcement of credibility. Confidence in the use of mild threat is likely to be increased by the awareness of the availability of more severe penalties which may be invoked should the initial gambit fail.

When we consider the case of third parties who may attempt authoritative control of conflict, we see that between the extreme alternatives of unlimited popular violence and of total indiscriminate suppression of all protest lies a very wide range indeed. In societies favoring substantial freedom and widespread participation in political processes, the agencies authorized to use violence—primarily the police and military—will be less likely to set off political conflicts involving violence or to escalate violence once it has appeared, if they are trained and organized to use finely graded measures of control. In general, the measures used to control violent demonstrations, riots, and other turbulence or assaults will be least likely to elicit further violence if they are highly selective and individualized, if they use warnings and minimal force, if intentions and limits are clear, and if action is quick, decisive, and quickly terminated.

But the instrumentalities of control, such as the police, are not neutral even in the hands of well-intentioned superordinate authorities. This is a fact worth remembering by persons who now seek to establish "local control" as a principle for organizing public agencies in metropolitan areas. They may find grounds for caution by examining the early history of urban violence in the United States. Highly localized police forces tended to be ethnically homogeneous—and highly partisan in enforcing the laws. "Moreover, since some of the rioting was political, the partisanship of the police led official force to be applied against one group, or protection to be withheld from another" (Wade, 1969, 10).

For social control to be accepted as *authoritative*, rather than merely as the rule of might, it must not be obviously and grossly arbitrary or biased (Eckhoff, 1966, 161).

Even when the authorities are acceptably neutral in their preferences among contending groupings, however, the effectiveness of threats and of negative sanctions as means of controlling or terminating conflicts is enormously varied; disputes concerning alleged effects rarely specify the relevant conditions under which diametrically opposite consequences may be expected.

At the level of the individual, a substantial amount of experimental research has explored the effects of direct punishment. For example:

Proposition 47: If undesired behavior is punished periodically rather than regularly, the punished behavior is less likely to reappear (Berelson and Steiner, 1964, 150-52).

Although both being punished for aggression and observing that others are punished tend to quickly reduce specific acts of aggression, the effects disappear rather quickly and tend to be specific rather than generalized. Hence the prevention through punishment of aggressive behavior, in general, requires close monitoring and frequent penalties. But frequent punishment increases frustration, and often supplies a punishing-aggressive personal model for emulation and identification. Accordingly, efforts to control aggression by extremely severe punishment ("counterviolence") *of particular individuals* often are ineffective and may increase the subsequent rate of aggression of other individuals of the same collectivity. For collective outbreaks, however, *evenhanded* and *certain* application of appropriate sanctions seems effective in controlling communal violence (Grimshaw, 1975, personal communication).

At the level of collective processes, any political program that intends to use and does use violence as a means will encounter the fact that conflict itself creates new conditions apart from its intended effects as an instrument of power. Conflict rarely, if at all, can be simply turned on and then turned off without further consequences that are intrinsic to the essential processes that constitute conflict.

When extremely violent actions taken by institutional agents of social control to suppress movements of protest (a) are vividly communicated to third parties who regard the protestors as having some legitimate basis for their protests, and (b) the assault appears to be directed to relatively inoffensive and helpless persons, the protest movement often gains adherents and sympathizers and the authorities lose adherents and sympathizers. This generalization is abundantly illustrated in the history of the civil rights struggles of the 1960s (Pinkney, 1969, 184-93). The proportions of the general public strongly supportive *and* strongly opposed increase, and the percentage of persons who are of neutral or moderate opinion decreases.

Effective use of sanctions depends importantly upon *appropriateness*— whether the imposition of sanctions is within a range of normative acceptance by a given population. Penalties quite clearly regarded by the relevant population as much more severe than required for deterrence, and hence as intended to hurt, as punitive or cruel retaliation, will arouse much resentment. Further, the recipients of punishment will receive sympathy from other individuals who have been complying with authoritative control, who are potentially vulnerable to such sanctions. For example, extralegal or extraordinary and disproportionate violence on the part of police or military forces against domestic protest and turbulence often produces new popular support for the cause of the protestors. The point has been illustrated in numerous instances, such as the Peterloo Massacre of 1819 in Manchester, the massacre of members of the French Commune of 1871, the violence of steel companies against workers in 1935, the use of cattle prods and police dogs against black demonstrators in Birmingham, Alabama in the 1960s. When the use of violence is far in excess of what would be expected on the basis of law, custom, and past experience, when it is highly visible and dramatic, and when the persons attacked represent a substantial body of popular sentiment in opposition to institutional authorities, the violence usually was "suicidal insofar as it transformed victims into martyrs who became symbols of the iniquity and callousness of the rulers" (Coser, 1966, 17). Such boomerang effects apply, of course, to partisans as well as to authorities.

Violent conflict probably is less likely than nonviolent conflict to result in the innovation, learning, and institutionalization of complex modes of resolving conflicts. This proposition is by no means self-evidently true or false. On the face of it, the hypothesis seems to be contradicted by the impressive elaboration of political procedures and organizations for resolving international wars and violent incidents, as well as by the indications that it was only after protracted and costly violence that a national system of collective bargaining was developed in the United States for dealing with oppositions and disagreements in labor-management relations. It is argued that there are many situations in which only the dramatic and extreme costs of violence are sufficient to focus attention and to instigate new modes of acting in relation to important and recurring oppositions and conflicts. But there are many other instances in which violence recurs with monotonous regularity without any important development of new and more sophisticated ways of avoiding or terminating the processes that lead to violence. Indeed, the example just cited of the apparent effect of violence in motivating new solutions to labor-management conflicts may be used to support the contrary argument. After all, a long history of destructive and bloody confrontations of employers and workers had produced no fundamentally new and effective modes of resolution during some three-quarters of a century before the New Deal reforms of the 1930s. Furthermore, it may be held, the new procedures and organizations were based not primarily on the experience of violence but more fundamentally on the slow accumulation of ideas, values, and techniques through nonviolent negotiation and bargaining.

Authoritative controls are necessary in many instances *if* conflict is to be resolved. But the use of authoritative sanctions is most effective in the long run when (1) they are applied sparingly only for clear violations of well-defined and easily understood rules that limit conflict, (2) both rules and sanctions have widely accepted cultural justifications, (3) alternatives are kept available whereby the parties can achieve a substantial degree of want-satisfaction when they forgo conflict.

13. Conditions Influencing Success or Failure of Attempts to Settle Conflicts

The possibilities for resolving any particular conflict always are affected by whether the proposed settlement is regarded as involving "issues of principle" and by whether the resolution is regarded as "establishing a precedent." The two considerations overlap but are not identical: decisions on matters of principle usually do set precedents for later decisions, but not always, and many precedents are highly specific or concrete and are not converted into generalized principles. Attempted resolutions that the parties regard as involving questions of principle are especially difficult because a principle typically implies a very great scope of possible implications. In other words, when a conflict comes to be interpreted as one of principle, one effect is to increase the magnitude of the stakes. The particular values over which the parties are struggling are augmented by the addition of a generalizable criterion which may be applicable to a wide range of future occasions: e.g., "the principle of collective bargaining," "the principle of racial quotas in university admissions," "the principle of faculty authority over changes in curriculum."

The question of setting precedents similarly increases the size of the stakes by emphasizing the likelihood that the type of settlement agreed upon or the procedures utilized in a present case will be used in future instances of disputes. For example, an organization may resist arbitration, even though it anticipates a favorable outcome in the immediate situation, for fear that acceptance now would establish the basis for continuing intervention by external authorities in future struggles.

> *Proposition 48:* Especially difficult to resolve, then, are conflicts that
> involve an issue of principle and the settlements of which at the same
> time are thought to establish a precedent for future settlements.

To insist that a dispute is an issue of principle that can be settled only by one's opponent accepting *our* principle while yielding *his* or *her* principle is to introduce rigidity and to court escalation. Insistence on a "victory of principle" may be used to solidify one's own constituency. It may be a deliberate way of showing the opponent that we have a fixed commitment that cannot be negotiated. But if one does not need to use it for such purposes, the insistence on principle merely makes negotiation and resolution difficult. The disadvantages can be reduced by decreasing the *emphasis* without giving up the principle. There are two main ways of reducing the stakes. One is to hold to our principle but not to insist that the opponent yield, e.g., we may tell our adversary that a particular proposal is consistent with his or her principle ("equality") as well as with ours ("freedom" or "self-determination"). A second mode of restriction is to interpret the dispute as a question of the application of a principle, i.e., does or does not the principle apply in this case? Thus "states rights" may be held to apply to traffic regulation but not to school desegregation.

But the same factors that produce the difficulty result in very large payoffs whenever a resolution actually is effected. Again, the American history of employer-union relationship provides an instructive illustration. So long as employers refused to accept collective bargaining in principle, every struggle over other issues tended to eventually gravitate toward this latent and overriding issue. The result was that particular conflicts often were characterized by bitterness, hostility, and violence out of all proportion to the particular ad hoc values in dispute. Once collective bargaining was explicitly accepted and institutionalized, there was a marked long-run reduction in the frequency, scale, and intensity of employer-union conflict as such. We believe that similar processes have occurred, although to a much more limited extent, in the development of regularized negotiations, legal procedures, and modes of mediation and adjudication in ethnic controversies.

Several more particularized propositions are implied by the considerations just summarized.

Proposition 49: The more easily divisible and transferable are the scarce objects of contention, the more likely it is that bargaining will occur and that resolutions will occur short of extreme violence.

If questions of religious or political *ideology* can be put aside for purposes of considering more particular questions of *values or norms*, resolutions of opposition will be favored. If differences of values or normative commitments can be put aside for purposes of considering questions of *allocations of resources or rewards*, the probability of agreement will be increased. If differences in claims for allocations can be *stated in monetary terms*, the likelihood of compromise is enhanced.

A clearly related rule is specified in the following proposition:

Proposition 50: Given that the total importance of the whole set of issues is approximately equal (in terms of the values and interests of the contending parties), the possibility of a nonviolent, mutually acceptable resolution of a dispute or other opposition will be the greater when the contention concerns many or several relatively small items rather than one or a few much more important matters.

However, when bargaining is at stalemate on a given issue, a resolution sometimes may be sought by bringing in another dispute between the parties as a means of "trading" a concession by A on issue X for a concession by B on issue Y. But, "the joining of issues as leverage or bargaining currency, even when constructively looking toward a negotiated agreement, tends to shift the focus away from the merits of a problem and to put relative bargaining power in issue" (Fisher, 1971, 161).

In negotiations that are more than simple bargaining over a single issue, there typically is no fixed and precise sum of predetermined values at stake (Ikle, 1964, 164-90). Rather, the stakes are defined and changed in the processes of bargaining—both the estimated level of valuation and the priority and preference orders change from moment to moment. What is a gain or a loss will be differently defined in the changing contexts of move and counter-move by the principals. The criteria of evaluation often are both vague and unstable, and there is a consequent pressure to find some grossly identifiable points of anchorage for judgment. An obvious referent for judging gain or loss is the status quo ante—the situation just preceding the present may be regarded as a break-even or zero point. Similarly, if events are thought to be moving in a given direction, a historical trend may be accepted as a bench mark. Frequently the break-even point is regarded as set by one's own initial expectations, or by one's opponent's estimated expectations, or by some point intermediate to the opposing claims and expectations.

We already have indicated why one may *sometimes* wish to avoid raising ("unnecessary") questions of principle and of precedent. We said that by keeping the issues as concrete and limited as possible, the stakes are minimized and long-run power implications are deemphasized, thereby enhancing the likelihood of agreement upon a settlement. But the opposite implication is also present: there may be occasions on which one will decide to "go for broke" by using the controversy at hand precisely as a device for raising an issue in principle. Presumably one will do this only when there are good grounds for believing that the total balance of power and of anticipated gains and losses of the parties would favor agreement. If one is mistaken, the effect will be to intensify the conflict, but at least we shall have been able to characterize in advance the nature of the risk entailed.

The feasibility of successful negotiations depends also on conditions indicated in the next three propositions (cf. Steiner, 1974).

> *Proposition 51:* In negotiations concerning any particular set of issues of contentions between two parties, the likelihood of mutually acceptable settlements will be the greater, the *less* the two parties agree upon the importance of each item. For if there is a reverse ordering of importance, the possibilities for bargaining tradeoffs are maximized.

> *Proposition 52:* In interactions between culturally different collectivities within a larger community or society, the likelihood of mutually accepted compromise between opposing or incompatible claims will be the greater:
>   (a) when the number of parties active in the process is small;
>   (b) when interaction is frequent between leaders, representatives, or prominent spokesmen of the respective formations;
>   (c) the less formalized the interactions;
>   (d) the less public the negotiations;
>   (e) the more stable the leadership structure;
>   (f) the longer the time between initiation of negotiations and some publicly conspicuous deadline for decision (e.g., expiration date of a prior agreement); and
>   (g) the more centralized the decision-making systems of the respective collectivities.

Successful agreements are more frequent when the total environing social environment encourages commonality of culture and reduces the salience of intergroup differences in beliefs, values, interests, and styles of life. For example:

> *Proposition 53:* The likelihood of successful resolution of conflicts is increased by educational and propaganda emphases upon characteristics and values *common* to various groups rather than upon intergroup differences (Williams, 1947, 64). However, the emphasis upon commonality will be subject to boomerang effects if excessive or unrealistic expectations are thereby created, and it will not be acceptable to advocates of cultural pluralism or cultural separatism.

Where cultural similarity is high, it facilitates the use of a great many varied social devices in the processes of solving conflicts to reduce tensions, to facilitate communication, and to increase areas of diffuse background agreement: humor, diversions (e.g., joint recreation), sharing external objects of interest, and positive regard. Although none of these approaches are sufficient to substantially change commitments to major stakes, they can serve to reduce nonrelevant interferences and to somewhat increase a mutual sense of trustworthiness. These advantages are not trivial.

Our discussion of this endless topic of conflict resolution must come to an end. We conclude that the success of efforts to settle conflicts primarily depends upon the basic causes of the conflict and the objectives of the parties. Of course, tactics do make a difference. There is, however, no simple virtue in the sheer fact of negotiation or of particular modes of bargaining. For instance, contrary to opinions of many statesmen and commentators, the sheer fact of continuing negotiations, even with no agreement in sight, does not seem very potent in preventing further conflict, including violence. However, continuing negotiations may prevent one or both of the principals from taking actions disadvantageous to the other, if: (1) the party thus restrained believes that if it took the action, the other principal would break off the negotiations; (2) the first party must regard a break in negotiations as carrying disadvantages greater than the advantages to be gained from the action it otherwise would take. In short, being engaged in negotiations is not in itself a substitute for violence, nor does it necessarily reduce the level of conflict. Negotiations serve as a restraint upon conflict if, and only if, one or both of the parties fears that a break in negotiations will result from its failure to be restrained and that the adverse results then would be greater than the costs of its restraint, or if the negotiations convey warnings that otherwise would not be effective (Ikle, 1964, 47-48). Of course we do not assume that negotiators, or third-party intervenors for that matter, are always rationally seeking effective means to attain well-defined goals. If, however, they are rational to any important degree, carefully chosen methods of conflict resolution often can be used to develop higher joint returns than the parties otherwise could gain.

Once more, however, we must remember that there are always costs, side-effects, or tradeoffs. Thus there do seem to be some fundamental incompatibilities between the characteristics of collectivities that favor nonviolent compromises and the characteristics that favor rapid learning and innovations in strategies and techniques of conflict-resolution. As Steiner (1974) has suggested, compromise solutions are favored by stable leadership, low participation of members, little time pressure, and small scope for new approaches in decision-making. These same conditions provide only weak incentives for learning, and minimize the amount of novel information, including feedback about the consequences of decisions. The net tendency will be to develop a routinized and simplified process and set of procedures for dealing with recurrent situations of disagreement or opposition.

Some "resolutions" of conflict are destructive: when the termination of an episode of conflict results in minus-sum outcomes or perpetuates conditions leading to unnecessary damage in the future. On the other hand, a particular conflict may be resolved in a way that increases consensus, increases mutually advantageous interdependence, and facilitates the integrative resolution of future clashes of interests or disagreements.

It is our view that human societies inevitably generate an important amount of disagreement, dissensus, opposition, and conflict. It seems likely also that a substantial proportion of the conflicts always will prove resistant to constructive resolutions. But the remaining cases, those that conceivably are objectively open to constructive resolutions, are extremely important, and offer a high-priority challenge to research, to imaginative social thinking, and to skillful innovations in social practices.

In lieu of a summary for this unavoidably lengthy discussion we add an Appendix on some possibly useful rules-of-practice for a benign third party who has an obligation to help resolve a conflict.

APPENDIX

Rules of Thumb for a Third Party Who Must Deal with Conflicts

There are circumstances in human affairs in which one may wish to activate or to escalate conflict, when no other course of action seems ethically acceptable or socially effective.

But many conflicts are mutually disadvantageous to the parties or to a larger community. If we wish to reduce, manage, regulate, or resolve such conflicts, how can we proceed? No set of rules will be applicable under all circumstances. There will always be unique features that need to be detected and taken into account. Nevertheless, there may be some value in a rough listing of do-it-yourself dicta for the third party who may be faced with a need to attempt some intervention in a situation of conflict. The following observations may be characterized as "informed folklore"—a set of notes from experience and research. They claim no final truth and are best used when accompanied by substantial doses of skepticism and humor.

Understood in this way, the following guidelines conceivably may be helpful:

1. "Keep weapons out of reach," that is, to the extent possible minimize the capacities of the opponents to directly hurt one another in the immediate situation. This may mean, literally, a prohibition against physical weapons. More commonly it will imply that the adversaries are somehow induced or constrained to accept negotiating rules against drastic threats in the context of discussion.

2. Use all the social and psychological devices you know of to keep both the conflict itself and the processes of conflict resolution from including highly personal charges and recriminations and the use of group epithets or abusive language.

3. Fractionate the conflict. If you have only one issue and the parties totally disagree on it, what hope is there? Usually the one Big Issue actually contains parts. It can be disaggregated. To increase the number of points that can be discussed is to open up possibilities for negotiations and tradeoffs.

4. Bring in factual evidence whenever possible. It may not be believed at first, but keep at it. The reference to "facts of the case" may eventually encourage some anchorage in realities, some reminder of the possibility of objective constraints on desires and solutions.

5. Translate as many issues as possible into money or into some other divisible and transferable terms. What is unique, unitary, and nontransferable is not a good object for bargaining compromises. If you can find "movable" items, prospects for agreements are enhanced.

6. Bring in trusted third parties for conciliation, fact-finding, mediation, arbitration, or adjudication.

For best results, such third-party intervenors in conflicts should be well known to the opponents, readily accessible, prestigeful, skilled, impartial, and discreet. They do not have to be super-persons, but it is essential that they be known for personal integrity and fairness.

7. Take the easiest problems first. There are exceptions: sometimes you have to first "go for broke" or nothing will be accomplished. But usually it is more effective to walk before you try to run.

8. Keep the very earliest exploratory discussions as informal as possible. If ethically proper and tactically feasible, keep the first tentative negotiations off the record and nonpublic. Participatory democracy can be a fine thing, but mass meetings are poor places for subtle explorations of complex issues. Everyone who has a legitimate interest in the outcomes should eventually have a chance to know what is being done. But genuine meeting of minds is facilitated by initial discussions in which people do not have to take public stands that lock them into premature commitments.

9. If you can avoid the appearance of nagging or dictating to the opponents, use all suitable occasions to unobtrusively remind the contending parties of common interests, shared values, or mutually advantageous interdependencies that they actually have.

10. Whenever possible, limit the immediate objects of discussion or bargaining to a few issues at a time. Avoid global packages in which "everything" has to be considered at once.

This guideline is consistent with the subdividing of issues mentioned in #3 above. Both approaches tend to reduce the stakes, and, hence, the risks in each attempted bargain or agreement, to increase the possibilities for trade-offs, to diversify the constituencies to which negotiators can appeal, and to encourage an emphasis on problem-solving rather than sheer "power" or "victory."

11. Continually explore possible shifts in the ways in which the parties conceive of the issues and how they evaluate or rank-order the various issues in relative importance. Do not assume that first positions will remain unchanged. Preferences often shift during negotiations.

12. Whenever it is possible and realistically justified, introduce information that validly shows that the long-run survival and security of the parties are not jeopardized by proposed procedures or agreements.

13. If one has the authority to effectively threaten an imposed settlement should the principals themselves not arrive at an agreement on their own responsibility, and it is ethically acceptable to do this, the nature of the imposed solution should be announced in advance. An announcement of an intended solution serves to produce restricted bargaining. Without such advance information, an unspecified threat only increases the difficulties in securing mutually acceptable agreements.

14. Without obtrusive nagging, call attention whenever appropriate to the negative consequences to the contending parties themselves of failure to regulate or resolve the conflict.

15. Keep talking. And then, try again. And then, keep talking.

P.S. A curious thing happened on the way to an agreement: by following these suggestions we implicitly told all parties that we respect them and ourselves—and, thereby, that we share a commitment to a certain kind of community.

Chapter 13

Realism and Utopia: The
Prospects for Social Maturity

*Repentance is extraordinarily difficult as long as the general view
prevails that anything that is wrong with anybody is always somebody
else's fault, and that is the official ideology of a large part of the world.*

Kenneth E. Boulding[1]

1. Some Matters of Perspective

In the last quarter of the twentieth century we look upon a world of rapid
population growth, present and impending famines, and ominous signs of
ecological threats. At the same time, we are continuously confronted with the
fact of numerous violent collective conflicts between nations and within them
in nearly every part of the world. Just when the beneficial possibilities of
technological development, increased knowledge, and more efficient social
organization had seemed most promising, the possibility of ever greater
catastrophes has come into the foreground. Is there a sane perspective that
can guide and steady our judgments—somewhere between Doomsday and
Utopia—as we review what we have learned about the possibilities for mutual
accommodation among racial and ethnic groups?

Sir Thomas More's *Utopia* described, in 1516, an imaginary island with a
perfect system of law, govenment, and other social arrangements. Utopia has
come to mean any visionary scheme for an ideal society. Utopias have an
important place in human affairs (Moore, 1966)—a place they share with
other ideals, hopes, and aspirations. A purely factual world in which things

just are as they are and have no aura of hopeful contingency whatsoever would be a dreary place for most of us. Utopias are of such stuff as values and aspirations are made of, and can be of great consequence in the actual world of the here and now.

On the other hand, realism refers to an attitude of appraisal that emphasizes the *actual* in projecting estimates of what is possible. In American society it often is held to be a good thing to be realistic and a bad thing to be utopian or visionary. But it is also generally believed by many persons that where there is no vision it is unlikely that there is a good society.

In this final chapter, we attempt to appraise the balance between narrow and time-bound realism and a more generous realism that respects facts past and present but also includes aspirations and contingencies in its view of possible developments of intergroup relations in the United States. To do this, we need to step back for a moment to place present urgencies in a long-range and basic perspective.

An essential characteristic of living things is that they are open systems, ceaselessly involved in boundary exchanges with environments. As energetic open systems, all living things have effects on the world. In a strict biological sense, therefore, people are inherently active, inevitably assertive. Unless they are effective in taking what they need from the environment — of air, water, food, space — they die. Without the assertiveness of sexual activity and subsistence-seeking the species dies. To live is to make claims upon the world. And the claims of different individuals and groups may be incompatible. In fact, they often are.

But without mutual accommodation and active cooperation, human beings would soon become extinct (Gaylin, 1976). Claims must be moderated and integrated if children are to survive, culture is to be preserved, and physical environments are to be managed.

So, opposition and conflict — cooperation and integration — are universal and simultaneously present aspects of life in society. Any realistic utopia, therefore, must allow for diversity, dissensus, conflict, and change. The Present can never fully bind the Future.

As Chapter 2 emphasized, actual social arrangements rarely meet our highest aspirations or most heroic standards. This is true of all human institutions and relationships. By most accounts it seems agreed that marriage in one or another of its many forms is an indispensible institution. At the same time, we are told by some marriage and family counselors that, even if only modestly demanding criteria are applied, perhaps 10-20 percent of contemporary American marriages could be rated as both stable and reasonably happy for both parties. Whatever estimate one may choose, it is clear that even the most universal and widely acclaimed social arrangements fall considerably short of fully successful outcomes, as judged by the norms accepted by most of the participants.

Furthermore, all so-called solutions to social problems create new problems. And situations of tragic social choice are common. They arise when any one of a set of feasible solutions to a problem of allocating benefits and disadvantages involves severe penalties in the long run. A solution is adopted to meet a current urgent problem, say, conscription to raise the necessary armed forces for war. Later, disadvantages are cumulatively felt, and the society shifts to volunteer forces. The new solution then proves to have drawbacks, e.g., excessive cost, unequal sacrifices, inadequacy to meet national needs in crisis — and one may see a return to conscription. When the effects are severe and impinge upon functionally crucial portions of the society, the most likely outcome is rotation or cycling of solutions. As one policy becomes increasingly intolerable, its opposite is chosen — only to generate eventually in its turn a different set of unacceptable disadvantages, deprivations, indignities, and ethical problems. Thus in the recent case of Community Action Programs in American cities, it has been noted that:

> The struggle of community action to reconcile contending ideals, its uneasy turning round upon its own arguments, are perhaps characteristic of any movement of reform in the face of fundamental dilemmas of social choice. . . . As community action evolved, it continually shifted its emphasis. Policy tended to move in a circle, turning from one alternative to another, as the drawbacks of each became apparent (Marris and Rein, 1967, 225-26).

Nor are such dilemmas confined to social behavior. Even with all the elaborate technology and accumulated knowledge of the physical sciences it is not yet possible to control earthquakes, volcanic eruptions, tidal waves, hurricanes, and many other enormously destructive natural processes. Even more significantly, biological and ecological processes (in which extremely complex side-effects of interventions are usual rather than unusual) further show the great recalcitrance of environmental conditions to purposive human control. Moreover, many physical and biological phenomena that have effects judged harmful to human beings are uncontrollable even though the phenomena have been exhaustively described and even though their causes are well understood.

In view of these facts, it would be most surprising were we to find that social processes were easier to manage than the biophysical environment. Suppose we have a wholly convincing explanation, backed by detailed and systematic empirical evidence, of the processes that result in urban residential segregation by socioeconomic strata and racial categories. Even with such valid and comprehensive knowledge we might find that the causes of the outcomes are so massive and so inaccessible to influence by any known social technology that only very limited control or management is feasible, at a particular time and place. Nevertheless the limitations upon the control of environments that can be attained through present knowledge do not at all imply that we should cease the effort to understand the physical, biological, and social worlds. Increased knowledge is, indeed, likely to be essential for human survival, let alone for enhancing the possibilities for value-realization.

Let us examine a fateful case in point: the problem of ethnic conflict in plural societies. When distinctive ethnic collectivities within a political society have developed separate and different institutions of marriage, family, religion, and property, and contend with one another for political control, the political society can be held together only by forceful regulation. Such coercive systems imply the domination of some ethnic group(s) over another or others (Rabushka and Shepsle, 1972, 15). From this observation, it is easy to infer that plural societies always must be politically unstable or else rigidly dictatorial. But we would say that what plural socieites show is *not* that ethnic diversity inevitably makes for instability of democratic polities. They do demonstrate that many of the processes of integration and conflict resolution that are most useful in societies with *a workable initial consensus* fail in a highly segmented society of great dissensus. In other words, the devices and institutions and procedures of education, persuasion, inducement, negotiation, and bargaining always have their limits.

In the very last paragraph of their book on plural societies Rabuska and Shepsle (1972, 217) say: "We ask, is the resolution of intense but conflicting preferences in the plural society manageable in a democratic framework? We think not." But this negative judgment rests in part upon the very *definition* of the problem—a definition in which plural societies were said to have especially sharp, rigid, and totalistic ethnic divisions. For less rigid pluralistic, rather than plural, societies such as the United States, the prospects need not include inevitable ethnic polarization so great as to disrupt a representative-democratic polity.

A workable pluralism is possible for one thing because, as we have seen in earlier chapters, the sharpness, strength, and permanency of ethnic boundaries are highly variable characteristics (Barth, 1969; LeVine and Campbell, 1972, Chapter 7; Das Gupta, 1974). Ethnic collectivities are not firmly fixed units; they emerge and disappear; their boundaries shift (and change in kind) not only over time but also from situation to situation. Racial categories and groupings similarly are not fixed historically but are made and unmade by social processes. The dynamic and multireferential qualities of "race" are convincingly shown by the consequences of racial intermixing—which have ranged from cultural assimilation under some conditions, to the development of rigid separation and elaborated ideologies of domination in other contexts.

A striking demonstration of the mutability of both "racial" conceptions and collective self-esteem has been described in the recent transformations of the people of Tristan da Cahuna (Munch, 1972). From a self-depreciating and socially atomistic condition, the islanders have developed substantial pride and self-assertion as a result of exile, of group success in winning a return to Tristan, and of external recognition and rewards for their maritime skills. (In the process, they changed their racial conception—no longer regarding themselves as "black.")

Remarkable changes in ethnic boundaries have occurred within the United States in this century, as we saw in Chapter 1. Peopled by the greatest intercontinental migrations in history, the public life and culture of this "nation of nations" have been profoundly shaped by the crisscrossing and overlapping of social categories based on ethnicity, religion, racial classifications, and socioeconomic strata. From more than three centuries of intricate historical experience of ethnicity in this society, some important lessons can be read.[2]

Proposition 1: First, ethnic alignments are highly specific and have changed dramatically from time to time (Higham, 1966, 237-58).

A striking feature of pre-1900 responses to immigrants was the diverse and changing pattern of antipathies and solidarities. The Alien and Sedition scare of 1798 concerned foreign radicals—but not foreign Catholics. The Know-Nothing Movement of the 1850s was directed against Catholics, ignored Jews, and included many northerners who were sympathetic to blacks. And so it went. No one ethnic, religious, or racial category was for long the dominant focus of nativistic prejudice or discrimination, with the peculiar exception of black Americans—who by 1900 were thoroughly "American." Indeed, throughout most of national history well into the twentieth century

ethnic tensions had been relatively discrete, and the prevailing theory of nationalism had been consonant with that fact. . . . So diverse were these tensions that no one tried to subsume them all under a single explanatory pattern (Higham, 1966, 241).

Proposition 2: Furthermore, there is substantial evidence that the more varied the social statuses and activities of members of an identifiable ethnic category, the less homogeneous and rigid are the stereotypes imposed on it.

It follows from the above considerations that maximum inaccuracy of group stereotypes is to be expected when ethnic groupings are spatially segregated, rarely interact directly, interact exclusively in dominant-subordinate relationships, and impinge upon one another in only one status or a few statuses or other social contexts. The contrasting conditions produce greater specificity and accuracy of collective characterizations.

Sheer spatial proximity is a crude indicator of actual ease of communication and often is negated by physical or social barriers. Functional proximity is what counts, i.e., the "cost" or the "ease" of engaging in interaction. The greater the functional proximity of an outgroup, the more salient it will be and the less likely it is to be regarded with indifference or neutrality. The effect of increased functional proximity, therefore, may be to increase either liking or disliking, harmonious or conflictful interaction. "Positive" outcomes will be heightened by similarity of values and beliefs, except when the similarity leads directly to increased competition for scarce goods. Dissimilarity will favor withdrawal or opposition—except when the differences are complementary, resulting in mutually rewarding interdependence.

An important specific example of these general points is occupational similarities and complementarities, as contrasted with occupational differences that carry built-in sources of competition and opposition. Thus attitudes and behavior between members of different ethnic groupings always will be strongly affected by the character of major occupations carried out and by the consequent relationships of trade and exchange, employer and employee, ruler and ruled, creditor and debtor, landlord and tenant, and so on. In general, the more diverse the occupations of the members of an ethnic grouping, the less distinctive will it be and the less will occupational stereotypes and evaluations be generalized as attributes of the entire ethnic category. Thus old-fashioned stereotypes of Swedes and Hungarians have practically disappeared, and old-fashioned stereotypes of Jews and blacks increasingly become patently unreal.

Proposition 3: Positive or negative orientations both affect and are affected by objective characteristics of collectivities.

Thus if a particular intergroup relationship is positive, for any cause, selectivity of attention and psychological leveling and sharpening will minimize divergent and unfavorably judged characteristics. And, if relationships are hostile and the other group is regarded as a threat, not only will negative traits be selectively noted and accentuated but even traits otherwise positively evaluated will be regarded unfavorably, e.g., ambition, intelligence, hard work.

Proposition 4: Thus stereotypes and evaluations are not fixed apart from the relationships and social contexts in which they develop. It follows that any collective actions that change relationships and contexts will affect beliefs, evaluations, and feelings.

Change can occur. It does occur. It often is difficult and complex—like the rest of life. But many desired changes in the direction of greater societal integration, lessened destructive conflict, and positive-sum intergroup accommodation have been achieved. Others are possible. We therefore repeat Lesson No. 1: It Can Be Done.

2. Aspirations and Allocations: Who Gets What, and Why?

An exclusive focus on ethnicity would prevent us from adequately understanding the large number of other politically active collectivities and the diversity of interests that must be articulated in the political arena. Accordingly, we have tried in the analyses in preceding chapters to see ethnic politics as a special case of generic processes.

In particular we have found in case after case that to say that there are economic and political *institutions* in a society is to say that there are sets of organized collectivities that have succeeded in having their interests in income, wealth, and power *vested*, i.e., their interests are protected by a *system of enforceable claims and norms of action*. Institutionalization thus signifies that particular interests are bound up with the maintenance of a given normative order. "Self-interest" and "social conformity" therefore point in the same direction.

> *Proposition 5:* By the same token, interests that are excluded from vesting under an institutional order at a particular time always meet resistance in any efforts to establish their own claims as rights.

The basis for the special resistance predicted by Proposition 5 is that the claims of the formerly excluded parties will be seen by the vested incumbants as encroaching upon legitimate claims of the established units—not merely as seeking a "better bargain" at the moment. Because the institutionalized system itself is the residue of many *interlocking*, mutually advantageous settlements, any change in the rules of the game to accommodate a new set of players, therefore, is likely to send multiple repercussions through many linkages. For all these reasons, the establishment of new institutionalized claims on the part of previously excluded parties typically will result only from a difficult and long struggle. Thus:

> Vesting excluded interests is a slow, arduous process, as organized labor discovered. . . . Success in one policy area, such as governmental regulation of collective bargaining, did not guarantee speedy acquisition of comparable influence for the working man in all functional areas. . . . If this was true for labor in national politics, blacks could expect at least

as much difficulty in city politics, if for no other reason than the comparative autonomy of large urban bureaucracies (Greenstone and Peterson, 1973, 290).

Struggles over vested interests, therefore, are especially crucial in plural societies. For, as originally noted by Furnivall, a plural society lacks the consensus that is required to generate a common social demand. His classic example has been paraphrased as follows:

> In a homogeneous society, the purchase of a cathedral provides an indivisible "public good," i.e., every citizen may benefit from its construction. In the plural society, however, the erection of a Chinese temple constitutes a "public bad" for Muslims; in a similar manner, Muslim mosques provide few or no benefits for Chinese. Therefore, in the plural society social demands often result in public expenditures with benefits for one community and opportunity costs for the others (Rabushka and Shepsle, 1972, 11).

Although this basic problem does exist, of course, in the United States, its acuteness has been lessened and is now lessened in two main ways: (1) by workable consensus on many common social demands, (2) by decentralized and nongovernmental allocations for many public goods (e.g., churches, hospitals, recreational facilities).

When there are clearly understood limits to the potential redistribution of power, authority, and other scarce resources that is likely to occur, there often emerges what Greenstone and Peterson (1973, 281-85) call "low-intensity pluralist politics." What this says in effect is that a *tacit prior settlement* of many of the terms of opposition and struggle is a prerequisite to consensual politics or to low-key bargaining. In Gamson's imagery (1975), the main articulated interests in the contention have become "insiders." Conversely, strongly conflictful politics occurs when a prior set of frozen bargains has excluded a collectivity or a set of interests whose advocates now demand influence and power. A new contender, in other words, attempts not only to enter the arena but to secure a place there as an established player. The double stake of the struggle then consists of (1) a set of immediate interests plus (2) a redistribution of influence and authority. When outsiders thus attempt to secure a place as insiders, the pluralist bargaining game is opened to a struggle over who will be the participants and what will be the rules.

Proposition 6: Because of the pluralism of interests among insiders and the resulting exigencies of tactics in bargaining, outsiders who seek access to crucial decision-making positions generally are in a stronger position when the collectivity has developed several organizations, each of which represents different emphases upon persuasion, inducements and constraints (Myrdal, 1944, 835; Williams, 1947, 75).

As we saw in Chapters 8 and 9 the effective political strategies of groups seeking to represent interests of low-income strata and disadvantaged ethnic minorities included coercive actions. Nevertheless whatever the tactics that may appear desirable from time to time, there is no practicable longer-range strategy that will not make use of *coalitions*, including coalitions with "non-ethnic" groupings (Comer, 1972, 219).

If and when a new collectivity actively seeks admission to the inner arenas of power and influence, a question its leaders must address is *how* representation is to be effected. For the *forms of representation* of *new* constituencies that seek effective access to authorities (or to establish alternative authorities) are not "mere formalities"—they can make real differences in outcome. The contrast with well-established groupings is sharp:

> The formal process by which corporations, labor unions, and professional associations are selected as representatives on official policy-making bodies probably has little effect on their subsequent behavior. . . . The multiplicity of access points available to higher-status groups reduces the significance of any one channel of influence. . . .
>
> Since low-status groups are likely to have significantly fewer alternative channels, the importance of any one is thereby enhanced. The representative's bargaining position vis-à-vis the agency he is trying to influence is weakened, and his bargaining position vis-à-vis the group he is representing is strengthened (Greenstone and Peterson, 1973, 197).
>
> *Proposition 7:* Accordingly, it is by winning power through organized action that a collectivity gains authority, and it is then by making binding decisions that new inducements can be created and persuasion can be reinforced to generate additional influence upon other authorities. The process is circular.

What has just been said concerning multiple organizations and diverse tactics, forms of representation, and the interplay of power and influence—all have been aptly illustrated in the post-1965 history of participation by blacks, Chicanos, Native Americans—and women—in American politics.

When bargaining must take place among a plurality of diverse groupings and associations it is typically a protracted, uneven, and complicated set of processes. Because bargaining implies compromises, if the processes are to continue from occasion to occasion, no one party is likely to be wholly satisfied with the outcome of all particular bargains. Settlements often turn out to be quickly undone. Coalitions may shift radically over relatively short periods of time. Eternal vigilance, therefore, is the price of enduring viability in the bargaining arena.

Proposition 8: Pluralistic bargaining, in short, necessarily represents incremental adjustments that have to be renegotiated from time to time.

Thus after some limited gains in the 1960s, newly articulate ethnic minorities met strong counterreactions during the Nixon years; it was then clear enough that such developments as revenue sharing and emphasis on local control in governmental programs did not mean sensitivity or responsiveness to the needs of poor people and ethnic minorities (Taylor, 1971).

Furthermore, bargaining is workable only between collectivities sufficiently well-organized to reach decisions that are enforceable among members. And bargaining implies some appreciable capacity to offer inducements or mount credible threats. Both conditions mean that established groupings have substantial advantages—they already are recognized players in an organized game.

Once new collective interests have been accepted into a system of pluralistic bargaining, however, the new bargaining unit has the opportunity to establish continuing advantages over and above the prior situation. Thus it can continuously defend its past gains as legitimate—as "institutionalized rights"—and also use its position to bargain for additional scarce values.

Proposition 9: A system of pluralistic bargaining thus works to the disadvantage of unorganized collectivities but may be a vehicle for important gains once an aspiring collectivity has established itself within the game.

The application to the special case of blacks in American cities has been formulated clearly by Greenstone and Peterson (1973, 314):

Once these black interests have been recognized as legitimate and become vested, the principle may then work to the blacks' benefit. . . . The success of the black struggle for equality depends in part on vesting black interests by controlling certain important community institutions, and then legitimatizing this new influence by appealing to the whites' . . . interest in preserving pluralist bargaining.

But effective representation and advocacy of collective interests cannot be a one-time thing. Political gains require political defenses and the struggles never end. For as Comer (1972, 214) notes:

The powerful do not "drop out." The fact that many blacks in the North took to the streets in the last decade rather than to the ballot boxes did not stop Congress from passing legislation that put money, power and control into the hands of state governments, North and South, all traditionally antagonistic to the cities and unsympathetic to the black community.

The resistance of vested interests and the interlocking of those interests help to account for a great deal of the problem of mutual accommodation among social collectivities and strata, e.g., the political difficulty of reducing inequalities of income and wealth. Really major changes in the distribution of income and wealth in national societies are very rare and with very few exceptions have occurred only under the drastic pressures of war, revolution, or catastrophic depression or inflation. On the other hand, the real incomes of most people in a society can be greatly increased by rising productivity—or, of course, decreased by diminishing productivity. Some limited, but still important, income redistribution can be achieved from time to time by changes in taxation and subsidies and other transfer payments, direct and indirect. But proposals for substantial and salient changes typically have aroused strong political resistance. Resistance appears to derive much of its force from a perhaps unperceived "divide and rule" syndrome: feelings of envy and relative deprivation among middle- and upper-lower-income strata lead to opposition to raising incomes of the poor (Thurow, 1973, 146-55); meanwhile the very rich continue to be very rich.

To propose solutions for social problems without considering the realities of power and authority is to be "utopian" in the worst sense—that is, both unrealistic and mistaken in one's estimates of consequences. Such prescribing sometimes ignores easily available evidence from prior social experience. Thus in the 1960s one "solution" proposed to deal with conflict in New York City's public schools was to turn the schools over to elected local boards in autonomous districts that would be racially or ethnically homogeneous. This approach, indeed, was encouraged by some philanthropic foundations and political officials. Nowhere in the public discussions, apparently, was there a careful review of the city's long and unhappy experience with decentralized "community control" systems in the nineteenth century. Local control then had proved to be an educational disaster and was rejected in favor of a more centralized system (Ravitch, 1974). The compromises of the 1960s barely prevented the city from plunging headlong into the conflictful and ineffectual system, which had once "flunked out" in the test of practical experience. Again, we are repeating one of our main messages: that both realistic goals and realistic tactics depend upon accurate diagnosis of complex societal settings.

No one who is interested in guiding social policies can afford to overlook how very common it is in collective social processes that: (1) the aggregation of individual rational decisions that maximize short-run interests (e.g., unlimited energy use; real-estate speculation) make everyone, or nearly everyone, worse off; (2) decisions that are contrary to such immediate interests of each individual member nevertheless are better or best for the whole collectivity, including the welfare of each individual in many settings. Social programs that ignore these fundamental characteristics of collective life almost always find the omission detrimental to their intended attainments.

3. Reflections on Pluralism, Governance, and Social Change

Institutions have not been conceived here as fixed, static entities but as recurring processes – as moving sets of statuses. Institutional norms . . . similarly have been regarded as rules that represent the outcomes of bargains, the resolutions of conflicts, the clarifications of ambiguities, the stabilization of competition, the consensual efforts to control power, the agreements to facilitate goal attainment (Williams, 1970, 620).

In the 146 years since Bolivia's independence, there have been 186 uprisings, resulting in more than 150 changes of government (Nash, 1974).

In spite of deep cleavages in its social structure, the United States is an ethnically pluralistic rather than a plural society. It is this basic pluralistic character that has allowed us to find so many examples of effective *specific* actions, short of violent revolutionary programs, in changing intergroup relations during recent decades.

But we have a society of increasingly large-scale and complex social units, and of increasing demands for performance and equity. To meet these demands, the increasingly large-scale and complex actions that would have to be taken for "adequate" regulation and direction are not possible (with the requisite resources and speed) unless there is a high degree of societal consensus, sustained over relatively long periods. As standards and expectations rise, however, consensus probably becomes more difficult to achieve. And as complexity increases, so do the occasions requiring collective decision and actions if major undesired consequences are to be avoided.

If conditions generally found to be humanly noxious are to be avoided, the "need" for purposive regulation of undesired effects of activities of social units increases at least as rapidly as societal complexity. Meanwhile the socio-technical requirements of effective regulation result in a lengthening of the future period which needs to be taken into account in planning. Also, there is a large increase in the lead-time required to bring into effective operation any large-scale collective program to counteract undesired conditions.

What is new in the highly industrialized megalopolitan society is not merely that high interdependence and social congestion make the actions of any one social unit externally costly or beneficial in ways not compensated for by direct payment or remuneration (Rosenberg, 1968). This situation has prevailed at one time or another in many densely settled villages and towns for millennia. What is unique is the addition of two new features: first, the units producing external effects have become very, very large; and, second, traditional social mechanisms for bringing nonmarket sanctions to bear have become ineffectual. In the village community, a man who created a public nuisance of some kind could quickly receive convincing negative feedback in the form of gossip, withdrawal of reciprocity, invoking of supernatural sanctions, social disapproval, and threats from personally significant individuals, and imposition of legal sanctions (Holt, 1965, 103-8). In many instances today, *none* of these mechanisms are effective in controlling actions of business firms, labor unions, illicit syndicates, and so on. For example, without explicit monitoring and suitable feedback, processes of ethnic discrimination and conflict can persist, even when the diffuse costs to the total society are very high. Uncontrolled market processes, as desirable as they are in many ways from an economic standpoint, often result in outcomes that are undesirable in terms of social values held by many members of the community concerning equity, justice, quality of life, and long-run survival of the social system. Uncontrolled processes of social conflict similarly can and do produce net negative outcomes in many instances. From these facts it follows that in developing and appraising social policy it is reasonable to give special attention to means of social regulation and control that may minimize constrictions of freedom while providing for equitable resolutions of oppositions and conflict.

Remember that we are not advocating utopia. We do not expect conflict or injustice or inefficiency to be abolished. We do not expect that a political society—even if we could calculate the ideal product—will ever be able to optimize the good of all its members. But we do think that some important gains in net well-being are possible.

4. An Illustrative Case: Governmental Action Concerning Employment and Union Membership

Legislation and executive action have been principal means in the attempt to reduce or eliminate ethnic-racial discrimination in the economic sectors of employment. One of the obvious points of intervention has been the unions, since routes of entry, age, education, and training requirements often have precluded the entrance of blacks, as have outright racial discrimination and exclusion from informal social networks (Granovetter, 1973, 1974) important to union affiliation.

Some of the earliest programs of the federal government aimed at increasing minority participation in the unionized construction industry were "outreach" programs. These programs provided recruitment services, tutorial aid in preparing for apprenticeship examinations, financial assistance, and follow-up services. Such programs must be classified as only "remedial," for they do nothing to change the *structural* barriers of union and industrial discrimination. Jobs are still limited and competitive in a scarce market, favoring overqualified and experienced white male applicants. Exclusionary qualifications for apprenticeship acceptance—such as age, education, special training, years of work, police record—remain in effect, and the goals for employment of minority-group members as set by federal guidelines or policies still permit practices that result in de facto concentration of the formerly excluded in the less desirable positions (Derryck, 1972).

More immediately effective than training and outreach programs in developing job opportunities have been the governmental programs aimed directly at discriminatory patterns. Economic sanctions (e.g., refusal to grant government contracts, conditional financing) can be used in such a manner that competition between contractors provides incentives for developing a program of positive inclusion of minorities. Whereas outreach programs accept the structural restrictions of unions and industry and "help industry out" by trying to help minorities meet those standards, the use of government legal and economic sanctions places the restrictions on business firms, which prove to be capable of helping themselves out by changing the structure of their employment practices.

Potentially effective means for thus challenging discrimination in industrial concerns and unionized employment exist in the form of laws, directives, and governmental agencies that have been mandated to generate and enforce anti-discrimination and affirmative action programs.[3] But there often is a formidable gap between program objectives and effective action. Implementation of such programs, it appears, often has been lacking or minimal. Federal agencies charged with monitoring compliance often do not have staffs adequate to conduct field investigations, meetings, and site inspections. Although all federal contracts have mandatory clauses regarding nondiscrimination, enforcement often has been minimal: "Contractors will readily agree to comply with the affirmative action clauses in federal contracts because they are totally aware of the historic failure of the agencies to use their sanctioning powers against the contractors" (Derryck, 1972, 16).

Yet properly administered programs prove that "success stories" are possible. The Cleveland Plan is one example:

> When strictly enforced, affirmative action does not have to be tokenism and voluntary compliance. Action in Cleveland is a perfect example. In the spring of 1967, all federal agencies acted in concert to enforce affirmative action requirements under Executive Order 11246. . . . Through the use of "manning tables" about 300 minority group people were committed to work on . . . construction. Of the 300 commitments, the Area Coordinator can already account for 255 persons who have worked in the mechanical trades on jobs as a result of "manning tables" over a three year period (Derryck, 1972, 17-18).

Under a similar plan in Philadelphia, an inventory in 1971 showed that the goals for minority employment had been met or exceeded for five of the six crafts included. The distinctive features of these two city-wide programs were: (1) coordinated action on the part of the implementing federal agencies (with adequate staff resources); (2) clear definition of the minority groups addressed; (3) assignment of direct responsibility to specific crafts lacking "significant minority representation"; (4) the requirement that an affirmative action program be submitted as part of a clearly outlined compliance process; (5) setting of binding goals for minority employment; (6) basing federal standards on a formula that took into account the state of the craft and its relation to minorities; (7) rejection of bids that failed to meet the standards set (enforcement of sanctions); and (8) carrying out a follow-up procedure to ensure compliance.

The net effect of these procedures was to change "the criterion of discrimination from specific intent in each case to numerical results" (Derryck, 1972, 18).

The burden of proof was thus shifted from the individual or group claiming discrimination to the union or contractor. Intent to discriminate is no longer the issue, but whether or not discrimination exists and whether affirmative integration has been achieved, or at least genuinely attempted.

5. Affirmative Action and Its Further Complications

Examples of the effectiveness of programs using legal and economic incentives and penalties in reducing long-established discriminatory barriers have commended "affirmative action" to many persons who believe in equality of opportunity. For remedying strongly entrenched discrimination, some positive action beyond merely nominal opening of employment and educational channels is indeed essential. At the same time, a realistic view must be alert to possible hazards and undesired effects, along with the desired outcomes. Thus although nondiscrimination and equal opportunity in employment are intended goals of civil rights legislation and administrative action of government, the methods by which nondiscrimination mandates are enforced may lead directly not only to preferential hiring but also to fixed quotas (van den Berghe, 1971; Seligman, 1973; Glazer, 1975; Stanfield, 1975).

To better understand the intense controversies that have arisen over affirmative action requirements it is helpful to review the recent historical background.

Recall that from 1954 until 1964, both the federal executive and the Congress agencies avoided any major commitment to desegregation of the public schools as initiated by the *Brown* decision in 1954. (The spasmodic and reluctant use of federal troops to counter open official defiance does not contradict the generalization.) In the face of highly organized and massive segregationist pressures, federal judges in the South after 1957 retreated to a position of approving long delays and token desegregation. The Supreme Court, too, had affirmed pupil-placement laws that sanctioned token desegregation. It was the lack of tight constraints in the Court's decisions that delegated major responsibility to the district courts. The wide latitude for interpretation provided by vague and ambiguous rulings left district judges exposed to strong and varied pressures to accommodate the new rulings to local practices and segregationist views.

Only with the decisive national actions represented by the Civil Rights Act of 1964 and the Voting Rights Act of 1965 was this impasse surmounted. During the subsequent years policies have moved from "civil rights" to "equal opportunity" to "affirmative action." It was the continuing lack of substantive equality of access to education and employment and the evasions and violations of new legal rules that led directly to administrative actions to ensure social change.

Policies of requiring inclusion of individuals from designated categories in education and in employment in proportion to their representation in some larger population have been labeled as affirmative actions, compensatory action, preferential (or benign) quotas, or reverse discrimination — according to the policy preferences of the labeler.[4] An illustrative case is the Department of Labor Order No. 4 (January 1970; revised, December 1971) under which it was not sufficient for employers to demonstrate nondiscrimination and "good faith" hiring; rather, employers were required to show results and to prove that their testing and other admission procedures were essentially related to job performance.

"Affirmative action" in employment, education, and other fields can take either a weak or a strong form. The so-called weak form need not necessarily be ineffective, for it can involve active search, recruitment, advertising, and special aids. However, the strong forms go further by mandating statistical requirements—in effect, minimal quotas. Under some circumstances, such requirements may result in displacement of achievement as a basis for admissions, hiring, promotions, and the like. When affirmative action takes a strong form, it sets goals for hiring based on estimates of potential recruits in selected populations in relation to anticipated total accessions. In practice it has been applied primarily to blacks, women, Spanish-surname, Native American, and Oriental-origin populations. When employment opportunities are regarded as a fixed number, affirmative action can evoke the charge that it involves discrimination against other population categories. Observe this complaint of a sociologist concerning university practices:

> Affirmative Action clearly requires violations of the U. S. Constitution and libertarian ideology. Without preferential treatment, "Affirmative Action" would be an empty slogan instead of a departure from recent federal policy. . . . Face it—the *intention* of Affirmative Action includes "discriminating against" white males—and what should we expect of its consequences? In short, Affirmative Action is a conspiracy to deprive of civil rights, and that is the main objection to it (Stanfield, 1975, 49).

Again we see that social changes, in their turn, affect evaluative criteria. Observe the case of "objective testing" as a procedure for appraising "merit." Various types of aptitude and performance tests have long been widely used in the United States in selecting and training individuals. One manifest goal has been to establish objective criteria of merit—to base "equality of opportunity" on universalistic tests of accomplishments and capabilities. Sharp challenges to testing and testing procedures have been appearing in recent years, based on the contention that paper-and-pencil tests of any kind work to the disadvantage of blacks and some other racial and ethnic minorities. Meanwhile, even as psychologists and psychometricians have intensified their long-standing efforts to improve reliability, validity, and consistency of use and interpretation, the courts are acting. The accumulating case decisions have raised the possibility of widespread abandonment of testing as a basis for employment and promotion (Holden, 1975).

Two criteria are involved in appraising the appropriateness of employee selection procedures in relation to Title VII of the Civil Rights Act of 1964 (and the Tower amendment thereto): (1) the procedures must be nondiscriminatory; (2) they must not have an "adverse impact," i.e., must not disqualify a disproportionate number of minority-group applicants. If a testing procedure is shown to have adverse impact, the employer may be required to show that the procedures and standards used are indeed specifically "job related."

The Supreme Court in *Griggs v. Duke Power Company* (1971) held that the employer's requirement of a high school education or a passing score on a standard IQ test resulted in disproportionate elimination of black applicants and had not been demonstrated to be validly job related. Subsequently, the Court ruled in *Moody v. Albermarle Paper Company* (1975) that the company's test validation procedures were inadequate and went on to state that if a valid test has adverse impact, an alternative procedure should be sought.

From the standpoint of the latest and best research, it is true, the tests involved in the two cases just cited were not particularly good. But the legal precedents that are being established may destroy uniform testing even of the best types and thus bring about a reversion to interviews. The latter practices are known to be highly unreliable, are likely to lead to informal quotas, and are open to intrusion of prejudices and particularistic favoritism. Further, recent validation studies indicate that the best job-related tests, in fact, do not discriminate against blacks—if anything they predict job performance somewhat more accurately for black than for white applicants.

The crux of the dilemmas we are reviewing is that *providing current equality of opportunity for individuals may nevertheless result in gross differentials in aggregate rewards for members of a previously disadvantaged social category*. Thus the phrase "equal employment opportunity" can come to mean not just evenhanded assessment of formal qualifications of individuals but proportionate representation of an entire social category in hiring, promotions, and other job-related conditions. With this shift in meaning, what is actually at issue is a categorical quota system, that is, substantive equality rather than formal equality of opportunity.

It is difficult to see how the rule of substantive equality ("equality of condition") can be tucked into the old rubric of equality of opportunity. A different principle, or set of principles, is being invoked. Essentially the newer thrust is based on an implicit doctrine of categorical compensation or "reparations": past disadvantages imposed upon entire strata or social collectivities are to be rectified by compensatory treatment in the present.

Carried to logically conceivable extremes, the "fair share" doctrines would mean that every category of individuals now disadvantaged by past discrimination could claim compensatory treatment. In that circumstance, there would appear to be no alternative to a comprehensive system of categorical goals or quotas. At most, current individual attainments would be of quite secondary importance.

We have long been familiar, of course, with remedial or compensatory programs to make opportunity really accessible to persons who have been disadvantaged by social environment. And the conception of social responsibility to reallocate and redistribute goods is likewise commonplace and is institutionalized to some extent in taxation policies, income transfers, and the provision of public goods and services.

When affirmative action is conceived as just such a remedial program, it poses no new issues in principle. It simply combines the principle of equality of opportunity with a sense of humanitarian obligation. But a new situation does emerge if and when affirmative action should become institutionalized on the basis of a formal right to *categorical allocations* of societal resources and rewards on the basis of ethnic membership, sex, age, or other status considerations. To the extent that such institutionalization should become permanent, the obvious outcome would be a rigid system of ascribed or assigned statuses. Then, the right of any particular individual to an education, to a job, to a political office, and so on would depend upon birth in or assignment to a fixed social category. The more explicit the categorical rules and the more extensive their application, the more likely it is that the result would be a new system of rigid group alignments.

As we have emphasized already, a society of ascribed status groupings contending for scarce resources and rewards is a *plural* society in which the processes of allocation and distribution necessarily become highly politicized. Such societies can, and do, exist, but it is difficult for them to retain an effective parliamentary democracy. To avoid the rigidity that arises from group claims and the consequent intensity of political conflict requires that individual qualities and attainments not be set aside as bases for social placement and reward. Affirmative action is compatible with a retained emphasis on individual achievement, although undoubtedly short-term compromises are unavoidable, so long as "quotas" are used as measures and instruments, not as fixed allocations. To the extent that status membership per se is used categorically and regardless of competitive performance, we invite subsequent political counteraction.

Millions of individuals in our society have been disadvantaged by reason of systematic violations of the very same criteria of universalism and achievement that are now being invoked to criticize affirmative action. Much of the criticism is correctly perceived by minorities as a sham, as a hypocritical response rendered blatant by the clear evidence of politicized status-based allocations of reward and privilege in the past to white males from high socioeconomic strata. It is also a valid observation that the recent movement toward enlarged opportunity and more evenhanded justice has been based in part upon appeals to principles to universalism and achievement. Universalistic norms take the individual—not a collectivity or social category—as the unit to which rules are to be applied. What would happen to minorities in the second round and subsequent political contests if group particularism were to become the primary basis of allocations of social rewards, rights, privileges, duties, obligations, immunities, and disabilities? To avoid extreme reactions, social policies will have to steer a delicate course between affirmative action needed to reduce effects of past discrimination and the continued use of universalistic criteria of performance.

6. The Case of Desegregation

We have just seen a few of the considerations that make remedial policies in the field of employment a complex matter. Similar considerations are found in efforts to eliminate racial and ethnic segregation.

Many myths about the consequences of desegregation have been conclusively shattered by the experiences of the years since World War II. We have recovered to some extent a lost segment of our history. We know that categorical racial segregation was neither necessary nor practicable in the pre-Civil War South. Nor did enforced public segregation develop quickly after Reconstruction—indeed, it required a full generation. Between the Bargain of 1876 (that returned political control of the South to white southerners) and the Supreme Court's endorsement of segregation in the *Plessy* case in 1896, public segregation was not a dominant system. As C. Vann Woodward (1957) has shown, for the first twenty years after Reconstruction, formal segregation was not salient in public life.

As we documented in Chapters 1 and 4, stable interracial integrated communities do exist in substantial numbers in the United States. One more example may be useful: a highly successful instance has been described in detail by Hesslink. In a rural county in southwestern Missouri containing 10 percent blacks, blacks and whites routinely participate in integrated mutually acceptable relations in schools, business and professions, public facilities, and political life. There are separate churches and residential clustering exists. Informal social relationships tend to be separate. But no discrimination is found in public social life, close relationships are formed among children, and blacks and whites interact easily and in a matter-of-fact way in everyday community affairs. The local community was first established by Quakers in the 1820s, who accepted and aided fugitive slaves from the South. The early establishment of economic and social equality has been maintained, under conditions of demographic and social stability. Long-term understandings and relationships protect the continuation of mutually satisfactory accommodations (Hesslink, 1968).

Current blockages of residential integration show that "class" often is more crucial than "race"—as, indeed, is true also of school desegregation. Of course there are local communities in which mixed-income residential areas and housing development have been successful. But generally, separation by income (rental) levels is the rule. Furthermore, much "income segregation" is maintained by local authorities' use of zoning and other forms of legal coercion. As we noted in Chapter 4, court actions to open local areas for racially mixed populations are in a state of rapid development, and decisive trends are difficult to discern (Hirschhorn, 1976, 387-88, 430). But "while there have been many successes in overturning one or another kind of denial to build— what seems to be determinative in preventing a major legal break-through is that while racial groups are constitutionally protected categories that cannot be excluded, income groups are not, and may be excluded" (Glazer, 1974, 108). Continued local resistance to opening up middle-income suburbs to housing for low-income families must be expected (Rothbart, 1976).

Outside of the South, where suburbs often include rural areas containing many low-income black families, the black population in suburbs differs from that in central cities in having higher incomes, higher occupational status, more home ownership, and lower percentage of households with female heads. Suburban black populations tend to be "middle class"; the suburbs are not new low-income ghettos. Further, within the heterogeneity of the central city the most recent years brought rising incomes among blacks and some desegregation of formerly all-white areas.

What seems clear amid all the complexity are three main points. First, strong legal provisions exist to bar racial or other categorical discrimination in housing and property transactions. The two main statuatory sources are the Civil Rights Act of 1866 and Title VIII of the Civil Rights Act of 1968 (Hirschhorn, 1976, 430-33). Under the latter provision, an aggrieved person may (1) file complaints with the Department of Housing and Urban Development, (2) bring a lawsuit in federal district court or in the appropriate state court; in addition, the attorney general may sue to enforce Title VIII under certain conditions (Hirschhorn, 1976, 433-35). Second, as Chapters 1 and 4 showed, residential desegregation is feasible and does occur, although it requires open housing and appropriate market conditions (e.g., relatively high income of minority families, in combination with available housing). Third, stable integration requires removal of real or imagined threats to property values, social status, and "quality of life."

In both residential and educational desegregation, we have noted repeatedly, the fact that the consequences are complex always implies that some will be desired by some persons, undesired by others. In all cases, we must seek to appraise *net* effects. Just as affirmative action in employment has mixed consequences, so integration of schools is not utopia. But desegregation has had numerous important successes, as we saw in Chapter 3. As new evidence continues to come in (St. John, 1975), an extensive inventory has accumulated of specific practicable means that have been used to make desegregation produce outcomes that will be positively valued by nearly all parents except those to whom segregation is a good in itself. As a further reminder of points covered in Chapter 3, we note as an illustration a detailed study of large samples of pupil histories as of 1970-71 and 1971-72 in the Philadelphia School District, which showed the following effects of racial mixing in the schools:

1. *"All elementary school students in the sample benefited in terms of achievement when they were in schools where the percentage of Blacks about equalled the percentage of non-Blacks. . . .*
2. *For Black and non-Black students in the junior high sample there is a very slight positive effect in attending schools ranging up to half Black"* (Summers and Wolfe, 1975, 16). (At higher levels of black proportions, blacks increase their learning but whites experience some learning declines.)
3. In the senior high samples, no significant impact on blacks or non-blacks was found but the narrow range of variation precludes any definitive assessment.

School integration can be and has been attained. Of course it will be attained only if the knowledge of effective means is used with skill and commitment. Where the commitment exists and the best available knowledge about educational procedures is used, we observe skillful adaptations of such techniques as team teaching, learning in interdependent groups, group rewards for group achievements, varied and differentiated materials and methods. In such cases, integrated schools in the long run can be made to produce effective learning (Summers and Wolfe, 1975), social skills and insights, and integrative norms and relationships. And in any case, desegregation in the American situation has been of incalculable but very great symbolic and legal significance. It was one of the more important early signals that institutional racism must be repudiated if major American values are to be preserved. In this sense:

> The primary value of the Supreme Court decision on school desegregation was not its contribution to education, but its embodiment of the doctrine that the government of the United States of America is in opposition to the theory of white supremacy. The climate of racism rises and falls with attitudes of government leaders toward the implementation of this policy (Comer, 1975, 215).

Strong positive leadership from national officials of government supporting policies of integration almost certainly would have greatly reduced the disturbances, ostensibly related to busing, in several large cities in the mid-1970s.

7. Pluralism and Assimilation

In spite of enormous costs in its earlier phases, ethnic assimilation in the United States has been accomplished on a scale to stagger imagination and in a manner that has protected the nation against the fiercer communal politics of most plural societies. Still more specifically — by the criteria not only of cultural assimilation but also of economic and political integration — certain parts of the society represent especially striking examples of what is possible in large-scale intergroup relations. Note these facts about the state of Hawaii:

1. Ninety percent of the citizens in 1970 were U.S.-born natives.
2. Nearly all are literate in English; 75 percent regard American English as their "mother tongue."
3. Incomes of Chinese-American and Japanese-American families are above those of whites; if military families are excluded, white incomes actually are lower than those of "pure" Hawaiians.
4. The public school system always has been integrated.
5. Interethnic marriages are over one-third of all marriages (38 percent in 1965).
6. Political participation is shared among the major ethnic groupings.

What has happened in Hawaii is to some degree unique, but the processes observable there demonstrate what is possible. Less dramatically and more slowly, ethnic groupings on the mainland also have blurred and merged. For example:

> Churches initially tended to be organized among people who came from the same community or region; their larger organizations were formed along national lines. Swedes, Norwegians, Danes, and Germans organized different Lutheran churches. German, Irish, Italian and Polish Catholics formed around their own language parishes and with churches named for their own national patron saints. Over the years these patterns changed. Individual parishes became more mixed in ethnic background, and nationality groupings gave way to broad denominational groupings. The change was slow but persistent (Hays, 1973, 11-12).

In general, we believe the following generalizations are valid.

1. The greater the mutual communication among the members of a social system, the greater the capacity to resist external pressure or internal conflict without disruption of the system of interaction.
2. In any group or society, the greater the range of role-experiences of the participants, the greater the identification with and commitment to the goals and values of the group or society as a whole.

3. The greater on the average the experience of each of the participants in a social system with the roles of others in the key communication points, the more rapid and effective will be the flow of communication.

4. The greater the integration of individuals into a primary ingroup (in terms of frequency of interaction and of identification with the group), the more attenuated will be the identification of the members with more inclusive groupings or systems.

5. The uncertainty of role-relations will be greatest in the role-intersections that occur least frequently, if the importance of the interaction is equal and the total number of persons involved is the same.

   Corollary: Infrequently occurring role-intersections tend not to be culturally transmitted and remain problematic with each new occurrence.

Modern national states are political associations successfully maintaining a claim to a monoply of certain kinds of binding decisions and especially those concerning the use of organized violence within a territory. To be successful, the claim must be recognized by other states that are in a position to contest it by force. Success also requires a relatively high degree of exclusive loyalty of the resident population. State authorities universally will be reluctant to accept large numbers of immigrants who continue to maintain strong loyalties to other nation-states. Thus it is to be expected that the status of resident aliens always is a delicate problem, and that state-societies are likely to exert influence to reduce or otherwise control the involvements and commitments of subjects and citizens to other nation-states. When ethnicity is identified with national origin, the symbolic link between "foreigner" and the image of "untrustworthy" or "subversive" sojourner is facilitated. Any condition that reduces the traditional imagery of threat will facilitate positive ethnic relations.

"Structural integration" may be a useful label for the condition, and the processes leading it, in which members of a culturally distinct group or category enter into unimpeded participation in economic, political, and general public life. The same label fits the anomalous case of a historically designated "racial" minority—black Americans.

Structural integration is favored, as a general rule with some exceptions, by both concrete similarity of culture (e.g., language, religion, material life-style) and by social isomorphism (Francis, 1952, 1954, 1956), e.g., level of formal education, urban experience, generic occupational skills and knowledge (e.g., working with people or things, degree of self-direction and self-discipline, complexity of knowledge required). Of the two, social isomorphism seems the more important, at least under the conditions found in twentieth-century industrialized societies. In the American experience the integration of immigrants was not greatly handicapped by a radically different background of language (Japanese, Czechoslovakian, Arabic, Greek, Hebrew), of religion (Shinto, Buddhist, Orthodox), or of initial life-styles. But unskilled, rural, uneducated immigrants will face great difficulties even if otherwise quite similar to the host society in general culture.

In the American case, the historical record shows that the peaks in nativistic, ethnocentric sentiments and in overt discrimination and conflict came on the heels of periods of very large influx of visibly different immigrants, or lagged behind only until the newcomers came into obvious and frequent competition with the "established" population.

Anti-Jewish reactions are especially instructive. Until the 1840s such responses were relatively rare and mild. The rapid growth of a new German Jewish population evoked a sharp increase in negative attitudes. A second wave of anti-Jewish sentiment came in the 1870s and after, as upwardly mobile Jews came into competition with "possessors of privilege" (Higham, 1966, 245). And occupational and educational discrimination became widespread from about 1916 through World War II as the sons and daughters of the first generation moved into business and professional arenas of competition. Similar patterns characterized responses to the Irish in the nineteenth and early twentieth centuries.

Anti-foreign and anti-immigration responses were affected deeply, of course, by changes in international relations, including wars. And the peaks of nativistic antipathy and discrimination tended to coincide with the valleys of economic depression. Fears of foreign influence and fears of being overwhelmed by competition were emphasized and played upon by every nativistic movement. Both fears were accentuated by rapid social change and by periods of international and domestic political crisis.

Much of the social structural bases of prejudices and discrimination against persons on the basis of national origins have disappeared or have been greatly weakened since the end of World War II. Although ethnicity remains durable and important, even the surface aspects of assimilation reduce visibility and provide relatively easy modes of public interaction. Lines of cleavage among hyphenated American sectors have become blurred and permeable, e.g., intermarriage is widespread. Although the absolute amount of immigration remains very high, the percentage of the population constituted by recent immigrants is no longer anywhere near the level that could reactivate anxieties of being "submerged in a sea of aliens." It seems likely that generalized prejudice is less and less crucial; specific policies and relationships correspondingly move to a central position.

The public salience of ethnicity, as well as the significance of ethnic origins in political and economic life, has fluctuated greatly from time to time. In spite of strong upsurges in recent years, the longer-term trends have been away from ethnic exclusiveness and toward greater cosmopolitanism.

> The persistence of some ethnic characteristics can conjure up notions of an unchanging ethnic world throughout American history. . . . But if we go beyond the impressions of the moment to the bench-marks of history, the overwhelming fact is the capacity of American society to erode ethnic characteristics and ethnic identity throughout its almost four centuries of invasion by immigrants (Hays, 1973, 15).

Recent developments in empirically grounded sociological and psychological theory throw serious doubt upon the easy assumption that close similarity of culture is either a necessary or a sufficient condition for mutually acceptable, harmonious intergroup relations. Much immigration policy in countries around the world has been based on exactly that assumption, which surely seems obviously true to common sense and has been very convincing in the realms of high national policies (Richmond, 1967, 3).

Yet the assumption, although it contains a partial truth, is fundamentally misleading. Similarity often does facilitate cooperation and solidarity: it does so primarily through the rewarding character of consensus as such, and through the reduction of interference-effects and mal-coordination of interaction. But the most important factor is not similarity per se but rather the circumstances which make it *rewarding*. And it is *interdependence* rather than *sheer similarity* that produces much of the essential collaboration in all complex societies. Both consensus and complementarity are important but we often can dispense with homogeneity in favor of mutually advantageous heterogeneity.

Furthermore, nominal similarity may be deceptive. Kimura (1957) has shown the disintegrative effects upon marriages of Japanese-American soldiers to Japanese brides of certain unfounded assumptions of cultural similarities. Richmond (1967, 265) documents the following nonobvious conclusion:

> However, the similarity between the British way of life and that of Canada, far from making it easier to absorb British immigrants in Canada, actually made it more difficult. British immigrants . . . were more likely to retain close links with their former country. . . . Those who retained the same occupational status as in their former country and who, therefore, had been compelled to make only a minimum adjustment to the Canadian way of life were more likely to identify closely with their former country.

Even at the level of small-scale working groups, complementarity of function often is more conducive to effective collaboration than is generalized similarity of status or of culture (Gross, 1956; Turk, 1963).

Human societies are complex networks of continually changing relationships. Their stability or change is the problematic outcome of diverse and subtle processes. Where effective collaborative functioning occurs, it is not the outcome of one master factor or process, such as "consensus" or "power." Rather it emerges from *varying combinations* of (1) cultural similarity and consensus; (2) advantageous interdependence, based on economic, political, and other types of differentiation; (3) power and authority; (4) interpersonal attachments and reciprocities. For a society such as the United States in the 1970s it would seem wise policy to refrain from insisting that any item of culture be made a matter of conformity unless dire necessity compels it.

> *Proposition 1:* At the same time, the political tranquility of this type of society depends upon the effective inclusion of all racial, ethnic, religious, and class elements of the population in a basic community of political and civil liberties, rights, and duties. Also, it can avoid serious internal cleavage and alienation only by agreement on reasonable limits of the exercise of power and by agreement on means of regulating and settling collective conflicts.

Some general implications of this line of analysis are fairly clear and basic. Ethnic attitudes and behavior are crucially shaped by, and acquire their human significance in, a definite societal setting. It is through intelligent and humane policies in our major institutions — political, economic, educational, medical, and so one — that many so-called ethnic problems will be exacerbated or reduced.

> *Proposition 2:* Above all, rewarding coexistence calls for creating and maintaining maximum opportunities for interethnic interaction in the joint accomplishment of shared objectives.

8. Social Change and Resistance in Intergroup Relations

It is "utopian" to expect that major changes in the relationships of ethnic collectivities will be equally welcome to all the persons affected. It is utopian to believe that moral exhortation alone will lead individuals to give up socially shared advantages. It is utopian to expect that merely offering correct information will drive out widely accepted misinformation (e.g., racial stereotypes).

It is realistic, however, to recognize that no set of social arrangements ever is immutable, that change is continuous, that denial of full membership in a societal community to large ethnic populations in a modern democracy spells trouble. It is realistic to search for ways to facilitate the less costly rather than the more costly types of social change. Even in the most far-reaching revolutions, life goes on from day to day and *specific* problems have to be met; generalized ideologies do not remove the necessity for thousands of detailed decisions for coping with the inescapable exigencies of social survival. Short of massive revolution, the generalization is even more cogent: limited reforms involve a continuous need to appraise sources of incentives to initiate or accept change, sources of resistance to change, and the consequences of change.

This is not the place for any extended discourse on the generic features of social change. Only a few central issues need attention.

The origins of change in intergroup relations very frequently have nothing to do with intergroup relations. This is a shorthand way of saying that racial and ethnic relations often are primarily shaped by values and interests that are "nonethnic"—changes in technology (the cotton gin; mass production techniques), in economic opportunities, in feasibility of suburban living, in international politics, and so on indefinitely.

Within the narrower class represented by changes originating in the facts of intergroup relations themselves, a primary locus of change lies in the socio-cultural conditions that produce organized reactions to collective *relative deprivation* (Williams, 1975b). In particular, organized efforts to change social allocations are favored when a large collectivity sees itself as arbitrarily blocked from achieving advantages enjoyed by other comparable collectivities.

Change in the positions of collectivities has effects both through differences in *sequences* and through *processes of comparison carried through time*.

Thus the same objective "reward" (or "penalty") will have different effects in different sequences. A succession of rewards produces lowered incremental value of added units (e.g., $+ + + +$), whereas the same positive stimulus produces higher gratification when it follows a series of negative stimuli (e.g, $- - - +$) (Gergen, 1969, 41-49).

Furthermore, changes in the relative positions of individuals and other social units always constitute social signals. Such signals not only indicate a current state of affairs but also affect expectations and aspirations. A special case of this signaling property is what Hirschman (1972, 2-6) calls the "tunnel effect." If two lines of automobiles are stopped in a tunnel and one finally begins to move, the initial reaction of drivers in the lane still stalled is not relative deprivation and resentment but relief and hope ("my turn will come soon"). Only if one's own movement is then inordinately delayed does the positive mood give way to frustration, irritation, moral outrage, and so on. Hirschman suggests, for example, that poor people in developing countries initially accept the existence of vast inequalities in income in the belief that eventually they themselves also will benefit from economic development. But the tunnel effect is temporary. If hope is deferred time after time, while others move ahead, disillusionment is likely to be marked and the sense of relative deprivation especially strong (cf. Zolberg, 1968).

Actual historical social movements typically represent a complex interaction of the factors we have examined. Cases in point are numerous. An almost classic large-scale instance is that of "actual gains and psychological losses" among black Americans between 1945 and 1965.

Open-class societies of increasing affluence tend also to experience an initial weakening of segmentary social structures and of insulating barriers to emulation and invidious comparisons (Duesenberry, 1967; Eisenstadt, 1971, 79).

Responses of relative deprivation are minimized by: slow social change, low geographic mobility, low education, little exposure to mass media, sharp boundaries between strata and among ethnic groups and local communities, low rates of upward and downward social mobility, and primary importance of kinship as a basis of social organization. Individualized relative deprivation will be high under the opposite set of conditions.

A sense of relative subordination, or fraternal deprivation, is likely to be maximized when distinctive strata and ethnic collectivities are preserved in a society of much mobility and mass communication that is marked by great inequalities and rapid social change. Such a society combines rapid change and high aspirations with rigid structural barriers. Therefore, highly segmented societies provide extremely hazardous conditions for political stability, especially when initial economic growth greatly widens and perpetuates inequalities among classes, regions, ethnic groupings, and the like.

> *Proposition 3:* Collective disturbance, rather than only individual
> resistance, protest, or conflict, will be the more likely, the greater the
> similarity of condition among those deprived and the sharper the
> contrast with some comparison-segment of the society (cf. Melson and
> Wolpe, 1970).

Any society that strongly institutionalizes criteria of technical performance but categorically excludes or discriminates against ascribed-status categories is inviting dissent and conflict.

A review of a wide range of data from many studies (Williams, 1975b) indicates that:

> *Proposition 4:* A sense of relative deprivation as a response to differen-
> tials in the social positions of collectivities is likely to be low when
> inequalities are stable, high when there are large and rapid changes.

"Adjustment" is the major type of response to large-scale, relatively constant inequalities that have existed over one or more generations. Resentment and protest are typical mass responses to large-scale inequalities under conditions of rapid change.

We suggest further that substantial *absolute* changes in societal levels of wealth, income, and power necessarily increase the prevalence of feelings of *relative* deprivation, except under some of the special circumstances of war and revolution. This occurs because large and rapid changes almost never affect all main collectivities and statuses in the same way or equally. Therefore, relative position acquires high visibility and those whose absolute or relative position is worsening will be aware of the differential rates of change. The effects will be greatest when relative worsening comes after enough stability that important segments of the society have built up firm expectations and claims.

But, as we have seen repeatedly in previous chapters, discontent alone is not sufficient to produce collective action. We have noted that unorganized and dispersed masses of discontented people are not in a position to generate effective political pressure. Only through communication and the subsequent emergence of leadership, authority, and division of functions—i.e., organization—can discontent be mobilized and focused into collective dissent, protest, and structured opposition. Revolutions, for example, require not only increased expectations and widespread frustration or threat but also that relative deprivation must be extended over a period long enough to activate organized protest and must strongly affect all or most of the main social formations supporting the political regime (Brinton, 1965; Davies, 1962; Janowitz, 1970; Williams, 1976). Furthermore, the main repressive forces of the regime (primarily the army and the police) must not be overwhelmingly active and committed to quelling any protest—otherwise one will have "abortive" rebellion that will be decisively crushed (Russell, 1974).

On the basis of the total pattern of findings and theories dealing with the effects of collective relative deprivation, the following hypotheses seem valid.

Proposition 5: The deprivations most likely to have the larger effects on subsequent attitudes and behavior involve collective social comparisons rather than only comparisons with internalized standards of the individual.

Proposition 6: Relative deprivations prominently involving power and prestige are more consequential for collective action than those involving primarily other types of scarce values.

Proposition 7: Major effects will be greatest when relative deprivations are (a) sudden, (b) involve widened absolute differences.

Proposition 8: Essential distinctions among types of behavioral outcomes include: (a) individualized adjustments and strivings, (b) primarily expressive short-term collective protest or rebellion, (c) sustained and organized collective action.

Proposition 9: The differential likelihood of the outcomes listed in number 8 a-b-c will be substantially affected by the relative resources and the degree of mobilization of dissenting and resisting collectivities and by the perceived efficacy of control of partisans and authorities over means of action.

Proposition 10: Discontented social elements are most likely to have a sense of high efficacy when (a) their objective resources have been increasing rapidly and (b) the opposing collectivities show weakness or irresolution, (c) intragroup communication is intensive, (d) intragroup consensus is high with regard to both grievances and locus of control.

It follows from the preceding ten hypotheses that a particular constellation of conditions will maximize the likelihood of organized protest and pressure for change.

Proposition 11: Maximum incentives for collective action will exist under the following conditions: (a) there is widespread and severe relative deprivation, especially in (b) prestige or social respect and in political power, which (c) occurs suddenly and results in an increased absolute gap between deprived and advantaged collectivities, when (d) the deprived collectivity is large, commands substantial economic and political resources, has recently increased in relative power, is internally cohesive and is linked by rapid and extensive communication, and when (e) the established regime and other control elements of the society have given signals of weakness, indecision, disunity, or actual encouragement of militant dissent.

In briefest summary, then, these are our reflections on an important set of *conditions producing pressures for change* in intergroup relations. The other side of the equation must also be examined: what are the *sources of resistance to change?* Again, the discussion will be as brief as possible.

Resistance to change may be heightened by ignorance, misinformation, sheer technical difficulties, a pervasive tendency to discount future benefits, or psychological rigidities of various kinds. We must pass over these factors with the mere mention at this time.

More important for present purposes are two closely related sets of conditions: (1) vested interests, (2) threat.[5]

"Interests" refer both to consummatory desires and goals and to the valued means for attaining gratifications. Although particular interests are enormously diverse, many of the most important can be identified readily: subsistence, safety, status. To say that interests are "vested" means that individuals regard certain interests as socially protected—as normal, legitimate, rightful, and properly secure. Examples include jobs, property ownership, political rights, established prestige-rank, pension claims, veterans' benefits, or long-continued subsidies or transfer payments.

Resistance to change seems to be maximized when it is perceived as a threat to one's vested interests. Authority, property, and income are particularly potent vested interests because they represent *generalized means* for obtaining a wide range of important gratifications, from hedonic satisfactions to the social fate of one's children or to the attainment of national purposes.

The bases of resistance to changes that affect vested interests may be summarized in another complex proposition (cf. Williams, 1968-69, 158-59).

Proposition 12:

(a) All social changes that are important (in terms of the values and interests of the social system affected) will redound to the advantage of some members of the society and to the (at least, relative) disadvantage of others. Effects are never wholly uniform.

(b) All long-continued enjoyment of the possession or use of scarce values—such as wealth, income, power, authority, safety, prestige— leads to some conviction of legitimacy on the part of the possessors of privilege. In short, "privilege" comes to be "right"; established advantages become vested interests.

(c) It follows, from (a) and (b), that important social changes always evoke some resistance, and that they are likely to increase the *immediate* likelihood of conflict, even though they may reduce or avoid more serious conflict later.

(d) Important social changes that are initiated, encouraged, or willingly accepted by the politically powerful or economically advantaged elements of a society are, for the most part, changes perceived to be advantageous to those elements. Changes that are particularly likely to be accepted with little resistance are those that produce immediate advantages to the powerful, while the disadvantages are absorbed primarily by unorganized, inarticulate, and hence politically ineffectual portions of the population.

These generalizations, we believe, fit the case of efforts in the United States to secure greater civil, political, educational, and economic rights and opportunities for members of racial, ethnic, or religious minorities (as well as for women, youths and children, the aged, and the handicapped). Supporters of reform typically are not the members of the advantaged groupings whose immediate interests are threatened. When threats are perceived to jobs, promotion, prestige, style of life, opportunities for children, or property values, even the most "liberal" frequently resist the specific change that is seen as threatening their own vested interests (Caditz, 1976; Rothbart, 1976).

A caution is necessary: vested interests incorporate *both* "interests" in the narrow sense of specific advantages (economic, sexual, prestige, power, etc.) *and* value-commitments. A person may accept even a change that reduces his or her immediate self-interest (e.g., increased taxes) on the basis of a value-commitment (e.g., justice or humanitarianism). And a person may reject a proposed change that threatens his or her immediate self-interest even though the change accords with his or her normal criteria of value-judgments, e.g., residential integration or school desegregation through busing. But the two other possibilities in which both self-interest and value-commitments point in the same direction are clear enough, and there are strong social and psychological incentives to move the ambivalent responses into these "congruent" combinations.

Self-Interest Is Favored or Threatened	Congruence with Commitments to Values and Norms	
	+	−
+	Welcomes change	Ambivalently accepts change
−	Ambivalently rejects change	Resists change

The practical implication of this analysis is direct and crucial.

Proposition 13: In general, if reforms of proposals for change are to have a reasonable chance of success, means must be found to avoid posing a *direct* threat of *important* loss to the population that must accept or tolerate the change.

As Rothbart (1976, 364) has illustrated the point: "It is unreasonable to expect whites [or blacks] to endorse social reforms that will cause them to lose their jobs or to suffer a precipitous drop in income. Although this 'principle' appears trivial in the extreme, it also appears to have been ignored in a significant number of instances." To avoid such threats often is difficult but sometimes is feasible — through diffusing any unavoidable costs or disadvantages over a large population, through building-in compensatory advantages, through mobilizing support from an unthreatened majority of the politically effective population. Wherever possible, proposed changes should seek to distribute benefits or minimize disadvantages beyond a narrow "minority" constituency. For example, a national program of job security or nonstigmatizing income maintenance, not limited by race or ethnic membership, may be sought rather than merely "affirmative action" for ethnic minorities. Analogous goals can be formulated for political participation, for residential and housing policies, for educational changes, and so on. The practical details always require blood, sweat, tears, and hard thinking, but the first step is to be clear about the bases of acceptance or resistance (Haberfeld, 1973; Sales, 1973).

9. The Prospects for an Integrated Multiethnic Society

Healthy black and white relationships do exist and their number can be enlarged. . . . These healthy alliances are made of the same stuff all healthy relationships are made of: give and take, sensitivity, mutual demands for trust and respect, and mutual responsibility of a quality that earns trust and respect (Comer, 1972, 219).

An important consequence of the prolonged experience of self-conscious struggle on the part of black people in the United States has been the development of an increasingly sophisticated political culture and organizational resources (Himes, 1973, Chapters 3, 6). It is evident that in any aspiring minority emerging from disadvantaged economic and political circumstances the continuing development of solidarity and of personal and collective discipline and competence is a high priority item in any program of change. Of equal importance on the side of would-be allies of such minority movement is the development of realistic and open relationships—purged so far as possible of false guilt, masochism, and "ego trips" (self-serving needs) (Comer, 1972, 203-8; Dixon and Foster, 1971).

A major part of the upward social mobility of blacks and of their increased integration into economic, political, and educational institutions is a direct result of the efforts of black people themselves—in spite of "white racism" and of "vested interests" of many whites and some blacks in segregated arrangements.

There have been some tendencies to look upon the idea of equality of opportunity as, at best, overly limited and outmoded or, at worst, as a sham and a diversion. We argue, to the contrary, that further movement toward such equality is crucial for the future and could not be repudiated without grave damage to the body politic.[6]

In all democratic societies, some people attach positive value to the principle of *equality*. And the same is true of the principle of *freedom*. But the two values are not the same, and under certain conditions, an emphasis on equality can lead to diminished freedom, and an extreme degree of individual freedom can lead to great inequality.

In all societies, institutions and relationships are governed to some extent both by the principle of *ascription* and by the contrary principle of *individual achievement* (performance). Under the principle of ascription, individuals' places in society are acquired on the basis of birth or by categorical assignment (as men or women; old or young; members of political parties; occupational classes; racial, ethnic, or religious categories, and the like).

The main emphasis in American conceptions of equality consistently has centered on equality of opportunity, as contrasted with equality of condition. The idea of equality of opportunity is so important and so attractive in American society because it represents a possibility of integrating the value of equality with the value of achievement. These partly contradictory values can be regarded as compatible if social rewards are based on meritorious performance and if the opportunity to compete is equally open to all. And the expression "to all" comes to have an increasingly inclusive meaning in a society of citizens rather than subjects.

During the civil rights era, determined effort cleared away many legal and some de facto barriers to full access and participation in the mainstream of American life. After the long period of suppression and enforced inequality from *Plessy* in 1896 to the 1950s, surely the changes of 1945-65 were remarkable, against any realistic historical criteria. But equality of opportunity is still a societal problem for two reasons. One is the reality of continued inequality of rights. The other lies in aspirations and expectations that make the speed of large-scale societal change altogether too slow for what are perceived as life-or-death needs of the present.

Discontent over the pace of change sometimes leads to the judgment that legal change is relatively ineffective, since de facto practices often persist. But it is essential to reject the notion that there is no difference between de jure and de facto segregation or discrimination, or, at least, that "one is just as bad as the other." American history indicates clearly that there are decisive differences. The primary lesson of that history is that inequalitarian systems are most resistant to change when supported by law. Both the influence of *legitimation and the monopolistic claim to exercise binding coercion* are entailed in de jure enforcement. The positive implication also holds true. The enactment or judicial establishment of rules favoring equal opportunity does not, of course, guarantee the intended outcome. (After all, violations and evasions occur to some important extent under nearly all social rules; otherwise, presumably, we would not require that rules be enforced.) But:

Proposition 14: The existence of laws protecting the rights of minorities and court decisions upholding these laws tend, in the long run, to decrease conflict over the rights involved. . . . Whenever there is sufficient flexibility in public attitudes, the abolition of legal discriminations and disabilities in the long run will reduce hostility and conflict (Williams, 1947, 73-74).

Thus far in American history, the establishment of political rights, civil rights, and civil liberties for portions of the national population formerly lacking these rights has been based on a set of values and beliefs present in the founding of the Republic. In every major instance, the rights newly established were already being exercised by the dominant elements of the political community and were then extended to a category of people hitherto denied those rights. In every major instance, the rights were actively sought and demanded against initial resistance (Meier and Rudwick, 1969). By struggling for safety, opportunity, and respect, minorities in the United States have continually recalled the whole society, politically, to the primary principles and the primary dilemmas of values in its institutions. In this way, all of us who now enjoy protections thus gained have benefited from the partisans.

10. Beyond Mutual Accommodation?

We have emphasized in this work that vested interests and established social structures often resist persuasion and inducement, and we have rejected the myth that disadvantaged low-power groups can dispense with threat and other means of constraint. But we have not seen indiscriminate threats nor diffuse violence as effective for purposive social change (Comer, 1972, 211-13). And we have analyzed a large number of modes of action that have some demonstrated efficacy in producing negotiations, reducing barriers and inequities, resolving conflicts, and creating bases upon which mutually gratifying sets of long-term relationships can be established. Respect and collaboration are not brotherly love, but they may be more practicable as goals of effort in intergroup relations in the United States as we move toward year 2000.

Denial or distortion of reality is a common defense against disliked information. It is by all odds the least adaptive and most dangerous of defenses. It has been widely illustrated in the United States—to deny that ethnic differences are important, that stigmatized people are competent and humanly valuable, that injustice exists (by one's own standards), to believe that problems will go away if ignored, that deprived minorities will forever remain subdued, that moral indignation alone will make ill-intentioned people behave well, that every undesired condition is someone's fault. A full listing would put too great a strain on both the reader's and the author's patience. When we speak here—advisedly and loosely—of "prospects for social maturity," we have in mind first and foremost the prospects for enhanced capacities in the American social system to *accept the observable realities of intergroup relations* as a basis for responsible public policies and actions.

Social maturity on the part of an individual person undoubtedly is difficult to define satisfactorily. But a reasonable conception would include characteristics we rather consistently observe in responsible and creative adults: awareness of self and others, ability to consider both short- and long-term needs and values, tolerance of imperfections in self and others, attention to actual conditions and probable consequences of action, self-regulation in terms of a system of values, enduring affirmation of life. Mature persons keep in touch with reality, control much of their own behavior in the service of a set of self-anchored values—and are able to be spontaneous and have fun when it is appropriate.

If some such set of characteristics can be accepted as a rough indication of viable personal maturity, we could look for similar patterns in the beliefs, values, norms, and actual social relationships that are prevalent in a given community or society. Social maturity in the field of intergroup relations could be taken to mean that the main institutions and forms of social organizations are responsive to environmental realities, both physical and social, and express relatively enduring commitments to a system of constitutive beliefs and values. But not mutual accommodation nor cooperation nor societal integration requires either complete consensus or unitary social control. The mature society, as we see it, would devote much attention and substantial resources to social integration, would accept the inevitability of disagreement, opposition, and conflict, and would develop institutionalized modes for expressing claims and grievances and for resolving conflicts.

At the same time that social life offers us opportunities and fulfillments, it presents limitations and constraints. Not everything we wish is possible. But many such things are possible.

We live in the time we have, and do that which is within our powers. Omnipotence is not part of the human condition, anymore than is earthly immortality. Yet no one would suppose that an active concern to strengthen health and preserve life is at all weakened by the inevitability of illness and death. The fact that some basic problems are not solvable, in our time and place, does not imply that we should give up in the face of problems that may be open to at least partial solutions. Erik Erikson has given a physician's view of psychological maturity as being evinced by a disinterested concern with life itself in the face of death itself. A similar attitude seems to us appropriate in dealing with the vicissitudes of social organization and change, of order and of conflict.

Notes

Notes

Chapter 1

1. The annual average for 1966-68 was 346,716; for 1969-72, 371,767; for 1973, over 400,000.

2. Proportion in integrated neighborhoods in 1967 as estimated from National Opinion Research Center data.

3. Proportion outside the South who reported in 1965 that they live or have lived on the same block with a black family.

4. Between 1968 and 1971, increased proportions of black persons in Detroit expressed preferences for all black or mostly black neighborhoods—*and* for mixed neighborhoods. The proportion who said it "makes no difference" declined sharply, from 35 to 18 percent (*Institute for Social Research Newsletter*, Spring 1974, 4).

5. Cf. Daniels, 1972, v: "Less than a generation ago, the accomplishments of the anti-Japanese movement were viewed as great deeds; its leaders held the highest places in the commonwealth (California). Today the last legal vestiges of anti-Orientalism have been wiped from the state's statute books, although *de facto* discrimination lingers on."

6. For a well-balanced review of the changes, both plus and minus, see Levitan, Johnston, Taggart (1975).

7. For cautions, however, concerning possibly misleading implications of conventional methods of comparing data on economic changes among whites and blacks, see Hill (1973).

8. Contrary to a pervasive current of pessimism among many American publicists and commentators in the 1970s, there are cogent arguments that the social and economic programs of the federal government in the 1960s actually did have substantial success in attaining their announced aims. See Levitan and Taggart (1976-77).

Chapter 2

1. The four sets of criteria, of course, describe the Parsonian AGIL model of system-problems: adaptation, goal-attainment, integration, and latency (pattern-maintenance and tension-management) (Parsons, 1966, 1971).

2. The following passage is adapted from the author's article in *Proceedings of the American Philosophical Society*, vol. 118, No. 3, 1970, pp. 217-18.

Chapter 3

1. Representating a classic example of decentralized particularism, the Boston School Committee is wholly independent of the mayor of Boston and of the governor of the Commonwealth of Massachusetts.

2. Note, for example, that in ordering a desegregation plan for Denver, Colorado, in 1974, Judge Doyle created by the court order itself a Community Education Council.

3. To appreciate the complexity, one has only to study the summaries of the voluminous literature presented in Miller and Dreger, eds., 1973; Weinberg, 1970; Pettigrew, 1971.

4. References consulted included: Lipset, 1967; Edwards, 1969; Kamens, 1972; Orum, 1972; Willie and McCord, 1972; Pifer, 1973; Porter, 1974; Wilburn, 1974; Egerton, 1974-75.

Chapter 4

1. The Supreme Court ruled in 1948 that restrictive covenants are nonenforceable in the courts (*Shelley v. Kraemer*). In 1968 the Court ruled that an 1866 law, under the authority of the Thirteenth Amendment, validly bars all private as well as public racial discrimination in sale or rental of real property.

2. Including the following: Gautreaux, 1967; Daley, 1970; Shannon, 1970; SASSO, 1970; Kennedy Park, 1971; Southern Burlington, 1972; Banks, 1972.

3. For example, United States Department of Labor. Office of Federal Contract Compliance. Revised Order 4 (February 5, 1970). "This Labor Department order requires a company with a federal contract operating in a community whose housing policies prevent the company from meeting its equal employment goals to take special corrective action which would promote housing opportunities congenial to successful recruitment of qualified minorities. Such action could entail relocation to another community or working on contract at branch facilities in communities with acceptable housing patterns" (Mary Vance, ed., 1974. *Council of Planning Librarians*, Exchange Bibliography #547, National Committee against Discrimination in Housing. Washington, D.C.: 23.)

For a comprehensive review of legislation and court decisions, see Hirschhorn, 1976.

4. Sections 804 and 813 of the Civil Rights Act of 1968. Further, the Supreme Court in *Jones v. Mayer* (June 1968) reaffirmed the 1866 Civil Rights Act, which says: "All citizens of the U.S. shall have the same right, in every state and territory, as is enjoyed by white citizens thereof to inherit, purchase, lease, sell, hold and convey real and personal property." See U.S. Code, Title 42, Section 1982.

5. For the case of the metropolitan areas of Maryland and Virginia surrounding Washington, D.C., see *The Washington Post*, May 18, 1975: "Black Rise by 110,000 in Suburbs—The pattern of an increasingly black city surrounded by increasingly white suburbs has been broken dramatically in the Washington area since 1970" (cf. Zeul, 1976).

6. For a large set of forthright additional recommendations see: Anthony Downs. 1973. *Opening up the Suburbs, an Urban Strategy for America*. New Haven: Yale University Press.

Chapter 5

1. This disadvantage holds regardless of whether the collectivity's welfare is defined as an aggregation of utilities of subunits or in terms of the functioning of the collectivity, as a whole, as a viable system.

2. Note the somber conclusion of Rabushka and Shepsle (1972) concerning the prospects for survival of parliamentary democracy in ethnically plural societies.

3. This section is adapted from J. M. Conforti, 1974.

Chapter 6

1. A common social-psychological conception holds that attitudes are "enduring, generalized, learned predispositions" that are directional and that have affective, cognitive, and conative (behavioral) components.

2. The Department of Defense maintains a highly active Race Relations Institute for training cadres of specialists who in turn will train officers and enlisted personnel. The Navy has carried out an especially widespread and comprehensive training effort in this field. See for example: System development corporation. 1974. *Navy Race Relations Education, Impact Analysis*. Vols. I and II. TM-(L)-5285/000/00. Santa Monica, California; also: *Racial Awareness Facilitator Training: Training Manual*. Navpers 15254 (preliminary) (n.d. – c. 1974).

3. Since this generalization was advanced in 1947, collective violence has become more common and perhaps less disapproved; however, the proposition still has a point, expecially for small and middle-size cities.

4. Striking effects on behavior can arise from the presence and example of total strangers – stopping to help a motorist, judging length of lines or autokinetic movement in a laboratory experiment, stopping for a "wait" signal, conforming to or violating rules and prohibitions (Abelson and Karlins, 1970, 42-48).

5. "Helping" may be defined as unilateral supplying of valued communication, services, goods, or other resources to another, in the absence of compulsion, threat, or an immediate agreement or understanding for later payment or exchange. It thus differs markedly from "cooperation," which consists of voluntary joint activity to achieve either common or mutually accepted or complementary goals. Studies of helping behavior include: Darley and Latane, 1970; Kaufman, 1970; Berkowitz and Macaulay, 1970; Batson and Darley, 1973; Gaertner in Katz (ed.), 1976.

6. For instance, in many of the early immigrant communities low trust for and lack of access to public agencies of finance and support led to mutual aid societies. The Chinese, Japanese, and Puerto Rican immigrants in particular had highly evolved and traditional revolving funds which enabled them to raise sufficient capital for small businesses and investments.

Chapter 7

1. See Gamson, 1968, 21-32: The latter case is not fully discussed in Gamson's treatment – the case in which neither party is an authority for the other, in the sense of making binding decisions for the larger collectivity represented by the relationship, and each is seeking to influence the other.

2. This study suggests that presence of a weapon may *either* increase *or* decrease aggressive behavior, depending upon whether in the past the person has associated reward or punishment with the symbolic context. (See also Leighton, 1946, 284).

3. Leighton, 1946, 284: *"In the control of human behavior, whether cooperative, apathetic or aggressive, punishment and reward are equally important. . . .* Punishment is most effective when it serves as a guide toward other types of behavior that are rewarded by relief from stress and opportunities to satisfy needs and desires."

4. Blalock says: "It is only under conditions where dominant-group reactions are not likely to materialize that pressure resources can be effectively used by a numerically small minority."

5. For a vivid, detailed description of the persistence and intensity of opposition to initial efforts toward racial desegregation in one southern city, see the first-hand account by Joseph Fichter of the struggle to desegregate the Catholic schools in New Orleans, 1948-56, in Chapter 3, "The Desegregation Project," 76-117, *One-Man Research*.

6. In the case of attempts to organize mass protests, demonstrations, and even more serious tumults, it is especially important to correctly appraise the willingness of police and of paramilitary and military forces to put down protests and uprisings. Without substantial disaffection within the agencies of political authority, effective rebellion is highly unlikely, and even large-scale attempts will be rare (Russell, 1974).

7. Compare this conclusion with Nieburg's observation that many incoherent acts of violence are exploited by insurgent elites as a means of improving their roles or imposing a larger part of their values upon a greater political system (1969, 81).

Chapter 8

1. Thomas C. Schelling, 1973. "Introduction," in Gene Sharp, *The Politics of Nonviolent Action*. Boston: Porter Sargent, p. xxi.

2. *The Random House Dictionary of the English Language*, College Edition, 1968, pp. 1298, 1338.

3. For example, no less than 73 percent of the whites and 52 percent of the blacks had participated in interracial religious organization activities (Jones and Long, 1965, 7-9).

Chapter 9

1. For a sympathetic but incisive and judicious critique of "nonviolence" as a total strategic commitment see Walton, 1971, especially Chapter 4, pp. 77-102.

2. In the small-scale instance of a two-party experiment, a threat to retaliate against noncooperation, when combined with a bid for cooperation and for cooperative reciprocity, increased the joint return of the parties.

3. That is as a guide to practical action rather than as, for example, a useful methodological assumption for scientific work.

Chapter 10

1. "The combination of a high degree of conflict of interest, great social distance, unfavorable personality types in the opponent group, absence of shared beliefs and moral standards, and unsympathetic third parties would make conversion exceedingly difficult."

2. Called *interactive competition* by Weigel, Wiser, and Cook, 1975.

3. These results were found for 5th and 6th grade pupils in desegregated schools in Austin, Texas, even after a busing program had been accompanied by riots in the high schools.

Chapter 11

1. There is no convincing evidence that the mandatory death sentence is an effective

deterrent or that the judicial moratorium on executions after 1967 affected homicide rates. There is evidence that blacks have been disproportionately penalized (data on over 5,000 state-imposed executions over a period of 104 years); blacks more often were executed for lesser offenses, at younger ages, and with appeals (Bowers, 1974).

2. We include blacks, Chicanos, and other Spanish-surname elements, substantial proportions of Asian-Americans, Native Americans, portions of several diverse white ethnic populations, e.g., low-income, working-class Polish-Americans. Nearly all major ethnic categories, of course, are strongly differentiated by income and occupation.

Chapter 12

1. An interesting and theoretically significant exception: the custom of "silent trade," which permits limited exchanges, that are of mutual advantage, between distrustful and potentially violent groups.

2. "The effectiveness of pressure is increased by keeping the objective narrow and making it easy for the adversary to back down" (Fisher, 1971, 166).

3. A third party seeking to resolve a conflict is by definition "interested" in producing peace. To a party who wishes to gain advantage through continuing the conflict, such a third party will not be regarded as impartial.

4. There are some instances, of course, in which one party is so strongly motivated to seek an all-out personal fight that the forbearance of an adversary only increases his/her fury (suggested by Allen D. Grimshaw).

5. Ikle (1968, 119) has made the useful suggestion that negotiations are more likely to be guided by varying *norms* rather than by *fixed rules* — such norms as avoidance of unambiguous lies, of invective, of explicit threats of physical violence, or of deliberate misconstruction of agreements in principle.

Chapter 13

1. Reviewing *Mankind at the Turning Point* (The Second Report to the Club of Rome) in *Science*. 1975. 187:1188.

2. Portions of pages 7-9 and 33-37 adapted from R. Williams. 1975. Attitudes and behavior toward immigrants and ethnic groups. *The New Immigration and the New Ethnicity, Social Policy and Social Theory in the 1970s*, eds. William S. Bernard and Judith Herman, 13-25. New York: American Immigration and Citizenship Conference.

3. Examples of these agencies include the Equal Employment Opportunity Commission, the Department of Justice, the National Labor Relations Board, and the Bureau of Apprenticeship and Training of the U.S. Department of Labor.

4. Title IV of the Civil Rights Act of 1964 has been administered under goals and guidelines formulated by the Department of Health, Education, and Welfare (under Executive Order 11246 of 1965 and 1969). The HEW guides, in effect, called for affirmative allocations, by any agency receiving federal grants and assistance, to handicapped minorities — blacks, Native Americans, Hispanics, some Asian-Americans, and women. Questions inevitably arose about the relation between the rectification of handicaps and the "equal protection of the laws" under the Fourteenth Amendment.

5. *Author's note:* Some thirty-five years of study of intergroup relations have left me with the impression that under most circumstances these are, indeed, the two most important factors to take into account in practical action.

6. Portions of the following pages, 404-5, have been adapted from Williams, 1973, in Rooney, ed., pp. 104-11.

Bibliography

Bibliography

Aaron, H. J. 1972. *Shelter and Subsidies, Who Benefits from Federal Housing Policies?* Washington, D.C.: The Brookings Institution. 238 pp.

Abelson, H. I., Karlins, M. 1970. *Persuasion, How Opinions and Attitudes Are Changed.* New York: Springer. 2nd. ed. 179 pp.

Adam, H. 1971. *Modernizing Racial Domination, The Dynamics of South African Politics.* Berkeley and Los Angeles: Univ. of Calif. Press. 203 pp.

Adam, H. 1973. The rise of black consciousness in South Africa. *Race.* 15:149-65.

Adamek, R. J., Lewis, J. M. 1975. Social control, violence and radicalization, behavioral data. *Soc. Probl.* 22:663-74.

Advisory Committee to the Department of Housing and Urban Development, Report of the Social Science Panel. 1972. *Freedom of Choice in Housing, Opportunities and Constraints.* Washington, D.C.: National Academy of Sciences-National Academy of Engineering. 62 pp.

Aellen, C., Lambert, W. E. 1969. Ethnic identification and personality, adjustments of Canadian adolescents of mixed English-French parentage. *Canadian. J. Behavioral Sci.* 1:69-86.

Ahlstrom, W. M., Havighurst, R. J. 1971. *400 Losers.* San Francisco: Jossey-Bass. 246 pp.

Aiken, M., Alford, R. R. 1970. Community structure and innovation, the case of urban renewal. *Am. Sociol. Rev.* 35:650-65.

Aiken, M., Demerath, N. J., III. 1968. Tokenism in the Delta. In *Our Children's Burden*, ed. R. W. Mack, 41-107. New York: Random House. 473 pp.

Alford, R. R. 1972. The political economy of health care, dynamics without change. *Politics and Society.* Winter: 127-64. (Reprinted as Warner Modular Publication. 1973. Reprint 96. 38 pp.)

Alker, H. A., Poppen, P. J. 1973. Personality and ideology in university students. *J. Pers.* 44:653-71.

Allport, G. W., Ross, J. M. 1967. Personal religious orientation and prejudice. *J. Pers. Soc. Psychol.* 5:432-43.

417

Althauser, Robert P., Spivack, S. S. 1975. *The Unequal Elites*. New York: Wiley-Interscience. 204 pp.

Altshuler, A. 1970. *Community Control, The Black Demand for Participation in Large American Cities*. New York: Pegasus. 240 pp.

Amalrik, A. 1970. *Will the Soviet Union Survive until 1984?* New York: Harper & Row. 93 pp.

Amir, Y. 1969. Contact hypothesis in ethnic relations. *Psychol. Bull.* 71:319-42.

Amir, Y. 1976. The role of intergroup contact in change of prejudice and ethnic relations. In *Towards the Elimination of Racism*, ed. P. A. Katz, 245-308. New York: Pergamon Press. 444 pp.

Amir, Y., Bisman, A., Rivner, M. 1973. Effects of interethnic contact on friendship choices in the military. *J. Cross-Cult. Psychol.* 4:361-73.

Anson, R. S. 1974. Southie is my home town. *New Times* (November 15):16-18, 21-24.

Ardrey, R. 1966. *The Territorial Imperative*. New York: Atheneum. 390 pp.

Armor, D. 1972. The evidence on busing. *Public Interest*. 28:612-41.

Aronson, E., Blaney, N., Stephan, C. 1975. Cooperation in the classroom, the jigsaw-puzzle model. Presented at the 83rd Ann. Meet. Am. Psychol. Assoc.

Aronson, E., Lindzey, G., eds. 1968-9. *Handbook of Social Psychology*, Vol. 2. Reading, Mass.: Addison-Wesley. 1226 pp.

Arrow, K. J. 1974. Limited knowledge and economic analysis. *Am. Econ. Rev.* 64:1-10.

Ashmore, R. D., Del Boca, F. K. 1976. Psychological approaches to understanding intergroup conflicts. In *Towards the Elimination of Racism*, ed. P. A. Katz, 73-123. New York: Pergamon Press. 444 pp.

Aurback, H. A., Coleman, J. R., Mausner, B. 1960. Restrictive and protective viewpoints of fair housing legislation, a comparative study of attitudes. *Soc. Probl.* 8:118-25.

Auspitz, J. L., Brown, C. W., Jr. 1974. What's wrong with politics. *Harpers*. 248:51-61.

Baden, M. A., Olsen, M. E. 1974. Legitimacy of social protest actions in the United States and Sweden. *J. Polit. Mil. Sociol.* 2:173-89.

Bailey, R., Jr. 1974. *Radicals in Urban Politics, The Alinsky Approach*. Chicago: Univ. Chicago Press. 187 pp.

Ball-Rokeach, S. J. 1973. Values and violence, a test of the subculture of violence thesis. *Am. Sociol. Rev.* 38:736-47.

Baltzell, E. D. 1966. *The Protestant Establishment, Aristocracy and Caste in America*. New York: Vintage. 429 pp.

Bandura, A., Ross, D., Ross, S. 1963. Imitation of film-mediated aggressive models. *J. Abnorm. Soc. Psychol.* 66:3-11.

Barnes, B. 1974. Groups seek removal of sex stereotyping from children's books. *Raleigh (N.C.) Times*. (October 18).

Barringer, H. R. 1968. School integration in Newark, the public schools. In *Our Children's Burden*, ed. R. W. Mack, 170-84. New York: Random House. 473 pp.

Barron, M. L. 1975. Recent developments in minority and race relations. *The Annals*. 420:125-76.

Barth, E. A. T., Noel, D. T. 1972. Conceptual frameworks for the analysis of race relations, an evaluation. *Soc. Forces*. 50:333-48.

Barth, F., ed. 1969. *Ethnic Groups and Boundaries, The Social Organization of Culture Differences*. Boston: Little, Brown. 153 pp.

Barton, A. H. 1968. The Columbia crisis, campus, Vietnam, and the ghetto. *Public Opin. Quart.* 32:333-51.

Barton, J., Cohen, B. P., Zelditch, M., Jr. 1966. Status characteristics and expectation states. In *Sociological Theories in Progress*, eds. J. Berger, M. Zelditch, Jr., B. Anderson, 29-46. Boston: Houghton-Mifflin.

Batson, C. D., Darley, J. M. 1973. From Jerusalem to Jericho, a study of situational and dispositional variables in helping behavior. *J. Person. Soc. Psychol.* 27:100-8.

Bavelas, A., Barrett, D. 1951. An experimental approach to organizational communications. *Personnel.* 27:366-71.

Bayton, J. A. 1941. The racial stereotypes of Negro college students. *J. Abnorm. Soc. Psychol.* 36:97-102.

Bayton, J. A., McAlister, L. B., Hamer, J. 1956. Race-class stereotypes *J. Negro Educ.* 25:75-8.

Beers, J. S., Reardon, F. J. 1974. Racial balancing in Harrisburg, achievement and attitudinal changes. *Integrated Educ.* 12:35-8.

Bendix, R. 1963. Concepts and generalizations in comparative sociological studies. *Am. Sociol. Rev.* 28:532-39.

Bendix, R. 1974. Inequality and social structure, a comparison of Marx and Weber. *Am. Sociol. Rev.* 39:149-61.

Benjamin, G. 1974. *Race Relations and the New York City Commission on Human Rights.* Ithaca, N.Y.: Cornell Univ. Press. 304 pp.

Bennett, D. C. 1973. Segregation and racial integration. *Annals Assoc. Am. Geographers.* 63-48-57.

Berelson, B., Steiner, G. A. 1964. *Human Behavior, An Inventory of Scientific Findings.* New York: Harcourt, Brace and World. 712 pp.

Berger, C. J. 1973. *Hart et al. v. Community School Board et al.—Report of the Special Master, Part I, The School Plan.* July.

Berger, M. 1952. *Equality By Statute, Legal Controls over Group Discrimination.* New York: Columbia Univ. Press. 238 pp.

Berk, R. A. 1972. The emergence of muted violence in crowd behavior, a case study of an almost riot. In *Collective Violence*, eds. J. F. Short, Jr., M. E. Wolfgang, 309-28. Chicago: Aldine-Atherton. 287 pp.

Berk, R. A. 1974. Performance measures, half full or half empty? *Soc. Sci. Quart.* 54: 762-4.

Berkowitz, L. 1968. Aggression, psychological aspects. In *Internat. Encycl. Soc. Sci.*, ed. D. L. Sills, Vol. 1, 168-174. New York: Macmillan and Free Press. 522 pp.

Berkowitz, L., Corwin, R., Hieronimus, R. 1963. Film violence and subsequent aggressive tendencies. *Pub. Opin. Quart.* 27:217-29.

Berkowitz, L., Macaulay, J. R., eds. 1970. *Altruism and Helping Behavior, Social Psychological Studies of Some Antecedents and Consequences.* New York: Academic Press. 290 pp.

Berson, L. 1974. Reading, writing, and ethnic infighting. Magazine section, *The Philadelphia Inquirer* (April 28):11.

Bettelheim, B., Janowitz, M. 1964. *Social Change and Prejudice.* New York: Free Press. 337 pp.

Betz, M. 1974. Riots and welfare, are they related? *Soc. Probl.* 21:345-55.

Billingsley, A. 1968. *Black Families in White America.* Englewood Cliffs, New Jersey: Prentice-Hall. 218 pp.

Blalock, H. M., Jr. 1967. *Toward a Theory of Minority-Group Relations.* New York: Wiley. 227 pp.

Blanchard, F. A., Adelman, L., Cook, S. W. 1975. The effect of group success and failure upon interpersonal attraction in cooperating interracial groups. *J. Pers. Soc. Psychol.* 31:120-30.

Blanchard, F. A., Weigel, R. H., Cook, S. W. 1975. The effect of relative competence of group members upon interpersonal attraction in cooperating interracial groups. *J. Pers. Soc. Psychol.* 32:519-30.

Block, J., Haan, N., Smith, M. B. 1968. Moral reasoning of young adults. *J. Pers. and Soc. Psychol.* 10:183-201.

Blood, R. O., Jr. 1968. *Northern Breakthrough.* Belmont, Calif.: Wadsworth. 157 pp.

Blumenthal, M., Kahn, R. L., Andrews, F. M., Head, K. B. 1972. *Justifying Violence, Attitudes of American Men.* Ann Arbor: Univ. of Mich. Press. 367 pp.

Bohannon, C. T. 1962. Antiguerrilla operations. *The Annals.* 341:19-29.

Bonacich, E., Goodman, R. F. 1972. *Deadlock in School Desegregation, A Case Study of Inglewood, California.* New York: Praeger. 118 pp.

Bontemps, A. 1975. National poll reveals startling new attitudes on interracial marriage. *Ebony.* 30:144-51.

Bopp, W. J. 1971. *The Police Rebellion, A Quest for Blue Power.* Springfield, Ill.: Charles C Thomas. 217 pp.

Borgatta, E. F. 1976. The concept of reverse discrimination and equality of opportunity. *Am. Sociologist.* 11:62-72.

Boulding, K. 1962. *Conflict and Defense, A General Theory.* New York: Harper and Bros. 349 pp.

Boulding, K. E. 1975. Mankind at the turning point. *Science.* 187:1188-89.

Bouma, G. 1970. *Is There a Religious Factor?* Ph.D. dissertation. Ithaca, New York: Cornell Univ. 157 pp.

Bowers, W. J. 1974. *Executions in America, Discrimination and Deterrence and an Inventory of 5,769 State-Imposed Executions.* Lexington, Mass.: D. C. Heath. 176 pp.

Bowser, B. P. 1975. *Black Political Class, The Formation of Political Attitudes among Blacks in New York City.* Ph.D. dissertation. Ithaca, New York: Cornell Univ. 258 pp.

Bracey, J. H., Jr., Meier, A., Rudwick, E., eds. 1970. *Black Nationalism in America.* Indianapolis and New York: Bobbs-Merrill. 568 pp.

Bradburn, N. M., Gockel, G. L., Sudman, S., Noel, J. R. 1971. *Side by Side, Integrated Neighborhoods in America.* Chicago: Quadrangle. 209 pp.

Bradburn, N. M., Sudman, S., Gockel, G. L., with Noel, J. R. 1970. *Racial Integration in American Neighborhoods.* Chicago: National Opinion Research Center. 599 pp.

Bradford, Z. B., Brown, F. J. 1973. *The United States Army in Transition.* Beverly Hills, Calif.: Sage Publications. 256 pp.

Braly, K., Katz, D. 1933. Racial stereotypes of one hundred college students. *J. Abnorm. Soc. Psychol.* 28:280-90.

Brehm, J. 1966. *A Theory of Psychological Reactance.* New York: Academic Press. 135 pp.

Bressler, M. 1960. The Myers case, an instance of successful racial invasion. *Soc. Probl.* 8:126-42.

Brinton, C. 1965. *Anatomy of Revolution.* New York: Vintage Books. 310 pp.

Britt, D., Galle, O. R. 1972. Industrial conflict and unionization. *Am. Sociol. Rev.* 37:46-57.

Brookover, W. B., Erickson, E. L. 1975. *Sociology of Education.* Homewood, Illinois: Dorsey. 425 pp.

Brooks, G. C., Jr., Merritt, M. S., Sedlacek, W. E. 1974. Quality of interracial interaction among university students. Study for the Cultural Study Center. (As reviewed in *Human Behavior*, 1975. 4:38.)

Brophy, I. N. 1946. The luxury of anti-Negro prejudice. *Public Opin. Quart.* 9:456-66.

Brown, B. R. 1971. Saving face. *Psychology Today.* 4:55-9, 86.

Brown, B. S., Albee, G. W. 1966. The effect of integrated hospital experiences on racial attitudes—a discordant note. *Soc. Probl.* 13:324-33.

Brown, S. 1973. Business brisk at housing center. *Oak Leaves.* December 12.

Buckley, W., Burns, T., and Meeker, L. D. 1974. Structural resolution of collective action problems. *Behav. Sci.* 19:277-97.

Bugansky, A. 1959. Certain factors in prejudice among inmates of three ethnic groups within a short-term penal institution. *Dissertation Abstracts.* 19:3360-1.

Bullock, S., III, Braxton, M. V. 1973. The coming of school desegregation, a before and after study of black and white student perceptions. *Soc. Sci. Quart.* 54:132-8.

Bullough, B. 1967. Alienation in the ghetto. *Am. J. Sociol.* 72:469-78.

Bureau of the Census. 1972. *Current Population Reports.* Series P-20: No. 85. Washington, D.C.: U.S. Dept. of Commerce.

Burke, Y. B. 1976. Report of interview. *Focus.* 4:3.

Burkey, R. M. 1971. *Racial Discrimination and Public Policy in the United States.* Lexington, Mass.: D. C. Heath. 144 pp.

Caditz, J. 1976. *White Liberals in Transition.* New York: Halstead Press (Wiley). c. 200 pp.

Cahn, E. 1968. Justice. In *International Encyclopedia of the Social Sciences*, ed. D. L. Sills, 8:341-7. New York: Macmillan and Free Press. 17 vols. 584 pp.

Cain, G. G., Watts, H. W. 1970. Problems in making policy inferences from the Coleman Report. *Am. Sociol. Rev.* 35:228-42.

Campbell, A. 1971. *White Attitudes toward Black People.* Ann Arbor, Mich., Inst. Soc. Res., Univ. of Michigan. 177 pp.

Campbell, A., Schuman, H. 1968. Racial attitudes in fifteen American cities. 1-67. *Supplemental Studies of the National Advisory Commission on Civil Disorders.* Washinton, D.C.: U.S. Govt. Printing Office. 248 pp.

Campbell, A., Schuman, H. 1970. *Racial Attitudes in Fifteen American Cities.* Ann Arbor, Mich.: Inst. Soc. Res., Univ. of Michigan. (4th printing): 67 pp.

Campbell, D. T., LeVine, R. A. 1972. *Ethnocentrism, Theories of Conflict, Ethnic Attitudes and Group Behavior.* New York: Wiley. 310 pp.

Caplow, T. 1953. The criteria of organizational success. *Soc. Forces.* 32:1-9.

Caplow, T., Forman, R. 1950. Neighborhood interaction in a homogeneous community. *Am. Sociol. Rev.* 15:357-66.

Carroll, Lewis (Charles L. Dodgson). *Through the Looking Glass.* In *The Annotated Alice.* New York: Clarkson N. Potter, Inc. p. 206. (345 pp.)

Chambliss, W. J. 1966. The deterrent influence of punishment. *Crime and Delinquency.* 12:70-5.

Chance, M. R. A. 1967. Resolution of social conflict in animals and man. In *Caste and Race, Comparative Approaches*, eds. A. de Reuck, J. Knight, 16-35. London: Churchill. 348 pp.

Chapin, F. S., Howell, J. T., Zehner, R. B. 1974. *Across the City Line, A White Community in Transition.* Lexington, Mass.: D. C. Heath. 249 pp.

Chiles, R. E. 1971. Techniques for lousing up the revolution. *Personnel & Guidance J.* 49:359-60.

Chirayath, V. 1974. *Voluntary Organizations in Action, the Development and Adminis-tration of United Way Budgets.* Ph.D. dissertation. Ithaca, New York: Cornell Univ. 184 pp.

Christenson, J. A., Yang, C. 1976. Dominant values in American society, an exploratory analysis. *Sociol. & Soc. Res.* 60:461-73.

Christmas, J. J. 1973. Self-concept and attitudes. In *Comparative Studies of Blacks and Whites in the United States*, ed. K. S. Miller, R. M. Dreger, 249-72. New York: Seminar Press. 572 pp.

Chudacoff, H. P. 1972. *Mobile Americans, Residential and Social Mobility in Omaha, 1800-1970.* New York: Oxford Univ. Press. 195 pp.

Clark, K. B., Clark, M. P. 1947. Racial identification and preference in Negro children. In *Readings in Social Psychology*, ed. T. M. Newcomb, E. L. Hartley, 169-78. New York: Holt. 672 pp.

Clark, K. E., Miller, G. A., eds. 1970. *Psychology, The Behavioral and Social Sciences Survey.* Englewood Cliffs, N.J.: Prentice-Hall, Inc. 146 pp.

Clark, T. N. 1968. Social stratification, differentiation, and integration. In *Community Structure and Decision-Making, Comparative Analyses*, ed. T. N. Clark, 25-44. San Francisco: Chandler. 498 pp.

Clore, G., Holtzman, W. H., Young, R. K. 1967. Further change in attitudes toward the Negro in a Southern University. In *Research Annual on Intergroup Relations*, eds. C. S. Greenblatt, M. M. Tumin, 20-21. New York: Praeger. 338 pp.

Coates, J. F. 1973. Urban violence—the pattern of disorder. *Annals.* 405:25-40.

Coch, L., French, J. R. F., Jr. 1948. Overcoming resistance to change. *Hum. Relations.* 1:512-32.

Coffman, T., Karlins, M., Walters, G. 1969. On the fading of social stereotypes, studies in three generations of college students. *J. Person. Soc. Psychol.* 13:1-16.

Cohen, D. K. 1974. Segregation, desegregation and *Brown*, a twenty-year retrospective. *Society.* 12:34-40.

Cohen, E. G. 1972. Interracial interaction disability. *Hum. Rels.* 25:9-24.

Cohen, E. G., Roper, S. S. 1972. Modification of interracial interaction disability, an application of status characteristic theory. *Am. Sociol. Rev.* 37:643-57.

Cole, L. A. 1976. *Blacks in Power, A Comparative Study of Black and White Elected Officials.* Princeton, N.J.: Princeton Univ. Press. 267 pp.

Coleman, J. 1957. *Community Conflict.* Glencoe, Ill.: The Free Press. 32 pp.

Coleman, J. S. 1971. *Resources for Social Change, Race in the United States.* New York: Wiley-Interscience. 109 pp.

Coleman, J. S., et al 1966. *Equality of Educational Opportunity.* Washington, D.C.: U.S. Govt. Printing Office. 737 pp.

Coles, R. 1967. *Children of Crisis, A Study of Courage and Fear.* Boston: Little, Brown. 401 pp.

Colle, R. D. 1967. *The Negro Image and the Mass Media.* Ph.D. dissertation. Ithaca, New York: Cornell Univ. 171 pp.

Colle, R. D. 1967. Color on t.v. *The Reporter.* November 30:23-25.

Collins, B. E., Raven, B. H. 1969. Group structure, attraction, coalitions, communication, power. In *Handbook of Social Psychology*, eds. G. Lindzey and E. Aronson, Vol. 4, 102-204. Reading, Mass.: Addison-Wesley. 694 pp.

Colson, E. 1953. Social control and vengeance in Plateau Tonga society. *Africa.* 23:119-211.

Comer, J. P. 1972. *Beyond Black and White.* New York: Quadrangle Books. 272 pp.

Conforti, J. M. 1974. Racial conflict in central cities, the Newark teachers' strike. *Society (Transaction: Soc. Sci. Mod. Soc.).* 12:22-33.

Contini, B. 1967. Threats and organizational design. *Behav. Sci.* 12:453-62.

Cook, S. W. 1970. Motives in a conceptual analysis of attitude-related behavior. In *1969 Nebraska Symposium on Motivation*, eds. W. J. Arnold, D. Levine, 179-231. Lincoln, Nebraska: Univ. Nebraska Press. 17:334 pp.

Cook, S. W., Walkley, R. P., Wilner, D. M. 1952. Residential proximity and intergroup relations in public housing projects. *J. Soc. Issues.* 8:45-69.

Cook, S. W., with Wrightsman, L. S., Wrightsman, S., Nottingham, J. 1971. *The Effects of Unintended Interracial Contact upon Racial Interaction and Attitude Change.* Final Report, Project No. 5-1320, Contract No. OEC-4-7-051320-0273 (Office of Education, U.S. Department of Health, Education, and Welfare), University of Colorado, Boulder. 98 pp.

Coser, L. A. 1956. *The Functions of Social Conflict.* New York: Free Press. 188 pp.

Coser, L. A. 1966. Some social functions of violence. *Annals.* 364:818.

Coser, L. A. 1967. *Continuities in the Study of Social Conflict.* New York: Free Press. 272 pp.

Cox, K. K. 1970. Changes in stereotyping of Negroes and whites in magazine advertisements. *Public Opin. Quart.* 33:603-6.

Crain, R. L. 1968. *The Politics of School Desegregation, Comparative Case Studies of Community Structure and Policy-Making.* Chicago: Aldine. 390 pp.

Crain, R. L. 1970. School integration and occupational achievement of Negroes. *Am. J. Sociol.* 75, Part 2:593-606.

Crain, R. L. 1971. School integration and the academic achievement of Negroes. *Sociol. Educ.* 44:1-26.

Crain, R. L., Weisman, C. S. 1972. *Discrimination, Personality, and Achievement—A Survey of Northern Blacks.* New York: Seminar Press. 225 pp.

Critchley, T. A. 1970. *The Conquest of Violence, Order and Liberty in Britain.* New York: Schocken. 226 pp.

Crombag, H. F. 1966. Cooperation and competition in means-interdependent triads, a replication. *J. Pers. Soc. Psychol.* 4:692-5.

Cuomo, M. 1974. *Forest Hills Diary, The Crisis of Low-Income Housing.* New York: Random House. 209 pp.

Dahl, R. 1970. *After the Revolution? Authority in a Good Society.* New Haven: Yale University Press. 171 pp.

Daniels, R. 1972. *The Politics of Prejudice, The Anti-Japanese Movement in California and the Struggle for Japanese Exclusion.* New York: Atheneum. 165 pp.

Danielson, M. N. 1976. The politics of exclusionary zoning in suburbia. *Polit. Sci. Quart.* 91:1-18.

Darden, J. T. 1973. *Afro-Americans in Pittsburgh, The Residential Segregation of a People.* Lexington, Mass.: D. C. Heath. 96 pp.

Darley, J., Latane, B. 1970. *The Unresponsive Bystander, Why Doesn't He Help?* New York: Appleton-Century Crofts. 131 pp.

Davies, J. 1962. Toward a theory of revolution. *Am. Sociol. Rev.* 27:5-19.

Dean, J. P., Rosen, A. 1955. *A Manual of Intergroup Relations.* Chicago: Univ. of Chicago Press. 193 pp.

Debevoise, E. W. 1968. *Report to Governor Nelson A. Rockefeller of the Governor's*

Committee to Review New York Laws and Procedure in the Area of Human Rights. New York: State of New York. 107 pp.

Demerath, N. J., III, Marwell, G., Aiken, T. 1971. *Dynamics of Idealism, White Activists in a Black Movement.* San Francisco: Jossey-Boss. 228 pp.

Derryck, D. A. 1972. *The Construction Industry, A Black Perspective.* Washington, D.C.: Joint Center for Political Studies. 40 pp.

Deutsch, M. 1949. An experimental study of the effects of cooperation and competition upon group process. *Hum. Relations.* 2:199-231.

Deutsch, M. 1959. Some factors affecting membership motivation in a group. *Hum. Relations.* 12:81-95.

Deutsch, M. 1969. Conflicts, productive and destructive. *J. Soc. Issues.* 25:7-41.

Deutsch, M. 1971. Conflict and its resolution. In *Conflict Resolution, Contributions of the Behavioral Sciences*, ed. C. G. Smith, 36-57. Notre Dame, Indiana: Univ. of Indiana Press. 553 pp.

Deutsch, M. 1973. *The Resolution of Conflict, Constructive and Destructive Processes.* New Haven and London: Yale Univ. Press. 420 pp.

Deutsch, M., Collins, M. E. 1951. *Interracial Housing, A Psychological Evaluation of a Social Experiment.* Minneapolis: Univ. of Minnesota Press. 173 pp.

Deutsch, M., Collins, M. E. 1958. The effects of public policy in housing projects upon interracial attitudes. In *Readings in Social Psychology*, eds. E. E. Maccoby, T. M. Newcomb, E. L. Hartley, 612-23. New York: Henry Holt. 674 pp.

deVos, G. 1966. Conflict, dominance and exploitation in human systems of segregation, some theoretical perspectives from the study of personality in culture. In *Conflict in Society*, eds. A. V. S. de Reuck and J. Knight, 60-81. London: J. & A. Churchill. 467 pp.

DeVries, D. L., Edwards, K. J. 1975. Student teams and learning games, their effects on cross-race and cross-sex interaction. *J. Educ. Psychol.* 66:741-9.

DeVries, D. L., Slavin, R. E. 1975. Effects of team competition on race relations in the classroom, further supportive evidence. Presented at the 83rd Ann. Meet. Am. Psychol. Assoc.

Dixon, V. J., Foster, B. G. 1971. *Beyond Black or White, An Alternate America.* Boston: Little, Brown. 140 pp.

Dobriner, W. 1958. Theory and research in the sociology of the suburbs. In *The Suburban Community*, ed. W. Dobriner, xiii-xxviii. New York: G. P. Putnam's Sons. 416 pp.

Dodson, J. 1960. Minority group housing in two cities. In *Studies in Housing and Minority Groups*, eds. N. Glazer, D. McEntire, 84-109. Berkeley: Univ. of Calif. Press. 228 pp.

Doob, L. W. 1970. *Resolving Conflict in Africa, The Fermeda Workshop.* New Haven: Yale Univ. Press. 209 pp.

Downs, A. 1973. *Opening up the Suburbs, An Urban Strategy for America.* New Haven: Yale Univ. Press. 219 pp.

Drucker, P. F. 1969. The sickness of government. *Public Int.* 14:3-23.

Duesenberry, J. S. 1967. *Income, Saving and the Theory of Consumer Behavior.* New York: Oxford Univ. Press. 128 pp.

Duncan, B., Schuman, H., Duncan, O. D. 1973. *Social Change in a Metropolitan Community.* New York: Russell Sage. 126 pp.

Duncan, O. D., Featherman, D. L., Duncan, B. 1972. *Socioeconomic Background and Achievement.* New York: Seminar Press. 284 pp.

Duster, T. 1968. Violence and civic responsibility. In *Our Children's Burden, Studies of Desegregation in Nine American Communities*, ed. R. W. Mack, 1-39. New York: Random House. 473 pp.

Dutton, J. M. and Walton, R. 1966. Interdepartmental conflict and cooperation, two contrasting studies. *Hum. Org.* 25:215.

Eckhoff, T. 1966. The mediator, the judge and the administrator in conflict-resolution. *Acta Sociologica.* 10:148-72.

Edwards, H. 1969. *Black Students.* New York: Free Press. 234 pp.

Edwards, H. 1973. *Sociology of Sport.* Homewood, Ill.: Dorsey. 395 pp.

Ehrlich, H. J. 1973. *The Social Psychology of Prejudice.* New York: Wiley-Interscience. 208 pp.

Eisenstadt, S. N. 1971. Continuities and changes in systems of stratification. In *Stability and Social Change*, eds. B. Barber, A. Inkeles, 61-81. Boston: Little, Brown. 451 pp.

Elder, G. H. 1970. Group orientations and strategies in racial change. *Soc. Forces.* 48:445-61.

Ellis, D. P., Weinir, P., Miller, L., III. 1971. Does the trigger pull the finger? An experimental test of weapons as aggression-eliciting stimuli. *Sociometry.* 34:453-65.

Enloe, C. H. 1973. *Ethnic Conflict and Political Development.* Boston: Little, Brown. 282 pp.

Erber, E., Prior, J. P. 1974. *Housing Allocation Planning, An Annotated Bibliography.* (#547). Monticello, Ill.: Council on Planning Librarians Exchange.

Esman, M. J. 1973. The management of communal conflict. *Public Policy.* 21:49-78.

Etzioni, A. 1966. *Studies in Social Change.* New York: Holt, Rinehart and Winston, Inc. 226 pp.

Evan, W. M. and MacDougall, J. A. 1967. Interorganizational conflict, a labor-management bargaining experiment. *J. Conflict. Resol.* 11:398-413.

Fainstein, N. J., Fainstein, S. S. 1974. *Urban Political Movements.* Englewood Cliffs, N.J.: Prentice-Hall. 271 pp.

Falk, R. A. 1968. Conflict of laws. In *International Encyclopedia of the Social Sciences*, ed. D. L. Sills, 3:246-53. New York: Macmillan and Free Press. 17 vols. 568 pp.

Farley, R. 1970. The changing distribution of Negroes within metropolitan areas, the emergence of black suburbs. *Am. J. Sociol.* 75:512-29.

Farley, R., Hermalin, A. I. 1973. The potential for residential integration in cities and suburbs, implications for the busing controversy. *Am. Sociol. Rev.* 38:595-610.

Farley, R., Taeuber, A. F. 1974. Racial segregation in the public schools. *Am. J. Sociol.* 79:888-905.

Feagin, J. R. 1971. White separatists and black separatists, a comparative analysis. *Soc. Problems.* 19:167-80.

Featherman, D. L., Hauser, R. M. 1976. Changes in the socioeconomic stratification of the races, 1962-1973. *Am. J. Sociol.* 82:621-51.

Fellman, D. 1968. Adjudication. I., Domestic. In *International Encyclopedia of the Social Sciences*, ed. D. L. Sills, 1:42-9. New York: Macmillan and Free Press. 17 vols. 522 pp.

Ferguson, C. K., Kelley, H. H. 1964. Significant factors in overevaluation of own group's product. *J. Abnorm. Soc. Psychol.* 69:223-8.

Ferson, J., Haltzman, W., Kelley, J. G. 1958. The measurement of attitudes toward the Negro in the South. *J. Soc. Psych.* 48:305-17.

Feshbach, S. 1956. The catharsis hypothesis and some consequences of interaction with aggressive and neutral play objects. *J. Pers.* 24:449-62.

Feshbach, S. 1961. The stimulating versus cathartic effects of a vicarious aggressive activity. *J. Abnorm. Soc. Psychol.* 63:381-5.

Festinger, L., Schacter, S., Bach, K. 1950. *Social Pressures in Informal Groups.* New York: Harper and Brothers. 240 pp.

Fichter, J. 1973. *One-Man Research, Reminiscences of a Catholic Sociologist.* New York: Wiley. 258 pp.

Fienberg, S. E. 1971. Randomization and social affairs, the 1970 draft lottery. *Science.* 171:255-61.

Firey, W. 1969. Limits to economy in crime and punishment. *Soc. Sci. Quart.* 50:72-77.

Fisher, R. 1971. Fractionating conflict. In *Conflict Resolution, Contributions of the Behavioral Sciences,* ed. C. G. Smith, 157-69. Notre Dame, Indiana: Univ. of Notre Dame Press. 553 pp.

Fishman, F. 1961. Some social and psychological determinants of intergroup relations in changing neighborhoods. *Soc. Forces.* 40:42-51.

Fiskin, J., Keniston, K., MacKinnon, C. 1973. Moral reasoning and political ideology. *J. Pers. Soc. Psychol.* 27:109-19.

Fleming, G. J., Haas, F. J. 1946. Personnel practices and wartime changes. *The Annals.* 244:48-56.

Foley, D. L. 1973. Institutional and contextual factors affecting the housing choices of minority residents. In *Segregation in Residential Areas,* eds. A. H. Hawley, V. P. Rock, 85-147. Washington, D.C.: National Academy of Sciences. 235 pp.

Ford, W. S. 1972. *Interracial Public Housing in a Border City.* Lexington, Mass.: D. C. Heath. 99 pp.

Ford. W. S. 1973. Interracial public housing in a border city, another look at the contact hypothesis. *Am. J. Sociol.* 78:1426-45.

Forman, R. E. 1971. *Black Ghettos, White Ghettos, and Slums.* Englewood Cliffs, N.J.: Prentice-Hall. 184 pp.

Francis, E. K. 1952. The adjustment of a peasant group to a capitalistic economy, the Manitoba Mennonites. *Rur. Sociol.* 17:218-28.

Francis, E. K. 1954. Variables in the formation of so-called 'minority groups'. *Am. J. Sociol.* 59:6-14.

Francis, E. K. 1956. Multiple intergroup relations in the upper Rio Grande region. *Am. Sociol. Rev.* 21:84-9.

Franklin, V. P. 1974. The persistence of school segregation in the urban North, an historical perspective. *J. Ethnic Studies.* 1:51-68.

Freeman, E., Meer, B. 1966. The impact of Negro neighbors on white home owners. *Soc. Forces.* 45:11-9.

Friedman, D. J. 1973. *White Militancy in Boston.* Lexington, Mass.: D. C. Heath. 176 pp.

Friedman, M. 1974. Review of C. H. Enloe, *Commentary.* 58:98.

Fuller, L. L. 1964. *The Morality of Law.* New Haven: Yale Univ. Press. 202 pp.

Fulton, R. L. 1960. *Russel Woods, A Study of a Neighborhood's Initial Response to Negro Invasion.* Ph.D. dissertation. Detroit: Wayne State Univ. 198 pp.

Gaertner, S. L. 1976. Nonreactive measures in racial attitude research, a focus on 'liberals'. In *Towards the Elimination of Racism,* ed. P. A. Katz, 183-212. New York: Pergamon. 444 pp.

Gamson, W. A. 1968. *Power and Discontent.* Homewood, Ill.: Dorsey. 208 pp.

Gamson, W. A. 1975. *The Strategy of Social Protest.* Homewood, Ill.: Dorsey. 217 pp.

Gamson, W. A., McEvoy, J. 1970. Police violence and its public support. *The Annals.* 391:97-110.

Gans, H. 1967. *The Levittowners, Ways of Life and Politics in a Suburban Community.* New York: Pantheon. 474 pp.

Gast, D. 1967. Minority Americans in children's literature. *Elem. English* 44:12-23.

Gaylin, W. 1976. *Caring.* New York: Alfred A. Knopf. 199 pp.

Geen, R. G., O'Neal., E. C. 1969. Activation of cue-elicited aggression by general arousal. *J. Pers. Soc. Psychol.* 11:289-92.

Gergen, K. J. 1969. *The Psychology of Behavior Exchange.* Reading, Mass.: Addison-Wesley. 113 pp.

Gilbert, G. M. 1951. Stereotype persistence and change among college students. (*J. Abnorm. Soc. Psychol.* 46:245-54.

Giles, M. W., Gatlin, D. S., Cataldo, E. F. 1974. The impact of busing on white flight. *Soc. Sci. Quart.* 55:493-501.

Glass, D. C., Henchy, T. 1968. Evaluation apprehension and the social facilitation of dominant and subordinate responses. *J. Person. Soc. Psychol.* 10:446-54.

Glazer, N. 1974. On 'opening up' the suburbs. *Public Interest.* 37:89-111.

Glazer, N. 1975. The exposed American Jew. *Commentary.* 59:25-30.

Glazer, N. 1976. *Affirmative Discrimination, Ethnic Inequality and Public Policy.* New York: Basic Books. 248 pp.

Glazer, N., Greeley, A. M., Patterson, O. Moynihan, D. P. 1974. What is ethnicity? *Bull. Am. Acad. Arts and Sci.* 27:16-35.

Glazer, N., McEntire, D., eds. 1960. *Studies in Housing and Minority Groups.* Berkeley and Los Angeles: Univ. of Calif. Press. 228 pp.

Glazer, N., Moynihan, D. P., eds. 1975. *Ethnicity, Theory and Experience.* Cambridge: Harvard Univ. Press. 531 pp.

Gluckman, M. 1954. *Rituals of Rebellion in Southeast Africa.* Manchester: Manchester Univ. Press. 36 pp.

Gluckman, M. 1956. *Custom and Conflict in Africa.* Glencoe, Ill.: Free Press. 173 pp.

Goering, J. M. 1971. The emergence of ethnic interests, a case of serendipity. *Soc. Forces.* 49:379-84.

Goering, J. M., Kahl, J. A. 1971. Stable workers, black and white. *Soc. Probl.* 18:306-18.

Goldblatt, H., Cromien, F. 1962. The effective reach of the Fair Housing Practices Law of the City of New York. *Soc. Probl.* 9:365-70.

Goldstein, J. H., Arms, R. L. 1971. Effects of observing athletic events on hostility. *Sociometry.* 34:83-90.

Gomberg, W. 1974. The problem of arbitration—the resolution of public sector disputes. *Proceed. Am. Phil. Soc.* 118:409-14.

Goodman, M. E. 1964. *Race Awareness in Young Children.* New York: Collier Books. 351 pp.

Gould, J. 1971. A sociological portrait, nationality and ethnicity. *New Society.* 18: 1281-4.

Grabosky, P. N., Rosenbloom, D. H. 1975. Racial and ethnic integration in the Federal Service. *Soc. Sci. Quart.* 56:71-84.

Graham, H. D. 1970. The paradox of American violence, a historical appraisal. *The Annals.* 391:74-82.

Graham, H. D., Gurr, T. R., eds. 1969. *Violence in America, Historical and Comparative Perspectives.* New York: American Library. 822 pp.

Granovetter, M. S. 1973. The strength of weak ties. *Am. J. Sociol.* 78:1360-80.

Granovetter, M. S. 1974. *Getting a Job, A Study of Contacts and Careers.* Cambridge, Mass.: Harvard Univ. Press. 179 pp.

Grant, W. V., Lind, C. G. 1976. *Digest of Educational Statistics, 1975 Edition*. Washington, D.C.: U.S. Govt. Printing Office. 199 pp.

Greeley, A. M. 1972. *That Most Distressful Nation, The Taming of the American Irish*. Chicago: Quadrangle. 281 pp.

Greeley, A. M., McCready, W. C. 1974. Does ethnicity matter? *Ethnicity*. 1:91-208.

Greeley, A. M., Sheatsley, P. B. 1971. Attitudes toward racial integration. *Sci. Am.* 225:13-19.

Greenberg, B. S., Mazingo, S. L. 1976. Racial issues in mass media institutions. In *Towards the Elimination of Racism*, ed. P. A. Katz, pp. 377-440. New York: Pergamon Press. 444 pp.

Greenberg, E. S. 1972. Black children, self-esteem and the liberation movement. *Politics and Society*. 2:293-307.

Greenfield, R. W. 1961. Factors associated with attitudes toward desegregation in a Florida residential suburb. *Soc. Forces*. 40:31-42.

Greenstone, J. D., Peterson, P. E. 1973. *Race and Authority in Urban Politics*. New York: Russell Sage. 364 pp.

Greer, A. L, Greer, S. 1974. *Neighborhood and Ghetto*. New York: Basic Books. 336 pp.

Greer, S. 1965. *Urban Renewal and American Cities, The Dilemma of Democratic Intervention*. Indianapolis: Bobbs-Merrill. 201 pp.

Grier, E., Grier, G. 1960. *Privately Developed Interracial Housing, An Analysis of Experience*. Berkeley, Los Angeles: Univ. of Calif. Press. 264 pp.

Grigsby, W., Rapkin, C. 1960. *The Demand for Housing in Racially Mixed Areas, A Study of the Nature of Neighborhood Change*. Berkeley, Los Angeles: Univ. of Calif. Press. 177 pp.

Grimshaw, A. D., ed. 1969. *Racial Violence in the United States*. Chicago: Aldine. 553.

Grimshaw, A. D. 1971. Review symposium, reports of the National Commission on the Causes and Prevention of Violence. *Am. Sociol. Rev.* 36:716-27.

Gross, E. 1956. Symbiosis and consensus as integrative factors in small groups. *Am. Sociol. Rev.* 21:174-9.

Guest, A. M., Zuiches, J. J. 1971. Another look at residential turnover in urban neighborhoods, a note on 'Racial change in a stable community' by Harvey Molotch. *Am. J. Sociol.* 77:457-67.

Gupta, J. D. 1974. Ethnicity, language demands and national development. *Ethnicity*. 1:65-72.

Gurin, P. et al. 1969. Internal-external control in the motivational dynamics of Negro youth. *J. Soc. Issues*. 25:29-54.

Gutman, H. G. 1976. *The Black Family in Slavery and Freedom, 1750-1925*. New York: Pantheon. 664.

Guttentag, M. 1972. Children in Harlem's community-controlled schools. *J. Soc. Issues*. 28:1-20.

Haas, J. E. 1972. Review symposium. (Of P. M. Blau and R. A. Schoenherr. 1971. *The Structure of Organizations*. New York: Basic Books. 445 pp.) *Contemp. Sociol.* 1:491.

Haberfeld, S. 1973. Strategies for structural change. *Race*. 14:443-63.

Hadden, J. K., Longino, C. F., Jr. 1974. *Gideon's Gang, A Case Study of the Church in Social Action*. Philadelphia: Pilgrim Press. 245 pp.

Hall, J. 1973. Up on Church Hill, remaking a neighborhood. *The Richmond (Va.) Mercury*. 1(42):1, 6-7.

Hamilton, D. L., Bishop, G. D. 1976. Attitudinal and behavioral effects of initial integration of white suburban neighborhoods. *J. Soc. Issues*. 32:47-67.

Hammond, J. L. 1974. Revival religion and anti-slavery politics. *Am. Sociol. Rev.* 39: 175-86.

Hampton, R. 1975. Social and economic causes and consequences of marital disruption. In *Five Thousand American Families, Patterns of Economic Progress.* Vol. III, eds. G. J. Duncan, J. N. Morgan. Ann Arbor, Mich.: Inst. Soc. Res., Univ. of Michigan. 490 pp.

Hardin, G. 1968. The tragedy of the commons. *Science.* 162:1243-8.

Harding, J., Hogrefe, R. 1952. Attitudes of white department store employees toward Negro co-workers. *J. Soc. Issues.* 8:18-28.

Harding, J. et al. 1954. Prejudice and ethnic relations. In *Handbook of Social Psychology,* vol. 2, ed. G. Lindzey, 1021-61. Cambridge, Mass.: Addison-Wesley.

Hare, A. P. 1952. Interaction and consensus in different groups. *Am. Sociol. Rev.* 17: 261-7.

Harrell, D. E. 1971. *White Sects and Black Men in the Recent South.* Nashville: Vanderbilt Univ. Press. 161 pp.

Harris, R. 1972. *Prejudice and Tolerance in Ulster.* Totowa, N. J.: Rowman and Littlefield. 234 pp.

Harrison, B. 1974. *Urban Economic Development, Suburbanization, Minority Opportunity, and the Condition of the Central City.* Washington, D.C.: The Urban Institute. 200 pp.

Harrison, G., Horowitz, A. R., von Furstenberg, G. M. 1974. *Patterns of Racial Discrimination, Volume I: Housing, Volume II: Employment and Income.* Lexington, Mass.: D. C. Heath.

Hauser, R. M., Featherman, D. L. 1973. Trends in the occupational mobility of U.S. men, 1962-1970. *Am. Sociol. Rev.* 38:302-10.

Hawley, A. H., Rock, V. P., eds. 1973. *Segregation in Residential Areas. Papers on Racial and Socioeconomic Factors in Choice of Housing.* Washington, D.C.: National Academy of Sciences. 235 pp.

Hays, S. P. 1973. The ebb and flow of ethnicity. *Pitt Magazine.* 29:9-15.

Hecht, J. L. 1974. The color tax in housing. *The Richmond (Va.) Mercury.* (November 13):2.

Heiss, J., Owens, S. 1972. Self-evaluations of blacks and whites. *Am. J. Sociol.* 78:360-70.

Helmreich, W. B. 1973. *The Black Crusaders, A Case Study of a Black Militant Organization.* New York: Harper & Row. 196 pp.

Helper, R. 1969. *Racial Policies and Practices of Real Estate Brokers.* Minneapolis: Univ. of Minnesota Press. 387 pp.

Hermalin, A. I., Farley, R. 1973. The potential for residential integration in cities and suburbs, implications for the busing controversy. *Am. Sociol. Rev.* 38:595-610.

Herrnstein, R. J. 1973. *IQ in the Meritocracy.* Boston: Little, Brown, 235 pp.

Hesslink, G. K. 1968. *Black Neighbors, Negroes in a Northern Rural Community.* Indianapolis: Bobbs-Merrill. 190 pp.

Higham, J. 1966. American anti-Semitism historically reconsidered. In *Jews in the Mind of America,* ed. C. H. Stember, 237-58. New York: Basic Books. 413 pp.

Hill, R. B. 1972. *The Strength of Black Families.* New York: Emerson Hall. 76 pp.

Hill, R. B. 1973. Benign neglect revisited, the illusion of black progress. Paper presented at the Annual Conference of the National Urban League, Washington, D.C. 11 pp. + tables.

Himes, J. S. 1973. *Racial Conflict in American Society.* Columbus, Ohio: Merrill. 205 pp.

Himmelfarb, M. 1974. Plural establishment. *Commentary.* 58:69-73.

Hirschhorn, E. 1976. Federal legal remedies for racial discrimination. In *Towards the Elimination of Racism*, ed. P. A. Katz, 377-440. New York: Pergamon. 444 pp.

Hirschman, A. O. 1972. The changing tolerance for income inequality in the course of economic development. Discussion paper No. 233 rev. Cambridge, Mass.: Harvard Institute of Economic Research. 25 pp.

Hoebel, E. Adamson. 1954. *The Law of Primitive Man, A Study in Comparative Legal Dynamics*. Cambridge, Mass.: Harvard Univ. Press. 357 pp.

Hoffman, L. R. 1958. Similarity of personality, a basis for interpersonal attraction? *Sociometry*. 21:300-8.

Holden, A. 1974. *The Bus Stops Here, A Study of School Desegregation in Three Cities*. New York: Agathon. 500 pp.

Holden, C. 1975. Employment testing, debate simmers in and out of court. *Science*. 190:35-9.

Holsti, K. J. 1966. Resolving international conflicts, a taxonomy of behavior and some figures on procedures. *J. Conflict. Resol.* 10:272-96.

Holt, R. J. 1965. A proposed structural-functional framework for political science. *The Annals*, Monograph, No. 5 (*Functionalism in the Social Sciences*, ed. D. Martindale): 84-110.

Homel, M. W. 1974. Race and schools in nineteenth century Chicago. *Integrated Educ.* 71:39-42.

Hope, J. 1952. Industrial integration of Negroes, the upgrading process. *Hum. Organ.* 11:5-14.

Howard, J. R. 1974. *The Cutting Edge, Social Movements and Social Change in America*. Philadelphia: Lippincott. 276 pp.

Hubbard, H. 1968. Five long hot summers and how they grew. *Public Interest*. 12:3-24.

Hudik, T. L., Wiley, M. G. 1974. Police-citizen encounters, a field test of exchange theory. *Soc. Probl.* 22:119-27.

Hulbary, W. E. 1975. Race, deprivation, and adolescent self-images. *Soc. Sci. Quart.* 56:105-14.

Humphrey, C. R., Zeul, C. R. 1971. The integration of blacks in suburban neighborhoods, a re-examination of the contact hypothesis. *Soc. Probl.* 18:462-74.

Hunt, C. L. 1960. Private integrated housing in a medium-sized Northern city. *Soc. Probl.* 7:196-209.

Hunter, A. 1974a. Community change, a stochastic analysis of Chicago's local communities, 1930-60. *Am. J. Sociol.* 79:923-47.

Hunter, A. 1974b. *Symbolic Communities, The Persistence and Change of Chicago's Local Communities*. Chicago: Univ. of Chicago Press. 288 pp.

Hurwitz, J. I., Zander, A. F., Hymovitch, B. 1953. Some effects of power on the relations among group members. In *Group Dynamics*, eds. D. Cartwright, A. Zander, 483-92. Evanston, Ill.: Row, Peterson & Co. 642 pp.

Hyman, H. H. 1969. Social psychology and race relations. In *Race and the Social Sciences*, ed. I. Katz, P. Guring, 3-48. New York: Basic Books. 387 pp.

Hyman, H. H., Reed, J. S. 1969. Black matriarchy reconsidered, evidence from secondary analysis of sample surveys. *Public Opin. Quart.* 33:346-54.

Hyman, H. H., Sheatsley, P. B. 1956. Attitudes toward desegregation. *Scientific American*. 195:35-9.

Hyman, H. H., Sheatsley, P. B. 1964. Attitudes toward desegregation. *Scientific American*. 211:16-23.

Ikle, F. 1964. *How Nations Negotiate*. New York: Praeger. 272 pp.

Ikle, F. C. 1968. Negotiation. In *International Encyclopedia of the Social Sciences*, ed. D. L. Sills, 11:117-20. New York: Macmillan and Free Press, 17 vols. 614 pp.

Irish, D. P. 1952. Reactions of Caucasian residents to Japanese-American neighbors. *J. Soc. Issues.* 8:10-17.

Irvine, S. 1973. Racial attitudes of American ministers. Paper presented at 81st annual meeting of Am. Psychol. Assn., Montreal.

Jackson, E. 1952. *Meeting of Minds.* New York: McGraw-Hill. 200 pp.

Jacobson, N. P. 1960. The problem of civilization. In *Social Change*, ed. J. E. Nordskog, 390-407. New York: McGraw Hill. 423 pp.

Janis, I. L., Katz, D. 1971. The reduction of intergroup hostility, research problems and hypotheses. In *Conflict Resolution, Contributions of the Behavioral Sciences*, ed. C. G. Smith, 219-32. Notre Dame, Indiana: Univ. of Notre Dame Press. 553 pp.

Janowitz, M. 1968. *Social Control of Escalated Riots.* Chicago: Univ. of Chicago Cntr. for Policy Study. 44 pp.

Janowitz, M. 1970. *Political Conflict, Essays in Political Sociology.* Chicago: Quadrangle. 271 pp.

Jeffries, V., Morris, R. T. 1968. Violence next door. *Soc. Forces.* 46:353-8.

Jencks, C. et al. 1972. *Inequality, A Reassessment of the Effect of Family and Schooling in America.* New York: Basic Books. 399 pp.

Jensen, J. A., Prothro, E, T. 1952. Comparison of some ethnic and white college students in the Deep South. *Soc. Forces.* 30:426-8.

Johnson, M. P., Sell, R. R. 1976. The cost of being black, a 1970 update. *Am. J. Sociol.* 82:183-90.

Johnson, P. B., Sears, D. O., McConahay, J. B. 1971. Black invisibility, the press, and the Los Angeles riot. *Am. J. Sociol.* 76:698-721.

Joint Center for Political Studies. 1973. *National Roster of Black Elected Officials.* Vol. III. Washington, D.C.: JCPS. 193 pp.

Jones, J. 1972. *Prejudice and Racism.* Reading, Mass.: Addison-Wesley. 196 pp.

Jones, L. W., Long, H. H. 1965. *The Negotiation of Desegregation in Ten Southern Cities.* Nashville, Tenn.: Fisk Univ., Race Rel. Dept., Am. Missionary Assoc. 38 pp.

Kahl, J. A., Goering, J. M. 1971. Stable workers, black and white. *Soc. Probl.* 18:306-18.

Kain, J. F., Persky, J. J. 1969. Alternatives to the gilded ghetto. *Public Interest.* 14:74-87.

Kamens, D. 1971. The college "charter" and college size, effects on occupational choice and attrition. *Sociol. Educ.* 44:270-96.

Kane, M. B. 1970. *Minorities in Textbooks.* Chicago: Quadrangle. 148 pp.

Kantrowitz, N. 1973. *Ethnic and Racial Segregation in the New York Metropolis, Residential Patterns among White Ethnic Groups, Blacks, and Puerto Ricans.* New York: Praeger. 122 pp.

Kaplan, H. 1963. *Urban Renewal Politics, Slum Clearance in Newark.* New York: Columbia Univ. Press. 219 pp.

Kardiner, A., Ovesey, L. 1951. *The Mark of Oppression, A Psychological Study of the American Negro.* New York: W. W. North. 396 pp.

Karlins, M., Coffman, T., Walters, G. 1969. On the fading of social stereotypes, studies in three generations of college students. *J. Pers. and Soc. Psych.* 13:1-16.

Katz, D. 1971. Group process and social integration, a system analysis of two movements of social protest. In *Conflict Resolution, Contributions of the Behavioral Sciences*, ed. C. G. Smith, 205-18. Notre Dame, Indiana: Univ. of Notre Dame Press. 553 pp.

Katz, I. 1964. Review of evidence relating to effects of desegregation on the performance of Negroes. *Am. Psychologist.* 19:381-99.

Katz, I. 1970. Experimental studies of Negro-white relationships. In *Advances in Experimental Social Psychology*, ed. L. Berkowitz. vol. 5. New York: Academic Press.

Katz, P. A. ed. 1976. *Towards the Elimination of Racism*. New York: Pergamon. 444 pp.

Kaufman, H. 1970. Some determinants of helping behavior. *Transact. New York Acad. Sciences.* Series II, 32:610-18.

Kawwa, T. 1968. A survey of some ethnic attitudes of some British secondary school pupils. *Brit. J. Soc. & Clin. Psychol.* 7:161-8.

Keeley, C. B. 1974. Immigration composition and population policy. *Science.* 185: 587-93.

Keesing's Research Report 4. 1970. *Race Relations in the U.S.A., 1954-1968.* New York: Scribner's Sons. 280 pp.

Kelley, J. 1974. The politics of school busing. *Congressional Record-Senate.* July 24: 5 13353-8.

Kelly, J. G., Ferson, J., Holtzman, W. 1958. The measurement of attitudes toward the Negro in the South. *J. Soc. Psychol.* 48:305-17.

Kephart, W. M. 1957. *Racial Factors and Urban Law Enforcement.* Philadelphia: Univ. of Pennsylvania Press. 209 pp.

Kerr. C. 1954. Industrial conflict and its mediation. *Am. J. Sociol.* 60:230-45.

Kerr, C., Siegel, A. 1954. The inter-industry propensity to strike, an international comparison. In *Industrial Conflict*, ed. A. Kornhauser, R. Dubin, A. M. Ross, 189-212. New York: McGraw-Hill. 551 pp.

Kershaw, J. A. with the assistance of Courant, P. N. 1970. *Government against Poverty.* Washington, D.C.: Brookings Inst. 174 pp.

Keyfitz N. 1973. Can inequality be cured? *Public Interest.* 31:91-101.

Killian, L. M. 1952. The effects of Southern white workers on race relations in Northern plants. *Am. Sociol. Rev.* 17:327-31.

Killian, L. M. 1958. *The Impossible Revolution? Black Power and the American Dream.* New York: Random House. 198 pp.

Killian, L. M., Grigg, C. 1964. *Racial Crisis in America.* Englewood Cliffs, N.J.: Prentice-Hall. 144 pp.

Kimura, Y. 1957. War brides in Hawaii and their in-laws. *Am. J. Sociol.* 63:70-6.

Kinloch, G. C. 1974. *The Dynamics of Race Relations, A Sociological Analysis.* New York: McGraw-Hill. 305 pp.

Kirby, D. J., Crain, R. L. 1974. The functions of conflict, school desegregation in 91 cities. *Soc. Sci. Quart.* 55:478-92.

Kirby, D. J., Harris, T. R., Crain, R. L., Rossell, C. H. 1973. *Political Strategies in Northern School Desegregation.* Lexington, Mass.: D. C. Heath. 262 pp.

Kitano, H. 1960. Housing of Japanese-Americans in the San Francisco Bay area. *Studies in Housing and Minority Groups*, eds. N. Glazer, D. McEntire, 178-97. Berkeley: Univ. of Calif. Press. 228 pp.

Klinberg, F. L. 1966. Predicting the termination of war, battle casualties and population losses. *J. Conflict. Resol.* 10:129-71.

Kolaja, J. 1968. Two processes, a new framework for the theory of participation in decision making. *Behavioral Sci.* 13:66-70.

Kriesberg, L. 1973. *The Sociology of Social Conflicts.* Englewood Cliffs, N.J.: Prentice-Hall. 300 pp.

Kronus, S. 1971. *The Black Middle Class.* Columbus, Ohio: Merrill. 182 pp.

Kuhn, J. W. 1968. Business unionism in a laboristic society. In *The Business of America*, ed. I. Berg, 284-310. New York: Harcourt, Brace and World, 437 pp.

Kupperman, R. H., Smith, H. A. 1972. Strategies of mutual deterrence. *Science.* 176: 18-23.

Kutner, B., Wilkins, C. A., Yarrow, P. R. 1952. Verbal attitudes and overt behavior involving racial prejudice. *J. Abnorm. Soc. Psychol.* 47:649-52.

Lambert, W. E., Tucker, G. R. 1973. The benefits of bilingualism. *Psych. Today.* 7:89-94.

Landers, J. 1967. Integration in the major metropolis. In *School Desegregation in the North, The Challenge and the Experience,* ed. T. B. Edwards, F. M. Wirt, 249-95. San Francisco: Chandler. 352 pp.

Lane, R. 1976. Criminal violence in America, the first hundred years. *The Annals.* 423: 1-13.

Lang, K., Lang, G. E. 1965. Resistance to school desegregation, a case study of backlash among Jews. *Sociol. Inquiry.* 35:94-106.

Langness, L. L. 1972. Violence in the New Guinea Highlands. In *Collective Violence,* eds. J. F. Short, Jr., M. E. Wolfgang, 171-85. Chicago: Aldine-Atherton. 287 pp.

LaPiere. 1934. Attitudes vs. actions. *Soc. Forces.* 12:230-7.

Larson, A. 1962. The role of law in building peace. In *Preventing World War III, Some Proposals,* eds. Q. Wright, W. M. Evan, M. Deutsch, 332-41. New York: Simon & Schuster. 460 pp.

Laue, J. H., and Cormick, G. W. In press. The ethics of intervention in community disputes. In *The Ethics of Social Intervention,* eds. H. Kelman, D. Warwick, G. Bermant. Washington: Hemisphere Publishing Co.

Lawrence, D. 1974. *Black Migrants, White Natives, A Study of Race Relations in Nottingham.* London: Cambridge Univ. Press. 251 pp.

Leacock, E. Deutsch, M., Fishman, J. A. 1959. The Bridgeview Study, a preliminary report. *J. Soc. Issues.* 15:30-7.

Leighton, A. 1946. *The Governing of Men.* Princeton, N.J.: Princeton Univ. Press. 404 pp.

Leites, N., Wolfe, C., Jr. 1970. *Rebellion and Authority, An Analytic Essay on Insurgent Conflicts.* Santa Monica, Calif.: Rand. 174 pp.

LeVine, R. A., Campbell, D. T. 1972. *Ethnocentrism, Theories of Conflict, Ethnic Attitudes and Group Behavior.* New York: Wiley. 310 pp.

Levinson, A. 1974. *The Working Class Majority.* New York: Coward, McCann & Goeghegan. 319 pp.

Levitan, S. A., Johnston, W. B., Taggart, R. 1975. *Still a Dream, The Changing Status of Blacks since 1960.* Cambridge, Mass.: Harvard Univ. Press. 381 pp.

Levitan, S. A. and Taggart, R. 1976-77. The Great Society did succeed. *Polit. Sci. Quart.* 91:601-18.

Levitt, T. 1973. *The Third Sector, New Tactics for a Responsive Society.* New York: Amacom. 182 pp.

Levy, C. J. 1968. *Voluntary Servitude, Whites in the Negro Movement.* New York: Appleton. 125 pp.

Levy, F. A., Meltsner, A. J., Wildavsky, A. 1974. *Urban Outcomes, Schools, Streets and Libraries.* Berkeley: Univ. of Calif. Press. 278 pp.

Lewis, R., St. John, N. 1974. The contribution of cross-racial friendship to minority group achievement in desegregated classrooms. *Sociometry.* 37:79-91.

Lieberson, S. 1963. *Ethnic Patterns in American Cities.* New York: Free Press of Glencoe. 230 pp.

Lieberson, S. 1973. Generational differences among blacks in the North. *Am. J. Sociol.* 79:550-65.

Lijphart, A. 1968. *The Politics of Accommodation, Pluralism and Democracy in the Netherlands.* Berkeley: Univ. of Calif. Press. 222 pp.

Likert, R. 1961. *New Patterns of Management.* New York: McGraw-Hill. 279 pp.

Lipset, S. M., ed. 1967. *Student Politics.* New York: Basic Books. 403 pp.

Lipset, S. M. 1974. Education and equality, Israel and the United States compared. *Society.* 11:56-66.

Lipsky, M. 1968. Protest as a political resource. *Am. Polit. Sci. Rev.* 62:1144-58.

Livernash, E. R. 1968. Labor relations. I. Collective bargaining. In *International Encyclopedia of the Social Sciences*, ed. D. L. Sills, 8:491-500. New York: Macmillan and Free Press. 17 vols. 584 pp.

Lohman, J. D., Reitzes, D. C. 1952. Note on race relations in mass society. *Am. J. Sociol.* 58:240-6.

Lohman, J. D., Reitzes, D. C. 1954. Deliberately organized groups and racial behavior. *Am. Sociol. Rev.* 19:342-4.

Lorenz, K. 1966. *On Aggression.* New York: Harcourt, Brace & World. 306 pp.

Lott, A. J., Lott, B. E. 1965. Group cohesiveness as interpersonal attraction, a review of relationships with antecedent and consequent variables. *Psychol. Bull.* 64:259-309.

Lundman, R. J. 1974. Routine police arrest practices, a commonwealth perspective. *Soc. Probl.* 22:127-41.

Mack, R. W., ed. 1968. *Our Children's Burden, Studies of Desegregation in Nine American Communities.* New York: Random House. 473 pp.

Mack, R. W., Snyder, R. C. 1957. The analysis of social conflict, toward an overview and synthesis. *J. Conflict. Resol.* 1:212-48.

MacKenzie, B. K. 1948. The importance of contact in determining attitudes toward Negroes. *J. Abnorm. Soc. Psychol.* 43:417-41.

Manns, A. 1973. Books for black children increasing. *Ithaca (N.Y.) Journal.* (December 28, 1973). Orig. from the *Washington Post.*

Marris, P., Rein, M. 1967. *Dilemmas of Social Reforms, Poverty and Community Action in the United States.* Chicago: Aldine. 309 pp.

Marris, R. 1968. Galbraith, Solow, and the truth about corporations. *Public Interest.* 11:37-46.

Martin, J. G., Franklin, C. W. 1973. *Minority Group Relations.* Columbus, Ohio: Merrill. 338 pp.

Marx, G. T. 1967. *Protest and Prejudice, A Study of Belief in the Black Community.* New York: 228 pp. Harper & Row.

Masters, S. H. 1975. *Black-White Income Differentials, Empirical Studies and Policy Implications.* New York: Academic Press. 204 pp.

Matthews, D. R, Prothro, J. W. 1963a. Social and economic factors and Negro voter registration. *Am. Polit. Sci. Rev.* 57:24-44.

Matthews, D. R., Prothro, J. W. 1963b. Political factors and Negro voter registration in the South. *Am. Polit. Sci. Rev.* 57:355-65.

Mayer, A. 1960. Russel Woods, change without conflict. In *Studies in Housing and Minority Groups*, eds. N. Glazer, D. McEntire, 198-220. Berkeley: Univ. of Calif. Press. 228 pp.

Mayer, R. R., King, C. E., Borders-Patterson, A., McCullough, J. S. 1974. *The Impact of School Desegregation in a Southern City, A Case Study in the Analysis of Educational Policy.* Lexington, Mass.: D. C. Heath. 143 pp.

Mayhew, L. H. 1971. Stability and change in legal systems. In *Stability and Social Change*, eds. B. Barber, A. Inkeles, 187-210. Boston: Little, Brown. 451 pp.

Maykovitch, M. K. 1972. Reciprocity in racial stereotypes, white, black and yellow. *Am. J. Sociol.* 77:876-97.

McKee, E. W. 1971. *To Die Game, the Story of the Lowry Band, Indian Guerrillas of Reconstruction.* Baton Rouge: Louisiana State Univ. Press. 282 pp.

Meade, A. 1972. The distribution of segregation in Atlanta. *Soc. Forces.* 51:182-92.

Meer, B., Freedman, E. 1966. The impact of Negro neighbors on white homeowners. *Soc. Forces.* 45:11-19.

Meier, A., Rudwick, E. 1969. The boycott movement against Jim Crow streetcars in the South, 1900-1906. *J. Am. Hist.* 4:756-75.

Meier, A. Rudwick, E. 1973. *CORE, A Study in the Equal Rights Movement, 1942-1968.* New York: Oxford Univ. Press. 563 pp.

Meketon, B. F. 1966. *The Effects of Integration upon the Negro Child's Response to Various Tasks and upon His Level of Self-Esteem.* Ph.D. dissertation. Lexington: Univ. of Kentucky. 136 pp.

Melson, R., Wolpe, H. 1970. Modernization and the politics of communalism, a theoretical perspective. *Am. Polit. Sci. Rev.* 64:1112-30.

Millen, J. S. 1973. Factors affecting racial mixing in residential areas. In *Segregation in Residential Areas,* eds. A. H. Hawley, V. P. Rock, 148-71. Washington, D.C.: National Academy of Sciences. 235 pp.

Miller, K. S., Dreger, R. M., eds. 1973. *Comparative Studies of Blacks and Whites in the United States.* New York: Seminar Press. 572.

Milstein, T. 1970. Black separatism and white conservatism, partners in deceit, perspective on the Panthers. *Commentary.* 50:35-43.

Minard, R. D. 1952. Race relationships in the Pocahontas coalfield. *J. Soc. Issues.* 8:29-44.

Molotch, H. L. 1972a. *Managed Integration, The Dilemmas of Doing Good in the City.* Berkeley, Los Angeles, London: Univ. of Calif. Press. 250 pp.

Molotch, H. L. 1972b. Why neighborhoods change, a reply to whom it may concern. *Am. J. Sociol.* 78:682-4.

Moore, C. H. 1970. The politics of urban violence, policy outcomes in Winston-Salem. *Soc. Sci. Quart.* 51:374-88.

Moore, W., Livermore, C. P., Galland, G. F., Jr. 1973. Woodlawn, the zone of destruc-. tion. *Public Interest.* 30:41-59.

Moore, W. E. 1966. The utility of utopias. *Am. Sociol. Rev.* 31:765-72.

Morris, D. C. 1970. White racial orientations toward Negroes in an urban context. Ph.D. dissertation. Columbus, Ohio: Ohio State University. 87 pp.

Morris, M. D. 1975. *The Politics of Black America.* New York: Harper & Row. 302 pp.

Morris, R. T., Jeffries, V. 1968. Violence next door. *Soc. Forces.* 46:353-8.

Moskos, C. C., Jr. 1966. Racial integration in the Armed Forces. *Am. J. Sociol.* 72:132-48.

Mosteller, F., Moynihan, D. P., eds. 1972. *On Equality of Educational Opportunity.* New York: Random House. 572 pp.

Mousnier, Roland (Trans. by P. Evans). 1973. *Social Hierarchies, 1450 to the Present.* New York: Schocken Books. 206 pp.

Moxley, R. L. 1973. Social solidarity, ethnic rigidity and differentiation in Latin American communities, a structural approach. *Rur. Sociol.* 38:439-61.

Moynihan, D. P. 1970. Policy vs. program in the 70s. *Public Interest.* 20:90-100.

Moynihan, D. P. 1974. Was Woodrow Wilson right? Morality and American foreign policy. *Commentary.* 57:25-31.

Mueller, C. 1971. Riot negotiations, conditions of successful bargaining in the ghetto riots of the 1960's. Ph.D. dissertation. Ithaca, N.Y.: Cornell Univ. 307 pp.

Muir, D. E. 1971. The first years of desegregation, patterns of acceptance of black students on a deep-South campus. *Soc. Forces.* 48:371-8.

Munch, P. A. 1972. Race and social relations in Tristan da Cahuna. In *The Blending of Races, Marginality and Identity in World Perspective*, eds. N. P. Gist, A. C. Dworkin, 265-281. New York: Wiley-Interscience. 289 pp.

Murray, P. T. 1971. Local draft board composition and institutional racism. *Soc. Probl.* 19:129-37.

Mussen, I., O'Hanlon, T., Winkel, G. H. 1974. *Black Families in White Neighborhoods, Experiences and Attitudes.* New York: Environmental Psychology Program, City Univ. of N.Y. Grad. Ctr. 52 pp.

Myrdal, G. with the assistance of R. Sterner and A. Rose. 1944. *An American Dilemma.* 2 vols. New York: Harper & Bros. 1483 pp.

Nadar, L., Metzger, D. 1963. Conflict resolution in two Mexican communities. *Am. Anthrop.* 65:584-92.

Nash, J. 1974. Ethics and politics in social science research. *Trans. N.Y. Acad. Sciences,* Series II. 36:497-510.

National Committee against Discrimination, Inc. 1974. *Trends in Housing.* 18:2.

National Committee against Discrimination in Housing and Urban Land Institute. 1974. *Fair Housing and Exclusionary Land Use, Historical Overview, Summary Litigation and a Comment with Research Bibliography.* Washington, D.C.: ULI Research Report 23.

Nelsen, H. M., Yokley, R. L., Nelsen, A. K., eds. 1971. *The Black Church in America.* New York: Basic Books. 375 pp.

Nelson, H. A. 1971. Leadership and change in an evolutionary movement, an analysis of change in the leadership structure of the Southern civil rights movement. *Soc. Forces.* 49:353-71.

Nieburg, H. L. 1969. *Political Violence, The Behavioral Process.* New York: St. Martin's Press. 184 pp.

Nonet, P. 1969. *Administrative Justice, Advocacy and Change in Government Agencies.* New York: Russell Sage. 274 pp.

Norris, D. F. 1973. *Police-Community Relations, A Program That Failed.* Lexington, Mass.: D. C. Heath. 136 pp.

Northrup, H. R. 1967. Industry's racial employment policies. In *Employment, Race and Poverty*, eds. A. M. Ross, H. Hill, 290-307. New York: Harcourt, Brace & World. 598 pp.

Novak, M. 1971. *The Rise of the Unmeltable Ethnics.* New York: Macmillan. 321 pp.

Oak Park Housing Center. 1973-4. *1973-4 Annual Report.* Oak Park, Illinois: Oak Park Housing Center.

Olsen, M. E. 1970. Social and political participation of blacks. *Am. Sociol. Rev.* 35:682-97.

Olson, M. 1965. *The Logic of Collective Action.* Cambridge, Mass.: Harvard Univ. Press. 176 pp.

Olweus, D. 1973. *Hackkycklinger och oversittare, Forskning om skolmobbning. (Bullies and Whipping Boys, Research on School Mobbing.)* Stockholm: Almquist and Wiksell. 239 pp.

Orbell, J. M., Sherrill, K. S. 1969. Racial attitudes and the metropolitan context, a structural analysis. *Public Opin. Quart.* 33:46-54.

O'Reilly, R. P. 1970. *Racial and Social Class Isolation in the Schools, Implications for Educational Policy and Programs.* New York: Praeger. 401 pp.

Orenstein, H. 1965. *Gaon, Conflict and Cohesion in an Indian Village.* Princeton, N.J.: Princeton Univ. Press. 341 pp.

Orum, A. M. 1966. A reappraisal of the social and political participation of Negroes. *Am. J. Sociol.* 72:32-46.

Orum, A. M. 1972. *Black Students in Protest, A Study of the Origins of the Black Student Movement.* Washington, D.C.: Am. Sociol. Assoc. 89 pp.

Osborne, W. 1967. *The Segregated Covenant, Race Relations and American Catholics.* New York: Herder and Herder. 252 pp.

Palmore, E., Whittington, F. J. 1970. Differential trends toward equality between whites and nonwhites. *Soc. Forces.* 49:108-17.

Palmore, E. B. 1955. The introduction of Negroes into white departments. *Human Org.* 14:27-8.

Parker, J. H. 1968. The integration of Negroes and whites in an integrated church setting. *Soc. Forces.* 46:359-66.

Parris, G., Brooks, L. 1971. *Blacks in the City, A History of the National Urban League.* Boston: Little, Brown. 534 pp.

Parsons, T. 1951. *The Social System.* Glencoe, Illinois: The Free Press. 575 pp.

Parsons, T. 1966. Full citizenship for the Negro American? a sociological problem. In *The Negro American*, eds. T. Parson, K. B. Clark, 709-54. Boston: Houghton Mifflin. 781 pp.

Parsons, T. 1966. *Societies, Evolutionary and Comparative Perspectives.* Englewood Cliffs, N.J.: Prentice-Hall. 120 pp.

Parsons, T. 1971. *The System of Modern Societies.* Englewood Cliffs, N.J.: Prentice-Hall. 152 pp.

Patterson, O. 1973. The moral crisis of the black American. *Public Interest.* 32:43-69.

Patterson, S. 1969. *Immigration and Race Relations in Britain, 1960-1967.* New York: Oxford Univ. Press. 460 pp.

Peltason, J. W. 1961. *Fifty-Eight Lonely Men, Southern Federal Judges and School Desegregation.* New York: Harcourt, Brace and World. 270 pp.

Peterson, W. 1971. *Japanese Americans, Oppression and Success.* New York: Random House. 268 pp.

Pettigrew, T. F. 1971. *Racially Separate or Together?* New York: McGraw-Hill. 371 pp.

Pettigrew, T. F. 1974. The case for the racial integration of the schools. In *Readings in Sociology*, eds. E. A. Schuler et al., 373-85. New York: Crowell Co., 5th ed. 788 pp.

Pettigrew, T. F., Cramer, M. R. 1959. The demography of desegregation. *J. Soc. Issues.* 15:61-71.

Pettigrew, T. F., Riley, R. T. 1972. Contextual models of school desegregation. In *Attitudes, Conflict and Social Change*, eds. B. T. King, E. McGinnies, 155-85. New York: Academic Press. 234 pp.

Phares, D. 1971. Racial change and housing values, transition in an inner suburb. *Soc. Sci. Quart.* 52:560-73.

Photiadis, J. D., Biggar, J. 1962. Religiosity, education, and ethnic distance. *Am. J. Sociol.* 67:666-72.

Pifer, A. 1973. *The Higher Education of Blacks in the United States.* New York: Carnegie Corporation of New York. 51 pp.

Pinkney, A. 1969. *Black Americans.* Englewood Cliffs, N.J.: Prentice-Hall. 226 pp.

Piven, F. F., Cloward, R. A. 1971. *Regulating the Poor, The Functions of Public Welfare.* New York: Pantheon. 389 pp.

Porter, J. 1976. *Ethnic Pluralism in Canada.* In *Ethnicity, Theory and Experience,* ed. N. Glazer, D. P. Moynihan, 267-304. Cambridge, Mass.: Harvard Univ. Press. 531 pp.

Porter, J. D. R. 1971. *Black Child, White Child, The Development of Racial Attitudes.* Cambridge, Mass.: Harvard Univ. Press. 178 pp.

Porter, J. N. 1974. Race, socialization and mobility in educational and early occupational attainment. *Am. Sociol. Rev.* 39:303-17.

President's Commission on Law Enforcement and the Administration of Justice. 1967. *The Challenge of Crime in a Free Society, A Report.* Washington, D.C.: U.S. Govt. Printing Office. 240 pp.

Pressman, J. L., Wildavsky, A. B. 1973. *Implementation—How Great Expectations in Washington Are Dashed in Oakland; Or, Why It's Amazing That Federal Programs Work at All, This Being a Saga of the Economic Development Administration as Told by Two Sympathetic Observers Who Hope to Build Morals on a Foundation of Ruined Hopes.* Berkeley, Calif.: Univ. of Calif. Press. 182 pp.

Preston, J. D., Robinson, J. W. 1974. On modification of interracial interaction. *Am. Sociol. Rev.* 29:283-5.

Quinley, H. E. 1974. *The Prophetic Clergy, Social Activism among Protestant Ministers.* New York: Wiley. 369 pp.

Rabbie, J. M., de Brey, J. H. C. 1971. The anticipation of intergroup cooperation and competition under private and public conditions. *Internat. J. Gp. Tensions.* 1:230-51.

Rabbie, J. M., Horwitz, M. 1969. The arousal of ingroup-outgroup bias by a chance win or loss. *J. Pers. Soc. Psychol.* 13:269-77.

Rabbie, J. M., Wilkins, G. 1971. Intergroup competition and its effect on intra- and intergroup relations. *European J. Soc. Psychol.* 1:215-34.

Rabushka, A., Shepsle, K. A. 1972. *Politics in Plural Societies, A Theory of Democratic Instability.* Columbus, Ohio: Merrill. 232 pp.

Rainwater, L. 1967. The lessons of Pruitt-Igoe. *Public Interest.* 8:116-26.

Rangel, C. B. 1974. The President and the Black Caucus. *Focus* 2 (September):4-5.

Rapkin, C., Grigsby, W. G. 1960. *The Demand for Housing in Racially Mixed Areas.* Berkeley, Los Angeles: Univ. of Calif. Press. 177 pp.

Rapoport, A. 1960. *Fights, Games, and Debates.* Ann Arbor: Univ. of Michigan Press. 400 pp.

Raven, B. H., Eachus, H. T. 1963. Cooperation and competition in means-interdependent triads. *J. Abnorm. Soc. Psychol.* 67:307-16.

Ravitch, D. 1974. *The Great School Wars, New York City, 1805-1973, A History of the Public Schools as a Battlefield of Social Change.* New York: Basic Books. 449 pp.

Reed, B. A. 1947. Accommodation between Negro and white employers in a West Coast aircraft industry, 1942-1944. *Soc. Forces.* 26:76-87.

Reed, J. S. 1972. Percent black and lynching, a test of Blalock's theory. *Soc. Forces.* 50:356-60.

Richmond, A. H. 1967. *Post-War Immigrants in Canada.* Toronto: Univ. of Toronto Press. 320 pp.

Ritterband, P., Silberstein, R. 1973. Group disorders in the public schools. *Am. Sociol. Rev.* 38:461-7.

Roberts, J. M. 1965. Oaths, autonomic ordeals, and power. *Am. Anthrop.* 67:186-212.

Roberts, S. O., Horton, C. P. 1973. Extent of and effects of school desegregation. In

Comparative Studies of Blacks and Whites in the United States, eds. K. S. Miller, R. M. Dreger, 295-323. New York: Seminar Press. 572 pp.

Robins, L. N. 1973. Review of W. H. Ahlstrom, R. J. Havighurst: *400 Losers. Am..J. Sociol.* 79:237.

Rogg, E. M. 1974. *The Assimilation of Cuban Exiles, The Role of Community and Class.* New York: Aberdeen Press. 241 pp.

Rogler, L. H. 1972. *Migrant in the City, The Life of a Puerto Rican Action Group.* New York: Basic Books. 251 pp.

Rokeach, M. 1973. *The Nature of Human Values.* New York: Free Press. 438 pp.

Rokeach, M., Kleijunas, P. 1972. Behavior as a function of attitude-toward-object and attitude-toward-situation. *J. Pers. Soc. Psych.* 22:194-201.

Roling, B. V. A. 1966. The role of law in conflict resolution. In *Conflict in Society*, eds. A. de Reuck, J. Knight, 328-50. London: Churchill. 467 pp.

Roof, W. C. 1974. Religious orthodoxy and minority prejudice, causal relationship or reflection of localistic world view? *Am. J. Sociol.* 80:643-64.

Rooney, C., ed. 1973. *Equal Opportunity in the United States, A Symposium on Civil Rights.* Austin, Texas: Univ. of Texas. 175 pp. (Essays by E. Warren, V. E. Jordan, R. Wilkins, and R. M. Williams.)

Rose, A. M., Atelsek, F. J., McDonald, L. R. 1953. Neighborhood reactions to isolated Negro residents. *Am. Sociol. Rev.* 18:497-507.

Rose, P. I. 1968. *The Subject Is Race, Traditional Ideologies and the Teaching of Race Relations.* New York: Oxford Univ. Press. 181 pp.

Rose, P. I., Rothman, S., Wilson, W. J., eds. 1973. *Through Different Eyes, Black and White Perspectives on American Race Relations.* London, New York: Oxford Univ. Press. 453 pp.

Rosenberg, N. 1968. Technology, economy and values. Unpublished paper. Program on Technology and Society. Cambridge, Mass.: Harvard University.

Rosenberg, M., Simmons, R. G. 1971. *Black and White Self-Esteem, The Urban School Child.* Washington, D.C.: Am. Sociol. Assoc. 160 pp.

Rosenwaike, I. 1973. Interethnic comparisons of educational attainment, an analysis based on Census data for New York City. *Am. J. Sociol.* 79:68-77.

Ross, A. M. 1968. Labor Relations. III. Settlement of industrial disputes. In *International Encyclopedia of the Social Sciences*, ed. D. L. Sills, 8:506-10. New York: Macmillan and Free Press. 17 vols. 584 pp.

Ross, J. C., Wheeler, R. 1967. Structural sources of threat to Negro membership in militant voluntary associations in a Southern city. *Soc. Forces.* 45:583-6.

Rossell, C. H. 1975-76. School desegregation and white flight. *Polit. Sci. Quart.* 90:675-95.

Rossi, P. H., Berk, R. A. 1972. Local political leadership and popular discontent in the ghetto. In *Collective Violence*, ed. J. F. Short, M. E. Wolfgang, 292-308. Chicago: Aldine-Atherton. 387 pp.

Rossi, P. H., Waite, E., Bose, C. E., Berke, R. E. 1974. The seriousness of crimes, normative structure and individual differences. *Am. Sociol. Rev.* 39:224-37.

Rothbart, M. 1976. Achieving racial equality, an analysis of resistance to social reform. In *Towards the Elimination of Racism*, ed. P. A. Katz, 341-75. New York: Pergamon. 444 pp.

Rowe, A. R., Tittle, C. R. 1973. Moral appeal, sanction threat, and deviance, an experimental test. *Soc. Probl.* 20:488-98.

Rozwenc, E. C., Schultz, D. P. 1964. *Conflict and Consensus in the American Revolution.* Boston: D. C. Heath. 65 pp.

Rubin, A., Segal, G. J. 1946. An industrial experiment. *The Annals.* 244:244-57.

Rubin, L. 1972. *Busing and Backlash, White against White in an Urban School District.* Berkeley, Calif.: Univ. of Calif. Press. 248 pp.

Ruchelman, L. 1974. *Police Politics, A Comparative Study of Three Cities.* Cambridge, Mass.: Ballinger. 118 pp.

Russell, D. E. H. 1974. *Rebellion, Revolution and Armed Forces.* New York: Academic Press. 210 pp.

Ryan, W., Sloan, A., Seferi, M., Weby, E. 1974. *All in Together, An Evaluation of Mixed Income Multi-Family Housing.* Boston: Summary Report of Mass. Housing Finance Agency Social Audit. 24 pp.

Rymph, R. C. Hadden, J. K. 1970. The persistence of regionalism in racial attitudes of Methodist clergy. *Soc. Forces.* 49:41-50.

St. John, N. 1973. Social psychological aspects of school desegregation. In *Urban Education Today, Rethinking Theory and Practice.* San Francisco: Jossey-Bass. 334 pp.

St. John, N. 1975. *School Desegregation, Outcomes for Children.* New York: Wiley-Interscience. 236 pp.

Saenger, G., Gilbert, E. 1950. Customer reactions to the integration of Negro sales personnel. *Int. J. Opin. Att. Res.* 4:57-76.

Sales, S. M. 1973. Threat as a factor in authoritarianism, an analysis of archival data. *J. Pers. Soc. Psychol.* 28:44-57.

Saltman, J. 1975. Implementing open housing laws through social action. *J. Appl. Behavioral Sci.* 11:39-61.

Saltzman, J. Z. 1971. *Open Housing as a Social Movement.* Lexington, Mass.: D. C. Heath. 213 pp.

Samuels, F. 1970. *The Japanese and the Haoles of Honolulu, Durable Group Interaction.* New Haven, Conn.: College and University Press. 206 pp.

Sattler, J. M. 1973. Racial experimenter effects. In *Comparative Studies of Blacks and Whites in the United States,* ed. K. S. Miller, R. M. Dreger, 7-32. New York: Seminar Press. 572 pp.

Scanzoni, J. H. 1971. *The Black Family in Modern Society.* Boston: Allyn & Bacon. 353 pp.

Schelling, T. C. 1960. *The Strategy of Conflict.* Cambridge, Mass.: Harvard Univ. Press. 309 pp.

Schelling, T. C. 1965. Strategic analysis and social problems. *Soc. Probl.* 12:267-79.

Schelling, T. C. 1971. On the ecology of micromotives. *Public Interest.* 25:59-98.

Schelling, T. C. 1973. Introduction. In *The Politics of Nonviolent Action*, Gene Sharp, xix-xxi. Boston: Porter Sargent. 902 pp.

Schermerhorn, R. A. 1970. *Comparative Ethnic Relations.* New York: Random House. 327 pp.

Schulman, G. I. 1974. Race, sex, and violence, a laboratory test of the sexual threat of the black male hypothesis. *Am. J. Sociol.* 79:1260-77.

Schurmann, F. 1971. On revolutionary conflict. In *Conflict Resolution, Contributions of the Behavioral Sciences,* ed. C. G. Smith, 261-71. Notre Dame, Indiana: Univ. of Notre Dame Press. 553 pp.

Schwartz, M. A. 1967. *Trends in White Attitudes toward Negroes.* Chicago: Nat. Opin. Res. Ctr. 134 pp.

Schwartz, R. D., Miller, J. C. 1964. Legal evolution and societal complexity. *Am. J. Sociol.* 70:159-69.

Sedlacek, W. E., Brooks, G. C., Mindus, L. A. 1973. Racial attitudes of white university students and their parents. *J. College Students Personnel.* 14:517-20.

Seligman, D. 1973. How 'equal opportunity' turned into employment quotas. *Fortune.* March:160-8.

Selznick, G., Steinberg, S. 1969. *The Tenacity of Prejudice, Anti-Semitism in Contemporary America.* New York: Harper & Row. 248 pp.

Sewell, W. H., Haller, A. O., Ohlendorf, G. W. 1970. The educational and early occupational status attainment process, replication and revision. *Am. Sociol. Rev.* 35:1014-27.

Sewell, W. H., Hauser, R. M. 1975. *Education, Occupation, and Earnings.* New York: Academic Press. 237 pp.

Sharp, G. 1973. *The Politics of Nonviolent Action.* Boston: Porter Sargent. 902 pp.

Sheatsley, P. B. 1966. White attitudes toward the Negro. *Daedalus.* Winter:217-38.

Shellow, R., Roemer, D. V. 1966. The riot that didn't happen. *Soc. Probl.* 14:221-33.

Shelly, H. P. 1954. Level of aspiration phenomenon in small groups. *J. Soc. Psychol.* 40:149-64.

Sherif, M. 1966. *In Common Predicament.* Boston: Houghton Mifflin. 192 pp.

Sherif, M., with Harvey, O. J., Hood, W. E., Sherif, C., White, B. J. 1961. *Intergroup Conflict and Cooperation, the Robber's Cave Experiment.* Norman, Oklahoma: Univ. of Oklahoma Book Exchange. 212 pp.

Short, J. F., Jr., Wolfgang, M. E., eds. 1972. *Collective Violence.* Chicago: Aldine-Atherton. 387 pp.

Shuval, J. T. 1962. The micro-neighborhood, an approach to ecological patterns of ethnic groups. *Soc. Probl.* 9:272-80.

Silver, J. 1966. *Mississippi, The Closed Society.* New York: Harcourt, Brace and World. 375 pp.

Simms, R. P. 1968. The Savannah story. In *Our Children's Burden*, ed. R. W. Mack, 109-40. New York: Random House. 473 pp.

Simpson, G. E., Yinger, J. M. 1972. *Racial and Cultural Minorities, An Analysis of Prejudice and Discrimination.* 4th ed. New York: Harper & Row. 775 pp.

Singer, D. 1966. Interracial attitudes of Negro and white fifth grade children in segregated schools. Ph.D. dissertation. New York: Columbia Univ., 141 pp.

Singer, L. 1962. Ethnogenesis and Negro-Americans today. *Soc. Res.* 29:419-32.

Smith, A., Downs, A., Lachman, M. L. 1973. *Achieving Effective Desegregation.* Lexington, Mass.: D. C. Heath. 248 pp.

Smith, F. T. 1944. *An Experiment in Modifying Attitudes toward the Negro.* New York: Teachers College, Columbia Univ. 135 pp.

Smith, H. S. 1972. *In His Image, But . . . , Racism in Southern Religion, 1780-1910.* Durham N.C.: Duke Univ. Press. 318 pp.

Smith, T. S. 1968. Conventionalization and control, an examination of adolescent crowds. *Am. J. Sociol.* 74:172-83.

Solomon, R. L. 1964. Punishment. *Am. Psychologist.* 19:239-53.

Spearman, R., Stevens, H. 1974. *A Step toward Equal Justice, Programs to Increase Black Lawyers in the South, 1969-1973.* New York: Carnegie Corp. of New York. 68 pp.

Spitz, D. 1974. Pure tolerance, a critique of criticism. *Dissent.* Spring:259-69.

Stack, C. B. 1974. *All Our Kin, Strategies for Survival in a Black Community.* New York: Harper & Row. 175 pp.

Stanfield, G. G. 1975. Reply to Jorgensen. *Am. Sociologist.* 10:49-50.

Star, S. A. 1967. An approach to the measurement of interracial tension. In *Contributions to Urban Sociology*, ed. E. W. Burgess, D. J. Bogue, 346-72. Chicago: Univ. of Chicago Press. 673 pp.

Stark, R. et al. 1971. *Wayward Sheperds, Prejudice and the Protestant Clergy.* New York: Harper & Row. 122 pp.

Stark W. 1965. Play-figures and play-forms, a functionalist approach. *Revista Internacional de Sociologia.* xxiii:365-75.

Steiner, J. 1974. *Amicable Agreement versus Majority Rule, Conflict Resolution in Switzerland.* Trans. A. Braendgaard and B. Braendgaard. Chapel Hill, N.C.: Univ. of North Carolina Press. 312 pp.

Stelzer, L. 1974. Institutionalizing conflict response, the case of school boards. *Soc. Sci. Quart.* 5:380-93.

Stember, C. H. 1961. *Education and Attitude Change.* New York: Institute of Human Relations Press. 182 pp.

Stember, C. H. et al. 1966. *Jews in the Mind of America.* New York: Basic Books. 413 pp.

Stone, C. N. 1976. *Economic Growth and Neighborhood Discontent, System Bias in the Urban Renewal Program of Atlanta.* Chapel Hill, N.C.: Univ. of North Carolina Press. 256 pp.

Storr, A. 1968. *Human Aggression.* New York: Atheneum. 127 pp.

Stouffer, S. A. 1955. *Communism, Conformity, and Civil Liberties.* Garden City, New York: Doubleday. 278 pp.

Streufert, S., Streufert, S. C. 1969. Effects of conceptual structure, failure and success on attribution of causality and interpersonal attitudes. *J. Pers. Soc. Psychol.* 11:138-47.

Suchman, E. A. et al. 1958. *Desegregation, Some Propositions and Research Suggestions.* New York: Anti-Defamation League of B'nai B'rith. 128 pp.

Summers, A. A., Wolfe, B. L. 1975. Which school resources help learning? Efficiency and equity in Philadelphia public schools. *Federal Reserve Bank of Philadelphia Business Review.* February:4-28.

Sundquist, J. L. 1973. Book review. *Polit. Sci. Quart.* 88:739.

Sutker, S., Sutker, S. S. 1974. *Racial Transition in the Inner Suburb, Studies of the St. Louis Area.* New York: Praeger. 250 pp.

Suttles, G. D. 1968. *The Social Order of the Slum, Ethnicity and Territory in the Inner City.* Chicago: Univ. of Chicago Press. 243 pp.

Suttles, G. D. 1972. *The Social Construction of Communities.* Chicago: Univ. of Chicago Press. 278 pp.

Swedner, H. 1971. *School Integration in Malmo.* Chicago: Integrated Education Associates. 51 pp.

System Development Corporation. 1974. *Navy Race Relations Education, Impact Analysis.* Vols. I and II. TM-(L)-5285/000/00. Santa Monica, Calif.

System Development Corporation. (n.d., c. 1974). *Racial Awareness Facilitator Training: Training Manual.* Navpers 15254 (preliminary).

Szymanski, A. 1974. Race, sex, and the U.S. working class. *Soc. Probl.* 21:706-25.

Taeuber, A., Taeuber, K. 1965. *Negroes in Cities, Residential Segregation and Neighborhood Change.* Chicago: Aldine. 284 pp.

Tajfel, H. 1970. Experiments in intergroup discrimination. *Scientific American.* 223:92-102.

Tanter, R. 1966. Dimensions of conflict behavior within and between nations, 1958-1960. *J. Conflict. Resol.* 10:44-64.

Taylor, W. L. 1971. *Hanging Together, Equality in an Urban Nation.* New York: Simon and Schuster. 348 pp.

Theil, H. 1964. *Optimal Decision Rules for Government and Industry.* Chicago: Rand-McNally. 364 pp.

Thibaut, J. W. 1950. An experimental study of the cohesiveness of underprivileged groups. *Human Relations.* 3:251-78.

Thibaut, J. W., Kelley, H. H. 1959. *The Social Psychology of Groups.* New York: Wiley. 313 pp.

Thomas, E. J. 1957. Effects of facilitative role interdependence on group functioning. *Human Relations.* 10:347-66.

Thompson, J. D. 1960. Organizational management of conflict. *Adm. Sci. Quart.* 4:389-409.

Thompson, R. A., Lewis, H., McEntire, D. 1960. Atlanta and Birmingham, a comparative study in Negro housing. In *Studies in Housing and Minority Groups*, eds. N. Glazer, D. McEntire, 13-83. Berkeley: Univ. of Calif. Press. 228 pp.

Thurow, L. 1972. Education and economic equality. *Public Interest.* 28:66-81.

Thurow, L. C. 1973. The political economy of income redistribution policies. *The Annals.* 409:146-55.

Timasheff, N. 1965. *War and Revolution.* New York: Sheed & Ward. 339 pp.

Timms, D. 1971. *The Urban Mosaic, Towards a Theory of Residential Differentiation.* New York: Cambridge Univ. Press. 277 pp.

Tittle, C. R. 1969. Crime rates and legal sanctions. *Soc. Probl.* 15:409-23.

Totenberg, N. 1974. Discriminating to end discrimination. *New York Times Magazine.* (April 14):9ff.

Triandis, H. C. 1972. The impact of social change on attitudes. In *Attitudes, Conflict and Social Change*, eds. B. T. King, E. McGinnies, 127-36. New York: Academic Press. 234 pp.

Trow, M. 1962. The democratization of higher education in America. *Eur. J. Sociol.* 3:231-62.

Tullock, G. 1969. An economic approach to crime. *Soc. Sci. Quart.* 50:59-71.

Tullock, G. 1974. Does punishment deter crime? *Public Interest.* 36:103-11.

Tunteng, P. K. 1973. Racism and the Montreal computer incident of 1969. *Race.* 14:229-40.

Turk, H. 1963. Social cohesion through variant values, evidence from medical role relations. *Am. Sociol. Rev.* 28:28-37.

Turner, R. H. 1969. The public perception of protest. *Am. Sociol. Rev.* 34:815-31.

Turner, R. H., Killian, L. M., eds. 1957. *Collective Behavior.* Englewood Cliffs, N.J.: Prentice-Hall. 547 pp.

Tyack, D. B. 1974. *The One Best System, A History of American Urban Education.* Cambridge, Mass.: Harvard Univ. Press. 353 pp.

Underhill, L., Coles, R., Baldwin, C., Whitney, T. W. 1974. *The Buses Roll.* New York: W. W. Norton. 112 pp.

U.S. Bureau of the Census. 1976. *Statistical Abstract of the United States, 1975.* Washington, D.C.: U.S. Govt. Printing Office. 1050 pp.

U.S. Commission on Civil Rights. 1968. *Political Participation.* Washington, D.C.: U.S. Govt. Printing Office. 256 pp.

van den Berghe, P. L. 1971. The benign quota, panacea or Pandora's box. *Am. Sociologist.* 6:40-3.

Vander Zanden, J. W. 1963. *American Minority Relations, The Sociology of Race and Ethnic Groups.* New York: Ronald Press. 470 pp.

Vanfossen, B. E. 1968. Variables related to resistance to desegregation in the South. *Soc. Forces.* 47:39-44.

Vickers, G. 1967. *Toward a Sociology of Management.* New York: Basic Books. 206 pp.

Wade, R. C. 1969. Violence in the cities, a historical view. *Urban Violence*, ed. C. V. Daley, 7-26. Chicago: Univ. of Chicago Center for Policy Study. 81 pp.

Wagner, C., Wheeler, L. 1969. Model, need, and cost effects in helping behavior. *J. Person. Soc. Psychol.* 12:111-16.

Walcott, H. F. 1974. *The African Beer Gardens of Bulawayo, Integrated Drinking in a Segregated Society.* New Brunswick, N.J.: Rutgers Cntr. Alcohol Studies. 261 pp.

Walter, B., Wirt, F. M. 1971. The political consequences of suburban variety. *Soc. Sci. Quart.* 52:746-67.

Walton, H., Jr. 1971. *The Political Philosophy of Martin Luther King, Jr.* Westport, Conn: Greenwood. 137 pp.

Walton, R. E. 1967. Third party roles in interdepartmental conflict. *Indus. Rel.* 7:29-30.

Walton, R. E., Dutton, J. M., Fitch, H. G. 1966. A study of conflict in the process, structure, and attitudes of lateral relationships. In *Some Theories of Organization*, eds. A. H. Rubenstein, C. J. Haberstroh, 444-65. Homewood, Ill.: R. D. Irwin and Dorsey Press. 722 pp.

Walton, R. E., McKersie, R. B. 1965. *A Behavioral Theory of Labor Negotiations, An Analysis of a Social Interaction System.* New York: McGraw-Hill. 437 pp.

Warren, E. 1973. Equal opportunity, the Constitution and the law. In *Equal Opportunity in the United States, A Symposium on Civil Rights*, ed. R. C. Rooney, 16-27. Austin, Texas: Lyndon B. Johnson School of Public Affairs. Univ. of Texas. 175 pp.

Washington, J. R. 1972. *Black Sects and Cults, The Power Axis in an Ethnic Ethic.* New York: Doubleday. 176 pp.

Watson, G. 1946. *Action for Unity.* New York: Harper & Bros. 164 pp.

Watson, G. L. 1973. Social structure and social movements, the Black Muslims in the U.S.A. and the Ras-Tafarians in Jamaica. *Brit. J. Sociol.* 24:188-204.

Wedge, B. 1968. Krushchev at a distance, a study of public personality. *Trans-action.* 5:27.

Weigel, R. H., Wiser, P. L., Cook, S. W. 1975. The impact of cooperative learning experiences on cross-ethnic relations and attitudes. *J. Soc. Issues.* 31:219-44.

Weinberg, M. 1970. *Desegregation Research, An Appraisal.* Bloomington, Indiana: Phi Delta Kappa. 2nd ed., 460 pp.

Weissbach, T. A. 1976. Laboratory controlled studies of change in racial attitudes. In *Toward the Elimination of Racism*, ed. P. A. Katz, 157-82. New York: Pergamon Press. 444 pp.

Wertzer, F. 1971. The effect of a shared stress situation on racial attitudes. Ph.D. dissertation. New York: Columbia Univ. (Univ. Microfilms, Ann Arbor, Mich. 1957. No. 57-1419).

Wheeler, L., Levine, L. 1967. Observer-model similarity in the contagion of aggression. *Sociometry.* 30:41-9.

Wilburn, A. Y. 1974. Careers in science and engineering for black Americans. *Science.* 184:1148-54.

Wilhoit, F. M. 1973. *The Politics of Massive Resistance.* New York: George Braziller. 320 pp.

Williams, J. A. 1971. The multifamily housing solution and housing type preferences. *Soc. Sci. Quart.* 52:543-59.

Williams, J. A., Nunn, C. Z., St. Peter, L. 1976. Origins of tolerance, findings from a replication of Stouffer's *Communism, Conformity, and Civil Liberties. Soc. Forces.* 55:394-408.

Williams, R. L., Byars, H. 1970. The effect of academic integration on the self-esteem of Southern Negro Students. *J. Soc. Psychol.* 80:183-8.

Williams, R. M., Jr. 1947. *The Reduction of Intergroup Tensions.* New York: *Soc. Sci. Res. Council.* 153 pp.

Williams, R. M., Jr., Dean, J. P., Suchman, E. A. 1964. *Strangers Next Door, Ethnic Relations in American Communities.* Englewood Cliffs, N.J.: Prentice-Hall. 434 pp.

Williams, R. M., Jr. 1965. Social change and social conflict, race relations in the United States, 1944-1964. *Sociol. Inquiry.* 35:8-25.

Williams, R. M., Jr. 1966. Some further comments on chronic controversies. *Am. J. Sociol.* 71:717-22.

Williams, R. M., Jr. 1968. Factors affecting reactions to public school desegregation in American communities. In *State of Knowledge Conference*, New York State Education Department, 1-40. Albany: Division of Intercultural Relations. 68 pp.

Williams, R. M., Jr. 1970. *American Society.* New York: Knopf. 639 pp.

Williams, R. M., Jr. 1971. Social Congestion and Social Conflict. All-college lecture, Mount Holyoke College: Processed. 38 pp.

Williams, R. M., Jr., 1973. Equal opportunity as a societal problem. In *Equal Opportunity in the United States, A Symposium on Civil Rights*, ed. R. C. Rooney, 104-11. Austin, Texas: Lyndon B. Johnson School of Public Affairs. Univ. of Texas. 175 pp.

Williams, R. M., Jr. 1974. Attitudes and behavior towards immigrants and ethnic groups. In *The New Immigration and the New Ethnicity, Social Policy and Social Theory in the 1970s*, eds. W. S. Bernard, J. Herman, 13-25. New York: Am. Immigration and Citizenship Conference. 67 pp.

Williams, R. M., Jr. 1975a. Race and ethnic relations. In *Annual Review of Sociology*, vol. 1, eds. A. Inkeles, J. Coleman, N. Smelser, 125-64. Palo Alto, Calif.: Annual Reviews, Inc. 479 pp.

Williams, R. M., Jr. 1975b. Relative deprivation. In *The Idea of Social Structure, Papers in Honor of Robert K. Merton*, ed. L. A. Coser, 355-78. New York: Harcourt Brace Jovanovich. 547 pp.

Williams, R. M., Jr. 1976. Relative deprivation versus power struggle? 'tension' and 'structural' explanations of collective conflict. *Cornell J. Soc. Rels.* 11:31-8.

Williams, R. M., Jr., Ryan, M. 1954. *Schools in Transition, Community Experiences in Desegregation.* Chapel Hill, N.C.: Univ. of North Carolina Press. 272 pp.

Willie, C. V. ed. 1970. *The Family Life of Black People.* Columbus, Ohio: Merrill. 341 pp.

Willie, C. V., McCord, A. S. 1972. *Black Students at White Colleges.* New York: Praeger. 110 pp.

Willie, C. V. 1976. *A New Look at Black Families.* Bayside, New York: General Hall, Inc. 211 pp.

Wilner, D. M., Price, R., Cook, S. W. 1952. Residential proximity and integration relations in public housing projects. *J. Soc. Issues.* 8:45-69.

Wilner, D. M., Walkley, R. P., Cook, S. W. 1955. *Human Relations in Interracial Housing, A Study of the Contact Hypothesis.* Minneapolis: Univ. of Minnesota Press. 167 pp.

Wilson, F. D., Day, R. C. 1974. White students' evaluation of a black student protest organization, a test of a model. *Soc. Sci. Quart.* 55:691-703.

Wilson, J. Q. 1968. Why are we having a wave of violence. *N. Y. Times Mag.* (May 19): 119.

Wilson, J. Q. 1975. The rise of the bureaucratic state. *Public Interest.* 41:77-103.

Wilson, W. 1970. Rank order of discrimination and its relevance to civil rights priorities. *J. Pers. Soc. Psychol.* 15:188-224.

Wilson, W., Chum, N., Kayatani, M. 1965. Projection, attraction and strategy choices in intergroup competition. *J. Person. Soc. Psychol.* 2:432-5.

Wilson, W., Kayatani, M. 1968. Intergroup attitudes and strategies in games between opponents of the same or of a different race. *J. Person. Soc. Psychol.* 9:24-30.

Wilson, W., Miller, N. 1961. Shifts in evaluation of participants following intergroup competition. *J. Abnorm. Soc. Psychol.* 63:428-32.

Wimberley, H. 1973. Legal evolution, one further step. *Am. J. Sociol.* 79:78-83.

Winder, A. E. 1952. White attitudes toward Negro-white interaction in an area of changing racial composition. *Am. Psychologist.* 7:330-1.

Wirt, F. M. 1970. *Politics of Southern Equality, Law and Social Change in a Mississippi County.* Chicago: Aldine. 335 pp.

Wolf, E. P. 1969. Community control of schools as an ideology and social mechanism. *Soc. Sci. Quart.* 50:713-22.

Wolf, E. P., Lebeaux, C. N. 1969. *Change and Renewal in an Urban Community.* New York: Praeger. 574 pp.

Wood, J. R. 1972. Unanticipated consequences of organizational coalitions, ecumenical cooperation and civil rights policy. *Soc. Forces.* 50:512-21.

Woodward, C. V. 1957. *The Strange Career of Jim Crow.* Fairlawn, N.J.: Oxford Univ. Press. 183 pp.

Woodward, J. W. 1944. The role of fictions in cultural organization. *Trans. N. Y. Acad. Sci.* Series II. 6:311-44.

Works, E. 1961. The prejudice-interaction hypothesis from the point of view of the Negro minority group. *Am. J. Sociol.* 67:47-52.

Wright, J. D. 1976. *The Dissent of the Governed, Alienation and Democracy in America.* New York: Academic Press. 318 pp.

Yancey, W. L. 1972. Going down home, family structure and the urban trap. *Soc. Sci. Quart.* 52:893-906.

Yancey, W. L., Rigsby, L., McCarthy, J. D. 1972. Social position and self-evaluation, the relative importance of race. *Am. J. Sociol.* 78:338-59.

Yinger, J. M. 1957. *Religion, Society and the Individual, An Introduction to the Sociology of Religion.* New York: Macmillan. 655 pp.

York, H. 1972. Technical exaggeration and the arms race. *Bull. Am. Acad. Arts and Sci.* 26:14.

Zander, A. 1971. *Motives and Goals in Groups.* New York: Academic Press. 212 pp.

Zawodny, J. W. 1962. Foreword. *The Annals.* 341:viii.

Zeitlin, M., Ewen, L. A., Ratcliff, R. E. 1974. "New princes" for old? The large corporation and the capitalist class in Chile. *Am. J. Sociol.* 80:87-123.

Zeul, C., Humphrey, C. R. 1971. The integration of black residents in suburban neighborhoods, a re-examination of the contact hypothesis. *Soc. Probl.* 18:462-74.

Zeul, C. Z. 1976. *Neighborhood Racial Composition and the House-Choice Process, Implications for Suburban Integration.* Ph.D. dissertation. Ithaca, N.Y.: Cornell Univ. 290 pp.

Zimbardo, P., Ebbesen, E. B. 1969. *Influencing Attitudes and Changing Behavior.* Reading, Mass.: Addison-Wesley. 179 pp.

Zimring, F. E. 1971. *Perspectives on Deterrence.* Washington, D.C.: (Ctr. Stud. Crime and Delinquency, Nat. Inst. Mental Health) U.S. Govt. Printing Office. 109 pp.

Zolberg, A. R. 1968. The structure of political conflict in the new states of tropical Africa. *Am. Polit. Sci. Rev.* 62:70-87.

Index

Index